Fast Reliable Algorithms for Matrices with Structure

Fast Reliable Algorithms for Matrices with Structure

Edited by

T. Kailath
Stanford University
Stanford, California

A. H. Sayed
University of California
Los Angeles, California

siam

Society for Industrial and Applied Mathematics
Philadelphia

Copyright © 1999 by Society for Industrial and Applied Mathematics.

10 9 8 7 6 5 4 3 2 1

All rights reserved. Printed in the United States of America. No part of this book may be reproduced, stored, or transmitted in any manner without the written permission of the publisher. For information, write to the Society for Industrial and Applied Mathematics, 3600 University City Science Center, Philadelphia, PA 19104-2688.

Library of Congress Cataloging-in-Publication Data

Fast reliable algorithms for matrices with structure / edited by T. Kailath, A.H. Sayed
        p. cm.
    Includes bibliographical references (p. -) and index.
    ISBN 0-89871-431-1 (pbk.)
    1. Matrices -- Data processing. 2. Algorithms. I. Kailath, Thomas. II. Sayed, Ali H.
QA188 .F38 1999
512.9'434 -- dc21   99-26368
                                                    CIP
                                                     rev.

siam is a registered trademark.

CONTRIBUTORS

Dario A. Bini
Dipartimento di Matematica
Università di Pisa
Pisa, Italy

Sheryl Branham
Dept. Math. and Computer Science
Lehman College
City University of New York
New York, NY 10468, USA

Richard P. Brent
Oxford University Computing Laboratory
Wolfson Building, Parks Road
Oxford OX1 3QD, England

Raymond H. Chan
Department of Mathematics
The Chinese University of Hong Kong
Shatin, Hong Kong

Shivkumar Chandrasekaran
Dept. Electrical and Computer Engineering
University of California
Santa Barbara, CA 93106, USA

Patrick Dewilde
DIMES, POB 5031, 2600GA Delft
Delft University of Technology
Delft, The Netherlands

Victor S. Grigorascu
Facultatea de Electronica and Telecomunicatii
Universitatea Politehnica Bucuresti
Bucharest, Romania

Thomas Kailath
Department of Electrical Engineering
Stanford University
Stanford, CA 94305, USA

Beatrice Meini
Dipartimento di Matematica
Università di Pisa
Pisa, Italy

Victor Y. Pan
Dept. Math. and Computer Science
Lehman College
City University of New York
New York, NY 10468, USA

Michael K. Ng
Department of Mathematics
The University of Hong Kong
Pokfulam Road, Hong Kong

Phillip A. Regalia
Signal and Image Processing Dept.
Inst. National des Télécommunications
F-91011 Evry cedex, France

Rhys E. Rosholt
Dept. Math. and Computer Science
City University of New York
Lehman College
New York, NY 10468, USA

Ali H. Sayed
Electrical Engineering Department
University of California
Los Angeles, CA 90024, USA

Paolo Tilli
Scuola Normale Superiore
Piazza Cavalieri 7
56100 Pisa, Italy

Ai-Long Zheng
Deptartment of Mathematics
City University of New York
New York, NY 10468, USA

CONTENTS

PREFACE		xiii
NOTATION		xv
1 DISPLACEMENT STRUCTURE AND ARRAY ALGORITHMS		1
Thomas Kailath		
1.1	Introduction	1
1.2	Toeplitz Matrices	2
1.3	Versions of Displacement Structure	6
1.4	Application to the Fast Evaluation of Matrix-Vector Products	12
1.5	Two Fundamental Properties	13
1.6	Fast Factorization of Structured Matrices	15
	1.6.1 Schur Reduction (Deflation)	15
	1.6.2 Close Relation to Gaussian Elimination	16
	1.6.3 A Generalized Schur Algorithm	17
	1.6.4 Array Derivation of the Algorithm	18
	1.6.5 An Elementary Section	23
	1.6.6 A Simple Example	24
1.7	Proper Form of the Fast Algorithm	25
	1.7.1 Positive Lengths	25
	1.7.2 Negative Lengths	26
	1.7.3 Statement of the Algorithm in Proper Form	26
	1.7.4 An Associated Transmission Line	27
	1.7.5 Shift-Structured ($F = Z$) Positive-Definite Matrices	27
	1.7.6 The Classical Schur Algorithm	28
	1.7.7 The Special Case of Toeplitz Matrices	30
1.8	Some Applications in Matrix Computation	30
	1.8.1 Going Beyond $F = Z$	31
	1.8.2 Simultaneous Factorization of T and T^{-1}	31
	1.8.3 QR Factorization of Structured Matrices	32
	1.8.4 Avoiding Back Substitution in Linear Equations	33
1.9	Look-Ahead (Block) Schur Algorithm	34
1.10	Fast Inversion of Structured Matrices	37
	1.10.1 Schur Construction (Inflation)	37
	1.10.2 Statement of the Fast Inversion Algorithm	39
	1.10.3 Algorithm Development	40
	1.10.4 An Example	41

	1.10.5 Proper Form of the Algorithm	42
	1.10.6 Application to Pick Matrices	44
	1.10.7 The Degenerate Case	44
1.11	Non-Hermitian Toeplitz-Like Matrices	45
1.12	Schur Algorithm for Hankel-Like Matrices	47
1.13	Structured Matrices and Pivoting	48
	1.13.1 Incorporating Pivoting into Generalized Schur Algorithms	49
	1.13.2 Transformations to Cauchy-Like Structures	50
	1.13.3 Numerical Issues	51
1.14	Some Further Issues	52
	1.14.1 Incorporating State-Space Structure	52
	1.14.2 Iterative Methods	53
	1.14.3 Interpolation Problems	54
	1.14.4 Inverse Scattering	55

2 STABILIZED SCHUR ALGORITHMS 57
Shivkumar Chandrasekaran and Ali H. Sayed

2.1	Introduction	57
2.2	Contributions and Problems	58
2.3	Related Works in the Literature	58
	2.3.1 Notation	60
	2.3.2 Brief Review of Displacement Structure	60
2.4	The Generalized Schur Algorithm	62
2.5	A Limit to Numerical Accuracy	64
2.6	Implementations of the Hyperbolic Rotation	65
	2.6.1 Direct Implementation	66
	2.6.2 Mixed Downdating	66
	2.6.3 The Orthogonal-Diagonal Procedure	67
	2.6.4 The H Procedure	68
2.7	Implementation of the Blaschke Matrix	69
	2.7.1 The Case of Diagonal F	69
	2.7.2 The Case of Strictly Lower Triangular F	70
2.8	Enforcing Positive Definiteness	71
2.9	Accuracy of the Factorization	71
2.10	Pivoting with Diagonal F	73
	2.10.1 A Numerical Example	74
	2.10.2 The Case of Positive F	74
	2.10.3 The Nonpositive Case	74
2.11	Controlling the Generator Growth	75
2.12	Solution of Linear Systems of Equations	75
	2.12.1 Computing the Matrix R	75
	2.12.2 Iterative Refinement	76
2.13	Enhancing the Robustness of the Algorithm	77
	2.13.1 Enhancing the OD Method	77
	2.13.2 Enhancing the H Procedure	78
	2.13.3 A Numerical Example	78
2.14	Results for the Positive-Definite Case	79
2.A	Pseudocode for the Stable Schur Algorithm	81

3 FAST STABLE SOLVERS FOR STRUCTURED LINEAR SYSTEMS 85
Ali H. Sayed and Shivkumar Chandrasekaran

- 3.1 Introduction — 85
- 3.2 Overview of the Proposed Solution — 86
- 3.3 The Generalized Schur Algorithm for Indefinite Matrices — 87
- 3.4 Fast QR Factorization of Shift-Structured Matrices — 90
  - 3.4.1 The Toeplitz Case — 91
  - 3.4.2 Other Augmentations — 92
- 3.5 Well-Conditioned Coefficient Matrices — 93
  - 3.5.1 Implementation of the Hyperbolic Rotation — 94
  - 3.5.2 Avoiding Breakdown — 95
  - 3.5.3 Error Analysis of the Last Steps — 96
  - 3.5.4 Summary — 97
  - 3.5.5 Solving the Linear System of Equations — 97
- 3.6 Ill-Conditioned Coefficient Matrices — 97
  - 3.6.1 Solving the Linear System of Equations — 98
  - 3.6.2 Conditions on the Coefficient Matrix — 99
- 3.7 Summary of the Algorithm — 99

4 STABILITY OF FAST ALGORITHMS FOR STRUCTURED LINEAR SYSTEMS 103
Richard P. Brent

- 4.1 Introduction — 103
  - 4.1.1 Outline — 104
  - 4.1.2 Notation — 105
- 4.2 Stability and Weak Stability — 105
  - 4.2.1 Gaussian Elimination with Pivoting — 106
  - 4.2.2 Weak Stability — 107
  - 4.2.3 Example: Orthogonal Factorization — 108
- 4.3 Classes of Structured Matrices — 108
  - 4.3.1 Cauchy and Cauchy-Like Matrices — 109
  - 4.3.2 Toeplitz Matrices — 109
- 4.4 Structured Gaussian Elimination — 109
  - 4.4.1 The GKO–Toeplitz Algorithm — 110
  - 4.4.2 Error Analysis — 111
  - 4.4.3 A General Strategy — 112
- 4.5 Positive-Definite Structured Matrices — 112
  - 4.5.1 The Bareiss Algorithm for Positive-Definite Matrices — 113
  - 4.5.2 Generalized Schur Algorithms — 113
- 4.6 Fast Orthogonal Factorization — 114
  - 4.6.1 Use of the Seminormal Equations — 115
  - 4.6.2 Computing Q Stably — 115
  - 4.6.3 Solution of Indefinite or Unsymmetric Structured Systems — 115
- 4.7 Concluding Remarks — 116

5 ITERATIVE METHODS FOR LINEAR SYSTEMS WITH MATRIX STRUCTURE 117
Raymond H. Chan and Michael K. Ng

- 5.1 Introduction — 117
- 5.2 The CG Method — 118

	5.3	Iterative Methods for Solving Toeplitz Systems	121
	5.3.1	Preconditioning	122
	5.3.2	Circulant Matrices	123
	5.3.3	Toeplitz Matrix-Vector Multiplication	124
	5.3.4	Circulant Preconditioners	125
	5.4	Band-Toeplitz Preconditioners	130
	5.5	Toeplitz-Circulant Preconditioners	132
	5.6	Preconditioners for Structured Linear Systems	133
	5.6.1	Toeplitz-Like Systems	133
	5.6.2	Toeplitz-Plus-Hankel Systems	137
	5.7	Toeplitz-Plus-Band Systems	139
	5.8	Applications	140
	5.8.1	Linear-Phase Filtering	140
	5.8.2	Numerical Solutions of Biharmonic Equations	142
	5.8.3	Queueing Networks with Batch Arrivals	144
	5.8.4	Image Restorations	147
	5.9	Concluding Remarks	149
	5.A	Proof of Theorem 5.3.4	150
	5.B	Proof of Theorem 5.6.2	151

6 ASYMPTOTIC SPECTRAL DISTRIBUTION OF TOEPLITZ-RELATED MATRICES 153
Paolo Tilli

6.1	Introduction	153
6.2	What Is Spectral Distribution?	153
6.3	Toeplitz Matrices and Shift Invariance	157
6.3.1	Spectral Distribution of Toeplitz Matrices	158
6.3.2	Unbounded Generating Function	162
6.3.3	Eigenvalues in the Non-Hermitian Case	163
6.3.4	The Szegő Formula for Singular Values	164
6.4	Multilevel Toeplitz Matrices	166
6.5	Block Toeplitz Matrices	170
6.6	Combining Block and Multilevel Structure	174
6.7	Locally Toeplitz Matrices	175
6.7.1	A Closer Look at Locally Toeplitz Matrices	178
6.7.2	Spectral Distribution of Locally Toeplitz Sequences	182
6.8	Concluding Remarks	186

7 NEWTON'S ITERATION FOR STRUCTURED MATRICES 189
Victor Y. Pan, Sheryl Branham, Rhys E. Rosholt, and Ai-Long Zheng

7.1	Introduction	189
7.2	Newton's Iteration for Matrix Inversion	190
7.3	Some Basic Results on Toeplitz-Like Matrices	192
7.4	The Newton–Toeplitz Iteration	194
7.4.1	Bounding the Displacement Rank	195
7.4.2	Convergence Rate and Computational Complexity	196
7.4.3	An Approach Using f-Circulant Matrices	198
7.5	Residual Correction Method	200
7.5.1	Application to Matrix Inversion	200
7.5.2	Application to a Linear System of Equations	201

		7.5.3	Application to a Toeplitz Linear System of Equations	201
		7.5.4	Estimates for the Convergence Rate	203
	7.6	Numerical Experiments		204
	7.7	Concluding Remarks		207
	7.A	Correctness of Algorithm 7.4.2		208
	7.B	Correctness of Algorithm 7.5.1		209
	7.C	Correctness of Algorithm 7.5.2		209

8 FAST ALGORITHMS WITH APPLICATIONS TO MARKOV CHAINS AND QUEUEING MODELS — 211
Dario A. Bini and Beatrice Meini

8.1	Introduction		211
8.2	Toeplitz Matrices and Markov Chains		212
	8.2.1	Modeling of Switches and Network Traffic Control	214
	8.2.2	Conditions for Positive Recurrence	215
	8.2.3	Computation of the Probability Invariant Vector	216
8.3	Exploitation of Structure and Computational Tools		217
	8.3.1	Block Toeplitz Matrices and Block Vector Product	218
	8.3.2	Inversion of Block Triangular Block Toeplitz Matrices	221
	8.3.3	Power Series Arithmetic	223
8.4	Displacement Structure		224
8.5	Fast Algorithms		226
	8.5.1	The Fast Ramaswami Formula	227
	8.5.2	A Doubling Algorithm	227
	8.5.3	Cyclic Reduction	230
	8.5.4	Cyclic Reduction for Infinite Systems	234
	8.5.5	Cyclic Reduction for Generalized Hessenberg Systems	239
8.6	Numerical Experiments		241

9 TENSOR DISPLACEMENT STRUCTURES AND POLYSPECTRAL MATCHING — 245
Victor S. Grigorascu and Phillip A. Regalia

9.1	Introduction		245
9.2	Motivation for Higher-Order Cumulants		245
9.3	Second-Order Displacement Structure		249
9.4	Tucker Product and Cumulant Tensors		251
9.5	Examples of Cumulants and Tensors		254
9.6	Displacement Structure for Tensors		257
	9.6.1	Relation to the Polyspectrum	258
	9.6.2	The Linear Case	261
9.7	Polyspectral Interpolation		264
9.8	A Schur-Type Algorithm for Tensors		268
	9.8.1	Review of the Second-Order Case	268
	9.8.2	A Tensor Outer Product	269
	9.8.3	Displacement Generators	272
9.9	Concluding Remarks		275

10 MINIMAL COMPLEXITY REALIZATION OF STRUCTURED MATRICES 277
Patrick Dewilde
- 10.1 Introduction 277
- 10.2 Motivation of Minimal Complexity Representations 278
- 10.3 Displacement Structure 279
- 10.4 Realization Theory for Matrices 280
  - 10.4.1 Nerode Equivalence and Natural State Spaces 283
  - 10.4.2 Algorithm for Finding a Realization 283
- 10.5 Realization of Low Displacement Rank Matrices 286
- 10.6 A Realization for the Cholesky Factor 289
- 10.7 Discussion 293

A USEFUL MATRIX RESULTS 297
Thomas Kailath and Ali H. Sayed
- A.1 Some Matrix Identities 298
- A.2 The Gram–Schmidt Procedure and the QR Decomposition 303
- A.3 Matrix Norms 304
- A.4 Unitary and J-Unitary Transformations 305
- A.5 Two Additional Results 306

B ELEMENTARY TRANSFORMATIONS 309
Thomas Kailath and Ali H. Sayed
- B.1 Elementary Householder Transformations 310
- B.2 Elementary Circular or Givens Rotations 312
- B.3 Hyperbolic Transformations 314

BIBLIOGRAPHY 321

INDEX 339

PREFACE

The design of fast and numerically reliable algorithms for large-scale matrix problems with structure has become an increasingly important activity, especially in recent years, driven by the ever-increasing complexity of applications arising in control, communications, computation, and signal processing.

The major challenge in this area is to develop algorithms that blend speed and numerical accuracy. These two requirements often have been regarded as competitive, so much so that the design of fast and numerically reliable algorithms for large-scale structured linear matrix equations has remained a significant open issue in many instances.

This problem, however, has been receiving increasing attention recently, as witnessed by a series of international meetings held in the last three years in Santa Barbara (USA, Aug. 1996), Cortona (Italy, Sept. 1996), and St. Emilion (France, Aug. 1997). These meetings provided a forum for the exchange of ideas on current developments, trends, and issues in fast and reliable computing among peer research groups. The idea of this book project grew out of these meetings, and the chapters are selections from works presented at the meetings. In the process, several difficult decisions had to be made; the editors beg the indulgence of participants whose contributions could not be included here.

Browsing through the chapters, the reader soon will realize that this project is unlike most edited volumes. The book is not merely a collection of submitted articles; considerable effort went into blending the several chapters into a reasonably consistent presentation. We asked each author to provide a contribution with a significant tutorial value. In this way, the chapters not only provide the reader with an opportunity to review some of the most recent advances in a particular area of research, but they do so with enough background material to put the work into proper context. Next, we carefully revised and revised again each submission to try to improve both clarity and uniformity of presentation. This was a substantial undertaking since we often needed to change symbols across chapters, to add cross-references to other chapters and sections, to reorganize sections, to reduce redundancy, and to try to state theorems, lemmas, and algorithms uniformly across the chapters. We did our best to ensure a uniformity of presentation and notation but, of course, errors and omissions may still exist and we apologize in advance for any of these. We also take this opportunity to thank the authors for their patience and for their collaboration during this time-consuming process. In all we believe the book includes a valuable collection of chapters that cover in some detail different aspects of the most recent trends in the theory of fast algorithms, with emphasis on implementation and application issues.

The book may be divided into four distinct parts:

1. The first four chapters deal with fast *direct* methods for the triangular factorization

of structured matrices, as well as the solution of structured linear systems of equations. The emphasis here is mostly on the generalized Schur algorithm, its numerical properties, and modifications to ensure numerical stability.

2. Chapters 5, 6, and 7 deal with fast *iterative* methods for the solution of structured linear systems of equations. The emphasis here is on the preconditioned conjugate gradient method and on Newton's method.

3. Chapters 8 to 10 deal with extensions of the notion of structure to the block case, the tensor case, and to the input-output framework. Chapter 8 presents fast algorithms for block Toeplitz systems of equations and considers applications in Markov chains and queueing theory. Chapter 9 studies tensor displacement structure and applications in polyspectral interpolation. Chapter 10 discusses realization theory and computational models for structured problems.

4. We have included two appendices that collect several useful matrix results that are used in several places in the book.

Acknowledgments. We gratefully acknowledge the support of the Army Research Office and the National Science Foundation in funding the organization of the Santa Barbara Workshop. Other grants from these agencies, as well as from the Defense Advanced Research Projects Agency and the Air Force Office of Scientific Research, supported the efforts of the editors on this project. We are also grateful to Professors Alan Laub of University of California Davis and Shivkumar Chandrasekaran of University of California Santa Barbara for their support and joint organization with the editors of the 1996 Santa Barbara Workshop. It is also a pleasure to thank Professors M. Najim of the University of Bordeaux and P. Dewilde of Delft University, for their leading role in the St. Emilion Workshop, and Professor D. Bini of the University of Pisa and several of his Italian colleagues, for the fine 1996 Toeplitz Workshop in Cortona.

October 1998

T. Kailath
Stanford, CA

A. H. Sayed
Westwood, CA

NOTATION

$\mathbb{N}$	The set of natural numbers.
$\mathbb{Z}$	The set of integer numbers.
$\mathbb{R}$	The set of real numbers.
$\mathbb{C}$	The set of complex numbers.
$\emptyset$	The empty set.
$\mathcal{C}_{2\pi}$	The set of 2π-periodic complex-valued continuous functions defined on $[-\pi, \pi]$.
$\mathcal{C}_0(\mathbb{R})$	The set of complex-valued continuous functions with bounded support in $\mathbb{R}$.
$\mathcal{C}_b(\mathbb{R})$	The set of bounded and uniformly continuous complex-valued functions over $\mathbb{R}$.
$.^T$	Matrix transposition.
$.^*$	Complex conjugation for scalars and conjugate transposition for matrices.
$a \triangleq b$	The quantity a is defined as b.
$\text{col}\{a, b\}$	A column vector with entries a and b.
$\text{diag}\{a, b\}$	A diagonal matrix with diagonal entries a and b.
$\text{tridiag}\{a, b, c\}$	A tridiagonal Toeplitz matrix with b along its diagonal, a along its lower diagonal, and c along its upper diagonal.
$a \oplus b$	The same as $\text{diag}\{a, b\}$.
$\hat{\imath}$	$\sqrt{-1}$
$\lceil x \rceil$	The smallest integer $m \geq x$.
$\lfloor x \rfloor$	The largest integer $m \leq x$.
0	A zero scalar, vector, or matrix.
I_n	The identify matrix of size $n \times n$.
$\mathcal{L}(x)$	A lower triangular Toeplitz matrix whose first column is x.
$\diamond$	The end of a proof, an example, or a remark.

$\|\cdot\|_2$	The Euclidean norm of a vector or the maximum singular value of a matrix.
$\|\cdot\|_1$	The sum of the absolute values of the entries of a vector or the maximum absolute column sum of a matrix.
$\|\cdot\|_\infty$	The largest absolute entry of a vector or the maximum absolute row sum of a matrix.
$\|\cdot\|_F$	The Frobenius norm of a matrix.
$\|\cdot\|$	Some vector or matrix norm.
$|A|$	A matrix with elements $|a_{ij}|$.
$\lambda_i(A)$	ith eigenvalue of A.
$\sigma_i(A)$	ith singular value of A.
$\kappa(A)$	Condition number of a matrix A, given by $\|A\|_2 \|A^{-1}\|_2$.
$\operatorname{cond}_k(A)$	Equal to $\|A\|_k \|A^{-1}\|_k$.
ε	Machine precision.
$O(n)$	A constant multiple of n, or of the order of n.
$O_n(\varepsilon)$	$O(\varepsilon c(n))$, where $c(n)$ is some polynomial in n.
$\widehat{\cdot}$	A computed quantity in a finite precision algorithm.
$\bar{\cdot}$	An intermediate exact quantity in a finite precision algorithm.
CG	The conjugate gradient method.
LDU	The lower-diagonal-upper triangular factorization of a matrix.
PCG	The preconditioned conjugate gradient method.
QR	The QR factorization of a matrix.

Chapter 1

DISPLACEMENT STRUCTURE AND ARRAY ALGORITHMS

Thomas Kailath

1.1 INTRODUCTION

Many problems in engineering and applied mathematics ultimately require the solution of $n \times n$ linear systems of equations. For small-size problems, there is often not much else to do except to use one of the already standard methods of solution such as Gaussian elimination. However, in many applications, n can be very large ($n \sim 1000, n \sim 1,000,000$) and, moreover, the linear equations may have to be solved over and over again, with different problem or model parameters, until a satisfactory solution to the original physical problem is obtained. In such cases, the $O(n^3)$ burden, i.e., the number of flops required to solve an $n \times n$ linear system of equations, can become prohibitively large. This is one reason why one seeks in various classes of applications to identify special or characteristic structures that may be assumed in order to reduce the computational burden. Of course, there are several different kinds of structure.

A special form of structure, which already has a rich literature, is sparsity; i.e., the coefficient matrices have only a few nonzero entries. We shall not consider this already well studied kind of structure here. Our focus will be on problems, as generally encountered in communications, control, optimization, and signal processing, where the matrices are not sparse but can be very large. In such problems one seeks further assumptions that impose particular patterns among the matrix entries. Among such assumptions (and we emphasize that they are always assumptions) are properties such as time-invariance, homogeneity, stationarity, and rationality, which lead to familiar matrix structures, such as Toeplitz, Hankel, Vandermonde, Cauchy, Pick, etc. Several fast algorithms have been devised over the years to exploit these special structures. The numerical (accuracy and stability) properties of several of these algorithms also have been studied, although, as we shall see from the chapters in this volume, the subject is by no means closed even for such familiar objects as Toeplitz and Vandermonde matrices.

In this book, we seek to broaden the above universe of discourse by noting that even more common than the *explicit* matrix structures, noted above, are matrices in which the structure is *implicit*. For example, in least-squares problems one often encounters products of Toeplitz matrices; these products generally are not Toeplitz, but on the other hand they are not "unstructured." Similarly, in probabilistic calculations the matrix of interest often is not a Toeplitz covariance matrix, but rather its inverse, which is rarely

Toeplitz itself, but of course is not unstructured: its inverse is Toeplitz. It is well known that $O(n^2)$ flops suffice to solve linear systems with an $n \times n$ Toeplitz coefficient matrix; a question is whether we will need $O(n^3)$ flops to invert a non-Toeplitz coefficient matrix whose inverse is known to be Toeplitz. When pressed, one's response clearly must be that it is conceivable that $O(n^2)$ flops will suffice, and we shall show that this is in fact true.

Such problems, and several others that we shall encounter in later chapters, suggest the need for a *quantitative* way of defining and identifying structure in (dense) matrices. Over the years we have found that an elegant and useful way is the concept of *displacement structure*. This has been useful for a host of problems apparently far removed from the solution of linear equations, such as the study of constrained and unconstrained rational interpolation, maximum entropy extension, signal detection, system identification, digital filter design, nonlinear Riccati differential equations, inverse scattering, certain Fredholm and Wiener–Hopf integral equations, etc. However, in this book we shall focus attention largely on displacement structure in matrix computations. For more general earlier reviews, we may refer to [KVM78], [Kai86], [Kai91], [HR84], [KS95a].

1.2 TOEPLITZ MATRICES

The concept of displacement structure is perhaps best introduced by considering the much-studied special case of a Hermitian Toeplitz matrix,

$$T = \begin{bmatrix} c_0 & c_{-1} & c_{-2} & \cdots & c_{-n+1} \\ c_1 & c_0 & c_{-1} & \cdots & c_{-n+2} \\ \vdots & \vdots & \ddots & \vdots & \vdots \\ c_{n-1} & c_{n-2} & \cdots & c_1 & c_0 \end{bmatrix}, \quad c_k = c^*_{-k}. \qquad (1.2.1)$$

The matrix T has constant entries along its diagonals and, hence, it depends only on n parameters rather than n^2. As stated above, it is therefore not surprising that many matrix problems involving T, such as triangular factorization, orthogonalization, and inversion, have solution complexity $O(n^2)$ rather than $O(n^3)$ operations. The issue is the complexity of such problems for inverses, products, and related combinations of Toeplitz matrices such as $T^{-1}, T_1 T_2, T_1 - T_2 T_3^{-1} T_4, (T_1 T_2)^{-1} T_3 \ldots$. As mentioned earlier, although these are not Toeplitz, they are certainly structured and the complexity of inversion and factorization may be expected to be not much different from that for a pure Toeplitz matrix, T. It turns out that the appropriate common property of all these matrices is not their "Toeplitzness," but the fact that they all have (low) *displacement rank* in a sense first defined in [KKM79a], [KKM79b] and later much studied and generalized. When the displacement rank is r, $r \leq n$, the solution complexity of the above problems turns out to be $O(rn^2)$. Now for some formal definitions.

The displacement of a Hermitian matrix $R = [r_{ij}]_{i,j=0}^{n-1} \in \mathbb{C}^{n \times n}$ was originally[1] defined in [KKM79a], [KKM79b] as

$$\nabla_Z R \triangleq R - ZRZ^*, \qquad (1.2.2)$$

---

[1] Other definitions will be introduced later. We may note that the concept was first identified in studying integral equations (see, e.g., [KLM78]).

Section 1.2. Toeplitz Matrices

where $*$ denotes Hermitian conjugation (complex conjugation for scalars) and Z is the $n \times n$ lower shift matrix with ones on the first subdiagonal and zeros elsewhere,

$$Z \triangleq \begin{bmatrix} 0 & & & & \\ 1 & 0 & & & \\ & 1 & 0 & & \\ & & \ddots & \ddots & \\ & & & 1 & 0 \end{bmatrix}. \qquad (1.2.3)$$

The product ZRZ^* then corresponds to shifting R downward along the main diagonal by one position, explaining the name *displacement* for $\nabla_Z R$. The situation is depicted in Fig. 1.1.

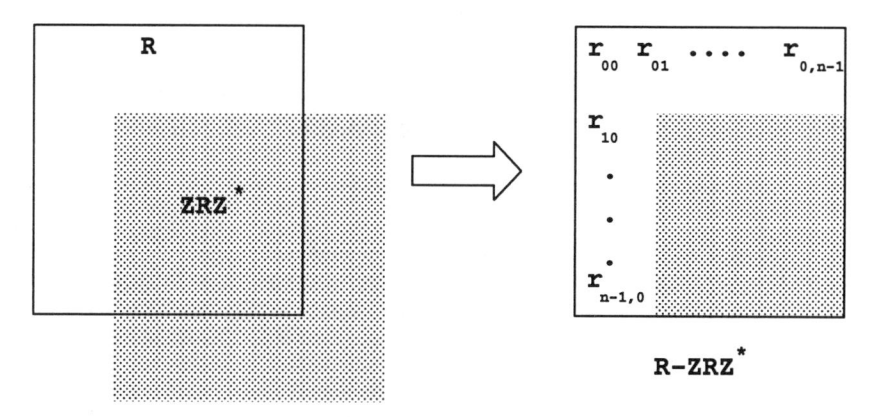

Figure 1.1. $\nabla_Z R$ is obtained by shifting R downward along the diagonal.

If $\nabla_Z R$ has (low) rank, say, r, *independent* of n, then R is said to be *structured* with respect to the displacement ∇_Z defined by (1.2.2), and r is called the *displacement rank* of R. The definition can be extended to non-Hermitian matrices, and this will be briefly described later. Here we may note that in the Hermitian case, $\nabla_Z R$ is Hermitian and therefore has further structure: its eigenvalues are real and so we can define the *displacement inertia* of R as the pair $\{p, q\}$, where p (respectively, q) is the number of strictly positive (respectively, negative) eigenvalues of $\nabla_Z R$. Of course, the displacement rank is $r = p + q$. Therefore, we can write

$$\nabla_Z R = R - ZRZ^* = GJG^*, \qquad (1.2.4)$$

where $J = J^* = (I_p \oplus -I_q)$ is a signature matrix and $G \in \mathbb{C}^{n \times r}$. The pair $\{G, J\}$ is called a ∇_Z-*generator* of R. This representation is clearly not unique; for example, $\{G\Theta, J\}$ is also a generator for any J-unitary matrix Θ (i.e., for any Θ such that $\Theta J \Theta^* = J$). This is because

$$G \underbrace{\Theta J \Theta^*}_{J} G^* = GJG^*.$$

Nonminimal generators (where G has more than r columns) are sometimes useful, although we shall not consider them here.

Returning to the Toeplitz matrix (1.2.1), it is easy to see that T has displacement rank 2, except when all c_i, $i \neq 0$, are zero, a case we shall exclude. Assuming

$c_0 = 1$, a generator for T is $\{x_0, y_0, (1 \oplus -1)\}$, where $x_0 = \text{col}\{1, c_1, \ldots, c_{n-1}\}$ and $y_0 = \text{col}\{0, c_1, \ldots, c_{n-1}\}$ (the notation $\text{col}\{\cdot\}$ denotes a column vector with the specified entries):

$$T - ZTZ^* = \begin{bmatrix} 1 & 0 \\ c_1 & c_1 \\ \vdots & \vdots \\ c_{n-1} & c_{n-1} \end{bmatrix} \begin{bmatrix} 1 & 0 \\ 0 & -1 \end{bmatrix} \begin{bmatrix} 1 & 0 \\ c_1 & c_1 \\ \vdots & \vdots \\ c_{n-1} & c_{n-1} \end{bmatrix}^*. \quad (1.2.5)$$

It will be shown later that if we define $T^\# \triangleq \tilde{I} T^{-1} \tilde{I}$, where $\tilde{I}$ denotes the reversed identity with ones on the reversed diagonal and zeros elsewhere, then $T^\#$ also has ∇_Z-displacement inertia $\{1, 1\}$. The product $T_1 T_2$ of two Toeplitz matrices, which may not be Hermitian, will be shown to have displacement rank ≤ 4. The significance of displacement rank with respect to the solution of linear equations is that the complexity can be reduced to $O(rn^2)$ from $O(n^3)$.

The well-known Levinson algorithm [Lev47] is one illustration of this fact. The best-known form of this algorithm (independently obtained by Durbin [Dur59]) refers to the so-called Yule–Walker system of equations

$$a_n T_n = \begin{bmatrix} 0 & 0 & \cdots & 0 & \sigma_n^2 \end{bmatrix}, \quad (1.2.6)$$

where $a_n = \begin{bmatrix} a_{n,n} & a_{n,n-1} & \cdots & a_{n,1} & 1 \end{bmatrix}$ and σ_n^2 are the $(n+1)$ unknowns and T_n is a positive-definite $(n+1) \times (n+1)$ Toeplitz matrix. The easily derived and now well-known recursions for the solution are

$$\begin{bmatrix} a_{i+1} \\ a_{i+1}^\# \end{bmatrix} = \begin{bmatrix} 1 & -\gamma_{i+1} \\ -\gamma_{i+1}^* & 1 \end{bmatrix} \begin{bmatrix} 0 & a_i \\ a_i^\# & 0 \end{bmatrix}, \quad a_0 = a_0^\# = 1, \quad (1.2.7)$$

where $\gamma_{i+1} = \delta_i / \sigma_i^2$,

$$\delta_i = a_{i,i} c_1 + a_{i,i-1} c_2 + \cdots + a_{i,1} c_i + c_{i+1}, \quad (1.2.8)$$

$$\sigma_{i+1}^2 = \sigma_i^2 [1 - |\gamma_{i+1}|^2], \quad \sigma_0^2 = c_0, \quad (1.2.9)$$

and

$$a_i^\# = \begin{bmatrix} 1 & a_{i,1}^* & \cdots & a_{i,i}^* \end{bmatrix}.$$

The above recursions are closely related to certain (nonrecursive[2]) formulas given by Szegő [Sze39] and Geronimus [Ger54] for polynomials orthogonal on the unit circle, as discussed in some detail in [Kai91]. It is easy to check that the $\{\gamma_i\}$ are all less than one in magnitude; in signal processing applications, they are often called reflection coefficients (see, e.g., [Kai85], [Kai86]).

While the Levinson–Durbin algorithm is widely used, it has limitations for certain applications. For one thing, it requires the formation of inner products and therefore is not efficiently parallelizable, requiring $O(n \log n)$ rather than $O(n)$ flops, with $O(n)$ processors. Second, while it can be extended to indefinite and even non-Hermitian Toeplitz matrices, it is difficult to extend it to non-Toeplitz matrices having displacement structure. Another problem is numerical. An error analysis of the algorithm in [Cyb80] showed that in the case of positive reflection coefficients $\{\gamma_i\}$, the residual error produced by the Levinson–Durbin procedure is comparable to the error produced

---
[2] They defined γ_i as $-a_{i+1,i+1}$.

Section 1.2. Toeplitz Matrices

by the numerically well-behaved Cholesky factorization [GV96, p. 191]. Thus in this special case the Levinson–Durbin algorithm is what is called *weakly stable*, in the sense of [Bun85], [Bun87]—see Sec. 4.2 of this book. No stability results seem to be available for the Levinson–Durbin algorithm for Toeplitz matrices with general $\{\gamma_i\}$.

To motivate an alternative (parallelizable and stable) approach to the problem, we first show that the Levinson–Durbin algorithm directly yields a (fast) triangular factorization of T_n^{-1}. To show this, note that stacking the successive solutions of the Yule–Walker equations (1.2.6) in a lower triangular matrix yields the equality

$$\begin{bmatrix} 1 & & & & \\ a_{11} & 1 & & & \\ a_{22} & a_{21} & 1 & & \\ \vdots & & & \ddots & \\ a_{n,n} & a_{n,n-1} & \cdots & & 1 \end{bmatrix} T_n \begin{bmatrix} 1 & & & & \\ a_{11} & 1 & & & \\ a_{22} & a_{21} & 1 & & \\ \vdots & & & \ddots & \\ a_{n,n} & a_{n,n-1} & \cdots & & 1 \end{bmatrix}^*$$

$$= \begin{bmatrix} \sigma_0^2 & \times & \times & \times & \times \\ & \sigma_1^2 & \times & \times & \times \\ & & \sigma_2^2 & \times & \times \\ & & & \ddots & \times \\ & & & & \sigma_n^2 \end{bmatrix},$$

which, using the Hermitian nature of T, yields the unique triangular factorization of the *inverse* of T_n:

(1.2.10)
$$T_n^{-1} = \begin{bmatrix} 1 & a_{11}^* & a_{22}^* & \cdots & a_{nn}^* \\ & 1 & a_{21}^* & \cdots & a_{n,n-1}^* \\ & & & \ddots & \vdots \\ & & & & 1 \end{bmatrix} D_n^{-1} \begin{bmatrix} 1 & & & & \\ a_{11} & 1 & & & \\ a_{22} & a_{21} & 1 & & \\ \vdots & & & \ddots & \\ a_{n,n} & a_{n,n-1} & \cdots & & 1 \end{bmatrix},$$

where $D_n = \text{diag}\{\sigma_0^2, \sigma_1^2, \ldots, \sigma_n^2\}$.

However, it is a fact, borne out by results in many different problems, that ultimately even for the solution of linear equations the (direct) triangular factorization of T rather than T^{-1} is more fundamental. Such insights can be traced back to the celebrated Wiener–Hopf technique [WH31] but, as perhaps first noted by Von Neumann and by Turing (see, e.g., [Ste73]), direct factorization is the key feature of the fundamental Gaussian elimination method for solving linear equations and was effectively noted as such by Gauss himself (though of course not in matrix notation).

Now a fast direct factorization of T_n cannot be obtained merely by inverting the factorization (1.2.10) of T_n^{-1}, because that will require $O(n^3)$ flops. The first fast algorithm was given by Schur [Sch17], although this fact was realized only much later in [DVK78]. In the meantime, a closely related direct factorization algorithm was derived by Bareiss [Bar69], and this is the designation used in the numerical analysis community. Morf [Mor70], [Mor74], Rissanen [Ris73], and LeRoux–Gueguen [LG77] also made independent rediscoveries.

We shall show in Sec. 1.7.7 that the Schur algorithm can also be applied to solve Toeplitz linear equations, at the cost of about 30% more computations than via the Levinson–Durbin algorithm. However, in return we can compute the reflection coefficients without using inner products, the algorithm has better numerical properties (see Chs. 2–4 and also [BBHS95], [CS96]), and as we shall show below, it can be elegantly and usefully extended by exploiting the concept of displacement structure. These generalizations are helpful in solving the many classes of problems (e.g., interpolation) mentioned earlier (at the end of Sec. 1.1). Therefore, our major focus in this chapter will be on what we have called generalized Schur algorithms.

First, however, let us make a few more observations on displacement structure.

1.3 VERSIONS OF DISPLACEMENT STRUCTURE

There are of course other kinds of displacement structure than those introduced in Sec. 1.2, as already noted in [KKM79a]. For example, it can be checked that

$$\text{rank}\,(Z_{-1}T - TZ) = 2, \tag{1.3.1}$$

where Z_{-1} denotes the circulant matrix with first row $\begin{bmatrix} 0 & \ldots & 0 & -1 \end{bmatrix}$. This fact has been used by Heinig [Hei95] and by [GKO95] to obtain alternatives to the Levinson–Durbin and Schur algorithms for solving Toeplitz systems of linear equations, as will be discussed later in this chapter (Sec. 1.13). However, a critical point is that because Z_{-1} is not triangular, these methods apply only to fixed n, and the whole solution has to be repeated if the size is increased even by one. Since many applications in communications, control, and signal processing involve continuing streams of data, recursive triangular factorization is often a critical requirement. It can be shown [LK86] that such factorization requires that triangular matrices be used in the definition of displacement structure, which is what we shall do henceforth.

One of the first extensions of definition (1.2.2) was to consider

$$\nabla_F R \triangleq R - FRF^*, \tag{1.3.2}$$

where, for reasons mentioned above, F is a lower triangular matrix; see [LK84], [CKL87]. One motivation for such extensions will be seen in Sec. 1.8. Another is that one can include matrices such as Vandermonde, Cauchy, Pick, etc. For example, consider the so-called Pick matrix, which occurs in the study of analytic interpolation problems,

$$P = \left[\frac{u_i u_i^* - v_j v_j^*}{1 - f_i f_j^*}\right]_{i,j=0}^{n-1},$$

where $\{u_i, v_i\}$ are row vectors of dimensions p and q, respectively, and f_i are complex points inside the open unit disc ($|f_i| < 1$). If we let F denote the diagonal matrix diag$\{f_0, f_1, \ldots, f_{n-1}\}$, then it can be verified that P has displacement rank $(p+q)$ with respect to F since

$$P - FPF^* = \begin{bmatrix} u_0 & v_0 \\ u_1 & v_1 \\ \vdots & \vdots \\ u_{n-1} & v_{n-1} \end{bmatrix} \begin{bmatrix} I_p & 0 \\ 0 & -I_q \end{bmatrix} \begin{bmatrix} u_0 & v_0 \\ u_1 & v_1 \\ \vdots & \vdots \\ u_{n-1} & v_{n-1} \end{bmatrix}^*.$$

In general, one can write for Hermitian $R \in \mathbb{C}^{n \times n}$,

$$\nabla_F R = R - FRF^* = GJG^*, \tag{1.3.3}$$

for some triangular $F \in \mathbb{C}^{n \times n}$, a signature matrix $J = (I_p \oplus -I_q) \in \mathbb{C}^{r \times r}$, and $G \in \mathbb{C}^{n \times r}$, with r independent of n. The pair $\{G, J\}$ will be called a ∇_F-generator

Section 1.3. Versions of Displacement Structure

of R. Because Toeplitz and, as we shall see later, several Toeplitz-related matrices are best studied via this definition, matrices with low ∇_F-displacement rank will be called *Toeplitz-like*. However, this is strictly a matter of convenience.

We can also consider non-Hermitian matrices R, in which case the displacement can be defined as

$$\nabla_{F,A} R \triangleq R - FRA^*, \tag{1.3.4}$$

where F and A are $n \times n$ lower triangular matrices. In some cases, F and A may coincide—see (1.3.7) below. When $\nabla_{F,A} R$ has low rank, say, r, we can factor it (nonuniquely) as

$$\nabla_{F,A} R = GB^*, \tag{1.3.5}$$

where G and B are also called generator matrices,

$$R - FRA^* = GB^*. \tag{1.3.6}$$

One particular example is the case of a non-Hermitian Toeplitz matrix $T = [c_{i-j}]_{i,j=0}^{n-1}$, which can be seen to satisfy

$$T - ZTZ^* = \begin{bmatrix} c_0 & 1 \\ c_1 & 0 \\ \vdots & \vdots \\ c_{n-1} & 0 \end{bmatrix} \begin{bmatrix} 1 & 0 \\ 0 & c_{-1}^* \\ \vdots & \vdots \\ 0 & c_{-n+1}^* \end{bmatrix}^*. \tag{1.3.7}$$

This is a special case of (1.3.6) with $F = A = Z$.

A second example is a Vandermonde matrix,

$$V = \begin{bmatrix} 1 & \alpha_1 & \alpha_1^2 & \cdots & \alpha_1^{n-1} \\ 1 & \alpha_2 & \alpha_2^2 & \cdots & \alpha_2^{n-1} \\ \vdots & \vdots & \vdots & & \vdots \\ 1 & \alpha_n & \alpha_n^2 & \cdots & \alpha_n^{n-1} \end{bmatrix}, \tag{1.3.8}$$

which can be seen to satisfy

$$\nabla_{F,Z} V = V - FVZ^* = \begin{bmatrix} 1 \\ 1 \\ \vdots \\ 1 \end{bmatrix} \begin{bmatrix} 1 & 0 & \cdots & 0 \end{bmatrix}, \tag{1.3.9}$$

where F is now the diagonal matrix $F = \text{diag}\{\alpha_1, \ldots, \alpha_n\}$.

Another common form of displacement structure, first introduced by Heinig and Rost [HR84], is what we call, again strictly for convenience, a Hankel-like structure. We shall say that a matrix $R \in \mathbb{C}^{n \times n}$ is Hankel-like if it satisfies a displacement equation of the form

$$FR - RA^* = GB^*, \tag{1.3.10}$$

for some lower triangular $F \in \mathbb{C}^{n \times n}$ and $A \in \mathbb{C}^{n \times n}$, and generator matrices $G \in \mathbb{C}^{n \times r}$ and $B \in \mathbb{C}^{n \times r}$, with r independent of n. When R is Hermitian, it is more convenient to express the displacement equation as

$$FR + RF^* = GJG^* \tag{1.3.11}$$

for some generator matrix $G \in \mathbb{C}^{n \times r}$ and signature matrix J that satisfies $J = J^*$ and $J^2 = I$. To avoid a notation explosion, we shall occasionally use the notation $\nabla_{F,A} R$ for both Toeplitz-like and Hankel-like structures.

As an illustration, consider a Hankel matrix, which is a symmetric matrix with real constant entries along the antidiagonals,

$$H = \begin{bmatrix} h_0 & h_1 & h_2 & \cdots & h_{n-1} \\ h_1 & h_2 & & \cdot & h_n \\ h_2 & & \cdot & & \vdots \\ \vdots & \cdot & & & \vdots \\ h_{n-1} & h_n & & \cdots & h_{2n-1} \end{bmatrix}. \quad (1.3.12)$$

It can be verified that the difference $ZH - HZ^*$ has rank 2 since

$$\hat{\imath}(ZH - HZ^*) = \hat{\imath} \cdot \begin{bmatrix} 0 & -h_0 & -h_1 & \cdots & -h_{n-2} \\ h_0 & & & & \\ h_1 & & O & & \\ \vdots & & & & \\ h_{n-2} & & & & \end{bmatrix}, \quad (1.3.13)$$

$$= \begin{bmatrix} 1 & 0 \\ 0 & h_0 \\ 0 & h_1 \\ \vdots & \vdots \\ 0 & h_{n-2} \end{bmatrix} \underbrace{\begin{bmatrix} 0 & -\hat{\imath} \\ \hat{\imath} & 0 \end{bmatrix}}_{J} \begin{bmatrix} 1 & 0 \\ 0 & h_0 \\ 0 & h_1 \\ \vdots & \vdots \\ 0 & h_{n-2} \end{bmatrix}^T.$$

We therefore say that H has displacement rank 2 with respect to the displacement operation (1.3.11) with $F = \hat{\imath} Z$ and J as above. Here, $\hat{\imath} = \sqrt{-1}$ and is introduced in order to obtain a J that satisfies the normalization conditions $J = J^*$, $J^2 = I$.

A problem that arises here is that H cannot be fully recovered from its displacement representation, because the entries $\{h_{n-1}, \ldots, h_{2n-2}\}$ do not appear in (1.3.14). This "difficulty" can be accommodated in various ways (see, e.g., [CK91b], [HR84], [KS95a]). One way is to border H with zeros and then form the displacement, which will now have rank 4. Another method is to form the $2n \times 2n$ (triangular) Hankel matrix with top row $\{h_0, \ldots, h_{2n-1}\}$; now the displacement rank will be two; however, note that in both cases the generators have the same number of entries. In general, the problem is that the displacement equation does not have a unique solution. This will happen when the displacement operator in (1.3.3)–(1.3.6) or (1.3.10)–(1.3.11) has a nontrivial nullspace or kernel. In this case, the generator has to be supplemented by some additional information, which varies from case to case. A detailed discussion, with several examples, is given in [KO96], [KO98].

Other examples of Hankel-like structures include Loewner matrices, Cauchy matrices, and Cauchy-like matrices, encountered, for example, in the study of unconstrained rational interpolation problems (see, e.g., [AA86], [Fie85], [Vav91]). The entries of an $n \times n$ Cauchy-like matrix R have the form

$$C_l = \left[\frac{u_i v_j^*}{f_i - a_j^*} \right]_{i,j=0}^{n-1},$$

Section 1.3. Versions of Displacement Structure

where u_i and v_j denote $1 \times r$ row vectors and the $\{f_i, a_i\}$ are scalars. The Loewner matrix is a special Cauchy-like matrix that corresponds to the choices $r = 2$, $u_i = \begin{bmatrix} \beta_i & 1 \end{bmatrix}$, and $v_i = \begin{bmatrix} 1 & -\kappa_i \end{bmatrix}$, and, consequently, $u_i v_j^* = \beta_i - \kappa_j^*$:

$$L_w = \left[\frac{\beta_i - \kappa_j^*}{f_i - a_j^*} \right]_{i,j=0}^{n-1}.$$

Cauchy matrices, on the other hand, arise from the choices $r = 1$ and $u_i = 1 = v_i$:

$$C = \left[\frac{1}{f_i - a_j^*} \right]_{i,j=0}^{n-1}.$$

It is easy to verify that a Cauchy-like matrix is Hankel-like since it satisfies a displacement equation of the form

$$FC_l - C_l A^* = \begin{bmatrix} u_0 \\ u_1 \\ \vdots \\ u_{n-1} \end{bmatrix} \begin{bmatrix} v_0 \\ v_1 \\ \vdots \\ v_{n-1} \end{bmatrix}^*, \qquad (1.3.14)$$

where F and A are diagonal matrices:

$$F = \text{diagonal}\{f_0, \ldots, f_{n-1}\}, \quad A = \text{diagonal}\{a_0, \ldots, a_{n-1}\}.$$

Hence, Loewner and Cauchy matrices are also Hankel-like. Another simple example is the Vandermonde matrix (1.3.8) itself, since it satisfies not only (1.3.9) but also

$$AV - VZ^* = \begin{bmatrix} \frac{1}{\alpha_1} \\ \frac{1}{\alpha_2} \\ \vdots \\ \frac{1}{\alpha_n} \end{bmatrix} \begin{bmatrix} 1 & 0 & \cdots & 0 \end{bmatrix}, \qquad (1.3.15)$$

where A is the diagonal matrix (assuming $\alpha_i \neq 0$)

$$A = \text{diagonal}\left\{\frac{1}{\alpha_1}, \ldots, \frac{1}{\alpha_n}\right\}.$$

Clearly, the distinction between Toeplitz-like and Hankel-like structures is not very tight, since many matrices can have both kinds of structure including Toeplitz matrices themselves (cf. (1.2.5) and (1.3.1)).

Toeplitz- and Hankel-like structures can be regarded as special cases of the generalized displacement structure [KS91], [Say92], [SK95a], [KS95a]:

$$\Omega R \Delta^* - FRA^* = GB^*, \qquad (1.3.16)$$

where $\{\Omega, \Delta, F, A\}$ are $n \times n$ and $\{G, B\}$ are $n \times r$. Such equations uniquely define R when the diagonal entries $\{\omega_i, \delta_i, f_i, a_i\}$ of the displacement operators $\{\Omega, \Delta, F, A\}$ satisfy

$$\omega_i \delta_j^* - f_i a_j^* \neq 0 \quad \text{for all } i, j. \qquad (1.3.17)$$

This explains the difficulty we had in the Hankel case, where the diagonal entries of $F = A = Z$ in (1.3.14) violate the above condition. The restriction that $\{\Omega, \Delta, F, A\}$ are lower triangular is the most general one that allows recursive triangular factorization (cf. a result in [LK86]). As mentioned earlier, since this is a critical feature in most of our applications, we shall assume this henceforth.

The Generating Function Formulation

We may remark that when $\{\Omega, \Delta, F, A\}$ are lower triangular Toeplitz, we can use generating function notation—see [LK84], [LK86]; these can be extended to more general $\{\Omega, \Delta, F, A\}$ by using divided difference matrices—see [Lev83], [Lev97]. The generating function formulation enables connections to be made with complex function theory and especially with the extensive theory of reproducing kernel Hilbert spaces of entire functions (deBranges spaces)—see, e.g., [AD86], [Dym89b], [AD92].

Let us briefly illustrate this for the special cases of Toeplitz and Hankel matrices, $T = [c_{i-j}]$, $H = [h_{i+j}]$. To use the generating function language, we assume that the matrices are semi-infinite, i.e., $i, j \in [0, \infty)$. Then straightforward calculation will yield, assuming $c_0 = 1$, the expression

$$T(z, w) \triangleq \sum_{i=0}^{\infty} \sum_{j=0}^{\infty} c_{i-j} z^i w^{*j} = \frac{c(z) + c^*(w)}{2(1 - zw^*)}, \quad (1.3.18)$$

where $c(z)$ is (a so-called Carathéodory function)

$$c(z) = 1 + 2 \sum_{i=1}^{\infty} c_j z^j.$$

The expression can also be rewritten as

$$T(z, w) = \frac{G_1(z) J_1 G_1^*(w)}{d_1(z, w)},$$

where

$$G_1(z) = \begin{bmatrix} \frac{c(z)+1}{2} & \frac{c(z)-1}{2} \end{bmatrix}, \quad J_1 = \begin{bmatrix} 1 & 0 \\ 0 & -1 \end{bmatrix}, \quad d_1(z, w) = 1 - zw^*.$$

In the Hankel case, we can write

$$H(z, w) \triangleq \sum_{i=0}^{\infty} \sum_{j=0}^{\infty} h_{i+1} z^i w^{*j} = \frac{zh(z) - w^* h^*(w)}{\hat{\imath}(z - w^*)} = \frac{G_2(z) J_2 G_2^*(w)}{d_2(z, w)},$$

where

$$G_2(z) = \begin{bmatrix} 1 & zh(z) \end{bmatrix}, \quad h(z) = \sum_{j=0}^{\infty} h_j z^j,$$

and

$$d_2(z) = \hat{\imath}(z - w^*), \quad J = \begin{bmatrix} 0 & -\hat{\imath} \\ \hat{\imath} & 0 \end{bmatrix}, \quad \hat{\imath} = \sqrt{-1}.$$

Generalizations can be obtained by using more complex $\{G(\cdot), J\}$ matrices and with

$$d(z, w) = \sum_{i=0}^{\infty} \sum_{j=0}^{\infty} d_{ij} z^i w^{*j}.$$

However, to admit recursive triangular factorization, one must assume that $d(z, w)$ has the form (see [LK86])

$$d(z, w) = a(z) a^*(w) - b(z) b^*(w).$$

Section 1.3. Versions of Displacement Structure

for some $\{a(z), b(z)\}$. The choice of $d(z,w)$ also has a geometric significance. For example, $d_1(z,w)$ partitions the complex plane with respect to the unit circle, as follows:

$$\Omega_o = \{z: 1 - |z|^2 = 0\}, \quad \Omega_+ = \{z: |z| > 1\}, \quad \Omega_- = \{z: |z| < 1\}.$$

Similarly, $d_2(z,w)$ partitions the plane with respect to the real axis. If we used $d_3(z,w) = z + w^*$, we would partition the plane with respect to the imaginary axis.

We may also note that the matrix forms of

$$d_1(z,w)R(z,w) = G_1(z)JG_1^*(w)$$

will be, in an obvious notation,

$$\mathcal{R} - \mathcal{Z}\mathcal{R}\mathcal{Z}^* = \mathcal{G}_1 J_1 \mathcal{G}_1^*, \tag{1.3.19}$$

while using $d_2(z,w)$ it will be

$$\hat{\imath}(\mathcal{Z}\mathcal{R} - \mathcal{R}\mathcal{Z}^*) = \mathcal{G}_2 J_2 \mathcal{G}_2^*. \tag{1.3.20}$$

Here, $\mathcal{Z}$ denotes the semi-infinite lower triangular shift matrix. Likewise, $\{\mathcal{R}, \mathcal{G}_1, \mathcal{G}_2\}$ denote semi-infinite matrices.

We shall not pursue the generating function descriptions further here. They are useful, inter alia, for studying root distribution problems (see, e.g., [LBK91]) and, as mentioned above, for making connections with the mathematical literature, especially the Russian school of operator theory. A minor reason for introducing these descriptions here is that they further highlight connections between displacement structure theory and the study of discrete-time and continuous-time systems, as we now explain briefly.

Lyapunov, Stein, and Displacement Equations

When $J = I$, (1.3.19) and (1.3.20) are the discrete-time and continuous-time Lyapunov equations much studied in system theory, where the association between discrete-time systems and the unit circle and continuous-time systems and half-planes, is well known. There are also well-known transformations (see [Kai80, p. 180]) between discrete-time and continuous-time (state-space) systems, so that in principle all results for Toeplitz-like displacement operators can be converted into the appropriate results for Hankel-like operators. This is one reason that we shall largely restrict ourselves here to the Toeplitz-like Hermitian structure (1.3.3); more general results can be found in [KS95a].

A further remark is that equations of the form (1.3.10), but with general right sides, are sometimes called Sylvester equations, while those of the form (1.3.6) are called Stein equations. For our studies, low-rank factorizations of the right side as in (1.3.10) and (1.3.6) and especially (1.3.11) and (1.3.3) are critical (as we shall illustrate immediately), which is why we call these special forms *displacement equations*.

Finally, as we shall briefly note in Sec. 1.14.1, there is an even more general version of displacement theory applying to "time-variant" matrices (see, e.g., [SCK94], [SLK94b], [CSK95]). These extensions are useful, for example, in adaptive filtering applications and also in matrix completion problems and interpolation problems, where matrices change with time but in such a way that certain displacement differences undergo only low-rank variations.

A Summary

To summarize, there are several ways to characterize the structure of a matrix, using for example (1.3.6), (1.3.10), or (1.3.16). However, in all cases, the main idea is to describe an $n \times n$ matrix R more compactly by $n \times r$ generator matrices $\{G, B\}$, with $r \ll n$. Since the generators have $2rn$ entries, as compared to n^2 entries in R, a computational gain of one order of magnitude can in general be expected from algorithms that operate on the generators directly.

The implications of this fact turn out to be far reaching and have connections with many other areas; see, e.g., [KS95a] and the references therein. In this chapter, we focus mainly on results that are relevant to matrix computations and that are also of interest to the discussions in the later chapters.

The first part of our presentation focuses exclusively on strongly regular Hermitian Toeplitz-like matrices, viz., those that satisfy

$$R - FRF^* = GJG^*, \quad J = J^*, \quad J^2 = I, \tag{1.3.21}$$

for some full rank $n \times r$ matrix G, with $r \ll n$, and lower triangular F. We also assume that the diagonal entries of F satisfy

$$1 - f_i f_j^* \neq 0 \quad \text{for all } i, j \tag{1.3.22}$$

so that (1.3.21) defines R uniquely. Once the main ideas have been presented for this case, we shall then briefly state the results for non-Hermitian Toeplitz-like and Hankel-like matrices. A more detailed exposition for these latter cases, and for generalized displacement equations (1.3.16), can be found in [Say92], [KS95a], [SK95a].

1.4 APPLICATION TO THE FAST EVALUATION OF MATRIX-VECTOR PRODUCTS

The evaluation of matrix-vector products is an important ingredient of several fast algorithms (see, e.g., Chs. 5 and 8), and we discuss it briefly here.

Consider an $n \times n$ Hermitian matrix R with (Toeplitz-like) displacement generator $\{Z, G, J\}$ as in (1.2.4). Given G, we can deduce an explicit representation for R in terms of the columns of G. Indeed, using the fact that Z is a nilpotent matrix, viz., $Z^n = 0$, we can check that the unique solution of (1.2.4) is

$$R = \sum_{i=0}^{n-1} Z^i GJG^* Z^{*i}. \tag{1.4.1}$$

Let us partition the columns of G into two sets $\{x_i\}_{i=0}^{p-1}$ and $\{y_i\}_{i=0}^{q-1}$,

$$G \triangleq \begin{bmatrix} x_0 & x_1 & \cdots & x_{p-1} & y_0 & y_1 & \cdots & y_{q-1} \end{bmatrix}, \quad p + q = r.$$

It is then easy to see that (1.4.1) is equivalent to the representation

$$R = \sum_{i=0}^{p-1} \mathcal{L}(x_i)\mathcal{L}^*(x_i) - \sum_{i=0}^{q-1} \mathcal{L}(y_i)\mathcal{L}^*(y_i), \tag{1.4.2}$$

where the notation $\mathcal{L}(x)$ denotes a lower triangular Toeplitz matrix whose first column is x, e.g.,

$$\mathcal{L}\left(\begin{bmatrix} a \\ b \\ c \end{bmatrix}\right) = \begin{bmatrix} a & 0 & 0 \\ b & a & 0 \\ c & b & a \end{bmatrix}.$$

Formula (1.4.2) expresses matrices R with displacement structure (1.2.4) in terms of products of triangular Toeplitz matrices. The special cases of Toeplitz matrices and their inverses and products are nice examples.

Among other applications (see, e.g., [KVM78]), the representation (1.4.2) can be exploited to speed up matrix-vector products of the form Ra for any column vector a. In general, such products require $O(n^2)$ operations. Using (1.4.2), the computational cost can be reduced to $O(rn \log 2n)$ by using the fast Fourier transform (FFT) technique. This is because, in view of (1.4.2), evaluating the product Ra involves evaluating products of lower or upper triangular *Toeplitz* matrices by vectors, which is equivalent to a convolution operation. For related applications, see [BP94], [GO94c], and Ch. 5.

1.5 TWO FUNDAMENTAL PROPERTIES

Two fundamental *invariance* properties that underlie displacement structure theory are

(a) invariance of displacement structure under inversion and

(b) invariance of displacement structure under Schur complementation.

Lemma 1.5.1 (Inversion). *If R is an $n \times n$ invertible matrix that satisfies (1.3.21) for some full rank $G \in \mathbb{C}^{n \times r}$, then there must exist a full rank matrix $H \in \mathbb{C}^{r \times n}$ such that*

$$R^{-1} - F^* R^{-1} F = H^* J H . \qquad (1.5.1)$$

Proof: The block matrix

$$\begin{bmatrix} R & F \\ F^* & R^{-1} \end{bmatrix}$$

admits the following block triangular decompositions (cf. App. A):

$$\begin{bmatrix} R & F \\ F^* & R^{-1} \end{bmatrix} = \begin{bmatrix} I & 0 \\ F^* R^{-1} & I \end{bmatrix} \begin{bmatrix} R & 0 \\ 0 & R^{-1} - F^* R^{-1} F \end{bmatrix} \begin{bmatrix} I & 0 \\ F^* R^{-1} & I \end{bmatrix}^*$$

$$= \begin{bmatrix} I & FR \\ 0 & I \end{bmatrix} \begin{bmatrix} R - FRF^* & 0 \\ 0 & R^{-1} \end{bmatrix} \begin{bmatrix} I & FR \\ 0 & I \end{bmatrix}^* .$$

Now Sylvester's law of inertia (see also App. A) implies that

$$\text{Inertia}\{R^{-1} - F^* R^{-1} F\} = \text{Inertia}\{R - FRF^*\}.$$

It follows from (1.3.21) that there must exist a full rank $r \times n$ matrix H such that (1.5.1) is valid.

$\diamond$

An immediate application of the above result is to verify that the inverse of a Toeplitz matrix also has displacement structure. Indeed, we know from (1.2.5) that for a Hermitian Toeplitz matrix T, Inertia $(T - ZTZ^*) = (1, 1)$. It then follows from Lemma 1.5.1 that the inertia of $(T^{-1} - Z^* T^{-1} Z)$ is also $(1, 1)$. But $\tilde{I} T^{-1} \tilde{I} = T^{-*}$ (since $\tilde{I} T \tilde{I} = T^*$) and $\tilde{I} Z^* \tilde{I} = Z$, where $\tilde{I}$ is the reverse identity matrix with ones on the antidiagonal and zeros elsewhere. Hence, Inertia $(T^{-*} - ZT^{-*}Z^*) = (1, 1)$, which shows that $T^{-*} - ZT^{-*}Z^*$ has rank 2 with one positive signature and one negative signature. This discussion underlies the famous Gohberg–Semencul formula.

It is worth noting that the result of Lemma 1.5.1 requires no special assumptions (e.g., triangularity) on the matrix F.

The second striking result of displacement structure theory is the following, first stated deliberately in vague terms:

The Schur complements of a structured matrix R inherit its displacement structure. Moreover, a so-called generalized Schur algorithm yields generator matrices for the Schur complements.

In this way, we can justify the low displacement rank property of the Toeplitz matrix combinations that we listed before in the introduction of Sec. 1.2, viz., $T_1 T_2$, $T_1 - T_2 T_3^{-1} T_4$, and $(T_1 T_2)^{-1} T_3$. Assuming for simplicity square matrices $\{T_1, T_2, T_3\}$, we note that these combinations are Schur complements of the following extended matrices, all of which have low displacement ranks (for suitable choices of F):

$$\begin{bmatrix} -T & I \\ I & 0 \end{bmatrix}, \quad \begin{bmatrix} -I & T_2 \\ T_1 & 0 \end{bmatrix}, \quad \begin{bmatrix} T_3 & T_4 \\ T_2 & T_1 \end{bmatrix}, \quad \begin{bmatrix} I & T_2 & 0 \\ T_1 & 0 & T_3 \\ 0 & I & 0 \end{bmatrix}. \tag{1.5.2}$$

More formally, the result reads as follows.

Lemma 1.5.2 (Schur Complementation). *Consider $n \times n$ matrices R and F. Assume that F is block lower triangular (F_1 and F_3 need not be triangular),*

$$F = \begin{bmatrix} F_1 & 0 \\ F_2 & F_3 \end{bmatrix},$$

partition R accordingly with F,

$$R = \begin{bmatrix} R_{11} & R_{12} \\ R_{21} & R_{22} \end{bmatrix},$$

and assume that R_{11} is invertible. Then

$$\text{rank}\,(R_{11} - F_1 R_{11} F_1^*) \leq \text{rank}\,(R - FRF^*), \tag{1.5.3}$$

$$\text{rank}\,(\Delta - F_3 \Delta F_3^*) \leq \text{rank}\,(R - FRF^*), \tag{1.5.4}$$

where $\Delta = R_{22} - R_{21} R_{11}^{-1} R_{12}$.

Proof: The first inequality follows immediately since R_{11} is a submatrix of R. For the second inequality we first note that

$$\text{rank}\,(R^{-1} - F^* R^{-1} F) = \text{rank}\,(R - FRF^*).$$

We now invoke a block matrix formula for R^{-1} (cf. App. A),

$$R^{-1} = \begin{bmatrix} R_{11}^{-1} + E\Delta^{-1} P & -E\Delta^{-1} \\ \Delta^{-1} P & \Delta^{-1} \end{bmatrix}, \quad E = R_{11}^{-1} R_{12}, \quad P = R_{21} R_{11}^{-1},$$

and observe that Δ^{-1} is a submatrix of R^{-1}. Hence,

$$\text{rank}\,(\Delta^{-1} - F_3^* \Delta^{-1} F_3) \leq \text{rank}\,(R^{-1} - F^* R^{-1} F).$$

But by the first result in the lemma we have

$$\text{rank}\,(\Delta - F_3 \Delta F_3^*) = \text{rank}\,(\Delta^{-1} - F_3^* \Delta^{-1} F_3).$$

Section 1.6.   Fast Factorization of Structured Matrices   15

We thus conclude that rank $(\Delta - F_3 \Delta F_3^*) \leq$ rank $(R - FRF^*)$.

$\diamond$

Hence, it follows from the statement of the lemma that if R has low displacement rank with respect to the displacement $R - FRF^*$, then its Schur complement Δ has low displacement rank with respect to the displacement $\Delta - F_3 \Delta F_3^*$. This result for $F = Z$ was first noted in [Mor80], and in its extended form it was further developed in the Ph.D. research of Delosme [Del82], Lev-Ari [Lev83], Chun [Chu89], Pal [Pal90], Ackner [Ack91], and Sayed [Say92].

1.6 FAST FACTORIZATION OF STRUCTURED MATRICES

The concept of Schur complements perhaps first arose in the context of triangular factorization of matrices. It was implicit in Gauss's work on linear equations and more explicit in the remarkable paper of Schur [Sch17]. In this section we consider afresh the problem of triangular factorization, which is basically effected by the Gaussian elimination technique, and show that adding displacement structure allows us to speed up the Gaussian elimination procedure. This will lead us to what we have called generalized Schur algorithms. We shall develop them here for the displacement structure (1.3.21) and later state variations that apply to non-Hermitian Toeplitz-like and also Hankel-like structures. More details on these latter cases can be found in [KS95a]. Our study of the special case (1.3.21) will be enough to convey the main ideas.

We start by reviewing what we shall call the Gauss–Schur reduction procedure.

1.6.1 Schur Reduction (Deflation)

The triangular decomposition of a matrix $R \in \mathbb{C}^{n \times n}$ will be denoted by

$$R = L D^{-1} L^*, \tag{1.6.1}$$

where $D = \mathrm{diag}\{d_0, d_1, \ldots, d_{n-1}\}$ is a diagonal matrix and the lower triangular factor L is normalized in such a way that the $\{d_i\}$ appear on its main diagonal. The nonzero part of the consecutive columns of L will be denoted by l_i. They can be obtained recursively as follows.

Algorithm 1.6.1 (Schur Reduction). *Given $R \in \mathbb{C}^{n \times n}$, start with $R_0 = R$ and repeat for $i = 0, 1, \ldots, n-1$:*

1. *Let l_i denote the first column of R_i and d_i denote the upper-left-corner element of R_i.*

2. *Perform the Schur reduction step:*

$$\begin{bmatrix} 0 & 0 \\ 0 & R_{i+1} \end{bmatrix} = R_i - l_i d_i^{-1} l_i^*. \tag{1.6.2}$$

The matrix R_i is known as the Schur complement of the leading $i \times i$ block of R.

$\diamond$

We therefore see that the Schur reduction step (1.6.2) *deflates* the matrix R_i by subtracting a rank 1 matrix from it and leads to a new matrix R_{i+1} that has one less row and one less column than R_i.

By successively repeating (1.6.2) we obtain the triangular factorization of R,

$$R = l_0 d_0^{-1} l_0^* + \begin{bmatrix} 0 & 0 \\ 0 & R_1 \end{bmatrix}, \quad R_1 \in \mathbb{C}^{n-1 \times n-1}$$

$$= l_0 d_0^{-1} l_0^* + \begin{bmatrix} 0 \\ l_1 \end{bmatrix} d_1^{-1} \begin{bmatrix} 0 \\ l_1 \end{bmatrix}^* + \begin{bmatrix} 0 & 0 \\ 0 & R_2 \end{bmatrix}, \quad R_2 \in \mathbb{C}^{n-2 \times n-2}$$

$$\vdots$$

$$= L D^{-1} L^*.$$

It is also easy to verify that a suitable partitioning of L and D provides triangular decompositions for the leading principal block of R and its Schur complement.

Lemma 1.6.1 (Partitioning of the Triangular Decomposition). *Assume that R, L, and D are partitioned as*

$$R = \begin{bmatrix} P_i & Q_i^* \\ Q_i & S_i \end{bmatrix} \begin{matrix} \}i \\ \}n-i \end{matrix}, \quad L = \begin{bmatrix} \bar{L}_i & 0 \\ \tilde{L}_i & L_i \end{bmatrix} \begin{matrix} \}i \\ \}n-i \end{matrix}, \quad D = \begin{bmatrix} \bar{D}_i & 0 \\ 0 & D_i \end{bmatrix} \begin{matrix} \}i \\ \}n-i \end{matrix}.$$

Then the leading principal block P_i and its Schur complement $R_i = S_i - Q_i P_i^{-1} Q_i^*$ admit the following triangular decompositions:

$$P_i = \bar{L}_i \bar{D}_i^{-1} \bar{L}_i^* \quad \text{and} \quad R_i = L_i D_i^{-1} L_i^*. \tag{1.6.3}$$

$\diamond$

1.6.2 Close Relation to Gaussian Elimination

The Schur reduction procedure is in fact the same as Gaussian elimination. To see this, consider the first step of (1.6.2):

$$\begin{bmatrix} 0 & 0 \\ 0 & R_1 \end{bmatrix} = R - l_0 d_0^{-1} l_0^*. \tag{1.6.4}$$

If we partition the entries of l_0 into $l_0 = \text{col}\{d_0, t_0\}$, where t_0 is also a column vector, then the above equality can be written as

$$R = \begin{bmatrix} 1 & 0 \\ t_0 d_0^{-1} & I_{n-1} \end{bmatrix} \begin{bmatrix} d_0 & \\ & R_1 \end{bmatrix} \begin{bmatrix} 1 & 0 \\ t_0 d_0^{-1} & I_{n-1} \end{bmatrix}^* \tag{1.6.5}$$

or, equivalently, as

$$\begin{bmatrix} 1 & 0 \\ -t_0 d_0^{-1} & I_{n-1} \end{bmatrix} R = \begin{bmatrix} d_0 & 0 \\ t_0 & R_1 \end{bmatrix}^*,$$

where I_{n-1} is the identity matrix of dimension $(n-1)$. This relation shows why (1.6.2), which we called Schur reduction, is closely related to Gaussian elimination. Schur reduction goes more explicitly toward matrix factorization. Note also that the above Schur reduction procedure can readily be extended to strongly regular non-Hermitian matrices to yield the so-called LDU decompositions (see, e.g., [KS95a]).

Section 1.6.   Fast Factorization of Structured Matrices   17

1.6.3 A Generalized Schur Algorithm

In general, Alg. 1.6.1 requires $\mathcal{O}(n^3)$ operations to factor R. However, when R has displacement structure, the computational burden can be significantly reduced by exploiting the fact that the Schur complements R_i all inherit the displacement structure of R.

Schur algorithms can be stated in two different, but equivalent, forms—via a set of equations or in a less traditional form as what we call an *array algorithm*. In the latter, the key operation is the triangularization by a sequence of elementary unitary or J-unitary operations of a prearray formed from the data at a certain iteration; the information needed to form the prearray for the next iteration can be read out from the entries of the triangularized prearray. No equations, or at most one or two very simple explicit equations, are needed. We first state a form of the algorithm, before presenting the derivation.

Algorithm 1.6.2 (A Generalized Schur Algorithm). *Given a matrix $R \in \mathbb{C}^{n \times n}$ that satisfies (1.3.21) and (1.3.22) for some full rank $G \in \mathbb{C}^{n \times r}$, start with $G_0 = G$ and perform the following steps for $i = 0, \ldots, n-1$:*

1. *Let g_i be the top row of G_i and let F be partitioned as*

$$F = \begin{bmatrix} \bar{F}_i & 0 \\ \tilde{F}_i & F_i \end{bmatrix} \begin{matrix} \}i \\ \}n-i \end{matrix} . \qquad (1.6.6)$$

   with column widths i and $n-i$. That is, F_i is obtained by ignoring the leading i rows and columns of F. Now compute l_i by solving the linear system of equations[3]

$$(I_{n-i} - f_i^* F_i) l_i = G_i J g_i^*. \qquad (1.6.7)$$

   Define the top element of l_i,

$$d_i = g_i J g_i^* / (1 - f_i f_i^*). \qquad (1.6.8)$$

2. *Form the prearray shown below and choose a $(d_i^{-1} \oplus J)$-unitary matrix Σ_i that eliminates the top row of G_i:*

$$\begin{bmatrix} F_i l_i & G_i \end{bmatrix} \Sigma_i = \begin{bmatrix} l_i & 0 \\ & G_{i+1} \end{bmatrix}. \qquad (1.6.9)$$

   This will give us a right-hand side as shown, where the matrix G_{i+1} can be used to repeat steps 1 and 2; a matrix Σ_i is $(d_i^{-1} \oplus J)$-unitary if

$$\Sigma_i (d_i^{-1} \oplus J) \Sigma_i^* = (d_i^{-1} \oplus J).$$

   Notice that G_{i+1} has one less row than G_i.

3. *Then the $\{l_i\}$ define the successive columns of L, $D = \text{diag}\{d_i\}$, and $R = L D^{-1} L^*$.*

$\diamond$

---

[3]F_i is not only triangular, but in many applications it is usually sparse and often diagonal or bidiagonal, so that (1.6.7) is easy to solve and (see (1.6.9)) $F_i l_i$ is easy to form. For example, whenever F is strictly lower triangular, say, $F = Z$ or $F = Z \oplus Z$, then $l_i = G_i J g_i^*$.

Remark 1. Unitary transformations can have several forms, which are discussed in App. B. A graphic depiction of the algorithm will be given in Sec. 1.6.6. When the matrix F is sparse enough (e.g., diagonal or bidiagonal), so that the total number of flops required for solving the linear system (1.6.7) is $\mathcal{O}(n-i)$, then the computational complexity of Alg. 1.6.2 is readily seen to be $\mathcal{O}(rn^2)$.

Remark 2. We shall show in Lemma 1.6.3 that the matrices $\{G_i\}$ that appear in the statement of the algorithm are in fact generator matrices for the successive Schur complements of R, viz.,

$$R_i - F_i G_i F_i^* = G_i J G_i^* . \tag{1.6.10}$$

Remark 3 (An Explicit Form). It can be shown that G_{i+1} can be obtained from G_i by an explicit calculation:

$$\begin{bmatrix} 0 \\ G_{i+1} \end{bmatrix} = \left\{ G_i + (\Phi_i - I_{n-i}) G_i \frac{J g_i^* g_i}{g_i J g_i^*} \right\} \Theta_i , \tag{1.6.11}$$

where Θ_i is any J-unitary matrix, and Φ_i is the so-called Blaschke–Potapov matrix

$$\Phi_i = (I_{n-i} - f_i^* F_i)^{-1}(F_i - f_i I_{n-i}) = (F_i - f_i I_{n-i})(I_{n-i} - f_i^* F_i)^{-1} . \tag{1.6.12}$$

Remark 4. Although the above statement is for Hermitian matrices that satisfy displacement equations of the form $R - FRF^* = GJG^*$, there are similar algorithms for non-Hermitian Toeplitz-like matrices and also for Hankel-like matrices (see Secs. 1.11 and 1.12). The discussion we provide in what follows for the Hermitian Toeplitz-like case highlights most of the concepts that arise in the study of structured matrices.

Remark 5 (Terminology). The ultimate conclusion is that the above generalized Schur algorithm is the result of combining displacement structure with Gaussian elimination in order to speed up the computations. We have called it *a* (rather than *the*) generalized Schur algorithm because there are many variations that can be obtained by different choices of the matrices $\{\Sigma_i, \Theta_i\}$ *and* for different forms of displacement structure. Generalized Schur algorithms for the general displacement (1.3.16) can be found in [KS91], [KS95a], [SK95a]. Finally, we mention that the classical (1917) Schur algorithm is deduced as a special case in Sec. 1.7.6.

1.6.4 Array Derivation of the Algorithm

The equation forms of the algorithm (i.e., (1.6.7) and (1.6.11)) can be derived in several different ways—see, e.g., [Lev83], [LK84], [LK92], [Say92], [KS95a], and the array-based algorithm deduced from it. Here we shall present a direct derivation of the array algorithm using minimal prior knowledge; in fact, we shall deduce the equation form from the array algorithm. The presentation follows that of [BSLK96], [BKLS98a].

The key matrix result is the next lemma. We first introduce some notation. Recall the factorization (1.6.1),

$$R = LD^{-1}L^*,$$

where L is lower triangular with diagonal entries d_i while $D = \text{diag}\{d_i\}$. Now let us define the upper triangular matrix

$$U \triangleq L^{-*}D \tag{1.6.13}$$

and write

$$R^{-1} = L^{-*}DL^{-1} = (L^{-*}D)D^{-1}(DL^{-1}) = UD^{-1}U^* . \tag{1.6.14}$$

Section 1.6. Fast Factorization of Structured Matrices

The factorization (1.6.14) is somewhat nontraditional since we use D^{-1} rather than D. That is, the same diagonal factor D^{-1} is used in the factorizations (1.6.1) and (1.6.14) for both R and R^{-1}. The reason for doing this will become clear soon.

Lemma 1.6.2 (Key Array Equation). *Consider a Toeplitz-like strongly regular and Hermitian matrix R with a full rank generator matrix $G \in \mathbb{C}^{n \times r}$, i.e., $R - FRF^* = GJG^*$. Then there must exist a $(D^{-1} \oplus J)$-unitary matrix Ω such that*

$$\begin{bmatrix} FL & G \\ U & 0 \end{bmatrix} \Omega = \begin{bmatrix} L & 0 \\ F^*U & H^* \end{bmatrix}, \quad \Omega(D^{-1} \oplus J)\Omega^* = (D^{-1} \oplus J). \quad (1.6.15)$$

Proof: Recall from Lemma 1.5.1 that there exists a full rank matrix H^* such that

$$R^{-1} - F^*R^{-1}F = H^*JH.$$

Hence, if we reconsider the block matrix

$$\begin{bmatrix} R & F \\ F^* & R^{-1} \end{bmatrix} \quad (1.6.16)$$

that appeared in the proof of Lemma 1.5.1 and use the displacement equations (1.3.21) and (1.5.1), we can rewrite the block triangular factorizations in the proof of the lemma as

$$\begin{bmatrix} R & F \\ F^* & R^{-1} \end{bmatrix} = \begin{bmatrix} FL & G \\ U & 0 \end{bmatrix} \begin{bmatrix} D^{-1} & 0 \\ 0 & J \end{bmatrix} \begin{bmatrix} FL & G \\ U & 0 \end{bmatrix}^* \quad (1.6.17)$$

$$= \begin{bmatrix} L & 0 \\ F^*U & H^* \end{bmatrix} \begin{bmatrix} D^{-1} & 0 \\ 0 & J \end{bmatrix} \begin{bmatrix} L & 0 \\ F^*U & H^* \end{bmatrix}^*. \quad (1.6.18)$$

The center matrix in both (1.6.17) and (1.6.18) is the same diagonal matrix $(D^{-1} \oplus J)$; it was to achieve this that we started with the nontraditional factorizations $R = LD^{-1}L^*$ and $R^{-1} = UD^{-1}U^*$, with D^{-1} in both factorizations.

The next step is to observe that, in view of the invertibility of L and U and the full rank assumption on G and H^*, the matrices

$$\begin{bmatrix} FL & G \\ U & 0 \end{bmatrix} \quad \text{and} \quad \begin{bmatrix} L & 0 \\ F^*U & H^* \end{bmatrix}$$

have full rank (equal to $n + r$). It then follows from Lemma A.4.3 in App. A that there must exist a $(D^{-1} \oplus J)$-unitary matrix Ω such that (1.6.15) holds.

$\diamond$

We shall focus first on the equality of the first block row in (1.6.15). The second block rows can be used as the basis for the derivation of an efficient algorithm for factoring R^{-1} and for determining H^*. We shall pursue this issue later in Sec. 1.10.

By confining ourselves to the first block row of (1.6.15), we note that there always exists a $(D^{-1} \oplus J)$-unitary matrix Ω that performs the transformation

$$\begin{bmatrix} FL & G \end{bmatrix} \Omega = \begin{bmatrix} L & 0 \end{bmatrix}. \quad (1.6.19)$$

The matrices $\{F, L, J\}$ are uniquely specified by R and the displacement equation $R - FRF^* = GJG^*$. There is flexibility in choosing G since we can also use $G\Theta$ for any J-unitary Θ, i.e., one that obeys $\Theta J\Theta^* = J = \Theta^*J\Theta$.

This freedom allows us to conjecture the following algorithmic consequence of (1.6.19): given any G, form a prearray as shown below in (1.6.20) and triangularize it in any way we wish by some $(D^{-1} \oplus J)$-unitary matrix Ω,

$$[\ FL \quad G\ ]\Omega = [\ X \quad 0\ ]. \tag{1.6.20}$$

Then we can identify $X = L$. Indeed, by forming the $(D^{-1} \oplus J)$-"norms" of both sides of (1.6.20), we obtain

$$[\ FL \quad G\ ]\underbrace{\Omega \begin{bmatrix} D^{-1} & 0 \\ 0 & J \end{bmatrix} \Omega^*}_{D^{-1} \oplus J} \begin{bmatrix} L^*F^* \\ G^* \end{bmatrix} = [\ X \quad 0\ ]\begin{bmatrix} D^{-1} & 0 \\ 0 & J \end{bmatrix}\begin{bmatrix} X^* \\ 0 \end{bmatrix}.$$

That is,

$$FLD^{-1}L^*F^* + GJG^* = XD^{-1}X^*.$$

Hence, it follows from (1.3.21) that $R = XD^{-1}X^*$. But $R = LD^{-1}L^*$, so by uniqueness we must have $X = L$.

Continuing with (1.6.19), at first it is of course difficult to see how (1.6.19) can be used to compute L and D when only F, G, and J are given, since the unknown quantity L appears on both sides of the equation. This apparent difficulty is resolved by proceeding *recursively*.

Thus note that the first column of L (and hence of FL) can be obtained by multiplying the displacement equation by the first unit column vector e_0 from the right,

$$LD^{-1}Le_0 - FLD^{-1}L^*F^*e_0 = GJG^*e_0,$$

or

$$l_0 - Fl_0 f_0^* = GJg_0^*, \quad l_0 = (I - Ff_0^*)^{-1}GJg_0^*,$$

where

$$g_0 = \text{the top row of } G.$$

The inverse exists by our solvability assumption (1.3.22), which ensured that the displacement equation has a unique solution.

Now we can find elementary transformations that successively combine the first column of FL with the columns of G so as to null out the top entries of G, i.e., to null out g_0. From (1.6.19) we see that the resulting postarray must have, say, the form

$$[\ FL \quad G\ ]\Omega_0 = \begin{bmatrix} l_0 & 0 & 0 \\ & F_1 l_1 & G_1 \end{bmatrix},$$

where F_1 and L_1 are (as defined earlier) obtained by omitting the first columns of F and L, and all the entries of G_1 are known.

Now we can prove that G_1 is such that $R_1 \triangleq L_1 D_1^{-1} L_1^*$ obeys

$$R_1 - F_1 R_1 F_1^* = G_1 J G_1^*, \tag{1.6.21}$$

where $D_1 = \text{diag}\{d_1, \ldots, d_{n-1}\}$. This equation allows us to determine the first column of $F_1 L_1$ and then proceed as above. To prove (1.6.21), it will be convenient to proceed more generally by considering the ith step of the recursion.

Section 1.6. Fast Factorization of Structured Matrices

For this purpose, we recall the partitioning

$$F = \begin{bmatrix} \bar{F}_i & 0 \\ \tilde{F}_i & F_i \end{bmatrix} \begin{matrix} \}i \\ \}n-i \end{matrix} \overbrace{\phantom{\bar{F}_i}}^{i} \overbrace{}^{n-i}, \qquad L = \begin{bmatrix} \bar{L}_i & 0 \\ \tilde{L}_i & L_i \end{bmatrix} \begin{matrix} \}i \\ \}n-i \end{matrix},$$

and therefore partition the pre- and postarrays accordingly:

$$\begin{bmatrix} FL & G \end{bmatrix} = \begin{bmatrix} \bar{F}_i \bar{L}_i & 0 & G \\ \tilde{F}_i \bar{L}_i + F_i \tilde{L}_i & F_i L_i & \end{bmatrix} \tag{1.6.22}$$

and

$$\begin{bmatrix} L & 0 \end{bmatrix} = \begin{bmatrix} \bar{L}_i & 0 & 0 \\ \tilde{L}_i & L_i & \end{bmatrix}. \tag{1.6.23}$$

After i iterations, the first i columns of the postarray are already computed, while the last $(n-i)$ columns of the prearray have not yet been modified. Therefore, the ith intermediate array must have the following form:

$$\begin{bmatrix} FL & G \end{bmatrix} \Omega_0 \Omega_1 \ldots \Omega_{i-1} = \begin{bmatrix} \bar{L}_i & 0 & 0 \\ \tilde{L}_i & F_i L_i & G_i \end{bmatrix}, \tag{1.6.24}$$

where G_i denotes the nontrivial element that appears in the upper-right-corner block.

All our results will now follow by using the fact that the prearray (1.6.22), the intermediate array (1.6.24), and the postarray (1.6.23) are all $(D^{-1} \oplus J)$ equivalent; i.e., their squares in the $(D^{-1} \oplus J)$ "metric" are all equal.

We first establish that the entry G_i in the intermediate array (1.6.24) is a generator matrix of the (leading) Schur complement R_i.

Lemma 1.6.3 (Structure of Schur Complements). *Let G_i be the matrix shown in (1.6.24). Then the Schur complement R_i satisfies the displacement equation*

$$R_i - F_i R_i F_i^* = G_i J G_i^*. \tag{1.6.25}$$

Proof: Since Ω and Ω_i are $(D^{-1} \oplus J)$-unitary, the second block rows of the postarray (1.6.23) and the intermediate array (1.6.24) must satisfy

$$\begin{bmatrix} \tilde{L}_i & F_i L_i & G_i \end{bmatrix} (\bar{D}_i^{-1} \oplus D_i^{-1} \oplus J) \begin{bmatrix} \tilde{L}_i & F_i L_i & G_i \end{bmatrix}^* = \begin{bmatrix} \tilde{L}_i & L_i & 0 \end{bmatrix} (\bar{D}_i^{-1} \oplus D_i^{-1} \oplus J) \begin{bmatrix} \tilde{L}_i & L_i & 0 \end{bmatrix}^*.$$

It follows immediately that

$$F_i (L_i D_i^{-1} L_i^*) F_i^* + G_i J G_i^* = (L_i D_i^{-1} L_i^*).$$

But we already know from (1.6.3) that $R_i = L_i D_i^{-1} L_i^*$, so (1.6.25) is established.
$\diamond$

From (1.6.25) it is easy to obtain a closed-form expression for l_i. In fact, equating the first columns on both sides of (1.6.25) leads to

$$l_i - F_i f_i^* l_i = G_i J g_i^*, \tag{1.6.26}$$

which is (1.6.7). The solvability condition (1.3.22) ensures that (1.6.7) has a unique solution for l_i.

Now recursion (1.6.9) follows by examining the transformation from the ith to the $(i+1)$th iteration, i.e., at the step that updates the right-hand side of (1.6.24). It can be succinctly described as

$$\left[\begin{array}{c|c} F_i l_i & G_i \end{array}\right] \Sigma_i = \left[\begin{array}{c|c} l_i & 0 \\ & G_{i+1} \end{array}\right], \tag{1.6.27}$$

where the irrelevant columns and rows of the pre- and postarrays (i.e., those rows and columns that remain unchanged) were omitted. Also, Σ_i is a submatrix of Ω_i, and it is $(d_i^{-1} \oplus J)$-unitary. We have argued above in (1.6.25) that the matrix G_{i+1} in (1.6.27) is a generator for the Schur complement R_{i+1}. This completes the proof of the array Alg. 1.6.2.

Explicit Equations

Although not needed for the algorithm, we can pursue the argument a bit further and deduce the explicit updating equation (1.6.11). To do this, we first identify the transformation Σ_i. To do this, note first that Σ_i is $(d_i^{-1} \oplus J)$-unitary, i.e., $\Sigma_i (d_i^{-1} \oplus J) \Sigma_i^* = (d_i^{-1} \oplus J)$. Therefore, the inverse of Σ_i is given by

$$\Sigma_i^{-1} = \left[\begin{array}{cc} d_i^{-1} & \\ & J \end{array}\right] \Sigma_i^* \left[\begin{array}{cc} d_i & \\ & J \end{array}\right].$$

It then follows from the array equation (1.6.27) that

$$\left[\begin{array}{cc} F_i l_i & G_i \end{array}\right] \left[\begin{array}{cc} d_i^{-1} & \\ & J \end{array}\right] = \left[\begin{array}{cc} l_i & 0 \\ & G_{i+1} \end{array}\right] \left[\begin{array}{cc} d_i^{-1} & \\ & J \end{array}\right] \Sigma_i^*. \tag{1.6.28}$$

If we denote the entries of Σ_i by

$$\Sigma_i = \left[\begin{array}{cc} a_i & b_i \\ c_i & s_i \end{array}\right], \tag{1.6.29}$$

where $a_i \in \mathcal{C}$, $b_i \in \mathcal{C}^{1 \times r}$, $c_i \in \mathcal{C}^{r \times 1}$, and $s_i \in \mathcal{C}^{r \times r}$, we conclude by equating the top row on both sides of (1.6.28) that we must have

$$a_i = f_i^*, \quad c_i = J g_i^*. \tag{1.6.30}$$

In other words, any $(d_i^{-1} \oplus J)$-transformation Σ_i that achieves (1.6.27) must be such that its entries $\{a_i, c_i\}$ are as above. In order to identify the remaining entries $\{b_i, s_i\}$, we note that in view of the $(d_i^{-1} \oplus J)$-unitarity of Σ_i, the entries $\{a_i, b_i, c_i, s_i\}$ must satisfy

$$\left[\begin{array}{cc} a_i & b_i \\ c_i & s_i \end{array}\right] \left[\begin{array}{cc} d_i^{-1} & 0 \\ 0 & J \end{array}\right] \left[\begin{array}{cc} a_i & b_i \\ c_i & s_i \end{array}\right]^* = \left[\begin{array}{cc} d_i^{-1} & 0 \\ 0 & J \end{array}\right]. \tag{1.6.31}$$

Lemma 1.6.4 (Identification of Σ_i). *Given $\{f_i, g_i, J\}$, all pairs $\{b_i, s_i\}$ that satisfy (1.6.31) are given by*

$$b_i^* = \Theta_i^* g_i^* d_i^{-1}, \tag{1.6.32}$$

$$s_i^* = \Theta_i^* \left[I - \frac{1+f_i^*}{1-f_i f_i^*} g_i^* d_i^{-1} g_i J \right] \tag{1.6.33}$$

for any J-unitary parameter Θ_i ($\Theta_i J \Theta_i^* = J$).

Section 1.6. Fast Factorization of Structured Matrices

Proof: It follows from (1.6.31) that

$$\begin{bmatrix} b_i \\ s_i \end{bmatrix} J \begin{bmatrix} b_i \\ s_i \end{bmatrix}^* = \begin{bmatrix} d_i^{-1}(1 - |f_i|^2) & -f_i^* d_i^{-1} g_i J \\ -J g_i^* d_i^{-1} f_i & J - J g_i^* d_i^{-1} g_i J \end{bmatrix}.$$

Using $d_i(1 - |f_i|^2) = g_i J g_i^*$, we can verify after some algebra that the right-hand side of the above expression can be factored as

$$\begin{bmatrix} b_i \\ s_i \end{bmatrix} J \begin{bmatrix} b_i \\ s_i \end{bmatrix}^* = \begin{bmatrix} d_i^{-1} g_i \\ I - \frac{1+f_i}{1-|f_i|^2} J g_i^* d_i^{-1} g_i \end{bmatrix} J \begin{bmatrix} d_i^{-1} g_i \\ I - \frac{1+f_i}{1-|f_i|^2} J g_i^* d_i^{-1} g_i \end{bmatrix}^*.$$

But the matrix $\begin{bmatrix} b_i \\ s_i \end{bmatrix}$ is full rank since Σ_i is full rank (due to its $(d_i^{-1} \oplus J)$-unitarity). Likewise, the matrix

$$\begin{bmatrix} d_i^{-1} g_i \\ I - \frac{1+f_i}{1-|f_i|^2} J g_i^* d_i^{-1} g_i \end{bmatrix}$$

is full rank since otherwise there would exist a nonzero vector x such that

$$\begin{bmatrix} d_i^{-1} g_i \\ I - \frac{1+f_i}{1-|f_i|^2} J g_i^* d_i^{-1} g_i \end{bmatrix} x = 0.$$

This implies that we must have $g_i x = 0$, which in turn implies from the equality of the second block row that $x = 0$. This contradicts the fact that x is nonzero.

Therefore, in view of the result of Lemma A.4.3, we conclude that there should exist a J-unitary matrix Θ_i such that

$$\begin{bmatrix} b_i \\ s_i \end{bmatrix} = \begin{bmatrix} d_i^{-1} g_i \\ I - \frac{1+f_i}{1-|f_i|^2} J g_i^* d_i^{-1} g_i \end{bmatrix} \Theta_i,$$

as desired.

◇

Substituting (1.6.30) and (1.6.33) into (1.6.27) yields (1.6.11).

1.6.5 An Elementary Section

A useful remark is to note that in (1.6.27), viz.,

$$\begin{bmatrix} F_i l_i & G_i \end{bmatrix} \begin{bmatrix} a_i & b_i \\ c_i & s_i \end{bmatrix} = \begin{bmatrix} l_i & 0 \\ & G_{i+1} \end{bmatrix},$$

we can regard the transformation Σ_i of (1.6.29) as the system matrix of a first-order state-space linear system; the rows of $\{G_i\}$ and $\{G_{i+1}\}$ can be regarded as inputs and outputs of this system, respectively, and the entries of $\{l_i, F_i l_i\}$ can be regarded as the corresponding current and future states.

Let $\Theta_i(z)$ denote the transfer function of the above linear system (with inputs from the left), viz.,

$$\Theta_i(z) = s_i + c_i(z^{-1} - f_i^*)^{-1} b_i.$$

Using (1.6.32) and (1.6.33), and simple algebra, shows that the above expression collapses to

$$\Theta_i(z) = \left[I_r + (B_i(z) - 1)\frac{Jg_i^*g_i}{g_iJg_i^*}\right]\Theta_i, \qquad (1.6.34)$$

where

$$B_i(z) = \frac{z - f_i}{1 - f_i^*z}. \qquad (1.6.35)$$

We therefore see that each step of the generalized Schur algorithm gives rise to a first-order section $\Theta_i(z)$. Such elementary sections have several useful properties. In particular, note that

$$g_i\Theta_i(f_i) = 0, \qquad (1.6.36)$$

which shows that $\Theta_i(z)$ has a transmission zero at f_i along the direction of g_i. This blocking property can be used, for example, to obtain efficient recursive solutions to rational interpolation problems (see, e.g., [SKLC94], [BSK94], [BSK99] and Sec. 1.14.3).

1.6.6 A Simple Example

To see how Alg. 1.6.2 works, we consider a simple example with $n=3$ and $r=2$. In this case the pre- and postarrays in (1.6.19) will have the following zero-patterns:

$$\begin{bmatrix} FL & G \end{bmatrix} = \begin{bmatrix} * & 0 & 0 & * & * \\ * & * & 0 & * & * \\ * & * & * & * & * \end{bmatrix}, \qquad \begin{bmatrix} L & 0 \end{bmatrix} = \begin{bmatrix} * & 0 & 0 & 0 & 0 \\ * & * & 0 & 0 & 0 \\ * & * & * & 0 & 0 \end{bmatrix}.$$

Using (1.6.7) for $i = 0$, viz.,

$$(I_n - f_0^*F)l_0 = GJg_0,$$

we can determine the first column l_0 of L and, consequently, the first column of FL. In this way, all the entries of the first column of the prearray are completely known. Also, the last two columns of the prearray are known since they are determined by G.

Hence, the $(1,2)$ block entry of the prearray (i.e., the top row of G) can be eliminated by pivoting with the top entry of the first column of FL. As a result, the first column of the prearray and its last two columns are linearly combined to yield the intermediate array shown below after the transformation Ω_0. The second and third columns of the prearray remain unchanged:

$$\begin{bmatrix} * & 0 & 0 & * & * \\ * & * & 0 & * & * \\ * & * & * & * & * \end{bmatrix} \xrightarrow{\Omega_0} \begin{bmatrix} * & 0 & 0 & 0 & 0 \\ * & * & 0 & * & * \\ * & * & * & * & * \end{bmatrix} \xrightarrow{\Omega_1} \begin{bmatrix} * & 0 & 0 & 0 & 0 \\ * & * & 0 & 0 & 0 \\ * & * & * & * & * \end{bmatrix} \xrightarrow{\Omega_2} \begin{bmatrix} * & 0 & 0 & 0 & 0 \\ * & * & 0 & 0 & 0 \\ * & * & * & 0 & 0 \end{bmatrix}.$$

We now proceed in a similar fashion to the next step. Using (1.6.7) for $i = 1$, viz.,

$$(I_{n-1} - f_1^*F_1)l_1 = G_1Jg_1,$$

we determine the l_1 and, consequently, the second column of FL. The second transformation Ω_1 can now be performed as shown above to yield G_2 (see below), and so on.

The rectangular boxes mark the entries to be eliminated at each step of the recursion by using elementary $(D^{-1} \oplus J)$-unitary transformations (scaled column permutations, Givens rotations, and Householder projections—see App. B). The square boxes mark the position of the pivot elements. The ultimate result of the recursion is that the $(1,2)$ block of the prearray is eliminated row by row.

1.7 PROPER FORM OF THE FAST ALGORITHM

A useful feature of the explicit form of the generator recursion (1.6.11) is that different choices of the arbitrary J-unitary matrix Θ_i can be more easily used to obtain different variants of the general algorithm, which can have different domains of usefulness. One of these is the so-called proper form.

This means that Θ_i is chosen so as to eliminate all elements of g_i with the exception of a single pivot element. This pivot has to be in the first p positions when $g_i J g_i^* > 0$ and in the last q positions when $g_i J g_i^* < 0$. (Note that the case $g_i J g_i^* = 0$ is ruled out by the strong regularity assumption on R. This is because $d_i \neq 0$ implies $g_i J g_i^* \neq 0$ by (1.6.8).)

1.7.1 Positive Lengths

When $g_i J g_i^* > 0$ holds, we can choose a J-unitary rotation Θ_i that would reduce g_i to the form

$$g_i \Theta_i = \begin{bmatrix} \delta_i & 0 & \cdots & 0 \end{bmatrix}, \qquad |\delta_i|^2 = g_i J g_i^*, \tag{1.7.1}$$

where we have chosen, without loss of generality, the nonzero entry to be in the leading position of the postarray. With this particular choice, the generator recursion (1.6.11) can be seen to collapse to

$$\begin{bmatrix} 0 \\ G_{i+1} \end{bmatrix} = G_i \Theta_i \begin{bmatrix} 0 & 0 \\ 0 & I_{r-1} \end{bmatrix} + \Phi_i G_i \Theta_i \begin{bmatrix} 1 & 0 \\ 0 & 0 \end{bmatrix}. \tag{1.7.2}$$

Likewise, the expressions (1.6.7) and (1.6.8) for l_i and d_i become

$$l_i = \delta_i^*(I_{n-i} - f_i^* F_i)^{-1} G_i \Theta_i \begin{bmatrix} 1 \\ 0 \end{bmatrix}, \qquad d_i = |\delta_i|^2/(1 - |f_i|^2). \tag{1.7.3}$$

Equation (1.7.2) yields the following simple statement for steps with $g_i J g_i^* > 0$:

1. Transform G_i into proper form with respect to its first column by using a J-unitary rotation Θ_i.

2. Multiply the first column by Φ_i and keep the rest of the columns unaltered.

The first step eliminates all entries in the first row of G_i except the pivot entry in the upper-left-corner position (see Fig. 1.2 below). The second step is needed to eliminate the pivot entry.

$$G_i = \begin{bmatrix} * & * & * \\ * & * & * \\ \vdots & \vdots & \vdots \\ * & * & * \end{bmatrix} \xrightarrow{\text{Step 1}} \begin{bmatrix} * & 0 & 0 \\ * & * & * \\ \vdots & \vdots & \vdots \\ * & * & * \end{bmatrix} \xrightarrow{\text{Step 2}} \begin{bmatrix} 0 & 0 & 0 \\ * & * & * \\ \vdots & \vdots & \vdots \\ * & * & * \end{bmatrix} = \begin{bmatrix} 0 \\ G_{i+1} \end{bmatrix}$$

Figure 1.2. Illustrating the proper form of the generator recursion.

Each step of (1.7.2) can also be depicted graphically as a cascade network of elementary sections, one of which is shown in Fig. 1.3; Θ_i is any J-unitary matrix that rotates

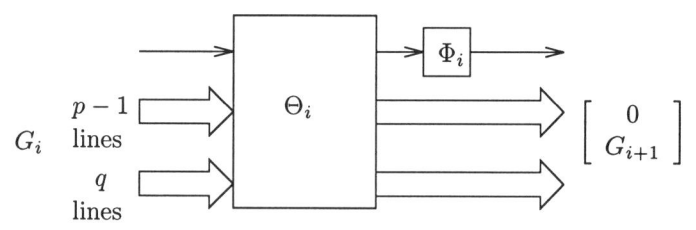

Figure 1.3. Proper form when $g_i J g_i^* > 0$.

the first row of the ith generator to $\begin{bmatrix} \delta_i & 0 \end{bmatrix}$. The rows of G_i enter the section one row at a time. The leftmost entry of each row is applied through the top line, while the remaining entries are applied through the bottom lines. The Blaschke–Potapov matrix Φ_i then acts on the entries of the top line. When $F_i = Z$, the lower shift matrix Φ_i collapses to $\Phi_i = Z$, a delay unit (see the discussion further ahead on shift-structured matrices). In general, note that the first row of each Φ_i is zero, and in this sense Φ_i acts as a generalized delay element. To clarify this, observe that when the entries of the first row of G_i are processed by Θ_i and Φ_i, the values of the outputs of the section will all be zero. The rows of G_{i+1} will start appearing at these outputs only when the second and higher rows of G_i are processed by the section.

1.7.2 Negative Lengths

A similar derivation holds for steps with $g_i J g_i^* < 0$. Now we choose a J-unitary matrix Θ_i so that

$$g_i \Theta_i = \begin{bmatrix} 0 & \ldots & 0 & \delta_i \end{bmatrix}, \qquad |\delta_i|^2 = -g_i J g_i^*, \tag{1.7.4}$$

where the nonzero entry in the postarray is chosen, again for convenience, to be at its last position.

Equation (1.6.11) now collapses to

$$\begin{bmatrix} 0 \\ G_{i+1} \end{bmatrix} = G_i \Theta_i \begin{bmatrix} I_{r-1} & 0 \\ 0 & 0 \end{bmatrix} + \Phi_i G_i \Theta_i \begin{bmatrix} 0 & 0 \\ 0 & 1 \end{bmatrix}. \tag{1.7.5}$$

Also, expressions (1.6.7) and (1.6.8) for l_i and d_i become

$$l_i = -\delta_i^* (I_{n-i} - f_i^* F_i)^{-1} G_i \Theta_i \begin{bmatrix} 0 \\ 1 \end{bmatrix}, \qquad d_i = |\delta_i|^2 / (1 - |f_i|^2). \tag{1.7.6}$$

Equation (1.7.5) admits the following simple interpretation:

1. Transform G_i into proper form with respect to its last column by using a J-unitary rotation Θ_i.

2. Multiply the last column by Φ_i and keep the rest of the columns unaltered.

1.7.3 Statement of the Algorithm in Proper Form

We collect the above results into the following statement.

Section 1.7. Proper Form of the Fast Algorithm

Algorithm 1.7.1 (Fast Algorithm in Proper Form). *Given a matrix $R \in \mathbb{C}^{n \times n}$ that satisfies (1.3.21) and (1.3.22) for some full rank $G \in \mathbb{C}^{n \times r}$, start with $G_0 = G$ and perform the following steps for $i = 0, \ldots, n-1$:*

1. Let g_i be the top row of G_i and let F_i be the submatrix obtained by deleting the leading i rows and columns of F.

2. If $g_i J g_i > 0$, then transform g_i to proper form according to (1.7.1), compute l_i and d_i using (1.7.3), and update G_i to G_{i+1} according to (1.7.2).

3. If $g_i J g_i < 0$, then transform g_i to proper form according to (1.7.4), compute l_i and d_i using (1.7.6), and update G_i to G_{i+1} according to (1.7.5).

$\diamond$

1.7.4 An Associated Transmission Line

We may return to the elementary section (1.6.34) and note that its form simplifies in the proper case. Assume $g_i J g_i^* > 0$ (a similar argument holds for $g_i J g_i^* < 0$). It then follows that (1.6.27) collapses to the form

$$\begin{bmatrix} F_i l_i & G_i \end{bmatrix} \begin{bmatrix} f_i^* & \frac{\delta_i}{d_i} \begin{bmatrix} 1 & 0 \end{bmatrix} \\ \Theta_i \begin{bmatrix} \delta_i \\ 0 \end{bmatrix} & \Theta_i \begin{bmatrix} -f_i & 0 \\ 0 & I_{r-1} \end{bmatrix} \end{bmatrix} = \begin{bmatrix} l_i & 0 \\ & G_{i+1} \end{bmatrix}, \quad (1.7.7)$$

which leads to the transfer matrix

$$\Theta_i(z) = \Theta_i \begin{bmatrix} -f_i & 0 \\ 0 & I_{r-1} \end{bmatrix} + \Theta_i \begin{bmatrix} \delta_i \\ 0 \end{bmatrix} (z^{-1} - f_i^*)^{-1} \frac{\delta_i}{d_i} \begin{bmatrix} 1 & 0 \end{bmatrix}$$

or, equivalently,

$$\Theta_i(z) = \Theta_i \begin{bmatrix} B_i(z) & 0 \\ 0 & I_{r-1} \end{bmatrix}, \quad B_i(z) = \frac{z - f_i}{1 - f_i^* z}. \quad (1.7.8)$$

Any $(p+q)$-row input to the above $\Theta_i(z)$ is processed by the rotation Θ_i first and then only the leading entry of the result is filtered by the all-pass function $B_i(z)$. This is represented schematically in Fig. 1.4, where the top line of the elementary section includes the factor $B_i(z)$.

When $F = Z$, the cascade of such sections is a classical discrete transmission line; it can be used to show that the generalized Schur algorithm gives a natural solution (and indicates several generalizations) of the classical inverse scattering problems (see, e.g., [BK87a], [BK87b], [CSK99]).

1.7.5 Shift-Structured ($F = Z$) Positive-Definite Matrices

Several simplifications occur when $F = Z$ and R is positive definite, say,

$$R - ZRZ^* = GJG^*, \quad R > 0. \quad (1.7.9)$$

To begin with, since the diagonal entries of Z are now zero, the expression (1.6.12) for Φ_i becomes simply $\Phi_i = Z$. (We continue to write Z, except when otherwise stated, to denote a shift matrix of any dimension.)

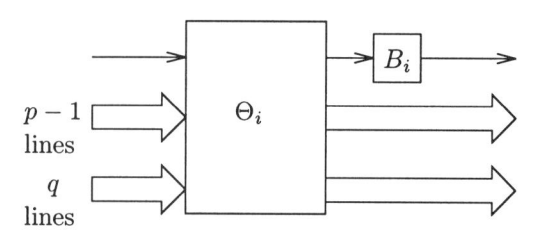

Figure 1.4. Elementary section $\Theta_i(z)$ when $g_i J g_i^* > 0$.

Moreover, since the f_i are now all zero, we conclude from (1.6.8) and from the positivity of the d_i that $g_i J g_i^* > 0$ always. This means that the proper form of the generalized Schur algorithm in this case becomes

$$\begin{bmatrix} 0 \\ G_{i+1} \end{bmatrix} = G_i \Theta_i \begin{bmatrix} 0 & 0 \\ 0 & I_{r-1} \end{bmatrix} + Z\, G_i \, \Theta_i \begin{bmatrix} 1 & 0 \\ 0 & 0 \end{bmatrix}. \qquad (1.7.10)$$

Likewise, the expressions (1.6.7) and (1.6.8) for l_i and d_i become

$$l_i = \delta_i^* G_i \Theta_i \begin{bmatrix} 1 \\ 0 \end{bmatrix}, \quad d_i = |\delta_i|^2. \qquad (1.7.11)$$

Equation (1.7.10) yields the following simple statements:

1. Transform G_i into proper form with respect to its first column by using a J-unitary rotation Θ_i.

2. Shift down the first column and keep the rest of the columns unaltered.

1.7.6 The Classical Schur Algorithm

In order to justify our earlier claim that Alg. 1.6.2 is a far-reaching generalization of the celebrated algorithm of Schur, we focus on a special subclass of (1.7.9), viz., matrices with displacement rank 2. Our objective is to verify that in this case the generator recursion (1.7.10) collapses to Schur's original algorithm [Sch17].

For this purpose, we shall now consider semi-infinite matrices $\mathcal{R}$ with semi-infinite generator matrices $\mathcal{G}$, say,

$$\mathcal{R} - Z\mathcal{R}Z^* = \mathcal{G} \begin{bmatrix} 1 & 0 \\ 0 & -1 \end{bmatrix} \mathcal{G}^*, \qquad (1.7.12)$$

where we shall denote the individual entries of $\mathcal{G}$ by

$$\mathcal{G} = \begin{bmatrix} x_{00} & y_{00} \\ x_{10} & y_{10} \\ x_{20} & y_{20} \\ x_{30} & y_{30} \\ \vdots & \vdots \end{bmatrix}.$$

We further associate with the columns of $\mathcal{G}$ two power series $x_0(z)$ and $y_0(z)$:

$$x_0(z) = x_{00} + x_{10}z + x_{20}z^2 + \cdots,$$
$$y_0(z) = y_{00} + y_{10}z + y_{20}z^2 + \cdots.$$

Section 1.7. Proper Form of the Fast Algorithm

(We assume $\mathcal{R}$ and $\mathcal{G}$ are such that these power series are well defined in some region of the complex plane.) Equivalently, these power series can be obtained by multiplying $\mathcal{G}$ from the left by $\begin{bmatrix} 1 & z & z^2 & z^3 & \cdots \end{bmatrix}$,

$$\begin{bmatrix} x_0(z) & y_0(z) \end{bmatrix} = \begin{bmatrix} 1 & z & z^2 & z^3 & \cdots \end{bmatrix} \mathcal{G}.$$

Now the first step of the generator recursion (1.7.10) takes the form

$$\begin{bmatrix} 0 \\ \mathcal{G}_1 \end{bmatrix} = \mathcal{G}_0 \, \Theta_0 \begin{bmatrix} 0 & 0 \\ 0 & 1 \end{bmatrix} + \mathcal{Z} \, \mathcal{G}_0 \, \Theta_0 \begin{bmatrix} 1 & 0 \\ 0 & 0 \end{bmatrix}, \qquad (1.7.13)$$

where we recall that the purpose of the J-unitary rotation Θ_0 is to annihilate y_{00}. This can be achieved by using a hyperbolic rotation of the form (cf. the discussion in App. B)

$$\Theta_0 = \frac{1}{\sqrt{1 - |\gamma_0|^2}} \begin{bmatrix} 1 & -\gamma_0 \\ -\gamma_0^* & 1 \end{bmatrix}, \quad \gamma_0 = \frac{y_{00}}{x_{00}} = \frac{y_0(0)}{x_0(0)}.$$

(The positive definiteness of $\mathcal{R}$ guarantees $|x_{00}|^2 - |y_{00}|^2 > 0$ and, hence, x_{00} cannot be zero.) After applying Θ_0 and then shifting down the first column, we obtain $\mathcal{G}_1$ by

$$\begin{bmatrix} 0 \\ \mathcal{G}_1 \end{bmatrix} = \begin{bmatrix} 0 & 0 \\ x_{11} & y_{11} \\ x_{21} & y_{21} \\ x_{31} & y_{31} \\ \vdots & \vdots \end{bmatrix}.$$

We also associate two power series with the nonidentically zero part of the columns of $\mathcal{G}_1$,

$$x_1(z) = x_{11} + x_{21}z + x_{31}z^2 + \cdots,$$
$$y_1(z) = y_{11} + y_{21}z + y_{31}z^2 + \cdots.$$

By multiplying both sides of (1.7.13) by $\begin{bmatrix} 1 & z & z^2 & z^3 & \cdots \end{bmatrix}$ from the left, and by noting that

$$\begin{bmatrix} 1 & z & z^2 & z^3 & \cdots \end{bmatrix} \mathcal{Z} = z \begin{bmatrix} 1 & z & z^2 & z^3 & \cdots \end{bmatrix},$$

we conclude that

$$\begin{bmatrix} zx_1(z) & zy_1(z) \end{bmatrix} = \begin{bmatrix} x_0(z) & y_0(z) \end{bmatrix} \Theta_0 \begin{bmatrix} z & 0 \\ 0 & 1 \end{bmatrix}.$$

This is a functional recursion that tells us how the power series of the successive generator matrices are related to each other.

The recursive procedure now continues as follows: compute γ_1 as the ratio of y_{11} and x_{11}, multiply the prearray $\mathcal{G}_1$ by Θ_1 in order to introduce a zero in the first entry of the second column of the postarray, shift down the first column of the postarray, and so on. In function form, for the ith step, we have

$$z \begin{bmatrix} x_{i+1}(z) & y_{i+1}(z) \end{bmatrix} = \begin{bmatrix} x_i(z) & y_i(z) \end{bmatrix} \Theta_i \begin{bmatrix} z & 0 \\ 0 & 1 \end{bmatrix}, \qquad (1.7.14)$$

where Θ_i is an elementary hyperbolic rotation determined by a coefficient γ_i,

$$\Theta_i = \frac{1}{\sqrt{1-|\gamma_i|^2}} \begin{bmatrix} 1 & -\gamma_i \\ -\gamma_i^* & 1 \end{bmatrix}, \quad \gamma_i = \frac{y_i(0)}{x_i(0)}. \tag{1.7.15}$$

If we introduce the (so-called scattering) function

$$s_i(z) \triangleq \frac{y_i(z)}{x_i(z)},$$

it then follows easily from (1.7.14) that $s_i(z)$ satisfies the recursion:

$$s_{i+1}(z) = \frac{1}{z} \frac{s_i(z) - \gamma_i}{1 - \gamma_i^* s_i(z)}, \quad \gamma_i = s_i(0). \tag{1.7.16}$$

This is the famous Schur recursion, which was originally derived for checking when power series are analytic and bounded by unity in the unit disc [Sch17]. We see that it follows as a special case of our earlier Alg. 1.6.2, which is in this sense a generalization of Schur's earlier work. Note that the generalization is in several respects: it allows for displacement ranks larger than 2, it allows for general lower triangular matrices F instead of the shift matrix Z, and it allows for strongly regular matrices R instead of positive-definite matrices R. The generalization also extends to non-Hermitian matrices and to other definitions of matrix structure (see further ahead and also [KS95a]). (The generating function language can continue to be used for certain forms of F—see [Lev97].)

1.7.7 The Special Case of Toeplitz Matrices

When the matrix R in (1.7.12) is a finite Hermitian Toeplitz matrix, $T = [c_{i-j}]_{i,j=0}^{n-1}$, with $c_0 = 1$, then it is easy to check that a generator matrix is given by

$$G^T = \begin{bmatrix} 1 & c_1 & \cdots & c_{n-1} \\ 0 & c_1 & \cdots & c_{n-1} \end{bmatrix}, \quad J = \begin{bmatrix} 1 & 0 \\ 0 & -1 \end{bmatrix}$$

(see (1.2.5)).

It turns out that in this case, the so-called Schur coefficients γ_i coincide with the reflection coefficients introduced in the Levinson–Durbin algorithm (1.2.7)–(1.2.9) for solving the Yule–Walker equations, which is why we used the same symbols for them. But, as noted earlier (at the end of Sec. 1.2), we can now present an alternative method of solving the Yule–Walker equations—we compute the $\{\gamma_i\}$ by the Schur algorithm and then directly use the recursions (1.2.7), thus circumventing the inner-product evaluations (1.2.8) of the Levinson–Durbin algorithm. This is sometimes called the hybrid method of solving the Yule–Walker equations—the algorithm can also be extended to solving Toeplitz linear equations with arbitrary right-hand sides, as will be shown in Sec. 1.8.4 below.

1.8 SOME APPLICATIONS IN MATRIX COMPUTATION

In the previous sections, we established that displacement structure is *invariant* under Schur complementation and derived a fast algorithm for recursively updating the generator matrices of the successive Schur complements of a structured matrix.

We also mentioned earlier that the above invariance property is very useful in handling combinations of structured matrices. Now that we have derived the fast algorithm,

Section 1.8. Some Applications in Matrix Computation 31

we can return to this earlier remark and demonstrate its usefulness by presenting a few examples. The examples we present here will also highlight the value of extending the the definition of displacement structure by replacing Z in (1.2.4) by more general (say, strictly lower) triangular matrices F in (1.3.21). Such extension allows us to handle, through a technique known as *embedding* [CKL87], [KC94], many matrix computation problems that involve combinations of structured matrices.

1.8.1 Going Beyond $F = Z$

A first application of the embedding idea is to note that T^{-1} is the Schur complement of the $(1,1)$ block in the Toeplitz block matrix

$$M = \begin{bmatrix} -T & I \\ I & 0 \end{bmatrix}. \quad (1.8.1)$$

Now by examining $M - Z_{2n} M Z_{2n}$, we can see that the displacement rank of M is less than or equal to 4, where we have employed the notation Z_{2n} to denote the $2n \times 2n$ lower shift matrix. Therefore, by Lemma 1.5.2, the rank of the Schur complement, T^{-1}, must also be less than or equal to 4. However, this is a weak conclusion, because we know from Lemma 1.5.1 that the displacement rank of T^{-1} is 2.

If we instead employ the definition

$$\nabla M = M - \begin{bmatrix} Z_n & 0 \\ 0 & Z_n \end{bmatrix} M \begin{bmatrix} Z_n & 0 \\ 0 & Z_n \end{bmatrix}^*, \quad (1.8.2)$$

where we use $F = (Z_n \oplus Z_n)$ in the definition $R - FRF^*$ rather than $F = Z_{2n}$, then it is easy to see that the displacement rank of M is now 2. In fact, the reader may wish to check that for a Hermitian Toeplitz matrix $T = [c_{i-j}]_{i,j=0}^{n-1}$, $c_0 = 1$, we obtain

$$M - FMF^* = GJG^*, \quad F = Z_n \oplus Z_n,$$

where $J = (1 \oplus -1)$ and

$$G^{\mathbf{T}} = \begin{bmatrix} 0 & c_1 & \cdots & c_{n-1} & 1 & 0 & \cdots & 0 \\ 1 & c_1 & \cdots & c_{n-1} & 1 & 0 & \cdots & 0 \end{bmatrix}^{\mathbf{T}}. \quad (1.8.3)$$

Soon we shall give more elaborate examples. However, from the embedding (1.8.1), we shall show how we can obtain several interesting results on both T and T^{-1}.

1.8.2 Simultaneous Factorization of T and T^{-1}

We shall see that by applying the generalized Schur algorithm to the matrix M in (1.8.1) we can not only determine (the generators of) T^{-1} but also simultaneously factor both T and T^{-1}. Thus consider the situation after we apply n steps of the generalized Schur algorithm (say Alg. 1.6.2 or, in proper form, Alg. 1.7.1) to the generator G of M, viz., (1.8.3). Of course, we shall then get a generator, say, $\{a, b\}$, of the Schur complement T^{-1} from which we can recover the matrix T^{-1} as

$$T^{-1} = \mathcal{L}(a)\mathcal{L}^*(a) - \mathcal{L}(b)\mathcal{L}^*(b).$$

Suppose that we also (or only) want the triangular factors of T^{-1}. One way to get these is to apply the Schur algorithm to the generator $\{a, b\}$. But in fact the factors of

T^{-1} are already available from the results of the first n steps of the generalized Schur algorithm applied to the generator of M.

To clarify this, assume we apply the first n recursive steps of the generalized Schur algorithm to a generator of the $2n \times 2n$ matrix M, with $F = (Z_n \oplus Z_n)$. This provides us with the first n columns and the first n diagonal entries of the triangular factors of M, which we denote by L_{2n} and D_{2n}. That is, we obtain the first n columns of L_{2n} and the first n entries of D_{2n} in the factorization $M = L_{2n} D_{2n}^{-1} L_{2n}^*$. Let us denote the leading $n \times n$ block of D_{2n} by D and let us partition the first n columns of L_{2n} into the form
$$\begin{bmatrix} L \\ U \end{bmatrix},$$
where L is $n \times n$ lower triangular and U is an $n \times n$ matrix that we shall soon see has to be upper triangular. It follows from the Schur reduction interpretation of Alg. 1.6.1 that we must have
$$\begin{bmatrix} -T & I \\ I & 0 \end{bmatrix} = M = \begin{bmatrix} L \\ U \end{bmatrix} D^{-1} \begin{bmatrix} L^* & U^* \end{bmatrix} + \begin{bmatrix} 0 & 0 \\ 0 & T^{-1} \end{bmatrix}.$$

By equating terms on both sides of the above equality we conclude that $U = L^{-*}D$, $-T^{-1} = UD^{-1}U^*$, and $-T = LD^{-1}L^*$. Hence, the first n recursive steps of the algorithm provide not only the triangular factorization of T but also the triangular factorization of T^{-1}. In fact, by examining the form (1.8.3) of the generator for the matrix M, the reader can check that the generalized Schur algorithm for the present problem (i.e., for M as in (1.8.1)) is exactly what we called a hybrid algorithm in Sec. 1.7.7.

Unfortunately, this nice embedding idea does not extend to a general F. To see this, consider again the simple example of a Pick matrix P,
$$P = \left[\frac{u_i u_i^* - v_j v_j^*}{1 - f_i f_j^*} \right]_{i,j=0}^{n-1}, \tag{1.8.4}$$

where the $\{u_i, v_i\}$ are row vectors of dimensions p and q, respectively, and the f_i are complex points inside the open unit disc ($|f_i| < 1$). Then with $F = \text{diag}\{f_0, f_1, \ldots, f_{n-1}\}$, we can check that P has ∇_F-displacement

$$P - FPF^* = \begin{bmatrix} u_0 & v_0 \\ u_1 & v_1 \\ \vdots & \vdots \\ u_{n-1} & v_{n-1} \end{bmatrix} \begin{bmatrix} I_p & 0 \\ 0 & -I_q \end{bmatrix} \begin{bmatrix} u_0 & v_0 \\ u_1 & v_1 \\ \vdots & \vdots \\ u_{n-1} & v_{n-1} \end{bmatrix}^*. \tag{1.8.5}$$

However, if we now construct the matrix M as before, i.e., as in (1.8.1) but with P instead of T, it is easy to check that $M - (F \oplus F)M(F \oplus F)^*$ does not have low rank since $(I - FF^*)$ is full rank in general.

A general method that overcomes this difficulty has recently been obtained and will be described in Sec. 1.10, where this example will be reconsidered.

1.8.3 QR Factorization of Structured Matrices

We now show how the displacement ideas can be used to suggest a fast algorithm for the QR factorization of structured matrices (with Q unitary and R upper triangular). This

Section 1.8. Some Applications in Matrix Computation

has been a much-studied problem, starting with the dissertation [Swe82]. Some later papers are those of [BBH86], [Cyb83], [Cyb87], [Swe84]. The displacement approach described below is much simpler, conceptually and algebraically.

Let X be an $n \times n$ matrix[4] that has low displacement rank with respect to the displacement $X - Z_n X Z_n^*$. Form the displacement of

$$M = \begin{bmatrix} -I & X & 0 \\ X^* & 0 & X^* \\ 0 & X & 0 \end{bmatrix}$$

with $F = Z_n \oplus Z_n \oplus Z_n$ and find a generator for M. A general procedure for doing this has been given in [Chu89], [KC94]; in many cases, e.g., when X is Toeplitz, one can obtain a generator of length 5 almost by inspection (see, e.g., the discussion in Sec. 3.4 of this book).

After n steps of the generalized Schur algorithm applied to a generator of M, we shall have a generator of

$$M_1 = \begin{bmatrix} X^*X & X^* \\ X & 0 \end{bmatrix}.$$

After another n steps, we shall have the partial triangularization (where L is $n \times n$ lower triangular and U is an $n \times n$ matrix)

$$M_1 = \begin{bmatrix} L \\ U \end{bmatrix} D^{-1} \begin{bmatrix} L^* & U^* \end{bmatrix} + \begin{bmatrix} 0 & 0 \\ 0 & -I \end{bmatrix}.$$

By equating terms on both sides of the above equality we conclude that

$$X^*X = (LD^{-*/2})(LD^{-*/2})^* \;,\; (UD^{-*/2})(LD^{-*/2})^* = X,$$

and $(UD^{-*/2})(UD^{-*/2})^* = I$. Therefore, we can identify

$$Q = UD^{-*/2}, \qquad R = (LD^{-*/2})^*$$

as the Q and R factors in the QR factorization of X. Here, D is a positive-definite diagonal matrix and $D^{1/2}$ denotes a diagonal matrix whose entries are the square roots of the diagonal entries of D. In summary, the QR factors of the structured matrix X can be obtained by applying the Schur recursion to a properly defined extended structured matrix M.

The above procedure may encounter numerical difficulties in finite precision implementations. However, in Sec. 3.1, it will be shown how to employ such embedding constructions to develop the first provably backward-stable algorithm for the solution of linear systems of equations with structured coefficient matrices (cf. [CS98]).

1.8.4 Avoiding Back Substitution in Linear Equations

The previous examples all involved the Schur algorithm for Hermitian matrices. Here is an example of a problem involving non-Hermitian matrices. The generalized Schur algorithm for non-Hermitian matrices is similar in nature to what we described in Sec. 1.6 and is covered in detail in [KS95a] (and briefly in Sec. 1.11). It is not necessary to know the exact algorithm to follow the present discussion.

---
[4]The argument also applies to rectangular matrices, say, $m \times n$.

Consider a linear system of equations of the form

$$Tx = b,$$

where T is an $n \times n$ strongly regular Hermitian Toeplitz matrix and b is a known column vector. One possibility for determining the entries of x is the following: compute the triangular factorization of T, say,

$$T = LD^{-1}L^*,$$

and then solve, via back substitution, the triangular system of equations in y and x,

$$LD^{-1}y = b \quad \text{and} \quad L^*x = y.$$

A major drawback of a back-substitution step is that it involves serial operations and does not lend itself to a parallelizable algorithm.

A way out of this is to employ a bordering (or embedding) technique (see, e.g., [KC94]). For this purpose, we define the extended (non-Hermitian) matrix

$$R = \begin{bmatrix} -T & b \\ I & 0 \end{bmatrix}$$

and note that the Schur complement of $-T$ in R is precisely $T^{-1}b$, which is equal to the desired solution x. Now the matrix R itself is also structured since T is Toeplitz. More precisely, we know that $T - ZTZ^*$ has rank 2 and it follows that

$$\begin{bmatrix} -T & b \\ I & 0 \end{bmatrix} - \begin{bmatrix} Z & \\ & Z \end{bmatrix} \begin{bmatrix} -T & b \\ I & 0 \end{bmatrix} \begin{bmatrix} Z & \\ & 0 \end{bmatrix}^* \quad \text{also has low rank.}$$

Therefore, after n steps of partial triangularization of R, we shall have a generator of its Schur complement, from which we can read out the solution x.

There are several other interesting examples and applications (see, e.g., [CXT94], [AS99]), but let us move on.

1.9 LOOK-AHEAD (BLOCK) SCHUR ALGORITHM

A standing assumption in all the preceding has been that the structured matrix R is strongly regular, i.e., all its leading minors are nonzero. However there are applications where we may have some poorly conditioned or even zero leading minors. In such cases, one can use the smallest nonsingular leading minor, or a well-conditioned leading minor of appropriate dimensions, in order to proceed with a block Schur complementation step. The use of such block pivoting has been studied by several authors trying to devise effective numerical algorithms for various classes of structured matrices (see, e.g., [CH92b], [Gut93], [Fre94], and the references therein).

There are also several theoretically interesting studies on the special case of Hankel matrices with zero minors (for which there is the celebrated Berlekamp–Massey algorithm [Mas69] and related studies of the so-called partial realization problem of system theory) and the less-studied problem for Toeplitz matrices (see [Pal90], [PK93], and the references therein).

Here we shall describe a very general algorithm that goes considerably beyond the results noted so far. The results appeared first in [SK95b], [Say92]; here we present an array-based derivation.

Section 1.9. Look-Ahead (Block) Schur Algorithm

Consider a Hermitian and invertible (but not necessarily strongly regular) matrix $R \in \mathbb{C}^{n \times n}$, and let η_0 denote the desired size of the leading invertible block, D_0, with respect to which a Schur complementation step is to be performed. The η_0 may stand for the size of the smallest nonsingular minor of R or, alternatively, for the size of a numerically well-conditioned block. If L_0 represents the first η_0 columns of R, then we can replace the earlier Schur complementation step (1.6.4) by the block step

$$R - L_0 D_0^{-1} L_0^* = \begin{bmatrix} 0_{\eta_0 \times \eta_0} & 0 \\ 0 & R_1 \end{bmatrix},$$

where R_1 is now an $(n - \eta_0) \times (n - \eta_0)$ matrix that is the Schur complement of D_0 in R. We are also being explicit about the dimensions of the leading zero block in the resulting matrix, viz., $\eta_0 \times \eta_0$.

The matrix L_0 is $n \times \eta_0$ with a leading $\eta_0 \times \eta_0$ block that is equal to D_0. If we further let η_1 denote the desired size of the leading invertible block of R_1 (denoted by D_1) and consider the corresponding first η_1 columns of R_1 (denoted by L_1), then we write for our second block step

$$R_1 - L_1 D_1^{-1} L_1^* = \begin{bmatrix} 0_{\eta_1 \times \eta_1} & 0 \\ 0 & R_2 \end{bmatrix},$$

where R_2 is an $(n - \eta_0 - \eta_1) \times (n - \eta_0 - \eta_1)$ matrix that is the Schur complement of D_1 in R_1. Repeating this block Schur reduction procedure, viz.,

$$\begin{bmatrix} 0_{\eta_i \times \eta_i} & 0 \\ 0 & R_{i+1} \end{bmatrix} = R_i - L_i D_i^{-1} L_i^*, \quad i \geq 0, \tag{1.9.1}$$

we clearly get, after, say, t steps,

$$R = L D^{-1} L^*$$

$$= L_0 D_0^{-1} L_0^* + \begin{bmatrix} 0_{\eta_0 \times \eta_1} \\ L_1 \end{bmatrix} D_1^{-1} \begin{bmatrix} 0_{\eta_0 \times \eta_1} \\ L_1 \end{bmatrix}^* + \begin{bmatrix} 0_{\eta_0 \times \eta_2} \\ 0_{\eta_1 \times \eta_2} \\ L_2 \end{bmatrix} D_2^{-1} \begin{bmatrix} 0_{\eta_0 \times \eta_2} \\ 0_{\eta_1 \times \eta_2} \\ L_2 \end{bmatrix}^* + \cdots,$$

where $D = (D_0 \oplus D_1 \oplus \ldots \oplus D_{t-1})$ is now *block* diagonal and the (nonzero parts of the) columns of the *block* lower triangular matrix L are $\{L_0, \ldots, L_{t-1}\}$. Here t is the number of reduction steps and, hence, $n = \sum_{i=0}^{t-1} \eta_i$.

The computational cost of this block reduction procedure is, as mentioned earlier, $O(n^3)$. By exploiting the structure of R we can reduce the computational cost by deriving an algorithm that operates on the successive generator matrices instead. So assume R satisfies (1.3.21) and (1.3.22). It is then clear that the same array equation (1.6.15) still holds, viz.,

$$\begin{bmatrix} FL & G \\ U & 0 \end{bmatrix} \Omega = \begin{bmatrix} L & 0 \\ F^*U & H^* \end{bmatrix}, \quad \Omega(D^{-1} \oplus J)\Omega^* = (D^{-1} \oplus J), \tag{1.9.2}$$

except that D and L are now *block* diagonal and *block* lower triangular, and U is such that $U = L^{-*}D$.

The same recursive argument that we employed in Sec. 1.6.4 shows that the basic recursion for the generators of the successive (block) Schur complements R_i now takes the form

$$\begin{bmatrix} F_i L_i & | & G_i \end{bmatrix} \Sigma_i = \begin{bmatrix} L_i & | & 0 \\ & & G_{i+1} \end{bmatrix}, \tag{1.9.3}$$

where L_i satisfies the equation

$$L_i - F_i L_i \hat{F}_i^* = G_i J \hat{G}_i^*, \qquad (1.9.4)$$

and $\hat{F}_i$ is the leading $\eta_i \times \eta_i$ block of F_i, which is now partitioned as

$$F_i = \begin{bmatrix} \hat{F}_i & 0 \\ \star & F_{i+1} \end{bmatrix}.$$

That is, F_{i+1} is now obtained by deleting the leading η_i rows and columns of F_i. Likewise, $\hat{G}_i$ denotes the top η_i rows of G_i and Σ_i is $(D_i^{-1} \oplus J)$-unitary. The quantities $\{\hat{F}_i, \hat{G}_i, L_i, D_i\}$ play the role of the quantities $\{f_i, g_i, l_i, d_i\}$ that we encountered earlier in Sec. 1.6.4.

If we denote the entries of Σ_i by

$$\Sigma_i = \begin{bmatrix} A_i & B_i \\ C_i & S_i \end{bmatrix}, \qquad (1.9.5)$$

where A_i is $\eta_i \times \eta_i$, B_i is $\eta_i \times r$, C_i is $r \times \eta_i$, and S_i is $r \times r$, we can verify that we must have

$$A_i = \hat{F}_i^*, \qquad C_i = J\hat{G}_i^*. \qquad (1.9.6)$$

To identify the remaining entries $\{B_i, S_i\}$, we note that in view of the $(D_i^{-1} \oplus J)$-unitarity of Σ_i, the entries $\{A_i, B_i, C_i, S_i\}$ must satisfy

$$\begin{bmatrix} A_i & B_i \\ C_i & S_i \end{bmatrix} \begin{bmatrix} D_i^{-1} & 0 \\ 0 & J \end{bmatrix} \begin{bmatrix} A_i & B_i \\ C_i & S_i \end{bmatrix}^* = \begin{bmatrix} D_i^{-1} & 0 \\ 0 & J \end{bmatrix}. \qquad (1.9.7)$$

Following the derivation in the proof of Lemma 1.6.4, we can use this relation to identify $\{B_i, S_i\}$ and obtain the following algorithm [Say92], [SK95b].

Algorithm 1.9.1 (Block or Look-Ahead Schur Algorithm). *Given a matrix $R \in \mathbb{C}^{n \times n}$ that satisfies (1.3.21) and (1.3.22) for some full rank $G \in \mathbb{C}^{n \times r}$, start with $F_0 = F$, $G_0 = G$ and perform the following steps:*

1. *At step i we have F_i and G_i. Let $\hat{G}_i$ denote the top η_i rows of G_i and let $\hat{F}_i$ denote the leading $\eta_i \times \eta_i$ block of F_i.*

2. *The ith triangular factors L_i and D_i are the solutions of the equations*

$$D_i = \hat{F}_i D_i \hat{F}_i^* + \hat{G}_i J \hat{G}_i^*, \qquad L_i = F_i L_i \hat{F}_i^* + G_i J \hat{G}_i^*. \qquad (1.9.8)$$

3. *Update the generator matrix G_i as follows:*

$$\begin{bmatrix} 0_{\eta_i \times r} \\ G_{i+1} \end{bmatrix} = \left\{ G_i + (\tau_i^* F_i - I_{n-\alpha_i}) L_i D_i^{-1} (I_{\eta_i} - \tau_i^* \hat{F}_i)^{-1} \hat{G}_i \right\} \Theta_i,$$

where Θ_i is an arbitrary J-unitary matrix and τ_i is an arbitrary unit-modulus scalar. Also, $\alpha_i = \sum_{k=0}^{i-1} \eta_k$.

The matrix G_i is a generator for R_i,

$$R_i - F_i R_i F_i^* = G_i J G_i^*,$$

which is the Schur complement of R with respect to its leading $\alpha_i \times \alpha_i$ block.

$\diamond$

We may remark that although block algorithms have often been used in connection with poorly conditioned matrices, Alg. 1.9.1 is quite general and has several other applications.

1.10 FAST INVERSION OF STRUCTURED MATRICES

Our discussion so far has been mainly concerned with the direct factorization problem, viz., that of computing the triangular factors of R. In Sec. 1.8.2 we saw how the embedding technique allowed us to employ the fast Schur algorithm for factoring the inverse of a Toeplitz matrix as well. We remarked, however, at the end of Sec. 1.8.2 that this technique does not extend readily to more general structured matrices. In fact, similar results for computing the triangular factors of the *inverse* matrix R^{-1} have not yet been obtained for the general case.

For Toeplitz matrices, as we mentioned in Sec. 1.2, the first and best-known algorithm for factoring the inverse is the celebrated Levinson–Durbin algorithm. Early attempts at extending this algorithm beyond the Toeplitz case were made in [FKML78], [Del82], [DGK85], [Lev83] but the formulas were rather complicated. After the (re)discovery of the Schur algorithm for directly factoring Toeplitz matrices rather than their inverses, it was realized by several authors (see [KH83], [Kai85]) that the Levinson–Durbin algorithm could be replaced by a two-step procedure: use the Schur algorithm to compute the so-called reflection coefficients, and then use a simple recursion to compute the triangular factors of the inverse; this is actually the hybrid algorithm of Sec. 1.8.2. This two-step procedure requires slightly more computation than the Levinson–Durbin algorithm on a serial machine, but it is significantly less expensive on a parallel machine. (This is because the classical Levinson–Durbin algorithm obtains the reflection coefficients via certain inner products, which cannot be parallelized in an efficient manner.) The hybrid method was extended in [Chu89] and [KC94] to invert matrices obeying displacement equations of the form $R - FRF^* = GJG^*$, where F had some *strictly* lower triangular structure. However, these extended algorithms generally require an intermediate array whose displacement rank can be larger than r.

In the recent works [BSLK96], [BKLS98a], [BKLS98b] we removed all the above-mentioned restrictions. In this section we provide an overview of the solution method. However, for simplicity of presentation, here we shall first assume that the following *nondegeneracy* condition holds (in addition to (1.3.22)):

$$i \neq j \implies f_i \neq f_j, \qquad i,j \in \{0,1,\ldots,n-1\}. \qquad (1.10.1)$$

This condition simplifies the derivation of the recursions for the factorization of the inverse of R; it is not needed for the direct factorization problem itself as we saw in the earlier section. The assumption, however, excludes the important cases of $F = Z$ or F strictly lower triangular; the general case is briefly discussed in Sec. 1.10.7.

1.10.1 Schur Construction (Inflation)

The Schur reduction procedure of Alg. 1.6.1 can be extended to the factorization of the inverse matrix. While we factored R before by recursively deflating it, we now factor R^{-1} by "inflation."

Recall that we expressed the triangular factorizations of R and R^{-1} in the somewhat nontraditional forms (cf. (1.6.1) and (1.6.14))

$$R = LD^{-1}L^*, \qquad R^{-1} = UD^{-1}U^*, \qquad (1.10.2)$$

where $D = \text{diag}\{d_0, d_1, \ldots, d_{n-1}\}$ and

$$LD^{-1}U^* = I_n. \qquad (1.10.3)$$

The nonzero parts of the columns of L are denoted by $\{l_j\}$ and of U are denoted by $\{u_j\}$.

Algorithm 1.10.1 (Schur Construction for Inversion). *Given $R \in \mathbb{C}^{n \times n}$, start with $\Delta_0 = [\ ]$ (the empty matrix) and repeat the following steps for $i = 0, 1, \ldots, n-1$:*

1. *Let l_i and d_i denote the first column and the upper-left-corner element of R_i. These can be evaluated via the Schur reduction of Alg. 1.6.1.*

2. *Given $\{l_0, l_1, \ldots, l_i\}$ and $\{d_0, d_1, \ldots, d_i\}$, compute u_i from the equation*

$$\sum_{j=0}^{i} \breve{l}_j d_j^{-1} \breve{u}_j^* = \begin{bmatrix} I_{i+1} & 0 \\ 0 & 0 \end{bmatrix},$$

where

$$\breve{l}_j = \begin{bmatrix} 0 \\ l_j \end{bmatrix} \begin{matrix} \}j \\ \}n-j \end{matrix}, \qquad \breve{u}_j = \begin{bmatrix} u_j \\ 0 \end{bmatrix} \begin{matrix} \}j+1 \\ \}n-j-1 \end{matrix}.$$

3. *Perform the Schur construction step*

$$\Delta_{i+1} = \begin{bmatrix} \Delta_i & 0 \\ 0 & 0 \end{bmatrix} + u_i d_i^{-1} u_i^*. \tag{1.10.4}$$

◇

Observe that while Alg. 1.6.1 involves *reduction* steps, i.e., rank 1 matrices are recursively subtracted at each step, the above algorithm involves *construction* steps in which rank 1 matrices are added to Δ_i (after bordering the matrix with zeros). Thus this procedure successively constructs the rows and columns of R^{-1}. The intermediate array Δ_i is the Schur complement of the trailing $(n-i) \times (n-i)$ block in R^{-1}. At the end of the procedure we obtain $\Delta_{n-1} = R^{-1}$. It is also immediate to verify the following result.

Lemma 1.10.1 (Partitioning of the Triangular Factorization). *If we partition R^{-1} and U as*

$$R^{-1} = \begin{bmatrix} W_i & V_i^* \\ V_i & T_i \end{bmatrix} \begin{matrix} \}i \\ \}n-i \end{matrix}, \qquad U = \begin{bmatrix} \bar{U}_i & \tilde{U}_i \\ 0 & U_i \end{bmatrix} \begin{matrix} \}i \\ \}n-i \end{matrix}$$

and let D be partitioned as before (after Alg. 1.6.1), then the trailing principal block T_i and its Schur complement $\Delta_i = W_i - V_i^* T_i^{-1} V_i$ admit the following triangular decompositions:

$$T_i = U_i D_i^{-1} U_i^*, \qquad \Delta_i = \bar{U}_i \bar{D}_i^{-1} \bar{U}_i^*.$$

Moreover, we also have that $R_i^{-1} = T_i$ and $\Delta_i^{-1} = P_i$.

◇

In other words, the inverse of the trailing principal block in R^{-1} is equal to the Schur complement of the leading principal block in R and vice versa: the inverse of the leading principal block in R is equal to the Schur complement of the trailing principal block in R^{-1}.

1.10.2 Statement of the Fast Inversion Algorithm

Just as for R_i, it turns out that Δ_i inherits the displacement structure of R, as we shall now proceed to show. Using this property, we shall also be able to reduce the cost of the above Schur reduction procedure from $O(n^3)$ to $O(n^2)$.

The algorithm we state below has one very important feature: it does not require that we know a priori a generator matrix H^* for R^{-1} to factor R^{-1}. Instead, it works directly with the given displacement description of R itself, namely, $\{F, G, J\}$, and constructs $\{H^*, U\}$! This will be achieved by recursively computing matrices $H_i \in \mathbb{C}^{i \times i}$ ($i = 0, 1, \ldots, n-1$) that are generators for the successive Δ_i,

$$\Delta_i - \bar{F}_i^* \Delta_i \bar{F}_i = H_i^* J H_i, \qquad (1.10.5)$$

where, according to (1.6.6), $\bar{F}_i$ is the leading $i \times i$ block of F,

$$F = \begin{bmatrix} \bar{F}_i & 0 \\ \tilde{F}_i & F_i \end{bmatrix} \begin{matrix} \}i \\ \}n-i \end{matrix} \overbrace{\phantom{\bar{F}_i}}^{i} \overbrace{}^{n-i}.$$

At this point, we encourage the reader to review Alg. 1.6.2 for the factorization of R, because it will be used here.

Algorithm 1.10.2 (Schur Algorithm for the Inverse Matrix). *Given a matrix $R \in \mathbb{C}^{n \times n}$ that satisfies (1.3.21), (1.3.22), and (1.10.1) for some full rank $G \in \mathbb{C}^{n \times r}$, start with $H_0 = [\ ]$ and repeat the following steps for $i = 0, \ldots, n-1$:*

1. *Let $\{l_i, d_i, g_i, G_i\}$ be defined and computed as in Alg. 1.6.2.*

2. *Let $\bar{F}_{i+1}$ and u_i be partitioned as*

$$\bar{F}_{i+1} = \begin{bmatrix} \bar{F}_i & 0 \\ \varphi_i & f_i \end{bmatrix}, \qquad u_i = \begin{bmatrix} \bar{u}_i \\ 1 \end{bmatrix}. \qquad (1.10.6)$$

Compute $\bar{u}_i$ by solving the linear system

$$(\bar{F}_i^* - f_i^* I_i) \bar{u}_i = H_i^* J g_i^* - \varphi_i^*. \qquad (1.10.7)$$

The nondegeneracy condition (1.10.1) ensures that (1.10.7) has a unique solution for $\bar{u}_i$.

3. *Apply the same transformation Σ_i as in (1.6.9) to the prearray shown below and obtain H_{i+1}^*:*

$$\begin{bmatrix} u_i & H_i^* \\ & 0 \end{bmatrix} \Sigma_i = \begin{bmatrix} \bar{F}_{i+1}^* u_i & H_{i+1}^* \end{bmatrix}. \qquad (1.10.8)$$

Notice that H_{i+1}^* has one more row than H_i^*.

$\diamond$

In fact, we can further show that H_{i+1}^* can be obtained from H_i^* explicitly via the equation

$$H_{i+1}^* = \left\{ \begin{bmatrix} H_i^* \\ 0 \end{bmatrix} + \begin{bmatrix} \Psi_i - I_i & 0 \\ 0 & 0 \end{bmatrix} \begin{bmatrix} H_i^* \\ 0 \end{bmatrix} \frac{J g_i^* g_i}{g_i J g_i^*} + \begin{bmatrix} \phi_i \\ 1 \end{bmatrix} g_i d_i^{-1} \right\} \Theta_i,$$

where Θ_i is any J-unitary matrix Θ_i and

$$\Psi_i = (\bar{F}_i^* - f_i^* I_i)^{-1}(I_i - f_i \bar{F}_i^*), \qquad (1.10.9)$$

$$\phi_i = -(\bar{F}_i^* - f_i^* I_i)^{-1} \varphi_i^*. \qquad (1.10.10)$$

1.10.3 Algorithm Development

The derivation of the algorithm follows from the array-based arguments that we employed earlier in Sec. 1.6.4. Recall that in that section we focused on the top block row of both the pre- and postarrays in (1.6.15). By further considering the effect of the rotation Ω on the second block row of both arrays, we are led to the above algorithm.

More explicitly, we already know from the argument that led to the array equation (1.6.15) that there exists a $(D^{-1} \oplus J)$-unitary matrix Ω such that

$$\begin{bmatrix} FL & G \\ U & 0 \end{bmatrix} \Omega = \begin{bmatrix} L & 0 \\ F^*U & H^* \end{bmatrix}. \qquad (1.10.11)$$

We used this equation earlier to argue recursively that by triangularizing the prearray

$$\begin{bmatrix} FL & G \end{bmatrix}$$

through a sequence of $(D^{-1} \oplus J)$-unitary rotations $\{\Omega_0, \Omega_1, \ldots, \Omega_{n-1}\}$ we obtain the generalized Schur procedure listed in Alg. 1.6.2. Now by applying these same rotations to the second block row in (1.10.11), viz.,

$$\begin{bmatrix} U & 0 \end{bmatrix},$$

we can justify Alg. 1.10.2.

For this purpose, we start by partitioning the pre- and postarrays as

$$\begin{bmatrix} FL & G \\ U & 0 \end{bmatrix} = \left[\begin{array}{cc|c} \bar{F}_i \bar{L}_i & 0 & \\ \tilde{F}_i \bar{L}_i + F_i \tilde{L}_i & F_i L_i & G \\ \hline \bar{U}_i & \tilde{U}_i & \\ 0 & U_i & 0 \end{array} \right] \qquad (1.10.12)$$

and

$$\begin{bmatrix} L & 0 \\ F^*U & H^* \end{bmatrix} = \left[\begin{array}{cc|c} \bar{L}_i & 0 & \\ \tilde{L}_i & L_i & 0 \\ \hline \bar{F}_i^* \bar{U}_i & \bar{F}_i^* \tilde{U}_i + \tilde{F}_i^* U_i & H^* \\ 0 & F_i^* U_i & \end{array} \right]. \qquad (1.10.13)$$

After i iterations, the first i columns of the postarray are already computed, while the last $(n-i)$ columns of the prearray have not yet been modified. Therefore, the ith intermediate array must have the following form:

$$\begin{bmatrix} FL & G \\ U & 0 \end{bmatrix} \Omega_0 \Omega_1 \ldots \Omega_{i-1} = \left[\begin{array}{cc|c} \bar{L}_i & 0 & 0 \\ \tilde{L}_i & F_i L_i & G_i \\ \hline \bar{F}_i^* \bar{U}_i & \tilde{U}_i & H_i^* \\ 0 & U_i & 0 \end{array} \right], \qquad (1.10.14)$$

where G_i and H_i^* denote the nontrivial elements that appear in the upper- and lower-right-corner blocks. Note that the prearray (1.6.22), the intermediate array (1.6.24), and the postarray (1.6.23) are all $(D^{-1} \oplus J)$-equivalent; i.e., their "squares" in the $(D^{-1} \oplus J)$ metric must be equal.

We already know from Lemma 1.6.3 that G_i is a generator matrix for the leading Schur complement R_i. Now, a similar conclusion follows for H_i^*. Indeed, note first that the matrix

$$\begin{bmatrix} G_i \\ H_i^* \end{bmatrix} \qquad (1.10.15)$$

Section 1.10. Fast Inversion of Structured Matrices 41

is $n \times r$ and must have full rank r. This is because the prearray in (1.6.24) has full rank $n+r$. Now since each of the Ω_j is invertible, we conclude that the postarray in (1.6.24) must also have full rank $n+r$. It then follows that (1.10.15) has full rank r.

Moreover, it also follows that the Schur complement Δ_i satisfies the displacement equation (1.10.5). This is obtained by comparing the *prearray* and the *intermediate array*. The "squared lengths" of the third block rows of (1.6.22) and (1.6.24) must be equal, i.e.,

$$[\bar{U}_i \ \tilde{U}_i \ 0](\bar{D}_i^{-1} \oplus D_i^{-1} \oplus J)[\bar{U}_i \ \tilde{U}_i \ 0]^*$$
$$= [\bar{F}_i^* \bar{U}_i \ \tilde{U}_i \ H_i^*](\bar{D}_i^{-1} \oplus D_i^{-1} \oplus J)[\bar{F}_i^* \bar{U}_i \ \tilde{U}_i \ H_i^*]^*.$$

Therefore,
$$(\bar{U}_i \bar{D}_i^{-1} \bar{U}_i^*) = \bar{F}_i^* (\bar{U}_i \bar{D}_i^{-1} \bar{U}_i^*) \bar{F}_i + H_i^* J H_i .$$

But since $\Delta_i = \bar{U}_i \bar{D}_i^{-1} \bar{U}_i^*$, we conclude that (1.10.5) holds.

We now establish (1.10.7) and the generator recursion of Alg. 1.10.2. Recall that we used (1.6.25) earlier to derive the closed-form expression (1.6.26) for l_i. Unfortunately, a similar argument using (1.10.5) cannot be used to determine u_i. This is because Δ_i involves $u_0, \ldots, u_{i-1}$ but not u_i. However, the $(D^{-1} \oplus J)$-unitary equivalence of the *intermediate* array and the *postarray* shows that the $(D^{-1} \oplus J)$-inner product of the second and third block rows of (1.6.23) and (1.6.24) must be equal, i.e.,

$$[\bar{F}_i^* \bar{U}_i \ \ \bar{F}_i^* \tilde{U}_i + \tilde{F}_i^* U_i \ \ H^*](\bar{D}_i^{-1} \oplus D_i^{-1} \oplus J) [\tilde{L}_i \ L_i \ 0]^*$$
$$= [\bar{F}_i^* \bar{U}_i \ \tilde{U}_i \ H_i^*](\bar{D}_i^{-1} \oplus D_i^{-1} \oplus J)[\tilde{L}_i \ F_i L_i \ G_i]^*.$$

This implies that
$$\bar{F}_i^* \tilde{U}_i D_i^{-1} L_i^* + \tilde{F}_i^* U_i D_i^{-1} L_i^* = \tilde{U}_i D_i^{-1} L_i^* F_i^* + H_i^* J G_i^* .$$

Equating the first columns on both sides leads to the equation
$$\bar{F}_i^* \bar{u}_i + \varphi_i^* = \bar{u}_i f_i^* + H_i^* J g_i^* ,$$

which validates (1.10.7). The nondegeneracy condition (1.10.1) ensures that (1.10.7) has a unique solution for $\bar{u}_i$.

Finally, by omitting the irrelevant columns and rows of the pre- and postarrays (i.e., those rows and columns that remain unchanged), we can write

$$\left[\begin{array}{c|c} F_i l_i & G_i \\ \hline u_i & H_i^* \\ & 0 \end{array}\right] \Sigma_i = \left[\begin{array}{c|c} l_i & 0 \\ & G_{i+1} \\ \hline \bar{F}_{i+1}^* u_i & H_{i+1}^* \end{array}\right], \quad (1.10.16)$$

where Σ_i is a submatrix of Ω_i as in (1.6.27). This establishes (1.10.8). Also, by using the parameters of Σ_i shown in Lemma 1.6.4, we obtain the generator recursion relating H_i^* and H_{i+1}^* (as stated after Alg. 1.10.2).

1.10.4 An Example

We return to the rotation example we considered in Sec. 1.6.6 with $n=3$ and $r=2$ and show how to incorporate the procedure for inverting R as well. In this case the pre- and postarrays will have the following zero-patterns:

$$\begin{bmatrix} FL & G \\ U & 0 \end{bmatrix} = \begin{bmatrix} * & 0 & 0 & * & * \\ * & * & 0 & * & * \\ * & * & * & * & * \\ \hline 1 & * & * & 0 & 0 \\ 0 & 1 & * & 0 & 0 \\ 0 & 0 & 1 & 0 & 0 \end{bmatrix}, \quad \begin{bmatrix} L & 0 \\ F^*U & H^* \end{bmatrix} = \begin{bmatrix} d_0 & 0 & 0 & 0 & 0 \\ * & d_1 & 0 & 0 & 0 \\ * & * & d_2 & 0 & 0 \\ \hline f_0^* & * & * & * & * \\ 0 & f_1^* & * & * & * \\ 0 & 0 & f_2^* & * & * \end{bmatrix}.$$

Using (1.6.7) for $i = 0$, viz.,

$$(I_n - f_0^* F)l_0 = GJg_0,$$

we can determine the first column l_0 of L and, consequently, the first column of FL. In this way, all the entries of the first column of the prearray are completely known. Also, the last two columns of the prearray are known since they are determined by G.

Hence, the $(1,2)$ block entry of the prearray (i.e., the top row of G) can be eliminated by pivoting with the top entry of the first column of FL. As a result, the first column of the prearray and its last two columns are linearly combined to yield the intermediate array shown below after the transformation Ω_0. The second and third columns of the prearray remain unchanged.

$$\begin{bmatrix} \boxed{*} & 0 & 0 & \boxed{* & *} \\ * & * & 0 & * & * \\ * & * & * & * & * \\ \hline 1 & * & * & 0 & 0 \\ 0 & 1 & * & 0 & 0 \\ 0 & 0 & 1 & 0 & 0 \end{bmatrix} \xrightarrow{\Omega_0} \begin{bmatrix} d_0 & 0 & 0 & 0 & 0 \\ * & \boxed{*} & 0 & \boxed{* & *} \\ * & * & * & * & * \\ \hline f_0^* & * & * & * & * \\ 0 & 1 & * & 0 & 0 \\ 0 & 0 & 1 & 0 & 0 \end{bmatrix}$$

$$\xrightarrow{\Omega_1} \begin{bmatrix} d_0 & 0 & 0 & 0 & 0 \\ * & d_1 & 0 & 0 & 0 \\ * & * & \boxed{*} & \boxed{* & *} \\ \hline f_0^* & * & * & * & * \\ 0 & f_1^* & * & * & * \\ 0 & 0 & 1 & 0 & 0 \end{bmatrix} \xrightarrow{\Omega_2} \begin{bmatrix} d_0 & 0 & 0 & 0 & 0 \\ * & d_1 & 0 & 0 & 0 \\ * & * & d_2 & 0 & 0 \\ \hline f_0^* & * & * & * & * \\ 0 & f_1^* & * & * & * \\ 0 & 0 & f_2^* & * & * \end{bmatrix}.$$

We now proceed in a similar fashion to the next step. Using (1.6.7) for $i = 1$, viz.,

$$(I_{n-1} - f_1^* F_1)l_1 = G_1 J g_1,$$

we determine the l_1 and, consequently, the second column of FL. Likewise, using (1.10.7) for $i = 1$ (in this case $\bar{F}_1 = f_0$),

$$(f_0^* - f_1^*)\bar{u}_1 = H_1^* J g_1^* - \varphi_1^*,$$

we determine $\bar{u}_1$. The second transformation Ω_1 can now be performed as shown above to yield G_2 and H_2, and so on.

The rectangular boxes mark the entries to be eliminated at each step of the recursion by using elementary $(D^{-1} \oplus J)$-unitary transformations. The square boxes mark the position of the pivot elements. The ultimate result of the recursion is that the $(1,2)$ block of the prearray is eliminated row by row ("reduction procedure"), while the $(2,2)$ block is filled up with nonzero elements ("construction procedure").

1.10.5 Proper Form of the Algorithm

Analogous to what we did in Sec. 1.7 for the recursion for the generators G_i, we can reduce the recursion for the H_i^* in Alg. 1.10.2 into proper form.

Section 1.10. Fast Inversion of Structured Matrices

Assume again that $g_i J g_i^* > 0$ and let Θ_i be a J-unitary matrix that rotates g_i to the form (1.7.1). Then it can be verified easily that the expression (1.10.7) for $\bar{u}_i$ reduces to

$$(\bar{F}_i^* - f_i^* I_i) \bar{u}_i = H_i^* \Theta_i \begin{bmatrix} \delta_i^* \\ 0 \end{bmatrix} - \varphi_i^*,$$

while the recursion for H_i^* reduces to

$$H_{i+1}^* = \begin{bmatrix} H_i^* \\ 0 \end{bmatrix} \Theta_i \begin{bmatrix} 0 & 0 \\ 0 & I_{r-1} \end{bmatrix} + \begin{bmatrix} \Psi_i & 0 \\ 0 & 0 \end{bmatrix} \begin{bmatrix} H_i^* \\ 0 \end{bmatrix} \Theta_i \begin{bmatrix} 1 & 0 \\ 0 & 0 \end{bmatrix} + \begin{bmatrix} \phi_i \\ 1 \end{bmatrix} [\sigma_i \ 0],$$

where we defined $\sigma_i \triangleq \delta_i / d_i$. The above equation has the following interpretation:

1. Multiply H_i^* by Θ_i.

2. Multiply the *first* column of $H_i^* \Theta_i$ by Ψ_i and keep the rest of the columns unaltered.

3. Attach a zero row to the bottom of the array.

4. Add the correction term $\sigma_i [\ \phi_i^* \ 1\ ]^*$ to the *first* column.

Note that initially H_i^* is in proper form. Multiplying the array by Θ_i will destroy this properness (see Fig. 1.5). After attaching a zero row to the bottom of the matrix and adding a correction term to the first column, the resulting matrix H_{i+1}^* will emerge in proper form again.

$$H_i^* = \begin{bmatrix} * & * & * \\ \vdots & \vdots & \vdots \\ * & * & * \\ * & 0 & 0 \end{bmatrix} \xrightarrow{\text{Steps 1-2}} \begin{bmatrix} * & * & * \\ \vdots & \vdots & \vdots \\ * & * & * \\ * & * & * \end{bmatrix}$$

$$\xrightarrow{\text{Step 3}} \begin{bmatrix} * & * & * \\ \vdots & \vdots & \vdots \\ * & * & * \\ * & * & * \\ 0 & 0 & 0 \end{bmatrix} \xrightarrow{\text{Step 4}} \begin{bmatrix} * & * & * \\ \vdots & \vdots & \vdots \\ * & * & * \\ * & * & * \\ * & 0 & 0 \end{bmatrix} = H_{i+1}^*$$

Figure 1.5. Proper form of the generator recursion for inversion.

When, on the other hand, $g_i J g_i^* < 0$ we let Θ_i be a J-unitary matrix that rotates g_i to the form (1.7.4). Then the expression for (1.10.7) $\bar{u}_i$ becomes

$$(\bar{F}_i^* - f_i^* I_i) \bar{u}_i = -H_i^* \Theta_i \begin{bmatrix} 0 \\ \delta_i^* \end{bmatrix} - \varphi_i^*,$$

and the recursion for H_i^* now reduces to

$$H_{i+1}^* = \begin{bmatrix} H_i^* \\ 0 \end{bmatrix} \Theta_i \begin{bmatrix} I_{r-1} & 0 \\ 0 & 0 \end{bmatrix} + \begin{bmatrix} \Psi_i & 0 \\ 0 & 0 \end{bmatrix} \begin{bmatrix} H_i^* \\ 0 \end{bmatrix} \Theta_i \begin{bmatrix} 0 & 0 \\ 0 & 1 \end{bmatrix} + \begin{bmatrix} \phi_i \\ 1 \end{bmatrix} [0 \ \sigma_i].$$

This equation has the following interpretation:

1. Multiply H_i^* by Θ_i.

2. Multiply the *last* column of $H_i^*\Theta_i$ by Ψ_i and keep the rest of the columns unaltered.

3. Attach a zero row to the bottom of the array.

4. Add the correction term $\sigma_i[\,\phi_i^*\ \ 1\,]^*$ to the *last* column.

1.10.6 Application to Pick Matrices

We reconsider the case of Pick matrices (1.8.4), which, as discussed at the end of Sec. 1.8.2, did not yield to the embedding technique for the factorization of the inverse matrix. More specifically, by starting with the matrix P in (1.8.4) and by using $F = \mathrm{diag}\{f_0, f_1, \ldots, f_{n-1}\}$, we saw that the extended matrix

$$M = \begin{bmatrix} -P & I \\ I & 0 \end{bmatrix}$$

did not have low displacement rank with respect to $M - (F \oplus F)M(F \oplus F)^*$ since $I - FF^*$ is full rank in general.

However, the fast inversion algorithm just derived overcomes this difficulty. Indeed, according to (1.8.5) we have

$$G = \begin{bmatrix} u_0 & v_0 \\ u_1 & v_1 \\ \vdots & \vdots \\ u_{n-1} & v_{n-1} \end{bmatrix}, \quad F = \begin{bmatrix} f_0 & & & \\ & f_1 & & \\ & & \ddots & \\ & & & f_{n-1} \end{bmatrix}.$$

Now Lemma 1.5.1 implies that

$$R^{-1} - F^* R^{-1} F = H^* J H$$

for some matrix $H \in \mathbb{C}^{r \times n}$. This means that R^{-1} is also a Pick matrix,

$$R^{-1} = \left[\frac{a_i a_j^* - b_i b_j^*}{1 - f_i^* f_j} \right]_{i,j=0}^{n-1},$$

where $[\,a_i\ \ b_i\,]$ denotes the ith row of H^*. It further follows from the diagonal structure of F that

$$\Phi_i = \mathrm{diag}\left\{ 0\ \ \frac{f_{i+1} - f_i}{1 - f_i^* f_{i+1}}\ \ \frac{f_{i+2} - f_i}{1 - f_i^* f_{i+2}}\ \ \cdots\ \ \frac{f_{n-1} - f_i}{1 - f_i^* f_{n-1}} \right\},$$

$$\Psi_i = \mathrm{diag}\left\{ \frac{1 - f_i f_0^*}{f_0^* - f_i^*}\ \ \frac{1 - f_i f_1^*}{f_1^* - f_i^*}\ \ \cdots\ \ \frac{1 - f_i f_{i-1}^*}{f_{i-1}^* - f_i^*} \right\},$$

$$\phi_i = 0.$$

The generator matrix H can then be determined by resorting to the fast inversion Alg. 1.10.2 (or to the proper form of Sec. 1.10.5).

1.10.7 The Degenerate Case

The derivation of the fast inversion algorithm of Sec. 1.10.2 was based on the nondegeneracy condition (1.10.1), viz., that the diagonal entries of F are distinct. This condition ensured that (1.10.7) had a unique solution for $\bar{u}_i$.

Section 1.11. Non-Hermitian Toeplitz-Like Matrices

In this section we show how to relax the nondegeneracy assumption (1.10.1). We do so by focusing on the case when F consists of a single Jordan block so that $f_0 = f_1 = \cdots = f_{n-1}$ holds:

$$F = \begin{bmatrix} f_0 & & & & \\ 1 & f_0 & & & \\ & 1 & f_0 & & \\ & & \ddots & \ddots & \\ & & & 1 & f_0 \end{bmatrix} = Z + f_0 I \qquad (1.10.17)$$

with $1-|f_0|^2 \neq 0$. This case clearly includes the special choice $F = Z$ (which corresponds to $f_0 = 0$). The argument we give here, however, can be extended easily to handle the more general case of a matrix F with multiple (or even repeated) Jordan blocks.

For a matrix F as in (1.10.17), it is easy to verify from (1.10.7) that all the entries of $\bar{u}_i$ can be determined uniquely from (1.10.7), except for the top entry of $\bar{u}_i$. We shall denote this top entry by ξ_i. This means that the fast inversion algorithm that we derived in Sec. 1.10 almost completely identifies the upper triangular factor U with the exception of its top row:

$$U = \begin{bmatrix} 1 & \xi_1 & \xi_2 & \cdots & \xi_{n-1} \\ & 1 & \times & \cdots & \times \\ & & 1 & \cdots & \times \\ & & & \ddots & \vdots \\ & & & & 1 \end{bmatrix}.$$

In the above expression, the symbol × denotes known entries. The unknown parameters $\{\xi_i\}$ can be identified by resorting to the fundamental equality (1.6.13), which provides an upper triangular system of linear equations in the $\{\xi_i\}$:

$$\begin{bmatrix} 1 & \xi_1 & \xi_2 & \cdots & \xi_{n-1} \end{bmatrix} D^{-1} L^* = \begin{bmatrix} 1 & 0 & 0 & \cdots & 0 \end{bmatrix}. \qquad (1.10.18)$$

Since the matrices $\{D, L\}$ can be determined without ambiguity from the recursions of the generalized Schur algorithm for the direct factorization problem, we can therefore use the above linear system of equations and determine the $\{\xi_i\}$.

More specifically, let L_{i+1} and D_{i+1} denote the leading $(i+1) \times (i+1)$ submatrices of L and D, respectively. Given $\{L_{i+1}, D_{i+1}\}$ and $\{\xi_1, \ldots, \xi_{i-1}\}$, we can determine ξ_i by solving

$$\begin{bmatrix} 1 & \xi_1 & \xi_2 & \cdots & \xi_i \end{bmatrix} D_{i+1}^{-1} L_{i+1}^* = \begin{bmatrix} 1 & 0 & 0 & \cdots & 0 \end{bmatrix}. \qquad (1.10.19)$$

Therefore, the only additional computation relative to Alg. 1.10.2 is the need to determine the top entries $\{\xi_i\}$ of the successive $\bar{u}_i$ as explained above. More can be said about the inversion algorithm in the degenerate case. We omit the discussion here and refer instead to [BSLK96], [BKLS98a], [BKLS98b].

1.11 NON-HERMITIAN TOEPLITZ-LIKE MATRICES

The derivation in the earlier sections was primarily devoted to Hermitian Toeplitz-like matrices R that satisfy displacement equations of the form $R - FRF^* = GJG^*$.

As mentioned before, we can also treat non-Hermitian Toeplitz-like matrices. Such matrices admit a triangular factorization of the form $R = LD^{-1}U$, where L is lower triangular and U is upper triangular with identical diagonal entries, and which are equal to those of D. In the Hermitian case, $U = L^*$. In what follows, we denote the (nonzero parts of the) columns and rows of L and U by $\{l_i, u_i\}$, respectively. (Observe that we are now using the letter U to denote the upper triangular factor of R and not of R^{-1}. We are also writing u_i to denote a row of U.)

We shall not repeat the derivation of the Schur algorithm in this context but will only state one of its forms; derivations can be found in [KS95a]. It will be noted that the general form of the recursions is still very similar to what we had in the Hermitian case, except that now we need to propagate two generator matrices. For reasons of space, we present only the more compactly described (explicit) equation forms.

Algorithm 1.11.1 (Non-Hermitian Toeplitz-Like Matrices). *Consider an $n \times n$ strongly regular matrix R with displacement structure*

$$R - FRA^* = GB^*,$$

where F and A are $n \times n$ lower triangular matrices whose diagonal entries are denoted by $\{f_i, a_i\}$, respectively, and G and B are $n \times r$ generator matrices. It is further assumed that

$$1 - f_j a_i^* \neq 0 \quad \text{for all } i, j.$$

Then the successive Schur complements of R satisfy

$$R_i - F_i R_i A_i^* = G_i B_i^*,$$

where $\{F_i, A_i\}$ are the submatrices obtained after deleting the first row and column of the corresponding $\{F_{i-1}, A_{i-1}\}$ and G_i and B_i are $(n-i) \times r$ generator matrices that satisfy the following recursions: start with $G_0 = G, B_0 = B, F_0 = F, A_0 = A$ and repeat for $i \geq 0$:

$$\begin{bmatrix} 0 \\ G_{i+1} \end{bmatrix} = \left[G_i + (\Phi_i - I_{n-i}) G_i \frac{b_i^* g_i}{g_i b_i^*} \right] \Theta_i,$$

$$\begin{bmatrix} 0 \\ B_{i+1} \end{bmatrix} = \left[B_i + (\Psi_i - I_{n-i}) B_i \frac{g_i^* b_i}{b_i g_i^*} \right] \Gamma_i,$$

(1.11.1)

where Θ_i and Γ_i are arbitrary matrices that satisfy $\Theta_i \Gamma_i^* = I$, g_i and b_i are the top rows of G_i and B_i, respectively, and

$$\Phi_i = (F_i - f_i I)(I - a_i^* F_i)^{-1}, \quad \Psi_i = (A_i - a_i I)(I - f_i^* A_i)^{-1}.$$

(1.11.2)

The triangular factors are given by

$$l_i = (I_{n-i} - a_i^* F_i)^{-1} G_i b_i^*, \quad u_i = g_i B_i^* (I_{n-i} - f_i A_i^*)^{-1}, \quad d_i = g_i b_i^* / (1 - f_i a_i^*).$$

$\Diamond$

Array forms of these recursions are also treated in [KS95a] and they can be described briefly as follows. Choose the parameters Θ_i and Γ_i to reduce g_i and b_i to the forms

$$g_i \Theta_i = \begin{bmatrix} 0 & \bar{x}_i & 0 \end{bmatrix} \quad \text{and} \quad b_i \Gamma_i = \begin{bmatrix} 0 & \bar{y}_i & 0 \end{bmatrix},$$

respectively, where the nonzero entries $\bar{x}_i$ and $\bar{y}_i$ are in the same column position, say, the jth position. (Generalizations of the Givens and Householder transformations can

Section 1.12. Schur Algorithm for Hankel-Like Matrices · 47

be obtained for finding $\{\Theta_i, \Psi_i\}$—see Sec. 4.4.3 of [KS95a].) Then it can be verified that the generator recursions collapse to

$$\begin{bmatrix} 0 \\ G_{i+1} \end{bmatrix} = \Phi_i G_i \Theta_i \begin{bmatrix} 0_{j \times j} & 0 & 0 \\ 0 & 1 & 0 \\ 0 & 0 & 0 \end{bmatrix} + G_i \Theta_i \begin{bmatrix} I_j & 0 & 0 \\ 0 & 0 & 0 \\ 0 & 0 & I_{r-j-1} \end{bmatrix},$$

$$\begin{bmatrix} 0 \\ B_{i+1} \end{bmatrix} = \Psi_i B_i \Gamma_i \begin{bmatrix} 0_{j \times j} & 0 & 0 \\ 0 & 1 & 0 \\ 0 & 0 & 0 \end{bmatrix} + B_i \Gamma_i \begin{bmatrix} I_j & 0 & 0 \\ 0 & 0 & 0 \\ 0 & 0 & I_{r-j-1} \end{bmatrix}, \quad (1.11.3)$$

where $d_i = (\bar{x}_i J_{jj} \bar{y}_i^*)/(1 - f_i a_i^*)$, and

$$l_i = (I_{n-i} - a_i^* F_i)^{-1} G_i \Theta_i J \begin{bmatrix} 0 \\ \bar{y}_i^* \\ 0 \end{bmatrix}, \quad u_i = \begin{bmatrix} 0 & \bar{x}_i & 0 \end{bmatrix} J \Gamma_i^* B_i^* (I - f_i A_i^*)^{-1}.$$

These algorithms are useful in studying (unconstrained) rational interpolation problems (see Sec. 1.14.3 and [BSK94], [BSK99]).

1.12 SCHUR ALGORITHM FOR HANKEL-LIKE MATRICES

To round out our discussions of generalized Schur algorithms, we finally consider the case of strongly regular Hankel-like matrices. As with the Toeplitz-like structure, the Hankel-like structure is also preserved under Schur complementation. Similar arguments will show that the following recursions hold—they are special cases of the general algorithm first derived in [KS91], [Say92] (see also [SK95a], [KS95b], Sec. 7.2.5 of [KS95a]), and are used in [GKO95].

Algorithm 1.12.1 (Schur Algorithm for Hankel-Like Matrices). *Consider an $n \times n$ strongly regular Hankel-like matrix that satisfies*

$$FR - RA^* = GB^*, \quad (1.12.1)$$

where the diagonal entries of the lower triangular matrices F and A are denoted by $\{f_i, a_i\}$, respectively, and satisfy

$$f_i - a_j^* \neq 0 \quad \text{for all } i, j. \quad (1.12.2)$$

Then the successive Schur complements R_i satisfy

$$F_i R_i - R_i A_i^* = G_i B_i^*, \quad (1.12.3)$$

where F_i and A_i are the submatrices obtained after deleting the first row and column of F_{i-1} and A_{i-1}, respectively, and G_i and B_i are $(n-i) \times r$ generator matrices that satisfy, along with l_i and u_i (the first column and row of R_i), the following recursions:

$$\begin{bmatrix} 0 \\ G_{i+1} \end{bmatrix} = \{G_i - l_i d_i^{-1} g_i\} \Theta_i, \quad (1.12.4)$$

$$\begin{bmatrix} 0 \\ B_{i+1} \end{bmatrix} = \{B_i - u_i^* d_i^{-*} b_i\} \Gamma_i, \quad (1.12.5)$$

where Θ_i and Γ_i are arbitrary parameters that satisfy $\Theta_i \Gamma_i^* = I$. Moreover,

$$d_i = \frac{g_i b_i^*}{f_i - a_i^*}, \qquad (1.12.6)$$

$$l_i = (F_i - a_i^* I_{n-i})^{-1} G_i b_i^*, \qquad (1.12.7)$$

$$u_i = g_i B_i^* (f_i I_{n-i} - A_i^*)^{-1}. \qquad (1.12.8)$$

$\diamond$

Remark 1. Array forms for these equations also exist and are discussed in [KS95a].

Remark 2. The condition (1.12.2) is necessary to guarantee a unique solution R of the displacement equation (1.12.1). It further guarantees that the expressions (1.12.6)–(1.12.8) are well defined and uniquely determine the quantities $\{d_i, l_i, u_i\}$. When (1.12.2) is violated, so that the inverses $(F_i - a_i^* I_{n-i})^{-1}$ and $(f_i I_{n-i} - A_i^*)^{-1}$ in (1.12.7) and (1.12.8) need not exist, then we need to determine the $\{d_i, l_i, u_i\}$ by solving the equations

$$(f_i - a_i^*) d_i = g_i b_i^*, \qquad (1.12.9)$$

$$(F_i - a_i^* I_{n-i}) l_i = G_i b_i^*, \qquad (1.12.10)$$

$$u_i (f_i I_{n-i} - A_i^*) = g_i B_i^*. \qquad (1.12.11)$$

The nonsingularity of $(F_i - a_i^* I_{n-i})$ and $(f_i I_{n-i} - A_i^*)$ would imply that these equations have many solutions $\{d_i, l_i, u_i\}$. For this reason, additional information (often known as coupling numbers) is needed to fully recover the $\{d_i, l_i, u_i\}$. These issues are not of major concern to us here since the fundamental equations (1.12.4) and (1.12.5) will be the same. More detailed discussions can be found in [KO96], [KO98] (see also [KS95a]).

1.13 STRUCTURED MATRICES AND PIVOTING

An issue that arises in the study of fast factorization algorithms is their numerical stability in finite precision implementations. It was mentioned in Sec. 1.6.2 that the Schur reduction procedure, which underlies the generalized Schur algorithm, is equivalent to the Gaussian elimination procedure, because the latter can be rewritten as

$$R = \begin{bmatrix} 1 & 0 \\ t_0 d_0^{-1} & I_{n-1} \end{bmatrix} \begin{bmatrix} d_0 & t_0^* \\ 0 & R_1 \end{bmatrix}.$$

Thus the generalized Schur algorithm amounts to combining Gaussian elimination with structure. Now it is well known (see, e.g., [GV96], [TB97], and Sec. 4.2.1) that Gaussian elimination in its purest form is numerically unstable (meaning that the error in the factorization $\hat{L}\hat{D}^{-1}\hat{L}^*$ can be quite large, where $\hat{L}$ and $\hat{D}$ denote the computed L and D, respectively). The instability often can be controlled by resorting to pivoting techniques, viz., by permuting the order of the rows, and perhaps columns, of the matrices before the Gaussian elimination steps.

In what is known as *complete pivoting*, a permutation matrix P_k is chosen at each iteration k so as to bring the maximal magnitude entry in the entire matrix R_k to the pivotal $(0,0)$th position. Such a procedure is computationally intensive since it requires many comparisons. A less-demanding procedure is *partial pivoting*. In this case, the permutation matrix P_k is chosen so as to bring at the kth step the maximal magnitude entry of the first column of R_k to the pivotal $(0,0)$th position. (Although partial pivoting often performs satisfactorily, there are several examples where the numerical accuracy of the factorization can still be poor—see, e.g., [Hig96].) In either case, complete or partial pivoting leads to the triangular factorization of a permuted verion of R, say, $PR = LD^{-1}L^*$.

Section 1.13. Structured Matrices and Pivoting

1.13.1 Incorporating Pivoting into Generalized Schur Algorithms

Unfortunately, pivoting can destroy matrix structure and thus can lead to a loss in computational efficiency. There are, however, matrices whose structure is unaffected by partial pivoting, e.g., Vandermonde and Cauchy matrices or even Cauchy-like matrices, as first noted and exploited by Heinig [Hei95].

Recall that Cauchy-like matrices are special cases of the class of Hankel-like matrices in that they satisfy displacement equations of the form

$$FR - RA^* = GB^*, \qquad (1.13.1)$$

where $\{F, A\}$ are now *diagonal*. Let P denote a permutation matrix that permutes the rows of R. Then $PP^T = I$ and we note that

$$(PFP^T) \cdot (PR) - (PR) \cdot A^* = (PG) \cdot B^*,$$

where PFP^T is still diagonal. We therefore see that the permuted matrix PR is still Cauchy-like with respect to the displacement operators $\{PFP^T, A\}$ and has generator matrices $\{PG, B\}$. In other words, partial pivoting does not destroy the Cauchy-like structure.

More generally, partial pivoting does not destroy the matrix structure as long as some displacement operators are diagonal, e.g.,

$$R - FRA^* = GB^* \quad \text{with } F \text{ diagonal only}, \qquad (1.13.2)$$
$$FR - RA^* = GB^* \quad \text{with } F \text{ diagonal only}, \qquad (1.13.3)$$
$$\Omega R\Delta^* - FRA^* = GB^* \quad \text{with } \Omega \text{ and } F \text{ diagonal only}. \qquad (1.13.4)$$

However, for definiteness, we continue our discussion here by focusing on the Cauchy-like case; similar arguments apply in the other cases—see, e.g., Sec. 2.10.

The following algorithm now follows immediately from Alg. 1.12.1 (and is used in [GKO95]); it incorporates partial pivoting into the generalized Schur algorithm for Cauchy-like matrices.

Algorithm 1.13.1. (Schur Algorithm for Cauchy-Like Matrices with Pivoting).
Consider an $n \times n$ strongly regular Cauchy-like matrix that satisfies

$$FR - RA^* = GB^* \qquad (1.13.5)$$

with diagonal $\{F, A\}$ whose entries satisfy $f_i - a_j^* \neq 0$ for all i, j. Start with $G_0 = G$, $B_0 = B$, $F_0 = F$, $A_0 = A$ and repeat for $i = 0, 1, \ldots$:

1. Determine $\{l_i, u_i\}$ from

$$l_i = (F_i - a_i^* I_{n-i})^{-1} G_i b_i^*, \qquad (1.13.6)$$
$$u_i = g_i B_i^* (f_i I_{n-i} - A_i^*)^{-1}. \qquad (1.13.7)$$

2. Determine the position of the maximal magnitude entry of l_i, say, at the jth position, and let P_i be the permutation matrix that exchanges it with the top entry of l_i. Let d_i be equal to this maximal entry.

3. Likewise, exchange the $(0,0)$th diagonal entry of F_i with its (j,j)th diagonal entry. Exchange also the first and the jth rows of G_i. At the end of this step, all three quantities $\{l_i, F_i, G_i\}$ have undergone permutation, but we continue to denote them by the same symbols.

4. *Now update the generator matrices* $\{G_i, B_i\}$ *using*

$$\begin{bmatrix} 0 \\ G_{i+1} \end{bmatrix} = \{G_i - l_i d_i^{-1} g_i\} \Theta_i, \tag{1.13.8}$$

$$\begin{bmatrix} 0 \\ B_{i+1} \end{bmatrix} = \{B_i - u_i^* d_i^{-*} b_i\} \Gamma_i, \tag{1.13.9}$$

where Θ_i *and* Γ_i *are arbitrary parameters that satisfy* $\Theta_i \Gamma_i^* = I$ *(e.g.,* $\Theta_i = \Gamma_i = I$*).*

◇

At the end of the procedure we obtain the triangular factorization

$$PR = LD^{-1}L^*,$$

where P is the combination of all the individual permutation matrices

$$P = P_0 \begin{bmatrix} 1 \\ & P_1 \end{bmatrix} \begin{bmatrix} I_2 \\ & P_2 \end{bmatrix} \cdots.$$

Remark 1. For Hermitian Cauchy-like matrices R, viz., those that satisfy $FR + RF^* = GJG^*$, partial pivoting destroys the symmetry. In such cases, one usually employs *diagonal pivoting*—see [KO98].

Remark 2. For the alternative cases (1.13.2)–(1.13.4), we simply incorporate steps similar to steps 2 and 3 above into the corresponding recursions (in array form or not).

1.13.2 Transformations to Cauchy-Like Structures

As noted above, incorporation of partial pivoting into the generalized Schur algorithm is possible for Cauchy-like, Hankel-like, Toeplitz-like, and even generalized structures with certain diagonal operators F or $\{F, \Omega\}$. But what about matrices not in these classes? Heinig had the nice idea that one could first transform them into matrices to which pivoting could be applied; in particular, he proposed transforming them to Cauchy-like matrices [Hei95]. (Transformations between different kinds of structured matrices were perhaps first proposed, in a different context, by Bini and Pan (see, e.g., [BP94] and the references therein).) We illustrate the procedure in the Toeplitz case.

Thus consider an $n \times n$ non-Hermitian Toeplitz matrix T. As mentioned at the beginning of Sec. 1.3, there are many forms of displacement structure even for the same matrix. In particular, T also has displacement rank 2 with respect to the displacement operation

$$\nabla_{\{Z_1, Z_{-1}\}} R = Z_1 R - R Z_{-1} = GB^*, \tag{1.13.10}$$

where Z_ϕ denotes the ϕ-circulant matrix

$$Z_\phi = \begin{bmatrix} 0 & 0 & \cdots & 0 & \phi \\ 1 & 0 & \cdots & \cdots & 0 \\ 0 & 1 & \ddots & & \vdots \\ \vdots & & \ddots & \ddots & \vdots \\ 0 & \cdots & 0 & 1 & 0 \end{bmatrix}.$$

Heinig [Hei95] showed that the above displacement equation can be transformed to Cauchy-like form as follows. The matrix Z_ϕ can be diagonalized by the scaled discrete Fourier matrix

$$\mathcal{F} = \frac{1}{\sqrt{n}} \left[\omega^{ij}\right]_{i,j=0}^{n-1},$$

with ω denoting the primitive nth root of unity. More specifically, it holds that

$$Z_\phi = (D_\phi^{-1} \mathcal{F}^*) D_{Z_\phi} (\mathcal{F} \cdot D_\phi) \qquad (1.13.11)$$

with

$$D_{Z_\phi} = \text{diag } \{\xi \omega^i\}_{i=0}^{n-1}, \quad D_\phi = \text{diag } \{\xi^i\}_{i=0}^{n-1},$$

where ξ is an arbitrary complex number satisfying $\xi^n = \phi$. Now define the transformed matrix

$$R = \mathcal{F} T D_{-1}^* \mathcal{F}^*.$$

Then R satisfies the Cauchy-like displacement equation

$$D_1 R - R D_{-1} = (\mathcal{F} G)(B D_{-1}^* \mathcal{F}^*).$$

Note that R is in general complex valued even when T is real valued. This increases the constant factors in the operation count due to the need for complex arithmetic. A study of this procedure, with several examples and extensions, can be found in [GKO95].

1.13.3 Numerical Issues

While the transformation-and-pivoting technique of the last two sections can be satisfactory in many situations, it still suffers from two problems. First, the method applies only to a fixed matrix size $n \times n$, and the whole solution has to be repeated if the size of the matrix is increased even by 1. Second, the procedure can still pose numerical problems because partial pivoting by itself is not sufficient to guarantee numerical stability even for slow algorithms (see, e.g., the discussion and examples in Ch. 4 by Brent).

A more direct approach to the numerical stability of the generalized Schur algorithm is to examine the steps of the algorithm directly and to stabilize them without resorting to transformations among matrix structures. This is pursued in Chs. 2, 3, and 4. For all practical purposes, the main conclusion of Chs. 2 and 4 is that the generalized Schur algorithm is numerically stable for a large class of positive-definite structured matrices. In Ch. 3, it is further shown how this conclusion can be extended to indefinite structured matrices.

Chapter 4 by Brent provides, among other results, an overview of the conclusions in [BBHS95]. This reference studied the stability of the generalized Schur algorithm for the subclass of positive-definite quasi-Toeplitz structured matrices ($F = Z$ and displacement rank 2) and established that the triangular factorization provided by the algorithm is in effect asymptotically stable regardless of the hyperbolic rotations. In [SD97b] it was further shown that for higher displacement ranks, special care is needed while implementing the rotations in order to still guarantee stable factorizations.

The results in [BBHS95] motivated Chandrasekaran and Sayed [CS96] to study the stability of the generalized Schur algorithm for a wider class of matrices, viz., positive-definite matrices R for which the shift structure matrix Z is replaced by a lower triangular F (as in the definition (1.3.21)). Their conclusions are reviewed in Ch. 2, where it is shown that, for all practical purposes, by incorporating a few enhancements to the algorithm, it yields backward-stable factorizations for a wide class of structured matrices.

This is a reassuring conclusion. However, it applies only to positive-definite structured matrices. In [CS98], Chandrasekaran and Sayed further showed how to employ the embedding ideas proposed in [KC94] to develop fast backward-stable solvers for linear systems of equations, say, $Tx = b$, with possibly indefinite and even nonsymmetric structured coefficient matrices T (see Ch. 3). This is achieved by transforming a problem that involves a nonsymmetric or indefinite structured matrix into an equivalent problem that involves sign-definite matrices only (either positive definite or negative definite). This is possible by introducing the larger matrix

$$M = \begin{bmatrix} T^*T & T^* \\ T & 0 \end{bmatrix}$$

and by observing that, regardless of T, the matrix M is always Hermitian. Moreover, its leading block is positive definite and the Schur complement with respect to it is negative definite (in fact, equal to $-I$). When T is structured, the matrix M also has structure and its factorization can be carried out efficiently by means of the generalized Schur algorithm. By factoring M fast and stably, the solution x of $Tx = b$ can be determined fast and stably. These results are reviewed in Ch. 3.

1.14 SOME FURTHER ISSUES

Although a wide range of results has already been addressed in this chapter, there are still several unmentioned results and applications. We give a brief outline of a few of these items here, some of which are treated at greater length in later chapters. Other items are covered in the article [KS95a].

1.14.1 Incorporating State-Space Structure

A very powerful and well-studied structure in system theory is state-space structure. A typical scenario is the following. We have a stochastic process $\{\mathbf{y}_i, i \geq 0\}$ having a model of the form

$$\begin{aligned} \mathbf{x}_{i+1} &= F_i \mathbf{x}_i + G_i \mathbf{u}_i, \\ \mathbf{y}_i &= H_i \mathbf{x}_i + \mathbf{v}_i, \end{aligned}$$

where $\{\mathbf{u}_i, \mathbf{v}_i\}$ are zero-mean white noise processes with covariance matrices

$$E \begin{bmatrix} \mathbf{u}_i \\ \mathbf{v}_i \end{bmatrix} \begin{bmatrix} \mathbf{u}_j^* & \mathbf{v}_j^* \end{bmatrix} = \begin{bmatrix} Q_i & S_i \\ S_i^* & R_i \end{bmatrix} \delta_{ij}.$$

The initial state, $\mathbf{x}_0$, is also assumed to be a zero-mean random variable with variance Π_0 and uncorrelated with $\{\mathbf{u}_i, \mathbf{v}_i\}$, i.e.,

$$E\mathbf{x}_0\mathbf{x}_0^* = \Pi_0, \quad E\mathbf{u}_i\mathbf{x}_0^* = 0, \quad E\mathbf{v}_i\mathbf{x}_0^* = 0, \quad i \geq 0.$$

The processes are vector valued, with $\{\mathbf{u}_i\}$ being q-dimensional, the states $\mathbf{x}_i$ being n-dimensional, and the measurement noise $\{\mathbf{v}_i\}$ and the output $\{\mathbf{y}_i\}$ being p-dimensional. It is assumed that $\{q, n, p\}$ are known, as are all the matrices $\{F_i, G_i, H_i, \Pi_0, Q_i, R_i, S_i\}$.

The solutions of many different problems associated with such models are closely related (see, e.g., [KSH99]) to the triangular factorization of the covariance matrix of the output process $\{\mathbf{y}_i\}$, say,

$$R_y = E\mathbf{y}\mathbf{y}^*, \quad \mathbf{y} \triangleq \text{col}\{\mathbf{y}_0, \mathbf{y}_1, \ldots, \mathbf{y}_{N-1}\}.$$

Although R_y is $N \times N$, and N is often very large, the fact that it is the covariance matrix of a process with an n-dimensional state-space model (where generally $n \ll N$) means that the triangular factorization should take fewer than the $O(N^3)$ flops required for an arbitrary $N \times N$ matrix. In fact, the flop count is $O(Nn^3)$, which is achieved via a so-called discrete-time Riccati recursion for an associated $n \times n$ matrix P_i; this is shown in books on state-space estimation and control (see, e.g., [KSH99] and the references therein).

When the model parameters are time invariant, it turns out that the $N \times N$ matrix R_y has displacement structure, with displacement rank $r \leq n$. In this case, the flop count can be reduced to $O(Nn^2)$ by developing an appropriate generalized Schur algorithm (see, e.g., [SLK94a]). The time-invariance assumption can actually be relaxed somewhat to allow a structured form of time variation, which is encountered, for example, in problems of adaptive filtering (see, e.g., [SK94a], [SK94b]). When displacement structure is present, the Riccati recursion is replaced by certain so-called generalized Chandrasekhar recursions, first introduced in [Kai73] and [MSK74]. The survey article [KS95a] gives an outline of how state-space structure can be combined with displacement structure.

In fact, the above studies inspired a generalization of the definition of displacement structure, for example, using equations of the form

$$\nabla_{F(t)} R(t) \stackrel{\Delta}{=} R(t) - F(t)R(t-\Delta)F^*(t). \qquad (1.14.1)$$

We refer to [SCK94], [SLK94b] for properties and applications of this extension.

The power of state-space representations makes it useful to seek to obtain them from input-output descriptions. For time-variant systems, this has been studied in [DV98]. In Ch. 10 of this volume, Dewilde describes how these ideas can be combined with displacement structure to obtain low-complexity approximations of matrices.

1.14.2 Iterative Methods

Existing methods for the solution of linear systems of equations of the form $Ax = b$ can be classified into two main categories: *direct* methods and *iterative* methods. A direct method or algorithm is primarily concerned with first obtaining the triangular or QR factors of A and then reducing the original equations $Ax = b$ to an equivalent triangular system of equations. The generalized Schur algorithm of this chapter leads to a direct method of solution.

An iterative method, on the other hand, starts with an initial guess for the solution x, say, x_0, and generates a sequence of approximate solutions, $\{x_k\}_{k\geq 1}$. The matrix A itself is involved in the iterations via matrix-vector products, and the major concern here is the speed of convergence of the iterations. To clarify this point, we note that we can rewrite the equation $Ax = b$ in the equivalent form

$$Cx = (C - A)x + b$$

for an arbitrary invertible matrix C. This suggests the following iterative scheme (see, e.g., [GV96]),

$$Cx_{i+1} = (C - A)x_i + b, \quad x_0 = \text{initial guess}. \qquad (1.14.2)$$

The convergence of (1.14.2) is clearly dependent on the spectrum of the matrix $I - C^{-1}A$. The usefulness of (1.14.2) from a practical point of view is very dependent on the choice for C. For Toeplitz matrices, Strang [Str86] proposed certain circulant preconditioners C, which allow the use of the FFT technique to carry out the computations in a numerically efficient and parallelizable manner.

A survey of this method, with emphasis on Toeplitz linear equations and many later developments, is provided by Chan and Ng in Ch. 5; closer study of the nullspaces of appropriate displacement operators leads to new families of preconditioners [KO96]. The study of spectral properties of Toeplitz matrices is important in this theory. In Ch. 6, Tilli provides a review of recent results in this area, especially for block Toeplitz matrices. Fast algorithms for block Toeplitz matrices are developed in Ch. 8 by Bini and Meini.

An iterative method that offers faster convergence rates than the above methods is based on the use of Newton iterations. In Ch. 7, Pan et al. describe how displacement structure ideas can be used to speed up the Newton iterations.

1.14.3 Interpolation Problems

Interpolation problems of various types have a long history in mathematics and in circuit theory, control theory, and system theory. Not surprisingly, this rich subject can be approached in many ways and in different settings, often involving a lot of quite abstract operator theory (see, e.g., the monographs [Hel87], [Dym89a], [FF90], [GS94]). For the rational case, we have the somewhat more concrete state-space approach of [BGR90].

In [Say92], [SK92], [SKLC94], a recursive approach to rational analytic interpolation problems has been proposed that relies on the displacement structure framework; it leads to a computationally efficient procedure that avoids matrix inversions. Reference [SKLC94] elaborates on connections with earlier works on the subject.

The basis for the approach of [SKLC94] is the generalized Schur algorithm of this chapter, which leads, as explained in Sec. 1.7.4, to a cascade of J-lossless first-order sections, each of which has an evident interpolation property. This is due to the fact that linear systems have "transmission zeros": certain inputs at certain frequencies yield zero outputs. More specifically, each section of the cascade can be seen to be characterized by a $(p+q) \times (p+q)$ rational transfer matrix, $\Theta_i(z)$, say, that has a left zero-direction vector g_i at a frequency f_i, viz.,

$$g_i \Theta_i(f_i) \equiv \begin{bmatrix} a_i & b_i \end{bmatrix} \begin{bmatrix} \Theta_{i,11} & \Theta_{i,12} \\ \Theta_{i,21} & \Theta_{i,22} \end{bmatrix}(f_i) = 0,$$

which makes evident (with the proper partitioning of the row vector g_i and the matrix function $\Theta_i(z)$) the following interpolation property: $a_i \Theta_{i,12} \Theta_{i,22}^{-1}(f_i) = -b_i$. This suggested to us that one way of solving an interpolation problem is to show how to construct an appropriate cascade so that the local interpolation properties of the elementary sections combine in such a way that the cascade yields a solution to the global interpolation problem. All possible interpolants can then be parametrized by attaching various loads to the right-hand side of the cascade system. Details are provided in [SKLC94], [KS95a], where different kinds of analytic interpolation problems are considered, including the problems of Carathéodory, Nevanlinna–Pick, and Hermite–Fejér. An application to the so-called four-block problem in H^∞-control can be found in [CSK94].

Actually, the arguments can also be extended to the very old class of unconstrained rational interpolation problems. These problems have a long history, associated with many classical results of Lagrange, Hermite, Prony, Padé, and other famous names. In [BSK94], [BSK99], we showed how the generalized Schur algorithm for non-Hermitian Toeplitz-like matrices [KS91], [Say92] (described in Sec. 1.11) can be used to give a recursive solution.

It is noteworthy that the solution of interpolation problems can be reduced to the de-

Section 1.14. Some Further Issues 55

termination of an appropriate fast matrix triangularization [SK92], [SKLC94], [BSK94]. This constructive view provides a nice complement to the many abstract formulations of the important topic of interpolation theory.

1.14.4 Inverse Scattering

An interesting interpretation of Schur's original recursion (1.7.16), when viewed in array form, is that it arises as the most natural way of solving the inverse scattering problem for discrete transmission lines (see [BK87b], [BK87a], [Kai87]). This interpretation gives a lot of insight into and suggests new results and new proofs for a surprisingly diverse set of problems. For example, references [BK87b], [BK87a] show how the transmission line picture gives nice interpretations of the classical Gelfand–Levitan, Marchenko, and Krein equations, and in fact yields various generalizations thereof; reference [BK87c] discusses discrete Schrödinger equations; see also [BCK88] and [RK84].

Define $\gamma_i^c = \sqrt{1-|\gamma_i|^2}$. Then the generator recursion of Schur's algorithm (cf. (1.7.13)) can be depicted graphically as a cascade of elementary sections as shown in Fig. 1.6.

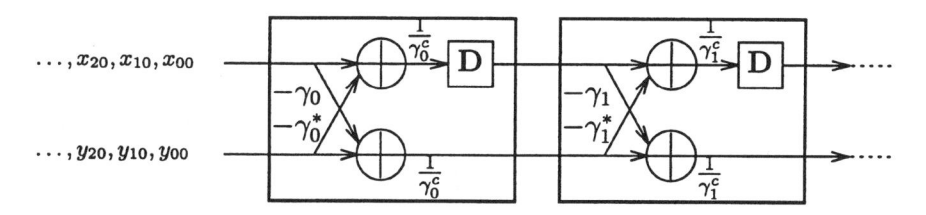

Figure 1.6. The feedforward structure (cascade network) associated with Schur's recursion.

By reversing the direction of flow in the lower line, we get a physical lossless discrete-time transmission line, as shown in Fig. 1.7, where each section is now composed of a unitary gain matrix Σ_i ($\Sigma_i \Sigma_i^* = I$) followed by a unit-time delay element,

$$\Sigma_i = \begin{bmatrix} \gamma_i^c & \gamma_i \\ -\gamma_i^* & \gamma_i^c \end{bmatrix}.$$

A physical motivation and derivation of a layered medium structure as in Fig. 1.7 can be given by showing that it corresponds to a discretization of the wave propagation (or telegrapher's) equations in an electromagnetic medium with varying local impedance; the relevant details can be found, for example, in [Kai87]. The name *reflection coefficients* for the Schur coefficients $\{\gamma_i\}$ arises from the picture in Fig. 1.7; at each section, a fraction γ_i of the incoming signal is reflected and the rest, γ_i^c, is transmitted.

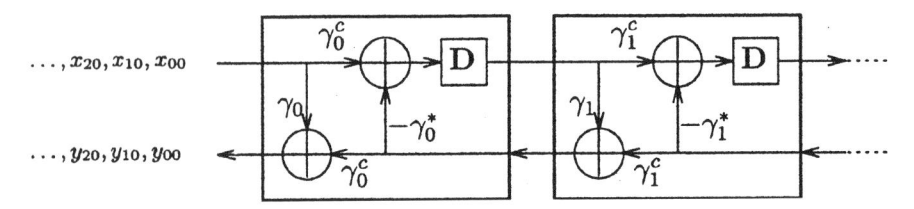

Figure 1.7. The feedback structure (transmission line) associated with Schur's recursion.

The so-called inverse-scattering problem that is associated with such layered media is the following: given an arbitrary pair of input-response sequences of a layered medium as in Fig. 1.7, say, $\{\ldots, x_{20}, x_{10}, x_{00}\}$ and $\{\ldots, y_{20}, y_{10}, y_{00}\}$, determine the medium (or reflection) parameters $\{\gamma_0, \gamma_1, \gamma_2, \ldots\}$, under the assumption that the line was initially quiescent. As mentioned above, this is a prototype of a famous problem, which has been attacked in many ways. The most widely known are methods using special choices of input sequences, based on which the inversion problem is shown to be equivalent to the solution of sets of linear equations, special forms of which are as famous as the Gelfand–Levitan, Marchenko, and Krein equations of classical inverse-scattering theory.

It turns out that a natural solution to the inverse scattering problem is Schur's array form (see [BK87b], [BK87a]). This fact leads to several useful applications in other areas including, among others, digital filter design and algebraic coding theory.

Chapter 2

STABILIZED SCHUR ALGORITHMS

Shivkumar Chandrasekaran

Ali H. Sayed

2.1 INTRODUCTION

As mentioned in Ch. 1, linear systems of equations are generally solved by resorting to the LDU factorization (or Gaussian elimination) of the coefficient matrix. But for indefinite or nonsymmetric matrices, the LDU factorization is well known to be numerically unstable if done without pivoting (see, e.g., [GV96], [Hig96], and also the discussion in Ch. 4). Moreover, since pivoting can destroy the structure of a matrix, it is not always possible to incorporate it immediately into a fast algorithm for structured matrices without potential loss of computational efficiency.

It was observed in [Hei95], however, that for Cauchy-like structured matrices, pivoting can be incorporated into fast factorization algorithms without reducing the computational efficiency of the algorithms (see the discussion in Sec. 1.13). This is because for such matrices, the displacement operators are diagonal and, therefore, column and row permutations do not destroy the Cauchy-like structure. The algorithm proposed in [Hei95] was of a hybrid type, involving Schur-type and Levinson-type operations. The technique was further used in [GKO95] to incorporate pivoting into the generalized Schur algorithm. This was achieved by first transforming different kinds of matrix structure into Cauchy-like structure and then using the so-called generator recursions of the Schur algorithm with *partial* pivoting. Sections 1.13 and 4.3 of this book review this approach to factorization.

While this transformation-and-pivoting addition to the generalized Schur algorithm can be satisfactory in many situations, it still suffers from two problems. First, the procedure can pose numerical problems because partial pivoting by itself is not sufficient to guarantee numerical stability even for slow algorithms (see, e.g., the discussion and examples in Ch. 4). It also seems difficult to implement *complete* pivoting in a fast algorithm without accruing a considerable loss of efficiency. Second, the transformation into a Cauchy-like structure makes it difficult to solve a linear system of equations of a higher order by relying on the solution of a linear system of equations of a smaller order. This is because once the size of the coefficient matrix is modified, say, by appending one more row and column to it, the transformation to Cauchy-like structures has to be applied afresh to the new extended matrix and the previous calculations therefore must be repeated. In this way, one of the major features of the generalized Schur algorithm is lost, viz., the possibility to solve a sequence of nested linear systems by exploiting the results of previous calculations (as already explained in Sec. 1.13.3).

2.2 CONTRIBUTIONS AND PROBLEMS

A more direct approach to the numerical stability of the generalized Schur algorithm is to examine the steps of the algorithm directly and to stabilize them without resorting to transformations among matrix structures. In this chapter we follow such a direct route to improving and ensuring the numerical stability of the generalized Schur algorithm and, as a by-product, we shall further devise in Ch. 3 a new numerically stable solver for linear systems of equations $Rx = b$, with structured coefficient matrices R. There are different notions of numerical stability in the literature. We follow the ones suggested in [Bun85], [Bun87] and reviewed in Ch. 4. More specifically, the error bounds we present for the algorithms developed here and in Ch. 3 will be such that they guarantee (backward) numerical stability in the sense defined in Ch. 4.

This chapter and the following one provide an overview of some recent results by the authors in [CS96], [CS98] and, for this reason, some derivations are not repeated here. The main ideas and conclusions, however, are emphasized. Also, complete descriptions of the algorithms are included for ease of reference.

Our exposition highlights three contributions:

1. We first show how to modify the generalized Schur algorithm of Ch. 1 in order to guarantee a fast *and* numerically stable triangular factorization procedure for positive-definite structured matrices R. For all practical purposes, the major conclusion of this chapter is that the generalized Schur algorithm, with certain modifications, is *backward stable* for a large class of structured matrices. This conclusion extends earlier work by [BBHS95] (see also Ch. 4) on the stability of a more specialized form of the algorithm. An overview of earlier works in this direction is provided in what follows.

2. Once it is shown how to obtain a provably stable implementation of the generalized Schur algorithm for positive-definite structured matrices, we then proceed to show in Ch. 3 how the result can be used to solve in a stable manner linear systems of equations with *indefinite* and possibly *nonsymmetric* structured coefficient matrices R. In other words, we show how to use the stability results of the positive-definite case to derive stable solvers even for the indefinite and nonsymmetric cases. This is achieved by exploiting in a suitable way the embedding techniques of [KC94], which are also described in Sec. 1.8.

3. We provide a detailed numerical analysis of the proposed algorithms.

2.3 RELATED WORKS IN THE LITERATURE

As already mentioned in Sec. 1.2, one of the most frequent structures, at least in signal processing applications, is the Toeplitz structure, with constant entries along the diagonals of the matrix. A classical algorithm for the Cholesky factorization of the *inverses* of such matrices is the Levinson algorithm [Lev47], [GV96], an error analysis of which has been provided by Cybenko [Cyb80]. He showed that, in the case of positive reflection coefficients, the residual error produced by the Levinson procedure is comparable to the error produced by the Cholesky factorization [GV96, p. 191]; i.e., the algorithm is weakly stable (cf. Sec. 4.5.1).

A related analysis has been carried out by Sweet [Swe82] for the Bareiss algorithm [Bar69], which was later recognized as being closely related to the algorithm of Schur [Sch17], [Kai86]; these are fast procedures for the Cholesky factorization of the Toeplitz matrix itself rather than its inverse (cf. Ch. 1 of this book). Sweet concluded that the Bareiss algorithm is asymptotically stable.

In recent work, Bojanczyk et al. [BBHS95] further extended and strengthened the conclusions of Sweet [Swe82] by employing elementary downdating techniques [APP88], [BBDH87], [BS88] that are also characteristic of array formulations of the Schur algorithm [KS95a], [SCK95]. They considered the class of quasi-Toeplitz matrices (viz., with a generator matrix G having two columns in the definition (1.2.4)—with $p = q = 1$), which includes the Toeplitz matrix as a special case, and provided an error analysis that established that the Schur algorithm for this class of matrices is asymptotically stable.

Contributions of Our Work

The results of Bojanczyk et al. [BBHS95] motivated us to take a closer look at the numerical stability of a generalized Schur algorithm [KS95a], [Say92], [SK95a] that applies to a more general class of structured matrices, viz., all positive-definite matrices R that satisfy displacement equations of the form $R - FRF^T = GJG^T$, where F is a stable lower triangular matrix (i.e., its diagonal entries have magnitude less than unity). This class clearly includes the case of quasi-Toeplitz matrices (by choosing $F = Z$). Several complications arise in this more general case when a matrix F is used rather than Z. In this chapter we provide an overview of the results of [CS96], where we propose several enhancements to the generalized Schur algorithm of Ch. 1 in order to ensure numerical stability while evaluating the Cholesky factor $\widehat{L}$ in the factorization $\widehat{L}\widehat{L}^T$. Hence, the current chapter is concerned with the numerical stability of the triangular factorization procedure.

Chapter 3, on the other hand, is concerned with the solution of linear systems of equations even for more general structured matrices (that need not be positive definite or even symmetric as above). More specifically, in Ch. 3 we use the stability results of the current chapter to develop a fast stable solver for linear systems of equations, $Tx = b$, with possibly indefinite or nonsymmetric structured coefficient matrices T [CS98].[5] As is well known, apart from the classical Gaussian elimination procedure, another way to solve the linear system of equations $Tx = b$ is to compute the QR factorization of the coefficient matrix T. For structured matrices, the computation has to be performed rapidly and several fast methods have been proposed earlier in the literature [BBH86], [CKL87], [Cyb83], [Cyb87], [Swe84], but none of them are numerically stable, especially since the resulting Q matrix is not guaranteed to be orthogonal (see Sec. 1.8.3 and also the discussion in Sec. 4.6).

In Ch. 3 we circumvent this difficulty by describing a new fast algorithm by the authors that provides a modified factorization for the coefficient matrix. The new algorithm relies on the observation that it is not really necessary to limit ourselves to LDU or QR factorizations of the coefficient matrix T in order to solve the linear system of equations $Tx = b$. If other factorizations for T can be obtained in a fast and stable manner, and if they are also useful for solving the linear system of equations, then these factorizations could be pursued as well. In fact, the new algorithm, rather than

---

[5] We are now denoting the coefficient matrix by T to distinguish it from the notation R for the R factor in the QR factorization of a matrix.

returning Q, returns two matrices Δ and Q such that Δ is triangular and the product $\Delta^{-1}Q$ is "numerically orthogonal"; it provides a factorization for the coefficient matrix T that is of the form

$$T = \Delta(\Delta^{-1}Q)R,$$

where we are now using R to denote an upper triangular matrix (just like the notation used to denote the R factor in the QR factorization of a matrix). The above factorization is in terms of three matrices $\{\Delta, Q, R\}$. The factorization is of course not unique, since we can replace Δ by any invertible matrix. The point, however, is that our algorithm returns that Δ that allows us to compensate for the fact that Q is not "numerically" orthogonal. More important, these factors are then used to solve $Tx = b$ both fast and in a backward-stable manner. The details are provided in Ch. 3.

2.3.1 Notation

In the discussion that follows we use $\|\cdot\|_2$ to denote the 2-norm of its argument (either Euclidean norm for a vector or maximum singular value for a matrix). We further assume, without loss of generality, that F is represented exactly in the computer. Also, the $\widehat{}$ notation denotes computed quantities, while the $\bar{}$ notation denotes intermediate exact quantities. We further let ε denote the machine precision and n the matrix size. We also use subscripted δ's to denote quantities bounded by machine precision in magnitude and we write $O_n(\varepsilon)$ to mean $O(\varepsilon c(n))$ for some polynomial $c(n)$ in n, which we usually do not specify. The special form of $c(n)$ depends on the norm used and on other details of the implementation.

We assume that in our floating point model, additions, subtractions, multiplications, divisions, and square roots are done to high relative accuracy, i.e.,

$$fl(x \circ y) = (x \circ y)(1 + \delta),$$

where $\circ$ denotes $+$, $-$, $\times$, or $\div$ and $|\delta| \leq \varepsilon$. The same is true for the square root operation. This is true for floating point processors that adhere to the IEEE standards.

2.3.2 Brief Review of Displacement Structure

A rather detailed exposition of displacement structure can be found in Ch. 1 of this book (and also in [KS95a] for more general non-Hermitian structures). Here we highlight only some of the basic equations and notation. We shall focus in this chapter, without loss of generality, on real-valued matrices. The analysis and results can be extended to the complex case.

We start with a symmetric matrix $R \in \mathbb{R}^{n \times n}$ that satisfies a displacement equation of the form

$$R - FRF^T = GJG^T \qquad (2.3.1)$$

with a "low" rank matrix G, say, $G \in \mathbb{R}^{n \times r}$ with $r \ll n$. Equation (2.3.1) uniquely defines R (i.e., it has a unique solution R) if and only if the diagonal entries of the lower triangular matrix F satisfy the condition

$$1 - f_i f_j \neq 0 \quad \text{for all } 0 \leq i, j \leq n - 1.$$

This uniqueness condition will be assumed throughout the chapter, although it can be relaxed in some instances—see Ch. 1 and also [KS95a].

As explained in Ch. 1, the pair (G, J) is said to be a generator pair for R since, along with F, it completely identifies R. Note, however, that while R has n^2 entries,

Section 2.3. Related Works in the Literature

the matrix G has nr entries and r is usually much smaller than n. Therefore, algorithms that operate on the entries of G, with the purpose of obtaining a triangular factorization for R, will generally be an order of magnitude faster than algorithms that operate on the entries of R itself. The generalized Schur algorithm is one such fast $O(rn^2)$ procedure, which receives as input data the matrices (F, G, J) and provides as output data the Cholesky factor of R.

The notion of structured matrices can also be extended to nonsymmetric matrices R. In this case, the displacement of R is generally defined with respect to two lower triangular matrices F and A (which can be the same, i.e., $F = A$—see (2.3.5)),

$$R - FRA^T = GB^T. \qquad (2.3.2)$$

Again, this displacement equation uniquely defines R if and only if the diagonal entries of F and A satisfy $1 - f_i a_j \neq 0$ for all i, j, a condition that will also be met in this chapter.

Several examples of matrices with displacement structure are given in Sec. 1.3, including Toeplitz, Hankel, Pick, Cauchy, and Vandermonde matrices. The concept is perhaps best illustrated by considering the much-studied special case of a symmetric Toeplitz matrix, $T = \left[t_{|i-j|}\right]_{i,j=0}^{n-1}$, $t_0 = 1$.

Let Z denote the $n \times n$ lower triangular shift matrix with ones on the first subdiagonal and zeros elsewhere (i.e., a lower triangular Jordan block with zero eigenvalues):

$$Z \triangleq \begin{bmatrix} 0 & & & \\ 1 & 0 & & \\ & \ddots & \ddots & \\ & & 1 & 0 \end{bmatrix}. \qquad (2.3.3)$$

It can be checked easily that the difference $T - ZTZ^T$ has displacement rank 2 (except when all $t_i, i \neq 0$, are zero) and a generator for T is $\{G, (1 \oplus -1)\}$, where

$$T - ZTZ^T = \begin{bmatrix} 1 & 0 \\ t_1 & t_1 \\ \vdots & \vdots \\ t_{n-1} & t_{n-1} \end{bmatrix} \begin{bmatrix} 1 & 0 \\ 0 & -1 \end{bmatrix} \begin{bmatrix} 1 & 0 \\ t_1 & t_1 \\ \vdots & \vdots \\ t_{n-1} & t_{n-1} \end{bmatrix}^T = GJG^T. \qquad (2.3.4)$$

Similarly, for a nonsymmetric Toeplitz matrix $T = [t_{i-j}]_{i,j=0}^{n-1}$, we can easily verify that the difference $T - ZTZ^T$ has displacement rank 2 and that a generator (G, B) for T is

$$T - ZTZ^T = \begin{bmatrix} t_0 & 1 \\ t_1 & 0 \\ \vdots & \vdots \\ t_{n-1} & 0 \end{bmatrix} \begin{bmatrix} 1 & 0 \\ 0 & t_{-1} \\ \vdots & \vdots \\ 0 & t_{-n+1} \end{bmatrix}^T = GB^T. \qquad (2.3.5)$$

This is a special case of (2.3.2) with $F = A = Z$. In particular, any matrix T (symmetric or not) for which $(T - ZTZ^T)$ has rank 2 is called *quasi Toeplitz*. For example, the inverse of a Toeplitz matrix is quasi Toeplitz (see Ch. 1). For higher displacement ranks, but still with $F = A = Z$, we shall say that the matrix is *shift structured*. For example, the product of two Toeplitz matrices is shift structured with displacement rank 4 (see, e.g., Ch. 1 and [KS95a]). Also, examples of structured matrices with diagonal $\{F, A\}$ in (2.3.2) are given in Ch. 1.

2.4 THE GENERALIZED SCHUR ALGORITHM

In this chapter we focus on symmetric positive-definite matrices R with displacement rank 2 with respect to a lower triangular matrix F, viz., matrices R that satisfy displacement equations of the form

$$R - FRF^T = \begin{bmatrix} u_0 & v_0 \end{bmatrix} \begin{bmatrix} 1 & 0 \\ 0 & -1 \end{bmatrix} \begin{bmatrix} u_0 & v_0 \end{bmatrix}^T, \qquad (2.4.1)$$

where u_0 and v_0 denote the $n \times 1$ column vectors of G and F is lower triangular with diagonal entries whose magnitude is less than unity. The results and conclusions can be extended easily to higher displacement ranks (and will be briefly mentioned in Sec. 3.1).

Recall also from Ch. 1 that since the generator matrix G is highly nonunique, it can always be in the so-called proper form

$$G = \begin{bmatrix} x & 0 \\ x & x \\ x & x \\ \vdots & \vdots \\ x & x \end{bmatrix}. \qquad (2.4.2)$$

That is, the top entry of v_1, v_{11}, can always be chosen to be zero. Indeed, assume that a generator G for R is found that does not satisfy this requirement, say,

$$G = \begin{bmatrix} u_{00} & v_{00} \\ x & x \\ \vdots & \vdots \\ x & x \end{bmatrix}.$$

It then follows from (2.4.1) that the $(0,0)$ entry of R, which is positive, is given by

$$[R]_{00} = \frac{|u_{00}|^2 - |v_{00}|^2}{1 - |f_0|^2} > 0.$$

Consequently, $|u_{00}| > |v_{00}|$ and a hyperbolic rotation Θ can always be found in order to reduce the row $\begin{bmatrix} u_{00} & v_{00} \end{bmatrix}$ to the form $\begin{bmatrix} \pm\sqrt{|u_{00}|^2 - |v_{00}|^2} & 0 \end{bmatrix}$ (see App. B). The matrix $G\Theta$ can then be used instead of G as a generator for R.

We now restate for convenience the generalized Schur algorithm in array form, which operates on the entries of (F, G, J) and provides the Cholesky factor of R. This statement is of course a special case of the algorithm derived in Sec. 1.7. We note, however, that we are now denoting the triangular factorization of the positive-definite R simply by $R = LL^T$ (rather than by $R = LD^{-1}L^T$ as in (1.6.1)).

Algorithm 2.4.1 (Generalized Schur Algorithm). *Consider a symmetric positive definite matrix $R \in \mathbb{R}^{n \times n}$ satisfying (2.4.1).*

- Input: *A stable lower triangular matrix F, a generator $G_0 = G$ in proper form, with columns denoted by u_0 and v_0, and $J = (1 \oplus -1)$.*

- Output: *The lower triangular Cholesky factor L of the unique symmetric positive-definite matrix R that satisfies (2.4.1), $R = LL^T$.*

Section 2.4. The Generalized Schur Algorithm

- Computation: *Start with (u_0, v_0), $F_0 = F$, and repeat for $i = 0, 1, \ldots, n-1$:*
  1. *Compute the matrix $\Phi_i = (F_i - f_i I)(I - f_i F_i)^{-1}$. Note that Φ_i is $(n-i) \times (n-i)$ lower triangular and that its first row is always zero.*
  2. *Form the prearray of numbers $\begin{bmatrix} \Phi_i u_i & v_i \end{bmatrix}$. Since $\begin{bmatrix} u_i & v_i \end{bmatrix}$ is assumed in proper form and since the first entry of $\Phi_i u_i$ is always zero, the prearray therefore has the form*
  $$\begin{bmatrix} 0 & 0 \\ \bar{G}_{i+1} & \end{bmatrix} \triangleq \begin{bmatrix} \Phi_i u_i & v_i \end{bmatrix}.$$
  That is, its top row is zero.
  3. *Apply a hyperbolic rotation Θ_i in order to annihilate the $(1,2)$ entry of $\bar{G}_{i+1}$, thus reducing it to proper form, say,*
  $$G_{i+1} \triangleq \begin{bmatrix} \times & 0 \\ \times & \times \\ \vdots & \vdots \\ \times & \times \end{bmatrix} = \bar{\bar{G}}_{i+1} \Theta_i = \underbrace{\begin{bmatrix} \times & \times \\ \times & \times \\ \vdots & \vdots \\ \times & \times \end{bmatrix}}_{\bar{G}_{i+1}} \Theta_i.$$

  We denote the resulting columns of G_{i+1} by $\{u_{i+1}, v_{i+1}\}$ and write, more compactly,
  $$G_{i+1} = \begin{bmatrix} u_{i+1} & v_{i+1} \end{bmatrix} = \bar{G}_{i+1} \Theta_i. \qquad (2.4.3)$$
  4. *The ith column of the Cholesky factor L is given by*
  $$l_i = \begin{bmatrix} 0 \\ \sqrt{1 - |f_i|^2}(I - f_i F_i)^{-1} u_i \end{bmatrix}, \qquad (2.4.4)$$
  where the top i entries are zero.
  5. *F_{i+1} is obtained by deleting the first row and column of F_i.*

⋄

After n steps, the algorithm provides the Cholesky decomposition
$$R = \sum_{i=0}^{n-1} l_i l_i^T. \qquad (2.4.5)$$

Recall also from Remark 2 after Alg. 1.6.2 that the successive matrices G_i that are obtained via the recursion have an interesting interpretation. Let R_i denote the Schur complement of R with respect to its leading $i \times i$ submatrix. That is, $R_0 = R$, R_1 is the Schur complement with respect to the $(0,0)$th top left entry of R, R_2 is the Schur complement with respect to the 2×2 top left submatrix of R, and so on. The matrix R_i is therefore $(n-i) \times (n-i)$. Then
$$R_i - F_i R_i F_i^T = G_i J G_i^T. \qquad (2.4.6)$$

In other words, G_i is a generator matrix for the ith Schur complement, which is also structured. Note that both G_i and $\bar{G}_i$ can be regarded as generator matrices for the ith Schur complement R_i.

2.5 A LIMIT TO NUMERICAL ACCURACY

Given a symmetric positive-definite matrix R (not necessarily structured), if its Cholesky factor is evaluated by any standard backward stable method that operates on the entries of R, e.g., by Gaussian elimination (see [GV96, Ch. 4] and also Ch. 1) the corresponding error bound is given by

$$\|R - \widehat{L}\widehat{L}^T\|_2 \leq O_n(\varepsilon)\|R\|_2,$$

where ε is the machine precision.

A fundamental question that needs to be answered then is the following: given (F, G, J) but not R, how accurately can we expect to be able to compute the Cholesky factorization of R *irrespective* of the algorithm used (*slow or fast*)? The example and discussion that follows justifies the following conclusion [CS96].

Lemma 2.5.1 (Limit of Accuracy). *Irrespective of the algorithm we use (slow or fast), if the input data is (F, G, J), for a general lower triangular F, we cannot expect a better bound than*

$$\|R - \widehat{L}\widehat{L}^T\|_2 \leq O_n(\varepsilon) \, \|(I - F \otimes F)^{-1}\|_2 \, \|u_0\|_2^2. \tag{2.5.1}$$

Proof: The claim is established in [CS96] by constructing a simple example. We highlight the main steps here.

To begin with, note that just representing (F, G) in finite precision already induces round-off errors. This fact in turn imposes limits on how accurate an algorithm that employs (F, G) can be.

Consider the following example. Let F be a stable diagonal matrix with distinct entries $\{f_i\}$ and assume f_0 is the largest in magnitude. Let the entries of the column vectors u_0 and v_0 be constructed as follows:

$$u_{i0} = \left(\frac{1}{2}\right)^{i-1}, \quad v_{i0} = \gamma f_i u_{i0}, \quad i \geq 1,$$

where γ is chosen such that $0 < \gamma < 1$. The unique matrix R that solves (2.4.1) for the given (F, u_0, v_0) can be shown to be symmetric positive definite.

When the data (u_0, v_0) are stored in finite precision, round-off errors are bound to occur. Let us assume that only a relative perturbation occurs in the first entry of u_0, while all other entries of u_0 and v_0 remain unchanged. That is, let us define the perturbed vectors $\widehat{u}_0$ and $\widehat{v}_0$ with

$$\widehat{u}_{00} = u_{00}(1 + \delta), \quad \widehat{u}_{i0} = u_{i0} \ \ i \geq 1, \quad \widehat{v}_0 = v_0,$$

where δ is a small number (for example, for round-off errors, $|\delta|$ is smaller than machine precision). We also assume that F is stored exactly. Hence, the only source of error we are assuming is in u_{00}.

An algorithm that is intended to factor R will in fact be factoring the matrix $\widehat{R}$ that is defined as the unique solution of the following displacement equation with the perturbed generator matrix,

$$\widehat{R} - F\widehat{R}F^T = \widehat{G}J\widehat{G}^T, \quad \widehat{G} = \begin{bmatrix} \widehat{u}_0 & \widehat{v}_0 \end{bmatrix}.$$

The difference between this matrix and the original matrix R is denoted by the error matrix $E = R - \widehat{R}$. How big can E be? It is easy to verify that E is the unique solution of

$$E - FEF^T = GJG^T - \widehat{G}J\widehat{G}^T = u_0 u_0^T - \widehat{u}_0 \widehat{u}_0^T.$$

Using this fact, it can be verified that [CS96]

$$\|E\|_2 \geq \frac{3}{4}|2\delta + \delta^2| \, \|(I - F \otimes F)^{-1}\|_2 \, \|u_0\|_2^2,$$

where $\otimes$ denotes the Kronecker product. This expression provides a *lower bound* on the norm of the error matrix. It is further argued in [CS96] that by choosing f_0 and γ sufficiently close to one, the norm of the original matrix R can be made much smaller than the above bound.

Hence, in general, we cannot expect the error norm, $\|R - \widehat{L}\widehat{L}^T\|$, for any algorithm (slow or fast) that uses (F, G, J) as input data (but not R) to be as small as $c_0|\delta|\|R\|$ for some constant c_0.

$\diamond$

The above perturbation analysis indicates the best accuracy that can be expected from *any* finite precision algorithm that uses the generator matrix as the input data. The issue now is to show that the generalized Schur algorithm can essentially achieve this bound if certain care is taken during its implementation. We shall show in this chapter that, in general, this requires that we incorporate four kinds of enhancement:

1. A careful implementation of the hyperbolic rotation Θ_i that is needed in each step of the algorithm (Sec. 2.6).

2. A careful implementation of the Blaschke-vector product $\Phi_i u_i$ that is also needed in each step of the algorithm (Sec. 2.7).

3. Enforcing positive definiteness of the successive Schur complements to avoid breakdown (Sec. 2.8).

4. Control of potential growth of the norms of the successive generator matrices (Sec. 2.11). We may remark that pivoting strategies can be useful in controlling generator growth when F is diagonal with norm close to unity.

For all practical purposes, the major conclusion (see Sec. 2.9) of the analysis will be that the modified Schur algorithm is a backward-stable procedure for a large class of positive-definite structured matrices.

2.6 IMPLEMENTATIONS OF THE HYPERBOLIC ROTATION

Each step (2.4.3) of the generalized Schur algorithm requires the application of a hyperbolic rotation Θ_i. The purpose of the rotation is to rotate the top row of the $\bar{G}_{i+1}$, which is the second row of the $[\,\Phi_i u_i \quad v_i\,]$, to proper form. If we denote the top row of $\bar{G}_{i+1}$ by

$$[\,(\Phi_i u_i)_1 \quad v_{i1}\,] \triangleq [\,\alpha_i \quad \beta_i\,],$$

then the expression for a hyperbolic rotation that transforms it to the form

$$[\,\pm\sqrt{|\alpha_i|^2 - |\beta_i|^2} \quad 0\,]$$

is given by

$$\Theta_i = \frac{1}{\sqrt{1-\rho_i^2}} \begin{bmatrix} 1 & -\rho_i \\ -\rho_i & 1 \end{bmatrix}, \quad \text{where } \rho_i = \frac{\beta_i}{\alpha_i}. \tag{2.6.1}$$

The positive definiteness of R guarantees $|\rho_i| < 1$.

Expression (2.4.3) shows that in infinite precision, the generator matrices G_{i+1} and $\bar{G}_{i+1}$ must satisfy the fundamental requirement

$$G_{i+1}JG_{i+1}^T = \bar{G}_{i+1}J\bar{G}_{i+1}^T. \qquad (2.6.2)$$

Obviously, this condition cannot be guaranteed in finite precision. But it turns out that with an appropriate implementation of the transformation (2.4.3), equality (2.6.2) can be guaranteed to within a "small" error. The need to enforce the condition in finite precision was first observed for the $F = Z$ case by Bojanczyk et al. [BBHS95].

2.6.1 Direct Implementation

A naive implementation of the hyperbolic transformation (2.4.3) can lead to large errors. Indeed, in finite precision, if we apply Θ_i directly to $\bar{G}_{i+1}$ we obtain a computed matrix $\widehat{G}_{i+1}$ such that [CS96]

$$\|\widehat{G}_{i+1}J\widehat{G}_{i+1}^T - \bar{G}_{i+1}J\bar{G}_{i+1}^T\|_2 \le O_n(\varepsilon)\,\|\bar{G}_{i+1}\|_2^2\,\|\Theta_i\|_2^2. \qquad (2.6.3)$$

But since $\|\Theta_i\|$ can be large, the computed quantities are not guaranteed to satisfy relation (2.6.2) to sufficient accuracy. This possibly explains the disrepute into which fast algorithms have fallen.

Interestingly though, Bojanczyk et al. [BBHS95] showed that for the special case $F = Z$ and displacement rank $r = 2$, the direct implementation of the hyperbolic rotation still leads to an asymptotically backward stable algorithm. This conclusion, however, does not hold for higher displacement ranks. Stewart and Van Dooren [SD97b] showed that for $F = Z$ and $r > 2$, the direct implementation of the hyperbolic rotation can be unstable.

We proceed to review alternative methods for implementing the hyperbolic rotation that can be used for general F, including $F = Z$, and also for higher displacement ranks.

2.6.2 Mixed Downdating

One possible way to ameliorate the above problem is to employ the mixed downdating procedure as suggested by Bojanczyk et al. [BBHS95], [BBDH87].

Assume we apply a hyperbolic rotation Θ to a row vector $\begin{bmatrix} x & y \end{bmatrix}$, say,

$$\begin{bmatrix} x_1 & y_1 \end{bmatrix} = \begin{bmatrix} x & y \end{bmatrix} \frac{1}{\sqrt{1-|\rho|^2}} \begin{bmatrix} 1 & -\rho \\ -\rho & 1 \end{bmatrix}. \qquad (2.6.4)$$

Then, more explicitly,

$$x_1 = \frac{1}{\sqrt{1-|\rho|^2}}\,[x - \rho y], \qquad (2.6.5)$$

$$y_1 = \frac{1}{\sqrt{1-|\rho|^2}}\,[-\rho x + y]. \qquad (2.6.6)$$

Solving for x in terms of x_1 from the first equation and substituting into the second equation we obtain

$$y_1 = -\rho x_1 + \sqrt{1-|\rho|^2}\,y. \qquad (2.6.7)$$

An implementation that is based on (2.6.5) and (2.6.7) is said to be in mixed downdating form. It has better numerical stability properties than a direct implementation of Θ as in (2.6.4).

Section 2.6. Implementations of the Hyperbolic Rotation

In the above mixed form, we first evaluate x_1 and then use it to compute y_1. We can obtain a similar procedure that first evaluates y_1 and then uses it to compute x_1. For this purpose, we solve for y in terms of y_1 from (2.6.6) and substitute into (2.6.5) to obtain

$$x_1 = -\rho y_1 + \sqrt{1 - |\rho|^2}\, x\,. \tag{2.6.8}$$

Equations (2.6.6) and (2.6.8) represent the second mixed form.

Using this scheme to implement the hyperbolic transformation (2.4.3) guarantees (cf. [BBHS95], [BBDH87])

$$\|\widehat{G}_{i+1} J \widehat{G}_{i+1}^T - \bar{G}_{i+1} J \bar{G}_{i+1}^T\|_2 \leq O_n(\varepsilon)\left(\|\bar{G}_{i+1}\|_2^2 + \|\widehat{G}_{i+1}\|_2^2\right).$$

This bound is sufficient, when combined with other modifications suggested in Secs. 2.7 and 2.11, to make the algorithm numerically reliable (Sec. 2.9).

2.6.3 The Orthogonal-Diagonal Procedure

An alternative scheme that was employed in [CS96] is based on using the singular value decomposition (SVD) representation of a hyperbolic rotation Θ. Its good numerical properties derive from the fact that the hyperbolic rotation is applied as a sequence of orthogonal and diagonal matrices, which we shall refer to as the orthogonal-diagonal (OD) procedure. Its other advantage is that it is a general technique that can be applied in other situations. It can be implemented with the same operation count as the mixed downdating algorithm of [BBHS95].

It is straightforward to verify that any hyperbolic rotation of the form (2.6.1) admits the following eigen(SVD-)decomposition:

$$\Theta_i = \frac{1}{\sqrt{2}}\begin{bmatrix} 1 & 1 \\ -1 & 1 \end{bmatrix} \begin{bmatrix} \sqrt{\frac{\alpha_i+\beta_i}{\alpha_i-\beta_i}} & 0 \\ 0 & \sqrt{\frac{\alpha_i-\beta_i}{\alpha_i+\beta_i}} \end{bmatrix} \begin{bmatrix} 1 & -1 \\ 1 & 1 \end{bmatrix} \frac{1}{\sqrt{2}} = Q_i D_i Q_i^T,$$

where the matrix

$$Q_i = \frac{1}{\sqrt{2}}\begin{bmatrix} 1 & 1 \\ -1 & 1 \end{bmatrix}$$

is orthogonal ($Q_i Q_i^T = I$).

If the eigendecomposition $Q_i D_i Q_i^T$ is now applied to the prearray $\bar{G}_{i+1}$ in (2.4.3), then it can be shown that the computed generator matrix $\widehat{G}_{i+1}$ satisfies [CS96]

$$(\widehat{G}_{i+1} + E_{2,i+1}) = (\bar{G}_{i+1} + E_{1,i+1})\Theta_i \tag{2.6.9}$$

and

$$\|\widehat{G}_{i+1} J \widehat{G}_{i+1}^T - \bar{G}_{i+1} J \bar{G}_{i+1}^T\|_2 \leq O_n(\varepsilon)\left(\|\bar{G}_{i+1}\|_2^2 + \|\widehat{G}_{i+1}\|_2^2\right)$$

with

$$\|E_{1,i+1}\|_2 \leq O_n(\varepsilon)\,\|\bar{G}_{i+1}\|_2, \quad \|E_{2,i+1}\|_2 \leq O_n(\varepsilon)\,\|\widehat{G}_{i+1}\|_2.$$

Algorithm 2.6.1 (The OD Procedure). *Given a hyperbolic rotation Θ with reflection coefficient $\rho = \beta/\alpha$, $|\rho| < 1$, and a prearray row vector $\begin{bmatrix} x & y \end{bmatrix}$, the postarray row vector $\begin{bmatrix} x_1 & y_1 \end{bmatrix}$ can be computed as follows:*

$$[\begin{array}{cc} x' & y' \end{array}] = [\begin{array}{cc} x & y \end{array}] \begin{bmatrix} 1 & 1 \\ -1 & 1 \end{bmatrix},$$

$$[\begin{array}{cc} x'' & y'' \end{array}] = [\begin{array}{cc} x' & y' \end{array}] \begin{bmatrix} \frac{1}{2}\sqrt{\frac{\alpha+\beta}{\alpha-\beta}} & 0 \\ 0 & \frac{1}{2}\sqrt{\frac{\alpha-\beta}{\alpha+\beta}} \end{bmatrix},$$

$$[\begin{array}{cc} x_1 & y_1 \end{array}] = [\begin{array}{cc} x'' & y'' \end{array}] \begin{bmatrix} 1 & -1 \\ 1 & 1 \end{bmatrix}.$$

◇

The above algorithm guarantees the error bounds

$$[\begin{array}{cc} \widehat{x}_1 + e_1 & \widehat{y}_1 + e_2 \end{array}] = [\begin{array}{cc} x + e_3 & y + e_4 \end{array}]\Theta$$

with

$$\|[\begin{array}{cc} e_1 & e_2 \end{array}]\|_2 \leq O_n(\varepsilon) \|[\begin{array}{cc} \widehat{x}_1 & \widehat{y}_1 \end{array}]\|_2, \quad \|[\begin{array}{cc} e_3 & e_4 \end{array}]\|_2 \leq O_n(\varepsilon) \|[\begin{array}{cc} x & y \end{array}]\|_2.$$

2.6.4 The H Procedure

Another method introduced in [CS96] is the following. Let $\rho = \beta/\alpha$ be the reflection coefficient of a hyperbolic rotation Θ,

$$\Theta = \frac{1}{\sqrt{1-\rho^2}} \begin{bmatrix} 1 & -\rho \\ -\rho & 1 \end{bmatrix},$$

with $|\rho| < 1$. Let $[\begin{array}{cc} x_1 & y_1 \end{array}]$ and $[\begin{array}{cc} x & y \end{array}]$ be the postarray and prearray rows, respectively:

$$[\begin{array}{cc} x_1 & y_1 \end{array}] = [\begin{array}{cc} x & y \end{array}]\Theta, \quad \text{with } |x| > |y|.$$

Algorithm 2.6.2 (The H Procedure). *Given a hyperbolic rotation Θ with reflection coefficient $\rho = \beta/\alpha$, $|\rho| < 1$, and a prearray $[\begin{array}{cc} x & y \end{array}]$ with $|x| > |y|$, the postarray $[\begin{array}{cc} x_1 & y_1 \end{array}]$ can be computed as follows:*

$$\begin{array}{l}
\text{If } \frac{\beta}{\alpha}\frac{y}{x} < 1/2 \\
\quad \text{then } \xi = 1 - \frac{\beta}{\alpha}\frac{y}{x} \\
\text{else} \\
\quad d_1 = \frac{|\alpha|-|\beta|}{|\alpha|}, \quad d_2 = \frac{|x|-|y|}{|x|} \\
\quad \xi = d_1 + d_2 - d_1 d_2 \\
\text{endif} \\
x_1 = \frac{|\alpha| x \xi}{\sqrt{(\alpha-\beta)(\alpha+\beta)}} \\
y_1 = x_1 - \sqrt{\frac{\alpha+\beta}{\alpha-\beta}}(x-y).
\end{array}$$

◇

Section 2.7. Implementation of the Blaschke Matrix   69

The advantage of the H procedure is that the computed quantities $\widehat{x}_1$ and $\widehat{y}_1$ will satisfy the equation
$$[\ \widehat{x}_1 + e'_1 \ \ \widehat{y}_1 + e'_2\ ] = [\ x\ \ y\ ]\Theta, \qquad (2.6.10)$$
where the error terms satisfy
$$|e'_1| \leq O_n(\varepsilon)|\widehat{x}_1|, \quad |e'_2| \leq O_n(\varepsilon)(|\widehat{x}_1| + |\widehat{y}_1|). \qquad (2.6.11)$$

Comparing with (2.6.9) we see that the prearray is not perturbed. Moreover, we shall show in Sec. 2.13.2 that by a slight modification we can further enforce that $|\widehat{x}_1| > |\widehat{y}_1|$, which is needed to prevent breakdown in the algorithm. (If $|x| < |y|$, then it can be seen that $[\ y\ \ x\ ]\Theta = [\ y_1\ \ x_1\ ]$. Therefore, without loss of generality, we considered above only the case $|x| > |y|$.)

The the H procedure requires $5n$ to $7n$ multiplications and $3n$ to $5n$ additions. It is therefore costlier than the OD procedure, which requires $2n$ multiplications and $4n$ additions. But the H procedure is forward stable (cf. (2.6.10)), whereas the OD method is only stable (cf. (2.6.9)).

From now on we shall denote by $\widehat{u}_{i+1}$ and $\widehat{v}_{i+1}$ the computed generator columns at step i, i.e., $\widehat{G}_{i+1} = [\ \widehat{u}_{i+1}\ \ \widehat{v}_{i+1}\ ]$, starting with $\bar{G}_i = [\ \Phi_i \widehat{u}_i\ \ \widehat{v}_i\ ]$.

2.7 IMPLEMENTATION OF THE BLASCHKE MATRIX

Each step of the Schur algorithm also requires multiplying the Blaschke matrix Φ_i by u_i. (Recall that the top entry of $\Phi_i u_i$ is always zero and, hence, can be ignored in the computation.) In this section, we consider the following two cases:

- F is stable and diagonal, in which case Φ_i itself is diagonal and its entries are given by
$$\left\{ \frac{f_j - f_i}{1 - f_i f_j} \right\}.$$

- F is strictly lower triangular, e.g., $F = Z$, $F = (Z \oplus Z)$, or other more involved choices. In these situations, the matrix Φ_i is equal to F_i itself since the f_i are all zero, $\Phi_i = F_i$.

2.7.1 The Case of Diagonal F

The goal of this section is to show how to compute $\Phi_i \widehat{u}_i$ to high componentwise relative accuracy (i.e., high relative accuracy for each component of the computed vector). Here, $\widehat{u}_i$ denotes the computed value of u_i.

The numerator of each diagonal entry of Φ_i can be computed to high relative accuracy as
$$fl(f_j - f_i) = (f_j - f_i)(1 + \delta_1).$$

Computing the denominator $x_{ij} \triangleq (1 - f_i f_j)$ to high relative accuracy is a bit trickier, as the following example shows.

Let $f_1 = f_2 = 0.998842$. Then in 6-digit arithmetic $1 - f_1 f_2 \approx 2.31500 \times 10^{-3}$, whereas the actual answer is $2.31465903600 \times 10^{-3}$. Therefore, the relative error is approximately 1.5×10^{-4}. Using the scheme given below, we find $1 - f_1 f_2 \approx 2.31466 \times 10^{-3}$. The relative error is now approximately 4.2×10^{-7}.

The scheme we use to compute x_{ij} is as follows:

If $f_i f_j < 1/2$
   then $x_{ij} = 1 - f_i f_j$
else
   $d_j = 1 - |f_j|, \quad d_i = 1 - |f_i|,$
   $x_{ij} = d_i + d_j - d_i d_j.$

It can be shown that this scheme ensures that x_{ij} is computed to high relative accuracy [CS96], viz., that
$$\widehat{x}_{ij} = x_{ij}(1 + 33\delta_{11}).$$
Knowing how to compute Φ_i to componentwise accuracy, and since Φ_i is diagonal, the entries of $\Phi_i \widehat{u}_i$ can be computed to componentwise high relative accuracy. More specifically,
$$fl\,(\Phi_i \widehat{u}_i)_k = (\Phi_i \widehat{u}_i)_k (1 + 72\delta_{12}). \tag{2.7.1}$$
We should remark that this scheme is not totally successful when F is a general triangular matrix (for example, when F is bidiagonal). A way around this difficulty will be addressed elsewhere. But for a strictly lower triangular F, the situation is far simpler as shown in the next subsection.

For now, let us consider how to compute the nonzero part of the l_i's. Define
$$\bar{l}_i \triangleq \begin{bmatrix} 0 \\ \sqrt{1 - f_i^2}\,(I - f_i F)^{-1} \widehat{u}_i \end{bmatrix} \tag{2.7.2}$$
with i leading zeros. We use the expression
$$\frac{\sqrt{(1 - f_i)(1 + f_i)}}{1 - f_i f_j}(\widehat{u}_i)_k$$
to evaluate the nonzero entries of $\bar{l}_i$, with the technique explained above for the denominator $(1 - f_i f_j)$. (The notation $(\widehat{u}_i)_k$ denotes the kth entry of $\widehat{u}_i$.) Then we can also show that the nonzero entries of $\bar{l}_i$ and $\widehat{l}_i$ satisfy
$$(\widehat{l}_i)_k = (\bar{l}_i)_k (1 + c_1(n)\delta_{13}) \tag{2.7.3}$$
for some polynomial in n, $c_1(n)$.

2.7.2 The Case of Strictly Lower Triangular F

When F is strictly lower triangular we obtain $\Phi_i = F_i$. Hence, here we use the standard matrix-vector multiplication to evaluate $\Phi_i u_i$ and the computed quantities will then satisfy [GV96]
$$\|fl(F_i \widehat{u}_i) - F_i \widehat{u}_i\|_2 \leq O_n(\varepsilon)\|F\|_2 \|\widehat{u}_i\|_2.$$
Moreover, since $f_i = 0$,
$$\bar{l}_i = \begin{bmatrix} 0 \\ \widehat{u}_i \end{bmatrix} = \widehat{l}_i. \tag{2.7.4}$$

2.8 ENFORCING POSITIVE DEFINITENESS

The computed successive Schur complements have to be positive definite to guarantee that the successive reflection coefficients are all strictly less than unity in magnitude. These facts can be enforced in finite precision by imposing a condition on the smallest eigenvalue of R and by introducing a computational enhancement during the evaluation of the reflection coefficients.

Define the matrix S_i that solves the displacement equation

$$S_i - F_i S_i F_i^T = \widehat{u}_i \widehat{u}_i^T - \widehat{v}_i \widehat{v}_i^T. \tag{2.8.1}$$

If the $\{\widehat{u}_i, \widehat{v}_i\}$ were exact and equal to $\{u_i, v_i\}$, then the S_i would correspond to the ith Schur complement R_i of R (cf. (2.4.6)). The matrix R_i is necessarily positive definite since R is positive definite. However, because we are now dealing with computed values rather than exact values, we need to guarantee that the computed generator columns $\{\widehat{u}_i, \widehat{v}_i\}$ define a positive-definite matrix S_i.

It was shown in [CS96] that this can be guaranteed by imposing a condition on the smallest eigenvalue of R, viz., by guaranteeing that R is sufficiently positive definite. Define

$$\bar{R} = \sum_{i=0}^{n-1} \bar{l}_i \bar{l}_i^T,$$

where the $\bar{l}_i$ are intermediate exact quantities computed via (2.7.2). Then we can ensure the positive definiteness of the computed Schur complements if

$$\lambda_{\min}(R) > O_n(\varepsilon) \|(I - F \otimes F)^{-1}\|_2 \, (2 + \|F\|_2^2) \left[\|\bar{R}\|_2 + \sum_{j=0}^{n-1} \|\widehat{u}_j\|_2^2 \right]. \tag{2.8.2}$$

The condition further guarantees, due to positive definiteness, that $|\Phi_i \widehat{u}_i|_2 > |\widehat{v}_i|_2$. (The inequality compares the second entries of $\Phi_i \widehat{u}_i$ and $\widehat{v}_i$.) This ensures that the reflection coefficients will be smaller than one in magnitude, a condition that we can enforce in finite precision as follows:

If $|fl(\Phi_i \widehat{u}_i)|_2 < |\widehat{v}_i|_2$ then
  set $fl(\Phi_i \widehat{u}_i)_2 = |\widehat{v}_i|_2 (1 + 3\varepsilon) \text{sign}(fl(\Phi_i \widehat{u}_i)_2)$.

This enhancement, along with condition (2.8.2), can be shown to guarantee that the algorithm will be completed without any breakdowns.

2.9 ACCURACY OF THE FACTORIZATION

Using the above enhancements (regarding the implementations of the hyperbolic rotation and the Blaschke-vector product and the enforcement of positivity), it was shown in [CS96] that the following error bound holds.

Theorem 2.9.1 (Error Bound). *Consider a symmetric positive-definite matrix $R \in \mathbb{R}^{n \times n}$ satisfying (2.4.1) and (2.8.2), with a stable diagonal or strictly lower triangular F.*

The generalized Schur algorithm, when implemented as detailed above (see also listing in App. 2.A), guarantees the following error bound:

$$\left\| R - \sum_{i=0}^{n-1} \widehat{l}_i \widehat{l}_i^T \right\|_2 \leq O_n(\varepsilon) \|(I - F \otimes F)^{-1}\|_2 \, (2 + \|F\|_2^2) \left[\|\bar{R}\|_2 + \sum_{j=0}^{n-1} \|\widehat{u}_j\|_2^2 \right]. \quad (2.9.1)$$

◇

The term $\|(I - F \otimes F)^{-1}\|_2$ in the error bound is expected from the perturbation analysis of Sec. 2.5. However, the presence of the norms of the successive generators makes the error bound larger than the bound suggested by the perturbation analysis, which depends only on the norm of the first generator matrix.

The natural question then is, How big can the norm of the generators be? We consider the following cases separately.

1. **F strictly lower triangular.** Using (2.4.4) we can verify that $\|u_i\|_2^2 \leq \|R\|_2$. It then follows that the error bound is as good as can be expected from the perturbation analysis of Sec. 2.5.

2. **F strictly lower triangular and contractive.** More can be said if F is further assumed to be contractive ($\|F\|_2 \leq 1$). To see this, we first note that the error bound in the case when F is strictly lower triangular can be rewritten as

$$\left\| R - \sum_{i=0}^{n-1} \widehat{l}_i \widehat{l}_i^T \right\|_2 \leq O_n(\varepsilon)(2 + \|F\|_2^2) \left(\sum_{i=1}^{n} \|F^i\|_2^2 \right) \left[\|\bar{R}\|_2 + \left(\sum_{i=0}^{n-1} \|\widehat{u}_i\|_2^2 \right) \right].$$

When F is contractive, this further implies that

$$\left\| R - \sum_{i=0}^{n-1} \widehat{l}_i \widehat{l}_i^T \right\|_2 \leq O_n(\varepsilon) \left[\|\bar{R}\|_2 + \left(\sum_{i=0}^{n-1} \|\widehat{u}_i\|_2^2 \right) \right].$$

But since we also have $\|u_i\|_2^2 \leq \|R\|_2$, we conclude that the factorization algorithm is backward stable.

This result applies to the important class of positive-definite quasi-Toeplitz matrices, which corresponds to $F = Z$. In this case, the above conclusion strengthens the result of Bojanczyk et al. [BBHS95], which states that for quasi-Toeplitz symmetric positive-definite matrices, the Schur algorithm is asymptotically backward stable. Our analysis shows that the modified algorithm proposed here is backward stable provided the smallest eigenvalue of the quasi-Toeplitz matrix satisfies

$$\lambda_{\min}(R) > O_n(\varepsilon) \left[\|\bar{R}\|_2 + \sum_{j=0}^{n-1} \|\widehat{u}_j\|_2^2 \right].$$

If F is strictly lower triangular but noncontractive, then the error norm can possibly depend on $\|(I - F \otimes F)^{-1}\|_2$, as shown in the previous case.

3. **F diagonal.** Using the fact that R is positive definite and (2.4.4), we can verify that

$$\|u_i\|_2^2 \leq \|(I - F \otimes F)^{-1}\|_2 \, (1 + \|F\|^2)^2 \, \|R\|_2. \quad (2.9.2)$$

This shows that the growth of the generators depends on $\|(I - F \otimes F)^{-1}\|_2$. This may suggest that the norm of the error can become very large when the magnitude of the diagonal entries of F becomes close to one. But this is not necessarily the case (see also the numerical example in the next section) since we can further strengthen the error bound as follows.

Define
$$\rho_{ji} = \frac{\widehat{v}_{ji}}{\widehat{u}_{ji}}.$$

It then holds in the diagonal case that

$$\left\| R - \sum_{i=0}^{n-1} \widehat{l}_i \widehat{l}_i^T \right\|_2 \leq O_n(\varepsilon) \frac{\sum_{i=1}^{n} \|\bar{R}_i\|_2}{1 - \max_{j,i} (\rho_{ji}^2)}, \tag{2.9.3}$$

where the $\bar{R}_i$ are defined by

$$\bar{R}_i = \sum_{j=0}^{i-1} \bar{l}_i \bar{l}_i^T + \begin{bmatrix} 0 & 0 \\ 0 & S_i \end{bmatrix}.$$

The bound (2.9.3) is independent of the $\{f_i\}$! In other words, if the coefficients $\rho_{j,i}$ defined above are sufficiently smaller than one, then the algorithm will still be backward stable irrespective of how close the $\{|f_i|\}$ are to one.

What does this say about the stability of the generalized Schur algorithm for a diagonal and stable F? Clearly, when the eigenvalues of F are sufficiently far from one the method has excellent numerical stability. The algorithm degrades as the eigenvalues of F get closer to one. This is to be expected from the perturbation analysis (whether we use a slow or a fast algorithm). However, if the generators grow rapidly (i.e., as fast as (2.9.2)), then the algorithm degrades faster than the rate predicted by the perturbation analysis.

Is there anything further we can do to ameliorate this problem? One thing we have not considered yet is pivoting, which is possible only when F is diagonal.

2.10 PIVOTING WITH DIAGONAL F

When F is diagonal it is possible to accommodate pivoting into the algorithm [Hei95]; it corresponds to reordering the f_j's, u_{ji}'s, and v_{ji}'s identically at the ith iteration of the algorithm. This has the effect of computing the Cholesky factorization of PRP^T, where P is the product of all the permutations that were carried out during the algorithm.

In finite precision, pivoting strategies are employed in classical Cholesky factorization algorithms when the positive-definite matrix is numerically singular. *In the context of the generalized Schur algorithm, the main motivation for pivoting should be to keep the norm of the generator matrices as small as possible* (see also Sec. 4.4.2). This is suggested by the expression for the error bound in (2.9.1), which depends on the norm of the generators. Note that this motivation has little to do with the size of the smallest eigenvalue of the matrix.

We would like to emphasize that pivoting is necessary only when the norm of F is very close to one, as otherwise the generators do not grow appreciably (cf. (2.9.2)).

2.10.1 A Numerical Example

The first question that arises then is whether there exists a pivoting strategy that guarantees a small growth in the norm of the generators. Unfortunately, we have numerical examples that show that irrespective of which pivoting strategy is employed, the norms of the generators may not exhibit significant reduction.

Consider the matrix R that satisfies the displacement equation $R - FRF^T = GJG^T$ with

$$G = \begin{bmatrix} 0.26782811166721 & 0.26782805810159 \\ 0.65586390188981 & -0.65586311485320 \\ 0.65268528182561 & 0.65268365011256 \\ 0.26853783287812 & -0.26853149538590 \end{bmatrix}, \quad J = \begin{bmatrix} 1 & 0 \\ 0 & -1 \end{bmatrix},$$

and
$$F = \text{diagonal}\{0.9999999, -0.9999989, 0.9999976, -0.9999765\}.$$

The matrix R is positive definite. Table 2.1 lists the values of the sum $\sum_{j=0}^{n-1} \|\widehat{u}_j\|_2^2$ (scaled by 10^{-6} and denoted by S) for all the 24 possible pivoting options of the rows of the generator matrix G. The results indicate that none of the pivoting options significantly reduces the size of the generators.

2.10.2 The Case of Positive F

This raises the next question: Is pivoting useful at all? It is useful when the entries of the F matrix are strictly positive (or negative). In this case, we permute the entries of F (and, correspondingly, the entries of u_1 and v_1) such that the diagonal of F is in increasing order in magnitude. Then it can be shown that [CS96]

$$\|\widehat{u}_i\|_2 \leq \|\bar{R}\|_2^{1/2},$$

which makes the first-order term of the upper bound on E depend only on the first power of $\|(I - F \otimes F)^{-1}\|_2$.

Table 2.1. Values of the scaled sum S for all 24 pivoting options.

1.	5.30	9.	0.41	17.	0.83
2.	5.30	10.	0.41	18.	0.83
3.	5.21	11.	0.40	19.	0.83
4.	5.21	12.	0.40	20.	0.83
5.	5.03	13.	0.40	21.	0.04
6.	5.03	14.	0.40	22.	0.04
7.	0.83	15.	0.04	23.	0.04
8.	0.83	16.	0.04	24.	0.04

2.10.3 The Nonpositive Case

When F is not positive, the example in Sec. 2.10.1 suggests that pivoting may not help in general. However, it may still be beneficial to try a heuristic pivoting strategy to control the growth of the generators. Ideally, at the ith iteration we should pick the row of the prearray $\bar{G}_{i+1}$ which would lead to the smallest (in norm) postarray G_{i+1}. Since there seems to be no efficient way to do this we suggest picking the row that leads to the smallest reflection coefficient (in magnitude) for the hyperbolic rotation Θ_i. As suggested by the example of Sec. 2.10.1, an alternate strategy would be to order the f_i's in increasing order of magnitude.

We may stress that pivoting is relevant *only* when the norm of F is very close to one, as indicated by the error bound (2.9.1) and by (2.9.2).

2.11 CONTROLLING THE GENERATOR GROWTH

We have shown before that the generators do not grow (i) if F is strictly lower triangular and contractive or (ii) if F is a positive diagonal matrix with increasing diagonal entries. We now show how to control the generator growth in general using an idea suggested by Gu [Gu95a].

It follows from (2.8.1) that

$$\|\widehat{G}_i J \widehat{G}_i^T\|_2 = \|S_i - F_i S_i F_i^T\|_2.$$

Let $W_i \Lambda_i W_i^T$ denote the eigendecomposition of $\widehat{G}_i J \widehat{G}_i^T$, where Λ_i is a 2×2 real diagonal matrix with $(\Lambda_i)_{11} > 0$ and $(\Lambda_i)_{22} < 0$. Then $W_i \sqrt{|\Lambda_i|}$ can be taken as a generator for S_i with the desirable property that

$$\left\|W_i \sqrt{|\Lambda_i|}\right\|_2^2 = \|\Lambda_i\|_2 = \|S_i - F_i S_i F_i^T\|_2 \leq \|S_i\|_2 \left(1 + \|F\|_2^2\right) \leq \|\bar{R}_i\|_2 \left(1 + \|F\|_2^2\right),$$

where $\|\bar{R}_i\|_2 \approx \|R\|_2$, to first order in ε.

Therefore, whenever the generator grows, i.e., $\|\widehat{G}_i\|_2^2$ becomes larger than a given threshold (say, $2\|R\|_2 (1 + \|F\|_2^2)$), we can replace it by $W_i \sqrt{|\Lambda_i|}$. This computation can be done in $O((n-i)r^2 + r^3)$ flops ($r = 2$ in the case under consideration) by first computing the QR factorization of $\widehat{G}_i$, say,

$$\widehat{G}_i = Q_i P_i, \quad Q_i Q_i^T = I,$$

and then computing the eigendecomposition of the 2×2 matrix $P_i J P_i^T$. We can then get W_i by multiplying Q_i by the orthogonal eigenvector matrix of $P_i J P_i^T$.

2.12 SOLUTION OF LINEAR SYSTEMS OF EQUATIONS

The analysis in the earlier sections suggests that for $\|F\|_2$ sufficiently close to one, the error norm can become large. However, if our original motivation is the solution of a linear system of equations, say, $Rx = b$, then the error can be improved by resorting to iterative refinement if the matrix R either is given or can be computed accurately from (F, G). In what follows we show that for a diagonal F, the matrix R can be evaluated to high relative accuracy if u_1 and v_1 are exact.

2.12.1 Computing the Matrix R

Given a positive-definite structured matrix R that satisfies

$$R - FRF^T = u_0 u_0^T - v_0 v_0^T$$

with F diagonal and stable, its entries can be computed to high relative accuracy as we explain below.

It follows from the displacement equation that

$$r_{ij} = \frac{u_{i0}u_{j0} - v_{i0}v_{j0}}{1 - f_i f_j} = \frac{u_{i0}u_{j0}\left(1 - \frac{v_{i0}}{u_{i0}}\frac{v_{j0}}{u_{j0}}\right)}{1 - f_i f_j},$$

where, by positive definiteness, the ratios

$$\frac{v_{i0}}{u_{i0}} \quad \text{and} \quad \frac{v_{j0}}{u_{j0}}$$

are strictly less than one.

The term $\xi = 1 - \frac{v_{i0}}{u_{i0}}\frac{v_{j0}}{u_{j0}}$ can be evaluated to high relative accuracy as explained earlier in Sec. 2.6.4, viz.,

$$\begin{aligned}
&\text{If } \tfrac{v_{i0}}{u_{i0}}\tfrac{v_{j0}}{u_{j0}} < 1/2 \\
&\quad \text{then } \xi = 1 - \tfrac{v_{i0}}{u_{i0}}\tfrac{v_{j0}}{u_{j0}} \\
&\text{else} \\
&\quad d_1 = \tfrac{|u_{i0}|-|v_{i0}|}{|u_{i0}|}, \ d_2 = \tfrac{|u_{j0}|-|v_{j0}|}{|u_{j0}|}, \\
&\quad \xi = d_1 + d_2 - d_1 d_2.
\end{aligned}$$

Likewise, we evaluate $\mu = (1 - f_i f_j)$ and then $r_{ij} = \frac{u_{i0}u_{j0}\xi}{\mu}$. This guarantees $\widehat{r}_{ij} = r_{ij}(1 + O_n(\varepsilon))$.

2.12.2 Iterative Refinement

If the factorization $\widehat{L}\widehat{L}^T$ is not too inaccurate, and if R is not too ill-conditioned, then it follows from the analysis in [JW77] that the solution $\widehat{x}$ of $Rx = b$ can be made backward stable by iterative refinement.

Algorithm 2.12.1 (Iterative Refinement). *Consider a symmetric positive-definite matrix $R \in \mathbb{R}^{n \times n}$ and let $\widehat{L}\widehat{L}^T$ be a computed Cholesky factorization for it. Let $\widehat{x}$ be a computed solution for $Rx = b$. The solution $\widehat{x}$ can be made backward stable as follows:*

$$\begin{aligned}
&\text{Set } \widehat{x}_0 = \widehat{x},\ r = b - R\widehat{x}_0 \\
&\text{repeat until } \|r\|_2 \le O_n(\varepsilon)\|R\|_2\,\|\widehat{x}\|_2 \\
&\quad \text{solve } \widehat{L}\widehat{L}^T \delta x = r \\
&\quad \text{set } \widehat{x}_i = \widehat{x}_{i-1} + \delta x \\
&\quad r = b - R\widehat{x}_i \\
&\text{end repeat.}
\end{aligned}$$

◊

2.13 ENHANCING THE ROBUSTNESS OF THE ALGORITHM

The performance and robustness of the generalized Schur algorithm can be improved by further enhancements.

Observe that the positive definiteness of R imposes conditions on the columns of the generator matrix:

- For a diagonal and stable F, a necessary condition for the positive definiteness of the matrix is that we must have

$$|\widehat{u}_{i+1}| > |\widehat{v}_{i+1}|, \qquad (2.13.1)$$

where the inequality holds componentwise.

- For a lower triangular contractive F, a necessary condition for positive definiteness is

$$\|u_i\|_2 \geq \|v_i\|_2.$$

- In all cases, the condition $|\Phi_i u_i|_{i+1} > |v_i|_{i+1}$ is required to ensure that the reflection coefficient of the hyperbolic rotation, Θ_i, is less than 1.

We have found that if all these necessary conditions are enforced explicitly, the algorithm is more reliable numerically. An example of this can be found in Sec. 2.13.3.

We now show how the OD and H methods can be modified to preserve the sign of the J-norm of each row of the prearray.

2.13.1 Enhancing the OD Method

The OD method can be enhanced to preserve the sign of the J-norm of the row to which it is applied. More specifically, if the jth row of the perturbed prearray has positive J-norm, then by adding a small perturbation to the jth row of the computed postarray we can guarantee a positive J-norm. If the jth row of the perturbed prearray does not have a positive J-norm, then in general there does not exist a small perturbation for the jth row of the postarray that will guarantee a positive J-norm. For such a row, the prearray must be perturbed to make its J-norm sufficiently positive and then the hyperbolic rotation must be reapplied by the OD method to that row. The new jth row of the postarray can now be made to have a positive J-norm by a small perturbation. The details are given in the algorithm below. For the case of a diagonal and stable F, all the rows of the prearray should have positive J-norm. The algorithm should enforce this property.

In the statement of the algorithm, $\begin{bmatrix} x & y \end{bmatrix}$ stands for a particular row of the prearray $\bar{G}_{i+1}$, $\begin{bmatrix} \widehat{x}_1 & \widehat{y}_1 \end{bmatrix}$ stands for the corresponding row of the postarray $\widehat{G}_{i+1}$, and Θ stands for the hyperbolic rotation. Here we are explicitly assuming that $|x| > |y|$, which is automatically the case when F is diagonal and stable. Otherwise, since $\begin{bmatrix} y & x \end{bmatrix} \Theta = \begin{bmatrix} y_1 & x_1 \end{bmatrix}$, the technique must be used with the elements of the input row interchanged.

Algorithm 2.13.1 (Enhanced OD Method).

>*Assumption:* $|x| > |y|$.
>*if* $|\widehat{x}_1| < |\widehat{y}_1|$
> $\gamma_1 = O_n(\varepsilon)(|\widehat{x}_1| + |\widehat{y}_1|)\,sign(\widehat{x}_1)$
> $\gamma_2 = O_n(\varepsilon)(|\widehat{x}_1| + |\widehat{y}_1|)\,sign(\widehat{y}_1)$
> *if* $|\widehat{x}_1 + \gamma_1| > |\widehat{y}_1 - \gamma_2|$ *then*
> $\widehat{x}_1 = \widehat{x}_1 + \gamma_1$
> $\widehat{y}_1 = \widehat{y}_1 - \gamma_2$
> *else*
> $\eta_1 = O_n(\varepsilon)(|x| + |y|)\,sign(x)$
> $\eta_2 = O_n(\varepsilon)(|x| + |y|)\,sign(y)$
> $\begin{bmatrix} \widehat{x}_1 & \widehat{y}_1 \end{bmatrix} = \begin{bmatrix} x + \eta_1 & y - \eta_2 \end{bmatrix} \Theta$ *(via the OD method)*
>   *if* $|\widehat{x}_1| > |\widehat{y}_1|$ *then* $\widehat{x}_1 = \widehat{x}_1$ *and* $\widehat{y}_1 = \widehat{y}_1$
>   *else*
> $\gamma_1 = O_n(\varepsilon)(|\widehat{x}_1| + |\widehat{y}_1|)\,sign(\widehat{x}_1)$
> $\gamma_2 = O_n(\varepsilon)(|\widehat{x}_1| + |\widehat{y}_1|)\,sign(\widehat{y}_1)$
> $\widehat{x}_1 = \widehat{x}_1 + \gamma_1$
> $\widehat{y}_1 = \widehat{y}_1 - \gamma_2$
>   *endif*
> *endif*
>*endif*

◇

2.13.2 Enhancing the H Procedure

Here again, $\begin{bmatrix} x & y \end{bmatrix}$ stands for a particular row of the prearray $\bar{G}_{i+1}$, and $\begin{bmatrix} \widehat{x}_1 & \widehat{y}_1 \end{bmatrix}$ stands for the corresponding row of the postarray. We shall again assume that $|x| > |y|$. If that is not the case then the procedure must be applied to $\begin{bmatrix} y & x \end{bmatrix}$, since $\begin{bmatrix} y & x \end{bmatrix}\Theta = \begin{bmatrix} y_1 & x_1 \end{bmatrix}$.

It follows from $|x| > |y|$ that

$$|\widehat{x}_1 + e_1|^2 - |\widehat{y}_1 + e_2|^2 > 0$$

for the H procedure. Therefore, by adding small numbers to $\widehat{x}_1$ and $\widehat{y}_1$ we can guarantee $|\widehat{x}_1| > |\widehat{y}_1|$.

Algorithm 2.13.2 (Enhanced H Method).

>*Assumption:* $|x| > |y|$.
>*Apply the hyperbolic rotation* Θ *to* $\begin{bmatrix} x & y \end{bmatrix}$ *using the H procedure.*
>*If* $|\widehat{x}_1| < |\widehat{y}_1|$ *then*
> $\widehat{y}_1 = |\widehat{x}_1|(1 - 3\varepsilon)\,sign(\widehat{y}_1)$.

◇

2.13.3 A Numerical Example

The following example exhibits a positive-definite matrix R for which a direct implementation of the generalized Schur algorithm, without the enhancements and modifications

Section 2.14. Results for the Positive-Definite Case 79

proposed herein, breaks down. On the other hand, the modified Schur algorithm enforces positive definiteness and avoids breakdown as the example shows. The data are as follows:

$$G = \begin{bmatrix} 0.29256168393970 & 0 \\ 0.28263551029525 & -0.10728616660709 \\ 0.09633626413940 & 0.01541380240248 \\ 0.06797943459994 & -0.02572176567354 \\ 0.55275012712414 & 0.22069874528633 \\ 0.42631253478657 & 0.06821000412583 \\ 0.50468895704517 & 0.20125628531328 \\ 0.23936358366577 & -0.09527653751206 \\ 0.14608901804405 & 0.02337424345679 \end{bmatrix},$$

$$F = \text{diag} \begin{bmatrix} 0.40000000000000 \\ 0.97781078411630 \\ -0.00000000433051 \\ 0.97646762001746 \\ -0.99577002371173 \\ 0.00000001005313 \\ -0.99285659894698 \\ 0.99789820799463 \\ -0.00000001100000 \end{bmatrix}.$$

A straightforward implementation of the generalized Schur algorithm (i.e., with a naive implementation of the hyperbolic rotation and the Blaschke matrix-vector multiply) breaks down at the eighth step and declares the matrix indefinite.

On the other hand, our implementation, using the enhanced H procedure and the enhanced Blaschke matrix-vector multiply, successfully completes the matrix factorization and yields a relative error

$$\frac{\|R - \widehat{L}\widehat{L}^T\|_2}{\varepsilon(1 - \|F\|_2^2)^{-2}\|R\|_2} \approx 0.15.$$

Furthermore, the relative backward error $\|R - \widehat{L}\widehat{L}^T\|_2/\|R\|_2$ is approximately 10^{-11} (using a machine precision of approximately 10^{-16}).

2.14 RESULTS FOR THE POSITIVE-DEFINITE CASE

The general conclusion is the following:

The modified Schur algorithm of this chapter is backward stable for a large class of positive-definite structured matrices. Generally, it is as stable as can be expected from the perturbation analysis of Sec. 2.5.

More specifically,

- If F is strictly lower triangular and contractive (e.g., $F = Z$), then the modified algorithm is backward stable with no generator growth.

- If F is stable, diagonal, and positive, then by reordering the entries of F in increasing order, there will be no generator growth and the algorithm will be as stable as can be expected from Sec. 2.5. In particular, it will be backward stable if $\|F\|_2$ is not too close to one (e.g., $\|F\|_2^2 \leq 1 - \frac{1}{n^2}$).

- In all other cases, we can use the technique outlined in Sec. 2.11 to control the generator growth and make the algorithm as stable as can be expected from Sec. 2.5. In particular, it is backward stable if $\|F\|_2$ is not too close to one (e.g., $\|F\|_2^2 \leq 1 - \frac{1}{n^2}$).

- If R is given or can be computed accurately (e.g., when F is diagonal), iterative refinement can be used to make the algorithm backward stable for the solution of linear equations.

As far as pivoting is concerned, in the diagonal F case, our analysis shows that it is necessary only when $\|F\|_2$ is very close to one.

- If F is positive (or negative), a good strategy is to reorder the entries of F in increasing order of magnitude.

- If F has both positive and negative entries, then our numerical example of Sec. 2.10.1 indicates that pivoting may not help in controlling the growth of the generators.

In our opinion, for positive-definite structured matrices, with diagonal or strictly lower triangular F, the stabilization of the generalized Schur algorithm is critically dependent on the following:

- Proper implementations of the hyperbolic rotations (using the OD or H procedures).

- Proper evaluation of the Blaschke matrix-vector product.

- Enforcing positive definiteness to avoid early breakdowns.

- Controlling the generator growth.

Acknowledgments

The authors wish to thank Professor Thomas Kailath for comments and feedback on an earlier draft of this chapter. They also gratefully acknowledge the support of the National Science Foundation; the work of A. H. Sayed was partially supported by awards MIP-9796147 and CCR-9732376, and the work of S. Chandrasekaran was partially supported by award CCR-9734290.

Section 2.A. Pseudocode for the Stable Schur Algorithm 81

APPENDIX FOR CHAPTER 2

2.A PSEUDOCODE FOR THE STABLE SCHUR ALGORITHM

We include here a listing of the stabilized Schur algorithm. The program assumes that the input matrix is positive definite and tries to enforce it. The algorithm listed here can be easily modified to test if a structured matrix is positive definite.[6]

The H Procedure

Input data: The ratio $beta/alpha$ represents the reflection coefficient, which is smaller than one in magnitude. Also, y/x is assumed to be smaller than one in magnitude.

Output data: The entries $\begin{bmatrix} x_1 & y_1 \end{bmatrix}$ that result by applying a hyperbolic rotation to $\begin{bmatrix} x & y \end{bmatrix}$, with $|x_1| > |y_1|$.

$function \begin{bmatrix} x1, & y1 \end{bmatrix} = h\_procedure(x, y, beta, alpha)$

```
        c = (beta * y)/(alpha * x);
        if c < 0.5
           xi = 1 - c;
        else
           d1 = (abs(alpha) - abs(beta))/abs(alpha);
           d2 = (abs(x) - abs(y))/abs(x);
           xi = d1 + d2 - d1 * d2;
        end
        x1 = (abs(alpha) * x * xi)/sqrt((alpha - beta) * (alpha + beta));
        y1 = x1 - sqrt((alpha + beta)/(alpha - beta)) * (x - y);
        if abs(x1) < abs(y1)
           y1 = abs(x1) * (1 - 3 * eps) * sign(y1)
        end
```

The Blaschke Matrix-Vector Product

We now list the program that computes $\Phi_i u_i$ for both a diagonal F and a strictly lower triangular F.

Remark. In contrast to the description of the generalized Schur algorithm in Alg. 2.4.1, the codes given here work with quantities $\{\Phi_i, u_i, v_i\}$ that are always n-dimensional. The indices also start at 1 rather than 0. Hence, $\{u_i, v_i\}$ are now taken as $n \times 1$ column vectors whose leading $(i-1)$ entries are zero. Also, Φ_i is taken as an $n \times n$ matrix. This convention is used for convenience of description.

- Input: An $n \times n$ stable and diagonal matrix F, a vector u, a vector v (such that $|v| < |u|$), and an index i ($1 \leq i \leq n$).

- Output: The matrix vector product $z = \Phi_i u$, where $\Phi_i = (I - f_i F)^{-1}(F - f_i I)$, and the vector $ub = (I - f_i F)^{-1} u$.

---

[6]The codes listed here are in a MATLAB-like language.

$function \begin{bmatrix} z, & ub \end{bmatrix} = blaschke\_1(F, u, v, i, n)$

$\quad ub = u;$
$\quad z = u;$
$\quad \text{for } j = i : n$
$\quad\quad \text{if } F(i,i) * F(j,j) < 0.5$
$\quad\quad\quad xi = 1/(1 - F(j,j) * F(i,i));$
$\quad\quad \text{else}$
$\quad\quad\quad d1 = 1 - \text{abs}(F(i,i));$
$\quad\quad\quad d2 = 1 - \text{abs}(F(j,j));$
$\quad\quad\quad xi = 1/(d1 + d2 - d1 * d2);$
$\quad\quad \text{end}$
$\quad\quad ub(j) = xi * z(j);$
$\quad\quad z(j) = (F(j,j) - F(i,i)) * ub(j);$
$\quad\quad \text{if } \text{abs}(z(j)) < \text{abs}(v(j))$
$\quad\quad\quad z(j) = \text{abs}(v(j)) * (1 + 3 * eps) * \text{sign}(z(j));$
$\quad\quad \text{end}$
$\quad \text{end}$

For a strictly lower triangular F we use the following.

Input data: An $n \times n$ strictly lower triangular matrix F, a vector u, a vector v (such that $|v| < |u|$), and an index i ($1 \le i \le n$).

Output data: The matrix–vector product $z = Fu$ and $ub = u$.

$function \begin{bmatrix} z, & ub \end{bmatrix} = blaschke\_2(F, u, v, i, n)$

$\quad ub = u;$
$\quad z = F * u;$
$\quad z(i) = 0;$
$\quad \text{if } \text{abs}(z(i+1)) < \text{abs}(v(i+1))$
$\quad\quad z(i+1) = \text{abs}(v(i+1)) * (1 + 3 * eps) * \text{sign}(z(i+1));$
$\quad \text{end}$

The Stable Schur Algorithm

We now list two versions of the stable modified Schur algorithm—one for diagonal stable F and the other for strictly lower triangular F.

Input data: An $n \times n$ diagonal and stable matrix F, a generator $G = \begin{bmatrix} u & v \end{bmatrix}$ in proper form (i.e., top entry of v is zero), with column vectors u, v.

Output data: A lower triangular Cholesky factor L such that $\|R - LL^T\|_2$ satisfies (2.9.1).

$function \ L = stable\_schur\_1(u, v, F)$

$\quad n = size(F, 1);$
$\quad \text{for } i = 1 : n - 1$

Section 2.A. Pseudocode for the Stable Schur Algorithm

$$\begin{bmatrix} u, & ub \end{bmatrix} = blaschke\_1(F, u, v, i, n);$$
$$L(:, i) = \text{sqrt}((1 - F(i,i)) * (1 + F(i,i))) * ub;$$
$$a = v(i+1);$$
$$b = u(i+1);$$
for $j = i + 1 : n$
$$\begin{bmatrix} u(j), & v(j) \end{bmatrix} = h\_procedure(u(j), v(j), a, b);$$
end
$$v(i+1) = 0;$$
end
$$L(n,n) = (1/\text{sqrt}((1 - F(n,n)) * (1 + F(n,n)))) * u(n);$$
$$L(1 : n-1, n) = zeros(n-1, 1);$$

- Input: An $n \times n$ strictly lower triangular matrix F, a generator $G = \begin{bmatrix} u & v \end{bmatrix}$ in proper form (i.e., top entry of v is zero), with column vectors u, v.

- Output: A lower triangular Cholesky factor L such that $\|R - LL^T\|_2$ satisfies (2.9.1).

$function \; L = stable\_schur\_2(u, v, F)$

$n = size(F, 1);$
for $i = 1 : n - 1$
$$\begin{bmatrix} u, & ub \end{bmatrix} = blaschke\_2(F, u, v, i, n);$$
$$L(:, i) = \text{sqrt}((1 - F(i,i)) * (1 + F(i,i))) * ub;$$
$$a = v(i+1);$$
$$b = u(i+1);$$
for $j = i + 1 : n$
  if $\text{abs}(u(j)) > \text{abs}(v(j))$
  $$\begin{bmatrix} u(j), & v(j) \end{bmatrix} = h\_procedure(u(j), v(j), a, b);$$
  else
  $$\begin{bmatrix} temp\_v, & temp\_u \end{bmatrix} = h\_procedure(v(j), u(j), a, b);$$
  $$v(j) = temp\_v; \; u(j) = temp\_u;$$
  endif
end
$$v(i+1) = 0;$$
end
$$L(n,n) = (1/\text{sqrt}((1 - F(n,n)) * (1 + F(n,n)))) * u(n);$$
$$L(1 : n-1, n) = zeros(n-1, 1);$$

Chapter 3

FAST STABLE SOLVERS FOR STRUCTURED LINEAR SYSTEMS

Ali H. Sayed

Shivkumar Chandrasekaran

3.1 INTRODUCTION

The derivation in Ch. 2 showed how to obtain a stable implementation of the generalized Schur algorithm for positive-definite structured matrices R and, also, how to solve $Rx = b$ when R is structured but still *positive definite*.

We now use this stable implementation of the Schur algorithm, and the same notation of Ch. 2, to solve in a stable manner linear systems of equations with possibly *indefinite* or even *nonsymmetric* structured coefficient matrices. In other words, we show how to use the stability results of the positive-definite case to derive stable solvers for the indefinite and nonsymmetric cases.

We shall focus on *shift-structured* coefficient matrices R, viz., those that satisfy displacement equations of the form

$$R - ZRZ^T = GB^T$$

for some (G, B). In fact, we shall denote the coefficient matrix throughout this chapter by T rather than R and write

$$T - ZTZ^T = GB^T. \qquad (3.1.1)$$

The notation T is chosen for two reasons. First, this class of matrices includes as a special case Toeplitz matrices (which correspond to a special choice for G and B—see (2.3.5)). However, our results apply not only to Toeplitz coefficient matrices but, more generally, to shift-structured matrices T (obtained for other choices of G and B and also for multicolumn G and B). Second, the notation T is also chosen to avoid confusion with the notation R for the R factor in the QR factorization of a matrix. Such QR factorizations will be repeatedly invoked in this chapter.

The coefficient matrix T is not required to be symmetric or positive definite. It is required only to be a structured matrix in the sense defined by (3.1.1). It can thus be indefinite or even nonsymmetric. Now given a linear system of equations $Tx = b$, one method for solving it fast is to compute the QR factorization of the coefficient matrix T rapidly. Several fast methods have been proposed for this purpose [BBH86], [CKL87], [Cyb83], [Cyb87], [Swe84] (see also Sec. 1.8.3) but none of them is numerically stable since the resulting Q matrix cannot be guaranteed to be orthogonal. In [CS98], however, the authors of this chapter showed how to circumvent this issue and derived an algorithm that is provably both fast *and* backward stable for solving $Tx = b$ for shift-structured matrices T that can be indefinite or even nonsymmetric.

The new algorithm relies on the observation that it is not really necessary to limit ourselves to only LDU or QR factorizations of the coefficient matrix T in order to solve the linear system of equations $Tx = b$. If other factorizations for T can be obtained in a fast and stable manner, and if they are also useful for solving the linear system of equations, then these factorizations should be pursued as well. In fact, the new algorithm, rather than returning Q, returns two matrices Δ and Q such that Δ is triangular and the product $\Delta^{-1}Q$ is "numerically orthogonal"; it provides a factorization for the coefficient matrix T that is of the form

$$T = \Delta(\Delta^{-1}Q)R.$$

This factorization is in terms of the three matrices $\{\Delta, Q, R\}$ and it is, of course, highly nonunique, since we can always replace Δ by any invertible matrix. The point, however, is that the new algorithm returns that particular Δ that allows us to compensate for the fact that Q is not numerically orthogonal. More important, these factors are then used to solve $Tx = b$ both fast and in a backward stable manner.

Our derivation is based on the following idea. We already know from the discussions in Ch. 2 how to develop a numerically reliable implementation of the generalized Schur algorithm for positive-definite structured matrices. This suggests that we should first transform a problem that involves a nonsymmetric or indefinite structured matrix T to an equivalent problem that involves sign-definite matrices only (either positive definite or negative definite). We achieve this by relying on a so-called embedding technique developed in [Chu89], [KC94] (see also Ch. 1). More specifically, we embed the square coefficient matrix T into a larger matrix of the form

$$M = \begin{bmatrix} T^T T & T^T \\ T & 0 \end{bmatrix}. \qquad (3.1.2)$$

The product $T^T T$ is *never* formed explicitly. This definition for M is just for explanation purposes since the algorithm itself will end up working with a generator matrix for M and not with the entries of M, and this generator for M can be found from a generator for T, without the need to form $T^T T$ (see Sec. 3.4).

Now observe that the leading block of M is positive definite and the Schur complement of M with respect to the $(1,1)$ block is negative definite (and equal to $-I$). The matrix M also turns out to be structured (e.g., M is shift structured when T is quasi Toeplitz). In this case, and with proper modifications, the stability results of Ch. 2 can be applied.

3.2 OVERVIEW OF THE PROPOSED SOLUTION

Once the matrices $\{\Delta, Q, R\}$ are obtained, they are used to solve for x efficiently by using the expression

$$x = R^{-1}(Q^T \Delta^{-T})\Delta^{-1} b. \qquad (3.2.1)$$

Note that in writing this expression we used the fact that $\Delta^{-1}Q$ is orthogonal and, hence, its inverse is the transpose matrix.

All computations in the above expression can be done in $O(n^2)$ operations, where n is the matrix dimension, and the algorithm turns out to be backward stable (cf. the definitions of stability in Ch. 4) in the sense that the computed solution $\widehat{x}$ is shown to satisfy an equation of the form

$$(T + \tilde{T})\widehat{x} = b,$$

where the norm of the error matrix $\tilde{T}$ satisfies

$$\|\tilde{T}\|_2 \leq O_n(\varepsilon) \|T\|_2 + O(\varepsilon^2),$$

where ε denotes machine precision.

The factorization for T is obtained as follows. We apply $2n$ steps of the generalized Schur algorithm to a generator of M in (3.1.2) and obtain its *computed* triangular factorization, which we partition in the form

$$\begin{bmatrix} \widehat{R}^T & 0 \\ \widehat{Q} & \Delta \end{bmatrix} \begin{bmatrix} \widehat{R} & \widehat{Q}^T \\ 0 & -\Delta^T \end{bmatrix},$$

where $\widehat{R}^T$ and Δ are $n \times n$ lower triangular matrices. The computed matrices $\{\widehat{R}, \widehat{Q}, \Delta\}$ are the quantities used in (3.2.1) to determine the computed solution $\widehat{x}$ in a backward stable manner.

From a numerical point of view, the above steps differ in a crucial way from the embeddings suggested in [Chu89], [KC94] and turn out to mark the difference between a numerically stable and a numerically unstable implementation. The discussion in [Chu89, pp. 37, 50, 52] and [KC94] is mainly concerned with fast procedures for the QR factorization of Toeplitz block and block Toeplitz matrices. It employs an embedding of the form

$$M = \begin{bmatrix} T^T T & T^T \\ T & I \end{bmatrix}, \tag{3.2.2}$$

where the identity matrix I in (3.2.2) replaces the zero matrix in our embedding (3.1.2). The derivation in [Chu89], [KC94] suggests applying n (rather than $2n$) steps of the generalized Schur algorithm to a generator of (3.2.2) and then using the resulting $\widehat{R}$ and $\widehat{Q}$ as the QR factors of T. However, numerical issues were not studied in [Chu89], [KC94], and it turns out that the above procedure *does not* guarantee a numerically orthogonal matrix $\widehat{Q}$ and therefore cannot be used to implement a stable solver for a linear system of equations $Tx = b$.

For this reason, we instead proposed in [CS98] to proceed with the previous embedding (3.1.2) since it seems difficult to obtain a stable algorithm that is based solely on the alternative embedding (3.2.2). We also apply $2n$ steps (rather than just n steps) of the generalized Schur algorithm to a generator of (3.1.2). This allows us to incorporate a correction procedure into the algorithm (by computing Δ), which is shown later to ensure backward stability when coupled with the other modifications that we discussed in Ch. 2 for stabilizing the generalized Schur algorithm.

3.3 THE GENERALIZED SCHUR ALGORITHM FOR INDEFINITE MATRICES

We described in Sec. 2.4 the array form of the Schur algorithm for symmetric positive definite structured matrices with displacement rank 2. Now, in view of the structure of

M, we shall need to apply the algorithm to a symmetric but possibly indefinite matrix with displacement rank larger than 2 with respect to a strictly lower triangular F, say,

$$M - FMF^T = GJG^T, \quad J = (I_p \oplus -I_q). \tag{3.3.1}$$

For this reason, and for ease of reference, we include here a statement of the algorithm for this particular case (this form is a special case of Alg. 1.7.1 of Ch. 1).

For displacement ranks larger than 2, we shall say that a generator matrix G is in *proper* form if its first nonzero row has a single nonzero entry, say, in the first column

$$G = \begin{bmatrix} x & 0 & 0 & 0 & 0 \\ x & x & x & x & x \\ x & x & x & x & x \\ \vdots & \vdots & \vdots & \vdots & \vdots \\ x & x & x & x & x \end{bmatrix} \tag{3.3.2}$$

or in the last column

$$G = \begin{bmatrix} 0 & 0 & 0 & 0 & x \\ x & x & x & x & x \\ x & x & x & x & x \\ \vdots & \vdots & \vdots & \vdots & \vdots \\ x & x & x & x & x \end{bmatrix}. \tag{3.3.3}$$

We note that in the statement below we are denoting the triangular factorization of a symmetric matrix M by $M = LDL^T$, where D is taken as a signature matrix (rather than $M = LD^{-1}L^T$ as in (1.6.1), where D is a diagonal matrix).

Algorithm 3.3.1 (Schur Algorithm for Indefinite Matrices). *Consider a symmetric strongly regular matrix $M \in \mathbb{R}^{n \times n}$ satisfying* (3.3.1).

- Input: *An $n \times n$ strictly lower triangular matrix F, an $n \times r$ generator $G_0 = G$, and $J = (I_p \oplus -I_q)$.*

- Output: *A lower triangular factor L and a signature matrix D such that $M = LDL^T$, where M is the solution of (3.3.1) (assumed $n \times n$).*

- Computation: *Start with $G_0 = G$, $F_0 = F$, and repeat for $i = 0, 1, \ldots, n-1$:*

    1. Let g_i denote the top row of G_i.
    2. If $g_i J g_i^T > 0$ (we refer to this case as a positive step):
        ⋄ Choose a J-unitary rotation Θ_i that converts g_i to proper form with respect to the first column, i.e.,

        $$g_i \Theta_i = \begin{bmatrix} x & 0 & 0 & 0 & 0 \end{bmatrix}. \tag{3.3.4}$$

        Let $\bar{G}_i = G_i \Theta_i$ (i.e., apply Θ_i to G_i).
        ⋄ The ith column of L, denoted by l_i, is obtained by appending i zero entries to the first column of $\bar{G}_i$,

        $$l_i = \begin{bmatrix} 0 \\ \bar{G}_i \begin{bmatrix} 1 \\ 0 \end{bmatrix} \end{bmatrix}. \tag{3.3.5}$$

        The ith signature is $d_i = 1$.

Section 3.3. The Generalized Schur Algorithm for Indefinite Matrices

⋄ Keep the last columns of $\bar{G}_i$ unchanged and multiply the first column by F_i, where F_i denotes the submatrix obtained by deleting the first i rows and columns of F. This provides a new matrix whose first row is zero (since F_i is strictly lower triangular) and whose last rows are the rows of the next generator matrix G_{i+1}, i.e.,

$$\begin{bmatrix} 0 \\ G_{i+1} \end{bmatrix} = \begin{bmatrix} F_i \bar{G}_i \begin{bmatrix} 1 \\ 0 \end{bmatrix} & \bar{G}_i \begin{bmatrix} 0 \\ I \end{bmatrix} \end{bmatrix}. \tag{3.3.6}$$

3. If $g_i J g_i^T < 0$ (we refer to this case as a negative step):

   ⋄ Choose a J-unitary rotation Θ_i that converts g_i to proper form with respect to the last column, i.e.,

$$g_i \Theta_i = \begin{bmatrix} 0 & 0 & 0 & 0 & x \end{bmatrix}. \tag{3.3.7}$$

   Let $\bar{G}_i = G_i \Theta_i$ (i.e., apply Θ_i to G_i).

   ⋄ The ith column of L, denoted by l_i, is obtained by appending i zero entries to the last column of $\bar{G}_i$,

$$l_i = \begin{bmatrix} 0 \\ \bar{G}_i \begin{bmatrix} 0 \\ 0 \\ 1 \end{bmatrix} \end{bmatrix}. \tag{3.3.8}$$

   The ith signature is $d_i = -1$.

   ⋄ Keep the first columns of $\bar{G}_i$ unchanged and multiply the last column by F_i. This provides a new matrix whose first row is zero (since F_i is strictly lower triangular) and whose last rows are the rows of the next generator matrix G_{i+1}, i.e.,

$$\begin{bmatrix} 0 \\ G_{i+1} \end{bmatrix} = \begin{bmatrix} \bar{G}_i \begin{bmatrix} I \\ 0 \end{bmatrix} & F_i \bar{G}_i \begin{bmatrix} 0 \\ 1 \end{bmatrix} \end{bmatrix}. \tag{3.3.9}$$

4. The case $g_i J g_i^T = 0$ is ruled out by the strong regularity of M.

⋄

Again, after n steps, the algorithm provides the triangular decomposition

$$M = \sum_{i=0}^{n-1} d_i l_i l_i^T \tag{3.3.10}$$

at $O(rn^2)$ computational cost (see Ch. 1). Moreover, the successive matrices G_i that are obtained via the algorithm can be interpreted as follows (recall Remark 2 after Alg. 1.6.2). Let M_i denote the Schur complement of M with respect to its leading $i \times i$ submatrix; then

$$M_i - F_i M_i F_i^T = G_i J G_i^T. \tag{3.3.11}$$

Hence, G_i constitutes a generator matrix for the ith Schur complement M_i, which is therefore structured. Note further that $\bar{G}_i$ is also a generator matrix for the same Schur complement M_i since, due to the J-unitarity of Θ_i, we have $\bar{G}_i J \bar{G}_i^T = G_i \Theta_i J \Theta_i^T G_i^T = G_i J G_i^T$. We now address the main issues of this chapter.

3.4 FAST QR FACTORIZATION OF SHIFT-STRUCTURED MATRICES

As mentioned in (3.1.1), we shall focus on matrices $T \in \mathbb{R}^{n \times n}$ that are shift structured and therefore satisfy a displacement equation of the form

$$T - ZTZ^T = GB^T \tag{3.4.1}$$

for some generator pair (G, B). Consider, for now, the following alternative definition of a $3n \times 3n$ augmented matrix:

$$M = \begin{bmatrix} -I & T & 0 \\ T^T & 0 & T^T \\ 0 & T & 0 \end{bmatrix}. \tag{3.4.2}$$

The matrix M is also structured (as shown below) with respect to $Z_n \oplus Z_n \oplus Z_n$, where Z_n denotes the $n \times n$ lower shift triangular matrix (denoted earlier by Z—here we include the subscript n in order to explicitly indicate the size of Z).

It can be easily verified that $M - (Z_n \oplus Z_n \oplus Z_n)M(Z_n \oplus Z_n \oplus Z_n)^T$ is low rank since

$$M - (Z_n \oplus Z_n \oplus Z_n)M(Z_n \oplus Z_n \oplus Z_n)^T = \begin{bmatrix} -e_1 e_1^T & GB^T & 0 \\ BG^T & 0 & BG^T \\ 0 & GB^T & 0 \end{bmatrix},$$

where $e_1 = \begin{bmatrix} 1 & 0 & \ldots & 0 \end{bmatrix}^T$ is a basis vector of appropriate dimension. A generator matrix for M, with $3n$ rows and $(2r+1)$ columns, can be seen to be

$$\mathcal{G} = \frac{1}{\sqrt{2}} \begin{bmatrix} G & -G & e_1 \\ B & B & 0 \\ G & -G & 0 \end{bmatrix}, \quad \mathcal{J} = \begin{bmatrix} I_r & \\ & -I_{r+1} \end{bmatrix}. \tag{3.4.3}$$

That is,

$$M - \mathcal{F}M\mathcal{F}^T = \mathcal{G}\mathcal{J}\mathcal{G}^T,$$

where $\mathcal{F} = (Z_n \oplus Z_n \oplus Z_n)$ and $(\mathcal{G}, \mathcal{J})$ are as above.

The $n \times n$ leading submatrix of M is negative definite (in fact, equal to $-I$). Therefore, the first n steps of the generalized Schur algorithm applied to $(\mathcal{F}, \mathcal{G}, \mathcal{J})$ will be negative steps (cf. step 3 of Alg. 3.3.1). These first n steps lead to a generator matrix, denoted by $\mathcal{G}_n$ (with $2n$ rows), for the Schur complement of M with respect to its leading $n \times n$ leading submatrix, viz.,

$$M_n - (Z_n \oplus Z_n)M_n(Z_n \oplus Z_n)^T = \mathcal{G}_n \mathcal{J} \mathcal{G}_n^T, \tag{3.4.4}$$

where M_n is $2n \times 2n$ and equal to (what we denoted earlier in (3.2.2) by M)

$$M_n = \begin{bmatrix} T^T T & T^T \\ T & 0 \end{bmatrix}. \tag{3.4.5}$$

Clearly, M and its Schur complement M_n are related via the Schur complement relation:

$$M = \begin{bmatrix} I \\ -T^T \\ 0 \end{bmatrix} (-I) \begin{bmatrix} I & -T^T & 0 \end{bmatrix} + \begin{bmatrix} 0 & 0 & 0 \\ 0 & T^T T & T^T \\ 0 & T & 0 \end{bmatrix}.$$

Section 3.4. Fast QR Factorization of Shift-Structured Matrices

Therefore, $(\mathcal{G}_n, \mathcal{J})$ is a generator for M_n with respect to $(Z_n \oplus Z_n)$, as shown by (3.4.4).

The leading $n \times n$ submatrix of M_n is now positive definite (equal to $T^T T$). Therefore, the next n steps of the generalized Schur algorithm applied to $(Z_n \oplus Z_n, \mathcal{G}_n, \mathcal{J})$ will be positive steps (cf. step 2 of Alg. 3.3.1). These steps lead to a generator matrix, denoted by $\mathcal{G}_{2n}$ (with n rows), for the Schur complement of M with respect to its leading $2n \times 2n$ leading submatrix, viz.,

$$M_{2n} - Z_n M_{2n} Z_n^T = \mathcal{G}_{2n} \mathcal{J} \mathcal{G}_{2n}^T,$$

where M_{2n} is now $n \times n$ and equal to $-I$.

Again, M_n and M_{2n} are related via a (block) Schur complementation step, written as

$$\begin{bmatrix} T^T T & T^T \\ T & 0 \end{bmatrix} = M_n = \begin{bmatrix} R^T \\ Q \end{bmatrix} (I) \begin{bmatrix} R & Q^T \end{bmatrix} + \begin{bmatrix} 0 & 0 \\ 0 & -I \end{bmatrix}, \quad (3.4.6)$$

where we have denoted the first n columns of the triangular factor of M_n by

$$\begin{bmatrix} R^T \\ Q \end{bmatrix}$$

with R an $n \times n$ upper triangular matrix and Q an $n \times n$ matrix. The R and Q matrices are thus obtained by splitting the first n columns of the triangular factor of M_n into a leading lower triangular block followed by a full matrix Q.

By equating terms on both sides of (3.4.6) we can explicitly identify R and Q as follows:

$$T^T T = R^T R, \quad T = QR, \quad QQ^T - I = 0.$$

These relations show that Q and R define the QR factors of the matrix T.

In summary, the above discussion shows the following: given a shift-structured matrix T as in (3.4.1), its QR factorization can be computed efficiently by applying $2n$ steps of the generalized Schur algorithm to the matrices $(\mathcal{F}, \mathcal{G}, \mathcal{J})$ defined in (3.4.3). The factors Q and R can be obtained from the triangular factors $\{l_i\}$ for $i = n, n+1, \ldots, 2n-1$.

Alternatively, if a generator matrix is directly available for M_n in (3.4.5) (see the discussion of the Toeplitz case below), then we need only apply n Schur steps to this generator matrix and read the factors Q and R from the resulting n columns of the triangular factor.

In what follows we shall establish, for convenience of exposition, the numerical stability of a fast solver for $Tx = b$ that starts with a generator matrix for the embedding (3.4.5) rather than the embedding (3.4.2). It will become clear, however, that the same conclusions will hold if we instead start with a generator matrix for the embedding (3.4.2).

The augmentation (3.4.2) was used in [Say92], [SK95b], and it is based on embedding ideas originally pursued in [Chu89], [KC94] (see other augmentations below).

3.4.1 The Toeplitz Case

In some cases it is possible to find an explicit generator matrix for M_n. This saves the first n steps of the generalized Schur algorithm.

For example, consider the case when T is a Toeplitz matrix (which is a special case of (3.4.1)) whose first column is $[t_0, t_1, \ldots, t_{n-1}]^T$ and whose first row is $[t_0, t_{-1}, \ldots, t_{-n+1}]$. Define the vectors

$$\begin{bmatrix} c_0 \\ \vdots \\ c_{n-1} \end{bmatrix} \triangleq \frac{T e_1}{\|T e_1\|_2}, \quad \begin{bmatrix} s_0 \\ \vdots \\ s_{n-1} \end{bmatrix} \triangleq T^T \begin{bmatrix} c_0 \\ \vdots \\ c_{n-1} \end{bmatrix}.$$

It can be verified that a generator matrix for M_n in (3.4.5) is the following [Chu89]:

$$M_n - (Z_n \oplus Z_n)M_n(Z_n \oplus Z_n)^T = \mathcal{G}_n \mathcal{J} \mathcal{G}_n^T,$$

where $\mathcal{J}$ is 5×5,

$$\mathcal{J} = \text{diag}[1, 1, -1, -1, -1],$$

and $\mathcal{G}_n$ is $2n \times 5$,

$$\mathcal{G}_n = \begin{bmatrix} s_0 & 0 & 0 & 0 & 0 \\ s_1 & t_{-1} & s_1 & t_{n-1} & 0 \\ \vdots & \vdots & \vdots & \vdots & \vdots \\ s_{n-1} & t_{-n+1} & s_{n-1} & t_1 & 0 \\ c_0 & 1 & c_0 & 0 & 1 \\ c_1 & 0 & c_1 & 0 & 0 \\ \vdots & \vdots & \vdots & \vdots & \vdots \\ c_{n-1} & 0 & c_{n-1} & 0 & 0 \end{bmatrix}.$$

3.4.2 Other Augmentations

It is possible to compute the QR factors of a structured matrix T satisfying (3.4.1) by using augmented matrices other than (3.4.2). For example, consider the $3n \times 3n$ augmented matrix

$$M = \begin{bmatrix} -I & T & 0 \\ T^T & 0 & T^T \\ 0 & T & I \end{bmatrix}, \quad (3.4.7)$$

where an identity matrix replaces the zero matrix in the (3,3) block entry of the matrix in (3.4.2). A generator matrix for M, with $3n$ rows and $(2r+2)$ columns, is now

$$\mathcal{G} = \frac{1}{\sqrt{2}} \begin{bmatrix} G & 0 & -G & e_1 \\ B & 0 & B & 0 \\ G & e_1 & -G & 0 \end{bmatrix}, \quad \mathcal{J} = \begin{bmatrix} I_{r+1} & \\ & -I_{r+1} \end{bmatrix}.$$

If T is Toeplitz, as discussed above, then the rank of $\mathcal{G}$ can be shown to reduce to $2r = 4$ [Chu89]. (This is in contrast to the displacement rank 5 that follows from the earlier embedding (3.4.2).)

After $2n$ steps of the generalized Schur algorithm applied to the above $(\mathcal{G}, \mathcal{J})$, we obtain the following factorization (since now $M_{2n} = 0$),

$$M = \begin{bmatrix} I & 0 \\ -T^T & R^T \\ 0 & Q \end{bmatrix} \begin{bmatrix} -I & 0 \\ 0 & I \end{bmatrix} \begin{bmatrix} I & 0 \\ -T^T & R^T \\ 0 & Q \end{bmatrix}^T,$$

from which we can again read the QR factors of T from the triangular factors $\{l_i\}$ for $i = n, \ldots, 2n-1$. This augmentation was suggested in [Chu89, p. 37] and [KC94].

However, from a numerical point of view, computing the QR factors of a structured matrix T using the generalized Schur algorithm on the augmented matrices M in (3.4.2) or (3.4.7) is not stable. The problem is that the computed Q matrix is not necessarily orthogonal. This is also true for other procedures for fast QR factorization [BBH86], [Cyb83], [Cyb87], [Swe84].

In the next section we show how to overcome this difficulty and develop a fast and stable algorithm for solving linear systems of equations with shift-structured coefficient matrices T. For this purpose, we proceed with the embedding suggested earlier in (3.4.2) since it seems difficult to obtain a stable algorithm that is based solely on the alternative embedding (3.4.7). The reason is that the embedding (3.4.2) allows us to incorporate a correction procedure into the algorithm in order to ensure stability.

We first derive a stable algorithm for a well-conditioned coefficient matrix and then modify it for the case when the coefficient matrix is ill-conditioned. The interested reader may consult the summary of the final algorithm in Sec. 3.7.

3.5 WELL-CONDITIONED COEFFICIENT MATRICES

In this section we develop a stable algorithm for the case of well-conditioned matrices T. A definition of what we mean by a well-conditioned matrix is given later (see (3.5.9)). Essentially this refers to matrices whose condition number is less than the reciprocal of the square root of the machine precision. Modifications to handle the ill-conditioned case are introduced later.

We start with an $n \times n$ (possibly nonsymmetric) shift-structured matrix T with displacement rank r,

$$T - Z_n T Z_n^T = G B^T, \qquad (3.5.1)$$

and assume we have available a generator matrix $\mathcal{G}$ for the $2n \times 2n$ augmented matrix

$$M = \begin{bmatrix} T^T T & T^T \\ T & 0 \end{bmatrix}; \qquad (3.5.2)$$

that is,

$$M - \mathcal{F} M \mathcal{F}^T = \mathcal{G} \mathcal{J} \mathcal{G}^T, \qquad (3.5.3)$$

where $\mathcal{F} = (Z_n \oplus Z_n)$. Note that, for ease of exposition, we have modified our notation. While we earlier denoted the above matrix M by M_n and its generator by $\mathcal{G}_n$ and used $\mathcal{F}$ to denote $(Z_n \oplus Z_n \oplus Z_n)$, we are now dropping the subscript n from $(M_n, \mathcal{G}_n)$ and are using $\mathcal{F}$ to denote the $2n \times 2n$ matrix $(Z_n \oplus Z_n)$.

We discussed in Sec. 3.4.1 an example where we showed a particular generator matrix $\mathcal{G}$ for the above M when T is Toeplitz. (We repeat that the error analysis of later sections will still apply if we instead start with the $3n \times 3n$ embedding (3.4.2) and its generator matrix (3.4.3).)

We indicated earlier (at the end of Sec. 3.4) that by applying n steps of the generalized Schur algorithm to the matrix M in (3.5.2) we can obtain the QR factorization of T from the resulting n columns of the triangular factors of M. But this procedure is not numerically stable since the resulting Q is not guaranteed to be unitary. To fix this problem, we propose some modifications. The most relevant modification we introduce now is to run the Schur algorithm for $2n$ steps on M rather than just n steps. As suggested in Ch. 2, we also need to be careful in the application of the hyperbolic rotations. In particular, we assume that the hyperbolic rotations are applied using one of the methods suggested in that chapter such as mixed downdating, the OD method, or the H procedure.

The matrix T is required only to be invertible. In this case, the leading submatrix of M in (3.5.2) is positive definite, and therefore the first n steps of the generalized Schur algorithm will be positive steps. Hence, the hyperbolic rotations needed for the first n steps will perform transformations of the form (3.3.4), where generators are transformed into proper form with respect to their first column. Likewise, the Schur complement of M with respect to its leading submatrix $T^T T$ is equal to $-I$, which is negative definite. This means that the last n steps of the generalized Schur algorithm will be negative steps. Hence, the hyperbolic rotations needed for the last n steps will perform transformations of the form (3.3.7), where generators are transformed into proper form with respect to their last column.

During a positive step (a similar discussion holds for a negative step), a generator matrix G_i will be reduced to proper form by implementing the hyperbolic transformation Θ_i as a sequence of orthogonal transformations followed by a 2×2 hyperbolic rotation (see also [SD97b]). The 2×2 rotation is implemented along the lines of [CS96] or Ch. 2, e.g., via mixed downdating [BBDH87], or the OD method, or the H procedure. Details are given below.

3.5.1 Implementation of the Hyperbolic Rotation

When the generalized Schur algorithm is applied to $(\mathcal{G}, \mathcal{F})$ in (3.5.3), we proceed through a sequence of generator matrices $(\mathcal{G}, \mathcal{G}_1, \mathcal{G}_2, \ldots)$ of decreasing number of rows $(2n, 2n-1, 2n-2, \ldots)$. Let g_i denote the top row of the generator matrix $\mathcal{G}_i$ at step i. In a positive step, it needs to be reduced to the form (3.3.4) via an $(I_p \oplus -I_q)$-unitary rotation Θ_i. We propose to perform this transformation as follows:

1. Apply a *unitary* (orthogonal) rotation (e.g., Householder—see App. B) to the first p columns of $\mathcal{G}_i$ so as to reduce the top row of these p columns into proper form,

$$g_i = \begin{bmatrix} x & x & x & x & x & x \end{bmatrix} \xrightarrow{unitary\ \Theta_{i,1}} \begin{bmatrix} x & 0 & 0 & x & x & x \end{bmatrix} = g_{i,1},$$

with a nonzero entry in the first column. Let

$$\mathcal{G}_{i,1} = \mathcal{G}_i \begin{bmatrix} \Theta_{i,1} & 0 \\ 0 & I \end{bmatrix} \qquad (3.5.4)$$

denote the modified generator matrix. Its last q columns coincide with those of $\mathcal{G}_i$.

2. Apply another *unitary* (orthogonal) rotation (e.g., Householder) to the last q columns of $\mathcal{G}_{i,1}$ so as to reduce the top row of these last q columns into proper form with respect to their last column,

$$g_{i,1} = \begin{bmatrix} x & 0 & 0 & x & x & x \end{bmatrix} \xrightarrow{unitary\ \Theta_{i,2}} \begin{bmatrix} x & 0 & 0 & 0 & 0 & x \end{bmatrix} = g_{i,2},$$

with a nonzero entry in the last column. Let

$$\mathcal{G}_{i,2} = \mathcal{G}_{i,1} \begin{bmatrix} I & 0 \\ 0 & \Theta_{i,2} \end{bmatrix} \qquad (3.5.5)$$

denote the modified generator matrix. Its first p columns coincide with those of $\mathcal{G}_{i,1}$.

3. Employ an elementary rotation Θ_i acting on the first and last columns (in mixed-downdating form or according to the OD or the H methods of Ch. 2) in order to annihilate the nonzero entry in the last column,

$$g_{i,2} = \begin{bmatrix} x & 0 & 0 & 0 & x \end{bmatrix} \xrightarrow{hyperbolic\ \Theta_{i,3}} \begin{bmatrix} x & 0 & 0 & 0 & 0 & 0 \end{bmatrix}.$$

Section 3.5. Well-Conditioned Coefficient Matrices

4. The combined effect of the above steps is to reduce g_i to the proper form (3.3.4) and, hence,

$$\bar{\mathcal{G}}_i = \mathcal{G}_i \begin{bmatrix} \Theta_{i,1} & 0 \\ 0 & I \end{bmatrix} \begin{bmatrix} I & 0 \\ 0 & \Theta_{i,2} \end{bmatrix} \Theta_{i,3}. \tag{3.5.6}$$

Expression (3.5.6) shows that, in infinite precision, the generator matrices $\mathcal{G}_i$ and $\bar{\mathcal{G}}_i$ must satisfy the fundamental requirement

$$\mathcal{G}_i \mathcal{J} \mathcal{G}_i^T = \bar{\mathcal{G}}_i \mathcal{J} \bar{\mathcal{G}}_i^T. \tag{3.5.7}$$

Obviously, this condition cannot be guaranteed in finite precision. But, as discussed in Ch. 2 and in [CS96], with the above implementation of the transformation (3.5.6) (as a sequence of two orthogonal transformations and a hyperbolic rotation in mixed, OD, or H forms), equality (3.5.7) can be guaranteed to within a "small" error, viz.,

$$\|\widehat{\bar{\mathcal{G}}}_i \mathcal{J} \widehat{\bar{\mathcal{G}}}_i^T - \mathcal{G}_i \mathcal{J} \mathcal{G}_i^T\|_2 \leq O_n(\varepsilon) \left(\|\widehat{\bar{\mathcal{G}}}_i\|_2^2 + \|\mathcal{G}_i\|_2^2 \right). \tag{3.5.8}$$

A similar analysis holds for a negative step, where the rotation Θ_i is again implemented as a sequence of two unitary rotations and one elementary hyperbolic rotation in order to guarantee the transformation (3.3.7). We forgo the details here.

We finally remark that in the algorithm, the incoming generator matrix $\mathcal{G}_i$ will in fact be the computed version, which we denote by $\widehat{\mathcal{G}}_i$. This explains why in the error analysis of the next section we replace $\mathcal{G}_i$ by $\widehat{\mathcal{G}}_i$ in the error bound (3.5.8).

Note also that we are implicitly assuming that the required hyperbolic rotation $\Theta_{i,3}$ exists. While that can be guaranteed in infinite precision, it is possible that in finite precision we can experience breakdowns.

3.5.2 Avoiding Breakdown

To avoid breakdown we need to guarantee that during the first n steps of the algorithm, the $\mathcal{J}$-unitary rotations Θ_i are well defined. This requires that the leading submatrices of the first n successive Schur complements remain positive definite, a condition that can be guaranteed by requiring T to be sufficiently well-conditioned [CS98], viz., by requiring that

$$\sigma_{\min}^2(T) > 2 O_n(\varepsilon) \sum_{j=0}^{n-1} \|\widehat{\mathcal{G}}_j\|_2^2. \tag{3.5.9}$$

We refer to a matrix T that satisfies the above requirement as being well conditioned. (The scalar multiple 2 is made explicit for convenience in later discussion.)

Now, after the first n steps of the generalized Schur algorithm applied to $(\mathcal{F}, \mathcal{G})$ in (3.5.3), we let

$$\begin{bmatrix} \widehat{R}^T \\ \widehat{Q} \end{bmatrix}$$

denote the computed factors that correspond to expression (3.4.6). We further define the matrix S_n that solves the displacement equation

$$S_n - Z_n S_n Z_n^T = \widehat{\mathcal{G}}_n \mathcal{J} \widehat{\mathcal{G}}_n^T. \tag{3.5.10}$$

Note that S_n is an $n \times n$ matrix, which in infinite precision would have been equal to the Schur complement—I (cf. (3.4.6)). We can now define

$$\widehat{M} = \begin{bmatrix} \widehat{R}^T \\ \widehat{Q} \end{bmatrix} \begin{bmatrix} \widehat{R} & \widehat{Q}^T \end{bmatrix} + \begin{bmatrix} 0 & 0 \\ 0 & S_n \end{bmatrix}. \tag{3.5.11}$$

We showed in [CS98] that the following error bound holds.

Theorem 3.5.1 (Error Bound). *The first n steps of the generalized Schur algorithm applied to $(\mathcal{F}, \mathcal{G})$ in (3.5.3), for a matrix T satisfying (3.5.9), and with the rotations Θ_i implemented as discussed in Sec. 3.5.1, guarantees the following error bound on the matrix $(M - \widehat{M})$ (with $\widehat{M}$ defined in (3.5.11)):*

$$\|M - \widehat{M}\|_2 \leq O_n(\varepsilon) \sum_{j=0}^{n-1} \|\widehat{\mathcal{G}}_j\|_2^2. \qquad (3.5.12)$$

$\diamond$

The natural question then is, How big can the norm of the generator matrices be? The following remark is motivated by an observation in [SD97b] that for matrices of the form $T^T T$, with T Toeplitz, there is no appreciable generator growth. Indeed, we showed in [CS98] that a first-order bound for the sum of the norms of the generators in (3.5.12) is given by

$$\sum_{i=0}^{n-1} \|\widehat{\mathcal{G}}_i\|_2^2 \leq 16n(1+n^2)(1+\|T\|_2+\|T^2\|_2) + O(\varepsilon^2). \qquad (3.5.13)$$

3.5.3 Error Analysis of the Last Steps

We now study the last n steps. Assume T satisfies the following normalization:

$$\|T\|_2 \leq \frac{1}{5}, \qquad (3.5.14)$$

which can always be guaranteed by proper scaling at the begining of the algorithm. We showed in [CS98] that under the well-conditioned assumption (3.5.9), the matrix S_n is guaranteed to be negative definite and well-conditioned. In particular, its condition number is at most 15.

Hence, we can proceed with the last n steps of the generalized Schur algorithm applied to $\widehat{\mathcal{G}}_n$, since $\widehat{\mathcal{G}}_n$ is a generator matrix for S_n:

$$S_n - Z_n S_n Z_n^T = \widehat{\mathcal{G}}_n \mathcal{J} \widehat{\mathcal{G}}_n^T.$$

All steps will now be negative steps. Hence, the discussion in Sec. 3.5.1 on the implementation of the hyperbolic rotations applies. The only difference will be that we make the generator proper with respect to its last column. In other words, the third step of that implementation should be modified as follows:

$$g_{i,2} = \begin{bmatrix} x & 0 & 0 & 0 & x \end{bmatrix} \xrightarrow{hyperbolic \; \Theta_{i,3}} \begin{bmatrix} 0 & 0 & 0 & 0 & x \end{bmatrix}. \qquad (3.5.15)$$

Let $-\Delta\Delta^T$ be the computed triangular factorization of S_n. It can be shown that

$$\|S_n - (-\Delta\Delta^T)\|_2 \leq O_n(\varepsilon) \sum_{i=n}^{2n-1} \|\widehat{\mathcal{G}}_i\|_2^2, \qquad (3.5.16)$$

where the norm of the generators $\{\widehat{\mathcal{G}}_i\}$ appearing in the above error expression can be shown to be bounded [CS98].

3.5.4 Summary

We have shown so far that if we apply $2n$ steps of the generalized Schur algorithm to the matrices $(\mathcal{F}, \mathcal{G})$ in (3.5.3), with proper implementation of the $\mathcal{J}$-unitary rotations (as explained in Sec. 3.5.1), then the error in the computed factorization of M is bounded as follows:

$$\left\| M - \begin{bmatrix} \widehat{R}^T & 0 \\ \widehat{Q} & \Delta \end{bmatrix} \begin{bmatrix} \widehat{R} & \widehat{Q}^T \\ 0 & -\Delta^T \end{bmatrix} \right\|_2 \leq O_n(\varepsilon) \sum_{i=0}^{2n-1} \|\widehat{\mathcal{G}}_i\|_2^2. \qquad (3.5.17)$$

We have also established (at least in infinite precision) that the norm of the generators is bounded. Therefore, the computed factorization is (at least asymptotically) backward stable with respect to M.

3.5.5 Solving the Linear System of Equations

We now return to the problem of solving the linear system of equations $Tx = b$, where T is a well-conditioned nonsymmetric shift-structured matrix (e.g., Toeplitz, quasi Toeplitz, product of two Toeplitz matrices).

We showed in [CS98] that $\Delta^{-1}\widehat{Q}$ is numerically orthogonal, viz.,

$$\|(\Delta^{-1}\widehat{Q})(\Delta^{-1}\widehat{Q})^T - I\|_2 \leq O_n(\varepsilon) \sum_{i=0}^{2n-1} \|\widehat{\mathcal{G}}_i\|^2,$$

and that

$$\|T - \widehat{Q}\widehat{R}\|_2 \leq O_n(\varepsilon) \sum_{i=0}^{2n-1} \|\widehat{\mathcal{G}}_i\|_2^2.$$

This shows that we can compute x by solving the nearby linear system

$$\Delta\Delta^{-1}\widehat{Q}\widehat{R}x = b$$

in $O(n^2)$ flops by exploiting the fact that $\Delta^{-1}\widehat{Q}$ is numerically orthogonal and Δ is triangular as follows:

$$\widehat{x} = \widehat{R}^{-1}(\widehat{Q}^T\Delta^{-T})\Delta^{-1}b. \qquad (3.5.18)$$

The fact that this scheme for computing x is backward stable will be established in the next section (see the remark after expression (3.6.6)).

3.6 ILL-CONDITIONED COEFFICIENT MATRICES

We now consider modifications to the algorithm when the inequality (3.5.9) is not satisfied by T. This essentially means that the condition number of T is larger than the square root of the reciprocal of the machine precision. We will refer to such matrices T as being ill-conditioned.

There are now several potential numerical problems, all of which have to be eliminated. First, the $(1,1)$ block of M can fail to factorize as it is not sufficiently positive definite. Second, even if the first n steps of the Schur algorithm are completed successfully, the Schur complement S_n of the $(2,2)$ block may no longer be negative definite, making the algorithm unstable. Third, the matrix Δ may no longer be well-conditioned, in which case it is not clear how one can solve the linear system $Tx = b$ in a stable manner. We now show how these problems can be resolved.

To resolve the first two problems we add small multiples of the identity matrix to the $(1,1)$ and $(2,2)$ blocks of M, separately:

$$M = \begin{bmatrix} T^T T + \alpha I & T \\ T^T & -\beta I \end{bmatrix}, \qquad (3.6.1)$$

where α and β are positive numbers that will be specified later. (We continue to use M for the new matrix in (3.6.1) for convenience of notation.) This leads to an increase in the displacement rank of M. For Toeplitz matrices the rank increases only by one and the new generators are given as follows:

$$M - (Z_n \oplus Z_n) M (Z_n \oplus Z_n)^T = \mathcal{G} \mathcal{J} \mathcal{G}^T, \qquad (3.6.2)$$

where $\mathcal{J}$ is 6×6,

$$\mathcal{J} = \text{diag}[1, 1, 1, -1, -1, -1], \qquad (3.6.3)$$

and $\mathcal{G}$ is $2n \times 6$,

$$\mathcal{G} = \begin{bmatrix} \sqrt{\alpha} & s_0 & 0 & 0 & 0 & 0 \\ 0 & s_1 & t_{-1} & s_1 & t_{n-1} & 0 \\ \vdots & \vdots & \vdots & \vdots & \vdots & \vdots \\ 0 & s_{n-1} & t_{-n+1} & s_{n-1} & t_1 & 0 \\ 0 & c_0 & 1 & c_0 & 0 & \sqrt{1+\beta} \\ 0 & c_1 & 0 & c_1 & 0 & 0 \\ \vdots & \vdots & \vdots & \vdots & \vdots & \vdots \\ 0 & c_{n-1} & 0 & c_{n-1} & 0 & 0 \end{bmatrix}. \qquad (3.6.4)$$

Had we started instead with the embedding (3.4.2) for more general shift-structured matrices, we would then modify the generators as explained later in the remark.

For suitably chosen α and β (see the statement of the algorithm in Sec. 3.7), it can be shown that in this case [CS98]

$$\left\| M - \begin{bmatrix} \widehat{R}^T & 0 \\ \widehat{Q} & \Delta \end{bmatrix} \begin{bmatrix} \widehat{R} & \widehat{Q}^T \\ 0 & -\Delta^T \end{bmatrix} \right\|_2 \leq \alpha + \beta + O_n(\varepsilon) \sum_{i=0}^{2n-1} \|\widehat{\mathcal{G}}_i\|_2^2,$$

where the norm of the generators is again bounded. Hence, we also obtain a backward-stable factorization of M.

Since Δ is no longer provably well-conditioned, we cannot argue that $\Delta^{-1}\widehat{Q}$ is numerically orthogonal. For this reason, we now discuss how to solve the linear system of equations $Tx = b$ in the ill-conditioned case.

3.6.1 Solving the Linear System of Equations

Note that if x solves $Tx = b$, then it also satisfies

$$\begin{bmatrix} T^T T & T^T \\ T & 0 \end{bmatrix} \begin{bmatrix} x \\ -b \end{bmatrix} = \begin{bmatrix} 0 \\ b \end{bmatrix}.$$

Using the above backward-stable factorization for M we can solve the above linear system of equations to get

$$\left(\begin{bmatrix} T^T T & T^T \\ T & 0 \end{bmatrix} + \widetilde{M} \right) \begin{bmatrix} \widehat{y} \\ \widehat{z} \end{bmatrix} = \begin{bmatrix} 0 \\ b \end{bmatrix}, \qquad (3.6.5)$$

Section 3.7. Summary of the Algorithm 99

where the error matrix $\tilde{M}$ satisfies

$$\|\tilde{M}\|_2 \leq \alpha + \beta + O_n(\varepsilon) \sum_{i=0}^{2n-1} \|\widehat{\mathcal{G}}_i\|_2^2 + O_n(\varepsilon) \left\| \begin{bmatrix} \widehat{R}^T & 0 \\ \widehat{Q} & \Delta \end{bmatrix} \right\|_2^2.$$

Note that $\widehat{y}$ is computed by the expression

$$R^{-1}\widehat{Q}^T \Delta^{-T} \Delta^{-1} b, \qquad (3.6.6)$$

which is identical to the formula (3.5.18) we obtained earlier by assuming $\Delta^{-1}\widehat{Q}$ is numerically orthogonal! Therefore, the subsequent error bound holds equally well for the well-conditioned case. It can be shown that the computed solution $\widehat{y}$ satisfies

$$(T + \tilde{T})\widehat{y} = b,$$

where the norm of the error matrix is bounded by

$$\|\tilde{T}\|_2 \leq 2(\alpha + \beta) + O_n(\varepsilon)[1 + \|T\|_2] + O(\varepsilon^2) \leq O_n(\varepsilon)\|T\|_2 + O(\varepsilon^2). \qquad (3.6.7)$$

3.6.2 Conditions on the Coefficient Matrix

For ease of reference, we list here the conditions imposed on the coefficient matrix T in order to guarantee a fast backward-stable solver of $Tx = b$:

1. $\|T\|_2$ is suitably normalized to guarantee $\|T\|_2 \approx 1$ (cf. (3.5.14)).

2. The condition number of T should essentially be less than the reciprocal of the machine precision.

Remark. Had we started instead with the embedding (3.4.2), we first perform n steps of the generalized Schur algorithm to get a generator matrix $\widehat{\mathcal{G}}_n$ for the computed version of the $2n \times 2n$ embedding (3.4.5). We then add two columns to $\widehat{\mathcal{G}}_n$ as follows:

$$\begin{bmatrix} \sqrt{\alpha} & & 0 \\ 0 & & 0 \\ 0 & & \sqrt{\beta} \\ \vdots & \widehat{\mathcal{G}}_{n+1} & \vdots \\ 0 & & 0 \\ 0 & & 0 \end{bmatrix},$$

where the entry $\sqrt{\beta}$ occurs in the nth row of the last column. The new first column has a positive signature and the new last column has a negative signature.

3.7 SUMMARY OF THE ALGORITHM

For convenience we summarize the algorithm here for the case of nonsymmetric Toeplitz systems. We hasten to add, however, that the algorithm also applies to more general shift-structured matrices T (other than Toeplitz, such as quasi Toeplitz or with higher displacement ranks, as demonstrated by the analysis in the earlier sections). The only difference will be in the initial generator matrix $\mathcal{G}$ and signature matrix $\mathcal{J}$ for M in (3.6.1) and (3.6.2). The algorithm will also be essentially the same, apart from an additional n Schur steps, if we instead employ the embedding (3.4.2).

- Input: A nonsymmetric Toeplitz matrix $T \in \mathbb{R}^{n \times n}$ and column vector $b \in \mathbb{R}^{n \times 1}$. The entries of the first column of T are denoted by $[t_0, t_1, \ldots, t_{n-1}]^T$, while the entries of the first row of T are denoted by $[t_0, t_{-1}, \ldots, t_{-n+1}]$.

- Output: A backward-stable solution of $Tx = b$.

- Algorithm:

- Normalize T and b. Since the Frobenius norm of T is less than

$$\gamma = \sqrt{n \sum_{i=-n+1}^{n-1} t_i^2},$$

we can normalize T by setting t_i to be $t_i/(5\gamma)$ for all i. Similarly, divide the entries of b by 5γ. In what follows, T and b will refer to these normalized quantities.

- Define the vectors

$$\begin{bmatrix} c_0 \\ \vdots \\ c_{n-1} \end{bmatrix} = \frac{Te_1}{\|Te_1\|_2}, \quad \begin{bmatrix} s_0 \\ \vdots \\ s_{n-1} \end{bmatrix} = T^T \begin{bmatrix} c_0 \\ \vdots \\ c_{n-1} \end{bmatrix}.$$

- Construct the 6×6 signature matrix $\mathcal{J} = \text{diag}[1, 1, 1, -1, -1, -1]$, and the $2n \times 6$ generator matrix $\mathcal{G}$,

$$\mathcal{G} = \begin{bmatrix} \sqrt{\alpha} & s_0 & 0 & 0 & 0 & 0 \\ 0 & s_1 & t_{-1} & s_1 & t_{n-1} & 0 \\ \vdots & \vdots & \vdots & \vdots & \vdots & \vdots \\ 0 & s_{n-1} & t_{-n+1} & s_{n-1} & t_1 & 0 \\ 0 & c_0 & 1 & c_0 & 0 & \sqrt{1+\beta} \\ 0 & c_1 & 0 & c_1 & 0 & 0 \\ \vdots & \vdots & \vdots & \vdots & \vdots & \vdots \\ 0 & c_{n-1} & 0 & c_{n-1} & 0 & 0 \end{bmatrix},$$

where the small positive numbers α and β are chosen as follows (by experimental tuning):

$$\alpha = n^{1/2} \varepsilon \|\mathcal{G}\|_2^2, \quad \beta = 4(2n)^{1/4} \varepsilon.$$

(If T is well-conditioned (say, $\kappa(T) < 1/\sqrt{\varepsilon}$), then we can set $\beta = 0 = \alpha$ and delete the first columns of $\mathcal{G}$ and $\mathcal{J}$, which then become $2n \times 5$ and 5×5, respectively.)

- Apply n steps of the generalized Schur algorithm starting with $\mathcal{G}_0 = \mathcal{G}$ and $\mathcal{F} = (Z_n \oplus Z_n)$ and ending with $\mathcal{G}_n$ and $\mathcal{F} = Z_n$. These are positive steps according to the description of Alg. 3.3.1 (step 2), where the successive generators are reduced to proper form relative to their first column. Note that this must be performed with care for numerical stability as explained in Sec. 3.5.1.

- Apply n more steps of the generalized Schur algorithm starting with $\mathcal{G}_n$. These are negative steps according to the description of Alg. 3.3.1 (step 3), where the successive generators are reduced to proper form relative to their last column. This also has to be performed with care as explained prior to (3.5.15).

Section 3.7. Summary of the Algorithm

Table 3.1. Complexity analysis of the fast algorithm.

During each iteration of the algorithm	Count in flops
Compute two Householder transformations	$3r$
Apply the Householder transformations	$4 \cdot i \cdot r$
Compute the hyperbolic transformation	7
Apply the hyperbolic transformation using OD	$6 \cdot i$
Shift columns	i
Total for $i = 2n - 1$ down to 0	$(14 + 8r)n^2 + 10nr + 21n$
Cost of 3 back-substitution steps	$3n^2$
Cost of matrix-vector multiplication	$2n^2$
Start-up costs	$n(24 \log n + r + 52)$
Total cost of the algorithm	$(19 + 8r)n^2$ $+ n(24 \log n + 11r + 73)$

- Each of the above $2n$ steps provides a column of the triangular factorization of the matrix M in (3.6.1), as described in Alg. 3.3.1 (steps 2 and 3). The triangular factor of M is then partitioned to yield the matrices $\{\widehat{R}, \widehat{Q}, \Delta\}$,

$$\begin{bmatrix} \widehat{R}^T & 0 \\ \widehat{Q} & \Delta \end{bmatrix},$$

where $\widehat{R}$ is upper triangular and Δ is lower triangular.

- The solution $\widehat{x}$ is obtained by evaluating the quantity

$$R^{-1}\widehat{Q}^T \Delta^{-T} \Delta^{-1} b$$

via a sequence of back substitutions and matrix-vector multiplications. The computed solution is backward stable. It satisfies $(T + \tilde{T})\widehat{x} = b$, where the norm of the error matrix is bounded by (3.6.7).

Operation Count

The major computational cost is due to the application of the successive steps of the generalized Schur algorithm. The overhead operations that are required for the normalization of T and for the determination of the generator matrix $\mathcal{G}$ amount at most to $O(n \log n)$ flops. Table 3.1 shows the number of flops needed at each step of the algorithm. (i denotes the iteration number and runs from $i = 2n$ down to $i = 1$.) The operation count given in the table assumes that, for each iteration, two Householder transformations are used to implement the reduction to the proper form of Sec. 3.5.1, combined with an elementary hyperbolic rotation in OD form.

The specific costs of the algorithm for the special case of Toeplitz matrices are the following:

1. For a well-conditioned Toeplitz matrix, the cost is $O(59n^2 + n(24 \log n + 128))$ operations.

2. For an ill-conditioned Toeplitz matrix, the cost is $O(67n^2 + n(24\log n + 139))$ operations.

Acknowledgments

The authors wish to thank Professor Thomas Kailath for comments and feedback on an earlier draft of this chapter. They also gratefully acknowledge the support of the National Science Foundation; the work of A. H. Sayed was partially supported by awards MIP-9796147 and CCR-9732376, and the work of S. Chandrasekaran was partially supported by award CCR-9734290.

Chapter 4

STABILITY OF FAST ALGORITHMS FOR STRUCTURED LINEAR SYSTEMS

Richard P. Brent

4.1 INTRODUCTION

This chapter surveys the numerical stability of some fast algorithms for solving systems of linear equations and linear least-squares problems with a low displacement rank structure. For example, the matrices involved may be Toeplitz or Hankel. We consider algorithms that incorporate pivoting without destroying the structure (cf. Sec. 1.13) and describe some recent results on the stability of these algorithms. We also compare these results with the corresponding stability results for the well-known algorithms of Schur–Bareiss and Levinson, and for algorithms based on the seminormal equations.

As is well known, the standard direct method for solving dense $n \times n$ systems of linear equations is Gaussian elimination with partial pivoting. The usual implementation requires arithmetic operations of order n^3.

In practice, linear systems often arise from some physical system and have a structure that is a consequence of the physical system. For example, time-invariant physical systems often give rise to *Toeplitz* systems of linear equations (Sec. 4.3.2). An $n \times n$ Toeplitz matrix is a dense matrix because it generally has n^2 nonzero elements. However, it is determined by only $O(n)$ parameters (in fact, by the $2n - 1$ entries in its first row and column). Similar examples are the Hankel, Cauchy, Toeplitz-plus-Hankel, and Vandermonde matrices (see, e.g., Sec. 1.3 of this book, as well as [GV96] and [GKO95]).

When solving such a structured linear system it is possible to ignore the structure, and this may have advantages if standard software is available and n is not too large. However, if n is large or if many systems have to be solved, perhaps with real-time constraints (e.g., in radar and sonar applications), then it is desirable to take advantage of the structure. The primary advantage to be gained is that the time to solve a linear system is reduced by a factor of order n to $O(n^2)$. Storage requirements may also be reduced by a factor of order n, to $O(n)$.

Most works concerned with algorithms for structured linear systems concentrate on the speed (usually measured in terms of the number of arithmetic operations required) and ignore questions of numerical accuracy. However, it is dangerous to use fast algorithms without considering their numerical properties. There is no point in obtaining an answer quickly if it is much less accurate than is justified by the data.

In this chapter we consider both the speed and the numerical properties of fast algorithms. Because there are many classes of structured matrices, and an ever-increasing number of fast algorithms, we cannot attempt to be comprehensive. Our aim is to introduce the reader to the subject, illustrate some of the main ideas, and provide pointers to the literature.

In this chapter, a "fast" algorithm will generally be one that requires $O(n^2)$ arithmetic operations, whereas a "slow" algorithm will be one that requires $O(n^3)$ arithmetic operations. Thus a fast algorithm should (in general) be faster than a slow algorithm if n is sufficiently large.

The subject of numerical stability and instability of fast algorithms is confused for several reasons:

1. Structured matrices can be very ill-conditioned [Tyr94b]. For example, the Hilbert matrix [Hil94], defined by $a_{ij} = 1/(i+j-1)$, is often used as an example of a very ill-conditioned matrix [FM67]. The Hilbert matrix is a Hankel matrix. Reversing the order of the rows gives a Toeplitz matrix. Even a stable numerical method cannot be expected to give an accurate solution when it is applied to a very ill-conditioned problem. Thus, when testing fast algorithms we must take the condition of the problem into account and not expect more than is reasonable.

2. The solution may be less sensitive to structured perturbations (i.e., perturbations that are physically plausible because they preserve the structure) than to general (unstructured) perturbations. The effect of rounding errors in methods that ignore the structure is generally equivalent to the introduction of unstructured perturbations. Ideally we should use a method that introduces only structured perturbations, but this property often does not hold or is difficult to prove, even for methods that take advantage of the structure to reduce the number of arithmetic operations.

3. The error bounds that can be proved are usually much weaker than those observed on "real" or "random" examples. Thus, methods that are observed to work well in practice cannot always be guaranteed, and it is hard to know if it is just the analysis that is weak or if the method fails in some rare cases. (A classical example of the latter phenomenon is given in Sec. 4.2.1.)

4. An algorithm may perform well on special classes of structured matrices, e.g., positive-definite matrices or Toeplitz matrices with positive reflection coefficients, but perform poorly or break down on broader classes of structured matrices.

4.1.1 Outline

Different authors have given different (and sometimes inconsistent) definitions of *stability* and *weak stability*. We follow Bunch [Bun85], [Bun87]. For completeness, our definitions are given in Sec. 4.2.

The concept of *displacement rank*, defined in Sec. 4.3 and also in Ch. 1 of this book, may be used to unify the discussion of many algorithms for structured matrices [KC94], [KKM79a], [KS95a]. It is well known that systems of n linear equations with a low displacement rank (e.g., Toeplitz or Hankel matrices) can be solved in $O(n^2)$ arithmetic operations. Asymptotically faster algorithms with time bound $O(n \log^2 n)$ exist [BGY80] but are not considered here because their numerical properties are generally poor and the constant factors hidden in the "O" notation are large [AG88].

For positive-definite Toeplitz matrices, the first $O(n^2)$ algorithms were introduced by Kolmogorov [Kol41], Wiener [Wie49], and Levinson [Lev47]. These algorithms are related to recursions of Szegő [Sze39] for polynomials orthogonal on the unit circle. Another class of $O(n^2)$ algorithms, e.g., the Bareiss algorithm [Bar69], is related to Schur's algorithm for finding the continued fraction representation of a holomorphic function in the unit disk [Sch17]. This class can be generalized to cover unsymmetric matrices and other low displacement rank matrices [KS95a]. In Sections 4.4–4.6 we consider the numerical stability of some of these algorithms. The GKO–Cauchy and GKO–Toeplitz algorithms are discussed in Sec. 4.4. The Schur–Bareiss algorithm for positive-definite matrices is considered in Sec. 4.5.1, and generalized Schur algorithms are mentioned in Sec. 4.5.2. In Sec. 4.6 we consider fast orthogonal factorization algorithms and the fast solution of structured least-squares problems. An embedding approach which leads to a stable algorithm for structured linear systems is mentioned in Sec. 4.6.3.

Algorithms for Vandermonde and many other classes of structured matrices are not considered here—we refer to Ch. 1. Also, we have omitted any discussion of fast "look-ahead" algorithms [CH92a], [CH92b], [FZ93a], [FZ93b], [Gut93], [GH93a], [GH93b], [HG93], [Swe93] because, although such algorithms often succeed in practice, in the worst case they require $O(n^3)$ operations.

Much work has been done on iterative methods for Toeplitz and related systems. Numerical stability is not a major problem with iterative methods, but the speed of convergence depends on a good choice of preconditioner. Iterative methods are considered in Chs. 5 and 7, so we do not consider them in detail here. However, it is worth noting that iterative refinement [JW77], [Wil65] can be used to improve the accuracy of solutions obtained by direct methods (see, e.g., Sec. 2.12.2).

4.1.2 Notation

In the following, R denotes an upper triangular or structured matrix, T is a Toeplitz or Toeplitz-like matrix, P is a permutation matrix, L is lower triangular, U is upper triangular, and Q is orthogonal. If A is a matrix with elements a_{jk}, then $|A|$ denotes the matrix with elements $|a_{jk}|$. In error bounds, ε is the machine precision [GV96], and $O_n(\varepsilon)$ means $O(\varepsilon f(n))$, where $f(n)$ is a polynomial in n. We usually do not try to specify the polynomial $f(n)$ precisely because it depends on the norm used to measure the error and on many unimportant details of the implementation. Also, the $\hat{}$ notation denotes computed quantities.

4.2 STABILITY AND WEAK STABILITY

In this section we give definitions of stability and weak stability of algorithms for solving linear systems. Consider algorithms for solving a nonsingular, $n \times n$ linear system $Ax = b$. To avoid trivial exceptional cases we always assume that $b \neq 0$.

The *condition number* $\kappa = \kappa(A)$ is defined to be the ratio σ_1/σ_n of the largest and smallest singular values of the matrix A (see [GV96] for a discussion of condition number and singular values). If κ is close to 1 we say that A is *well-conditioned*, and if κ is large we say that A is *ill-conditioned*. The meaning of "large" is a little flexible, but $\kappa > 1/\varepsilon$ is certainly large and, depending on the circumstances, we may regard $\kappa > 1/\sqrt{\varepsilon}$ as large.

There are many definitions of numerical stability in the literature, for example, [Bjo87], [Bjo91], [BBHS95], [BS91], [Bun85], [Cyb80], [GV96], [JW77], [MW80], [Pai73], [Ste73]. Definitions 4.2.1 and 4.2.2 are taken from Bunch [Bun87].

Definition 4.2.1 (Stable Algorithm). *An algorithm for solving linear equations is stable for a class of matrices $\mathcal{A}$ if for each A in $\mathcal{A}$ and for each b the computed solution $\widehat{x}$ to $Ax = b$ satisfies $\tilde{A}\widehat{x} = \tilde{b}$, where $\tilde{A}$ is close to A and $\tilde{b}$ is close to b.*
◇

Definition 4.2.1 says that, for stability, the *computed* solution has to be the *exact* solution of a problem that is close to the original problem. This is the classical *backward stability* of Wilkinson [Wil61], [Wil63], [Wil65]. We interpret "close" to mean close in the relative sense in some norm, i.e.,

$$\|\tilde{A} - A\|/\|A\| = O_n(\varepsilon), \quad \|\tilde{b} - b\|/\|b\| = O_n(\varepsilon).$$

It is well known that the perturbation in A can be absorbed into the perturbation in b, since

$$A\widehat{x} = \tilde{b} + (A - \tilde{A})\widehat{x}.$$

Alternatively, the perturbation in b can be absorbed into the perturbation in A, since

$$(\tilde{A} - \|\widehat{x}\|_2^{-2}(\tilde{b} - b)\widehat{x}^T)\widehat{x} = b.$$

Thus, it is not necessary to permit perturbations of both A and b in Definition 4.2.1.

Note that the matrix $\tilde{A}$ is not required to be in the class $\mathcal{A}$. For example, $\mathcal{A}$ might be the class of nonsingular Toeplitz matrices, but $\tilde{A}$ is not required to be a Toeplitz matrix. If we require $\tilde{A} \in \mathcal{A}$ we get what Bunch [Bun87] calls *strong stability*. For a discussion of the difference between stability and strong stability for Toeplitz algorithms, see [GK93], [GKX94], [HH92], [Var92].

Stability does not imply that the computed solution $\widehat{x}$ is close to the exact solution x, unless the problem is well-conditioned. Provided $\kappa\varepsilon$ is sufficiently small, stability implies that

$$\|\widehat{x} - x\|/\|x\| = O_n(\kappa\varepsilon). \tag{4.2.1}$$

For more precise results, see Bunch [Bun87] and Wilkinson [Wil61].

4.2.1 Gaussian Elimination with Pivoting

To provide a basis for comparison when we quote error bounds for fast methods, and to give an example of a method for which the error bounds are necessarily more pessimistic than what is usually observed, it is worthwhile to consider briefly the classical method of Gaussian elimination (see also Sec. 1.6.2). Wilkinson [Wil61] shows that

$$\|\tilde{A} - A\|/\|A\| = O_n(g\varepsilon),$$

where $g = g(n)$ is the "growth factor." g depends on whether partial or complete pivoting is used. In practice g is usually moderate, even for partial pivoting. However, a well-known example shows that $g(n) = 2^{n-1}$ is possible for partial pivoting, and it has been shown that examples where $g(n)$ grows exponentially with n may occasionally arise in applications, e.g., for linear systems arising from boundary value problems [HH89].

Even for complete pivoting, it has not been *proved* that $g(n)$ is bounded by a polynomial in n. Wilkinson [Wil61] showed that $g(n) \leq n^{(\log n)/4 + O(1)}$, and Gould [Gou91]

Section 4.2. Stability and Weak Stability

showed that $g(n) > n$ is possible for $n > 12$; there is still a large gap between these results. Thus, to ensure that Gaussian elimination satisfies Definition 4.2.1, we must restrict $\mathcal{A}$ to the class of matrices for which g is $O_n(1)$. In practice this is not a serious problem, except in certain safety-critical real-time applications, because g can be computed easily and cheaply as the computation proceeds. In the unlikely event that g is large, the result can be checked by an independent computation using a more stable (but slower) method.

4.2.2 Weak Stability

Although stability is desirable, it is more than we can prove for many useful algorithms. Thus, following Bunch [Bun87], we define the (weaker, but still useful) property of *weak stability*.

Definition 4.2.2 (Weak Stability). *An algorithm for solving linear equations is weakly stable for a class of matrices $\mathcal{A}$ if for each well-conditioned A in $\mathcal{A}$ and for each b the computed solution $\widehat{x}$ to $Ax = b$ is such that $\|\widehat{x} - x\|/\|x\|$ is small.*

◊

In Def. 4.2.2, we take "small" to mean $O_n(\varepsilon)$ and "well-conditioned" to mean that $\kappa(A)$ is $O_n(1)$, i.e., is bounded by a polynomial in n. From (4.2.1), stability implies weak stability. It may happen that we cannot prove the inequality (4.2.1), but we can prove the weaker inequality

$$\|\widehat{x} - x\|/\|x\| = O_n(\kappa^2 \varepsilon).$$

Clearly, in such a case, the method is weakly stable.

Define the *residual vector r* by

$$r \stackrel{\Delta}{=} A\widehat{x} - b. \qquad (4.2.2)$$

We refer to $r/\|b\|$ as the *normalized residual*. It is easy to compute and gives an indication of how well the numerical method has performed—we would be unhappy if the the size of the normalized residual was large, and in general the smaller it is the better. It is important to realize that a small normalized residual does not necessarily mean the that computed solution $\widehat{x}$ is accurate. If the condition number $\kappa(A)$ is large, then $\widehat{x}$ might not agree with the "correct" solution x to any significant figures, although the normalized residual is very small. The residual and the solution error satisfy the following well-known inequalities [Wil63]:

$$\frac{1}{\kappa}\frac{\|r\|}{\|b\|} \leq \frac{\|\widehat{x} - x\|}{\|x\|} \leq \kappa\frac{\|r\|}{\|b\|}. \qquad (4.2.3)$$

Thus, for *well-conditioned* A, $\|\widehat{x} - x\|/\|x\|$ is small if and only if $\|r\|/\|b\|$ is small. This observation leads to an alternative definition of weak stability.

Definition 4.2.3 (Equivalent Condition). *An algorithm for solving linear equations is weakly stable for a class of matrices $\mathcal{A}$ if for each well-conditioned A in $\mathcal{A}$ and for each b the computed solution $\widehat{x}$ to $Ax = b$ is such that $\|A\widehat{x} - b\|/\|b\|$ is small.*

◊

If we can prove that
$$||A\hat{x} - b||/||b|| = O_n(\varepsilon),$$
then the method is stable; if we can prove that
$$||A\hat{x} - b||/||b|| = O_n(\kappa\varepsilon),$$
then the method is (at least) weakly stable.

4.2.3 Example: Orthogonal Factorization

To illustrate the concepts of stability and weak stability, consider computation of the Cholesky factor R of $A^T A$,[7] where A is an $m \times n$ matrix of full rank n. For simplicity we assume that $||A^T A||$ is of order unity. A good $O(mn^2)$ algorithm is to compute the QR factorization
$$A = QR$$
of A using Householder or Givens transformations [GV96] (see also App. B). It can be shown [Wil63] that the computed matrices $\widehat{Q}$, $\widehat{R}$ satisfy
$$\tilde{A} = \tilde{Q}\widehat{R}, \tag{4.2.4}$$
where $\tilde{Q}^T \tilde{Q} = I$, $\widehat{Q}$ is close to $\tilde{Q}$, and $\tilde{A}$ is close to A. Thus, the algorithm is stable in the sense of backward error analysis. Note that $||A^T A - \widehat{R}^T \widehat{R}||$ is small, but $||\widehat{Q} - Q||$ and $||\widehat{R} - R||/||R||$ are not necessarily small. Bounds on $||\widehat{Q} - Q||$ and $||\widehat{R} - R||/||R||$ depend on $\kappa(A)$ and are discussed in [Gol65], [Ste77], [Wil65].

A different algorithm is to compute (the upper triangular part of) $A^T A$ and then compute the Cholesky factorization of $A^T A$ by the usual (stable) algorithm. The computed result $\widehat{R}$ is such that $\widehat{R}^T \widehat{R}$ is close to $A^T A$. However, this does not imply the existence of $\tilde{A}$ and $\tilde{Q}$ such that (4.2.4) holds (with $\tilde{A}$ close to A and some $\tilde{Q}$ with $\tilde{Q}^T \tilde{Q} = I$) unless A is well-conditioned [Ste79]. By analogy with Definition 4.2.3 above, we may say that Cholesky factorization of $A^T A$ gives a *weakly stable* algorithm for computing R, because the "residual" $A^T A - \widehat{R}^T \widehat{R}$ is small.

4.3 CLASSES OF STRUCTURED MATRICES

We consider structured matrices R that satisfy displacement equations of the form[8]
$$\nabla_{\{F,A\}}(R) = FR - RA^T = GB^T, \tag{4.3.1}$$
where F and A have some simple structure (usually lower triangular or banded, with three or fewer full diagonals), G and B are $n \times \alpha$, and α is some fixed integer. The pair of matrices (G, B) is called an $\{F, A\}$-*generator* of R.

The number α is called the *displacement rank* of R with respect to the displacement operation (4.3.1). We are interested in cases where α is small (say, at most 4). For a discussion of the history and some variants of (4.3.1), see Ch. 1 of this book and [KS95a].

---

[7]In this subsection, the symbol R denotes an upper triangular matrix.
[8]We now use the letter R to denote a structured matrix and the letter A to denote a displacement operator.

4.3.1 Cauchy and Cauchy-Like Matrices

Particular choices of F and A lead to definitions of basic classes of matrices (see also Sec. 1.3). Thus, for a Cauchy matrix, $\alpha = 1$,

$$R = C(\mathbf{t}, \mathbf{s}) \triangleq \left[\frac{1}{t_j - s_k}\right]_{jk},$$

we have

$$F = D_t \triangleq \mathrm{diag}(t_1, t_2, \ldots, t_n),$$

$$A = D_s \triangleq \mathrm{diag}(s_1, s_2, \ldots, s_n),$$

and

$$G^T = B^T = [1, 1, \ldots, 1].$$

As a natural generalization, we can take G and B to be any $n \times \alpha$ rank-α matrices, with F and A as above. Then a matrix R satisfying (4.3.1) is said to be a *Cauchy-like* matrix.

4.3.2 Toeplitz Matrices

For a Toeplitz matrix $R = T = [t_{jk}] = [a_{j-k}]$, we can take $\alpha = 2$,

$$F = Z_1 \triangleq \begin{bmatrix} 0 & 0 & \cdots & 0 & 1 \\ 1 & 0 & & & 0 \\ 0 & 1 & & & \vdots \\ \vdots & & \ddots & & \vdots \\ 0 & \cdots & 0 & 1 & 0 \end{bmatrix}, \quad A^T = Z_{-1} \triangleq \begin{bmatrix} 0 & 0 & \cdots & 0 & -1 \\ 1 & 0 & & & 0 \\ 0 & 1 & & & \vdots \\ \vdots & & \ddots & & \vdots \\ 0 & \cdots & 0 & 1 & 0 \end{bmatrix},$$

$$G^T = \begin{bmatrix} 1 & 0 & \cdots & 0 \\ a_0 & a_{1-n} + a_1 & \cdots & a_{-1} + a_{n-1} \end{bmatrix}, \quad (4.3.2)$$

and

$$B^T = \begin{bmatrix} a_{n-1} - a_{-1} & \cdots & a_1 - a_{1-n} & a_0 \\ 0 & \cdots & 0 & 1 \end{bmatrix}. \quad (4.3.3)$$

We can generalize to *Toeplitz-like* matrices by taking G and B to be general $n \times \alpha$ rank-α matrices, $\alpha \geq 2$. We can also choose other matrices $\{F, A\}$ for the Toeplitz case (see Ch. 1).

4.4 STRUCTURED GAUSSIAN ELIMINATION

Let an input matrix, R_1, have the partitioning

$$R_1 = \begin{bmatrix} d_1 & \mathbf{w}_1^T \\ \mathbf{y}_1 & \tilde{R}_1 \end{bmatrix}.$$

The first step of normal Gaussian elimination is to premultiply R_1 by (see also Sec. 1.6.2 for a related discussion)

$$\begin{bmatrix} 1 & 0 \\ -\mathbf{y}_1/d_1 & I \end{bmatrix},$$

which reduces it to
$$\begin{bmatrix} d_1 & \mathbf{w}_1^T \\ 0 & R_2 \end{bmatrix},$$
where
$$R_2 = \tilde{R}_1 - \mathbf{y}_1 \mathbf{w}_1^T / d_1$$
is the *Schur complement* of d_1 in R_1. At this stage, R_1 has the factorization
$$R_1 = \begin{bmatrix} 1 & 0 \\ \mathbf{y}_1/d_1 & I \end{bmatrix} \begin{bmatrix} d_1 & \mathbf{w}_1^T \\ 0 & R_2 \end{bmatrix}.$$

One can proceed recursively with the Schur complement R_2, eventually obtaining a factorization $R_1 = LU$.

As discussed in Sec. 1.5, the key to *structured* Gaussian elimination is the fact that the displacement structure is preserved under Schur complementation and that the generators for the Schur complement of R_{k+1} can be computed from the generators of R_k in $O(n)$ operations (see also Sec. 1.12).

Row or column interchanges destroy the structure of matrices such as Toeplitz matrices. However, if F is diagonal (which is the case for Cauchy- and Vandermonde-type matrices), then *the structure is preserved under row permutations* (recall the discussion in Sec. 1.13). This observation leads to the *GKO–Cauchy* algorithm of [GKO95] for fast factorization of Cauchy-like matrices with partial pivoting (see Sec. 1.13.1). The idea of using pivoting in a hybrid Schur–Levinson algorithm for Cauchy-like systems was introduced by Heinig [Hei95]. There have been several variations on the idea in recent papers [GKO95], [Gu95a], [Ste98].

4.4.1 The GKO–Toeplitz Algorithm

Heinig [Hei95] showed that, if T is a Toeplitz-like matrix with $\{Z_1, Z_{-1}^T\}$-generators (G, B), then
$$R \triangleq \mathcal{F} T D^* \mathcal{F}^*$$
is a Cauchy-like matrix, where
$$\mathcal{F} \triangleq \frac{1}{\sqrt{n}} \left[e^{2\pi \hat{\imath} (j-1)(k-1)/n} \right]_{1 \leq j, k \leq n}, \quad \hat{\imath} = \sqrt{-1},$$
is the discrete Fourier transform (DFT) matrix,
$$D = \mathrm{diag}\left(1, e^{\pi \hat{\imath}/n}, \ldots, e^{\pi \hat{\imath}(n-1)/n}\right),$$
and the generators of T and R are simply related. In fact, it is easy to verify that
$$\nabla_{\{D_f, D_a\}}(R) = (\mathcal{F}G)(B^T D^* \mathcal{F}^*), \qquad (4.4.1)$$
where
$$D_f \triangleq D^2 = \mathrm{diag}\left(1, e^{2\pi \hat{\imath}/n}, \ldots, e^{2\pi \hat{\imath}(n-1)/n}\right)$$
and
$$D_a \triangleq e^{\pi \hat{\imath}/n} D_f = \mathrm{diag}\left(e^{\pi \hat{\imath}/n}, e^{3\pi \hat{\imath}/n}, \ldots, e^{(2n-1)\pi \hat{\imath}/n}\right).$$

Thus, the (D_f, D_a) generator of R is $(\mathcal{F}G, \mathcal{F}DB)$.

Section 4.4. Structured Gaussian Elimination

The transformation $T \leftrightarrow R$ is perfectly stable because $\mathcal{F}$ and D are unitary. Note that R is (in general) complex even if T is real. This increases the constant factors in the time bounds, because complex arithmetic is required.

Heinig's observation was exploited in [GKO95] (see Sec. 1.13.1): R can be factored as $R = P^T LU$ using the GKO–Cauchy algorithm. Thus, from the factorization

$$T = \mathcal{F}^* P^T LU F D,$$

a linear system involving T can be solved in $O(n^2)$ operations. The full procedure of conversion to Cauchy form, factorization, and solution requires $O(n^2)$ complex operations.

Other structured matrices, such as Hankel, Toeplitz-plus-Hankel, Vandermonde, Chebyshev–Vandermonde, etc., can be converted to Cauchy-like matrices in a similar way (e.g., [GKO95], [KO95]).

4.4.2 Error Analysis

Because GKO–Cauchy and GKO–Toeplitz involve partial pivoting, we might guess that their stability would be similar to that of Gaussian elimination with partial pivoting. Unfortunately, there is a flaw in this reasoning. During GKO–Cauchy the *generators* have to be transformed, and the partial pivoting does not ensure that the transformed generators are small.

Sweet and Brent [SB95] show that significant generator growth can occur if all the elements of GB^T are small compared with those of $|G| \cdot |B^T|$. This cannot happen for ordinary Cauchy matrices because $\alpha = 1$ and the successive generator matrices, G_k and B_k, have only one column and one row, respectively. However, it can happen for higher displacement-rank Cauchy-like matrices, even if the original matrix is well-conditioned.

For example, taking $\alpha = 2$,

$$G = [\mathbf{a}, \mathbf{a} + \mathbf{f}], \qquad B = [\mathbf{a} + \mathbf{e}, -\mathbf{a}],$$

where $\|\mathbf{a}\|$ is of order unity and $\|\mathbf{e}\|$ and $\|\mathbf{f}\|$ are very small, we see that all the elements of $GB^T = \mathbf{a}\mathbf{e}^T - \mathbf{f}\mathbf{a}^T$ are very small compared with those of $|G||B^T|$. Moreover, because $\mathbf{a}$, $\mathbf{e}$, and $\mathbf{f}$ can be arbitrary except for their norms, the original Cauchy-type matrix is in general well-conditioned. The problem is that the *generators* are ill-conditioned, being close to lower-rank matrices.

There are corresponding examples for Toeplitz-type matrices, easily derived using the correspondence between generators of Toeplitz-type and Cauchy-type matrices discussed in Sec. 4.4.1. However, in the strictly Toeplitz case the special form of the matrices B and G in (4.3.2) and (4.3.3) imposes additional constraints, which appear to rule out this kind of example. However, it is still possible to give examples where the normalized solution error grows like κ^2 and the normalized residual grows like κ, where κ is the condition number of the Toeplitz matrix: see Sweet and Brent [SB95, §5.2]. Thus, the GKO–Toeplitz algorithm is (at best) weakly stable.

It is easy to think of modified algorithms that avoid the examples given above and by Sweet and Brent [SB95], but it is difficult to prove that they are stable in all cases. Stability depends on the worst case, which may be rare and hard to find by random sampling.

The problem with the original GKO algorithm is growth in the generators. Gu [Gu95a] suggested exploiting the fact that the generators are not unique. Recall the displacement equation (4.3.1). Clearly we can replace G by GM and B^T by $M^{-1}B^T$, where M is any invertible $\alpha \times \alpha$ matrix, because this does not change the product GB^T. This holds similarly at later stages of the GKO algorithm. Gu [Gu95a] proposes taking M to orthogonalize the columns of G (that is, at each stage perform an orthogonal factorization of the generators—see also Sec. 2.11). Stewart [Ste98] proposes a (cheaper) LU factorization of the generators. This avoids examples of the type given above. In both cases, clever pivoting schemes give error bounds analogous to those for Gaussian elimination with partial pivoting.

The error bounds obtained by Gu and Stewart involve a factor K^n, where K depends on the ratio of the largest to smallest modulus elements in the Cauchy matrix

$$\left[\frac{1}{t_j - s_k}\right]_{jk}.$$

Although this is unsatisfactory, it is similar to the factor 2^{n-1} in the error bound for Gaussian elimination with partial pivoting. As mentioned in Sec. 4.2.1, the latter factor is extremely pessimistic, which explains why Gaussian elimination with partial pivoting is popular in practice [Hig96]. Perhaps the bounds of Gu and Stewart are similarly pessimistic, although practical experience is not yet extensive enough to be confident of this. Stewart [Ste98] gives some interesting numerical results suggesting that his scheme works well, but more numerical experience is necessary before a definite conclusion can be reached.

4.4.3 A General Strategy

It often happens that there is a choice of

1. a fast algorithm that usually gives an accurate result but occasionally fails (or at least cannot be proved to succeed every time), or

2. an algorithm that is guaranteed to be stable but is slow.

In such cases, a good strategy may be to use the fast algorithm but then check the normalized residual $||A\hat{x} - b||/||b||$, where $\hat{x}$ is the computed solution of the system $Ax = b$. If the normalized residual is sufficiently small (say at most 1000ε) we can accept $\hat{x}$ as a reasonably good solution. In the rare cases that the normalized residual is not sufficiently small we can can use the slow but stable algorithm. (Alternatively, if the residual is not too large, one or two iterations of iterative refinement may be sufficient and faster [JW77], [Wil65]—see also Sec. 2.12.2.)

An example of this general strategy is the solution of a Toeplitz system by Gu or Stewart's modification of the GKO algorithm. We can use the $O(n^2)$ algorithm, check the residual, and resort to iterative refinement or a slow but stable algorithm in the (rare) cases that it is necessary. Computing the residual takes only $O(n \log n)$ arithmetic operations.

We now turn our attention to another class of methods.

4.5 POSITIVE-DEFINITE STRUCTURED MATRICES

An important class of algorithms, typified by the algorithm of Bareiss [Bar69], finds an LU factorization of a Toeplitz matrix T and (in the symmetric case) is related to the classical algorithm of Schur [Bur75], [Goh86], [Sch17] (see also Ch. 1).

It is interesting to consider the numerical properties of these algorithms and compare them with the numerical properties of the Levinson–Durbin algorithm, which essentially finds an LU factorization of T^{-1}.

4.5.1 The Bareiss Algorithm for Positive-Definite Matrices

Bojanczyk, Brent, de Hoog, and Sweet (BBHS) have shown in [BBHS95], [Swe82] that the numerical properties of the Bareiss algorithm are similar to those of Gaussian elimination (*without* pivoting). Thus, the algorithm is stable for positive-definite symmetric Toeplitz matrices. In fact, the results of [BBHS95] establish stability for the larger class of quasi-Toeplitz positive-definite matrices. (For a definition of this class, see Ch. 1.)

The result of [BBHS95, Sec. 5] is that the computed upper triangular factor $\widehat{U}$ of the positive-definite matrix T satisfies the backward error bound

$$\|T - \widehat{U}^T\widehat{U}\|_2/t_0 = O(n^2\varepsilon) , \qquad (4.5.1)$$

where t_0 is a normalizing factor (a diagonal element of T), provided the Cholesky downdating is done using the "mixed downdating" scheme [BBDH87]. If "hyperbolic downdating" is used, then the bound (4.5.1) increases to $O(n^3\varepsilon)$, although numerical experiments reported in [BBHS95, Sec. 7] did not demonstrate much difference between the two forms of downdating. (Different forms of downdating are equivalent to different implementations of hyperbolic rotations.) The same numerical experiments showed that Cholesky factorization usually gave a slightly more accurate solution, but a slightly larger residual, than the fast algorithm using either form of downdating.

The Levinson–Durbin algorithm can be shown to be weakly stable for bounded n, and numerical results by [Var93], [BBHS95], and others suggest this is all we can expect. Thus, the Bareiss algorithm is (generally) better numerically than the Levinson–Durbin algorithm. For example, the numerical results reported in [BBHS95, Sec. 7] for three ill-conditioned positive-definite Toeplitz matrices (the Prolate matrix [Var93] and two matrices whose reflection coefficients have alternating signs) indicate that the Levinson–Durbin algorithm typically gives solution errors more than twice as large as the other algorithms (Bareiss with two forms of downdating and Cholesky), and residual errors 4×10^3 to 5×10^5 as large. The condition numbers of the test matrices ranged from 3×10^{14} to 8×10^{15}, and the machine precision was $\varepsilon = 2^{-53} \simeq 10^{-16}$; for better conditioned matrices the differences between the methods are generally less apparent.

Cybenko [Cyb80] showed that if the so-called reflection coefficients (see Sec. 1.2) are all positive, then the Levinson–Durbin algorithm for solving the Yule–Walker equations (a positive-definite Toeplitz system with a special right-hand side) is stable. Unfortunately, Cybenko's result usually is not applicable, because most positive-definite Toeplitz matrices (e.g., the examples just quoted) do not satisfy the restrictive condition on the reflection coefficients.

4.5.2 Generalized Schur Algorithms

The Schur algorithm can be generalized to factor a large variety of structured matrices [KC94], [KS95a] (see Ch. 1). For example, suitably generalized Schur algorithms apply to block Toeplitz matrices, Toeplitz block matrices, and matrices of the form T^TT, where T is rectangular Toeplitz.

It is natural to ask to what extent the stability results of [BBHS95] can be generalized. This has been considered in recent papers by Stewart and Van Dooren [SD97b] and by Chandrasekaran and Sayed [CS96] (see also Chs. 2 and 3 of this book).

Stewart and Van Dooren [SD97b] generalized the results of BBHS to matrices with similar structure but displacement rank larger than 2. They showed that for higher displacement ranks one has to be careful to implement the hyperbolic rotations properly. If they are implemented correctly (e.g., as recommended in [BBDH87]), then a backward error bound of the same form as (4.5.1) holds. In contrast, as mentioned in Sec. 4.5.1, one does not have to be so careful when the displacement rank is 2 because a result of the same form as (4.5.1), albeit with an extra power of n, holds for other implementations of hyperbolic rotations. (Of course, the error bound will certainly fail for a *sufficiently bad* implementation of hyperbolic rotations.)

Chandrasekaran and Sayed [CS96] studied a significantly more general Schur-like algorithm. (Their results are discussed in Chs. 2 and 3 of this book.) They dropped the assumption that the matrices F, A of Sec. 4.3.2 are shift matrices Z, although the corresponding matrices still have to satisfy certain restrictions. This extra generality causes significant complications in the error analysis and appears to make the Schur algorithm even more sensitive to the method of implementing hyperbolic rotations. Provided these hyperbolic rotations and certain "Blaschke factors" (see Sec. 1.6 for a description of these factors) are implemented correctly, a backward stability result similar to that of BBHS can be established. The interested reader is referred to [CS96] (and also Ch. 2) for details.

The overall conclusion is that the generalized Schur algorithm is stable for positive-definite symmetric (or Hermitian) matrices, *provided* the hyperbolic rotations and the Blaschke factors (if any) in the algorithm are implemented correctly.

We now drop the assumption of positive definiteness, and even (temporarily) the assumption that the matrix T is square, and we consider fast algorithms for orthogonal factorization.

4.6 FAST ORTHOGONAL FACTORIZATION

In an attempt to achieve stability without pivoting, and to solve $m \times n$ least squares problems $(m \geq n)$, it is natural to consider algorithms for computing an orthogonal factorization

$$T = QU \qquad (4.6.1)$$

of an $m \times n$ Toeplitz matrix T. We assume that T has full rank n. For simplicity, in the time bounds we assume $m = O(n)$ to avoid functions of both m and n.

The first $O(n^2)$ (more precisely, $O(mn)$) algorithm for computing the factorization (4.6.1) was introduced by Sweet [Swe82]. Unfortunately, Sweet's algorithm is unstable—see [LQ87].

Other $O(n^2)$ algorithms for computing the matrices Q and U or U^{-1} were given by Bojanczyk, Brent, and de Hoog (BBH) [BBH86], Chun, Kailath, and Lev-Ari [CKL87], Cybenko [Cyb87], and Qiao [Qia88], but none of them has been shown to be stable, and in several cases examples show that they are unstable.

It may be surprising that fast algorithms for computing an orthogonal factorization (4.6.1) are unstable. The classical $O(n^3)$ algorithms are stable because they form Q as a product of elementary orthogonal matrices (usually Givens or Householder matrices [Gol65], [GV96], [Wil65]). Unlike the classical algorithms, the $O(n^2)$ algorithms do not form Q in a numerically stable manner as a product of matrices that are (close to) orthogonal. This observation explains both their speed and their instability!

For example, the algorithms of [BBH86] and [CKL87] depend on Cholesky downdating, and numerical experiments show that they do not give a Q that is close to orthogonal. This is not too surprising, because Cholesky downdating is known to be a sensitive numerical problem [BBDH87], [Ste79]. Perhaps it is more surprising that the authors of [BBHS95] were able to use an error analysis of a form of downdating in their analysis of the Bareiss algorithm (but only in the positive-definite case)—see Sec. 4.5.1.

Section 4.6. Fast Orthogonal Factorization 115

4.6.1 Use of the Seminormal Equations

It can be shown that, provided the Cholesky downdates are implemented in a certain way (analogous to the condition for the stability of the Schur algorithm for $\alpha > 2$, discussed in Sec. 4.5.2), the BBH algorithm computes U in a weakly stable manner [BBH95]. In fact, the computed upper triangular matrix $\widehat{U}$ is about as good as can be obtained by performing a Cholesky factorization of $T^T T$, so

$$\|T^T T - \widehat{U}^T \widehat{U}\| / \|T^T T\| = O_m(\varepsilon).$$

Thus, by solving

$$\widehat{U}^T \widehat{U} x = T^T b$$

(the so-called seminormal equations) we have a *weakly stable* algorithm for the solution of general full-rank Toeplitz least-squares problems. In the case $m = n$, this gives a weakly stable algorithm for the solution of Toeplitz linear systems $Tx = b$ in $O(n^2)$ operations. The solution can be improved by iterative refinement if desired [GW66]. Weak stability is achieved because the computation of Q is avoided. The disadvantage of this method is that, by implicitly forming $T^T T$, the condition of the problem is effectively squared. If the condition number $\kappa = \kappa(T)$ is in the range

$$\frac{1}{\sqrt{\varepsilon}} \leq \kappa \leq \frac{1}{\varepsilon},$$

then it usually will be impossible to get any significant figures in the result (iterative refinement may fail to converge) without reverting to a slow but stable orthogonal factorization algorithm. One remedy is to use double-precision arithmetic, i.e., replace ε by ε^2, but this may be difficult if ε already corresponds to the maximum precision implemented in hardware.

Another way of computing the upper triangular matrix U, but not the orthogonal matrix Q, in (4.6.1) is to apply a generalized Schur algorithm to $T^T T$. This method also squares the condition number.

4.6.2 Computing Q Stably

It seems difficult to give a satisfactory $O(n^2)$ algorithm for the computation of Q in the factorization (4.6.1). The algorithm suggested in [BBH86] is unsatisfactory, as are all other fast algorithms known to us. In Sec. 4.6.1 we sidestepped this problem by avoiding the computation of Q, but in some applications Q is required. We leave the existence of a fast, stable algorithm for the computation of Q as an open question.

4.6.3 Solution of Indefinite or Unsymmetric Structured Systems

Using a modification of the embedding approach pioneered by Chun and Kailath [Chu89], [KC94] and Chandrasekaran and Sayed [CS98] gives a stable algorithm to compute a factorization of the form (see Ch. 3 of this book)

$$T = \Delta(\Delta^{-1}Q)U \qquad (4.6.2)$$

in terms of three matrices $\{\Delta, Q, U\}$, where Δ is a lower triangular matrix that compensates for the fact that Q is not numerically orthogonal. (Of course, the factorization (4.6.2) is not unique.) The motivation of [CS98] was to give a backward-stable algorithm for general square Toeplitz or quasi-Toeplitz systems (symmetric but not positive definite, or possibly unsymmetric). For details of the stability analysis, we refer to [CS98] and Ch. 3.

The algorithm of [CS98] can be used to solve linear equations but not least-squares problems (because T has to be square). Because the algorithm involves embedding the $n \times n$ matrix T in a $2n \times 2n$ matrix

$$\begin{bmatrix} T^T T & T^T \\ T & 0 \end{bmatrix},$$

the constant factors in the operation count are moderately large: $59n^2 + O(n \log n)$, which should be compared to $8n^2 + O(n \log n)$ for BBH and the seminormal equations (a weakly stable method, as discussed in Sec. 4.6.1). These operation counts apply for $m = n$: see [BBH95] for operation counts of various algorithms when $m \geq n$.

4.7 CONCLUDING REMARKS

Although this survey has barely scratched the surface, we hope the reader who has come this far is convinced that questions of numerical stability are amongst the most interesting, difficult, and useful questions that we can ask about fast algorithms for structured linear systems. It is not too hard to invent a new fast algorithm, but to find a new stable algorithm is more difficult, and to *prove* its stability or weak stability is a real challenge!

Acknowledgments

A preliminary version of this review appeared in [Bre97]. Thanks to Greg Ammar, Adam Bojanczyk, James Bunch, Shiv Chandrasekaran, George Cybenko, Paul Van Dooren, Lars Eldén, Roland Freund, Andreas Griewank, Ming Gu, Martin Gutknecht, Georg Heinig, Frank de Hoog, Franklin Luk, Vadim Olshevsky, Haesun Park, A. H. Sayed, Michael Stewart, Douglas Sweet, and James Varah for their assistance, and especially to A. H. Sayed for his detailed comments on a draft of this chapter.

Chapter 5

ITERATIVE METHODS FOR LINEAR SYSTEMS WITH MATRIX STRUCTURE

Raymond H. Chan

Michael K. Ng

5.1 INTRODUCTION

So far in the book, only direct methods for the solution of linear systems of equations $Ax = b$ have been discussed. These methods involve computing a factorization for the coefficient matrix A, say, an LDU or a QR factorization, and then solving for the unknown vector x by solving triangular systems of equations.

There is another class of methods, known as *iterative methods*, where the solution x is approximated by successive iterates x_k starting from an initial guess x_0. A major algorithm in this regard is the so-called conjugate gradient (CG) method. However, its convergence rate, as we shall demonstrate in Sec. 5.2, is dependent on the clustering of the eigenvalues of the coefficient matrix A; the more clustered the eigenvalues are the faster the convergence of x_k to x.

For this reason, one way to speed up the convergence of the CG method is to precondition the original system. This corresponds to choosing a matrix P and solving instead the equivalent system $P^{-1}Ax = P^{-1}b$. The preconditioner P is chosen such that the spectrum of the new coefficient matrix $P^{-1}A$ has better clustering properties than that of A. This condition, in addition to other requirements on the matrix P, such as ease of computations with P, results in the so-called preconditioned conjugate gradient (PCG) method. The method allows us to solve $n \times n$ structured linear systems in $O(n \log n)$ operations and is therefore attractive for large-scale problems.

This chapter provides a survey of some of the latest developments on PCG methods for the solution of $n \times n$ linear systems of equations with structured coefficient matrices, such as Toeplitz, Toeplitz-like, Toeplitz-plus-Hankel, and Toeplitz-plus-band matrices. Several preconditioning techniques are discussed for different classes of structured matrices. Application examples are also included. We start with a review of the classical CG method.

5.2 THE CG METHOD

The CG method was invented in the 1950s [HS52] as a direct method for solving Hermitian positive-definite systems. It has been widely used in the last 20 years as an iterative method.

Let us consider the linear system of equations $Ax_t = b$, where $A \in \mathbb{C}^{n \times n}$ is a nonsingular Hermitian positive-definite matrix and $b \in \mathbb{C}^{n \times 1}$. Consider further the quadratic cost function

$$\phi(x) \triangleq x^* A x - x^* b. \tag{5.2.1}$$

The minimizer of $\phi(x)$ over $x \in \mathbb{C}^{n \times 1}$ easily can be seen to satisfy $Ax - b = 0$ and, hence, coincides with the solution x_t of the linear system of equations $Ax_t = b$.

Given an initial guess $x_0 \in \mathbb{C}^{n \times 1}$ for x_t and the corresponding initial residual $r_0 = b - Ax_0$, the kth iterate $x_k \in \mathbb{C}^{n \times 1}$ of the CG method is determined by minimizing $\phi(x)$ over all vectors x in the subspace $x_0 + \mathbf{K}_k$, where $\mathbf{K}_k$ is the kth Krylov subspace

$$\mathbf{K}_k \triangleq \operatorname{span}(r_0, A r_0, \ldots, A^{k-1} r_0), \quad k = 1, 2, \ldots.$$

By this we mean that the minimization in the kth step is performed over all vectors x that can be expressed in the form

$$x = x_0 + \sum_{j=0}^{k-1} \alpha_j A^j r_0 \tag{5.2.2}$$

for some coefficients $\{\alpha_j\}$. If we now introduce the norm

$$\|x\|_A \triangleq \sqrt{x^* A x},$$

then it can be shown that minimizing $\phi(x)$ over $x_0 + \mathbf{K}_k$ is the same as minimizing $\|x_t - x\|_A$ over $x_0 + \mathbf{K}_k$,

$$\min_{x \in x_0 + \mathbf{K}_k} \|x_t - x\|_A \quad \Longrightarrow \quad x_k.$$

Using (5.2.2), we can write

$$x_t - x = x_t - x_0 - \sum_{j=0}^{k-1} \alpha_j A^j r_0.$$

But since $r_0 = b - Ax_0 = A(x_t - x_0)$, we obtain

$$x_t - x = x_t - x_0 - \sum_{j=0}^{k-1} \alpha_j A^{j+1} (x_t - x_0) = p(A)(x_t - x_0),$$

where the polynomial

$$p(z) \triangleq 1 - \sum_{j=0}^{k-1} \alpha_j z^{j+1}$$

has degree k and satisfies $p(0) = 1$. Therefore, our minimization problem becomes

$$\min_{p \in \mathbf{P}_k, p(0)=1} \|p(A)(x_t - x_0)\|_A \quad \Longrightarrow \quad x_k, \tag{5.2.3}$$

Section 5.2. The CG Method

where $\mathbf{P}_k$ is the set of polynomials of degree k.

Now, the spectral theorem for Hermitian positive-definite matrices asserts that $A = U\Lambda U^*$, where U is a unitary matrix whose columns are the eigenvectors of A and Λ is a diagonal matrix with the positive eigenvalues of A on the diagonal. Since $UU^* = U^*U = I$, we have $A^j = U\Lambda^j U^*$ and, consequently, $p(A) = Up(\Lambda)U^*$.

Define the square root factor $A^{1/2} \triangleq U\Lambda^{1/2}U^*$. Then

$$\|p(A)x\|_A = \|A^{1/2}p(A)x\|_2 \leq \|p(A)\|_2 \cdot \|x\|_A,$$

where $\|\cdot\|_2$ denotes the Euclidean norm of a vector argument or the maximum singular value of a matrix argument.

Together with (5.2.3), this inequality implies that

$$\|x_t - x_k\|_A \leq \|x_t - x_0\|_A \left(\min_{\substack{p \in \mathbf{P}_k \\ p(0) = 1}} \max_{\lambda \in \sigma(A)} |p(\lambda)| \right). \tag{5.2.4}$$

Here $\sigma(A)$ is the set of all eigenvalues of A. Clearly, if $k = n$, we can choose p to be the nth degree polynomial that vanishes at all the eigenvalues $\lambda \in \sigma(A)$ with $p(0) = 1$. Then the maximum in the right-hand side of (5.2.4) will be zero and we have the following result (see [AB84, p. 24]).

Theorem 5.2.1 (A Property of the CG Method). *Let A be a Hermitian positive-definite matrix of size n. Then the CG algorithm (described below in more detail) finds the solution of $Ax = b$ within n iterations in the absence of any round-off errors.*
◇

In most applications, the number of unknowns n is very large. In these cases, it is better to regard the CG approach as an iterative method and to terminate the iteration when some specified error tolerance is reached. The usual implementation of the CG method is to find, for a given ϵ, a vector x so that $\|b - Ax\|_2 \leq \epsilon \|b\|_2$. We have the following statement (see, e.g., [GV96]).

Algorithm 5.2.1 (The CG Algorithm). *Consider a Hermitian positive-definite linear system of equations $Ax = b$. The inputs of the CG algorithm are the right-hand side b, a routine that computes the action of A on a vector, and an initial guess x_0, which will be overwritten by the subsequent iterates x_k. We limit the number of iterations to kmax and return the solution x_k and the residual norm ρ_k.*

$CG(x, b, A, \epsilon, kmax)$

1. Start with $r = b - Ax_0$, $\rho_0 = \|r\|_2^2$, $k = 1$.

2. Do while $\sqrt{\rho_{k-1}} > \epsilon\|b\|_2$ and $k < kmax$:

    if $k = 1$ then $q = r$
    else
    $\beta = \rho_{k-1}/\rho_{k-2}$ and $q = r + \beta q$
    $w = Aq$

$$\alpha = \rho_{k-1}/q^*w$$
$$x = x + \alpha q$$
$$r = r - \alpha w$$
$$\rho_k = \|r\|_2^2$$
$$k = k + 1.$$

◇

Note that the matrix A itself need not be formed or stored; only a routine for matrix-vector products Aq is required. Now we consider the cost. We need to store only four vectors x, w, q, and r. Each iteration requires a single matrix-vector product (to compute $w = Aq$), two scalar products (one for q^*w and one to compute $\rho_k = \|r\|_2^2$), and three operations of the form $ax + y$, where x and y are vectors and a is a scalar. Thus, besides the matrix-vector multiplication, each iteration of Alg. 5.2.1 requires $O(n)$ operations, where n is the size of the matrix A.

For $k \leq n$, the convergence rate of the CG method can be determined by the condition number $\kappa(A)$ of the matrix A, where $\kappa(A) = \lambda_{\max}(A)/\lambda_{\min}(A)$, the ratio between the largest eigenvalue of A and the smallest eigenvalue of A. In fact, by choosing the polynomial p in (5.2.4) to be the kth degree Chebyshev polynomial, one can establish the following theorem (see [AB84, p. 26]).

Theorem 5.2.2 (Convergence of the CG Method). *Let A be Hermitian positive definite with condition number $\kappa(A)$. Then the kth iterate x_k of the CG method satisfies*

$$\|x_t - x_k\|_A \leq 2 \|x_t - x_0\|_A \left(\frac{\sqrt{\kappa(A)} - 1}{\sqrt{\kappa(A)} + 1} \right)^k. \tag{5.2.5}$$

◇

The above theorem shows that the convergence rate of the CG method is linear, viz.,

$$\frac{\|x_t - x_k\|_A}{\|x_t - x_0\|_A} \leq 2r^k,$$

where $r < 1$. We note that if we have more information about the distribution of the eigenvalues of the matrix A, then we can obtain a better bound for the error as the following theorem shows.

Let us consider a special case where the eigenvalues of A are clustered around 1, i.e., except for the outlying eigenvalues, all eigenvalues are in the interval $[1 - \epsilon, 1 + \epsilon]$, where $\epsilon < 1$ is a small positive number. Then the CG method will converge very fast.

Corollary 5.2.1 (The Case of Clustered Eigenvalues). *Consider the same setting as Theorem 5.2.2. If the eigenvalues of A are such that*

$$0 < \delta \leq \lambda_1 \leq \cdots \leq \lambda_i \leq 1 - \epsilon \leq \lambda_{i+1} \leq \cdots \leq \lambda_{n-j} \leq 1 + \epsilon \leq \lambda_{n-j+1} \leq \cdots \leq \lambda_n,$$

then

$$\frac{\|x_t - x_k\|_A}{\|x_t - x_0\|_A} \leq 2 \left(\frac{1+\epsilon}{\delta} \right)^i \epsilon^{k-i-j}, \quad k \geq i + j. \tag{5.2.6}$$

◇

Section 5.3. Iterative Methods for Solving Toeplitz Systems

This result suggests that the performance of the CG method is greatly influenced by the distribution of the eigenvalues of the coefficient matrix. In this chapter we are primarily interested in structured coefficient matrices, such as Toeplitz or Toeplitz-like. For this reason, in the next section we start with the Toeplitz case and review some basic facts about its spectral distribution. (These are covered in some detail in Ch. 6.) We then use this discussion to motivate the use of, and the need for, preconditioners.

5.3 ITERATIVE METHODS FOR SOLVING TOEPLITZ SYSTEMS

When A is a Toeplitz matrix, we shall denote it by T. In fact, we shall be more explicit and write T_n instead of T to emphasize the fact that it is an $n \times n$ matrix. It turns out that there is a close relationship between the spectrum of T_n and its so-called generating function as we now explain.

Let $\mathcal{C}_{2\pi}$ denote the set of all 2π-periodic continuous complex-valued functions defined on $[-\pi, \pi]$. For any $f \in \mathcal{C}_{2\pi}$, let

$$t_k \triangleq \frac{1}{2\pi}\int_{-\pi}^{\pi} f(\theta)e^{-\hat{\imath}k\theta}d\theta, \quad k = 0, \pm 1, \pm 2, \ldots, \quad \hat{\imath} \triangleq \sqrt{-1}, \qquad (5.3.1)$$

be the so-called Fourier coefficients of f. For all $n \geq 1$, let T_n be the $n \times n$ Toeplitz matrix with entries $t_{j,k} = t_{j-k}$, $0 \leq j, k < n$, i.e.,

$$T_n = \begin{bmatrix} t_0 & t_{-1} & \cdots & t_{2-n} & t_{1-n} \\ t_1 & t_0 & t_{-1} & & t_{2-n} \\ \vdots & t_1 & t_0 & \ddots & \vdots \\ t_{n-2} & & \ddots & \ddots & t_{-1} \\ t_{n-1} & t_{n-2} & \cdots & t_1 & t_0 \end{bmatrix}. \qquad (5.3.2)$$

The function f is called the *generating function* of the sequence of Toeplitz matrices $\{T_n\}$ [GS84]. If f is a real-valued function, we have

$$t_{-k} = t_k^*, \quad k = 0, \pm 1, \pm 2, \ldots, \qquad (5.3.3)$$

where the symbol $*$ denotes complex conjugation. It follows that the $\{T_n\}$ are Hermitian matrices. Note further that when f is an even real-valued function, the matrices $\{T_n\}$ are real symmetric.

We may remark that in several practical applications, the generating function f is readily available. Typical examples of generating functions are the kernels of Wiener–Hopf equations (see [GF74, p. 82]), the functions that describe the amplitude characteristics of recursive digital filters (see [CC82]), the spectral density functions of stationary stochastic processes (see [GS84, p. 171]), and the point-spread functions in image deblurring (see [Jai89, p. 269]).

The following statement clarifies the connection between the spectrum of T_n and its generating function f, as discussed in Sec. 6.3.1. The proof of the theorem can be found in [GS84] (see also Thm. 6.3.2).

Theorem 5.3.1 (Spectra and Generating Functions). *Let f be a 2π-periodic continuous real-valued function. Then the spectrum $\lambda(T_n)$ of T_n satisfies*

$$\lambda(T_n) \subseteq [f_{\min}, f_{\max}] \quad \text{for all} \quad n \geq 1, \qquad (5.3.4)$$

where $f_{\min}$ and $f_{\max}$ are the minimum and maximum values of f, respectively. Moreover, the eigenvalues $\lambda_j(T_n)$, $j = 0, 1, \ldots, n-1$, are equally distributed as $f(2\pi j/n)$, i.e.,

$$\lim_{n\to\infty} \frac{1}{n} \sum_{j=0}^{n-1} \left[g(\lambda_j(T_n)) - g\left(f\left(\frac{2\pi j}{n}\right)\right) \right] = 0 \qquad (5.3.5)$$

for any continuous function g defined on $[-\pi, \pi]$.

$\diamondsuit$

To illustrate the theorem, consider the one-dimensional discrete Laplacian matrix (encountered in Sec. 6.3)
$$T_n = tridiag[-1, 2, -1].$$
Its generating function is $2 - 2\cos(\theta)$. Its eigenvalues are given by

$$\lambda_j(T_n) = 4\sin^2\left(\frac{\pi j}{n+1}\right) = 2 - 2\cos\left(\frac{2\pi j}{n}\right), \quad 1 \leq j \leq n.$$

For $n = 32$, the eigenvalues of T_n are depicted in Fig. 5.1.

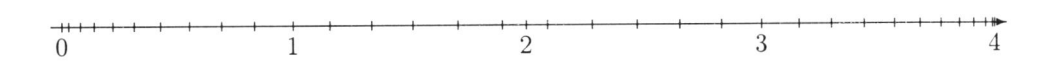

Figure 5.1. Spectrum of one-dimensional discrete Laplacian.

5.3.1 Preconditioning

We saw earlier in Sec. 5.2 that the convergence rate of the CG method for the solution of a system of linear equations $A_n x = b$ depends partly on how clustered the spectra of the sequence of matrices $\{A_n\}$ are. Here, by the clustering of the spectra of a sequence of matrices we mean the following (where I_n denotes the $n \times n$ identity matrix).

Definition 5.3.1 (Clustered Spectra). *A sequence of matrices $\{A_n\}_{n=1}^{\infty}$ is said to have clustered spectra around 1 if, for any given $\epsilon > 0$, there exist positive integers n_1 and n_2 such that for all $n > n_1$, at most n_2 eigenvalues of the matrix $A_n - I_n$ have absolute value larger than ϵ.*

$\diamondsuit$

The equal distribution of the eigenvalues of Hermitian Toeplitz matrices indicates that the eigenvalues will not be clustered in general. For this reason, one way to speed up the convergence rate of the CG method is to precondition the Toeplitz system of equations. This means that instead of solving $T_n x = b$, we solve the preconditioned system

$$P_n^{-1} T_n x = P_n^{-1} b \qquad (5.3.6)$$

for some so-called preconditioner matrix P_n that we choose. The preconditioner P_n should be chosen according to the following criteria:

… Section 5.3. Iterative Methods for Solving Toeplitz Systems

1. It should be possible to construct P_n within $O(n \log n)$ operations.

2. It should be possible to solve a linear system of equations with coefficient matrix P_n, say, $P_n v = y$, in $O(n \log n)$ operations.

3. The spectrum of $P_n^{-1} T_n$ should be clustered or the condition number $\kappa(P_n^{-1} T_n)$ of the preconditioned matrix should be close to 1 (cf. Thm. 5.2.2 and Cor. 5.2.1).

The statement of the PCG algorithm is now the following.

Algorithm 5.3.1 (The PCG Algorithm). *Consider a Hermitian positive-definite linear system of equations $Ax = b$. The inputs of the PCG algorithm are the right-hand side b, a routine that computes the action of A on a vector, a preconditioner P, and an initial guess x_0, which will be overwritten by the subsequent iterates x_k. We limit the number of iterations to kmax and return the solution x_k and the residual norm ρ_k.*

PCG $(x, b, A, P, \epsilon, kmax)$

1. $r = b - Ax$, $\rho_0 = \|r\|_2^2$, $k = 1$.

2. Do while $\sqrt{\rho_{k-1}} > \epsilon \|b\|_2$ and $k < kmax$

   $z = P^{-1} r$ (or solve $Pz = r$)
   $\tau_{k-1} = z^* r$
   if $k = 1$ then $\beta = 0$ and $q = z$
   else
   $\beta = \tau_{k-1}/\tau_{k-2}$ and $q = z + \beta q$
   $w = Aq$
   $\alpha = \tau_{k-1}/q^* w$
   $x = x + \alpha q$
   $r = r - \alpha w$
   $\rho_k = \|r\|_2^2$
   $k = k + 1$.

$\diamond$

In the next three subsections, we review three different kinds of preconditioner that have been developed for Toeplitz systems and that satisfy the above three criteria. We first provide a brief discussion of circulant matrices.

5.3.2 Circulant Matrices

A circulant matrix is a Toeplitz matrix whose rows are circular shifts of one another. More specifically, an $n \times n$ circulant matrix C_n has the form

$$C_n = \begin{bmatrix} c_0 & c_{-1} & \cdots & c_{2-n} & c_{1-n} \\ c_1 & c_0 & c_{-1} & & c_{2-n} \\ \vdots & c_1 & c_0 & \ddots & \vdots \\ c_{n-2} & & \ddots & \ddots & c_{-1} \\ c_{n-1} & c_{n-2} & \cdots & c_1 & c_0 \end{bmatrix}, \qquad (5.3.7)$$

where
$$c_{-k} = c_{n-k} \quad \text{for} \quad 1 \leq k \leq n-1. \tag{5.3.8}$$
Circulant matrices have the important property that they are diagonalized by the Fourier matrix F_n, i.e.,
$$C_n = F_n^* \Lambda_n F_n, \tag{5.3.9}$$
where the entries of F_n are given by
$$[F_n]_{j,k} = \frac{1}{\sqrt{n}} e^{2\pi i j k/n}, \quad 0 \leq j, k \leq n-1,$$
and Λ_n is a diagonal matrix holding the eigenvalues of C_n [Dav79, p. 73]. The matrix F_n is unitary, i.e., $F_n F_n^* = F_n^* F_n = I_n$.

Moreover, multiplying a vector x by F_n, say, $F_n x$, results in a column vector whose entries compose the DFT of x. It is well known that, due to the special structure of F_n, products of the form $F_n x$ can be computed in $O(n \log n)$ operations by employing the FFT algorithm [CT65].

Now using (5.3.9), we note that the first column of F_n is $\frac{1}{\sqrt{n}}\text{col}\{1, 1, \ldots, 1\}$. Hence,
$$F_n C_n \text{col}\{1, 0, \ldots, 0\} = \frac{1}{\sqrt{n}} \Lambda_n \text{col}\{1, 1, \ldots, 1\}. \tag{5.3.10}$$

That is, the entries of Λ_n can be obtained in $O(n \log n)$ operations by taking the FFT of the first column of C_n. In fact, expression (5.3.10) shows that the diagonal entries λ_k of Λ_n are given by
$$\lambda_k = \sum_{j=0}^{n-1} c_j e^{2\pi i j k/n}, \quad k = 0, \ldots, n-1. \tag{5.3.11}$$

Once Λ_n is obtained, products of the form $C_n y$ and $C_n^{-1} y$, for any vector y, can be computed by FFTs in $O(n \log n)$ operations using (5.3.9).

5.3.3 Toeplitz Matrix-Vector Multiplication

In each PCG iteration, one matrix-vector multiplication $T_n y$ is needed. This can be computed by FFTs by first embedding T_n into a $2n \times 2n$ circulant matrix, i.e.,
$$\begin{bmatrix} T_n & B_n \\ B_n & T_n \end{bmatrix} \begin{bmatrix} y \\ 0 \end{bmatrix} = \begin{bmatrix} T_n y \\ \times \end{bmatrix}, \tag{5.3.12}$$
where (see Strang [Str86])
$$B_n = \begin{bmatrix} 0 & t_{n-1} & \cdots & t_2 & t_1 \\ t_{1-n} & 0 & t_{n-1} & & t_2 \\ \vdots & t_{1-n} & 0 & \ddots & \vdots \\ t_{-2} & & \ddots & \ddots & t_{n-1} \\ t_{-1} & t_{-2} & \cdots & t_{1-n} & 0 \end{bmatrix}.$$

Then we can carry out the multiplication in (5.3.12) by using the decomposition (5.3.9). The matrix-vector multiplication $T_n y$ thus requires $O(2n \log(2n))$ operations. It follows that the total number of operations per iteration of Algorithm CG in this case is of $O(n \log n)$ operations.

5.3.4 Circulant Preconditioners

In 1986, Strang [Str86] and Olkin [Olk86] independently proposed the use of circulant matrices to precondition Hermitian Toeplitz matrices in CG iterations. Part of their motivation was to exploit the fact that circulant matrices can be inverted rather fast.

Strang's Preconditioner

For an $n \times n$ Hermitian Toeplitz matrix T_n, Strang's circulant preconditioner [Str86] is defined to be the matrix that copies the central diagonals of T_n and reflects them around to complete the circulant requirement. For T_n given by (5.3.2), the diagonals s_j of Strang's preconditioner $S_n = [s_{k-\ell}]_{0 \le k,\ell < n}$ are given by

$$s_j = \begin{cases} t_j & 0 \le j \le \lfloor n/2 \rfloor, \\ t_{j-n} & \lfloor n/2 \rfloor < j < n, \\ s_{n+j} & 0 < -j < n. \end{cases} \qquad (5.3.13)$$

Here the notation $\lfloor \frac{n}{2} \rfloor$ denotes the largest integer $m \le \frac{n}{2}$.

The approach developed in the following convergence proof (Thms. 5.3.2 and 5.3.3 and Cor. 5.3.1) of Strang's preconditioned system have been adapted by other authors to establish the convergence proof of other circulant preconditioned systems. The main idea of the proof is to show that the preconditioned matrices $S_n^{-1} T_n$ can be written in the form $I_n + L_n + U_n$, where I_n is the $n \times n$ identity matrix, L_n is a matrix of low rank, and U_n is a matrix of small ℓ_2-norm. It will follow in this case that the PCG method, when applied to the preconditioned system, converges superlinearly.

The first step of the proof on the clustered spectra of $S_n^{-1} T_n$ is to show that S_n and S_n^{-1} are uniformly bounded in ℓ_2-norm for a subclass of generating functions [Cha89a].

Theorem 5.3.2 (Uniform Boundedness of S_n and S_n^{-1}). *Let f be a positive real-valued function in the Wiener class; i.e., its Fourier coefficients are absolutely summable,*

$$\sum_{k=0}^{\infty} |t_k| < \infty.$$

Then, for large n, the circulants S_n and S_n^{-1} are uniformly bounded in ℓ_2-norm.

Proof: By (5.3.11), the jth eigenvalue of S_n is equal to

$$\lambda_j(S_n) = \sum_{k=1-m}^{m} t_k e^{2\pi i j k/n},$$

where $m = \lfloor n/2 \rfloor$. Since, for $\theta \in [-\pi, \pi]$, the infinite series $\sum_{k=-\infty}^{\infty} t_k e^{ik\theta}$ is absolutely convergent, then for any given $\epsilon > 0$, there exists N such that for $n \ge N$,

$$\left| \sum_{k \le 1-m, k > m} t_k e^{ik\theta} \right| < \epsilon.$$

We note that

$$\lambda_j(S_n) = \sum_{k=1-m}^{m} t_k e^{2\pi i jk/n} - f\left(\frac{2\pi j}{n}\right) + f\left(\frac{2\pi j}{n}\right)$$

$$\geq f_{\min} - \left| \sum_{k \leq 1-m, k > m} t_k e^{ik\theta} \right|$$

$$= f_{\min} - \epsilon.$$

Since f is positive, $f_{\min} \geq \delta > 0$. The result follows.

$\diamondsuit$

The second step of the proof is to establish the clustering of the spectra of $S_n - T_n$ [Cha89a].

Theorem 5.3.3 (Clustered Spectra). *Let f be a real-valued function in the Wiener class. Let $\{T_n\}$ be the sequence of Hermitian Toeplitz matrices generated by f. Then the spectra of $S_n - T_n$ are clustered around zero for large n.*

Proof: For simplicity, we assume here and in the following that n is odd, i.e., $n = 2m+1$ for some m. The case where $n = 2m$ can be treated similarly.

Clearly $L_n \triangleq S_n - T_n$ is a Hermitian Toeplitz matrix with entries $l_{ij} = l_{i-j}$ given by

$$l_k = \begin{cases} 0 & 0 \leq k \leq m, \\ t_{k-n} - t_k & m < k < n, \\ l_{-k}^* & 0 < -k < n. \end{cases} \quad (5.3.14)$$

Since f is in the Wiener class, for all given $\epsilon > 0$, there exists an $N > 0$ such that $\sum_{k=N+1}^{\infty} |t_k| < \epsilon$. Let $U_n^{(N)}$ be the $n \times n$ matrix obtained from L_n by replacing the $(n-N) \times (n-N)$ leading principal submatrix of L_n by the zero matrix. Therefore, the entries of $U_n^{(N)}$ are zero except at its last N columns and last N rows. Hence $\text{rank}(U_n^{(N)}) \leq 2N$.

Let $W_n^{(N)} \triangleq M_n - U_n^{(N)}$. The leading $(n-N) \times (n-N)$ block of $W_n^{(N)}$ is the leading $(n-N) \times (n-N)$ principal submatrix of L_n; hence this block is a Toeplitz matrix, and it is easy to see that the maximum absolute column sum of $W_n^{(N)}$ is attained at the first column (or the $(n-N-1)$th column) of $W_n^{(N)}$. Thus

$$\|W_n^{(N)}\|_1 = \sum_{k=m+1}^{n-N-1} |b_k| = \sum_{k=m+1}^{n-N-1} |t_{k-n} - t_k| \leq \sum_{k=N+1}^{n-N-1} |t_k| < \epsilon.$$

Since $W_n^{(N)}$ is Hermitian, we have $\|W_n^{(N)}\|_\infty = \|W_n^{(N)}\|_1$. Thus

$$\|W_n^{(N)}\|_2 \leq (\|W_n^{(N)}\|_1 \cdot \|W_n^{(N)}\|_\infty)^{\frac{1}{2}} < \epsilon.$$

Hence the spectrum of $W_n^{(N)}$ lies in $(-\epsilon, \epsilon)$. By the Cauchy interlace theorem [Par80, p. 192] (see also App. A), we see that at most $2N$ eigenvalues of $L_n = S_n - T_n$ have absolute values exceeding ϵ.

$\diamondsuit$

Section 5.3. Iterative Methods for Solving Toeplitz Systems

Using the fact that $S_n^{-1}T_n$ is similar to $S_n^{-1/2}T_nS_n^{-1/2}$, along with the result of Thm. 5.3.2 and the equality

$$S_n^{-1/2}T_nS_n^{-1/2} = I_n + S_n^{-1/2}(T_n - S_n)S_n^{-1/2},$$

we conclude that the spectra of $S_n^{-1}T_n$ are clustered around 1 for large n.

It follows easily from Thms. 5.3.2 and 5.3.3 that the CG method, when applied to solving the preconditioned system

$$S_n^{-1}T_nx = S_n^{-1}b,$$

converges superlinearly for large n in the sense specified below (see [CS89]).

Corollary 5.3.1 (Superlinear Convergence). *Let f be a positive real-valued function in the Wiener class. Let $\{T_n\}$ be the sequence of Toeplitz matrices generated by f. Then for any given $\epsilon > 0$, there exists a constant $c(\epsilon) > 0$ such that the error vector e_k of the PCG method at the kth iteration satisfies*

$$\frac{|||x - x_k|||}{|||x - x_0|||} \leq c(\epsilon)\epsilon^k, \tag{5.3.15}$$

where x is the true solution of the linear system of equations $T_nx = b$ and x_k is the kth iterate of the PCG method. Moreover, the notation $||| \cdot |||$ stands for the weighted norm

$$|||v|||^2 \triangleq v^* S_n^{-1/2} T_n S_n^{-1/2} v.$$

◊

If extra smoothness conditions are imposed on the generating function f (or on the sequence $\{t_k\}$), we can get more precise estimates on how $|||x - x_k|||$ in (5.3.15) goes to zero [Cha89a].

Theorem 5.3.4 (Smooth Generating Functions). *Let f be an $(\ell+1)$-times differentiable real-valued function with $f^{(\ell+1)} \in L^1[-\pi, \pi]$, where $\ell > 0$ (i.e., $|t_j| \leq \hat{c}/j^{\ell+1}$ for some constant $\hat{c}$ and therefore f is in the Wiener class). Then there exists a constant c which depends only on f and ν, such that for large n,*

$$\frac{|||x - x_{2q}|||}{|||x - x_0|||} \leq \frac{c^q}{((q-1)!)^{2\ell}}. \tag{5.3.16}$$

Proof: See App. 5.A. ◊

Other precise estimates on how $|||x - x_k|||$ in (5.3.15) goes to zero under different smoothness conditions can be found in [Tre90], [KK93b], [KK93c], [CY92].

T. Chan's Preconditioner

For an $n \times n$ Toeplitz matrix T_n, T. Chan's circulant preconditioner $C(T_n)$ is defined as the minimizer of

$$\|C_n - T_n\|_F \tag{5.3.17}$$

over all $n \times n$ circulant matrices C_n [Cha88]. Here $\| \cdot \|_F$ denotes the Frobenius norm. In [Cha88], the matrix $C(T_n)$ is called an *optimal* circulant preconditioner because it minimizes (5.3.17).

Theorem 5.3.5 (T. Chan's Preconditioner). *The jth diagonals of $C(T_n)$ are given by*

$$c_j = \begin{cases} \dfrac{(n-j)t_j + j t_{j-n}}{n}, & 0 \le j < n, \\ c_{n+j}, & 0 < -j < n, \end{cases} \quad (5.3.18)$$

which are simply the average of the diagonals of T_n, with the diagonals being extended to length n by a wrap-around procedure.

Proof: Since the Frobenius norm is a unitary-invariant norm, the minimizer of $\|C_n - T_n\|_F$ over all C_n of the form $C = F^*\Lambda F$, Λ a diagonal matrix, is attained at $F_n\Delta_n F_n^*$. Here Δ_n is a diagonal matrix with diagonal entries

$$[\Delta_n]_{j,j} = [F_n T_n F_n^*]_{j,j} \equiv \lambda_j, \quad j = 1,\ldots,n.$$

It is now immediate to verify that the entries of $C(T_n)$ are given by (5.3.18). $\diamond$

By using (5.3.11) and (5.3.18), we further see that the eigenvalues $\lambda_k(C(T_n))$ of $C(T_n)$ in (5.3.18) are given by

$$\lambda_k(C(T_n)) = \sum_{j=-n+1}^{n-1} t_j \left(1 - \frac{|j|}{n}\right) e^{2\pi i j k/n}, \quad k = 0,\ldots,n-1. \quad (5.3.19)$$

For the performance of $C(T_n)$ as preconditioners for Hermitian Toeplitz matrices T_n, it is shown in [Cha89b] that under the Wiener class assumptions of Thm. 5.3.3 (i.e., f is a positive function with absolutely summable Fourier coefficients), the spectra of $C(T_n) - T_n$ and $S_n - T_n$ are asymptotically the same as n tends to infinity, i.e., $\lim_{n\to\infty} \|C(T_n) - S_n\|_2 = 0$. Hence, $C(T_n)$ works as well for Wiener class functions as S_n does.

Theorem 5.3.6 (Performance of T. Chan's Preconditioner). *Let f be a real-valued function in the Wiener class. Let $\{T_n\}$ be the sequence of Toeplitz matrices generated by f. Then*

$$\lim_{n\to\infty} \rho\left(S_n - C(T_n)\right) = 0,$$

where $\rho(\cdot)$ denotes the spectral radius.

Proof: By (5.3.13) and (5.3.18), it is clear that $L_n \stackrel{\triangle}{=} S_n - C(T_n)$ is circulant with entries

$$l_k = \begin{cases} \dfrac{k}{n}(t_k - t_{n-k}), & 0 \le k \le m, \\ \dfrac{n-k}{n}(t_{n-k} - t_k), & m \le k < n. \end{cases}$$

Here, for simplicity, we are still assuming $n = 2m$. Using the fact that the jth eigenvalue $\lambda_j(L_n)$ of L_n is given by $\sum_{k=0}^{n-1} b_k e^{2\pi i j k/n}$, we have

$$\lambda_j(B_n) = 2\sum_{k=1}^{m-1} \frac{k}{n}(t_k - t_{n-k})\cos(2\pi j k/n).$$

Section 5.3. Iterative Methods for Solving Toeplitz Systems

This implies

$$\rho(B_n) \leq 2 \sum_{k=1}^{m-1} \frac{k}{n}|t_k| + 2 \sum_{k=m+1}^{n-1} |t_k|.$$

Since f is in the Wiener class, for all $\epsilon > 0$, we can always find an $M_1 > 0$ and an $M_2 > M_1$ such that

$$\sum_{k=M_1+1}^{\infty} |t_k| < \epsilon/6 \quad \text{and} \quad \frac{1}{M_2} \sum_{k=1}^{M_1} k|t_k| < \epsilon/6.$$

Thus for all $m > M_2$,

$$\rho(B_n) < \frac{2}{M_2} \sum_{k=1}^{M_1} k|t_k| + 2 \sum_{k=M_1+1}^{m-1} |t_k| + 2 \sum_{k=m+1}^{\infty} |t_k| < \epsilon.$$

◇

For an $n \times n$ general non-Toeplitz matrix A_n, the circulant minimizer $C(A_n)$ of $\|C_n - A_n\|_F$ still can be defined and obtained easily by taking the arithmetic average of the entries of A_n, i.e., its diagonals are given by [Tyr92b]

$$c_\ell = \frac{1}{n} \sum_{j-k=\ell(\bmod\ n)} a_{j,k}, \quad \ell = 0, \ldots, n-1. \tag{5.3.20}$$

Therefore, T. Chan's preconditioner is particularly useful in solving non-Toeplitz systems arising from the numerical solutions of elliptic partial differential equations [CC92] and Toeplitz least-squares problems arising from signal and image processing [CNP94a], [CNP93], [CNP94b], [CO94], [NP96]. Convergence results for T. Chan's preconditioner have been established for these problems (see [CN96]). One good property of T. Chan's preconditioner is that it preserves the positive definiteness of a given matrix [Tyr92b], [CJY91a].

Theorem 5.3.7 (Positive-Definiteness Property). *If A_n is Hermitian positive definite, then $C(A_n)$ is Hermitian and positive definite. Moreover, we have*

$$\lambda_{\min}(A_n) \leq \lambda_{\min}(C(A_n)) \leq \lambda_{\max}(C(A_n)) \leq \lambda_{\max}(A_n). \tag{5.3.21}$$

Proof: By (5.3.20), it is clear that $C(A_n)$ is Hermitian when A_n is Hermitian. Moreover, since the Frobenius norm is a unitary-invariant norm, we conclude as before that the minimizer of $\|C_n - A_n\|_F$ is attained at $F_n \Delta_n F_n^*$. Here Δ_n is a diagonal matrix with diagonal entries

$$[\Delta_n]_{j,j} = [F_n A_n F_n^*]_{j,j} \equiv \lambda_j, \quad j = 1, \ldots, n.$$

Suppose that $\lambda_j = \lambda_{\min}(C(A_n))$ and $\lambda_k = \lambda_{\max}(C(A_n))$. Let e_j and e_k denote the jth and the kth unit vectors, respectively. Since A_n is Hermitian, we have

$$\lambda_{\max}(C(A_n)) = \lambda_k = \frac{e_k^* F_n A_n F_n^* e_k}{e_k^* e_k} \leq \max_{x \neq 0} \frac{x^* F_n A_n F_n^* x}{x^* x}$$

$$= \max_{x \neq 0} \frac{x^* A_n x}{x^* x} = \lambda_{\max}(A_n).$$

Similarly,

$$\lambda_{\min}(A_n) = \min_{x \neq 0} \frac{x^* A_n x}{x^* x} = \min_{x \neq 0} \frac{x^* F_n A_n F_n^* x}{x^* x} \leq \frac{e_j^* F_n A_n F_n^* e_j}{e_j^* e_j}$$
$$= \lambda_j = \lambda_{\min}(C(A_n)).$$

From the inequality above, we can easily see that $C(A_n)$ is positive definite when A_n is positive definite.

◇

5.4 BAND-TOEPLITZ PRECONDITIONERS

In this section we consider Hermitian Toeplitz matrices T_n that are generated by nonnegative 2π-periodic real-valued functions. We first recall that a function f is said to have a νth-order zero at θ_0 if $f(\theta_0) = 0$ and ν is the smallest positive integer such that $f^{(\nu)}(\theta_0) \neq 0$ and $f^{(\nu+1)}(\theta)$ is continuous in a neighborhood of θ_0. With the knowledge of the order of f at its minimum, we can give a better estimate of the spectrum of T_n than that in (5.3.4) [Cha91].

Theorem 5.4.1 (Spectrum of T_n). *Suppose that $f(\theta) - f_{\min}$ has a unique zero of order 2ν on $[-\pi, \pi]$. Let $\{T_n\}$ be the sequence of Hermitian Toeplitz matrices generated by f. Then for all $n > 0$, we have*

$$\lambda_{\min}(T_n) \leq d_1 f_{\min} + d_2 n^{-2\nu},$$

and the condition number $\kappa(T_n)$ of T_n satisfies

$$\kappa(T_n) \geq \frac{d_3 n^{2\nu}}{d_4 + f_{\min} n^{2\nu}},$$

where $\{d_i\}_{i=1}^4$ are some constants independent of n.

◇

Thus when $f_{\min} = 0$, the condition number of T_n is not uniformly bounded and the Toeplitz matrix T_n is ill-conditioned. It was shown in [Tyr95] that Strang's preconditioner will fail in this case. More specifically, if f is such that its μth derivative $f^{(\mu)}$ is piecewise continuous and has a bounded derivative on each continuity interval, the number of outlying eigenvalues of $S_n^{-1} T_n$ is of $O(n^{\nu/(\nu+\mu)})$. Here ν is the order of f at the zero.

Instead of finding other possible circulant preconditioners, it was suggested in [Cha91] to use band-Toeplitz matrices as preconditioners. The motivation behind using band-Toeplitz matrices is to approximate the generating function f by trigonometric polynomials of fixed degree rather than by convolution products of f with some kernels. The advantage here is that trigonometric polynomials can be chosen to match the zeros of f, so that the preconditioned method still works when f has zeros [Cha91], [CN93a].

Theorem 5.4.2 (Band-Toeplitz Preconditioner). *Let f be a nonnegative piecewise continuous real-valued function defined on $[-\pi, \pi]$. Suppose that $f(\theta) - f_{\min}$ has a unique*

Section 5.4. Band-Toeplitz Preconditioners

zero of order 2ν at $\theta = \theta_0$. Let $\{T_n\}$ be the sequence of Toeplitz matrices generated by f. Let $\{E_n\}$ be the sequence of Toeplitz matrices generated by the function

$$b_\nu(\theta) = [2 - 2\cos(\theta - \theta_0)]^\nu + f_{\min}. \tag{5.4.1}$$

Then $\kappa(E_n^{-1}T_n)$ is uniformly bounded for all $n > 0$.

Proof: We can assume without loss of generality that $\theta_0 = 0$. Let G_n be generated by $f(\theta + \theta_0)$. The function $f(\theta + \theta_0) - f_{\min}$ has a zero at $\theta = 0$ and

$$G_n = V_n^* T_n V_n,$$

where $V_n = \text{diag}(1, e^{-i\theta_0}, e^{-2i\theta_0}, \ldots, e^{-i(n-1)\theta_0})$ (see [Cha89b, Lemma 2]).

By assumption, there exists a neighborhood N of 0 such that f is continuous in N. Define

$$F(\theta) \triangleq \frac{f(\theta)}{(2 - 2\cos\theta)^\nu + f_{\min}}.$$

Clearly F is continuous and positive for $\theta \in N \setminus \{0\}$. Since

$$\lim_{\theta \to 0} F(\theta) = \begin{cases} 1, & f_{\min} > 0, \\ \dfrac{f^{(2\nu)}(0)}{(2\nu)!}, & f_{\min} = 0, \end{cases}$$

is positive, F is a continuous positive function in N. Since f is piecewise continuous and positive almost everywhere in $[-\pi, \pi] \setminus N$, we see that F is a piecewise continuous function with a positive essential infimum in $[-\pi, \pi]$. Hence there exist constants $b_1, b_2 > 0$ such that $b_1 \leq F(\theta) \leq b_2$ almost everywhere in $[-\pi, \pi]$. Without loss of generality, we assume that $b_2 \geq 1 \geq b_1$. Then we have

$$b_1 \leq \frac{u^* T_n u}{u^* E_n u} \leq b_2$$

for any n-vector u. Hence $\kappa(E_n^{-1} T_n) \leq b_2/b_1$, which is independent of n. $\diamond$

We note that E_n is a band-Toeplitz matrix with bandwidth $2\nu + 1$ and its diagonals can be obtained by using Pascal's triangle. We remark that

$$2 - 2\cos(\theta) = -e^{-i\theta}(1 - e^{i\theta})^2 = -(e^{-i\theta} + 2 - e^{i\theta}).$$

Hence by the binomial theorem,

$$[2 - 2\cos(\theta)]^\nu = \sum_{k=-\nu}^{\nu} a_k^{(\nu)} e^{ik\theta},$$

where

$$a_j^{(\nu)} = a_{-j}^{(\nu)} = (-1)^j \binom{2l}{\nu + j}$$

are the binomial coefficients of $(-1)^\nu (1 - e^{i\theta})^{2\nu}$. Hence the diagonals of E_n can be obtained easily from the Pascal triangle.

The band system $E_n y = z$ can be solved by using any band matrix solver (see, e.g., [GV96], [Wri91]). The cost of factorizing E_n is about $\frac{1}{2}\nu^2 n$ operations, and then each subsequent solve requires an extra $(2\nu + 1)n$ operations. Hence the total number of operations per iteration is of $O(n \log n)$ as ν is independent of n.

When $f_{\min} = 0$, the band preconditioner improves the condition number from $\kappa(S_n^{-1} T_n) = O(n^{2\nu})$ to $\kappa(E_n^{-1} T_n) = O(1)$. Since the number of iterations required to attain a given tolerance ϵ is bounded by [AB84, p. 26]

$$\frac{1}{2}\sqrt{\kappa(E_n^{-1} T_n)} \log\left(\frac{2}{\epsilon}\right) + 1,$$

the overall work required to attain the given tolerance is reduced from $O(n^{\nu+1} \log n)$ to $O(n \log n)$ operations. As for the storage, we just need an $n \times (2\nu + 1)$ matrix to hold the factors of the preconditioner E_n. Thus, the overall storage requirement in the CG method is about $(8 + \nu)n$. Finally, we remark that similar results hold when there are multiple points on $[-\pi, \pi]$ where f takes on its minimum value [Cha91].

5.5 TOEPLITZ-CIRCULANT PRECONDITIONERS

The main idea behind Thm. 5.4.2 is to approximate the given nonnegative generating function f by trigonometric polynomials that match the zeros of f. Clearly, any function g that matches the zeros of f and gives rise to Toeplitz matrices that are easily invertible can be considered too. This idea is exploited in [DiB95], [DFS93], [CT94], [CC96b]. In [CC96b], products of circulant matrices and band-Toeplitz matrices are considered as preconditioners for Toeplitz systems generated by nonnegative functions. The band-Toeplitz part of these *Toeplitz-circulant preconditioners* is to match the zeros of the given function, and the circulant part is to speed up the convergence rate of the algorithm. Instead of using powers of $2 - 2\cos\theta$ as in (5.7.1) to generate the band-Toeplitz part of the preconditioner, reference [CC96b] considers using powers of $1 - e^{i\theta}$. This results in preconditioners that can handle complex-valued generating functions with zeros of arbitrary order.

Theorem 5.5.1 (Toeplitz-Circulant Preconditioner). *Suppose that $f(z)$ is of the form*

$$f(z) = \left\{\prod_j (z - z_j)^{\ell_j}\right\} h(z), \quad \text{with} \quad z = e^{i\theta},$$

where z_j are the roots of $f(z)$ on $|z| = 1$ with order ℓ_j and $h(z)$ is a nonvanishing function on $|z| = 1$. Let $\{T_n\}$, $\{E_n\}$, and $\{G_n\}$ be sequences of Toeplitz matrices generated by f, $\prod_j (z - z_j)^{\ell_j}$, and h, respectively. Then the sequence of matrices $C(G_n) E_n^{-1} T_n$ has singular values clustered around 1 for all sufficiently large n.

Proof: By expanding the product $\prod_j (z - z_j)^{\ell_j}$ we see that the Toeplitz matrix E_n is a lower triangular matrix with bandwidth equal to $(\ell+1)$, where $\ell = \sum_j \ell_j$. Moreover, its main diagonal entry is 1 and therefore it is invertible for all n. We see that the matrix $T_n - E_n G_n$ only has nonzero entries in the first $l + 1$ rows. Hence it is clear that

$$T_n = E_n G_n + L_1,$$

where rank $L_1 \leq \ell + 1$. Therefore,

$$C(G_n)^{-1}E_n^{-1}T_n = C(G_n)^{-1}E_n^{-1}(E_n G_n + L_1) = C(G_n)^{-1}G_n + L_2, \quad (5.5.1)$$

where rank $L_2 \leq \ell$.

Since $h(z)$ has no zeros on $|z| = 1$, the matrices $C(G_n)^{-1}G_n$ have clustered singular values. In particular, we can write $C(G_n)^{-1}G_n = I + L_3 + U$, where U is a small norm matrix and rank L_3 is fixed independent of n. Hence (5.5.1) becomes

$$E_n^{-1}C(G_n)^{-1}T_n = I + L_4 + U,$$

where the rank of L_4 is again fixed independent of n. By using the Cauchy interlace theorem [Par80, p. 192] (see App. A) on

$$(E_n^{-1}C(G_n)^{-1}T_n)^*(E_n^{-1}C(G_n)^{-1}T_n) = (I + L_4 + U)^*(I + L_4 + U),$$

it is straightforward to show that $E_n^{-1}C(G_n)^{-1}T_n$ has singular values clustered around 1.

$\diamond$

In each iteration of the PCG method, we have to solve a linear system of the form $E_n C(G_n) y = r$. We first claim that $E_n C(G_n)$ is invertible for large n. As mentioned above, the Toeplitz matrix E_n is invertible for all n. Since h is a Wiener class function and has no zeros on $|z| = 1$, the invertibility of $C(G_n)$ for large n is guaranteed by Thm. 5.3.7. Hence $C(G_n)E_n$ is invertible for large n. Let us consider the cost of solving the system

$$C(G_n)E_n y = r.$$

As the matrix E_n is a lower triangular matrix with bandwidth $(\ell + 1)$, the system involving E_n can be solved by forward substitution and the cost is $O(\ell n)$ operations. Given any vector x, the matrix-vector product $C(G_n)x$ can be done by using FFTs in $O(n \log n)$ operations. Thus the system $C(G_n)E_n y = r$ can be solved in $O(n \log n) + O(\ell n)$ operations.

5.6 PRECONDITIONERS FOR STRUCTURED LINEAR SYSTEMS

We now study preconditioners for more general kinds of matrix structure.

5.6.1 Toeplitz-Like Systems

Let Z_n denote the $n \times n$ lower shift matrix whose entries are zero everywhere except for the 1's on the first subdiagonal, i.e.,

$$Z_n = \begin{bmatrix} 0 & 0 & \cdots & & 0 & 0 \\ 1 & 0 & 0 & & & 0 \\ \vdots & 1 & 0 & & \ddots & \vdots \\ 0 & & \ddots & & \ddots & 0 \\ 0 & 0 & \cdots & & 1 & 0 \end{bmatrix}.$$

Let A_n be an $n \times n$ structured matrix with respect to Z_n (cf. definition (1.2.4) in Ch. 1), say,

$$\nabla_{Z_n} A_n = A_n - Z_n A_n Z_n^* = GJG^*,$$

for some $n \times r$ generator matrix G and $r \times r$ signature matrix $J = (I_p \oplus -I_q)$. If we partition the columns of G into two sets $\{x_i\}_{i=0}^{p-1}$ and $\{y_i\}_{i=0}^{q-1}$,

$$G = \begin{bmatrix} x_0 & x_1 & \cdots & x_{p-1} & y_0 & y_1 & \cdots & y_{q-1} \end{bmatrix}, \quad p+q=r,$$

then we know from the representation (1.4.2) that we can express A_n as a linear combination of lower triangular Toeplitz matrices,

$$A_n = \sum_{i=0}^{p-1} \mathcal{L}_n(x_i)\mathcal{L}_n^*(x_i) - \sum_{i=0}^{q-1} \mathcal{L}_n(y_i)\mathcal{L}_n^*(y_i). \tag{5.6.1}$$

Here, the subscript n in $\mathcal{L}_n$ denotes the size $(n \times n)$ of the matrix.

For example, if $T_{m,n}$ is an $m \times n$ Toeplitz matrix with $m \geq n$, then $T_{m,n}^* T_{m,n}$ is in general not a Toeplitz matrix. However, $T_{m,n}^* T_{m,n}$ does have a small displacement rank, $r \leq 4$, and a displacement representation for $T_{m,n}^* T_{m,n}$ is

$$T_{m,n}^* T_{m,n} = \mathcal{L}_n(x_0)\mathcal{L}_n(x_0)^* - \mathcal{L}_n(y_0)\mathcal{L}_n(y_0)^* + \mathcal{L}_n(x_1)\mathcal{L}_n(x_1)^* - \mathcal{L}_n(y_1)\mathcal{L}_n(y_1)^*,$$

where

$$\begin{aligned} x_0 &= T_{m,n}^* T_{m,n} e_1 / \|T_{m,n} e_1\|, \\ x_1 &= [0, t_{-1}, t_{-2}, \ldots, t_{1-n}]^*, \\ y_0 &= Z_n Z_n^* x_0, \\ y_1 &= [0, t_{m-1}, t_{m-2}, \ldots, t_{m-n+1}]^*. \end{aligned}$$

For structured matrices as in (5.6.1), it was suggested in [CNP94b], [Huc94] to define the *displacement preconditioner* to be the circulant approximation of the factors in the displacement representation of A_n; i.e., the circulant approximation C of A_n is

$$C(A_n) = \sum_{i=0}^{p-1} C(\mathcal{L}_n(x_i))C^*(\mathcal{L}_n(x_i)) - \sum_{i=0}^{q-1} C(\mathcal{L}_n(y_i))C^*(\mathcal{L}_n(y_i)).$$

Here, $C(X_n)$ denotes the optimal $n \times n$ circulant approximation to X_n in the Frobenius norm; see (5.3.18). In the following, we assume that the generating function f of $T_{m,n}$ is in the Wiener class; i.e., the diagonals of $T_{m,n}$ are absolutely summable:

$$\sum_{j=-\infty}^{\infty} |t_j| \leq \gamma < \infty. \tag{5.6.2}$$

For the case of $T_{m,n}^* T_{m,n}$, it can be verfied that we can write

$$T_{m,n}^* T_{m,n} = T + \mathcal{L}_n(x_1)\mathcal{L}_n^*(x_1) - \mathcal{L}_n(y_1)\mathcal{L}_n^*(y_1), \tag{5.6.3}$$

where T is a Hermitian Toeplitz matrix with

$$T e_1 \equiv \begin{bmatrix} t_0 \\ t_1 \\ \vdots \\ t_{n-1} \end{bmatrix} = T_{m,n}^* T_{m,n} e_1. \tag{5.6.4}$$

Section 5.6. Preconditioners for Structured Linear Systems

Using this representation, it was proposed in [CNP94b] to define the displacement preconditioner for $T_{m,n}^* T_{m,n}$ to be P_n:

$$P_n = C(T) + C(\mathcal{L}_n(x_1))C^*(\mathcal{L}_n(x_1)).$$

In the following, we show that P_n is a good preconditioner.

For simplicity, we will denote by U_i Hermitian matrices with small rank and by V_i Hermitian matrices with small norm. More precisely, given any $\epsilon > 0$, there exist integers N and $M > 0$ such that when n, the size of the matrices U_i and V_i, is larger than N, the rank of U_i is bounded by M and $||V_i||_2 < \epsilon$.

Lemma 5.6.1 (A Decomposition Result). *It holds that*

$$\mathcal{L}_n(y_1)\mathcal{L}_n^*(y_1) = U_1 + V_1. \tag{5.6.5}$$

Proof: Since the sequence $\{t_j\}_{j=-\infty}^{\infty}$ is absolutely summable, for any given ϵ, we can choose $N > 0$ such that

$$\sum_{j>N} |t_j| < \epsilon.$$

Partition $\mathcal{L}_n(y_1)$ as $R_N + W_N$, where the first N columns of R_N are the first N columns of $\mathcal{L}_n(y_1)$ with the remaining columns zero vectors. Then R_N is a matrix of rank N and

$$||W_N||_1 = \sum_{j=m-n+N+1}^{m-1} |t_j| \leq \sum_{j=N+1}^{m-1} |t_j| < \epsilon.$$

Thus

$$\mathcal{L}_n(y_1)\mathcal{L}_n^*(y_1) = (R_N + W_N)(R_N + W_N)^* = U_1 + V_1,$$

where

$$\operatorname{rank} U_3 = \operatorname{rank}(R_N W_N^* + W_N R_N^* + R_N R_N^*) \leq 2N$$

and

$$||V_3||_2 \leq ||W_N W_N^*||_2 \leq \epsilon^2.$$

$\diamond$

We note from Lemma 5.6.1 that it suffices to show that the matrix

$$P_n - T_{m,n}^* T_{m,n} = \{C(T) - T\} + \{C(\mathcal{L}_n(x_1))C^*(\mathcal{L}_n(x_1)) - \mathcal{L}_n(x_1)\mathcal{L}_n^*(x_1)\} + \mathcal{L}_n(y_1)\mathcal{L}_n^*(y_1)$$

is the sum of a matrix of low rank and a matrix of small norm [CNP94b].

Theorem 5.6.1 (Displacement Preconditioner). *Let f be a function in the Wiener class. Then the spectra of $P_n - T_{m,n}^* T_{m,n}$ are clustered around zero for large n.*

Proof: The generating function of $T_{m,n}$ is in the Wiener class; therefore, the generating function of T is also in the Wiener class. In fact,

$$||Te_1||_1 = ||T_{m,n}^* T_{m,n} e_1||_1 \leq ||T_{m,n}^*||_1 ||T_{m,n} e_1||_1 \leq \gamma^2 < \infty. \tag{5.6.6}$$

According to Thm. 5.3.3, we have

$$C(T) - T = U_2 + V_2. \tag{5.6.7}$$

Next we show that
$$C(\mathcal{L}(x_1))C^*(\mathcal{L}(x_1)) - \mathcal{L}(x_1)\mathcal{L}^*(x_1) = U_3 + V_3. \tag{5.6.8}$$

The generating function of $\mathcal{L}_n(x_1)$ is given by
$$g(\theta) = \sum_{j=-\infty}^{-1} t_j e^{ij\theta}, \tag{5.6.9}$$

which is a function in the Wiener class. Equation (5.6.8) now follows by Lemma 5 of [CNP94a] or using the arguments in Thm. 5.3.3. Combining (5.6.7), (5.6.8), and (5.6.5), we see that
$$P_n - T_{m,n}^* T_{m,n} = C(T) - T + C(\mathcal{L}_n(x_1))C^*(\mathcal{L}_n(x_1)) - \mathcal{L}_n(x_1)\mathcal{L}_n^*(x_1) + \mathcal{L}_n(y_1)\mathcal{L}_n^*(y_1)$$

is the sum of a matrix of low rank and a matrix of small norm.

$\diamond$

In order to show that $\|P_n^{-1}\|_2$ is uniformly bounded, we need the following two lemmas. These two lemmas state some properties of the optimal circulant preconditioner for non-Hermitian Toeplitz matrices. Their proofs can be found in [CY93] and [CJY91b], respectively.

Lemma 5.6.2 (Norm Bounds for the Optimal Preconditioner). *Let $f \in \mathcal{C}_{2\pi}$. Let $\{T_n\}$ be a sequence of Toeplitz matrices generated by f. Then we have*
$$\|C(T_n)\|_2 \leq 2\|f\|_\infty, \quad n = 1, 2, \ldots.$$

Moreover, if f has no zeros, i.e.,
$$|f|_{\min} \equiv \min_{\theta \in [-\pi, \pi]} |f(\theta)| > 0,$$

then, for all sufficiently large n, we also have
$$\|C(T_n)^{-1}\|_2 \leq 2 \left\| \frac{1}{f} \right\|_\infty.$$

$\diamond$

Lemma 5.6.3 (A Limit Result). *Let $\{T_n\}$ be a sequence of Toeplitz matrices with generating function in the Wiener class. Then*
$$\lim_{n \to \infty} \|C(T_n)C(T_n)^* - C(T_n T_n^*)\|_2 = 0.$$

$\diamond$

We now are ready to show that $\|P_n^{-1}\|_2$ is uniformly bounded [CNP94b].

Theorem 5.6.2 (Uniform Boundedness of P_n^{-1}). *Let the generating function f of $T_{m,n}$ be a Wiener class function that satisfies*
$$\min_{\theta \in [-\pi, \pi]} |f(\theta)| \geq \delta > 0. \tag{5.6.10}$$

Then $\|P_n\|_2 \leq 6\gamma^2$ for all n and $\|P_n^{-1}\|_2$ is uniformly bounded for n sufficiently large.

Section 5.6. Preconditioners for Structured Linear Systems   137

Proof: See App. 5.B.

$\diamond$

By combining the above results we can show that the spectra of the preconditioned matrices $P_n^{-1} T_{m,n}^* T_{m,n}$ are clustered around 1. Thus the CG method, when applied to solving the preconditioned system, converges superlinearly. Numerical experiments in [CNP94b] show the effectiveness of the preconditioners for Toeplitz least-squares problems.

5.6.2 Toeplitz-Plus-Hankel Systems

The systems of linear equations with Toeplitz-plus-Hankel coefficient matrices arise in many signal processing applications. For example, the inverse scattering problem can be formulated as Toeplitz-plus-Hankel systems of equations [GL55]. A Hankel matrix is one with constant elements along its antidiagonals, say, $[H_n]_{i,j} = h_{n+1-i-j}$,

$$H_n = \begin{bmatrix} h_0 & h_1 & \cdots & h_{n-2} & h_{n-1} \\ h_1 & h_2 & \cdot\cdot\cdot & \cdot\cdot\cdot & h_n \\ \vdots & \cdot\cdot\cdot & \cdot\cdot\cdot & \cdot\cdot\cdot & \vdots \\ h_{n-2} & \cdot\cdot\cdot & \cdot\cdot\cdot & \cdot\cdot\cdot & h_{2n-2} \\ h_{n-1} & h_n & \cdots & h_{2n-2} & h_{2n-1} \end{bmatrix}. \quad (5.6.11)$$

Let J_n be an $n \times n$ matrix with 1's along the secondary diagonal and zeros elsewhere, i.e.,

$$J_n = \begin{bmatrix} 0 & 0 & \cdots & 0 & 1 \\ 0 & 0 & \cdot\cdot\cdot & 1 & 0 \\ \vdots & \cdot\cdot\cdot & \cdot\cdot\cdot & \cdot\cdot\cdot & \vdots \\ 0 & 1 & \cdot\cdot\cdot & \cdot\cdot\cdot & 0 \\ 1 & 0 & \cdots & 0 & 0 \end{bmatrix}.$$

It is easy to see that the product of J_n and H_n and the product of H_n and J_n both give Toeplitz matrices:

$$J_n H_n = \begin{bmatrix} h_{n-1} & h_n & \cdots & h_{2n-2} & h_{2n-1} \\ h_{n-2} & h_{n-1} & h_n & & h_{2n-2} \\ \vdots & h_{n-2} & h_{n-1} & \ddots & \vdots \\ h_1 & & \ddots & \ddots & h_n \\ h_0 & h_1 & \cdots & h_{n-2} & h_{n-1} \end{bmatrix},$$

or

$$H_n J_n = \begin{bmatrix} h_{n-1} & h_{n-2} & \cdots & h_1 & h_0 \\ h_n & h_{n-1} & h_{n-2} & & h_1 \\ \vdots & h_n & h_{n-1} & \ddots & \vdots \\ h_{2n-2} & & & \ddots & h_{-1} \\ h_{2n-1} & h_{2n-2} & \cdots & h_n & h_{n-1} \end{bmatrix}.$$

(We remark that premultiplying J_n to a vector v corresponds to reversing the order of the elements in v.) Since

$$H_n v = H_n J_n J_n v$$

and $H_n J_n$ is a Toeplitz matrix, the Hankel matrix-vector products $H_n v$ can be done in $O(n \log n)$ using FFTs as shown in as in Sec. 5.3.3.

A Toeplitz-plus-Hankel matrix can be expressed as $A_n = T_n + H_n = T_n + J_n J_n H_n$. Given circulant preconditioners $C_n^{(1)}$ and $C_n^{(2)}$ for Toeplitz matrices T_n and $J_n H_n$, respectively, it was proposed in [KK93a] to use

$$P_n = C_n^{(1)} + J_n C_n^{(2)} \tag{5.6.12}$$

as a preconditioner for the Toeplitz-plus-Hankel matrix $T_n + H_n$.

With the equality $J_n^2 = I_n$ and (5.6.12), we have

$$P_n z = C_n^{(1)} z + J_n C_n^{(2)} J_n J_n z = v, \tag{5.6.13}$$

which is equivalent to

$$J_n P_n z = J_n C_n^{(1)} J_n J_n z + C_n^{(2)} z = J_n v. \tag{5.6.14}$$

Since $C_n^{(1)}$ and $C_n^{(2)}$ are circulant,

$$J_n C_n^{(1)} J_n = C_n^{(1)T} \quad \text{and} \quad J_n C_n^{(2)} J_n = C_n^{(2)T}.$$

By multiplying (5.6.13) with $C_n^{(1)T}$ and (5.6.14) with $C_n^{(2)T}$, we can write the difference between the two resulting equations as

$$(C_n^{(1)T} C_n^{(1)} - C_n^{(2)T} C_n^{(2)}) z = C_n^{(1)T} v - C_n^{(2)T} J_n v. \tag{5.6.15}$$

The solution of $z = P_n^{-1} v$ can also be determined from (5.6.15). We note that the matrix $C_n^{(1)T} C_n^{(1)} - C_n^{(2)T} C_n^{(2)}$ is circulant and therefore that $P_n^{-1} v$ can be found efficiently via FFT with $O(n \log n)$ operations.

For Toeplitz matrices T_n and $J_n H_n$ generated by rational functions, it was shown in [KK93a] that the spectra of the preconditioned Toeplitz-plus-Hankel matrices are clustered around 1.

Theorem 5.6.3 (Preconditioned Toeplitz-plus-Hankel Matrices). *Let $T_n + H_n$ be a real symmetric $n \times n$ matrix. Let the generating functions of T_n and $J_n H_n$ be*

$$f_1(\theta) = \frac{f_{1,a}(\theta)}{f_{1,b}(\theta)} + \frac{f_{1,c}(\theta)}{f_{1,d}(\theta)} = \frac{\sum_{k=0}^{\alpha_1} a_{1,k} e^{-\hat{i}k\theta}}{\sum_{k=0}^{\beta_1} b_{1,k} e^{-\hat{i}k\theta}} + \frac{\sum_{k=0}^{\gamma_1} c_{1,k} e^{\hat{i}k\theta}}{\sum_{k=0}^{\delta_1} d_{1,k} e^{\hat{i}k\theta}}$$

and

$$f_2(\theta) = \frac{f_{2,a}(\theta)}{f_{2,b}(\theta)} + \frac{f_{2,c}(\theta)}{f_{2,d}(\theta)} = \frac{\sum_{k=0}^{\alpha_2} a_{2,k} e^{-\hat{i}k\theta}}{\sum_{k=0}^{\beta_2} b_{2,k} e^{-\hat{i}k\theta}} + \frac{\sum_{k=0}^{\gamma_2} c_{2,k} e^{\hat{i}k\theta}}{\sum_{k=0}^{\delta_2} d_{2,k} e^{\hat{i}k\theta}}$$

with $a_{i,\alpha_i} b_{i,\beta_i} c_{i,\gamma_i} d_{i,\delta_i} \neq 0$, $b_{i,0} = 1$, $d_{i,0} = 1$, polynomials $f_{i,a}(\theta)$ and $f_{i,b}(\theta)$, and $f_{i,c}(\theta)$ and $f_{i,d}(\theta)$ have no common zeros. If

$$||\lambda_k(C_n^{(1)})|^2 - |\lambda_k(C_n^{(2)})|^2| \geq \mu > 0, \quad 1 \leq k \leq n,$$

where μ is a constant independent of n, then the spectra of $P_n^{-1}(T_n + H_n)$ are clustered around 1 and the number of outliers is bounded by

$$\eta = \max\{\max\{\alpha_1, \beta_1\} + \beta_2, \max\{\alpha_2, \beta_2\} + \beta_1\}$$
$$+ \max\{\max\{\gamma_1, \delta_1\} + \delta_2, \max\{\gamma_2, \delta_2\} + \delta_1\} - \eta_c,$$

where η_c is the number of common zeros in $f_{1,b} f_{1,d}$ and $f_{2,b} f_{2,d}$.

◇

Section 5.7. Toeplitz-Plus-Band Systems

Using Thm. 5.3.3, the following result can be established.

Theorem 5.6.4. *Let $T_n + H_n$ be a real symmetric $n \times n$ matrix. Let the generating functions of T_n and $J_n H_n$ be f_1 and f_2, respectively. Let f_1 and f_2 be functions in the Wiener class. If*

$$||\lambda_k(C_n^{(1)})|^2 - |\lambda_k(C_n^{(2)})|^2| \geq \mu > 0, \quad 1 \leq k \leq n,$$

where μ is a constant independent of n, then the spectra of $P_n^{-1}(T_n + H_n)$ are clustered around 1.

Proof: Recall from (5.6.15) that $P_n z = v$ is equivalent to

$$(C_n^{(1)T} C_n^{(1)} - C_n^{(2)T} C_n^{(2)})z = C_n^{(1)T} v - C_n^{(2)T} J_n v.$$

For any given n, $\|C_n^{(1)}\|_1$ and $\|C_n^{(2)}\|_\infty$ are both bounded. As a consequence, $\|C_n^{(1)T}\|_2$ is also bounded. Similar results hold for $C_n^{(2)T}$. Thus the right-hand sides of (5.6.15) are bounded. Under the assumption, the magnitude of any eigenvalue of $(C_n^{(1)T} C_n^{(1)} - C_n^{(2)T} C_n^{(2)})$ is also bounded. Therefore, $\|P_n^{-1}\|_2$ is bounded and the preconditioner P is invertible.

According to the definitions, the difference matrix $P_n - T_n - H_n$ can be written as

$$P_n - T_n - H_n = (C_n^{(1)} - T_n) + J_n(C_n^{(2)} - J_n H_n).$$

By Theorem 5.3.3, the spectra of the matrices $C_n^{(1)} - T_n$ and and $C_n^{(2)} - J_n H_n$ are clustered around zero for large n. Hence the result follows.

◇

With the above spectral properties of preconditioned Toeplitz-plus-Hankel matrices, various preconditioned iterative methods including GMRES and CGS [Saa96] can be applied effectively. These Toeplitz-plus-Hankel systems can be solved in a finite number of iterations independent of n so that total operations required are $O(n \log n)$.

5.7 TOEPLITZ-PLUS-BAND SYSTEMS

In this subsection, we consider the solution of systems of the form $(T_n + B_n)x = b$, where T_n is an $n \times n$ Hermitian Toeplitz matrix and B_n is an $n \times n$ Hermitian band matrix with bandwidth $2b + 1$ independent of n. These systems appear in solving Fredholm integrodifferential equations of the form

$$L\{x(\theta)\} + \int_\alpha^\beta K(\phi - \theta)x(\phi)d\phi = b(\theta).$$

Here $x(\theta)$ is the unknown function to be found, $K(\theta)$ is a convolution kernel, L is a differential operator, and $b(\theta)$ is a given function. After discretization, K will lead to a Toeplitz matrix, L to a band matrix, and $b(\theta)$ to the right-hand side vector [DM85, p. 343]. Toeplitz-plus-band matrices also appear in signal processing literature and have been referred to as peripheral innovation matrices [CKM82].

Unlike Toeplitz systems, there exist no fast direct solvers for solving Toeplitz-plus-band systems. It is mainly because the displacement rank of the matrix $T_n + B_n$

can take any value between 0 and n. Hence, fast Toeplitz solvers that are based on small displacement rank of the matrices cannot be applied. CG methods with circulant preconditioners do not work for Toeplitz-plus-band systems either. In fact, Strang's circulant preconditioner is not even defined for non-Toeplitz matrices. T. Chan's circulant preconditioner, while defined for $T_n + B_n$, does not work well when the eigenvalues of B_n are not clustered; see [CN93a]. Also, the matrix $C(T_n) + B_n$ cannot be used as a preconditioner for it cannot be inverted easily.

In [CN93a] it was proposed to use the matrix $E_n + B_n$ to precondition $T_n + B_n$, where E_n is the band-Toeplitz preconditioner.

Theorem 5.7.1 (Toeplitz-plus-Band Preconditioner). *Let f be a nonnegative piecewise continuous real-valued function defined on $[-\pi, \pi]$. Let T_n be generated by f. Suppose that $f(\theta) - f_{\min}$ has a unique zero of order 2ν at $\theta = \theta_0$. Let $\{E_n\}$ be the sequence of Toeplitz matrices generated by the function*

$$b_\nu(\theta) = [2 - 2\cos(\theta - \theta_0)]^\nu + f_{\min}. \quad (5.7.1)$$

Then $\kappa((E_n + B_n)^{-1}(T_n + B_n))$ is uniformly bounded for all $n > 0$. ◇

Note that E_n is a band matrix with bandwidth $2\nu + 1$ and its diagonals can be obtained by using Pascal's triangle. The band system $(E_n + B_n)y = z$ can be solved by using any band matrix solver (see, e.g., [GV96], [Wri91]). Let

$$\gamma = \max\{\nu, b\}.$$

The cost of factorizing $E_n + B_n$ is about $\frac{1}{2}\gamma^2 n$ operations, and then each subsequent solve requires an extra $(2\gamma + 1)n$ operations. Hence, the total number of operations per iteration is of $O(n \log n)$ as ν is independent of n. The number of iterations required to attain a given tolerance ϵ is bounded by

$$\frac{1}{2}\sqrt{\kappa((E_n + B_n)^{-1}(T_n + B_n))} \log\left(\frac{2}{\epsilon}\right) + 1;$$

see, for instance, [AB84, p. 26]. The overall work required to attain the given tolerance is reduced from $O(n^{\nu+1} \log n)$ to $O(n \log n)$ operations. As for the storage, we just need an $n \times (2\gamma + 1)$ matrix to hold the factors of the preconditioner $E_n + B_n$. Thus, the overall storage requirement in the CG method is about $(8 + \gamma)n$.

5.8 APPLICATIONS

We now provide a brief overview of several examples where structured matrices of the form studied earlier in this chapter arise.

5.8.1 Linear-Phase Filtering

Finite impulse response linear-phase filters are commonly used in signal processing. Such filters are especially important for applications where frequency dispersion due to nonlinear phase is harmful, such as in speech processing. In this case, the impulse responses of the filters can be found by solving a Toeplitz-plus-Hankel least-squares problem of the form

$$\min_b \|d - (T + H)b\|_2,$$

where $T+H$ is a rectangular Toeplitz-plus-Hankel matrix; see [Mar80], [Mar81], [Mar82], [Yag91], [HY93]. The coefficient matrix of the corresponding normal equations can be written as

$$(T+H)^*(T+H) = \tilde{T}_n + \tilde{H}_n - V_n^{(1)} - V_n^{(2)} - V_n^{(3)} - V_n^{(4)},$$

where $\tilde{T}_n$ is a Toeplitz matrix, $\tilde{H}$ is a Hankel matrix, and $\{V_n^{(i)}\}_{i=1}^4$ are non-Toeplitz and non-Hankel matrices. In [Ng94], the optimal circulant preconditioner $C(\tilde{T}_n)$ is used as a preconditioner for the problem.

This preconditioner is different from that proposed in [KK93a] for Toeplitz-plus-Hankel systems and which we studied earlier. The preconditioner in [KK93a] basically corresponds to combining the circulant approximations of the Toeplitz and Hankel matrices. Also, under the assumptions in [KK93a], the spectrum of the Hankel matrix is not clustered around zero.

The motivation behind the preconditioner $C(\tilde{T}_n)$ suggested above is that the Toeplitz matrix $\tilde{T}_n$ is a sample autocorrelation matrix, which intuitively should be a good estimate of the autocorrelation matrix of the corresponding discrete-time stationary process, provided that a sufficiently large number of data samples is used. Moreover, under practical signal processing assumptions, the spectrum of the Hankel matrix $\tilde{H}_n$ is clustered around zero. Hence it suffices to approximate $\tilde{T}_n$ by a circulant preconditioner.

To prove convergence, the following practical assumptions on the random process are made [Ng94] (for instance, an autoregressive (AR) progress):

- The process is stationary with constant mean μ.

- The spectral density function of the process is positive and in the Wiener class.

- There exist positive constants β_1 and β_2 such that

$$\text{Var}\left(\frac{1}{m}\sum_{j=1}^{m-k} x(j)\right) \leq \frac{\beta_1}{m}, \quad k = 0, 1, 2, \ldots, m-1,$$

and

$$\text{Var}\left(\frac{1}{m}\sum_{j=1}^{m-k} [x(j) - \mu][x(j+k) - \mu]\right) \leq \frac{\beta_2}{m}, \quad k = 0, 1, 2, \ldots, m-1.$$

Here, the notation $\text{Var}(\cdot)$ denotes the variance of the random variable. We note that the positiveness of the spectral density function can be guaranteed by the causality of the process [BD91, p. 85], whereas the absolute summability of the autocovariances can be assured by the invertibility of the process [BD91, p. 86]. With these assumptions, it can be shown that the spectra of the preconditioned matrices $C(\tilde{T}_n)^{-1}((T+H)^*(T+H))$ are clustered around 1 with probability 1, provided that a sufficiently large number of data samples is taken [Ng94].

Theorem 5.8.1 (Spectra for Preconditioned Toeplitz-plus-Hankel). *Let the discrete-time process satisfy the above assumptions. Then for any given $\epsilon > 0$ and $0 < \eta < 1$, there exist positive integers ρ_1 and ρ_2 such that for $n > \rho_1$, the probability that at most ρ_2 eigenvalues of the matrix $I - c(\tilde{T}_n)^{-1}((T+H)^*(T+H))$ have absolute value greater than ϵ is greater than $1 - \eta$, provided that $m = O(n^{3+\nu})$ with $\nu > 0$.*

◊

Hence, when we apply the CG method to the preconditioned system, the method converges superlinearly with probability 1. Since the data matrix $T + H$ is an $m \times n$ rectangular matrix, the normal equations and the circulant preconditioner can be formed in $O(m \log n)$ operations. Once they are formed, the cost per iteration of the PCG method is $O(n \log n)$ operations. Therefore, the total work for obtaining the filter coefficients to a given accuracy is of $O((m + n) \log n)$.

5.8.2 Numerical Solutions of Biharmonic Equations

Boundary value problems for the biharmonic equation in two dimensions arise in the computation of the Airy stress function for plane stress problems [Mus53] and in steady Stokes flow of highly viscous fluids [Mil68, Ch. 22]. The integral equations method is a popular choice for the numerical solution of these equations [GGM92]. The application of conformal mapping to this problem, although classical, is less well known [Mus53]. Unlike the Laplace equation, the biharmonic equation is not preserved under conformal transplantation. However, a biharmonic function and its boundary values can be represented in terms of the analytic Goursat functions, and this representation can be transplanted with a conformal map to a computational region, such as a disk, an ellipse, or an annulus, where the boundary value problem can be solved more easily.

We wish to find a function $u = u(\eta, \mu)$ that satisfies the biharmonic equation

$$\Delta^2 u = 0$$

for $\zeta = \eta + \hat{\imath}\mu \in \Omega$, where Ω is a region with a smooth boundary Γ and u satisfies the boundary conditions

$$u_\eta = G_1 \quad \text{and} \quad u_\mu = G_2$$

on Γ. The solution u can be represented as

$$u(\zeta) = \text{Re}(\zeta^* \phi(\zeta) + \chi(\zeta)),$$

where $\phi(\zeta)$ and $\chi(\zeta)$ are analytic functions in Ω, known as the *Goursat functions*. Letting $G = G_1 + \hat{\imath}G_2$, the boundary conditions become

$$\phi(\zeta) + \zeta(\phi'(\zeta))^* + (\psi(\zeta))^* = G(\zeta), \quad \zeta \in \Gamma, \tag{5.8.1}$$

where $\psi(\zeta) = \chi'(\zeta)$. The problem is to find ϕ and ψ satisfying (5.8.1).

Let $\zeta = f(z)$ be the conformal map from the unit disc to Ω, fixing $f(0) = 0 \in \Omega$. Then with

$$d(z) \triangleq f(z)/(f'(z))^*, \quad \phi(z) \triangleq \phi(f(z)), \quad \psi(z) \triangleq \psi(f(z)), \quad G(z) \triangleq G(f(z)),$$

(5.8.1) transplants to the unit disc as

$$\phi(z) + d(z)(\phi'(z))^* + (\psi(z))^* = G(z), \quad |z| = 1. \tag{5.8.2}$$

Let

$$\phi(z) = \sum_{k=1}^{\infty} a_k z^k \quad \text{and} \quad \psi(z) = \sum_{k=0}^{\infty} b_k z^k.$$

The problem now is to find the a_k's and the b_k's. For $|z| = 1$, define the Fourier series

$$d(z) \triangleq f(z)/(f'(z))^* = \sum_{k=-\infty}^{\infty} h_k z^k, \quad G(z) = \sum_{k=-\infty}^{\infty} A_k z^k. \tag{5.8.3}$$

Substituting (5.8.3) into (5.8.2) gives a linear system of equations for the a_k's and b_k's,

$$a_j + \sum_{k=1}^{\infty} k a_k^* h_{k+j-1} = A_j, \quad j = 1, 2, 3, \ldots, \tag{5.8.4}$$

$$\overline{b}_j + \sum_{k=1}^{\infty} k a_k^* h_{k-j-1} = A_{-j}, \quad j = 0, 1, 2, \ldots. \tag{5.8.5}$$

If (5.8.4) is solved for the a_k's, then the b_k's can be computed easily from (5.8.5). These systems are derived in [Mus53]. We note that the coefficient matrix of the (infinite) linear system in (5.8.4) is of the form $I + HD$, where I is the identity matrix, D is a diagonal matrix, and H is a Hankel matrix. We remark that HD actually can be represented as a compact operator with a one-dimensional null space; see [CDH97].

In [CDH97], the linear system in (5.8.4) was truncated after n terms and solved efficiently using the CG method (up to the null vector). To solve the discrete system, the major computations that are required at each iteration are the matrix-vector products $H_n v$ for arbitrary vectors v. We note that the Hankel matrix-vector products $H_n v$ can be done in $O(n \log n)$ using FFTs.

For the convergence rate of the CG method, estimates are given in [CDH98] for the decay rates of the eigenvalues of the compact operators when the boundary curve is analytic or in a Hölder class. These estimates are used to give detailed bounds for the r-superlinear convergence which do not depend on the right-hand side. It follows that the CG method, when applied to solve this kind of Hankel system, converges sufficiently fast [CDH98].

Theorem 5.8.2. *Assume that the coefficient matrix A_∞ in the infinite linear system (5.8.4) is positive semidefinite with exactly one null vector v. Let*

$$v \triangleq [v_1, v_2, \ldots, v_n, v_{n+1}, \ldots]^T,$$
$$v^{(n)} \triangleq [v_1, v_2, \ldots, v_n]^T,$$
$$v^{(n)\perp} \triangleq \{x \in \mathbb{R}^{n \times 1} \text{ such that } x^T v^{(n)} = 0\}.$$

Then, for large n, the error vector $x - x_q$ at the qth step of the CG method applied to $v^{(n)\perp}$ satisfies the following estimates.

(i) *If Γ is analytic, there is an r, $0 < r < 1$, such that*

$$|||x - x_{4q}||| \leq C^q r^{q^2} |||x - x_0|||.$$

(ii) *If Γ is of class $C^{l+1,\alpha}$, $l \geq 2$, $0 < \alpha < 1$, then*

$$|||x - x_{4q}||| \leq \frac{C^q}{((q-1)!)^{2(l-2+\alpha)}} |||x - x_0|||.$$

Here C is a constant that depends on the conformal map and the notation $||| \cdot |||$ stands for

$$|||v|||^2 \triangleq v^* A v.$$

◇

The proof follows closely that of Thm. 5.3.4. In case A_∞ is not semidefinite we can solve the normal equations by the CG method. It is clear that $(I_n + A_n)^2$ will then be positive definite on $\underline{v}^{(n)\perp}$. A similar result for the normal equations can be established. For a discussion of the numerical conformal mapping methods used, see [CDH97].

5.8.3 Queueing Networks with Batch Arrivals

In this subsection, we consider using the PCG method with the Toeplitz-circulant preconditioners of Sec. 5.5 for solving the stationary probability distribution vectors for Markovian queueing models with batch arrivals. This kind of queueing system occurs in many applications, such as telecommunication networks [Oda91] and loading dock models [Sei90]. We will see that the generator matrices of these systems have a near-Toeplitz structure and preconditioners are constructed by exploiting this fact.

Let us first introduce the following queueing parameters. (Definitions of queueing theory terminologies used below can be found in [Coo72].) The input of the queueing system will be an exogenous Poisson batch arrival process with mean batch interarrival time λ^{-1}. For $k \geq 1$, denote λ_k to be the batch arrival rate for batches with size k. We note that

$$\lambda_k = \lambda p_k, \qquad (5.8.6)$$

where p_k is the probability that the arrival batch size is k. Clearly we have

$$\sum_{k=1}^{\infty} \lambda_k = \lambda. \qquad (5.8.7)$$

The number of servers in the queueing system will be denoted by s. The service time of each server is independent of the others and is exponentially distributed with mean μ^{-1}. The waiting room is of size $(n - s - 1)$ and the queueing discipline is blocked customers cleared. If the arrival batch size is larger than the number of waiting places left, then only part of the arrival batch will be accepted; the other customers will be treated as overflows and will be cleared from the system.

By ordering the state-space lexicographically, i.e., the ith variable corresponds to the state where there are $(i - 1)$ customers in the system, the queueing model can be characterized by the infinitesimal generator matrix

$$A_n = \begin{bmatrix} \lambda & -\mu & 0 & 0 & 0 & \cdots & 0 \\ -\lambda_1 & \lambda+\mu & -2\mu & 0 & 0 & \cdots & 0 \\ -\lambda_2 & -\lambda_1 & \lambda+2\mu & \ddots & \ddots & & \vdots \\ \vdots & -\lambda_2 & \ddots & \ddots & -s\mu & \ddots & \\ & \vdots & \ddots & \ddots & \lambda+s\mu & \ddots & 0 \\ -\lambda_{n-2} & -\lambda_{n-3} & & \vdots & & \lambda+s\mu & -s\mu \\ -r_1 & -r_2 & -r_3 & \cdots & -r_{s+1} & \cdots & s\mu \end{bmatrix},$$

where r_i are such that each column sum of A_n is zero [Sei90].

Clearly A_n has zero column sum, positive diagonal entries, and nonpositive off diagonal entries. Moreover, the matrix A_n is irreducible. In fact, if $\lambda_i = 0$ for all $i = 1, \ldots, n - 2$, then $r_1 = \lambda$ and the matrix is irreducible. If the λ_i's are not all zero, say, λ_j is the first nonzero λ_i, then $r_{n-j} = \lambda$, and hence A_n is also irreducible. From Perron and Frobenius theory [Var63, p. 30], A_n has a one-dimensional nullspace with a positive null vector.

The stationary probability distribution vector p of the queueing system is the normalized null vector of the generator matrix A_n given above. Much useful information about the queueing system, such as the blocking probability and the expected waiting time of customers, can be obtained from p. Since A_n has a one-dimensional nullspace,

Section 5.8. Applications

p can be found by deleting the last column and the last row of A_n and solving the $(n-1) \times (n-1)$ reduced linear system $Q_{n-1} y = (0, \ldots, 0, s\mu)^T$. After obtaining y, the distribution vector p can then be obtained by normalizing the vector $(y^T, 1)^T$.

Thus let us concentrate on solving nonhomogeneous systems of the form

$$Q_n x = b, \qquad (5.8.8)$$

where

$$Q_n = \begin{bmatrix} \lambda & -\mu & 0 & 0 & 0 & \cdots & 0 \\ -\lambda_1 & \lambda+\mu & -2\mu & 0 & 0 & \cdots & 0 \\ -\lambda_2 & -\lambda_1 & \lambda+2\mu & \ddots & \ddots & & \vdots \\ \vdots & -\lambda_2 & \ddots & \ddots & -s\mu & \ddots & \\ & \vdots & \ddots & \ddots & \lambda+s\mu & \ddots & 0 \\ -\lambda_{n-2} & -\lambda_{n-3} & & \ddots & \ddots & \ddots & -s\mu \\ -\lambda_{n-1} & -\lambda_{n-2} & & \cdots & -\lambda_2 & -\lambda_1 & \lambda+s\mu \end{bmatrix}. \qquad (5.8.9)$$

Notice that if all of the λ_i, $i = 1, \ldots, n-1$, are zeros, then Q_n will be a bidiagonal matrix and can be inverted easily. Therefore, in the following, we assume that at least one of the λ_i is nonzero. Then clearly, Q_n^T is an irreducibly diagonally dominant matrix. In particular, if the system (5.8.8) is solved by classical iterative methods such as the Jacobi or the Gauss–Seidel methods, both methods will converge for arbitrary initial guesses; see for instance [Var63, Thm. 3.4].

We see that the costs per iteration of the Jacobi and the Gauss–Seidel methods are $O(n \log n)$ and $O(n^2)$, respectively. The memory requirement is $O(n)$ for both methods. We remark that the system (5.8.8) can also be solved by Gaussian elimination in $O(n^2)$ operations with $O(n^2)$ memory. In the remainder of this subsection, we are interested in solving (5.8.8) by the PCG method. We will see that the cost per iteration of the method is $O(n \log n)$ and the memory requirement is $O(n)$, the same as those of the Jacobi method.

However, we are able to show that if s is independent of n, then with the Toeplitz-circulant preconditioner, the PCG method converges superlinearly for all sufficiently large n. In particular, the method converges in a finite number of steps independent of the queue size n. Therefore, the total cost of finding the steady-state probability distribution is $O(n \log n)$ operations.

We observe that in the single server case, i.e., when $s = 1$, the matrix Q_n given above differs from a lower Hessenberg Toeplitz matrix by only its $(1,1)$ entry. In general, Q_n can be written as

$$Q_n = T_n + R_n, \qquad (5.8.10)$$

where T_n is a Toeplitz matrix

$$T_n = \begin{bmatrix} \lambda+s\mu & -s\mu & 0 & 0 & 0 & \cdots & 0 \\ -\lambda_1 & \lambda+s\mu & -s\mu & 0 & 0 & \cdots & 0 \\ -\lambda_2 & -\lambda_1 & \lambda+s\mu & \ddots & \ddots & & \vdots \\ \vdots & -\lambda_2 & \ddots & \ddots & -s\mu & \ddots & \\ & \vdots & \ddots & \ddots & \lambda+s\mu & \ddots & 0 \\ -\lambda_{n-2} & & & \ddots & \ddots & \ddots & -s\mu \\ -\lambda_{n-1} & -\lambda_{n-2} & & \cdots & -\lambda_2 & -\lambda_1 & \lambda+s\mu \end{bmatrix}$$

and R_n is a matrix of rank s.

From the above expression for T_n, we see that T_n is generated by $g(z)$ given by

$$g(z) = -s\mu \frac{1}{z} + \lambda + s\mu - \sum_{k=1}^{\infty} \lambda_k z^k \qquad (5.8.11)$$

with $z = e^{i\theta}$. We note that by (5.8.7), $g(z)$ belongs to the Wiener class of functions defined on the unit circle $|z| = 1$. Unfortunately, it is also clear from (5.8.11) and (5.8.7) that $g(z)$ has a zero at $z = 1$. If we examine the real part of $g(z)$ on the unit circle $|z| = 1$, we see that

$$\text{Re}\{g(z)\} = -s\mu \cos\theta + \lambda + s\mu - \sum_{k=1}^{\infty} \lambda_k \cos(k\theta) \geq s\mu - s\mu \cos\theta.$$

Hence the zeros of $g(z)$ can only occur at $z = 1$. In particular, we can write

$$g(z) = (z-1)^\ell b(z), \qquad (5.8.12)$$

where ℓ is the order of the zero of $g(z)$ at $z = 1$ and $b(z)$ will have no zeros on the unit circle.

Using the idea developed in Sec. 5.5, we define the preconditioner for Q_n as

$$P_n = E_n C(G_n), \qquad (5.8.13)$$

where E_n and G_n are the Toeplitz matrices generated by $(z-1)^\ell$ and $b(z)$, respectively, and $C(G_n)$ is the optimal circulant approximation of G_n.

Let us consider cases where the quotient function $b(z)$ is a Wiener class function and $b(z)$ has no zeros on $|z| = 1$. We note first that if the radius of convergence ρ of the power series $\sum_{k=1}^{\infty} \lambda_k z^k$ in (5.8.11) is greater than 1, then $g(z)$ and hence $b(z)$ are analytic functions in a neighborhood of $|z| = 1$; see Conway [Con73, p. 31]. In particular, $b(z)$ will be a Wiener class function and $b(z)$ has no zeros on $|z| = 1$. A formula for computing ρ is given by [Con73, p. 31]

$$\frac{1}{\rho} = \limsup |\lambda_j|^{1/j}. \qquad (5.8.14)$$

Next we consider the case $\ell = 1$ in more depth. By straightforward division of $g(z)$ in (5.8.11) by $(z-1)$, we have

$$b(z) = s\mu \frac{1}{z} - \lambda - \sum_{k=1}^{\infty} \left(\lambda - \sum_{j=1}^{k} \lambda_j \right) z^k. \qquad (5.8.15)$$

Therefore, by (5.8.6) and (5.8.7),

$$b(1) = s\mu - \sum_{k=0}^{\infty} \sum_{j=k+1}^{\infty} \lambda_j = s\mu - \lambda \sum_{k=0}^{\infty} k p_k = s\mu - \lambda \mathcal{E}(B), \qquad (5.8.16)$$

where $\mathcal{E}(B)$ is the expected value of the arrival batch size. Thus if $s\mu \neq \lambda \mathcal{E}(B)$ then $b(1) \neq 0$ and hence $\ell = 1$. Moreover, if $\mathcal{E}(B) < \infty$, then $b(z)$ is again a Wiener class function and $b(z)$ has no zeros on $|z| = 1$. Clearly from (5.8.15), the first n Laurent coefficients of $b(z)$, i.e., $\sum_{j=1}^{k} \lambda_j - \lambda$, $k = 1, 2, \ldots, n$, can be computed recursively in $O(n)$ operations. Hence by using (5.3.18), $c(G_n)$ and also P_n can be constructed in $O(n)$ operations [CC96b].

Section 5.8. Applications 147

Theorem 5.8.3 (Singular Values of $P_n^{-1}Q_n$). *Let $b(z)$ be defined as in (5.8.12) and the number of servers s in the queue be independent of the queue size n. Then the sequence of preconditioned matrices $P_n^{-1}Q_n$ has singular values clustered around 1 for large n.*

Proof: By (5.8.10) and (5.8.13),
$$P_n^{-1}Q_n = C(G_n)^{-1}E_n^{-1}(T_n + R_n) = C(G_n)^{-1}E_n^{-1}T_n + L_n,$$
where rank $L_n \leq s$. Using Thm. 5.5.1, we can show that the sequence of matrices $C(G_n)^{-1}E_n^{-1}T_n$ has singular values clustered around 1 for all sufficiently large n. Therefore, the matrix $P_n^{-1}Q_n$ has singular values clustered around 1 for sufficiently large n.
$\diamond$

It follows from standard convergence theory of the PCG method (see Sec. 5.3) applied to the normal equations $(P_n^{-1}Q_n)^*(P_n^{-1}Q_n)x = (P_n^{-1}Q_n)^*P_n^{-1}b$ that the method will converge superlinearly and, in particular, in a finite number of steps independent of n. In each iteration of the PCG method, the main computational cost consists of solving a linear system $P_n y = r$ and multiplying Q_n to some vector r. We first recall from Sec. 5.5 that the cost of solving $P_n y = r$ is of $O(n \log n) + O(\ell n)$ operations. To compute $Q_n r$, we make use of the partitioning (5.8.10). Note that R_n in (5.8.10) is a matrix containing only $2s-1$ nonzero entries; we therefore need $O(s)$ operations for computing $R_n r$. Since T_n is a Toeplitz matrix, $T_n r$ can be computed in $O(n \log n)$ operations by embedding T_n into a $2n \times 2n$ circulant matrix [Str86]. Hence $Q_n r$ can be obtained in $O(n \log n)$ operations. Thus the number of operations required for each iteration of the PCG method is of order $O(n \log n)$.

Finally, we consider the memory requirement. We note that besides some n-vectors, we have to store only the first column (or eigenvalues) of the matrices E_n and $C(G_n)$ but not the whole matrices. Thus we need $O(n)$ memory for the PCG method.

We remark that circulant-type preconditioners have also been used in solving Markovian network with overflow [CCW96] and Markov-modulated Poisson process queueing systems [CCZ97]. Further discussions on applications of queueing theory can be found in Ch. 8.

5.8.4 Image Restorations

Image restoration refers to the removal or reduction of degradations (or blur) in an image using a priori knowledge about the degradation phenomena; see for instance [Jai89]. When the quality of the images is degraded by blurring and noise, important information remains hidden and cannot be directly interpreted without numerical processing. In operator notation, the form of the image restoration problem is given as

$$z = \mathcal{A}u + \eta = \int_{-\infty}^{\infty}\int_{-\infty}^{\infty} a(\xi,\delta;\alpha,\beta)u(\alpha,\beta)d\alpha d\beta + \eta, \qquad (5.8.17)$$

where the operator $\mathcal{A}$ represents the degradation, z is the observed image, and η represents an additive noise. Given z and $\mathcal{A}$ and possibly the statistics of the noise vector η, the problem is to compute an approximation to the original signal u. In the digital implementation of (5.8.17), the integral is discretized using some quadrature rule to obtain the discrete scalar model

$$z(i,j) = \sum_{k=1}^{N}\sum_{l=1}^{N} a(i,j;k,l)u(k,l) + \eta(i,j).$$

Writing this in matrix-vector notation, we obtain the linear algebraic form of the image restoration problem,
$$z = Au + \eta, \tag{5.8.18}$$
where z, η, and u are N^2–vectors and A is an $N^2 \times N^2$ matrix.

Writing the point-spectrum function (PSF) as $a(\xi, \delta; \alpha, \beta)$ provides the most general description of the imaging system. This representation allows the PSF to vary with position in both the image and object planes. In this case the PSF is said to be *spatially variant*. If we assume the PSF is spatially variant, then the matrix A in (5.8.18) has no special structure. Thus computing a solution to (5.8.18), in this case, can be very expensive.

In many cases, though, the PSF acts uniformly across the image and object planes. That is, the PSF is independent of position and, hence, becomes a function of only $\xi - \alpha$ and $\delta - \beta$. In this case the PSF is said to be *spatially invariant* and is written as
$$a(\xi, \delta; \alpha, \beta) = a(\xi - \alpha, \delta - \beta).$$
Thus the image model (5.8.17) is written as
$$z(\xi, \delta) = \int_{-\infty}^{\infty} \int_{-\infty}^{\infty} a(\xi - \alpha, \delta - \beta) u(\alpha, \beta) d\alpha d\beta + \eta(\xi, \delta), \tag{5.8.19}$$
where the integral in (5.8.19) is a two-dimensional convolution. The inverse problem of recovering u is thus a two-dimensional *deconvolution problem*. In the discrete implementation, (5.8.19) becomes
$$z = Au + \eta,$$
where the matrix A is now a block Toeplitz matrix with Toeplitz blocks, i.e., BTTB. The image restoration problem, with a spatially invariant PSF, can be reduced to solving an ill-conditioned BTTB system.

Because of the ill-conditioning of $\mathcal{A}$, naively solving $\mathcal{A}u = z$ will lead to extreme instability with respect to noise in the observed image; see [Jai89]. The method of *regularization* can be used to achieve stability for these problems [AE87]. In the classical *Tikhonov regularization* [Gro84], stability is attained by introducing a regularization functional $\mathcal{R}$, which restricts the set of admissible solutions. Since this causes the regularized solution to be biased, a scalar μ, called a regularization parameter, is introduced to control the degree of bias. Specifically, the regularized solution is computed as
$$\min_u \|\mathcal{A}u - z\|_2^2 + \mu \mathcal{R}(u), \tag{5.8.20}$$
where $\mathcal{R}(\cdot)$ is a certain functional which measures the irregularity of u in a certain sense. When $\mathcal{R}(f) = \|\mathcal{D}_k f\|_2^2$, where $\mathcal{D}_k$ is the kth-order differential operator, it forces the solution to have a small kth-order derivative. Notice that if the discretization of the differential operator is a Toeplitz matrix, then in digital implementation (5.8.20) reduces to a block Toeplitz least-squares problem. For these Toeplitz least-squares problems, different preconditioners that are based on the circulant approximations were considered in [CNP94a], [CNP93], [CNP96]. In [CNP96], [NPT96], restoration of real images by using the circulant PCG algorithm has been carried out.

The algorithms for deblurring and noise removal have been based on least squares. The output of these least-squares-based algorithms will be a continuous or smooth function, which obviously cannot be a good approximation to the original image if the original image contains edges. To overcome this difficulty, a technique based on the minimization of the *"total variation norm"* subject to some noise and blurring constraints is proposed in [ROF92]. The idea is to use as a regularization function the so-called total variation norm

$$TV(f) = \int_\Omega |\nabla f|\, dxdy = \int_\Omega \sqrt{\left(\frac{\partial f}{\partial x}\right)^2 + \left(\frac{\partial f}{\partial y}\right)^2}\, dxdy.$$

The solution to (5.8.20) with $R(f) = TV(f)$ can have discontinuities, thus allowing us to recover the edges of the original image from the blurred and noisy data. At a stationary point of (5.8.20), the gradient vanishes, giving

$$g(u) \triangleq \mathcal{A}^*(\mathcal{A}u - z) - \alpha \nabla \cdot \left(\frac{\nabla u}{|\nabla u|}\right) = 0, \quad x \in \Omega, \quad (5.8.21)$$

$$\frac{\partial u}{\partial n} = 0, \quad x \in \partial\Omega.$$

The second term in g is obtained by taking the gradient of $\alpha \int_\Omega |\nabla u| dx$ and then applying integration by parts from which a Neumann boundary condition results. Since the gradient equation of (5.8.20) is nonlinear, the fixed point (FP) iteration was employed in [VO96] to solve this nonlinear gradient equation. The FP iteration will produce a sequence of approximations x_k to the solution x and can be expressed as

$$(T^*T + \mu L(x_k))x_{k+1} = T^*b, \quad k = 0, 1, \ldots. \quad (5.8.22)$$

The coefficient matrices T and L correspond to the discretization of the convolution operator and the elliptic operator, respectively, in the gradient equation (5.8.21). In [CCW95], the optimal cosine transform-based preconditioner was used to precondition the linear system. Numerical results showed that this preconditioner works very well. However, we remark that it is still an active research area to find a good preconditioner for the linearized equation (5.8.22).

5.9 CONCLUDING REMARKS

The CG method coupled with a suitable preconditioner can solve a large class of $n \times n$ linear systems with matrix structure in $O(n \log n)$ operations. This chapter summarizes some of the developments of this iterative method for solving Toeplitz-like, Toeplitz-plus-Hankel, and Toeplitz-plus-band systems in the past few years. The results show that the method in some instances works better than traditional methods used specifically for these problems. In practical applications, many linear systems with matrix structure arise. For instance, in image processing, the restoration of images in nonlinear space-invariant systems involves the solution of Toeplitz-like-plus-band systems; see [TP91]. Iterative methods provide attractive alternatives to solving these large-scale linear systems with matrix structure.

APPENDICES FOR CHAPTER 5

5.A PROOF OF THEOREM 5.3.4

We remark that from the standard error analysis of the CG method (Sec. 5.2), we have

$$|||x - x_k||| \leq [\min_{P_k} \max_{\lambda} |P_k(\lambda)|\,] \, |||x - x_0|||, \tag{5.A.1}$$

where the minimum is taken over polynomials P_k of degree k with constant term 1 and the maximum is taken over the spectrum of $S_n^{-1/2} T_n S_n^{-1/2}$. In the following, we estimate the minimum in (5.A.1). We first note that the assumptions on f imply that

$$|t_j| \leq \frac{\hat{c}}{|j|^{l+1}} \quad \text{for all} \quad j,$$

where $\hat{c} = \|f^{(l+1)}\|_{L^1}$ (see, e.g., [Kat76, p. 24]). Hence,

$$\sum_{j=k+1}^{n-k-1} |t_j| \leq \hat{c} \sum_{j=k+1}^{n-k-1} \frac{1}{|j|^{l+1}} \leq \hat{c} \int_k^\infty \frac{dx}{x^{l+1}} \leq \frac{\hat{c}}{k^l} \quad \text{for all} \quad k \geq 1.$$

As in Thm. 5.3.3, we write

$$L_n = W_n^{(k)} + U_n^{(k)} \quad \text{for all} \quad k \geq 1,$$

where $U_n^{(k)}$ is the matrix obtained from L_n by replacing the $(n-k) \times (n-k)$ principal submatrix of L_n by a zero matrix. Using the arguments in Thm. 5.3.3, we see that $\text{rank}(U_n^{(k)}) \leq 2k$ and $\|W_n^{(k)}\|_2 \leq \hat{c}/k^l$ for all $k \geq 1$. Now consider

$$S_n^{-\frac{1}{2}} L_n S_n^{-\frac{1}{2}} = S_n^{-\frac{1}{2}} W_n^{(k)} S_n^{-\frac{1}{2}} + S_n^{-\frac{1}{2}} U_n^{(k)} S_n^{-\frac{1}{2}} \equiv \tilde{W}_n^{(k)} + \tilde{U}_n^{(k)}.$$

By Thm. 5.3.3, we have, for large n, $\text{rank}(\tilde{U}_n^{(k)}) \leq 2k$ and

$$\|\tilde{W}_n^{(k)}\|_2 \leq \|S_n^{-1}\|_2 \|W_n^{(k)}\|_2 \leq \frac{\tilde{c}}{k^l} \quad \text{for all} \quad k \geq 1$$

with $\tilde{c} = \hat{c}/f_{\min}$.

Next we note that $W_n^{(k)} - W_n^{(k+1)}$ can be written as the sum of two rank-1 matrices of the form

$$W_n^{(k)} - W_n^{(k+1)} = u_k v_k^* + v_k u_k^* = \frac{1}{2}(w_k^+ w_k^{+*} - w_k^- w_k^{-*}) \quad \text{for all} \quad k \geq 0.$$

Here u_k is the $(n-k)$th unit vector

$$v_k = [l_{n-k-1}, \ldots, l_1, l_0/2, 0, \ldots, 0]^T$$

with l_j given by (5.3.14), and $w_k^\pm = u_k \pm v_k$. Hence by letting $z_k^\pm = S_n^{-\frac{1}{2}} w_k^\pm$ for $k \geq 0$, we have

$$\begin{aligned}
S_n^{-\frac{1}{2}} L_n S_n^{-\frac{1}{2}} &= \tilde{W}_n^{(0)} = \tilde{W}_n^{(k)} + \frac{1}{2} \sum_{j=0}^{k-1} (z_j^+ z_j^{+*} - z_j^- z_j^{-*}) \\
&= \tilde{W}_n^{(k)} + V_k^+ - V_k^- \quad \text{for all} \quad k \geq 1, \tag{5.A.2}
\end{aligned}$$

where $V_k^\pm \equiv \frac{1}{2} \sum_{j=0}^{k-1} z_j^\pm z_j^{\pm *}$ are positive semidefinite matrices of rank k.

Let us order the eigenvalues of $\tilde{W}_n^{(0)}$ as

$$\mu_0^- \leq \mu_1^- \leq \cdots \leq \mu_1^+ \leq \mu_0^+.$$

Section 5.B. Proof of Theorem 5.6.2   151

By applying the Cauchy interlace theorem (cf. App. A) and using the bound of $||\tilde{W}_n^{(k)}||_2$ in (5.A.2), we see that for all $k \geq 1$, there are at most k eigenvalues of $\tilde{W}_n^{(0)}$ lying to the right of $\tilde{c}/k^l$, and there are at most k of them lying to the left of $-\tilde{c}/k^l$. More precisely, we have

$$|\mu_k^{\pm}| \leq ||\tilde{W}_n^{(k)}||_2 \leq \frac{\tilde{c}}{k^l} \quad \text{for all} \quad k \geq 1.$$

Using the identity

$$S_n^{-\frac{1}{2}} A_n S_n^{-\frac{1}{2}} = I_n + S_n^{-\frac{1}{2}} L_n S_n^{-\frac{1}{2}} = I_n + \tilde{W}_n^{(0)},$$

we see that if we order the eigenvalues of $S_n^{-\frac{1}{2}} A_n S_n^{-\frac{1}{2}}$ as

$$\lambda_0^- \leq \lambda_1^- \leq \cdots \leq \lambda_1^+ \leq \lambda_0^+, \tag{5.A.3}$$

then $\lambda_k^{\pm} = 1 + \mu_k^{\pm}$ for all $k \geq 0$ with

$$1 - \frac{\tilde{c}}{k^l} \leq \lambda_k^- \leq \lambda_k^+ \leq 1 + \frac{\tilde{c}}{k^l} \quad \text{for all} \quad k \geq 1. \tag{5.A.4}$$

For $\lambda_0^{\pm}$, the bounds are obtained from Thm. 5.3.1:

$$\frac{f_{\min}}{f_{\max}} \leq \lambda_0^- \leq \lambda_0^+ \leq \frac{f_{\max}}{f_{\min}}. \tag{5.A.5}$$

Having obtained the bounds for $\lambda_k^{\pm}$, we can now construct the polynomial that will give us a bound for (5.A.1). Our idea is to choose P_{2q} that annihilates the q extreme pairs of eigenvalues. Thus consider

$$p_k(x) = \left(1 - \frac{x}{\lambda_k^+}\right)\left(1 - \frac{x}{\lambda_k^-}\right) \quad \text{for all} \quad k \geq 1.$$

Between those roots $\lambda_k^{\pm}$, the maximum of $|p_k(x)|$ is attained at the average $x = \frac{1}{2}(\lambda_k^+ + \lambda_k^-)$, where by (5.A.3), (5.A.4), and (5.A.5) we have

$$\max_{x \in [\lambda_k^-, \lambda_k^+]} |p_k(x)| = \frac{(\lambda_k^+ - \lambda_k^-)^2}{4\lambda_k^+ \lambda_k^-} \leq \left(\frac{2\tilde{c}}{k^l}\right)^2 \cdot \left(\frac{f_{\max}}{2f_{\min}}\right)^2 = \left(\frac{\tilde{c} f_{\max}}{f_{\min}}\right)^2 \cdot \frac{1}{k^{2l}} \quad \text{for all} \quad k \geq 1.$$

Similarly, for $k = 0$, we have, by using (5.A.5),

$$\max_{x \in [\lambda_0^-, \lambda_0^+]} |p_0(x)| = \frac{(\lambda_0^+ - \lambda_0^-)^2}{4\lambda_0^+ \lambda_0^-} \leq \frac{(f_{\max}^2 - f_{\min}^2)^2}{4 f_{\min}^4}.$$

Hence the polynomial $P_{2q} = p_0 p_1 \cdots p_{q-1}$, which annihilates the q extreme pairs of eigenvalues, satisfies

$$|P_{2q}(x)| \leq \frac{c^q}{((q-1)!)^{2l}} \tag{5.A.6}$$

for some constant c that depends only on f and l. This holds for all $\lambda_k^{\pm}$ in the inner interval between λ_{q-1}^- and λ_{q-1}^+, where the remaining eigenvalues are located. Equation (5.3.16) now follows directly from (5.A.1) and (5.A.6).

5.B PROOF OF THEOREM 5.6.2

We note that

$$||P_n||_2 \leq ||C(T)||_2 + ||C(\mathcal{L}(x_1))C^*(\mathcal{L}_n(x_1))||_2 \leq ||T||_2 + ||C(\mathcal{L}_n(x_1))||_2^2.$$

It follows from (5.6.6) that

$$||T||_2 \leq ||T||_1 \leq 2||Te_1||_1 \leq 2\gamma^2.$$

On the other hand, using Lemma 5.6.2, we have

$$\|C(\mathcal{L}_n(x_1))\|_2 \leq 2\|g\|_\infty,$$

where g is the generating function of $\mathcal{L}_n(x_1)$ given in (5.6.9). Thus

$$\|C(\mathcal{L}_n(x_1))\|_2 \leq 2 \left\| \sum_{j=-\infty}^{-1} t_j e^{ij\theta} \right\|_\infty \leq 2\gamma.$$

Since the generating function g of $\mathcal{L}_n(x_1)$ is in the Wiener class, it follows from Lemma 5.6.3 that given any $\epsilon > 0$,

$$C(\mathcal{L}_n(x_1))C^*(\mathcal{L}_n(x_1)) - C^*(\mathcal{L}_n(x_1)\mathcal{L}_n(x_1)) = V_4,$$

where $\|V_4\|_2 < \epsilon$, provided that the size n of the matrix is sufficiently large [CJY91b]. Hence

$$\begin{aligned} P_n &= C(T) + C(\mathcal{L}_n(x_1))C^*(\mathcal{L}_n(x_1)) = C(T) + C^*(\mathcal{L}_n(x_1)\mathcal{L}_n(x_1)) + V_4 \\ &= C(T + \mathcal{L}_n(x_1)\mathcal{L}_n^*(x_1)) + V_4 = C(T_{m,n}^* T_{m,n} + \mathcal{L}_n(y_1)\mathcal{L}_n^*(y_1)) + V_4, \end{aligned}$$

where the last equality follows from (5.6.3). Write

$$T_{m,n} = \begin{bmatrix} T_1 \\ T_2 \end{bmatrix},$$

where T_1 is the $n \times n$ submatrix of $T_{m,n}$. The matrices $T_{m,n}$ and T_1 have the same generating function f and $T_{m,n}^* T_{m,n} = T_1^* T_1 + T_2^* T_2$.

Since f by assumption is in the Wiener class,

$$C(T_1^* T_1) = C(T_1)^* C(T_1) + V_5,$$

where $\|V_5\|_2 \leq \epsilon$ if n is sufficiently large. Thus

$$\begin{aligned} P_n &= C(T_{m,n}^* T_{m,n} + \mathcal{L}_n(y_1)\mathcal{L}_n^*(y_1)) + V_4 \\ &= C(T_1^* T_1 + T_2^* T_2 + \mathcal{L}_n(y_1)\mathcal{L}_n^*(y_1)) + V_4 \\ &= C(T_1)^* C(T_1) + C(T_2^* T_2 + \mathcal{L}_n(y_1)\mathcal{L}_n^*(y_1)) + V_4 + V_5. \end{aligned} \quad (5.\text{B}.1)$$

Observe that

$$\{\lambda_{\min}[C(T_1)^* C(T_1)]\}^{-1} = \|[C(T_1)^* C(T_1)]^{-1}\|_2 = \|C(T_1)^{-1}\|_2^2 \leq 4 \left\| \frac{1}{f} \right\|_\infty^2,$$

where the last inequality follows from Lemma 5.6.2. Thus by (5.6.10),

$$\lambda_{\min}[C(T_1)^* C(T_1)] \geq \frac{\delta^2}{4}.$$

Since $T_2^* T_2 + \mathcal{L}_n(y_1)\mathcal{L}_n^*(y_1)$ is a positive semidefinite matrix, $C(T_2^* T_2 + \mathcal{L}_n(y_1)\mathcal{L}_n^*(y_1))$ is also a positive semidefinite matrix. Thus we conclude from (5.B.1) that

$$\lambda_{\min}\{P\} \geq \lambda_{\min}[C(T_1)^* C(T_1)] - \|V_4\|_2 - \|V_5\|_2 \geq \frac{\delta^2}{4} - 2\epsilon.$$

The lemma follows by observing that ϵ is chosen arbitrarily and δ depends only on f and not on n.

Chapter 6

ASYMPTOTIC SPECTRAL DISTRIBUTION OF TOEPLITZ-RELATED MATRICES

Paolo Tilli

6.1 INTRODUCTION

As mentioned in Ch. 5, the convergence rate of the CG algorithm is dependent on the clustering of the eigenvalues of the coefficient matrix A (assumed symmetric and positive definite); the more clustered the eigenvalues, the faster the convergence of the iterates x_k to the solution x of the linear system $Ax = b$.

The purpose of the current chapter is to provide an overview of several old and new spectral distribution results for matrices in view of their relevance to the performance of iterative methods. In particular, it will be seen that for Toeplitz matrices, the eigenvalues are not necessarily clustered. Hence, the convergence rate of the (classical) CG method when applied to a Toeplitz system of equations will not be satisfactory, as already seen in Ch. 5. This is one reason for incorporating preconditioning into the CG algorithm to improve the spectral distribution of the resulting coefficient matrix. We thus have a demonstration of the value of the results on spectral distribution of this chapter.

6.2 WHAT IS SPECTRAL DISTRIBUTION?

In many applications it is customary to deal with a sequence of matrices A_n arising from several discretizations of the same underlying mathematical problem. For example, one may have to approximate a boundary value problem by finite differences: after reducing to a discrete problem over a mesh of n points, one has to solve a linear system with a matrix A_n of order n (for reasons that we will soon make clear, such matrices are likely to have some Toeplitz-related structure). On solving such linear systems by iterative methods (for instance, by the CG method; see [Tyr97] and also Ch. 5), a qualitative knowledge of eigenvalues or singular values of the involved matrices plays a crucial role, since the convergence rate of the most popular iterative methods is strictly connected with some spectral properties of the matrices themselves.

Suppose A_n is $n \times n$ Hermitian and positive definite, and let $\lambda_j(A_n)$, $j = 1, 2, \ldots, n$, denote its eigenvalues, labeled in nondecreasing order. Then it is well known that the convergence rate of the CG method crucially depends on the quantity (see Sec. 5.2)

$$\kappa(A_n) = \frac{\lambda_n(A_n)}{\lambda_1(A_n)},$$

i.e., the condition number of A_n with respect to the operator norm induced on matrices by the Euclidean norm on vectors. (We recall that if A_n is not assumed to be positive definite but merely nonsingular, then $\kappa(A_n)$ equals the ratio of the largest to the smallest singular value of A_n; moreover, we agree to let $\kappa(A_n) = +\infty$ when A_n is singular.) More precisely, letting $e_h = \|x - x_h\|_2$, where x is the solution to a linear system $A_n x = b$, x_h is the vector obtained after h iterations of the CG method starting from any vector x_0, and $\|\cdot\|_2$ is the Euclidean vector norm, we can prove (see [Tyr97] and also Thm. 5.2.2) that the error e_h satisfies the estimate

$$e_h \leq 2\sqrt{\kappa(A_n)}\left(\frac{\sqrt{\kappa(A_n)} - 1}{\sqrt{\kappa(A_n)} + 1}\right)^h e_0.$$

From the above equation we see that the CG method is fast when $\kappa(A_n)$ is close to 1 (observe that it always holds that $\kappa(A_n) \geq 1$). Therefore, to predict the behavior of the CG method, we should have an estimate of the quantity $\kappa(A_n)$, and this can be achieved, in principle, by numerically computing the largest and the smallest eigenvalues of A_n.

Nevertheless, in many cases the CG method is quite fast although the ratio λ_n/λ_1 is large; for example, this nice feature is apparent from numerical experiments when the ratio λ_n/λ_1 is large but the ratio λ_n/λ_2 is close to 1. Indeed, one can prove [Tyr97] that after h iterations the following estimate also holds:

$$e_h \leq 2\,\kappa(A_n)^{\frac{3}{2}}\left(\frac{\sqrt{\lambda_n/\lambda_2} - 1}{\sqrt{\lambda_n/\lambda_2} + 1}\right)^{h-1} e_0.$$

Observe that one can think of the ratio λ_n/λ_2 as the condition number of the matrix A_n restricted to the subspace generated by the eigenvectors relative to the eigenvalues λ_j, $j \geq 2$.

The convergence rate of the CG method was studied in detail in [AL86], [SV86], and it was proved that, for any natural number $k \ll n$, after a certain number of iterations depending on k, the method behaves as if the first k and the last k eigenvalues of the matrix were not present; in some sense, the ill-conditioning due to the first and the last k eigenvalues slows down the convergence rate only during the first iterations.

From these considerations we see that, to predict the behavior of the CG method, it is necessary to have some information about the spectra of the involved matrices and, in particular, to know the behavior of the first and the last k eigenvalues for large values of k, not only for $k = 1$.

To achieve this information, an explicit computation of the eigenvalues of A_n is not practicable for at least two different reasons. First, the required computational cost would be much higher than that for solving a linear system with the same matrix (which was the original task). Furthermore, in a preliminary analysis even the size of the matrix might be unknown: indeed, one might need qualitative information only on

Section 6.2. What Is Spectral Distribution?

the spectrum of A_n for all large values of n and not for a single n. (This is clear if, for example, n is the number of grid points in a finite difference problem and may have to be increased to achieve a better approximation.)

Some typical questions one might want to answer concerning the matrices A_n are the following:

1. Are the condition numbers bounded as $n \to \infty$?

2. If the matrices are ill-conditioned when n is large, are there many small singular values or just a few?

3. More generally, how are eigenvalues and singular values distributed on the real line?

The theory of the asymptotic spectral distribution is a useful tool in trying to answer all the above questions. The underlying idea is, in principle, quite simple: instead of taking into account every single eigenvalue or singular value, one adopts a global approach by studying the asymptotic behavior, as $n \to \infty$, of averages of the kind

$$\Sigma_n(\lambda, F) \triangleq \frac{1}{n} \sum_{j=1}^{n} F(\lambda_j(A_n)),$$

where F is a given function (called the *test function*) and λ_j are the eigenvalues of A_n. One can also study singular values by investigating the averages

$$\Sigma_n(\sigma, F) \triangleq \frac{1}{n} \sum_{j=1}^{n} F(\sigma_j(A_n)),$$

where σ_j are the singular values.

The knowledge of $\lim_{n \to \infty} \Sigma_n(\lambda, F)$ or $\lim_{n \to \infty} \Sigma_n(\sigma, F)$ for a suitable choice of the test function F may provide interesting information, as we can see from the following example.

Example. Suppose that each A_n is Hermitian and positive definite. Letting $F(x) = \log x$, one obtains
$$\Sigma_n(\lambda, F) = \log(\det A_n)^{\frac{1}{n}},$$
from which it follows
$$\lim_{n \to \infty} \det(A_n)^{\frac{1}{n}} = \exp\left(\lim_{n \to \infty} \Sigma_n(\lambda, F)\right)$$
provided, of course, the limit exists. In this case, we can compute the limit of the geometric mean of the eigenvalues.

Observe that, in the more general case where the matrices are merely assumed to be normal (i.e., $A_n^* A_n = A_n A_n^*$), it holds that
$$\lim_{n \to \infty} |\det A_n|^{\frac{1}{n}} = \exp\left(\lim_{n \to \infty} \Sigma_n(\sigma, F)\right).$$

◇

Sometimes one has also to deal with nonsquare matrices (such as in the least-squares problem; see [CNP93], [GR70], [Tyr97]). The notion of eigenvalue in this case would not make sense, while singular values are well defined. We recall that, if a matrix A has n_1 rows and n_2 columns, then it has $\min\{n_1, n_2\}$ singular values, which coincide with the square roots of the eigenvalues of AA^* or A^*A, according to whether $n_1 \leq n_2$ or $n_1 > n_2$ (throughout, A^* denotes the complex conjugate transpose of A).

Given a matrix A of order $n_1 \times n_2$ and a test function F defined on the real line, we define
$$\Sigma(\sigma, A, F) \triangleq \frac{1}{\min\{n_1, n_2\}} \sum_{j=1}^{\min\{n_1,n_2\}} F(\sigma_j(A)),$$
where $\sigma_j(A)$ are the singular values of A. If, moreover, A is Hermitian and has order n, we also define
$$\Sigma(\lambda, A, F) \triangleq \frac{1}{n} \sum_{j=1}^{n} F(\lambda_j(A)),$$
where $\lambda_j(A)$ are the (necessarily real) eigenvalues of A.

Observe that $\Sigma(\sigma, A, F)$ is the average of F over the singular values of A, whereas $\Sigma(\lambda, A, F)$ is the average over the eigenvalues.

The theory of the asymptotic spectral distribution, in its most general form, deals with the following problem.

Problem 6.2.1 (Spectral Distribution). *Given a family of matrices $\{A_\alpha\}_{\alpha \in S}$, where S is a partially ordered set of indices, find a class $\mathcal{T}$ of test functions F, defined on the real line, such that the limit*
$$\lim_{\alpha \to \infty} \Sigma(\sigma, A_\alpha, F) \tag{6.2.1}$$
exists for all $F \in \mathcal{T}$ and compute the limit explicitly in terms of F.

If, moreover, each A_α is Hermitian, then do the same concerning the limits
$$\lim_{\alpha \to \infty} \Sigma(\lambda, A_\alpha, F). \tag{6.2.2}$$

$\Diamond$

It is clear that if one wants to retrieve some nontrivial information from the limits (6.2.1) and (6.2.2), the class of test functions $\mathcal{T}$ must be, in some sense, wide; for example, the class of all constant functions surely works for any sequence of matrices A_α, but in this case the knowledge of (6.2.1) and (6.2.2) will provide no information at all. In the next sections, we will mainly consider test functions from the space $\mathcal{C}_0(\mathbb{R})$ of all continuous functions with a bounded support (we recall that a function has compact support if and only if it vanishes outside some bounded interval) or from the space $\mathcal{C}_b(\mathbb{R})$ of all bounded and uniformly continuous functions. (In both cases, the test functions are defined over $\mathbb{R}$ and are complex valued.) Both $\mathcal{C}_0(\mathbb{R})$ and $\mathcal{C}_b(\mathbb{R})$ are large enough for many purposes; observe, however, that $\mathcal{C}_0(\mathbb{R}) \subset \mathcal{C}_b(\mathbb{R})$ and the inclusion is strict, as one can see by considering any (nonidentically vanishing) continuous periodic function.

Observe further that in the above statement of the problem, we did not specify the nature of the set of indices S, and hence what $\lim_{\alpha \to \infty}$ means may depend on the context. Of course, the case where $S = \mathbb{N}$ is the set of natural numbers is the simplest one and, in this case, $\lim_{\alpha \to \infty}$ has the usual meaning. However, the case where A_n is a sequence of matrices of order n is not the only one that may occur when S is the set of natural numbers; for example, each A_n might be an $n \times n$ block matrix with $k \times k$ blocks, where k is a fixed natural number, or even an $n \times n$ block matrix with $h \times k$ blocks. (Nonsquare matrices are natural, for example, in dealing with least-squares problems.)

Section 6.3. Toeplitz Matrices and Shift Invariance 157

The reason why we do not restrict ourselves to the case where S is the set of natural numbers is the following. In many cases, it may be convenient to partition a matrix into $n_1 \times n_1$ blocks, partition each of these blocks into $n_2 \times n_2$ further blocks, and so on, with p nesting block levels. In this situation, it is natural to let $S = \mathbf{N}^p$ be the set of all multi-indices of the kind $(n_1, \ldots, n_p)$, where each entry n_i is a positive natural number, and label each matrix as $A_{\mathbf{n}}$, where $\mathbf{n} = (n_1, \ldots, n_p)$. In this case, (6.2.1) and (6.2.2) are to be understood as

$$\lim_{\substack{n_1 \to \infty \\ \vdots \\ n_p \to \infty}} \Sigma(\sigma, A_{\mathbf{n}}, F) \quad \text{and} \quad \lim_{\substack{n_1 \to \infty \\ \vdots \\ n_p \to \infty}} \Sigma(\lambda, A_{\mathbf{n}}, F),$$

respectively. In other words, each single entry n_i of the multi-index $\mathbf{n}$ (and not only its magnitude) has to approach infinity. This situation is natural when one deals with multilevel Toeplitz matrices, which will be discussed later on.

6.3 TOEPLITZ MATRICES AND SHIFT INVARIANCE

Let us begin with a simple example, which shows a typical problem where Toeplitz matrices are involved. Consider the boundary value problem

$$\begin{cases} -u''(x) = b(x) & \text{if } 0 < x < 1, \\ u(0) = 0, \\ u(1) = 0 \end{cases} \quad (6.3.1)$$

and suppose we want to approximate it by finite differences. The idea behind the method of finite differences is that of replacing the derivatives of the unknown function u at a point x with a suitable linear combination of the values u attains at some nearby points. If u is smooth enough, Taylor's formula yields

$$u(x+h) = u(x) + hu'(x) + \frac{h^2}{2}u''(x) + \frac{h^3}{6}u'''(x) + O(h^4),$$

$$u(x-h) = u(x) - hu'(x) + \frac{h^2}{2}u''(x) - \frac{h^3}{6}u'''(x) + O(h^4),$$

where the symbol $O(\epsilon)$ denotes a quantity that is infinitesimal of order at least ϵ, as ϵ tends to zero. After adding and solving with respect to $u''(x)$, we obtain

$$u''(x) = \frac{u(x-h) - 2u(x) + u(x+h)}{h^2} + O(h^2). \quad (6.3.2)$$

Letting

$$h = \frac{1}{n+1}, \quad u_j = u(jh), \quad b_j = b(jh), \quad j = 0, 1, \ldots, n+1,$$

we can replace the continuous problem (6.3.1) by a linear system of n equations in n unknowns. Indeed, forcing (6.3.2) at $x = jh$, $j = 1, \ldots, n$, and disregarding the terms $O(h^2)$ yields

$$\begin{cases} -u_{j-1} + 2u_j - u_{j+1} = h^2 b_j, & j = 1, \ldots, n, \\ u_0 = 0, \\ u_{n+1} = 0, \end{cases} \quad (6.3.3)$$

which is a discrete analogue of (6.3.1). Observe that (6.3.3) can be written in matrix form as

$$\begin{bmatrix} 2 & -1 & & \\ -1 & 2 & \ddots & \\ & \ddots & \ddots & -1 \\ & & -1 & 2 \end{bmatrix} \begin{bmatrix} u_1 \\ u_2 \\ \vdots \\ u_n \end{bmatrix} = h^2 \begin{bmatrix} b_1 \\ b_2 \\ \vdots \\ b_n \end{bmatrix}. \tag{6.3.4}$$

Let T_n denote the above coefficient matrix, which has order n. It is clear that, whatever n is, T_n has the same entry 2 along the main diagonal, the entry -1 along the two secondary diagonals, and zeros elsewhere. The property of having the same entry along each diagonal characterizes Toeplitz matrices: T_n is therefore a Toeplitz matrix.

As we have seen, T_n (more precisely, T_n/h^2) is a reasonable discrete analogue of the differential operator

$$u \mapsto \mathcal{D}u, \quad \mathcal{D}u = -\frac{d^2}{dx^2}u. \tag{6.3.5}$$

Two questions arise naturally: Why does T_n have a Toeplitz structure? Why just the numbers $(-1, 2, -1)$?

The answer to the second question is simple: the numbers $(-1, 2, -1)$ are the coefficients of the linear combination (6.3.2) used to approximate the second derivative. Indeed, another finite difference scheme (e.g., a five-point one instead of the three-point one above) would lead to different entries in the resulting matrices. The reader is referred to [Col60] for a discussion of many other schemes suitable to approximate the second derivative and more general differential operators.

The answer to the first question is related to the fact that T_n approximates a differential operator with constant coefficients. More precisely, any differential operator $\mathcal{D}$ with constant coefficients, such as (6.3.5), is *shift invariant*; that is, if $\mathcal{T}_h$ is the shift operator acting on functions as

$$\mathcal{T}_h u(x) = u(x - h),$$

then $\mathcal{D}$ and $\mathcal{T}_h$ turn out to commute for all h. (The underlying reason is easy: the set of all shifts is an Abelian group, and differentiation is naturally defined in terms of shifts.)

It is therefore natural to expect that any discrete analogue of a differential operator with constant coefficients should be, in some sense, shift invariant. Indeed, this is what actually happens: all the n equations in (6.3.3) can be obtained from one another, simply by shifting the unknowns. There is indeed only one single pattern of equation, associated with the numbers $(-1, 2, -1)$, which must hold at each of the n points of the grid $\{x_j\}$. This sort of shift invariance is better understood through the matrix representation (6.3.4), where the jth row of the matrix is associated with the jth equation in (6.3.3); the $(j+1)$th row of the matrix is then equal to the jth row, shifted to the right by one position. In short, the shift invariance of the initial problem (6.3.1) is, in some sense, inherited by the discrete model (6.3.4), and this reflects into the Toeplitz structure of the resulting matrix.

We recall that the shift invariance of Toeplitz matrices can be also exploited in order to devise efficient algorithms for Toeplitz-related matrices by means of the theory of displacement structure (see, e.g., Ch. 1 and [KS95a]).

6.3.1 Spectral Distribution of Toeplitz Matrices

In the theory of spectral distribution, we are not interested in a single Toeplitz matrix, but in a whole sequence $\{T_n\}_{n=1}^{\infty}$ (which, for simplicity, we shall continue to denote

Section 6.3. Toeplitz Matrices and Shift Invariance

by T_n), such that T_n is a principal submatrix of T_{n+1}. Letting $T_n = \{a_{j-i}\}_{i,j=1}^{n}$, we have that the sequence T_n is uniquely determined by the bi-infinite sequence of complex numbers $\{a_j\}_{j=-\infty}^{+\infty}$. One may think of each T_n as an $n \times n$ section of the infinite Toeplitz matrix $T = \{a_{j-i}\}_{i,j=1}^{+\infty}$, yet we shall not deal with infinite-dimensional Toeplitz operators here.

It is customary to associate the sequence T_n with an integrable function f, defined over the interval $(-\pi, \pi)$; more precisely, f is the function whose Fourier coefficients are just the a_j's; in formulas, we have

$$a_j = \frac{1}{2\pi}\int_{-\pi}^{\pi} f(\theta)\, e^{-\hat{\imath} j\theta}\, d\theta, \quad j = 0, \pm 1, \pm 2, \ldots, \tag{6.3.6}$$

where $\hat{\imath}$ is the imaginary unit. It is easy to see that, given a sequence of complex numbers $\{a_j\}$, a function f satisfying (6.3.6) will not, in general, exist. For example, from the Riemann–Lebesgue lemma (see [Edw82]) it follows that a necessary condition for such an f to exist is that $\lim_{|j|\to\infty} a_j = 0$, but this condition is still far from being sufficient: unfortunately, there is no characterization of the sequences $\{a_j\}$ that are the Fourier coefficients of an integrable function f. (This problem is a difficult one; the interested reader is referred to the book of Edwards [Edw82] for more details on Fourier series.)

We can overcome this difficulty by choosing the inverse approach: we start from an integrable function $f\colon (-\pi,\pi) \mapsto \mathbb{C}$, we consider its Fourier coefficients according to (6.3.6), and we build the sequence of Toeplitz matrices

$$T_n(f) = \begin{pmatrix} a_0 & a_1 & \cdots & a_{n-1} \\ a_{-1} & \ddots & \ddots & \vdots \\ \vdots & \ddots & \ddots & a_1 \\ a_{-n+1} & \cdots & a_{-1} & a_0 \end{pmatrix} \in \mathbb{C}^{n\times n}. \tag{6.3.7}$$

We say that $T_n(f)$ is the sequence of Toeplitz matrices *generated* by f, and we call f the *generating function*.

The spectral theory of Toeplitz matrices, which started with the pioneering work of the Hungarian mathematician Gabor Szegő, relates many properties of the matrices $T_n(f)$ to some properties of f as a function.

From (6.3.6), one immediately finds $T_n(f)^* = T_n(f^*)$; therefore, we have the following.

Proposition 6.3.1 (Hermitian Toeplitz Matrices). *The matrices of the sequence $T_n(f)$ are all Hermitian if and only if f is a real-valued function.*

◇

The keystone of the asymptotic spectral theory of Hermitian Toeplitz matrices is a celebrated result due to Szegő, which we state here in its original formulation [GS84].

Theorem 6.3.1 (Asymptotic Distribution Result). *Suppose $f\colon (-\pi,\pi) \mapsto \mathbb{R}$ is a measurable bounded function, and let T_n be the sequence of Hermitian Toeplitz matrices generated by f; then for any function F, continuous on $[\inf f, \sup f]$, it holds that*

$$\lim_{n\to\infty} \frac{1}{n}\sum_{j=1}^{n} F\bigl(\lambda_j(T_n)\bigr) = \frac{1}{2\pi}\int_{-\pi}^{\pi} F\bigl(f(\theta)\bigr)\, d\theta, \tag{6.3.8}$$

where $\lambda_j(T_n)$, $j = 1, \ldots, n$, are the eigenvalues of T_n.

$\diamond$

In the Szegő theorem the numbers $\inf f$ and $\sup f$ denote the essential infimum and the essential supremum of the function f over its domain. The word "essential" means that we disregard sets of null Lebesgue measure; more precisely, the number $\sup f$ is the smallest real number c such that $f(\theta) \leq c$ holds for all $\theta \in (-\pi, \pi)$ except, at most, on a subset of null Lebesgue measure (the existence of such a number follows from the fact that f is supposed to be bounded), and a dual definition holds for $\inf f$. Disregarding null measure sets is natural when one is concerned with quantities depending on the integral of a function f; indeed, changing the values of f over a null measure subset of its domain will not affect the value of its Lebesgue integral. For example, if $f(\theta) = g(\theta)$ for all θ except on a null measure set, then the Fourier coefficients of f and g are the same, and hence the matrices $T_n(f)$ and $T_n(g)$ coincide. Therefore, all properties concerning the generating function f (such as "f is positive," "f is real valued," and so on) will be tacitly assumed to hold "almost everywhere," that is, everywhere except possibly over a null measure subset of the domain of f.

The limit relation (6.3.8) is known as the Szegő formula. Its importance lies in that it provides, in one stroke, a lot of information concerning the asymptotic behavior of the eigenvalues of T_n. Throughout, we will discuss some recent extensions of the Szegő formula, also concerning matrices that are not Toeplitz in the usual sense but that are closely related to Toeplitz matrices. The Szegő formula can be considered a classic result, which has been generalized and extended by so many authors and in so many directions that taking into account all the contributions is no easy task and is perhaps impossible; among the many relevant papers and books, here we mention [Avr88], [GS84], [HH77], [Par86], [BS90], [Til98a], [Til98b], [Tyr96a], [TZ97], [Wid74], [Wid80], [Wid75].

Example. Consider the generating function

$$f(\theta) = 2 - 2\cos\theta. \tag{6.3.9}$$

An elementary computation of the integrals (6.3.6) shows that the Fourier coefficients of f are

$$a_j = \begin{cases} 2 & \text{if } j = 0, \\ -1 & \text{if } j = \pm 1, \\ 0 & \text{otherwise.} \end{cases}$$

Therefore, the Toeplitz matrix $T_n(f)$ coincides with the matrix in (6.3.4). It turns out that the eigenvalues of T_n can be computed explicitly; they are

$$\lambda_j(T_n) = 2 - 2\cos\frac{j\pi}{n+1}, \quad j = 1, \ldots, n, \tag{6.3.10}$$

as one can prove by checking that, for $j = 1, \ldots, n$, the vector whose ith component is $\sin(\frac{ij\pi}{n+1})$ is an eigenvector of T_n, relative to the eigenvalue $\lambda_j(T_n)$.

It is clear that the range $[\inf f, \sup f]$ is the interval $[0, 4]$; according to the assumptions of Thm. 6.3.1, let F be continuous over $[0, 4]$. Using (6.3.10), we can make the summation in (6.3.8) more explicit, and the Szegő formula (6.3.8) simplifies to

$$\lim_{n\to\infty} \frac{1}{n} \sum_{j=1}^{n} F\left(2 - 2\cos\frac{j\pi}{n+1}\right) = \frac{1}{2\pi} \int_{-\pi}^{\pi} F(2 - 2\cos\theta)\, d\theta. \tag{6.3.11}$$

Section 6.3. Toeplitz Matrices and Shift Invariance   161

Observe that, in this very special case, the above relation could be obtained without the aid of the Szegő theorem; indeed, the left-hand side is just a Riemann sum of the continuous and bounded function $F(2 - 2\cos \pi t)$, and therefore it converges to

$$\int_0^1 F(2 - 2\cos \pi t)\, dt.$$

Finally, letting $x = \pi t$ and observing that $\cos x = \cos(-x)$, it is easily seen that the last integral coincides with the integral in (6.3.11).

◇

In the above theorem, the test function F is supposed to be defined (and continuous) over the interval $[\inf f, \sup f]$, and this assumption assures that the integral in the right-hand side of (6.3.8) makes sense; on the other hand, in the left-hand side of (6.3.8) F is evaluated at the eigenvalues of T_n. For this to make sense, the spectrum of each T_n should lie inside the interval $[\inf f, \sup f]$; indeed, we have the following [GS84].

Theorem 6.3.2 (Bounds for Eigenvalues). *Suppose f is real valued and bounded and let T_n be the set of Hermitian Toeplitz matrices generated by f. Then, for any natural number n, if λ is an eigenvalue of T_n, it holds that*

$$\inf f \leq \lambda \leq \sup f. \tag{6.3.12}$$

Moreover, if $\lambda = \inf f$ or $\lambda = \sup f$, then f is constant.

◇

In other words, if f is not constant then the inequalities in (6.3.12) are strict and the spectrum of T_n actually lies inside the open interval $(\inf f, \sup f)$; if, on the other hand, f is constant, then the problem is trivial since each T_n is a scalar multiple of the identity matrix.

In the Szegő formula, the assumption that the test functions are continuous cannot be dropped, as we show in the following example.

Example. Suppose f is defined according to

$$f(\theta) = \begin{cases} 0 & \text{if} \quad -\pi < \theta \leq 0, \\ 1 & \text{if} \quad 0 < \theta < \pi. \end{cases}$$

Then f is clearly bounded, $\inf f = 0$, and $\sup f = 1$. Consider the test function

$$F(y) = \begin{cases} 0 & \text{if} \quad 0 \leq y < 1, \\ 1 & \text{if} \quad y = 1, \end{cases}$$

which is continuous over the interval $[\inf f, \sup f] = [0, 1]$ except for $y = 1$. Since f is not constant, by Thm. 6.3.2 the eigenvalues of each T_n lie in the open interval $(0, 1)$; therefore, for all n we have

$$\frac{1}{n}\sum_{j=1}^n F(\lambda_j(T_n)) = 0.$$

On the other hand, the integral

$$\frac{1}{2\pi}\int_{-\pi}^{\pi} F(f(\theta))\, d\theta = \frac{1}{\pi}F(0) + \frac{1}{\pi}F(1) = \frac{1}{\pi}$$

is nonzero and hence F is not a suitable test function in the Szegő formula; that is, (6.3.8) does not hold with this choice of F. We remark, however, that F is discontinuous only at one point over $[\inf f, \sup f]$.

◇

The Szegő formula opens up many interesting questions:

- What can we say if f is not bounded but merely integrable?

- What can we say if f is not real but complex valued?

- What can we say about singular values?

We shall examine the above three items in some detail in the following sections.

6.3.2 Unbounded Generating Function

Perhaps the most unpleasant assumption in the classic Szegő theorem 6.3.1 is the boundedness of the generating function f. In 1996, Tyrtyshnikov [Tyr96a] gave a new proof of the Szegő formula based on approximation by circulant matrices; curiously enough, his proof by no means rested on the boundedness of f, but had in the space L^2 its natural environment. For $p \geq 1$, we denote by L^p the vector space of all functions defined over $(-\pi, \pi)$ such that $|f|^p$ is integrable; we recall that L^p is a Banach space if endowed with the natural norm

$$\|f\|_{L^p} \triangleq \left(\int_{-\pi}^{\pi} |f(x)|^p \, dx \right)^{\frac{1}{p}}.$$

It is customary to denote by L^∞ the space of all essentially bounded functions, which is a Banach space with the so-called (essential) sup norm (see [Edw82] for more details).

Since the interval $(-\pi, \pi)$ has finite measure, by the Cauchy–Schwartz inequality we obtain the (strict) inclusion $L^p \subset L^q$ whenever $p \geq q$. In view of this fact, we can say that Tyrtyshnikov [Tyr96a] extended the Szegő theorem from L^∞ to L^2; the results from [Tyr96a], however, left open the question of whether the Szegő formula is valid for an arbitrary $f \in L^1$.

This problem was first solved in [TZ97], where the Szegő formula was proved for $f \in L^1$ and when the test functions are from $\mathcal{C}_0(\mathbb{R})$.

A short and elementary proof of the Szegő formula in the L^1 case (which, moreover, allows all test functions from $\mathcal{C}_b(\mathbb{R})$; see the discussion after the statement of Prob. 6.2.1) can be found in [Til98c]. Following [Til98c], the Tyrtyshnikov–Zamarashkin theorem reads as follows.

Theorem 6.3.3 (Szegő Formula, L^1 Case). *Suppose $f \colon (-\pi, \pi) \mapsto \mathbb{R}$ is integrable, and let T_n be the sequence of Hermitian Toeplitz matrices generated by f; then for any test function F from $\mathcal{C}_b(\mathbb{R})$ it holds that*

$$\lim_{n \to \infty} \frac{1}{n} \sum_{j=1}^{n} F(\lambda_j(T_n)) = \frac{1}{2\pi} \int_{-\pi}^{\pi} F(f(\theta)) \, d\theta, \qquad (6.3.13)$$

where $\lambda_j(T_n)$, $j = 1, \ldots, n$, are the eigenvalues of T_n.

◇

Section 6.3. Toeplitz Matrices and Shift Invariance   163

This theorem should be considered as the ultimate version of the classic Szegő formula, as long as one considers sequences of Toeplitz matrices associated with a generating function f; indeed, the assumption $f \in L^1$ cannot be weakened any further since, if f is not integrable, then the Fourier coefficients in (6.3.6) are not well defined.

6.3.3 Eigenvalues in the Non-Hermitian Case

Now let us drop the assumption that f is real valued. Can we find some sort of Szegő formula in this case?

A look at (6.3.8) suggests that when f is complex valued (and hence some T_n may fail to be Hermitian), then F should be defined on some domain of the complex plane, for example, in the disk of radius $\sup |f|$, in order that the right-hand side of (6.3.8) makes sense.

The following simple example shows that the matter is much more subtle than might be expected.

Example. Consider $f(\theta) = r\, e^{\hat{\imath}\theta}$, where r is any positive real number. It is easy to see that, in this case,

$$T_n(f) = \begin{bmatrix} 0 & r & & \\ & 0 & \ddots & \\ & & \ddots & r \\ & & & 0 \end{bmatrix}_{n \times n} \tag{6.3.14}$$

and hence the eigenvalues of T_n are all null. Therefore, (6.3.8) would reduce to

$$F(0) = \frac{1}{2\pi} \int_{-\pi}^{\pi} F(r\, e^{\hat{\imath}\theta})\, d\theta. \tag{6.3.15}$$

It is easy to see that (6.3.15) does not hold for all continuous F, since the right-hand side only depends on the values of $F(z)$ when $|z| = r$, which may have nothing to do with $F(0)$ (see [Til98a] for more details).

$\diamondsuit$

From the above example it is clear that if we want to extend the Szegő formula to the non-Hermitian case, then each admittable test function F should at least satisfy (6.3.15); that is, the mean value over a circle should equal the value at the center. It is well known (see, for example, [GT83]) that this property, known as the mean property, is typical of (indeed, it characterizes) harmonics functions, that is, functions such that $\triangle u = 0$, where $\triangle$ is the Laplace operator. If F is defined over the complex plane, then we say that F is harmonic if, letting

$$u(x, y) = F(x + \hat{\imath} y),$$

the bivariate function $u(x, y)$ is harmonic in the usual sense, that is, if

$$\triangle u = \frac{\partial^2 u}{\partial x^2} + \frac{\partial^2 u}{\partial y^2} = 0.$$

This definition is natural since it says that F is harmonic if it is regarded as a function of two real variables (namely, the real and imaginary part of the complex variable).

Curiously, it turns out that the Szegő formula can be extended to the case where f is complex valued if (and only if!) the test functions are harmonic; more precisely, the following result holds [Til98a].

Theorem 6.3.4 (Complex-Valued f). *Suppose $f\colon (-\pi, \pi) \mapsto \mathbb{C}$ is bounded, and let T_n be the set of Toeplitz matrices generated by f. Then for any function F, harmonic in an open convex set containing the range of f, it holds that*

$$\lim_{n \to \infty} \frac{1}{n} \sum_{j=1}^{n} F(\lambda_j(T_n)) = \frac{1}{2\pi} \int_{-\pi}^{\pi} F(f(\theta))\, d\theta. \tag{6.3.16}$$

Conversely, if F is continuous in an open set $\mathcal{O} \subseteq \mathbb{C}$ and is such that (6.3.16) holds for any bounded f whose range is inside $\mathcal{O}$, then F is harmonic inside $\mathcal{O}$.

◇

The fact that (6.3.16) does not hold (in general) when F is not harmonic prevents (6.3.16) from having a great practical interest, since the class of harmonic test functions is too restricted, and hence (6.3.16) does not help to understand, for example, where the eigenvalues are actually clustered.

On the other hand, the last part of the theorem states that we cannot do better; that is, the class of harmonic functions is the largest class of test functions that comply with the Szegő formula in the complex case. Perhaps some new tool other than the Szegő formula should be introduced to investigate the distribution, on the complex plane, of the eigenvalues of non-Hermitian Toeplitz matrices.

6.3.4 The Szegő Formula for Singular Values

When f is complex valued, the lack of a satisfactory Szegő formula for eigenvalues is in some sense compensated by a full Szegő formula for singular values. According to [Til98c], it reads as follows.

Theorem 6.3.5 (Szegő Formula for Singular Values). *Suppose $f\colon (-\pi, \pi) \mapsto \mathbb{C}$ is integrable, and let T_n be the sequence of (nonnecessarily Hermitian) Toeplitz matrices generated by f; then for any function F, uniformly continuous and bounded over $\mathbb{R}$, it holds that*

$$\lim_{n \to \infty} \frac{1}{n} \sum_{j=1}^{n} F(\sigma_j(T_n)) = \frac{1}{2\pi} \int_{-\pi}^{\pi} F(|f(\theta)|)\, d\theta, \tag{6.3.17}$$

where $\sigma_j(T_n)$ are the singular values of T_n.

◇

The above theorem is essentially due to Avram [Avr88] and Parter [Par86] who proved it under very restrictive assumptions on f; later, it was extended by Tyrtyshnikov [Tyr96a] to the case $f \in L^2$ and by Tyrtyshnikov and Zamarashkin [TZ97] to the case $f \in L^1$, while Tilli [Til98c] proved it in the above formulation.

The analogy with the Szegő formula (6.3.8) is apparent: it suffices to replace eigenvalues with singular values in the left-hand side and $f(\theta)$ with $|f(\theta)|$ in the right-hand side. Indeed, the above result is known as the Szegő formula for singular values.

Section 6.3. Toeplitz Matrices and Shift Invariance   165

However, one fundamental difference between the eigenvalues and the singular values setting should be pointed out: Thm. 6.3.2 has no analogue for singular values. In other words, in the light of Thm. 6.3.2, it might be expected that the singular values of $T_n(f)$ all lie in the interval $[\inf |f|, \sup |f|]$, but this is not true in general.

Example. Consider the generating function and the sequence of associated Toeplitz matrices of the first example of Sec. 6.3.3. In this case, since $|f(\theta)| = r$ for all θ, the interval $[\inf |f|, \sup |f|]$ reduces to the single point $\{r\}$, but $T_n(f)$ (which is given by (6.3.14)) has always one null singular value, which therefore lies outside $[\inf |f|, \sup |f|]$.
$\diamond$

The last example shows that the estimate from below $\sigma \geq \inf |f|$ does not generally hold; nevertheless, the one from above is always true [Til98a].

Theorem 6.3.6 (Upper Bound for Singular Values). *Suppose that $f: (-\pi, \pi) \mapsto \mathbb{C}$ is bounded, and let T_n be the sequence of Toeplitz matrices generated by f. Then, for any natural number n, if σ is a singular value of T_n it holds that*

$$\sigma \leq \sup |f|. \qquad (6.3.18)$$

Moreover, if we denote by $\gamma_\epsilon(n)$ the number of singular values of T_n that are smaller than $\inf |f| - \epsilon$, then for all $\epsilon > 0$ it holds that

$$\lim_{n \to \infty} \frac{\gamma_\epsilon(n)}{n} = 0. \qquad (6.3.19)$$
$\diamond$

The last part of the theorem states that the set $[\inf |f|, \sup |f|]$ is a "general cluster" for the singular values of T_n (the notion of general cluster was introduced by Tyrtyshnikov in [Tyr96a]); roughly speaking it means that, although the interval $[\inf |f|, \sup |f|]$ does not necessarily contain all the singular values of each T_n, the number of "outliers" is $o(n)$ as $n \to \infty$. (The notation $o(n)$ denotes a quantity such that $o(n)/n \to 0$ as $n \to \infty$.)

Now suppose that $|f(\theta)| \geq \delta$ for some $\delta > 0$; from the results stated so far, it is clear that T_n might be ill-conditioned (or even singular, according to the last example) as $n \to \infty$, since T_n might have some small singular values closer and closer to zero. In the light of what we said in the introduction about the convergence rate of the CG method it is important to estimate (in terms of n) how many singular values of T_n are less than $\inf |f|$ or, keeping the notation of the last theorem, estimate the quantity $\gamma_\epsilon(n)$.

When f is continuous, we can prove the following [ST98].

Theorem 6.3.7 (Estimate of $\gamma_\epsilon(n)$). *Suppose that $f: (-\pi, \pi) \mapsto \mathbb{C}$ is continuous; then for all $\epsilon > 0$ there exists a constant $C_\epsilon > 0$ such that*

$$\gamma_\epsilon(n) \leq C_\epsilon \quad \text{for all } n. \qquad (6.3.20)$$
$\diamond$

According to the terminology introduced by Tyrtyshnikov [Tyr96a], the above theorem says that if f is continuous, then the interval $[\inf |f|, \sup |f|]$ is a *proper* cluster for the singular values of T_n.

6.4 MULTILEVEL TOEPLITZ MATRICES

Suppose we want to approximate by finite differences the Laplace equation

$$\begin{cases} \dfrac{\partial^2 u}{\partial x^2} + \dfrac{\partial^2 u}{\partial y^2} = -b(x,y) & \text{if } (x,y) \in \Omega, \\ u(x,y) = 0 & \text{if } (x,y) \in \partial\Omega, \end{cases} \qquad (6.4.1)$$

where $\Omega \subset \mathbb{R}^2$ is the open square defined by

$$(x,y) \in \Omega \iff 0 < x < 1, \quad 0 < y < 1,$$

and $\partial\Omega$ is its boundary.

Given a natural number $m \geq 1$, consider the mesh of points

$$\{(x_i, y_j)\}, \quad x_i = i\delta, \quad y_j = j\delta, \quad i,j = 0, 1, \ldots, m+1,$$

where $\delta = 1/(m+1)$ is the mesh size. We want to replace the differential equation (6.4.1) with a system of finite difference equations, one for each point of the mesh. Let us set

$$u_{i,j} = u(x_i, y_j), \quad b_{i,j} = b(x_i, y_j).$$

The boundary condition becomes

$$u_{i,j} = 0 \quad \text{if} \quad i \in \{0, m+1\} \quad \text{or} \quad j \in \{0, m+1\}. \qquad (6.4.2)$$

If (x_i, y_j) is an interior point of the mesh, then the Laplacian can be approximated by

$$-\left(\frac{\partial^2 u}{\partial x^2} + \frac{\partial^2 u}{\partial y^2}\right)(x_i, y_j) = \frac{1}{\delta^2}(4u_{i,j} - u_{i-1,j} - u_{i+1,j} - u_{i,j-1} - u_{i,j+1}) + O(\delta^2).$$

(The above formula is known as the five-points approximation to the Laplacian and can be obtained by reasoning as in the unidimensional case discussed in Sec. 6.3.) Disregarding the term $O(\delta^2)$ and recalling (6.4.2), we obtain a linear system of m^2 equations in m^2 unknowns:

$$4u_{i,j} - u_{i-1,j} - u_{i+1,j} - u_{i,j-1} - u_{i,j+1} = \delta^2 b_{i,j}, \quad i,j = 1, \ldots, m. \qquad (6.4.3)$$

It is convenient to partition the unknowns $\{u_{i,j}\}_{i,j=1}^m$ into m vectors as

$$u_j \in \mathbb{R}^m, \quad u_j = \begin{bmatrix} u_{1,j} \\ u_{2,j} \\ \vdots \\ u_{m,j} \end{bmatrix}, \quad j = 1, \ldots, m,$$

and do the same with the right-hand sides of (6.4.3):

$$b_j \in \mathbb{R}^m, \quad b_j = \begin{bmatrix} b_{1,j} \\ b_{2,j} \\ \vdots \\ b_{m,j} \end{bmatrix}, \quad j = 1, \ldots, m.$$

Section 6.4. Multilevel Toeplitz Matrices

The linear system of (6.4.3) then can be written blockwise as

$$\begin{bmatrix} B & -I_m & & \\ -I_m & B & \ddots & \\ & \ddots & \ddots & -I_m \\ & & -I_m & B \end{bmatrix} \begin{bmatrix} u_1 \\ u_2 \\ \vdots \\ u_m \end{bmatrix} = \begin{bmatrix} b_1 \\ b_2 \\ \vdots \\ b_m \end{bmatrix}, \qquad (6.4.4)$$

where I_m is the identity matrix of order m and the matrix B is given by

$$B = \begin{bmatrix} 4 & -1 & & \\ -1 & 4 & \ddots & \\ & \ddots & \ddots & -1 \\ & & -1 & 4 \end{bmatrix}, \qquad B \in \mathbb{R}^{m \times m}.$$

We find out that the matrix of the linear system (6.4.4) has order $m^2 \times m^2$, it has an $m \times m$ blockwise Toeplitz structure, and each block is an ordinary Toeplitz matrix of order m. We can say that the Toeplitz structure of the matrix has two nesting levels; for this reason, such a matrix is called a two-level Toeplitz matrix.

Matrices of this kind are quite common in many applications. The one above has a two-level Toeplitz structure, and each level has order m; more generally, one can consider matrices with a p-level Toeplitz structure, where the order of the ith level is a given natural number n_i, $i = 1, \ldots, p$. We now want to investigate this structure in more detail.

Given a multi-index $\mathbf{n} = (n_1, \ldots, n_p)$, a p-level Toeplitz matrix $T_\mathbf{n}$ of size $\mathbf{n}$ is defined recursively as follows. If $p = 1$, then it is a customary Toeplitz matrix of order n_1. If $p > 1$, then $T_\mathbf{n}$ can be partitioned into $n_1 \times n_1$ blocks,

$$T_\mathbf{n} = \begin{pmatrix} B_0 & B_1 & \cdots & B_{n_1-1} \\ B_{-1} & \ddots & \ddots & \vdots \\ \vdots & \ddots & \ddots & B_1 \\ B_{-n_1+1} & \cdots & B_{-1} & B_0 \end{pmatrix}, \qquad (6.4.5)$$

and each block B_j is a $(p-1)$-level Toeplitz matrix of size $(n_2, \ldots, n_p)$.

In other words, $T_\mathbf{n}$ has an outermost block Toeplitz structure of order n_1, each block is itself a block Toeplitz matrix of order n_2, and so on, down to the innermost block level, made of ordinary Toeplitz matrices of order n_p.

As an example, for $p = 2$, $n_1 = 3$, and $n_2 = 2$, the generic two-level Toeplitz matrix of order $\mathbf{n} = (3, 2)$ has the following structure:

$$T_{(3,2)} = \begin{bmatrix} \begin{bmatrix} a_{0,0} & a_{0,1} \\ a_{0,-1} & a_{0,0} \end{bmatrix} & \begin{bmatrix} a_{1,0} & a_{1,1} \\ a_{1,-1} & a_{1,0} \end{bmatrix} & \begin{bmatrix} a_{2,0} & a_{2,1} \\ a_{2,-1} & a_{2,0} \end{bmatrix} \\ \begin{bmatrix} a_{-1,0} & a_{-1,1} \\ a_{-1,-1} & a_{-1,0} \end{bmatrix} & \begin{bmatrix} a_{0,0} & a_{0,1} \\ a_{0,-1} & a_{0,0} \end{bmatrix} & \begin{bmatrix} a_{1,0} & a_{1,1} \\ a_{1,-1} & a_{1,0} \end{bmatrix} \\ \begin{bmatrix} a_{-2,0} & a_{-2,1} \\ a_{-2,-1} & a_{-2,0} \end{bmatrix} & \begin{bmatrix} a_{-1,0} & a_{-1,1} \\ a_{-1,-1} & a_{-1,0} \end{bmatrix} & \begin{bmatrix} a_{0,0} & a_{0,1} \\ a_{0,-1} & a_{0,0} \end{bmatrix} \end{bmatrix},$$

where the $a_{i,j}$ are arbitrary complex numbers. This definition of a p-level Toeplitz matrix is easy to understand but hard to handle; an equivalent but more suitable definition is via the tensor product. Given two matrices, A of order $n_1 \times m_1$ and B of order $n_2 \times m_2$, the tensor product of A and B is defined by

$$A \otimes B = \begin{pmatrix} a_{1,1}B & \cdots & a_{1,m_1}B \\ \vdots & \cdots & \vdots \\ a_{n_1,1}B & \cdots & a_{n_1,m_1}B \end{pmatrix} \in \mathbb{C}^{n_1 m_1 \times n_2 m_2}. \qquad (6.4.6)$$

It is easy to see that if A has some structure (e.g., it is a Toeplitz matrix), then $A \otimes B$ inherits the same structure at a block level (e.g., it is a block Toeplitz matrix). We can exploit this observation in order to handle p-level Toeplitz matrices more easily.

The set of all Toeplitz matrices of order $n \times n$ is clearly a vector space of dimension $2n - 1$, and the natural basis is provided by the matrices $J_n^{(l)}$, $l = 0, \pm 1, \ldots, \pm(n-1)$, where $J_n^{(l)}$ denotes the matrix of order n whose (i,j) entry equals 1 if $j - i = l$ and equals zero otherwise.

The reader can check that the set of all p-level Toeplitz matrices of a given order $\mathbf{n} = (n_1, \ldots, n_p)$ is a vector space of dimension $(2n_1 - 1) \cdots (2n_p - 1)$, whose natural basis is given by the matrices

$$J_{n_1}^{(j_1)} \otimes \cdots \otimes J_{n_p}^{(j_p)}, \quad j_i = 0, \pm 1, \ldots, \pm(n_i - 1), \quad i = 1, \ldots, p.$$

Therefore, any p-level Toeplitz matrix $T_\mathbf{n}$, where $\mathbf{n} = (n_1, \ldots, n_p)$, can be uniquely written as

$$T_\mathbf{n} = \sum_{j_1=-n_1+1}^{n_1-1} \cdots \sum_{j_p=-n_p+1}^{n_p-1} J_{n_1}^{(j_1)} \otimes \cdots \otimes J_{n_p}^{(j_p)} a_{j_1,\ldots,j_p}, \qquad (6.4.7)$$

where the complex numbers $a_{j_1,\ldots,j_p}$ are suitable entries of the matrix.

As in the one-level (ordinary Toeplitz) case, it is natural to consider the sequence of p-level Toeplitz matrices generated by a function f; in order to have a natural correspondence between the coefficients $a_{j_1,\ldots,j_p}$ in (6.4.7) and the Fourier coefficients of the generating function, we can see that f should be a funcion of p independent variables. Usually, such an f is defined over the p-cube $(-\pi, \pi)^p$, and its Fourier coefficients are

$$a_{j_1,\ldots,j_p} = \frac{1}{(2\pi)^p} \int_{-\pi}^{\pi} \cdots \int_{-\pi}^{\pi} f(\theta_1, \ldots, \theta_p) e^{-i(j_1 \theta_1 + \cdots + j_p \theta_p)} d\theta_1 \cdots d\theta_p. \qquad (6.4.8)$$

Given f depending on p variables as above, we can consider the family of p-level Toeplitz matrices $T_\mathbf{n}(f)$ generated by the Fourier coefficients of f, according to (6.4.7) and (6.4.8). Again, the function f is referred to as the generating function.

All the distribution theorems discussed in Sec. 6.3.2 have an analogue in the p-level case; for instance, it is easily checked that the $T_\mathbf{n}$ are all Hermitian if and only if the generating function is real valued.

Concerning the asymptotic distribution of the eigenvalues when f is real valued, Thm. 6.3.3 extends in a natural way to handle p-level Toeplitz matrices.

Theorem 6.4.1 (Szegő Formula for Eigenvalues, p-Level Case). *Suppose that $f: (-\pi, \pi)^p \mapsto \mathbb{R}$ is integrable, and let $T_\mathbf{n}$ be the sequence of Hermitian p-level Toeplitz matrices generated by f; then for any function F, uniformly continuous and bounded over $\mathbb{R}$, it holds that*

$$\lim_{\substack{n_1 \to \infty \\ \vdots \\ n_p \to \infty}} \frac{1}{n_1 \cdots n_p} \sum_{j=1}^{n_1 \cdots n_p} F(\lambda_j(T_\mathbf{n})) \qquad (6.4.9)$$

Section 6.4. Multilevel Toeplitz Matrices

$$= \frac{1}{(2\pi)^p} \int_{-\pi}^{\pi} \cdots \int_{-\pi}^{\pi} F\bigl(f(\theta_1, \ldots, \theta_p)\bigr) \, d\theta_1 \cdots d\theta_p,$$

where $\lambda_j(T_\mathbf{n})$ are the eigenvalues of $T_\mathbf{n}$.

◇

Also, Thm. 6.3.5 has a natural analogue in the multilevel case.

Theorem 6.4.2 (Szegö Formula for Singular Values, p-Level Case). *Suppose f: $(-\pi, \pi)^p \mapsto \mathbb{C}$ is integrable, and let $T_\mathbf{n}$ be the sequence of (nonnecessarily Hermitian) p-Toeplitz matrices generated by f; then for any function F, uniformly continuous and bounded over $\mathbb{R}$, it holds that*

$$\lim_{\substack{n_1 \to \infty \\ \vdots \\ n_p \to \infty}} \frac{1}{n_1 \cdots n_p} \sum_{j=1}^{n_1 \cdots n_p} F\bigl(\sigma_j(T_\mathbf{n})\bigr) \quad (6.4.10)$$

$$= \frac{1}{(2\pi)^p} \int_{-\pi}^{\pi} \cdots \int_{-\pi}^{\pi} F\bigl(|f(\theta_1, \ldots, \theta_p)|\bigr) \, d\theta_1 \cdots d\theta_p,$$

where $\sigma_j(T_\mathbf{n})$ are the singular values of $T_\mathbf{n}$.

◇

The last two theorems are mainly due to Tyrtyshnikov [Tyr96a] and Tyrtyshnikov and Zamarashkin [TZ97]; an elementary proof can be found in [Til98c].

We stress that in (6.4.9) and (6.4.10) all the entries n_i of the multi-index $\mathbf{n}$ simultaneously tend to infinity. The next example shows that this requirement cannot be dropped in general; that is, letting the size of $T_\mathbf{n}$ tend to infinity (instead of each single entry) is not sufficient for (6.4.9) and (6.4.10) to hold. (It is clear that, if all the n_i's tend to infinity, then in particular the size of $T_\mathbf{n}$ tends to infinity).

Example. If $p = 2$ and $f(\theta_1, \theta_2) = 2 - 2\cos(\theta_1)$, then it is easy to check that

$$T_{(n_1, n_2)}(f) = T_{n_1}(g) \otimes I_{n_2}, \quad (6.4.11)$$

where

$$g = g(\theta_1) = 2 - 2\cos(\theta_1),$$

$T_{n_1}(g)$ is the one-level Toeplitz matrix of order n_1 generated by $g(\theta_1)$, and I_{n_2} is the identity matrix of order n_2. Then the $n_1 n_2$ eigenvalues of $T_\mathbf{n}$ coincide with the n_1 eigenvalues of $T_{n_1}(g)$, each with multiplicity equal to n_2. (This follows from (6.4.11) and from some elementary properties of the tensor product.)

Therefore, in this case (6.4.9) reduces to

$$\lim_{\substack{n_1 \to \infty \\ n_2 \to \infty}} \frac{1}{n_1 n_2} \sum_{j=1}^{n_1 n_2} F\bigl(\lambda_j(T_{(n_1, n_2)})\bigr)$$

$$= \frac{1}{(2\pi)^2} \int_{-\pi}^{\pi} \int_{-\pi}^{\pi} F\bigl(f(\theta_1, \theta_2)\bigr) \, d\theta_1 \, d\theta_2 = \frac{1}{2\pi} \int_{-\pi}^{\pi} F\bigl(g(\theta_1)\bigr) \, d\theta_1. \quad (6.4.12)$$

If we replace the above limit, which involves both n_1 and n_2, with $\lim_{n_2 \to \infty}$, letting $n_1 = 1$, then we obtain

$$\lim_{n_2 \to \infty} \frac{1}{n_2} \sum_{j=1}^{n_2} F\big(\lambda_j(T_{(1,n_2)})\big) = \lim_{n_2 \to \infty} \frac{1}{n_2} \sum_{j=1}^{n_2} F\big(\lambda_j(T_1(g) \otimes I_{n_2})\big)$$

$$= \lim_{n_2 \to \infty} \frac{1}{n_2} \sum_{j=1}^{n_2} F\big(\lambda_j(2I_{n_2})\big) = F(2),$$

which is easily checked since $T_1(g)$ is a scalar and equals 2. It is clear that, in general, $F(2)$ does not equal the integral in (6.4.12).

◇

Unlike the distribution theorems of Sec. 6.3.2, Thm. 6.3.7 does not extend to the case where $p > 1$, as seen by the following example.

Example. Suppose $p > 1$, and let

$$f(\theta_1, \ldots, \theta_p) = e^{\mathrm{i}(\theta_1 + \cdots + \theta_p)}.$$

Then all the Fourier coefficients $a_{j_1,\ldots,j_p}$ are null, except for $a_{1,\ldots,1}$, which equals 1. Therefore, (6.4.7) simplifies to

$$T_{\mathbf{n}} = J_{n_1}^{(1)} \otimes \cdots \otimes J_{n_p}^{(1)}.$$

Since the first column of $J_{n_1}^{(1)}$ is null, from the above equation we see that the first $n_2 \cdots n_p$ columns of $T_{\mathbf{n}}$ are null, and hence at least $n_2 \cdots n_p$ singular values of $T_{\mathbf{n}}$ are null. This means that Thm. 6.3.7 does not hold if $p > 1$, since in our example $\inf |f| = 1$, yet the number of null singular values of $T_{\mathbf{n}}$ cannot be bounded by any constant.

◇

6.5 BLOCK TOEPLITZ MATRICES

Suppose one wants to approximate the following convolution operator T with a matrix-valued kernel:

$$(Tu)(x) = \int_0^1 F(x - y) u(y) \, dy, \quad x \in [0, 1], \tag{6.5.1}$$

where

$$F \colon [-1, 1] \mapsto \mathbb{R}^{h \times k}, \quad u \colon [0, 1] \mapsto \mathbb{R}^k, \quad Tu \colon [0, 1] \mapsto \mathbb{R}^h.$$

The operator T transforms k-vector-valued functions into h-vector-valued functions over $[0, 1]$. If we sample the kernel F at the points $\{\pm x_j\}$, where

$$x_j = \frac{j}{n-1}, \quad j = 0, 1, \ldots, n-1,$$

and we let

$$(Tu)_j = (Tu)(x_j), \quad u_j = u(x_j), \quad j = 0, 1, \ldots, n-1,$$

by replacing the integral with a finite summation we obtain the approximation

$$Tu(x_i) \approx \frac{1}{n-1} \sum_{j=0}^{n-1} F(x_i - x_j) u_j, \quad i = 0, 1, \ldots, n-1. \tag{6.5.2}$$

Section 6.5. Block Toeplitz Matrices

Building the vectors

$$u = \begin{bmatrix} u_0 \\ u_1 \\ \vdots \\ u_{n-1} \end{bmatrix}, \quad Tu = \begin{bmatrix} (Tu)_0 \\ (Tu)_1 \\ \vdots \\ (Tu)_{n-1} \end{bmatrix},$$

the system (6.5.2) can be written in compact form as

$$(n-1)Tu = F_n u,$$

where the matrix F_n is given by

$$F_n = \begin{pmatrix} F(0) & F(1) & \cdots & F(n-1) \\ F(-1) & F(0) & \ddots & \vdots \\ \vdots & \ddots & \ddots & F(1) \\ F(-n+1) & \cdots & F(-1) & F(0) \end{pmatrix}.$$

The matrix F_n has an $n \times n$ block Toeplitz structure, where each block has order $h \times k$ (according to the assumptions on the kernel F). On the other hand, the blocks have no particular structure. (They are a sampling of the matrix-valued function F, which satisfies no structure assumption.)

Matrices with such a structure are called block Toeplitz matrices and are frequently encountered in many applications such as signal processing, Markov chains (see, e.g., Ch. 8 of this volume), or integral equations. Therefore, it would be desirable to have Szegő-like formulas for block Toeplitz matrices.

To make things precise, a block Toeplitz matrix of order n with $h \times k$ blocks is one that can be partitioned into blocks according to

$$T_n = \begin{pmatrix} A_0 & A_1 & \cdots & A_{n-1} \\ A_{-1} & \ddots & \ddots & \vdots \\ \vdots & \ddots & \ddots & A_1 \\ A_{-n+1} & \cdots & A_{-1} & A_0 \end{pmatrix} \in \mathbb{C}^{hn \times kn}, \quad A_j \in \mathbb{C}^{h \times k}. \tag{6.5.3}$$

We caution the reader against confusing the notion of a multilevel Toeplitz matrix with the more general one of a block Toeplitz matrix. A p-level Toeplitz matrix (with $p > 1$) is a block Toeplitz matrix, but its blocks are themselves block Toeplitz matrices (more precisely, they are $(p-1)$-level Toeplitz matrices and so on, recursively); on the other hand, in (6.5.3) the blocks A_j are not required to have any structure. (Indeed, they are not even required to be square matrices.)

We can think of a block Toeplitz matrix such as T_n in (6.5.3) as an ordinary Toeplitz matrix whose entries are matrices of a given size $h \times k$. It is therefore easy to extend the notion of generating function to the case of block Toeplitz matrices: if the blocks have size $h \times k$, it is natural to consider a function f defined over $(-\pi, \pi)$, taking values in the space of $h \times k$ matrices. In other words, for all $\theta \in (-\pi, \pi)$, $f(\theta)$ is a matrix with h rows and k columns. The Fourier coefficients of f are defined in a natural way as

$$A_j = \frac{1}{2\pi} \int_{-\pi}^{\pi} f(\theta) e^{-ij\theta} d\theta, \quad j = 0, \pm 1, \pm 2, \ldots, \quad a_j \in \mathbb{C}^{h \times k}. \tag{6.5.4}$$

Then the block Toeplitz matrix of order n generated by f can be written suitably as

$$T_n(f) = \sum_{j=-n+1}^{n-1} J_n^{(j)} \otimes A_j. \qquad (6.5.5)$$

Observe that, in the particular case where $h = k = 1$, the above definition reduces to that of ordinary Toeplitz matrices; moreover, the notation is consistent.

Before discussing some possible extensions of the Szegő formula to block Toeplitz matrices, some remarks are needed. Observe that the notion of eigenvalue is meaningless when $h \neq k$ (that is, when $T_n(f)$ is not a square matrix); on the other hand, singular values make sense also in the nonsquare case. The main difficulty, however, is of a different nature. Suppose $h = k$, and assume that $f(\theta)$ is Hermitian for all x, so that $T_n(f)$ is also Hermitian; if we want to extend the Szegő formula to the block case, what should we put in the right-hand side of (6.3.8)? Of course $F(f(\theta))$ makes no sense, since F is defined on the real line and $f(\theta)$ is a matrix. The following example suggests how (6.3.8) should be modified when f is matrix valued.

Example. Suppose f_1 and f_2 are real-valued functions defined over $(-\pi, \pi)$, let $h = k = 2$, and define the matrix-valued function

$$f(\theta) = \begin{pmatrix} f_1(\theta) & 0 \\ 0 & f_2(\theta) \end{pmatrix}, \quad \theta \in (-\pi, \pi). \qquad (6.5.6)$$

According to (6.5.5), each $T_n(f)$ is a square matrix of order $2n$. Let Π_{2n} be the permutation matrix of order $2n$ which acts on a vector $v = (v_1, \ldots, v_{2n})^t$ according to

$$\Pi_{2n} v = (v_1, v_3, \ldots, v_{2n-1}, v_2, v_4, \ldots, v_{2n})^t.$$

An elemetary computation shows that

$$\Pi_{2n} T_n(f) \Pi_{2n}^t = \begin{pmatrix} T_n(f_1) & 0 \\ 0 & T_n(f_2) \end{pmatrix}, \qquad (6.5.7)$$

where $T_n(f_i)$ is the ordinary Toeplitz matrix of order n generated by f_i. (Recall that each f_i is scalar valued.) In other words, by a suitable permutation of rows and columns $T_n(f)$ is reduced to the direct sum of two ordinary Toeplitz matrices of order n. The reason why this can be done is very easy to see: the permutation matrix Π_{2n} simply sorts rows and columns in such a way that the Fourier coefficients of f_1 are placed in the upper left block of order n, those of f_2 are placed in the lower right block of order n, and the remaining null entries (which amount to $2n^2$) fill the two off-diagonal blocks of order n.

Since permutation matrices are unitary, it follows from (6.5.7) that the $2n$ eigenvalues of $T_n(f)$ result from the union of the eigenvalues of $T_n(f_1)$ with those of $T_n(f_2)$. As a consequence, for any test function F, we have

$$\frac{1}{2n} \sum_{j=1}^{2n} F\bigl(\lambda_j(T_n(f))\bigr) = \frac{1}{2n} \sum_{j=1}^{n} F\bigl(\lambda_j(T_n(f_1))\bigr) + \frac{1}{2n} \sum_{j=1}^{n} F\bigl(\lambda_j(T_n(f_2))\bigr).$$

Taking the limit as $n \to \infty$, from the Szegő formula separately applied to $T_n(f_1)$ and $T_n(f_2)$, we obtain

$$\lim_{n \to \infty} \frac{1}{2n} \sum_{j=1}^{2n} F\bigl(\lambda_j(T_n(f))\bigr) = \frac{1}{2\pi} \int_{-\pi}^{\pi} \frac{1}{2} \bigl(F(f_1(\theta)) + F(f_2(\theta))\bigr) \, d\theta.$$

Section 6.5. Block Toeplitz Matrices 173

Since for all $\theta \in (-\pi, \pi)$ the two numbers $f_1(\theta)$ and $f_2(\theta)$ are just the two eigenvalues of $f(\theta)$, the above formula can be rewritten suggestively as

$$\lim_{n \to \infty} \frac{1}{2n} \sum_{j=1}^{2n} F\Big(\lambda_j(T_n(f))\Big) = \frac{1}{2\pi} \int_{-\pi}^{\pi} \frac{1}{2} \sum_{j=1}^{2} F\Big(\lambda_j(f_1(\theta))\Big) d\theta.$$

◇

This example suggests how the right-hand side of the Szegő formula should be modified in the case of block Toeplitz matrices: in place of $F(f(\theta))$ (which makes no sense if $f(\theta)$ is a matrix), we use the average of F over the eigenvalues of $f(\theta)$.

However, we stress that the technique used in the above example cannot be used in general. Indeed, the block splitting (6.5.7) strongly rests on the diagonal structure of f given by (6.5.6). When f is not diagonal (that is, in the general case) the trick used in the above example is bound to fail.

Although the technique used in the last example cannot be applied in general, by means of more sophisticated tools the following theorem can be proved (see [TM99], [MT96], [Til98c]).

Theorem 6.5.1 (Szegő Formula for Hermitian Block Toeplitz Matrices). *Suppose $f: (-\pi, \pi) \mapsto \mathbb{C}^{h \times h}$ is a matrix-valued integrable function such that $f(\theta)$ is Hermitian for all x, and let T_n be the sequence of Hermitian block Toeplitz matrices generated by f. Then for any function F, uniformly continuous and bounded over $\mathbb{R}$, it holds that*

$$\lim_{n \to \infty} \frac{1}{nh} \sum_{j=1}^{nh} F(\lambda_j(T_n)) = \frac{1}{2\pi} \int_{-\pi}^{\pi} \frac{1}{h} \sum_{j=1}^{h} F\Big(\lambda_j(f(\theta))\Big) d\theta, \quad (6.5.8)$$

where $\lambda_j(T_n)$ are the eigenvalues of T_n and $\lambda_j(f(\theta))$ are those of $f(\theta)$.

◇

In the above theorem, the assumption that f is integrable obviously means that each entry of f is integrable in the usual sense.

It is easy to see that, in the particular case where $h = 1$, f reduces to a real-valued function and Thm. 6.5.1 reduces to Thm. 6.3.3.

Concerning singular values, we can drop not only the assumption that $f(\theta)$ is Hermitian but even the assumption that it is a square matrix.

Theorem 6.5.2. (Szegő Formula for Non-Hermitian Block Toeplitz Matrices). *Suppose that the function $f: (-\pi, \pi) \mapsto \mathbb{C}^{h \times k}$ is integrable, let T_n be the sequence of block Toeplitz matrices generated by f, and let $d = \min\{h, k\}$; then for any function F, uniformly continuous and bounded over $\mathbb{R}$, it holds that*

$$\lim_{n \to \infty} \frac{1}{nd} \sum_{j=1}^{nd} F(\sigma_j(T_n)) = \frac{1}{2\pi} \int_{-\pi}^{\pi} \frac{1}{d} \sum_{j=1}^{d} F\Big(\sigma_j(f(\theta))\Big) d\theta, \quad (6.5.9)$$

where $\sigma_j(T_n)$ are the singular values of T_n and $\sigma_j(f(\theta))$ are those of $f(\theta)$.

◇

A simple proof of the last two theorems can be found in [Til98c] (see also [Til98a], [Til96], [MT96]).

6.6 COMBINING BLOCK AND MULTILEVEL STRUCTURE

Starting from ordinary Toeplitz matrices (the generating function f is univariate and scalar valued), we have so far discussed p-level Toeplitz matrices (when f is p-variate and scalar valued) and block Toeplitz matrices (when f is univariate and matrix valued). It is therefore natural to consider block multilevel Toeplitz matrices (BMTMs), that is, the case where the generating function f is simultaneously multivariate and matrix valued.

For natural numbers $p, h, k \geq 1$, suppose the function $f \colon (-\pi, \pi)^p \mapsto \mathbb{C}^{h \times k}$ is integrable over the cube $(-\pi, \pi)^p$. Then the Fourier coefficients of f are $h \times k$ matrices defined according to

$$A_{j_1, \ldots, j_p} = \frac{1}{(2\pi)^p} \int_{-\pi}^{\pi} \cdots \int_{-\pi}^{\pi} f(\theta_1, \ldots, \theta_p) \, e^{-\hat{\imath}(j_1 \theta_1 + \cdots + j_p \theta_p)} \, d\theta_1 \cdots d\theta_p, \quad (6.6.1)$$

$$A_{j_1, \ldots, j_p} \in \mathbb{C}^{h \times k}, \quad j_1, \ldots, j_p = 0, \pm 1, \pm 2, \ldots.$$

Given a multi-index $\mathbf{n} = (n_1, \ldots, n_p)$, we can define the block p-level Toeplitz matrix $T_\mathbf{n}(f)$ generated by f as

$$T_\mathbf{n} = \sum_{j_1 = -n_1 + 1}^{n_1 - 1} \cdots \sum_{j_p = -n_p + 1}^{n_p - 1} J_{n_1}^{(j_1)} \otimes \cdots \otimes J_{n_p}^{(j_p)} \otimes A_{j_1, \ldots, j_p}. \quad (6.6.2)$$

It is immediate to see that $T_\mathbf{n}$ has $h \, n_1 \cdots n_p$ rows and $k \, n_1 \cdots n_p$ columns; therefore, it is a square matrix if and only if $h = k$.

Observing that the transpose conjugate sequence $T_\mathbf{n}(f)^*$ is generated by the transpose conjugate function f^*, one can easily prove the following.

Proposition 6.6.1 (Hermitian Matrices $T_\mathbf{n}(f)$). *All the matrices $T_\mathbf{n}(f)$ are Hermitian if and only if the generating function f is Hermitian valued.*

◇

It turns out that the Szegő formulas for singular values and eigenvalues can be extended to the case of BMTMs. (In the case of eigenvalues, by virtue of Proposition 6.6.1, we have to suppose that $h = k$ and that f is Hermitian valued.)

Theorem 6.6.1 (Szegő Formula for Hermitian BMTMs). *Suppose*

$$f \colon (-\pi, \pi)^p \mapsto \mathbb{C}^{h \times h}$$

is integrable and Hermitian valued, and let $T_\mathbf{n}$ be the sequence of Hermitian block p-level Toeplitz matrices generated by f; then for any function F, uniformly continuous and bounded over $\mathbb{R}$, it holds that

$$\lim_{\substack{n_1 \to \infty \\ \vdots \\ n_p \to \infty}} \frac{1}{h \, n_1 \cdots n_p} \sum_{j=1}^{h \, n_1 \cdots n_p} F(\lambda_j(T_\mathbf{n}))$$

$$= \frac{1}{(2\pi)^p} \int_{-\pi}^{\pi} \cdots \int_{-\pi}^{\pi} \frac{1}{h} \sum_{j=1}^{h} F\Big(\lambda_j\big(f(\theta_1, \ldots, \theta_p)\big)\Big) \, d\theta_1 \cdots d\theta_p,$$

Section 6.7. Locally Toeplitz Matrices   175

where $\lambda_j(T_\mathbf{n})$ are the eigenvalues of $T_\mathbf{n}$ and $\lambda_j\big(f(\theta_1,\ldots,\theta_p)\big)$ are those of $f(\theta_1,\ldots,\theta_p)$. ◇

Theorem 6.6.2 (Szegő Formula for Non-Hermitian BMTMs). *Suppose*

$$f\colon (-\pi,\pi)^p \mapsto \mathbb{C}^{h\times k}$$

is integrable; let $T_\mathbf{n}$ be the sequence of BMTMs generated by f, and let $d = \min\{h,k\}$; then for any function F, uniformly continuous and bounded over $\mathbb{R}$, it holds that

$$\lim_{\substack{n_1\to\infty \\ \vdots \\ n_p\to\infty}} \frac{1}{dn_1\cdots n_p} \sum_{j=1}^{dn_1\cdots n_p} F\big(\sigma_j(T_\mathbf{n})\big) \qquad (6.6.3)$$

$$= \frac{1}{(2\pi)^p} \int_{-\pi}^{\pi}\cdots\int_{-\pi}^{\pi} \frac{1}{d}\sum_{j=1}^{d} F\big(\sigma_j(f(\theta_1,\ldots,\theta_p))\big)\,d\theta_1\cdots d\theta_p,$$

where $\sigma_j(T_\mathbf{n})$ are the singular values of $T_\mathbf{n}$ and $\sigma_j\big(f(\theta_1,\ldots,\theta_p)\big)$ are those of $f(\theta_1,\ldots,\theta_p)$. ◇

The proofs of the above two theorems can be found in [Til98c]. It is worth observing that they embrace, as particular cases, all the extensions of the Szegő formula we have discussed so far; indeed, letting $p = 1$ we obtain the distribution results of Sec. 6.5, letting $h = k = 1$ we obtain the results of Sec. 6.4, while letting $p = h = k = 1$ we obtain the results of Sec. 6.3.1.

6.7 LOCALLY TOEPLITZ MATRICES

In Sec. 6.3 we discussed how Toeplitz matrices arise quite naturally when a problem has some kind of shift invariance; in particular, we discussed the example of the boundary value problem (6.3.1) which leads to Toeplitz matrices since the associated differential operator has constant coefficients.

This section is devoted to describing, quite informally indeed, the notion of a "locally Toeplitz" structure, which was introduced in [Til98b].

Consider the Sturm–Liouville problem

$$\begin{cases} -\big(a(x)u'(x)\big)' = b(x) & \text{if } 0 < x < 1, \\ \quad u(0) = 0, \\ \quad u(1) = 0. \end{cases} \qquad (6.7.1)$$

There are many ways to discretize the above equation via finite differences over the grid $\{j/(n+1)\}_{j=1}^n$, and the interested reader is referred to the classical book of Collatz [Col60]. However, a rather standard approach (see [Col60], [FS95]) leads to a linear system of the kind

$$\begin{bmatrix} \alpha_0+\alpha_1 & -\alpha_1 & & & \\ -\alpha_1 & \alpha_1+\alpha_2 & \ddots & & \\ & \ddots & \ddots & & \\ & & & & -\alpha_{n-1} \\ & & & -\alpha_{n-1} & \alpha_{n-1}+\alpha_n \end{bmatrix} \begin{bmatrix} u_1 \\ u_2 \\ \vdots \\ u_n \end{bmatrix} = h^2 \begin{bmatrix} b_1 \\ b_2 \\ \vdots \\ b_n \end{bmatrix}, \qquad (6.7.2)$$

where
$$h = \frac{1}{n+1}, \quad \alpha_j = a\left(\frac{h}{2} + jh\right), \quad u_j = u(jh), \quad b_j = b(jh). \tag{6.7.3}$$

Let us briefly explain how this linear system of equations is obtained. (This is but a heuristic explanation meant as a motivation; for a rigorous approach, see [Col60].) For any small number θ, $0 < \theta \ll 1$, from Taylor's formula we obtain

$$a(x)u'(x) \approx F(x), \quad \text{where} \quad F(x) \triangleq a(x)\frac{u(x+\theta) - u(x-\theta)}{2\theta}. \tag{6.7.4}$$

As a consequence, from Taylor's formula (now applied to $F(x)$) we obtain

$$-\frac{F(x+\theta) - F(x-\theta)}{2\theta} \approx -\bigl(a(x)u'(x)\bigr)'. \tag{6.7.5}$$

Substituting this approximation into (6.7.1), we obtain

$$-a(x-\theta)u(x-2\theta) + \bigl(a(x-\theta) + a(x+\theta)\bigr)u(x) - a(x+\theta)u(x+2\theta) = 4\theta^2 b(x).$$

Finally, letting $h = 1/(n+1)$, $\theta = h/2$, and forcing the last equation for $x = jh$, $j = 1, \ldots, n$, yields the linear system (6.7.2).

It is immediate to see that (6.7.2) reduces to (6.3.4) if $a(x) = 1$; this is quite natural, since the differential problem (6.7.1) (which has, in general, nonconstant coefficients depending on $a(x)$) also reduces to (6.3.1) when $a(x) = 1$, that is, when it has constant coefficients.

Observe that, if $a(x)$ is not identically constant, then for sufficiently large n there will exist several pairs (i, j) such that $\alpha_i \neq \alpha_j$, and hence the matrix in (6.7.2) will have no Toeplitz structure.

Nevertheless, some structural connection between the matrix in (6.3.4) and that in (6.7.2) is apparent. Indeed, putting mathematical rigor aside for a while, we can intuitively associate the jth row in (6.3.4) with the triplet $(-1, 2, -1)$ and, similarly, associate the jth row in (6.7.2) with the triplet $(-\alpha_{j-1}, \alpha_{j-1} + \alpha_j, -\alpha_j)$. Now shift by one position from the jth to the $(j+1)$th row and see how the triplets change. In (6.3.4), we have

$$(-1, 2, -1) \mapsto (-1, 2, -1) \quad \text{(Toeplitz structure)},$$

whereas in (6.7.2) we have

$$(-\alpha_{j-1}, \alpha_{j-1} + \alpha_j, -\alpha_j) \mapsto (-\alpha_j, \alpha_j + \alpha_{j+1}, -\alpha_{j+1}) \quad \text{(what structure?)}.$$

Suppose that $a(x)$ is smooth, say, differentiable or Lipschitz continuous; then, recalling (6.7.3), the last transition can be rewritten as

$$(-\alpha_{j-1}, \alpha_{j-1} + \alpha_j, -\alpha_j) \mapsto (-\alpha_{j-1}, \alpha_{j-1} + \alpha_j, -\alpha_j) + O\left(\frac{1}{n}\right).$$

In other words, when n is very large, while moving from the jth to the $(j+1)$th row the triplet varies by a very small quantity, whereas in the Toeplitz case it does not vary at all. By (6.7.3), the triplet associated with the jth row in (6.7.2) can be written as

$$(-\alpha_{j-1}, \alpha_{j-1} + \alpha_j, -\alpha_j) = a\left(\frac{j}{n}\right)(-1, 2, -1) + O\left(\frac{1}{n}\right).$$

Section 6.7. Locally Toeplitz Matrices

Disregarding the term $O(1/n)$ and moving from the first to the last row in (6.7.2), we can identify the triplet $(-\alpha_{j-1}, \alpha_{j-1} + \alpha_j, -\alpha_j)$ with the triplet $(-1, 2, -1)$ multiplied by the coefficient (or *weight*) $a(j/n)$, which almost continuously varies from $a(0)$ to $a(1)$. A matrix with this structure is called *locally Toeplitz* (a precise definition, however, will be given in the next section). In fact, in the matrix (6.7.2) we can find a new type of Toeplitz structure that is not global (indeed, if $|a(1) - a(0)|$ is large, then the triplet $(-\alpha_1, \alpha_1 + \alpha_2, -\alpha_2)$ in the second row of (6.7.2) will have nothing to do with the triplet $(-\alpha_{n-2}, \alpha_{n-2} + \alpha_{n-1}, -\alpha_0)$ in the $(n-1)$th row) but only *local*; that is, when $k \ll n$ any two triplets of the kind

$$(-\alpha_{j-1}, \alpha_{j-1} + \alpha_j, -\alpha_j) = a\left(\frac{j}{n}\right)(-1, 2, -1) + O\left(\frac{1}{n}\right)$$

and

$$(-\alpha_{j+k-1}, \alpha_{j+k-1} + \alpha_{j+k}, -\alpha_{j+k-1}) = a\left(\frac{j+k}{n}\right)(-1, 2, -1) + O\left(\frac{1}{n}\right)$$

will be almost equal, since the quantity

$$\left| a\left(\frac{j+k}{n}\right) - a\left(\frac{j}{n}\right) \right|$$

will be very small (for example, it will be $O(k/n)$ if $a(x)$ is Lipschitz continuous).

Recalling the example following Thm. 6.3.1, the triplet $(-1, 2, -1)$ is made of the nonzero Fourier coefficients of the function $f(\theta) = 2 - 2\cos\theta$, which is the generating function of the Toeplitz matrix in (6.3.4). By analogy, we can say that the locally Toeplitz matrix in (6.7.2) has $f(\theta)$ as generating function and $a(x)$ as *weight function* (all this will be made rigorous in the next section); intuitively, we can think of $f(\theta)$ as providing the underlying Toeplitz structure $(-1, 2, -1)$, by means of its Fourier coefficients, whereas $a(x)$ determines how this Toeplitz structure changes from row to row, by means of the sampling $a(j/n)$, $j = 1, 2, \ldots, n$.

If T_n denotes the Toeplitz matrix in (6.3.4), then from the Szegő formula (see the example following Thm. 6.3.1) we obtain

$$\lim_{n \to \infty} \frac{1}{n} \sum_{j=1}^{n} F(\lambda_j(T_n)) = \frac{1}{2\pi} \int_{-\pi}^{\pi} F(2 - 2\cos\theta)\, d\theta. \tag{6.7.6}$$

Now let A_n denote the locally Toeplitz matrix in (6.7.2); what can we say about the asymptotic distribution of the eigenvalues of A_n? In the next sections we will see that, since A_n is locally Toeplitz with $f(\theta)$ as generating function and $a(x)$ as weight function, then the following generalized Szegő formula holds:

$$\lim_{n \to \infty} \frac{1}{n} \sum_{j=1}^{n} F(\lambda_j(A_n)) = \frac{1}{2\pi} \int_{0}^{1} \int_{-\pi}^{\pi} F(a(x)(2 - 2\cos\theta))\, d\theta\, dx. \tag{6.7.7}$$

Observe that, if $a(x) = 1$, then integration with respect to x can be omitted and (6.7.7) reduces to the Szegő formula (6.7.6); on the other hand, as we have already observed, if $a(x) = 1$ then A_n reduces to T_n. In view of this, (6.7.7) can be thought of as a *weighted* Szegő formula, with $a(x)$ as weight function.

The spectral distribution of A_n is completely determined by two functions, $a(x)$ and $f(\theta)$, which are independent of each other: indeed, the former comes from the differential problem (6.7.1) and has nothing to do with finite differences, whereas the latter depends only on the finite difference scheme adopted to discretize the problem. (Indeed, the triplet $(-1, 2, -1)$ comes from the approximation schemes (6.7.4) and (6.7.5), which hold for any choice of a in (6.7.1).)

6.7.1 A Closer Look at Locally Toeplitz Matrices

Given matrices A and B we denote by $A \otimes B$ the tensor product defined by (6.4.6) and denote by $A \oplus B$ the 2×2 block diagonal matrix with A and B as diagonal blocks; as usual, we agree to let $A \otimes B \oplus C = (A \otimes B) \oplus C$. Moreover, we denote by $\|A\|_F$ the Frobenius norm of A, defined as

$$\|A\|_F \triangleq \sqrt{\sum_{i=1}^{m}\sum_{j=1}^{n} |a_{ij}|^2}, \quad A \in \mathbb{C}^{m \times n}, \quad A = \{a_{ij}\}.$$

Given a function $a\colon [0,1] \to \mathbb{C}$ and a positive integer m, we set

$$D_m(a) = \operatorname{diag}[a(j/m)]_{j=1}^{m}; \tag{6.7.8}$$

that is, $D_m(a)$ is the diagonal matrix of order m whose entries are the values of the function a on the mesh $\{j/m\}_{j=1}^{m}$.

We denote by O_k the null matrix of order k. Given two functions

$$a\colon [0,1] \to \mathbb{C}, \quad f\colon [-\pi, \pi] \to \mathbb{C}, \tag{6.7.9}$$

and two positive integers $n > m$, we define the matrix-valued operator LT_n^m as follows:

$$\mathrm{LT}_n^m(a, f) = D_m(a) \otimes T_{\lfloor n/m \rfloor}(f) \oplus O_{n \bmod m}. \tag{6.7.10}$$

In the last equation $\lfloor n/m \rfloor$ is the integer part of n/m and $n \bmod m$ denotes the remainder $n - m \lfloor n/m \rfloor$ (it is understood that the null block is not present if n is a multiple of m).

We stress that $\mathrm{LT}_n^m(a, f)$ is a matrix of order n, with block diagonal structure. More precisely, it consists of m blocks of order $\lfloor n/m \rfloor$ and one null block of order $n \bmod m$ to match the size. Moreover, the jth diagonal block is the Toeplitz matrix of order $\lfloor n/m \rfloor$ generated by the function

$$f_j^{(m)}(\theta) = a(j/m)\,f(\theta).$$

Bearing in mind the above notation, we are in a position to give a precise definition of locally Toeplitz structure. The reader is referred to [Til98b] for more details.

Definition 6.7.1 (Locally Toeplitz Sequences). *A sequence of matrices A_n, where $A_n \in \mathbb{C}^{n \times n}$, is said to be* locally Toeplitz *with respect to a pair of functions (a, f) satisfying (6.7.9) if f is integrable and, for all sufficiently large $m \in \mathbf{N}$, there exists $n_m \in \mathbf{N}$ such that the following splittings hold:*

$$A_n = \mathrm{LT}_n^m(a, f) + R_{n,m} + N_{n,m} \quad \text{for all } n > n_m \tag{6.7.11}$$

with

$$\operatorname{rank} R_{n,m} \leq c(m), \quad \frac{1}{\sqrt{n}}\|N_{n,m}\|_F \leq \omega(m), \tag{6.7.12}$$

where $c(m)$ and $\omega(m)$ are functions of m and $\lim_{m \to \infty} \omega(m) = 0$.

◇

Section 6.7. Locally Toeplitz Matrices

Given a sequence of matrices A_n, we will simply write

$$A_n \xrightarrow{\text{LT}} (a, f)$$

to indicate that (the sequence) A_n is locally Toeplitz with respect to a and f. It is understood that each A_n has order n, that a is defined over $[0, 1]$, and that f is defined over $[-\pi, \pi]$ and is integrable; moreover, both a and f are supposed to be complex valued, unless otherwise specified. We call a the *weight function* and f the *generating function*; moreover, in the splittings (6.7.11), the matrices $R_{n,m}$ are called *rank corrections*, while $N_{n,m}$ are called *norm corrections*.

In the last section we claimed that the matrix A_n in (6.7.2) is locally Toeplitz; in light of the above definition, this was not quite correct, since being locally Toeplitz is a property not of a single matrix but of a whole sequence of matrices $\{A_n\}$ (which, for simplicity of notation, still will be denoted by A_n). In other words, given a single matrix A_n, it makes no sense to ask if it is locally Toeplitz. Nevertheless, if a sequence $\{A_n\}$ is locally Toeplitz and $A \in \{A_n\}$, we will improperly say that "A is a locally Toeplitz matrix." This should not cause confusion, provided one bears in mind the above definition.

With each locally Toeplitz sequence of matrices A_n a pair of functions (a, f) is associated, each of which plays a different role. Intuitively, we regard $a(x)$ as a *weight function*, and $f(\theta)$ as a *generating function* in the usual Toeplitz sense. The idea underlying the splittings (6.7.11) is that each matrix A_n has, up to small-rank and small-norm corrections, a sort of local Toeplitz structure modeled on $T_n(f)$, varying along each diagonal according to the weight function a.

Pondering over Def. 6.7.1 for a while, the reader will realize that it gives a precise mathematical meaning to the intuitive remarks of the previous section. In particular, by explicitly building the splittings (6.7.11), the reader may check that $A_n \xrightarrow{\text{LT}} (a, f)$, where A_n is the matrix in (6.7.2), $a(x)$ is the weight function in (6.7.3), and f is as in the example following Thm. 6.3.1.

On trying to prove that $A_n \xrightarrow{\text{LT}} (a, f)$ when A_n is given by (6.7.2), the reader will find out that building the splittings (6.7.11) can be a very difficult task. (However, with the aid of some more theory, the claim $A_n \xrightarrow{\text{LT}} (a, f)$ can be proved without explicitly building the splittings (6.7.11), as we will see in the example following Cor. 6.7.2). Therefore, we will state some theorems that can serve as a tool for generating nontrivial locally Toeplitz sequences or for proving that a given sequence is locally Toeplitz.

Theorem 6.7.1 (Toeplitz Matrices are Locally Toeplitz). *If $f \colon [-\pi, \pi] \mapsto \mathbb{C}$ is square integrable and $T_n(f)$ is the sequence of Toeplitz matrices generated by f, then $T_n(f)$ is a locally Toeplitz with f as generating function and $a(x) = 1$ as weight function, that is,*

$$T_n(f) \xrightarrow{\text{LT}} (1, f).$$

$\diamondsuit$

Observe that, by virtue of the last theorem, the notion of locally Toeplitz sequence extends that of Toeplitz sequences of matrices.

Another nontrivial class of locally Toeplitz sequences is provided by the following example.

Example (**Sampling Matrices**). Suppose $a(x)$ is continuous over $[0,1]$, and consider the sequence of diagonal matrices

$$\Lambda_n(a) = \operatorname{diag}\left[a\left(\frac{1}{n+1}\right), a\left(\frac{2}{n+1}\right), \ldots, a\left(\frac{n}{n+1}\right)\right] \tag{6.7.13}$$

for $n \geq 1$. We claim that

$$\Lambda_n(a) \xrightarrow{\mathrm{LT}} (a, 1). \tag{6.7.14}$$

To prove this, we explicitly build the splittings (6.7.11). Let us set

$$R_{n,m} = O_n, \quad N_{n,m} = \Lambda_n(a) - \mathrm{LT}_n^m(a, 1).$$

The rank condition in (6.7.12) is trivially satisfied letting $c(m) = 0$. Concerning the norm condition in (6.7.12), we observe that $N_{n,m}$ is a diagonal matrix of order n, whose generic diagonal element can be expressed as $a(x) - a(y)$, with $|x - y| \leq 4/m$; therefore, the Frobenius norm of $N_{n,m}$ cannot exceed $\sqrt{n}\,\theta(4/m)$, where θ is the modulus of continuity of a:

$$\theta(\epsilon) = \sup_{\substack{0 \leq x, y \leq 1 \\ |x-y| \leq \epsilon}} |a(x) - a(y)|. \tag{6.7.15}$$

Since $\lim_{\epsilon \to 0} \theta(\epsilon) = 0$ (this follows from elementary analysis, since a is continuous over $[0,1]$ and hence uniformly continuous), the norm estimate in (6.7.12) is satisfied by letting $\omega(m) = \theta(4/m)$.

$\diamond$

According to Thm. 6.7.1 and the example above we observe that, in a sense which we will soon make clear, Toeplitz sequences and sampling sequences are orthogonal: indeed, the former are locally Toeplitz with weight function $a(x) = 1$, whereas the latter are locally Toeplitz with generating function $f(\theta) = 1$.

Under certain reasonable assumptions, the termwise product of two locally Toeplitz sequences is also locally Toeplitz. In the following theorem, we denote by $\|A\|_2$ the spectral norm of the matrix A, that is, the largest among its singular values [Til98b].

Theorem 6.7.2 (**Product of Two Sequences**). *Suppose $A_n \xrightarrow{\mathrm{LT}} (a, f)$ and $\tilde{A}_n \xrightarrow{\mathrm{LT}} (\tilde{a}, \tilde{f})$, where $a, \tilde{a}, f, \tilde{f}$ are bounded functions. If there exists a constant $C > 0$ such that*

$$\|N_{n,m}\|_2 \leq C \tag{6.7.16}$$

holds in the splittings (6.7.11), then it holds that

$$A_n \tilde{A}_n \xrightarrow{\mathrm{LT}} (a\tilde{a}, f\tilde{f}), \quad \tilde{A}_n A_n \xrightarrow{\mathrm{LT}} (a\tilde{a}, f\tilde{f}). \tag{6.7.17}$$

$\diamond$

It can be shown (see [Til98b]) that the additional assumption (6.7.16) is always satisfied by a sequence of Toeplitz matrices $T_n(f)$, provided f is bounded. As a consequence, when the generating functions are bounded, the product of a locally Toeplitz sequence with Toeplitz sequences is also locally Toeplitz; in particular, the product of any number of Toeplitz sequences is locally Toeplitz. (Observe that, in general, the product of two Toeplitz matrices is not a Toeplitz matrix.)

Section 6.7. Locally Toeplitz Matrices 181

Corollary 6.7.1 (Product of Toeplitz Matrices). *Suppose $A_n \xrightarrow{LT} (a, f)$, where a and f are bounded. If $p_1, \ldots, p_j$ and $q_1, \ldots, q_k$ are all bounded functions, then letting*

$$B_n = T_n(p_1) \cdots T_n(p_j) A_n T_n(q_1) \cdots T_n(q_k)$$

it holds that

$$B_n \xrightarrow{LT} (a, p_1 \cdots p_j f q_1 \cdots q_k).$$

◇

Observing that $I_n \xrightarrow{LT} (1, 1)$ (where I_n is the identity matrix of order n) we obtain the following.

Corollary 6.7.2 (Product of Toeplitz Matrices). *Suppose $f_1, \ldots, f_k$ are bounded functions. Then it holds that*

$$T_n(f_1) \cdots T_n(f_k) \xrightarrow{LT} (1, f_1 \cdots f_k).$$

◇

As an application of the above corollary, in the following example we show that the matrices in (6.7.2) are locally Toeplitz, as we claimed in the last section.

Example. Suppose $a(x)$ is continuous over $[0, 1]$ and let A_n be defined according to (6.7.2). We want to prove that the sequence A_n is locally Toeplitz with respect to the pair of functions (a, f), where $f(\theta) = 2 - 2 \cos \theta$.
For $q(\theta) = e^{i\theta} - 1$, consider the bidiagonal Toeplitz matrices

$$T_n(q) = \begin{pmatrix} -1 & 1 & & \\ & \ddots & \ddots & \\ & & \ddots & 1 \\ & & & -1 \end{pmatrix}_{n \times n}.$$

A direct computation shows that

$$A_n = T_n^*(q) \Lambda_n(a) T_n(q) + a\left(\frac{1}{2(n+1)}\right) e_1 e_1^*, \tag{6.7.18}$$

where Λ_n is the sampling matrix (6.7.13) and $e_1 = (1, 0, \ldots, 0)^*$ is the first vector of the canonical basis of $\mathbb{R}^n$. In particular, the difference

$$A_n - T_n^*(q) \Lambda_n(a) T_n(q)$$

has rank at most 1 for all n and hence, in order to show $A_n \xrightarrow{LT} (a, 2 - 2 \cos \theta)$, it suffices to show

$$T_n^*(q) \Lambda_n T_n(q) \xrightarrow{LT} (a, 1, 2 - 2 \cos \theta).$$

Since trivially $T_n^*(q) = T_n(q^*)$, from Thm. 6.7.1 and the example following it we obtain

$$\Lambda_n(a) \xrightarrow{LT} (a, 1), \quad T_n(q) \xrightarrow{LT} (1, q), \quad T_n^*(q) \xrightarrow{LT} (1, q^*),$$

and hence from Cor. 6.7.1 it follows that

$$T_n^*(q) \Lambda_n T_n(q) \xrightarrow{LT} (a, q^* q).$$

Finally, it suffices to observe that $q^*(\theta) q(\theta) = 2 - 2 \cos \theta$.

◇

6.7.2 Spectral Distribution of Locally Toeplitz Sequences

It turns out that locally Toeplitz sequences have singular values and (in the Hermitian case) eigenvalues nicely distributed, according to weighted Szegő formulas of the type (6.7.7).

Concerning singular values, the following result can be proved [Til98b].

Theorem 6.7.3 (Weighted Szegő Formula for Singular Values). *Suppose the sequence of matrices A_n is such that $A_n \xrightarrow{LT} (a, f)$, where a is a piecewise continuous weight function. Then for any test function F, continuous with bounded support, it holds that*

$$\lim_{n \to \infty} \frac{1}{n} \sum_{j=1}^{n} F[\sigma_j(A_n)] = \frac{1}{2\pi} \int_0^1 \int_{-\pi}^{\pi} F(|a(x)f(\theta)|) \, d\theta \, dx. \qquad (6.7.19)$$

$\diamond$

Example. We know from the last example that the matrices A_n in (6.7.2) are locally Toeplitz with respect to the pair (a, f), where a is given by (6.7.1) and $f(\theta) = 2 - 2\cos\theta$. Therefore, using Thm. 6.7.3 we are able to compute the asymptotic distribution of the singular values of the matrices A_n, as follows:

$$\lim_{n \to \infty} \frac{1}{n} \sum_{j=1}^{n} F(\sigma_j(A_n)) = \frac{1}{2\pi} \int_0^1 \int_{-\pi}^{\pi} F\big[|a(x)(2 - 2\cos\theta)|\big] \, d\theta \, dx. \qquad (6.7.20)$$

We remark that the above formula holds also when $a(x)$ in (6.7.1) is not real but complex valued, since Thm. 6.7.3 does not require the involved matrices to be Hermitian.

$\diamond$

Example. Consider $\Lambda_n(a)$ given by (6.7.13). Since $\Lambda_n(a)$ is diagonal, its singular values are

$$\left|a\left(\frac{1}{n+1}\right)\right|, \left|a\left(\frac{2}{n+1}\right)\right|, \ldots, \left|a\left(\frac{n}{n+1}\right)\right|.$$

If a is continuous, we know from the example following Thm. 6.7.1 that $\Lambda_n(a) \xrightarrow{LT} (a, 1)$. Therefore, Thm. 6.7.3 can be applied, and (6.7.19) reduces to

$$\lim_{n \to \infty} \frac{1}{n} \sum_{j=1}^{n} F\left(\left|a\left(\frac{j}{n+1}\right)\right|\right) = \int_0^1 F(|a(x)|) \, dx;$$

that is, the Riemann sums of the continuous function $F(|a(x)|)$ converge to its Lebesgue integral.

$\diamond$

Given a square matrix A, we let

$$\operatorname{Re} A = \frac{1}{2}(A + A^*), \quad \operatorname{Im} A = \frac{1}{2\hat{\imath}}(A - A^*).$$

Observe that $\operatorname{Re} A$ and $\operatorname{Im} A$, respectively, reduce to the usual notion of real and imaginary part when A has order 1 (i.e., when A is a complex number): therefore, we say that $\operatorname{Re} A$ and $\operatorname{Im} A$ are the real and, respectively, the imaginary part of the matrix A. (It is easily seen that $\operatorname{Re} A$ and $\operatorname{Im} A$ are always Hermitian matrices.)

Concerning the eigenvalues of a locally Toeplitz sequence, it is possible to prove a weighted Szegő formula for the eigenvalues of the real and the imaginary part of the sequence and of the sequence itself when it is Hermitian [Til98b].

Section 6.7. Locally Toeplitz Matrices

Theorem 6.7.4 (Weighted Szegö Formulas for Eigenvalues). *Suppose a sequence of matrices A_n satisfies $A_n \xrightarrow{LT} (a, f)$, and suppose the weight function a is piecewise continuous. Then for all test functions F, continuous with a bounded support, it holds that*

$$\lim_{n \to \infty} \frac{1}{n} \sum_{j=1}^{n} F[\lambda_j(\operatorname{Re} A_n)] = \frac{1}{2\pi} \int_0^1 \int_{-\pi}^{\pi} F[\operatorname{Re} a(x) f(\theta)] \, d\theta \, dx, \qquad (6.7.21)$$

$$\lim_{n \to \infty} \frac{1}{n} \sum_{j=1}^{n} F[\lambda_j(\operatorname{Im} A_n)] = \frac{1}{2\pi} \int_0^1 \int_{-\pi}^{\pi} F[\operatorname{Im} a(x) f(\theta)] \, d\theta \, dx. \qquad (6.7.22)$$

If, moreover, each A_n is Hermitian, then it holds that

$$\lim_{n \to \infty} \frac{1}{n} \sum_{j=1}^{n} F[\lambda_j(A_n)] = \frac{1}{2\pi} \int_0^1 \int_{-\pi}^{\pi} F[a(x) f(\theta)] \, d\theta \, dx. \qquad (6.7.23)$$

◇

The right-hand sides of (6.7.19) and (6.7.23) can be thought of as weighted versions of the right-hand sides of (6.3.17) and (6.3.13); in particular, when $a(x) = 1$ the integrals in (6.7.19) and (6.7.23) reduce to those in (6.3.17) and (6.3.13), respectively. This analogy is more than a formal one; indeed, according to Thm. 6.7.1, if f is square integrable, then $T_n(f) \xrightarrow{LT} (1, f)$. In view of this, when f is square integrable, Thm. 6.3.5 can be obtained as a corollary of Thm. 6.7.3 and, similarly, Thm. 6.3.3 can be obtained as a corollary of Thm. 6.7.4.

Example. Let us consider again the matrices A_n in (6.7.2). Suppose that $a(x)$ is complex valued and continuous, and define the two real-valued functions u, v according to

$$a(x) = v(x) + \hat{\imath} w(x), \quad v(x) = \operatorname{Re} a(x), \quad w(x) = \operatorname{Im} a(x).$$

From the example following Cor. 6.7.2 we know $A_n \xrightarrow{LT} (a, f)$, where $f(\theta) = 2 - 2\cos\theta$. Therefore, applying Thm. 6.7.4, from (6.7.21) and (6.7.22) we obtain

$$\lim_{n \to \infty} \frac{1}{n} \sum_{j=1}^{n} F\big(\lambda_j(\operatorname{Re} A_n)\big) = \frac{1}{2\pi} \int_0^1 \int_{-\pi}^{\pi} F\big[v(x)(2 - 2\cos\theta)\big] \, d\theta \, dx,$$

$$\lim_{n \to \infty} \frac{1}{n} \sum_{j=1}^{n} F\big(\lambda_j(\operatorname{Im} A_n)\big) = \frac{1}{2\pi} \int_0^1 \int_{-\pi}^{\pi} F\big[w(x)(2 - 2\cos\theta)\big] \, d\theta \, dx.$$

In the particular case where a is real valued (so that A_n is Hermitian), from (6.7.23) we have

$$\lim_{n \to \infty} \frac{1}{n} \sum_{j=1}^{n} F\big(\lambda_j(A_n)\big) = \frac{1}{2\pi} \int_0^1 \int_{-\pi}^{\pi} F\big[a(x)(2 - 2\cos\theta)\big] \, d\theta \, dx.$$

◇

Suppose a sequence of Hermitian matrices A_n is locally Toeplitz with respect to a pair of functions (a, f); then, according to Thm. 6.7.4, formula (6.7.23) holds for all F. The right-hand side of (6.7.23) deserves some remarks: indeed, the test function F is defined on the real line, and hence $F(z)$ makes sense only when z is a real number;

on the other hand, in Thm. 6.7.4 there seems to be no assumption on a and f as to a guarantee that the product $a(x)f(\theta)$ is real.

However, it turns out that the assumption that each A_n is Hermitian forces the product function
$$(x, \theta) \mapsto a(x)\, f(\theta)$$
to be real valued almost everywhere (with respect to the bidimensional Lebesgue measure) over the rectangle $[0,1] \times [-\pi, \pi]$, and hence the integral in (6.7.23) is well defined.

This fact can be easily proved with the aid of the following result [Til98b].

Theorem 6.7.5 (Uniqueness of Representation). *Suppose that a sequence of matrices A_n can be split, in two different ways, as the sum of p locally Toeplitz sequences*
$$A_n = \sum_{i=1}^{p} A_n^{(i)} = \sum_{i=1}^{p} \widehat{A}_n^{(i)}, \quad n = 1, 2, \ldots,$$
$$A_n^{(i)} \xrightarrow{\text{LT}} (a_i, f_i), \quad \widehat{A}_n^{(i)} \xrightarrow{\text{LT}} (\hat{a}_i, \hat{f}_i), \quad i = 1, 2, \ldots, p,$$
where all the weight functions are piecewise continuous and the generating functions are integrable. Then for all $(y,x) \in [0,1] \times [-\pi,\pi]$, except at most on a subset of null measure, it holds that
$$\sum_{i=1}^{p} a_i(x)\, f_i(\theta) = \sum_{i=1}^{p} \hat{a}_i(x)\, \hat{f}_i(\theta). \tag{6.7.24}$$
$\diamond$

In particular, if $A_n \xrightarrow{\text{LT}} (a, f)$ and A_n is Hermitian, then trivially $A_n^* \xrightarrow{\text{LT}} (a^*, f^*)$ and hence also $A_n \xrightarrow{\text{LT}} (a^*, f^*)$. Therefore, the sequence A_n is locally Toeplitz with respect to the two pairs of functions (a, f) and (a^*, f^*). From the previous theorem, applied with $p = 1$, we obtain that
$$a(x)f(\theta) = a^*(x)f^*(\theta)$$
or, which is the same, that $a(x)f(\theta)$ is a real number for almost every pair $(x, \theta) \in [0, 1] \times [-\pi, \pi]$, so that the integral in (6.7.23) makes sense. Observe, however, that from the fact that $a(x)f(\theta)$ is real almost everywhere it does not follows that $a(x)$ and $f(\theta)$ are real valued. (For example, both a and f might always take imaginary values.)

In many applications, it often happens that we need to deal with a sequence of matrices that perhaps is not locally Toeplitz but can be split into the the sum of a certain number of locally Toeplitz sequences. In this case, the following results (which generalize the last two theorems) can be applied [Til98b].

Theorem 6.7.6 (Sum of Locally Toeplitz Matrices). *Suppose that a sequence of matrices A_n can be split as the sum of p locally Toeplitz sequences*
$$A_n = \sum_{i=1}^{p} A_n^{(i)}, \quad n = 1, 2, \ldots,$$
$$A_n^{(i)} \xrightarrow{\text{LT}} (a_i, f_i), \quad i = 1, 2, \ldots, p,$$

Section 6.7. Locally Toeplitz Matrices 185

where each a_i is piecewise continuous. Then for all $F \in \mathcal{C}_0$ it holds that

$$\lim_{n \to \infty} \frac{1}{n} \sum_{j=1}^{n} F[\sigma_j(A_n)] = \frac{1}{2\pi} \int_0^1 \int_{-\pi}^{\pi} F\left(\left|\sum_{i=1}^{p} a_i(x) f_i(\theta)\right|\right) d\theta \, dx. \qquad (6.7.25)$$

$\diamond$

Theorem 6.7.7 (Spectral Distribution Results). *Under the same assumptions and notation as in the previous theorem, for all $F \in \mathcal{C}_0$ it holds that*

$$\lim_{n \to \infty} \frac{1}{n} \sum_{j=1}^{n} F[\lambda_j(\mathrm{Re}\, A_n)] = \frac{1}{2\pi} \int_0^1 \int_{-\pi}^{\pi} F\left[\mathrm{Re} \sum_{i=1}^{p} a_i(x) f_i(\theta)\right] d\theta \, dx,$$

$$\lim_{n \to \infty} \frac{1}{n} \sum_{j=1}^{n} F[\lambda_j(\mathrm{Im}\, A_n)] = \frac{1}{2\pi} \int_0^1 \int_{-\pi}^{\pi} F\left[\mathrm{Im} \sum_{i=1}^{p} a_i(x) f_i(\theta)\right] d\theta \, dx.$$

If, moreover, each A_n is Hermitian, then it also holds that

$$\lim_{n \to \infty} \frac{1}{n} \sum_{j=1}^{n} F[\lambda_j(A_n)] = \frac{1}{2\pi} \int_0^1 \int_{-\pi}^{\pi} F\left[\sum_{i=1}^{p} a_i(x) f_i(\theta)\right] d\theta \, dx. \qquad (6.7.26)$$

$\diamond$

Unlike Toeplitz sequences, the sum of two locally Toeplitz sequences may fail to be locally Toeplitz; therefore, the last two theorems by no means follow as consequences of Thms. 6.7.3 and 6.7.4.

Observe that when A_n is Hermitian, the integral in (6.7.26) is well defined, since the sum

$$\sum_{i=1}^{p} a_i(x) f_i(\theta)$$

is a real number almost everywhere. (This can be proved without difficulty relying on Thm. 6.7.5, reasoning in exactly the same way as we did for the case $p = 1$.)

Example (Algebra Generated by Toeplitz Sequences). In [Tyr94a], Tyrtyshnikov proved that the singular values of a finite product of Toeplitz sequences are distributed as the magnitude of the product of their generating functions; that is,

$$\lim_{n \to \infty} \frac{1}{n} \sum_{j=1}^{n} F\Big(\sigma_j\big(T_n(f_1) \cdots T_n(f_p)\big)\Big) = \frac{1}{2\pi} \int_{-\pi}^{\pi} F\big(|f_1(\theta) \cdots f_p(\theta)|\big) d\theta$$

whenever all the f_i's are bounded. Observe that we can obtain this result as a consequence of Cor. 6.7.2 and Thm. 6.7.3; moreover, we can extend it to handle all sequences in the algebra generated by Toeplitz sequences, as follows.

Let $\mathcal{T}$ be the vector space of all Toeplitz sequences $T_n(f)$ with a bounded generating function f, and let $\mathcal{A}$ be the algebra of sequences generated by $\mathcal{T}$. It is clear that any sequence $A_n \in \mathcal{A}$ can be written as

$$A_n = \sum_\alpha \prod_\beta T_n(f_{\alpha\beta}), \quad f_{\alpha\beta} \in L_\infty.$$

(If necessary, one can let $f_{\alpha\beta} = 1$ for some indices α, β, observing that the identity matrix $T_n(1)$ does not affect the products.) From Cor. 6.7.2 we know that, for each α,

$$\prod_\beta T_n(f_{\alpha\beta}) \xrightarrow{LT} \left(1, \prod_\beta f_{\alpha\beta}\right),$$

and hence from Thm. 6.7.6 (omitting integration with respect to x, since $a(x) = 1$) we can conclude that

$$\lim_{n\to\infty} \frac{1}{n} \sum_{j=1}^n F\left(\sigma_j\left(\sum_\alpha \prod_\beta T_n(f_{\alpha\beta})\right)\right) = \frac{1}{2\pi} \int_{-\pi}^{\pi} F\left(\left|\sum_\alpha \prod_\beta f_{\alpha\beta}(\theta)\right|\right) d\theta.$$

Concerning eigenvalues, in a similar way from Thm. 6.7.7 we obtain

$$\lim_{n\to\infty} \frac{1}{n} \sum_{j=1}^n F\left(\lambda_j\left(\operatorname{Re}\sum_\alpha \prod_\beta T_n(f_{\alpha\beta})\right)\right) = \frac{1}{2\pi} \int_{-\pi}^{\pi} F\left(\operatorname{Re}\sum_\alpha \prod_\beta f_{\alpha\beta}(\theta)\right) d\theta,$$

$$\lim_{n\to\infty} \frac{1}{n} \sum_{j=1}^n F\left(\lambda_j\left(\operatorname{Im}\sum_\alpha \prod_\beta T_n(f_{\alpha\beta})\right)\right) = \frac{1}{2\pi} \int_{-\pi}^{\pi} F\left(\operatorname{Im}\sum_\alpha \prod_\beta f_{\alpha\beta}(\theta)\right) d\theta.$$

◇

6.8 CONCLUDING REMARKS

From the results discussed in this chapter it appears that the theory of the spectral distribution of Toeplitz-related matrices is quite well developed; however, the research in this field is far from being exhausted. There are, in fact, many interesting questions that deserve a deeper investigation.

If $f : (-\pi, \pi) \mapsto \mathbb{R}$ is measurable and bounded, then the Szegő formula implies (see [GS84]) that

$$\lim_{n\to\infty} \lambda_k(T_n) = \inf f, \qquad (6.8.1)$$

$$\lim_{n\to\infty} \lambda_{n+1-k}(T_n) = \sup f \qquad (6.8.2)$$

for any natural number k. In other words, for any k, the smallest k eigenvalues of T_n tend to $\inf f$, whereas the largest k eigenvalues tend to $\sup f$, as n tends to infinity. Observe that, according to Thm. 6.3.2, all the eigenvalues of any T_n lie inside the interval $[\inf f, \sup f]$. Moreover, since T_n is a principal submatrix of T_{n+1}, the minimax principle (see, for example, [HJ85]) implies that the sequence $\{\lambda_k(T_n)\}_n$ is nonincreasing for any fixed k, and therefore the existence of the limit in (6.8.1) is trivial. (A similar argument applies to (6.8.2).)

A question that arises quite naturally is, How fast is the convergence in (6.8.1) and (6.8.2)?

In the case where $\inf f = 0$ and f has a unique zero the convergence rate of $\lambda_1(T_n)$ is strictly connected with the order of the zero; roughly speaking, if f is sufficiently smooth in a neighborhood of the zero and if the zero has a finite order $\theta \geq 2$, it can be proved that $\lambda_k(T_n)$ is $O(1/n^\theta)$ (see [GS84], [HH77], and Ch. 5).

Section 6.8. Concluding Remarks

Example. Consider $f(\theta) = 2 - 2\cos\theta$. Then $f(\theta) \geq 0$, $\inf f = 0$, and $f(\theta) = 0$ only at $\theta = 0$. From Taylor's expansion we obtain

$$f(\theta) = 2 - 2\left(1 - \frac{\theta^2}{2} + O(\theta^4)\right) = \theta^2 + O(\theta^4),$$

and therefore $\theta = 0$ is a zero of order two. On the other hand, we know from the example following Thm. 6.3.1 that

$$\lambda_k(T_n) = 2 - 2\cos\frac{k\pi}{n+1}.$$

When k is fixed and n is large, again from Taylor's formula we obtain

$$\lambda_k(T_n) = 2 - 2\left(1 - \frac{k\pi^2}{2(n+1)^2} + O\left(\frac{k^4}{n^4}\right)\right) = \pi^2\frac{k^2}{n^2} + O\left(\frac{k^4}{n^4}\right)$$

and hence, for fixed k, $\lambda_k(T_n)$ is $O(1/n^2)$.

$\diamond$

Knowing how fast $\lambda_1(T_n)$ tends to $\inf f$ as $n \to \infty$ is important in applications, especially when $\inf f = 0$ and $0 < \sup f < +\infty$; indeed, in this case we know from Thm. 6.3.2 that each T_n is positive definite and hence

$$\kappa(T_n) = \frac{\lambda_n(T_n)}{\lambda_1(T_n)} \leq \frac{\sup f}{\lambda_1(T_n)}.$$

Therefore, knowing how fast $\lambda_1(T_n)$ tends to zero allows one to estimate the condition number of T_n.

It would be desirable to obtain precise estimates on the behavior of $\lambda_k(T_n)$ in more general cases, for example, when f is not a smooth function, or when it is multivariate, matrix valued, and so on. Also the behavior of $\sigma_k(T_n)$ should be investigated in more detail. (For some new results in this direction, see [BG97] and the references therein.)

We remark that, on investigating such questions as the behavior of the kth eigenvalue or singular value of a sequence of matrices, a Szegő-type formula alone is not sufficient, since it provides only global information on the asymptotic spectra of the involved matrices; in other words, investigating the behavior of the kth eigenvalue requires a finer analysis of the spectrum.

To conclude, we recall that there are several classes of structured matrices, in addition to Toeplitz matrices, that can be associated with the Fourier coefficients of a generating function; among such classes, we mention Hankel and circulant matrices (see [Ioh82], [Dav79], and Ch. 1).

For sequences of Hankel or circulant matrices some Szegő-type formulas hold, and a spectral theory similar to that of Toeplitz matrices can be developed (see, for example, [Tyr96a], [Til97a]); in view of that, the importance of a general theory for the spectral distribution of a sequence of matrices is apparent. The first step explicitly taken in this direction is by Tyrtyshnikov, in the fundamental paper [Tyr96a].

Chapter 7

NEWTON'S ITERATION FOR STRUCTURED MATRICES

Victor Y. Pan

Sheryl Branham

Rhys E. Rosholt

Ai-Long Zheng

7.1 INTRODUCTION

Preconditioned conjugate gradient (PCG) methods are quite effective for the solution of a large class of Toeplitz and Toeplitz-like linear systems of equations. In a few iterations, they provide an approximate solution and then improve the approximation with linear convergence rate (cf. the discussions in Chs. 5 and 6). While this performance is sufficient in several applications, there are many cases where it is still desirable to compute a highly accurate solution at a faster convergence rate, assuming that a rough initial approximation has been computed by a PCG algorithm. Alternatively, any Toeplitz or Toeplitz-like linear system of equations can be solved effectively by known direct methods (e.g., [AG88], [Bun85], [GKO95], [Gu95a], and also Chs. 1–3 of this book). The references [GKO95], [Gu95a] extend the general approach of [Pan90] to yield practical Toeplitz and Toeplitz-like solvers, but in many cases the computed solution must be refined to counter the effect of rounding errors.

In this chapter we rely on the techniques of [Pan93a], [Pan93b], [Pan92a], [Pan90], [PZHD97], and on their variations, to compute the desired refinement by means of Newton's iteration. We describe and analyze four quadratically convergent algorithms for the refinement of rough initial approximations to the inverses of $n \times n$ nonsingular Toeplitz and Toeplitz-like matrices and to the solutions of nonsingular Toeplitz and Toeplitz-like linear systems of n equations. Our first two modifications of Newton's iteration (Algs. 7.4.1 and 7.4.2) exploit the displacement structure of the input matrices to simplify the computations. Our third and fourth modifications (Algs. 7.5.1 and 7.5.2) rely on the inversion formulas known for Toeplitz matrices and simplify the first two algorithms. By exploiting matrix structure, each iteration step requires $O(n \log n)$ operations.

Algorithm 7.4.1 is a little more costly to perform but yields convergence under substantially milder assumptions on the initial approximation than Alg. 7.4.2. Algorithm 7.5.2 runs roughly twice as fast as Alg. 7.5.1 and does not require any stronger initial assumptions. Algorithms 7.4.1 and 7.5.1 are more convenient to apply when the triangular Toeplitz representation is used for the input and output matrices, whereas Algs. 7.4.2 and 7.5.2 are more convenient to apply when a factor-circulant (f-circulant) representation is used. As we will point out later, some of our algorithms can be extended to other classes of structured matrices.

We may mention that all four algorithms require an initial approximation that lies sufficiently close to the desired solution (see (7.4.6), (7.4.11), (7.5.9)), since otherwise the iterations may converge too slowly or even diverge. A partial remedy can be obtained by means of homotopy techniques (cf. our remark at the end of Sec. 7.4.2 and also the discussion in [Pan92a]).

Algorithms 7.4.1 and 7.4.2 are presented as Newton's iteration for matrix inversion and Algs. 7.5.1 and 7.5.2 as residual correction for linear systems. In Sec. 7.5 we show the equivalence of Newton's iteration and residual correction in our cases. Furthermore, the inversion and linear system solving are closely related in the Toeplitz and Toeplitz-like cases, where a displacement generator of the inverse matrix A^{-1} is produced by the solution of two or a few linear systems $A\mathbf{x} = \mathbf{b}_i$ and the solution to $A\mathbf{x} = \mathbf{b}$ is immediately obtained from a displacement generator of A^{-1}. Since the approximation to the inverse is improved together with the improvement of its displacement generator in each recursive step, our residual correction processes converge quadratically, rather than linearly. Newton's iteration has an algebraic version [Pan92b], [BP93], [BP94, pp. 189–190] that we will not cover here.

7.2 NEWTON'S ITERATION FOR MATRIX INVERSION

Newton's iteration is a major tool for solving a nonlinear equation $f(x) = 0$. Let x_0 be an initial approximation to a solution x. Then the iteration successively produces a sequence of iterates

$$x_{i+1} = x_i - \frac{f(x_i)}{f'(x_i)}, \qquad (7.2.1)$$

with errors $e_i = |x_i - x|$, $i = 0, 1, \ldots$. If $f(x)$ is smooth enough in a neighborhood of x and if e_0 is small enough, then the approximations converge to the solution with quadratic convergence rate [Atk78], i.e.,

$$e_{i+1} \approx \frac{f''(x)}{2f'(x)} e_i^2, \qquad i = 0, 1, \ldots. \qquad (7.2.2)$$

For example, suppose that we wish to apply Newton's iteration to approximate $1/t$ for a given positive binary t of the form

$$t = 2^e (0.t_1 t_2 t_3 \ldots)_2,$$

where e is an integer, $t_1 = 1$, and $t_i \in \{0,1\}$ for $i \geq 2$. By choosing $x_0 = 2^{-e}$ and $f(x) = t - 1/x$, we obtain

$$0 < |1 - tx_0| = 1 - (0.t_1 t_2 \ldots)_2 \leq 1/2,$$

and Newton's iteration takes the form

$$x_i = x_{i-1}(2 - tx_{i-1}), \qquad i = 1, 2, \ldots.$$

Section 7.2. Newton's Iteration for Matrix Inversion

It follows that
$$1 - tx_i = 1 - 2tx_{i-1} + (tx_{i-1})^2 = (1 - tx_{i-1})^2.$$

Recursively, we obtain that $0 < 1 - tx_i = (1 - tx_0)^{2^i} \leq 2^{-2^i}$. Therefore,

$$0 < \frac{1}{t} - x_i \leq \frac{2^{-2^i}}{t},$$

and the iteration very rapidly (quadratically) converges to $1/t$.

Assume $t = (0.101)_2 = 1/2 + 1/8$. Then the results of performing four steps of Newton's iteration on a computer with 8-decimal precision are shown in Table 7.1 (where the values of $1 - tx_4$ and $1/t - x_4$ are shown without several decimal digits lost at the stage of the subtraction of $tx_4 = 0.99999999$ from 1).

Table 7.1. Newton's iteration for the reciprocal of 5/8.

i	x_i	$1 - tx_i$	$1/t - x_i$
0	1.0000000e + 00	3.7500000e − 01	6.0000000e − 01
1	1.3750000e + 00	1.4062500e − 01	2.2500000e − 01
2	1.5683594e + 00	1.9775391e − 02	3.1640649e − 02
3	1.5993743e + 00	3.9106607e − 04	6.2572956e − 04
4	1.5999998e + 00	1.3411045e − 07	2.3841858e − 07

Remark. According to [Boy68], and despite Newton's name, the origin of this iteration can be traced back four millennia, when the ancient Babylonians applied it in rudimentary form to solve quadratic equations. For the solution of polynomial equations of higher degree, the iteration was routinely used by Chinese and Arab mathematicians in medieval times. Among European predecessors of Newton, F. Viéte should be mentioned. The present-day version of Newton's iteration was given by Joseph Raphson in 1690. We use Newton's name to be consistent with the commonly accepted (although inaccurate) terminology.

Newton's iteration can also be effectively applied to some matrix equations of the form $f(X) = 0$, where X is now a matrix rather than a scalar. We demonstrate this fact by considering the inversion of an $n \times n$ nonsingular matrix A by Newton's method. The idea of using Newton's method for such an application can be traced back to [Sch33]; a more recent treatment can be found in [PS91].

Assume that a matrix A is given along with an initial approximation $-X_0$ to its inverse A^{-1} satisfying the bound

$$\tau = ||I + X_0 A|| = ||I - (-X_0)A|| < 1$$

for some positive τ and some fixed matrix norm. The initial approximation $-X_0$ to A^{-1} can be obtained by some other computational procedure, for example, by a PCG algorithm, by an exact solution algorithm (see, e.g., the discussions in Ch. 1 and also [GKO95], [Gu95a]), or by the homotopy algorithm of [Pan92a]. By choosing $f(X) = A + X^{-1}$, Newton's iteration becomes

$$X_{i+1} = X_i(2I + AX_i) = (2I + X_i A)X_i, \quad i = 0, 1, \ldots. \tag{7.2.3}$$

(Here, we deviated slightly from the customary notation of Newton's iteration by writing $-X_i$ instead of X_i to denote the computed approximations to the inverse matrix A^{-1}.)

It follows from (7.2.3) that
$$I + X_{i+1}A = (I + X_iA)^2 = (I + X_{i-1}A)^4 = \cdots = (I + X_0A)^{2^{i+1}}.$$
Consequently,
$$\|I + X_iA\| = \|I - (-X_i)A\| \leq \tau^{2^i}$$
so that the norm of the residual matrix $I + X_iA$ is bounded from above by τ^{2^i}. This establishes quadratic convergence of the iteration. Moreover, given a desired residual norm bound $\epsilon > 0$, the bound
$$\|I + X_iA\| < \epsilon \qquad (7.2.4)$$
is guaranteed in $\lceil \log_2(\frac{\log \epsilon}{\log \tau}) \rceil$ recursive steps (7.2.3), where $\lceil x \rceil$ stands for the smallest integer not exceeded by x. We also deduce from (7.2.4) that
$$\|A^{-1} + X_i\| \leq \|I + X_iA\| \cdot \|A^{-1}\| < \epsilon \|A^{-1}\|,$$
and it follows that
$$\frac{\|A^{-1} - (-X_i)\|}{\|A^{-1}\|} < \epsilon$$
so that the matrix $-X_i$ approximates A^{-1} with a relative error norm less than ϵ.

Each step of the iteration (7.2.3) involves the multiplication of A by X_i, the addition of 2 to all the diagonal entries of the product (which takes n additions), and the premultiplication of the resulting matrix by X_i. The most costly steps are the two matrix multiplications, each taking n^3 multiplications and $n^3 - n^2$ additions for a pair of general $n \times n$ input matrices A and X_0.

The next example demonstrates the advantage of the quadratic convergence rate over the linear convergence rate.

Example (Comparison with Linearly Convergent Schemes). Let $\tau = 1/2$ and $\epsilon = 10^{-6}$. Then 5 iteration steps (7.2.3) suffice to compute the matrix X_5 satisfying the bounds $\|I + X_5A\| < \epsilon$ and $\|A^{-1} - (-X_5)\| < \epsilon \|A^{-1}\|$. On the other hand, assume any linearly convergent scheme such as Jacobi's or Gauss–Seidel's iteration is used (cf. [GV96, p. 510]), where for the same input, the norm of the error matrix of the computed approximation to A^{-1} decreases by a factor of 2 in each iteration step. Then the error norm decreases to below 2^{-i-1} in i iteration steps, so that it takes 19 steps to ensure the bound (7.2.4) for $\epsilon = 10^{-6}$.
$\diamond$

7.3 SOME BASIC RESULTS ON TOEPLITZ-LIKE MATRICES

When A and X_0 are structured matrices, say Toeplitz or Toeplitz-like matrices, the computations required for Newton's iteration can be carried out more efficiently. First, however, let us review some basic facts about Toeplitz-like matrices and introduce some notation that will be useful in what follows. More details can be found in Ch. 1.

As defined in Ch. 1, a matrix $R \in \mathbb{R}^{n \times n}$ is said to be *Toeplitz-like* if its displacement $\nabla_Z R = R - ZRZ^T$ has low rank, say, $r \ll n$, where Z is the lower triangular shift matrix,
$$Z = \begin{bmatrix} 0 & & & \\ 1 & 0 & & \\ & \ddots & \ddots & \\ & & 1 & 0 \end{bmatrix}.$$

Section 7.3. Some Basic Results on Toeplitz-Like Matrices 193

(Here and hereafter, W^T denotes the transpose of a matrix or a vector W.) Hence there exist (so-called generator) matrices G and $H \in \mathbb{R}^{n \times r}$ such that

$$R - ZRZ^T = GH^T. \tag{7.3.1}$$

It is further shown in Ch. 1 that if a nonsingular matrix R satisfies a displacement equation of the form (7.3.1), then its inverse satisfies a similar equation of the form

$$R^{-1} - Z^T R^{-1} Z = CD^T \tag{7.3.2}$$

for some (generator) matrices C and $D \in \mathbb{R}^{n \times r}$. Notice that the roles of $\{Z, Z^T\}$ are switched. To distinguish between these two kinds of displacement equation, we shall use the notation (cf. [KKM79a])

$$\nabla_+(R) \triangleq R - ZRZ^T, \qquad \nabla_-(R) \triangleq R - Z^T RZ. \tag{7.3.3}$$

That is, we write $\nabla_+(R)$ instead of $\nabla_Z R$ and $\nabla_-(R)$ for the other displacement where Z^T comes first. We also denote the corresponding generator matrices by $G_+, H_+, G_-, H_- \in \mathbb{R}^{n \times r}$,

$$\nabla_+(R) = R - ZRZ^T = G_+ H_+^T, \quad \nabla_-(R) = R - Z^T RZ = G_- H_-^T. \tag{7.3.4}$$

The following basic facts are immediate (see Ch. 1 and also [KKM79a]).

Lemma 7.3.1 (A Basic Fact). *Given matrices $G, H \in \mathbb{R}^{n \times r}$, there exist a unique matrix T_+ and a unique matrix T_- satisfying*

$$\nabla_+(T_+) = T_+ - ZT_+Z^T = GH^T,$$
$$\nabla_-(T_-) = T_- - Z^T T_- Z = GH^T.$$

Indeed, T_+ and T_- are given by

$$T_+ = \sum_{i=1}^r \mathcal{L}(\mathbf{a}_i)\mathcal{L}^T(\mathbf{b}_i), \qquad T_- = \sum_{i=1}^r \mathcal{L}^T(\tilde{I}\mathbf{a}_i)\mathcal{L}(\tilde{I}\mathbf{b}_i),$$

where $\mathbf{a}_i$ and $\mathbf{b}_i$ denote the ith columns of G and H, respectively, $\mathcal{L}(\mathbf{v})$ denotes a lower triangular Toeplitz matrix whose first column is $\mathbf{v}$, and $\tilde{I}$ denotes the (reflection) matrix with ones on the antidiagonal and zeros elsewhere; that is, $\tilde{I} = (i_{g,h})_{g,h=0}^{n-1}$, $i_{g,h} = 1$ if $g + h = n - 1$, $i_{g,h} = 0$ otherwise, so that $\tilde{I}[v_0, v_1, \ldots, v_{n-1}]^T = [v_{n-1}, \ldots, v_0]^T$ for any vector $[v_0, v_1, \ldots, v_{n-1}]^T$.

◇

Lemma 7.3.2 (Properties of the Displacement Operators). *The displacement operators ∇_- and ∇_+ satisfy the following properties for any nonsingular matrix R and for any pair of $n \times n$ matrices X and Y:*

(a) $\mathrm{rank}[\nabla_+(R)] = \mathrm{rank}[\nabla_-(R^{-1})]$.

(b) $\mathrm{rank}[\nabla_-(XY)] \leq \mathrm{rank}[\nabla_-(X)] + \mathrm{rank}[\nabla_-(Y)] + 1$.

(c) *Given two pairs of generator matrices of lengths a and b for $\nabla_-(X)$ and $\nabla_-(Y)$, respectively, a pair of generator matrices of length at most $a + b + 1$ for $\nabla_-(XY)$ can be computed using $O(nab \log n)$ flops.*

(d) *Given a pair of generator matrices of length r for $\nabla_+(X)$, a pair of generator matrices of length $\bar{r} \le r+2$ for $\nabla_-(X)$ can be computed using $O(nr \log n)$ flops.*

Proof: For parts (a) and (d) see Ch. 1, [KKM79a], and pp. 176–178 of [BP94]. For part (b), we first write

$$\nabla_-(X) = X - Z^T X Z = G_X H_X^T, \quad \nabla_-(Y) = Y - Z^T Y Z = G_Y H_Y^T.$$

Then

$$\begin{aligned}\nabla_-(XY) &= XY - Z^T XYZ \\ &= XY - Z^T XZY + Z^T XZY - Z^T XZZ^T YZ + Z^T XZZ^T YZ - Z^T XYZ \\ &= \nabla_-(X)Y + Z^T XZ\nabla_-(Y) + Z^T X(ZZ^T - I)YZ.\end{aligned}$$

We also observe that $ZZ^T - I = -\mathbf{e}_0 \mathbf{e}_0^T$, where $\mathbf{e}_0^T = [1, 0, \ldots, 0]^T$ is a unit coordinate vector. Therefore, we can write $\nabla_-(XY) = G_{XY} H_{XY}^T$, where

$$G_{XY} = [G_X \quad Z^T XZ G_Y \quad -Z^T X\mathbf{e}_0], \quad H_{XY} = [Y^T H_X \quad H_Y \quad Z^T Y^T \mathbf{e}_0].$$

These expressions provide a generator (G_{XY}, H_{XY}) for $\nabla_-(XY)$ via the three generators: (G_X, H_X) of the displacement $\nabla_-(X)$, (G_Y, H_Y) of the displacement $\nabla_-(Y)$, and $(-Z^T X \mathbf{e}_0, Z^T Y^T \mathbf{e}_0)$ of the rank 1 matrix $Z^T X(ZZ^T - I)YZ$. This establishes part (b).

Finally, observe that the computation of G_{XY} and H_{XY} requires the multiplication of X by ZG_Y and of Y^T by H_X. By estimating the computational cost of these multiplications, and by applying Lemma 7.3.1 and recalling that an $n \times n$ Toeplitz matrix can be multiplied by a vector in $O(n \log n)$ flops (cf. Sec. 1.4), we establish part (c).

◇

7.4 THE NEWTON–TOEPLITZ ITERATION

We now describe the first version of Newton's iteration (7.2.3) in the Toeplitz-like case. Until the end of Sec. 7.4.2, we shall assume that both A and X_0 are structured matrices with

$$\operatorname{rank}[\nabla_+(A)] = \operatorname{rank}[\nabla_-(A^{-1})] = r, \quad \operatorname{rank}[\nabla_-(X_0)] = r_0$$

and that the matrices A and X_0 are given with their respective ∇_--generators of minimum length $\bar{r}$ and r_0, respectively, where $\bar{r} \le r + 2$ by Lemma 7.3.2(d) and r and r_0 are small relative to n. Then, in view of the above results, a displacement generator for X_k having length at most $\bar{r}_k = 2^k r_0 + (2^k - 1)(\bar{r} + 3)$ can be computed at the overall cost of $O(n(\bar{r}_{k-1} + \bar{r})\bar{r}_{k-1} \log n)$ flops, $k = 1, 2, \ldots$. The values $\bar{r}_k$ and $\sum_{i=0}^{k-1}(\bar{r}_i + \bar{r})\bar{r}_i$ have orders of 2^k and 4^k, respectively, so that the iteration (7.2.3) soon becomes quite costly.

In some cases, a few steps (7.2.3) may already suffice for the refinement of a given approximation X_0 to A^{-1}, and then the overall computational cost is small enough. If one needs many steps (7.2.3), then the techniques of the next two sections will help us to control the growth of the generator length and the computational cost.

Let us outline these techniques. By assumption, $\operatorname{rank}(\nabla_-(A^{-1})) = r$. Hence the matrices $-X_i$, which approximate A^{-1} closely for larger i, have a nearby matrix of ∇_--displacement rank r for larger i. This fact suggests the following approach to decreasing the computational cost of the iterative scheme (7.2.3): shift from X_i to a nearby matrix

Section 7.4. The Newton–Toeplitz Iteration

Y_i having displacement rank at most r and then restart the iteration with Y_i instead of X_i.

The advantage of this modification is the decrease of the computational cost at the ith Newton's step and at all subsequent steps. The disadvantage is a possible deterioration of the approximation, since we do not know A^{-1}, and the transition from X_i to Y_i may occur in a wrong direction. Both X_i and Y_i, however, lie close to A^{-1} and, therefore, to each other. The latter observation enables us to bound the deterioration of the approximation relative to the current approximation error, so that the quadratic improvement in the error bound at the next step of Newton's iteration will immediately compensate for such a deterioration. Moreover, the transition from X_i to a nearby matrix Y_i of a small displacement rank can be achieved at a low computational cost. We will supply more details in the next two sections.

7.4.1 Bounding the Displacement Rank

To estimate the errors of the approximations of A^{-1} by X_i and Y_i, we first recall the following basic result (cf. [GV96, pp. 72, 230]).

Lemma 7.4.1 (Optimal Matrix Approximation). *Given a matrix W of rank n, it holds that*

$$\sigma_r = \min_{\text{rank }(B) \leq r} ||W - B||_2;$$

that is, the error in the optimal choice of an approximant of W whose rank does not exceed r is equal to the rth singular value of W. Moreover, the condition number of W is equal to the ratio σ_1/σ_n.

◇

The reader may assume below that the numbers r and r_0 are small ($\bar{r} = r = 2$ for a Toeplitz matrix A) and that r_i is not much larger than r, say, $r_i \leq 3r + 3$. Hereafter, until the end of Sec. 7.4.2, we will use the displacement $\nabla_-(R) = R - Z^T R Z$.

Algorithm 7.4.1 (Bounding the Displacement Rank of Newton's Iterates). *The following procedure bounds the displacement rank of the successive iterates as follows.*

- **Input:** *A positive integer $r = \text{rank}(\nabla_+(A)) = \text{rank}(\nabla_-(A^{-1}))$ and a displacement generator $\{G_i, H_i\}$, of length at most $r_i \geq r$, for a matrix X_i, such that $\nabla_-(X_i) = G_i H_i^T$.*

- **Output:** *A displacement generator of length at most r for a matrix Y_i such that*

$$||Y_i + A^{-1}||_2 \leq (1 + 2n(r_i - r))\, ||X_i + A^{-1}||_2.$$

- **Computations:**

    1. *Compute the SVD of the displacement $\nabla_-(X_i) = U_i \Sigma_i V_i^T$. This step is not costly (cf. [Pan93b]) since it is performed for $G_i H_i^T$, where $G_i, H_i \in \text{real}^{n \times r_i}$, and since r_i is small.*

    2. *Set to zero the $r_i - r$ smallest singular values of $\nabla_-(X_i)$ in the matrix in Σ_i, thus turning Σ_i into a diagonal matrix of rank r.*

3. Compute and output the matrices $\bar{G}_i$ and $\bar{H}_i$ obtained from the matrices $U_i\Sigma_i$ and V_i, respectively, by deleting their last $r_i - r$ columns.

◇

The overall computational cost of this algorithm is $O(n\, r_i^2)$ flops. Of course, this covers only the computations that are part of a single step of Newton's iteration.

Now let $Y_i \in \mathbb{R}^{n \times n}$ denote the unique matrix defined by the ∇_--generator $\{\bar{G}_i, \bar{H}_i\}$. The accuracy of the above algorithm is implied by the following result of [Pan93a], [Pan93b], [Pan92a], which shows that the matrix Y_i approximates A^{-1} almost as well as X_i does.

Theorem 7.4.1 (Accuracy of Approximation). *It holds that*

$$\|Y_i + A^{-1}\|_2 \leq (1 + 2(r_i - r)n)\|X_i + A^{-1}\|_2. \tag{7.4.1}$$

Proof: The proof of this basic result was given in [Pan93a], [Pan93b], [Pan92a] and relies on the following observations. The matrices A^{-1} and $-X_i$ closely approximate each other; therefore, so do their ∇_--displacements, $\nabla_-(A^{-1})$ and $\nabla_-(X_i)$. Since the approximation of $\nabla_-(X_i)$ by $\nabla_-(Y_i)$ is optimal by Lemma 7.4.1, we have

$$\|\nabla_-(Y_i) - \nabla_-(X_i)\|_2 \leq \|\nabla_-(A^{-1}) + \nabla_-(X_i)\|_2.$$

The map from the ∇_--displacements $\nabla_-(Y_i), \nabla_-(X_i), \nabla_-(A^{-1})$ back to the matrices Y_i, X_i, A^{-1} may change this bound by at most a factor of $1 + 2(r_i - r)n$.

◇

We may now modify Newton's iteration (7.2.3) by incorporating the construction of Alg. 7.4.1. Let a matrix A and an initial approximation X_0 of A^{-1} be given with their ∇_--generators of length $\bar{r} \leq r + 2$ and r_0, respectively. We recursively compute the matrices $Y_0, X_1, Y_1, X_2, \ldots$, satisfying

$$X_{i+1} = Y_i(2I + AY_i) = (2I + Y_iA)Y_i, \ i = 0, 1, \ldots, \tag{7.4.2}$$

where Y_i denotes the output matrix of Alg. 7.4.1 applied to X_i. Thus, for each i, we first apply Alg. 7.4.1 to the matrix X_i followed by the computation of the matrix X_{i+1} based on (7.4.2). Since Y_i is a Toeplitz-like matrix represented with its displacement generator of length at most r, the overall computational cost is $O(nr^2 \log n)$ for each step of (7.4.2).

7.4.2 Convergence Rate and Computational Complexity

Define
$$p(i) \triangleq \|I + Y_iA\|_2, \ i = 0, 1, \ldots. \tag{7.4.3}$$

We then deduce from (7.4.2) that $I + X_{i+1}A = (I + Y_iA)^2$, so that

$$\|I + X_{i+1}A\|_2 \leq p^2(i), \quad \|A^{-1} + X_{i+1}\|_2 \leq p^2(i)\|A^{-1}\|_2.$$

Here and hereafter, we write $p^h(i)$ to denote $(p(i))^h$. By Thm. 7.4.1, we obtain

$$\|A^{-1} + Y_{i+1}\|_2 \leq (1 + 2(r_i - r)n)\|A^{-1} + X_{i+1}\|_2 \leq (1 + 2(r_i - r)n)p^2(i)\|A^{-1}\|_2$$

Section 7.4. The Newton–Toeplitz Iteration

and hence

$$\begin{aligned} p(i+1) &= \|I + Y_{i+1}A\|_2 \\ &\leq \|A^{-1} + Y_{i+1}\|_2 \|A\|_2 \\ &\leq (1 + 2(r_i - r)n)p^2(i)\|A^{-1}\|_2\|A\|_2 \\ &= (1 + 2(r_i - r)n)\kappa(A)p^2(i), \end{aligned}$$

where $\kappa(A)$ denotes the condition number of A and is equal to $\|A\|_2\|A^{-1}\|_2$. Therefore, for a positive b, the inequality

$$(1 + 2(r_i - r)n)\kappa(A)p^{1-b}(i) \leq 1 \quad \text{for all } i \tag{7.4.4}$$

implies a convergence rate of $1 + b$, that is, it implies the bound

$$p(i+1) \leq p^{1+b}(i) \quad \text{for all } i. \tag{7.4.5}$$

By observing that rank $[\nabla_-(R + I)] \leq 1 + $ rank $[\nabla_-(R)]$ for any matrix R and by applying Lemma 7.3.2(c) to the matrices of (7.4.2), we obtain that

$$r_i - r \leq r + \bar{r} + 3, \quad \bar{r} \leq r + 2,$$

where the length of the ∇_--generators of Y_i and A is at most r and $\bar{r}$, respectively. If $p(i) \leq 1$ and $p(i)$ satisfies (7.4.4), then (7.4.5) implies that $p(i+1) \leq p(i)$. Thus it suffices to assume (7.4.4) with $p(i)$ replaced by $p(0)$ and $r_i - r$ replaced by $r + \bar{r} + 3$. The results are summarized below (cf. [Pan93a], [Pan93b], [Pan92a]).

Theorem 7.4.2 (Convergence Rate). *Let* rank$[\nabla_-(A^{-1})] \leq r$ *and let the matrices X_0 and A be given with their ∇_--displacement generators of length $r_0 \leq r$ and $\bar{r} \leq r+2$, respectively. Let*

$$(1 + 2(r + \bar{r} + 3)n)\kappa(A)p^{1-b}(0) \leq 1 \tag{7.4.6}$$

for $p(0)$ of (7.4.3) (for $i = 0$) and for some fixed positive $b < 1$. Then, for $i \geq 0$ we have

$$\text{rank}\,(\nabla_-(Y_i)) \leq r, \quad \text{rank}\,(\nabla_-(X_i)) \leq 2r + \bar{r} + 3,$$

$$\|X_i + A^{-1}\|_2 = \|(-X_i) - A^{-1}\|_2 \leq (p(0))^{(1+b)^i}\|A^{-1}\|_2,$$

and the matrices $Y_1, X_1, Y_2, X_2, \ldots, Y_i, X_i$ can be computed at the overall cost of $O(inr^2 \log n)$ flops.

◇

We can see that unless the matrix A has a very large condition number (that is, unless A is very ill-conditioned), (7.4.6) is a mild assumption on the residual norm $p(0)$. This assumption is sufficient to ensure a rapid improvement of the initial approximation of A^{-1} by $-X_0$ at a low computational cost of $O(inr^2 \log n)$ flops. Therefore, the bound $p_i = \|I + X_i A\|_2 \leq \epsilon \kappa(A)$ is ensured already in

$$i = \left\lceil \log_{(1+b)} \left(\frac{\log p(0)}{-\log \epsilon} \right) \right\rceil \tag{7.4.7}$$

Newton–Toeplitz steps (7.4.2).

Remark. If the initial approximation X_0 does not satisfy the bound (7.4.6), various homotopy techniques can be remedies. The most straightforward remedy is to apply our algorithm recursively to compute the matrices

$$A_i^{-1} = (A_0 + t_i(A - A_0))^{-1} \text{ for } i = 0, 1, \ldots, K,$$

where A_0 is a readily invertible matrix, $t_0 = 0$, $t_K = 1$, and a sufficiently large natural K and an increasing sequence $t_0, t_1, \ldots, t_K$ are chosen to ensure rapid convergence of our algorithm in each recursive step. Similar treatment can be applied to other algorithms of this chapter, and we refer the reader to [Pan92a] for a particular application of homotopy techniques to the design of fast Toeplitz-like solvers.

7.4.3 An Approach Using f-Circulant Matrices

We now present an alternative Newton–Toeplitz iteration by using other displacement operators. Indeed, as already noted in Ch. 1, the displacement structure of Toeplitz-like matrices can be represented in terms of other operators, e.g.,

$$\nabla_f(A) \triangleq A - Z_f A Z_{1/f}^T, \qquad (7.4.8)$$

where $f \neq 0$ is a scalar and Z_f is a unit f-circulant matrix,

$$Z_f = \begin{bmatrix} 0 & \cdots & 0 & f \\ 1 & 0 & & 0 \\ \vdots & \ddots & \ddots & \vdots \\ 0 & & 1 & 0 \end{bmatrix} = Z + f\mathbf{e}_0 \mathbf{e}_{n-1}^T.$$

Here and hereafter, $\mathbf{e}_0 = [1, 0, \ldots, 0]^T$ and $\mathbf{e}_{n-1} = [0, \ldots, 0, 1]^T$ denote two unit coordinate vectors. (Circulant matrices are 1-circulant.)

Since $Z_f = Z + f\mathbf{e}_0\mathbf{e}_{n-1}^T$, we have

$$\text{rank}[\nabla_f(A) - \nabla_-(A)] \leq 2, \quad \text{rank}[\nabla_f(A) - \nabla_g(A)] \leq 2$$

for any triple (A, f, g). Lemmas 7.3.1 and 7.3.2 are easily extended (cf. [GO92] and also pp. 182–195 of [BP94]), and so is Alg. 7.4.1. In particular, we will use the next result.

Lemma 7.4.2 (Matrix Representation). *If $e \neq f$, $e \neq 0$ (say, $f = 1$, $e = -1$), and if*

$$\nabla_f(A) = GH^T = \sum_{i=1}^r \mathbf{a}_i \mathbf{b}_i^T,$$

then we have

$$A = Z_{f,lc}(A\mathbf{e}_{n-1}) + \frac{e}{e-f} \sum_{i=1}^r Z_f(\mathbf{a}_i) Z_{1/e}^T(\mathbf{b}_i),$$

where

$$Z_f(\mathbf{v}) \triangleq \sum_{i=0}^{n-1} v_i Z_f^i$$

Section 7.4. The Newton–Toeplitz Iteration 199

denotes the f-circulant matrix with first column $\mathbf{v} = [v_0, \ldots, v_{n-1}]^T$, and $Z_{f,lc}(\mathbf{v})$ denotes the f-circulant matrix with last column $\mathbf{v}$.

◇

The complication due to the extra term $Z_{f,lc}(A\mathbf{e}_{n-1})$ in the representation of Lemma 7.4.2 (versus the one of Lemma 7.3.1) is compensated by the simplification of the multiplication of the matrices $Z_f(\mathbf{v})$ by a vector versus the same operation with the matrices $\mathcal{L}(\mathbf{v})$ or $\mathcal{L}^T(\mathbf{v})$. (The former multiplication requires roughly twice fewer flops than the latter.)

The matrices Z_f are nonsingular, and we may use the operators $\nabla^f(A) = Z_f^{-1}A - AZ_{1/f}^T$ instead of $\nabla_f(A)$ (cf. [HR84], [Pan92b]). This enables a distinct version of Newton's iteration, which we will demonstrate next. (Note that a generator $\{G, H\}$ for $\nabla_f(A)$ immediately turns into the generator $Z_f^{-1}G, H$ for $\nabla^f(A)$ and vice versa.) In particular, Lemma 7.4.2 turns into the following result.

Lemma 7.4.3 (Alternative Representation). *If $e \neq f$, $e \neq 0$ (say, $f = 1$, $e = -1$), and if*

$$\nabla^f(A) = GH^T = \sum_{i=1}^r \mathbf{a}_i \mathbf{b}_i^T,$$

then we have

$$A = Z_{f,lc}(A\mathbf{e}_{n-1}) + \frac{e}{e-f} \sum_{i=1}^r Z_f(Z_f \mathbf{a}_i) Z_{1/e}^T(\mathbf{b}_i),$$

where $Z_f(\mathbf{v})$ and $Z_{f,lc}(\mathbf{v})$ are defined as in Lemma 7.4.2.

◇

For our numerical tests, we chose $f = 1$ and $e = -1$, although other choices of f and e with $f \neq e$, $e \neq 0$ are also possible. (Moreover, the operators ∇^f can be replaced by $\nabla^+(A) = ZA - AZ$ or $\nabla^-(A) = Z^T A - AZ^T$, to which Lemma 7.4.2 is easily extended; see p. 184 of [BP94].)

Now suppose that $\nabla^f(A) = GH^T$, write $X = -A^{-1}$, and deduce that $\nabla^f(X) = G_X H_X^T = X\nabla^f(A)X = XGH^T X$ so that

$$G_X = XG, \quad H_X^T = H^T X. \tag{7.4.9}$$

Indeed,

$$\begin{aligned} X\nabla^f(A)X &= XZ_f^{-1}AX - XAZ_{1/f}^T X \\ &= -XZ_f^{-1} + Z_{1/f}^T X \\ &= Z_f^{-1}X - XZ_{1/f}^T \\ &= \nabla^f(X), \end{aligned}$$

where the second-to-last equation follows because $Z_{1/f}^T = Z_f^{-1}$.

Next, based on (7.4.9) and Lemmas 7.4.2 and 7.4.3 we will modify Alg. 7.4.1. (To distinguish from Alg. 7.4.1, we use the notation $\tilde{X}_i$ rather than X_i for the computed approximations to $X = -A^{-1}$, $i = 1, 2, \ldots$, and, as in the case of Alg. 7.4.1, we assume that an initial approximation $\tilde{X}_0$ is given from outside, in this case in the form of the ∇^f-displacement generator matrices G_0, H_0, and the last column vector $\tilde{X}_0 \mathbf{e}_{n-1}$.)

Algorithm 7.4.2. (Bounding the Displacement Rank of Newton's Iterates).
The procedure below bounds the displacement rank of the successive iterates as follows.

- Input: A complex f, $|f| = 1$, a natural $\tilde{r}$, and two matrices A and $\tilde{X}_i$ given with their ∇^f-displacement generators, $G = G_A$, $H = H_A$ and $G_i = G_{\tilde{X}_i}$, $H_i = H_{\tilde{X}_i}$, respectively, both of length at most $\tilde{r}$, and with their last columns, $A\mathbf{e}_{n-1}$ and $\tilde{X}_i\mathbf{e}_{n-1}$, respectively.

- Output: A ∇^f-displacement generator $\{G_{i+1}, H_{i+1}\}$ of length at most $\tilde{r}$ for a matrix $\tilde{X}_{i+1}$ and its last column $\tilde{X}_{i+1}\mathbf{e}_{n-1}$ satisfying
$$\tilde{p}(i+1) = \|I + \tilde{X}_{i+1}A\|_1$$
$$\leq \tilde{p}^2(i)\operatorname{cond}_1(A)(1 + 0.5r\|G\|_1\|H^T\|_1\|X\|_1(2 + \tilde{p}^2(i))) \quad (7.4.10)$$
(cf. Remark in App. 7.A, and where $\operatorname{cond}_1(A)$ denotes $\|A\|_1\|A^{-1}\|_1$).

- Computations: Apply Lemma 7.4.3 to express A and $\tilde{X}_i$ through the input parameters. Then compute and output the vector
$$\tilde{X}_{i+1}\mathbf{e}_{n-1} = \tilde{X}_i(2I + A\tilde{X}_i)\mathbf{e}_{n-1}$$
and the matrices
$$G_{i+1} = \tilde{X}_i(2I + A\tilde{X}_i)G, \quad H_{i+1}^T = H^T\tilde{X}_i(2I + A\tilde{X}_i).$$

$\diamond$

Lemma 7.4.3 reduces the computations of Alg. 7.4.2 to a sequence of $6\tilde{r}(2\tilde{r} + 1)$ multiplications of $n \times n$ h-circulant matrices by vectors for $h = f$ and $h = 1/e$, $2(3\tilde{r}+1)\tilde{r}$ additions and subtractions of n-dimensional vectors, and $6\tilde{r}$ multiplications of such vectors by $e/(e - f)$, that is, to $O(\tilde{r}^2 n \log n)$ flops. Note that the computation of SVDs is not required in this case.

In App. 7.A, we prove that the output satisfies the bound (7.4.10). This bound immediately implies both accuracy of the algorithm and convergence of $\tilde{X}_i$ to X with the rate $1 + b$ for a positive $b < 1$ provided that

$$\tilde{p}^{1-b}(0)\operatorname{cond}_1(A)(1 + 0.5r\|G\|_1\|H^T\|_1\|X\|_1(1 + \tilde{p}^2(0))) \leq 1, \quad (7.4.11)$$

which extends (7.4.6) and Thm. 7.4.2. The comparison with (7.4.6) shows that a little stronger upper bound on the error norm of the initial approximation is needed now for the convergence of the refinement process, but if such a stronger bound is achieved, then the computation by Alg. 7.4.2 is simpler since the displacement rank of Newton's iterates is controlled more directly, without involving the SVDs of the displacements.

7.5 RESIDUAL CORRECTION METHOD

7.5.1 Application to Matrix Inversion

Newton's iteration is a special case (where $l = 2$) of the following more general residual correction algorithm:
$$X_{i+1,l} = (I + R_i + R_i^2 + \cdots + R_i^{l-1})X_{i,l},$$
where $R_i = I + X_{i,l}A$. It can be easily deduced [IK66, p. 82] that $R_{i+1} = R_i^l$ and, therefore, $p_i = \|I + X_{i,l}A\| \leq p_{i-1}^l \leq p_0^{l^i}$. It is a tedious but straightforward exercise to extend our Algs. 7.4.1 and 7.4.2 and their analysis to the case of $l > 2$. (See [IK66] for some advantages of choosing $l = 3$ in the case of a general unstructured matrix A.)

7.5.2 Application to a Linear System of Equations

Newton's method can be applied to the solution of a fixed linear system of equations as well. If X_i and $\mathbf{w}_i$ denote the current approximations to the matrix $X = -A^{-1}$ and to the solution $\mathbf{w} = A^{-1}\mathbf{b}$ of a linear system $A\mathbf{w} = \mathbf{b}$, respectively (computed in i recursive steps), then the next approximation,

$$\mathbf{w}_{i+1} = \mathbf{w}_i + X_i(A\mathbf{w}_i - \mathbf{b}), \tag{7.5.1}$$

satisfies $\mathbf{w} - \mathbf{w}_{i+1} = (I + X_iA)(\mathbf{w} - \mathbf{w}_i)$. Consequently, for any fixed operator norm (for matrices and vectors), we have

$$\|\mathbf{w} - \mathbf{w}_{i+1}\| \leq p(i)\|\mathbf{w} - \mathbf{w}_i\|, \quad p(i) = \|I + X_iA\|. \tag{7.5.2}$$

Actually, (7.5.1) is just a restriction of Newton's iteration (7.2.3). Indeed, postmultiply (7.2.3) by the vector $\mathbf{b}$, substitute $-\mathbf{w}_{i+1}$ for $X_{i+1}\mathbf{b}$ and $-\mathbf{w}_i$ for $X_i\mathbf{b}$, and obtain $-\mathbf{w}_{i+1} = X_{i+1}\mathbf{b} = X_i\mathbf{b} + X_i(I + AX_i)\mathbf{b} = -\mathbf{w}_i + X_i(\mathbf{b} + AX_i\mathbf{b}) = -\mathbf{w}_i + X_i(\mathbf{b} - A\mathbf{w}_i)$. Therefore, $\mathbf{w}_{i+1} = \mathbf{w}_i + X_i(A\mathbf{w}_i - \mathbf{b})$, which agrees with (7.5.1).

In application to general linear systems, the matrix X_i is invariant in i and residual correction converges linearly, but in the Toeplitz case we will obtain quadratic convergence because we will correct the matrix X_i simultaneously with $\mathbf{w}_i$.

7.5.3 Application to a Toeplitz Linear System of Equations

Let A be a Toeplitz matrix, $A = T = [t_{i,j}]$, $t_{i,j} = t_{i-j}$ for all i and j. In this case, we can simplify the above Newton-based recursion by relying on two known formulas that express the inverse $-X = T^{-1}$ via the solution of two Toeplitz linear systems,

$$T\mathbf{y} = \mathbf{e}_0, \quad T\mathbf{x} = \mathbf{t},$$

where $\mathbf{t} = [w, at_1 + bt_{1-n}, at_2 + bt_{2-n}, \ldots, at_{n-1} + bt_{-1}]^T$ for three fixed scalars, w, a, and b. Each of these two expressions for the inverse relates the two equations of (7.5.1) for $\mathbf{b} = \mathbf{e}_0$ and $\mathbf{b} = \mathbf{t}$ to each other and to the matrix $-X = T^{-1}$.

In particular, to extend Alg. 7.4.1 in this way, we will use the following known formula (cf. p. 136 of [BP94] and the second remark at the end of this section):

$$-X = T^{-1} = \mathcal{L}(\mathbf{x})\mathcal{L}^T(Z\tilde{I}\mathbf{y}) - \mathcal{L}(\mathbf{y})\mathcal{L}^T(Z\tilde{I}\mathbf{x} - \mathbf{e}_0), \tag{7.5.3}$$

where $\mathbf{t} = [w, t_{1-n}, \ldots, t_{-1}]^T$, t_{i-j}, denotes the (i,j)th entry of T; w is any fixed scalar, say, $w = 0$ or $w = \max_{i,j}|t_{i-j}|$; and $\tilde{I}$ is the reflection matrix, defined in Lemma 7.3.1. Due to this expression and to (7.5.1), we may update the approximation X_i to X as follows.

Algorithm 7.5.1 (Residual Correction for a Toeplitz System). *The following procedure updates the estimates X_i:*

- Input: *A Toeplitz matrix T and the approximations X_i to $X = -T^{-1}$, $\mathbf{x}_i$ to $\mathbf{x} = T^{-1}\mathbf{t}$, and $\mathbf{y}_i$ to $\mathbf{y} = T^{-1}\mathbf{e}_0$.*

- Output: *New approximations X_{i+1}, $\mathbf{x}_{i+1}$, and $\mathbf{y}_{i+1}$.*

- Computations (cf. (7.5.1) for $A = T$ and (7.5.2)): *Compute and output*

$$\mathbf{x}_{i+1} = \mathbf{x}_i + X_i(T\mathbf{x}_i - \mathbf{t}),$$

$$\mathbf{y}_{i+1} = \mathbf{y}_i + X_i(T\mathbf{y}_i - \mathbf{e}_0),$$

where we set

$$-X_{i+1} = \mathcal{L}(\mathbf{x}_{i+1})\mathcal{L}^T(Z\tilde{I}\mathbf{y}_{i+1}) - \mathcal{L}(\mathbf{y}_{i+1})\mathcal{L}^T(Z\tilde{I}\mathbf{x}_{i+1} - \mathbf{e}_0). \tag{7.5.4}$$

◇

Algorithm 7.5.1 can be applied recursively for $i = 0, 1, \ldots$ provided that some initial approximations $\mathbf{x}_0, \mathbf{y}_0$, and X_0 to $\mathbf{x}, \mathbf{y}$, and X, respectively, are available. Furthermore, if just some initial approximations $\mathbf{x}_0$ and $\mathbf{y}_0$ are available, we may substitute $\mathbf{x} = \mathbf{x}_0$ and $\mathbf{y} = \mathbf{y}_0$ on the right-hand side of (7.5.3) and choose the resulting matrix as $-X_0$.

By using the operator ∇^f and (7.4.8), we may modify (7.5.3) and Alg. 7.5.1 to replace the lower triangular Toeplitz matrices $\mathcal{L}(\mathbf{x})$ and $\mathcal{L}(\mathbf{y})$ by f-circulant matrices and the upper triangular Toeplitz matrices $\mathcal{L}^T(ZJ\mathbf{y})$ and $\mathcal{L}^T(ZJ\mathbf{x} - \mathbf{e}_0)$ by $(1/e)$-circulant matrices. This can be also viewed as the specialization of Alg. 7.4.2 to solving a Toeplitz linear system of equations. Namely, instead of (7.5.3), we will use the following result [GO92] (cf. the second remark at the end of this section and [AG89] for the case where $f = -e = 1$ and T is a Hermitian Toeplitz matrix).

Theorem 7.5.1 (Inverse of a Toeplitz Matrix). *Let $T = (t_{i,j})_{i,j=0}^{n-1}$ be a Toeplitz matrix, $t_{i,j} = t_{i-j}$, $i,j = 0, 1, \ldots, n-1$. Let e, f, and w be three scalars, $e \neq 0$, $ef \neq 1$. Let two vectors $\mathbf{x}$ and $\mathbf{y}$ satisfy the linear systems of equations $T\mathbf{y} = \mathbf{e}_0$, $T\mathbf{x} = \mathbf{t}(e,w)$, where $\mathbf{t}(e,w) = [w, t_1 - et_{1-n}, t_2 - et_{2-n}, \ldots, t_{n-1} - et_{-1}]^T$. Then T is a nonsingular matrix and*

$$-X = T^{-1} = \frac{1}{1-ef}\left[Z_f(\mathbf{y})Z_{1/e}(\mathbf{x}) - Z_f(\mathbf{x} - (1-ef)\mathbf{e}_0)Z_{1/e}(\mathbf{y})\right],$$

where $Z_g(\mathbf{v})$ denotes the g-circulant matrix with first column $\mathbf{v}$ (cf. Lemma 7.4.2). ◇

Now we will modify Alg. 7.5.1 as follows.

Algorithm 7.5.2 (Residual Correction for a Toeplitz System). *The following modifications should be incorporated into Alg. 7.5.1.*

(a) *Include the scalars e, f, and w of Thm. 7.5.1 (say, write $f = -e = 1$, $w = 0$) in the input set of the algorithm.*

(b) *Let $\mathbf{x}_i$ and $\mathbf{x}_{i+1}$ approximate $T^{-1}\mathbf{t}(e,w)$, rather than $T^{-1}\mathbf{t}$; in particular, replace $\mathbf{t}$ by $\mathbf{t}(e,w)$ in the expression $\mathbf{x}_{i+1} = \mathbf{x}_i + X_i(T\mathbf{x}_i - \mathbf{t})$.*

(c) *Replace the expression (7.5.4) for $-X_{i+1}$ by the following expression (based on Thm. 7.5.1):*

Section 7.5. Residual Correction Method 203

$$-X_{i+1} = \frac{1}{1-ef}\left[Z_f(\mathbf{y}_{i+1})Z_{1/e}(\mathbf{x}_{i+1}) - Z_f(\mathbf{x}_{i+1} - (1-ef)\mathbf{e}^{(0)})Z_{1/e}(\mathbf{y}_{i+1})\right]. \tag{7.5.5}$$

◇

Since multiplication of a matrix $Z_f(\mathbf{v})$ by a vector is roughly twice as fast as multiplication of $\mathcal{L}(\mathbf{v})$ or $\mathcal{L}^T(\mathbf{v})$ by a vector, Alg. 7.5.2 is roughly twice as fast as Alg. 7.5.1.

Remark 1. To use (7.5.3)–(7.5.5) and Thm. 7.5.1 more efficiently, one may normalize the vector $\mathbf{x}_0$ by scaling the input matrix T or just change e and f so as to bring the norm $||\mathbf{x}_0||$ close to $|1-ef| \cdot ||\mathbf{e}_0|| = |1-ef|$.

Remark 2. Various modifications of the inversion formula (7.5.3) and, consequently, of Alg. 7.5.1 are possible. In particular, one may express the matrices $x_{0,0}X$ and (if $x_{0,0} \neq 0$) then $X = -T^{-1} = (x_{i,j})$ via the columns $\mathbf{y} = X\mathbf{e}_0$ and $\mathbf{x} = X\mathbf{e}_{n-1}$ based on the celebrated Gohberg–Semencul formula (cf. [BP94, p. 135] and [GO92]). We choose (7.5.3) rather than the latter formula to avoid the division by $x_{0,0}$, since such a divisor may vanish or may have too small a magnitude even for well-conditioned input matrices T. Similar comments apply to the inversion formulas of Thm. 7.5.1 and Alg. 7.5.2 of this section. The expressions of Thm. 7.5.1 are closely related to the ones of Lemma 7.4.2 in the case of a nonsingular Toeplitz matrix A.

7.5.4 Estimates for the Convergence Rate

Since Algs. 7.5.1 and 7.5.2 are the specializations of Algs. 7.4.1 and 7.4.2, the estimates for the convergence rates of Algs. 7.4.1 and 7.4.2 can be extended to Algs. 7.5.1 and 7.5.2. Next, however, we will estimate the convergence rates of Algs. 7.5.1 and 7.5.2 directly. Let us write

$$e(i) = \max\{||\mathbf{x}_i - \mathbf{x}||_1/||\mathbf{x}||_1, \ ||\mathbf{y}_i - \mathbf{y}||_1/||\mathbf{y}||_1\}.$$

By combining the latter definition and the norm bounds (7.5.2) for $\mathbf{w} = \mathbf{x}$ and $\mathbf{w} = \mathbf{y}$, we immediately deduce that

$$||\mathbf{x}_{i+1} - \mathbf{x}||_1 \leq p(i)||\mathbf{x}_i - \mathbf{x}||_1 \leq p(i)e(i)||\mathbf{x}||_1, \tag{7.5.6}$$

$$||\mathbf{y}_{i+1} - \mathbf{y}||_1 \leq p(i)||\mathbf{y}_i - \mathbf{y}||_1 \leq p(i)e(i)||\mathbf{y}||_1, \tag{7.5.7}$$

and, consequently,

$$||\mathbf{x}_{i+1}||_1 \leq (1+p(i)e(i))||\mathbf{x}||_1, \quad ||\mathbf{y}_{i+1}||_1 \leq (1+p(i)e(i))||\mathbf{y}||_1 \tag{7.5.8}$$

for $p(i)$ of (7.5.2). In Apps. 7.B and 7.C we derive the following bounds.

Lemma 7.5.1 (Error Bounds). *The following bounds hold:*

(a) *If Alg. 7.5.1 is applied, then*

$$E_{i+1} = ||X - X_{i+1}||_1 \leq p(i)e(i)||\mathbf{y}||_1(2(n-1)(2+p(i)e(i))||\mathbf{x}||_1 + 1).$$

(b) *If Alg. 7.5.2 is applied and if $f = -e = 1$ in (7.5.5) and in Thm. 7.5.1, then*

$$E_{i+1} = ||X - X_{i+1}||_1 \leq p(i)e(i)||\mathbf{y}||_1(||\mathbf{x}||_1(1+p(i)e(i))+1).$$

◇

We also have the bound $p(i+1) \leq \|A\|_1 E_{i+1}$, and by (7.5.2), $e(i+1) \leq p(i)e(i)$. By applying Lemma 7.5.1, we obtain that

$$p(i+1) \leq p(i)e(i)\|A\|_1\|\mathbf{y}\|_1(2(n-1)(2+p(i)e(i))\|\mathbf{x}\|_1+1)$$

and

$$p(i+1) \leq p(i)e(i)\|A\|_1\|\mathbf{y}\|_1(\|\mathbf{x}\|_1(1+p(i)e(i))+1),$$

where Algs. 7.5.1 and 7.5.2 are applied, respectively. Let us write

$$\nu = \|\mathbf{y}\|_1(2(n-1)(2+p(0)e(0))\|\mathbf{x}\|_1+1)$$

if Alg. 7.5.1 is applied and

$$\nu = \|\mathbf{y}\|_1(\|\mathbf{x}\|_1(1+p(0)e(0))+1)$$

if Alg. 7.5.2 is applied. In both cases, we have $p(i+1) \leq p(i)e(i)\|A\|_1\nu$, provided that $p(i)e(i) \leq p(0)e(0)$ for all i.

Now suppose that $p(0)$ and $e(0)$ are sufficiently small such that

$$p(0) < \rho, \ e(0)\|A\|_1\nu < \rho, \tag{7.5.9}$$

for a fixed $\rho < 1$. Then we obtain that

$$p(1) \leq p(0)e(0)\|A\|_1\nu < p(0)\rho < \rho^2$$

so that $p(1)e(1) < \rho^2 p(0)e(0) < p(0)e(0)$. Recursively, we obtain by induction that

$$p(i+1) \leq p(i)e(i)\|A\|_1\nu \leq p(i)(e(i)/e(0))e(0)\|A\|_1\nu$$
$$\leq (e(i)/e(0))p(i)\rho$$
$$< \rho^{2^{i+1}-1}p(0) < \rho^{2^{i+1}}$$

and

$$e(i+1) \leq p(i)e(i) < \rho^{2^{i+1}-1}e(0).$$

This implies quadratic convergence with the base ρ assuming the initial upper bounds (7.5.9) on $e(0)$ and $p(0)$, which extend the respective bounds of (7.4.6) and (7.4.10) to the Toeplitz case.

7.6 NUMERICAL EXPERIMENTS

The four algorithms developed in this chapter were tested using MATLAB, a software package marketed by The Math Works, Inc., of Massachusetts. In the first group of experiments, the input matrices A were generated as 100×100 Toeplitz matrices whose first columns and first rows were filled with random entries chosen from a uniform distribution on the interval $-1 < \alpha_{i,j} < 1$. To generate an initial approximation X_0 to $-A^{-1}$, we first numerically computed the actual inverse matrix $-X$ and then perturbed its entries by adding some small random values. To generate the perturbations, we first composed 100×100 matrices with random entries chosen under a normal distribution with mean zero and variance one and then scaled the values by a noise factor. We used a noise factor of 0.001 for Algs. 7.4.1, 7.5.1, and 7.5.2. Algorithm 7.4.2 requires a closer initial approximation to the solution to yield quadratic convergence, so we decreased

Section 7.6. Numerical Experiments 205

the noise factor in its test to 0.0001. Once the noise matrix was obtained, we added it to the actual inverse.

We then tested the algorithms, running a group of 40 tests for each algorithm. In most cases rapid convergence was achieved, with four exceptions in the second group, one exception in the third group, and one exception in the fourth group. To test the convergence rate, we computed the column norm $p(i) = ||AX_i + I||_1$ of the residual matrix $R_i = AX_i + I$ obtained in the ith iteration step. Sample test results are presented in Tables 7.2–7.8. We also supplied the value

$$\text{cond}_1(A) = ||A||_1 ||A^{-1}||_1.$$

We let $f = -e = 1$ in Algs. 7.4.2 and 7.5.2, and we performed Algs. 7.5.1 and 7.5.2 for vectors **t** with $w = 0$.

Table 7.2. Tests for inputs of class 1 for Alg. 7.4.1.

	Sample Test 1	Sample Test 2	Sample Test 3
$\text{cond}_1(A)$	$2.024643e + 004$	$1.365480e + 005$	$2.223065e + 004$
r_0	$1.932960e - 002$	$1.990289e - 002$	$2.206516e - 002$
r_1	$5.822783e - 005$	$3.102183e - 005$	$8.922756e - 005$
r_2	$9.966761e - 011$	$1.277523e - 010$	$8.006189e - 010$
r_3	$8.220646e - 013$	$8.420042e - 012$	$1.920519e - 012$

Table 7.3. Tests for inputs of class 1 for Alg. 7.4.2.

	Sample Test 1	Sample Test 2	Sample Test 3
$\text{cond}_1(A)$	$3.274079e + 003$	$5.836559e + 003$	$3.425782e + 003$
r_0	$4.392883e - 003$	$2.053855e - 002$	$1.876769e - 002$
r_1	$4.999007e - 005$	$3.952711e - 003$	$2.661747e - 003$
r_2	$9.924380e - 009$	$3.011774e - 004$	$7.458110e - 005$
r_3	$2.121324e - 012$	$9.710310e - 007$	$1.452111e - 007$
r_4		$2.223482e - 011$	$2.891295e - 011$

Table 7.4. Tests for inputs of class 1 for Alg. 7.5.1.

	Sample Test 1	Sample Test 2	Sample Test 3
$\text{cond}_1(A)$	$3.032816e + 003$	$7.932677e + 003$	$2.836675e + 003$
r_0	$7.205510e - 001$	$7.046618e - 001$	$1.330095e - 001$
r_1	$6.074104e - 002$	$7.454610e - 002$	$3.528652e - 003$
r_2	$8.190064e - 004$	$1.608024e - 003$	$3.643328e - 006$
r_3	$2.160530e - 007$	$1.015745e - 006$	$4.971280e - 012$
r_4	$7.357363e - 013$	$4.453048e - 012$	

The results of these computations fell into three classes. The first class, represented in Tables 7.2–7.5, shows the computations where rapid convergence was observed immediately. The second class, represented in Tables 7.6–7.8, shows the computations with the input matrices for which iteration initially stumbled and then, after a certain number of steps, s, started to converge rapidly. In fact, we observed only 4 such cases of

Table 7.5. Tests for inputs of class 1 for Alg. 7.5.2.

	Sample Test 1	Sample Test 2	Sample Test 3
$\text{cond}_1(A)$	$1.727930e+003$	$2.435048e+003$	$3.248792e+003$
r_0	$2.246859e-001$	$5.085527e-001$	$6.194036e-001$
r_1	$9.875483e-003$	$4.438413e-002$	$7.533096e-002$
r_2	$2.864990e-005$	$4.116238e-004$	$1.865356e-003$
r_3	$2.354060e-010$	$4.307276e-008$	$1.342796e-006$
r_4	$1.764283e-013$	$3.781741e-013$	$1.848549e-012$

Table 7.6. Tests for inputs of class 2 for Alg. 7.4.2.

	Sample Test 1	Sample Test 2	Sample Test 3
$\text{cond}_1(A)$	$4.637187e+003$	$5.763326e+003$	$1.349509e+003$
s	4	2	1
r_0	$6.170632e-003$	$1.021014e-003$	$9.937866e-003$
r_1	$7.897623e-004$	$5.588185e-005$	$1.241422e-005$
r_2	$1.426298e-005$	$1.621575e-007$	$2.137849e-009$
r_3	$4.577198e-009$	$7.528647e-012$	$6.846061e-012$
r_4	$2.713013e-011$		

Table 7.7. Tests for inputs of class 2 for Alg. 7.5.1.

	Sample Test 1	Sample Test 2	Sample Test 3
$\text{cond}_1(A)$	$2.042839e+004$	$1.483413e+004$	$1.044744e+004$
s	3	2	2
r_0	$3.699548e-001$	$9.831201e-002$	$8.105060e-002$
r_1	$6.345701e-002$	$4.084126e-003$	$2.120317e-003$
r_2	$1.766525e-003$	$7.245445e-006$	$1.247355e-006$
r_3	$1.372439e-006$	$2.563352e-011$	$3.775972e-011$
r_4	$3.605207e-011$		

Table 7.8. Tests for inputs of class 2 for Alg. 7.5.2.

	Sample Test 1
$\text{cond}_1(A)$	$2.000268e+004$
s	3
r_0	$1.097395e-001$
r_1	$5.196420e-003$
r_2	$1.226878e-005$
r_3	$8.729462e-011$

40 in the tests of Alg. 7.4.2 ($s \leq 4$), 3 cases of 40 in the tests of Alg. 7.5.1 ($s = 2$), and 1 case of 40 in the tests of Alg. 7.5.2 ($s = 3$). In the third class of inputs, the iteration showed no sign of convergence even after 10 Newton steps. Only 6 such cases occured in all 160 tests. We display the results for 3 samples in the first class and 2 samples in the second class, in which case we display the $p(i)$ after s steps of stumbling. In all tables, the results are displayed only until convergence, up to the step after which the roundoff errors started to exceed the approximation errors.

In some experiments the iteration seemed to converge irregularly, in the sense that the residual norm exceeded 1 initially but the iteration still converged. The apparent reason is that the bound

$$||I + AX_{i+1}|| \leq ||I + AX_i||^2$$

can be a strict inequality rather than an equation.

On the other hand, the residual norm sometimes decreased more slowly than quadratically. This is immediately explained by the influence of the stage of adjusting the matrices to Toeplitz format, for Algs. 7.5.1 and 7.5.2, to the selected Toeplitz-like format, for Alg. 7.4.2, and to their representation with shorter displacement generators for Alg. 7.4.1. With these comments in mind, the test results are quite consistent with the theoretical estimates for the convergence rate.

7.7 CONCLUDING REMARKS

The algorithms based on Newton's iteration–residual correction run very fast for structured matrices, are easy to code, and allow their effective parallel implementation (cf. [BP94]). We note that the techniques discussed in this chapter and used in [Pan93a], [Pan93b], [Pan92a] can be extended to other classes of structured matrices such as Cauchy-like and Vandermonde-like (Vandermonde-type) matrices [Pan90], [PZHD97].

Acknowledgments

This work was supported by NSF grant CCR 9625344 and by PSC CUNY awards 667340 and 668365. The chapter was written by Pan, who was joined by Branham and Rasholt in Sec. 7.6 and by Zheng in Secs. 7.3 and 7.4.

APPENDICES FOR CHAPTER 7

7.A CORRECTNESS OF ALGORITHM 7.4.2

Our goal is to prove (7.4.10). We will start with an informal argument. Write

$$\hat{X}_{i+1} = \tilde{X}_i(2I + A\tilde{X}_i) \tag{7.A.1}$$

and immediately obtain that $I + A\hat{X}_{i+1} = (I + A\tilde{X}_i)^2$, and, consequently,

$$\|I + A\hat{X}_{i+1}\| = \tilde{p}^2(i).$$

Therefore, for small $\tilde{p}(i)$ we have $\hat{X}_{i+1} \approx X$, and by extending (7.4.9) we write

$$G_{\hat{X}_{i+1}} \triangleq \hat{X}_{i+1}G = \tilde{X}_i(2I + A\tilde{X}_i)G = G_{\tilde{X}_{i+1}},$$
$$H^T_{\hat{X}_{i+1}} \triangleq H^T\hat{X}_{i+1} = H^T\tilde{X}_i(2I + A\tilde{X}_i) = H_{\tilde{X}_{i+1}},$$

and, therefore, $\tilde{X}_{i+1} \approx \hat{X}_{i+1} \approx X$.

Next we will formally deduce (7.4.10). Substitute (7.A.1) into the equations of Alg. 7.4.2 and rewrite them as follows:

$$\tilde{X}_{i+1}\mathbf{e}_{n-1} = \hat{X}_{i+1}\mathbf{e}_{n-1}, \quad G_{i+1} = \hat{X}_{i+1}G, \quad H^T_{i+1} = H^T\hat{X}_{i+1}.$$

Combine these equations with those of (7.4.9) and obtain that

$$G_X - G_{i+1} = (X - \hat{X}_{i+1})G,$$
$$H^T_X - H^T_{i+1} = H^T(X - \hat{X}_{i+1}),$$
$$X\mathbf{e}_{n-1} - \tilde{X}_{i+1}\mathbf{e}_{n-1} = (X - \hat{X}_{i+1})\mathbf{e}_{n-1}.$$

Let us next estimate $\|X - \hat{X}_{i+1}\|_1$. We have $X - \hat{X}_{i+1} = (I + \hat{X}_{i+1}A)A^{-1} = (I + \tilde{X}_iA)^2A^{-1}$. Recall that $\|I + \tilde{X}_iA\|_1 = \tilde{p}(i)$ and obtain that

$$\|X - \hat{X}_{i+1}\|_1 \le \|A^{-1}\|_1\tilde{p}^2(i),$$
$$\|G_X - G_{i+1}\|_1 \le \|A^{-1}\|_1\tilde{p}^2(i)\|G\|_1,$$
$$\|H^T_X - H^T_{i+1}\|_1 \le \|A^{-1}\|_1\tilde{p}^2(i)\|H^T\|_1,$$
$$\|X\mathbf{e}_{n-1} - \tilde{X}_{i+1}\mathbf{e}_{n-1}\|_1 \le \|A^{-1}\|_1\tilde{p}^2(i).$$

We also observe that $\|Z^T_h(\mathbf{v})\|_1 \le \|Z_h(\mathbf{v})\|_1 = \|\mathbf{v}\|_1$ for $|h| = 1$ and any vector $\mathbf{v}$ of dimension n.

Now, by applying Lemma 7.4.2 to $A = X$ and $A = \tilde{X}_{i+1}$ for $f = -e$ and recalling that $|f| = 1$, we deduce that

$$\|X - \tilde{X}_{i+1}\|_1 \le \|(X - \tilde{X}_{i+1})\mathbf{e}_{n-1}\|_1$$
$$+ 0.5r(\|G_X - G_{i+1}\|_1\|H^T_X\|_1 + \|G_{i+1}\|_1\|H^T_X - H^T_{i+1}\|_1)$$
$$\le \|A^{-1}\|_1\tilde{p}^2(i)(1 + 0.5r\|G\|_1\|H^T_X\|_1 + \|G_{i+1}\|_1\|H^T\|_1).$$

Substitute the expression for H^T_X from (7.4.9) and for G_{i+1} from Alg. 7.4.2 and obtain that

$$\|X - \tilde{X}_{i+1}\|_1 \le \|A^{-1}\|_1\tilde{p}^2(i)(1 + 0.5r\|G\|_1\|H^T\|_1(\|X\|_1 + \|\hat{X}_{i+1}\|_1)).$$

Since $\|I + \hat{X}_{i+1}A\|_1 \le \tilde{p}^2(i)$, we also have

$$\|X - \hat{X}_{i+1}\|_1 \le \tilde{p}^2(i)\|A^{-1}\|_1 = \tilde{p}^2(i)\|X\|_1, \quad \|\hat{X}_{i+1}\|_1 \le \|X\|_1(1 + \tilde{p}^2(i)). \tag{7.A.2}$$

Therefore,

$$\tilde{p}(i+1) = \|I + \tilde{X}_{i+1}A\|_1$$
$$\le \|X - \tilde{X}_{i+1}\|_1\|A\|_1$$
$$\le \tilde{p}^2(i)\text{cond}_1(A)(1 + 0.5r\|G\|_1\|H^T\|_1\|X\|_1(2 + \tilde{p}^2(i))).$$

This proves the bound (7.4.10).

Section 7.B. Correctness of Algorithm 7.5.1   209

Remark. By (7.A.2), $\|X\|_1 \le \|\hat{X}_{i+1}\|_1/(1-\tilde{p}^2(i))$. Therefore, the right-hand side of (7.4.10) can be expressed entirely in terms of the values given as the input or made available in the process of performing Alg. 7.4.2.

7.B CORRECTNESS OF ALGORITHM 7.5.1

We now prove the result of Lemma 7.5.1(a). Let $E_{i+1} = \|X - X_{i+1}\|_1$ and substitute the expressions for $-X$ and $-X_{i+1}$ from (7.5.3) and (7.5.4) to obtain that

$$\begin{aligned}E_{i+1} &= \|\mathcal{L}(\mathbf{x}_{i+1})\mathcal{L}^T(Z\tilde{I}\mathbf{y}_{i+1}) - \mathcal{L}(\mathbf{x})\mathcal{L}^T(Z\tilde{I}\mathbf{y}) \\ &\quad + \mathcal{L}(\mathbf{y})\mathcal{L}^T(Z\tilde{I}\mathbf{x} - \mathbf{e}_0) - \mathcal{L}(\mathbf{y}_{i+1})L^T(Z\tilde{I}\mathbf{x}_{i+1} - \mathbf{e}_0)\|_1 \\ &= \|(\mathcal{L}(\mathbf{x}_{i+1}) - \mathcal{L}(\mathbf{x}))\mathcal{L}^T(Z\tilde{I}\mathbf{y}_{i+1}) + \mathcal{L}(\mathbf{x})(L^T(Z\tilde{I}\mathbf{y}_{i+1}) - \mathcal{L}^T(Z\tilde{I}\mathbf{y})) \\ &\quad + (\mathcal{L}(\mathbf{y}) - \mathcal{L}(\mathbf{y}_{i+1}))\mathcal{L}^T(Z\tilde{I}\mathbf{x} - \mathbf{e}_0) \\ &\quad + \mathcal{L}(\mathbf{y}_{i+1})(\mathcal{L}^T(Z\tilde{I}\mathbf{x} - \mathbf{e}_0) - \mathcal{L}^T(Z\tilde{I}\mathbf{x}_{i+1} - \mathbf{e}_0))\|_1 .\end{aligned}$$

Now recall that $\mathcal{L}(\mathbf{u}) - \mathcal{L}(\mathbf{v}) = \mathcal{L}(\mathbf{u} - \mathbf{v})$ and $\|BC + UV\|_1 \le \|B\|_1\|C\|_1 + \|U\|_1\|V\|_1$ for any choice of four matrices B, C, U, V and two vectors $\mathbf{u}$ and $\mathbf{v}$, and deduce that

$$\begin{aligned}E_{i+1} &= \|\mathcal{L}(\mathbf{x}_{i+1} - \mathbf{x})\mathcal{L}^T(Z\tilde{I}\mathbf{y}_{i+1}) + \mathcal{L}(\mathbf{x})\mathcal{L}^T(Z\tilde{I}(\mathbf{y}_{i+1} - \mathbf{y})) \\ &\quad + \mathcal{L}(\mathbf{y} - \mathbf{y}_{i+1})\mathcal{L}^T(Z\tilde{I}\mathbf{x} - \mathbf{e}_0) + \mathcal{L}(\mathbf{y}_{i+1})\mathcal{L}^T(Z\tilde{I}(\mathbf{x} - \mathbf{x}_{i+1}))\|_1 \\ &\le \|\mathcal{L}(\mathbf{x}_{i+1} - \mathbf{x})\|_1 \|\mathcal{L}^T(Z\tilde{I}\mathbf{y}_{i+1})\|_1 + \|\mathcal{L}(\mathbf{x})\|_1 \|\mathcal{L}^T(Z\tilde{I}(\mathbf{y}_{i+1} - \mathbf{y}))\|_1 \\ &\quad + \|\mathcal{L}(\mathbf{y} - \mathbf{y}_{i+1})\|_1 \|\mathcal{L}^T(Z\tilde{I}\mathbf{x} - \mathbf{e}_0)\|_1 + \|\mathcal{L}(\mathbf{y}_{i+1})\|_1 \|\mathcal{L}^T(Z\tilde{I}(\mathbf{x} - \mathbf{x}_{i+1}))\|_1.\end{aligned}$$

Now observe that

$$\|\mathcal{L}(\mathbf{u})\|_1 \le \|\mathbf{u}\|_1, \quad \|\mathcal{L}^T(\mathbf{u})\|_1 \le n\|\mathbf{u}\|_1, \quad \|\mathcal{L}^T(Z\mathbf{u})\|_1 \le (n-1)\|\mathbf{u}\|_1,$$
$$\|\mathcal{L}^T(Z\mathbf{u} - \mathbf{e}_0)\|_1 = 1 + \|\mathcal{L}^T(Z\mathbf{u})\|_1 \le 1 + (n-1)\|\mathbf{u}\|_1$$

for any vector $\mathbf{u}$ of dimension n. Substitute these bounds and obtain that

$$\begin{aligned}E_{i+1} &\le \|\mathbf{x}_{i+1} - \mathbf{x}\|_1(n-1)\|\mathbf{y}_{i+1}\|_1 + \|\mathbf{x}\|_1(n-1)\|\mathbf{y}_{i+1} - \mathbf{y}\|_1 \\ &\quad + \|\mathbf{y} - \mathbf{y}_{i+1}\|_1((n-1)\|\mathbf{x}\|_1 + 1) + \|\mathbf{y}_{i+1}\|_1(n-1)\|\mathbf{x} - \mathbf{x}_{i+1}\|_1.\end{aligned}$$

Substitute the bounds (7.5.6) and (7.5.7) and deduce that

$$E_{i+1} \le p(i)e(i)(\|\mathbf{x}\|_1 2(n-1)(\|\mathbf{y}_{i+1}\|_1 + \|\mathbf{y}\|_1)) + \|\mathbf{y}\|_1).$$

Substitute (7.5.8) and arrive at the result of Lemma 7.5.1(a).

7.C CORRECTNESS OF ALGORITHM 7.5.2

We now prove the result of Lemma 7.5.1(b). Again let $E_{i+1} = \|X - X_{i+1}\|_1$ and substitute the expressions for $-X$ and $-X_{i+1}$ from Thm. 7.5.1 and (7.5.5) to obtain that

$$\begin{aligned}2E_{i+1} &= \|Z_1(\mathbf{y}_{i+1})Z_{-1}(\mathbf{x}_{i+1}) - Z_1(\mathbf{x}_{i+1} - 2\mathbf{e}_0)Z_{-1}(\mathbf{y}_{i+1}) \\ &\quad - Z_1(\mathbf{y})Z_{-1}(\mathbf{x}) + Z_1(\mathbf{x} - 2\mathbf{e}_0)Z_{-1}(\mathbf{y})\|_1 \\ &= \|(Z_1(\mathbf{y}_{i+1}) - Z_1(\mathbf{y}))Z_{-1}(\mathbf{x}_{i+1}) + Z_1(\mathbf{y})(Z_{-1}(\mathbf{x}_{i+1}) - Z_{-1}(\mathbf{x})) \\ &\quad + Z_1(\mathbf{x} - 2\mathbf{e}_0)(Z_{-1}(\mathbf{y}) - Z_{-1}(\mathbf{y}_{i+1})) \\ &\quad + (Z_1(\mathbf{x} - 2\mathbf{e}_0) - Z_1(\mathbf{x}_{i+1} - 2\mathbf{e}_0))Z_{-1}(\mathbf{y}_{i+1})\|_1.\end{aligned}$$

Now observe that $Z_h(\mathbf{u}) - Z_h(\mathbf{v}) = Z_h(\mathbf{u} - \mathbf{v})$, $\|Z_g(\mathbf{u})\|_1 = \|\mathbf{u}\|_1$ for any pair of scalars g and h, where $|g| = 1$, and any pair of vectors $\mathbf{u}$ and $\mathbf{v}$ of dimension n. Substitute these relations and deduce that

$$\begin{aligned}
2E_{i+1} &= ||Z_1(\mathbf{y}_{i+1} - \mathbf{y})Z_{-1}(\mathbf{x}_{i+1}) + Z_1(\mathbf{y})Z_{-1}(\mathbf{x}_{i+1} - \mathbf{x}) \\
&\quad + Z_1(\mathbf{x} - 2\mathbf{e}_0)Z_{-1}(\mathbf{y} - \mathbf{y}_{i+1}) + Z_1(\mathbf{x} - \mathbf{x}_{i+1})Z_{-1}(\mathbf{y}_{i+1})||_1 \\
&\leq ||Z_1(\mathbf{y}_{i+1} - \mathbf{y})||_1 ||Z_{-1}(\mathbf{x}_{i+1})||_1 + ||Z_1(\mathbf{y})||_1 ||Z_{-1}(\mathbf{x}_{i+1} - \mathbf{x})||_1 \\
&\quad + ||Z_1(\mathbf{x} - 2\mathbf{e}_0)||_1 ||Z_{-1}(\mathbf{y} - \mathbf{y}_{i+1})||_1 + ||Z_1(\mathbf{x} - \mathbf{x}_{i+1})||_1 ||Z_{-1}(\mathbf{y}_{i+1})||_1 \\
&= ||\mathbf{y}_{i+1} - \mathbf{y}||_1 ||\mathbf{x}_{i+1}||_1 + ||\mathbf{y}||_1 ||\mathbf{x}_{i+1} - \mathbf{x}||_1 \\
&\quad + ||\mathbf{x} - 2\mathbf{e}_0||_1 ||\mathbf{y} - \mathbf{y}_{i+1}||_1 + ||\mathbf{x} - \mathbf{x}_{i+1}||_1 ||\mathbf{y}_{i+1}||_1.
\end{aligned}$$

Substitute (7.5.6)–(7.5.8) and the trivial bound $||\mathbf{x} - 2\mathbf{e}_0||_1 \leq 2 + ||\mathbf{x}||_1$ and obtain that

$$\begin{aligned}
2E_{i+1} &\leq p(i)e(i)(||\mathbf{y}||_1 ||\mathbf{x}_{i+1}||_1 + ||\mathbf{y}||_1 ||\mathbf{x}||_1 + ||\mathbf{x} - 2\mathbf{e}_0||_1 ||\mathbf{y}||_1 + ||\mathbf{x}||_1 ||\mathbf{y}_{i+1}||_1) \\
&\leq 2p(i)e(i)((1 + p(i)e(i))||\mathbf{x}||_1 + 1)||\mathbf{y}||_1,
\end{aligned}$$

which immediately implies the result of Lemma 7.5.1(b).

Chapter 8

FAST ALGORITHMS WITH APPLICATIONS TO MARKOV CHAINS AND QUEUEING MODELS

Dario A. Bini

Beatrice Meini

8.1 INTRODUCTION

A very meaningful application where the exploitation of the Toeplitz-like structure plays a fundamental role in devising advanced and effective algorithms arises in the field of queueing theory (see, e.g., [BM96a], [BM96b], [BM97b], [BM97a], [BM98a], [Mei97b]). This chapter provides an overview of this application area.

Many problems in queueing theory are modeled by Markov chains of M/G/1 type [Neu89], which are characterized in terms of transition probability matrices P that have a lower block Hessenberg structure and, except for their first block column, a block Toeplitz structure. Moreover, these transition matrices are generally infinite dimensional and the block entries may have a considerable size. Examples of real-world situations where such models are encountered include the analysis of telephone networks with multiple types of traffic (voice, data, video, multimedia) [GHKT94], as well as the analysis of metropolitan queueing models [ALM97].

The main computational burden in this kind of application consists of solving a homogeneous linear system of equations of the form

$$P^T \pi = \pi,$$

where π is the probability invariant vector of the chain and the symbol T denotes matrix transposition.

A related problem arises in the computation of an approximate nonnegative solution G to the matrix equation

$$X = \sum_{i=0}^{+\infty} X^i A_i = A_0 + X A_1 + X^2 A_2 + X^3 A_3 + \cdots$$

for given $m\times m$ nonnegative matrices A_i such that $\sum_{i=0}^{+\infty} A_i^T$ is stochastic. This problem can be reduced to the computation of the top-leftmost block entry of the infinite block matrix $(I-Q)^{-1}$, where I denotes the identity operator and

$$Q = \begin{bmatrix} A_1 & A_0 & & & \bigcirc \\ A_2 & A_1 & A_0 & & \\ A_3 & A_2 & A_1 & A_0 & \\ \vdots & \ddots & \ddots & \ddots & \ddots \end{bmatrix}$$

is an infinite block Toeplitz matrix in block Hessenberg form. The knowledge of G allows us to recover an arbitrary number of components of the vector $\boldsymbol{\pi}$ by means of a well-known tool in Markov chains known as the Ramaswami formula [Neu89], [Ram88].

The purpose of this chapter is to provide an overview of the most recent efficient algorithms for matrix problems with such block Toeplitz and Hessenberg structures.

8.2 TOEPLITZ MATRICES AND MARKOV CHAINS

In this section we recall the basic concepts related to Markov chains, describe the main computational problems, and present the most recurrent matrix structures arising in applications.

Let $\mathbf{N}$ denote the set of nonnegative integers.

Definition 8.2.1 (Markov Chains). *A homogeneous discrete-time Markov chain with discrete (finite or infinite) state space $\mathcal{S} = \{x_i,\ i \in \boldsymbol{E}\}$, $\boldsymbol{E} \subset \mathbf{N}$, is a discrete-time stochastic process $\{X_n, n \in \mathbf{N}\}$ such that*

$$\mathrm{Prob}\{X_{n+1}=x_j|X_0=x_{i_0},X_1=x_{i_1},\ldots,X_{n-1}=x_{i_{n-1}},X_n=x_i\}$$
$$= \mathrm{Prob}\{X_{n+1}=x_j|X_n=x_i\}=p_{i,j} \quad \textit{for all} \quad n\in\mathbf{N}, i,j,i_0,\ldots,i_{n-1}\in\boldsymbol{E}.$$

That is, the state of the system at time $n+1$ depends only on the state of the system at time n.

$\diamondsuit$

The scalar $p_{i,j}$, called the transition probability, represents the probability of making a transition from state x_i to state x_j when the time parameter increases from n to $n+1$ for any integer n.

The matrix $P = (p_{i,j})$, called the transition probability matrix, is a (finite or infinite) stochastic matrix, i.e.,

$$p_{i,j} \geq 0 \quad \text{and} \quad \sum_{j \in \boldsymbol{E}} p_{i,j} = 1 \qquad (8.2.1)$$

for any $i \in \boldsymbol{E}$.

A relevant problem in the study of Markov chains is to compute a nonnegative vector $\boldsymbol{\pi} = \mathrm{col}\{\pi_0, \pi_1, \pi_2, \pi_3, \ldots\}$ such that

$$P^T\boldsymbol{\pi} = \boldsymbol{\pi}, \quad \sum_i \pi_i = 1. \qquad (8.2.2)$$

Such a vector is called the probability invariant vector and, under suitable conditions, exists and is unique. In this case, the Markov chain is said to be positive recurrent and it holds that

$$\lim_{n\to+\infty} \mathrm{Prob}\{X_n=x_i\} = \pi_i ,$$

Section 8.2. Toeplitz Matrices and Markov Chains

whatever the initial state distribution $(\text{Prob}\{X_0 = x_i\})_i$ of the chain is.

In most cases, the matrix P (possibly infinite) is strongly structured. One such example occurs for Markov chains of M/G/1 type that arise in queueing models [Neu89]. For these chains, the transition probability matrix is infinite and has the form

$$P^T = \begin{bmatrix} B_1 & A_0 & & & \bigcirc \\ B_2 & A_1 & A_0 & & \\ B_3 & A_2 & A_1 & A_0 & \\ \vdots & \vdots & \ddots & \ddots & \ddots \end{bmatrix}, \qquad (8.2.3)$$

where A_i, B_{i+1}, $i \geq 0$, are $m \times m$ nonnegative matrices such that $\sum_{i=0}^{+\infty} A_i^T$ and $\sum_{i=1}^{+\infty} B_i^T$ are stochastic. That is, P^T is in block Hessenberg form and the submatrix obtained by removing its first block column is block Toeplitz.

Another example arises in the study of so-called quasi-birth-death (QBD) problems [Neu89], where the matrix P, in addition to the M/G/1 structure, is also block tridiagonal. That is, P is uniquely defined by the blocks A_0, A_1, A_2, B_1, B_2.

More general M/G/1 type Markov chains, called non-skip-free in [GHT97], are defined by transition matrices of the form

$$P^T = \begin{bmatrix} B_{1,1} & \cdots & B_{1,k} & A_0 & & & \bigcirc \\ B_{2,1} & \cdots & B_{2,k} & A_1 & A_0 & & \\ B_{3,1} & \cdots & B_{3,k} & A_2 & A_1 & A_0 & \\ \vdots & & \vdots & \vdots & \vdots & \ddots & \ddots \end{bmatrix}, \qquad (8.2.4)$$

where A_i, $B_{i+1,j}$, $i \geq 0$, $j = 1, \ldots, k$, are $m \times m$ nonnegative matrices such that $\sum_{i=0}^{+\infty} A_i^T$ and $\sum_{i=1}^{+\infty} B_{i,j}^T$, $j = 1, \ldots, k$, are stochastic. This class of transition matrices can be regarded as special cases of the block Hessenberg form (8.2.3) by partitioning the matrix P^T in (8.2.4) into blocks $\mathcal{A}_i$, $\mathcal{B}_i$ of dimension $p = mk$, where

$$\mathcal{A}_0 = \begin{bmatrix} A_0 & O & \cdots & O \\ A_1 & A_0 & \ddots & \vdots \\ \vdots & \ddots & \ddots & O \\ A_{k-1} & \cdots & A_1 & A_0 \end{bmatrix},$$

$$\mathcal{A}_i = \begin{bmatrix} A_{ik} & A_{ik-1} & \cdots & A_{ik-k+1} \\ A_{ik+1} & A_{ik} & \ddots & \vdots \\ \vdots & \ddots & \ddots & A_{ik-1} \\ A_{ik+k-1} & \cdots & A_{ik+1} & A_{ik} \end{bmatrix}, \quad i \geq 1, \qquad (8.2.5)$$

and

$$\mathcal{B}_i = \begin{bmatrix} B_{(i-1)k+1,1} & B_{(i-1)k+1,2} & \cdots & B_{(i-1)k+1,k} \\ B_{(i-1)k+2,1} & B_{(i-1)k+2,2} & \cdots & B_{(i-1)k+2,k} \\ \vdots & \vdots & & \vdots \\ B_{ik,1} & B_{ik,2} & \cdots & B_{ik,k} \end{bmatrix}, \quad i \geq 1.$$

M/G/1 type Markov chains have been introduced and thoroughly investigated in [Neu89]. However, no explicit attempt has been made to exploit matrix structure in developing efficient algorithms.

Similar structures arise in the case of finite Markov chains or where the infinite matrix P^T is replaced by a finite stochastic matrix obtained by cutting P^T to a finite (large) size and by adjusting the last row to preserve the stochastic nature of the matrix. In this case the resulting structure becomes

$$P^T = \begin{bmatrix} B_1 & A_0 & & & \bigcirc \\ B_2 & A_1 & A_0 & & \\ \vdots & \vdots & \ddots & \ddots & \\ B_{n-1} & A_{n-2} & \cdots & A_1 & A_0 \\ C_n & C_{n-1} & \cdots & C_2 & C_1 \end{bmatrix}. \quad (8.2.6)$$

For block tridiagonal matrices, like the ones arising from QBD problems, P is then uniquely defined by the blocks A_0, A_1, A_2, B_1, B_2, C_1, C_2.

8.2.1 Modeling of Switches and Network Traffic Control

An example of a general M/G/1 Markov chain of the type (8.2.4) arises in the modeling of the behavior of switches with multiple types of traffic (voice, data, video, and multimedia) [GHKT94], [KR86].

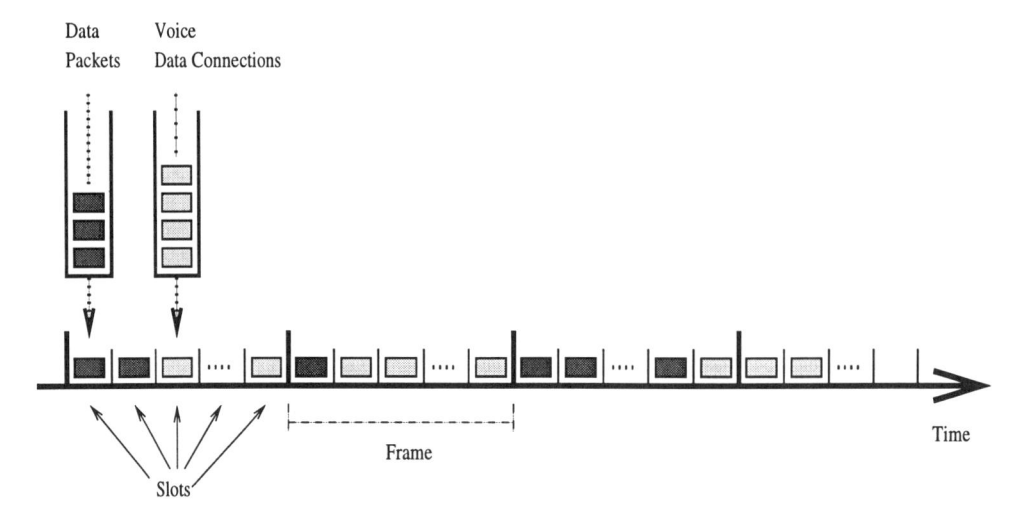

Figure 8.1. Voice-data multiplexor.

Indeed, consider a voice-data multiplexor where voice and data traffic are multiplexed over a single channel [GHKT94], [KR86], [LM85], [SVS83] and where time is divided into slots (see Fig. 8.1). The time slots are aggregated into frames of k slots each. There are at most $m - 1 \leq k$ voice connections actively transmitting during a time frame, and voice connections become active or inactive at the beginning of a frame. The number of active voice connections per frame is governed by an m state Markov chain having an irreducible aperiodic transition matrix $Q = (Q_{r,s})$, $r, s = 0, \ldots, m-1$, where $Q_{r,s}$ is the probability to switch from r active voice connections in the previous frame to s active voices connections in the present frame. Each active voice connection occupies one slot of time during a frame, and the remaining slots are allocated to data packets. Each data packet is one slot in length. The arrival process of data packets is

Section 8.2. Toeplitz Matrices and Markov Chains

governed by a generating function $R(z)$, and packets that arrive during a frame can be transmitted only in subsequent frames. There is an infinite buffer for data packets.

Let u_n be the random variable representing the number of buffered data packets at the beginning of the nth frame and v_n the random variable representing the number of active connections at the beginning of the nth frame. Then $X_n = (u_n, v_n)$ is a two-dimensional Markov chain with states (i,j), $i = 0, 1, \ldots$, $j = 0, \ldots, m-1$. This is a Markov chain of the M/G/1 type (8.2.4), where the blocks A_i and $B_{i,j}$ are defined in terms of matrix power series in the following way:

$$A(z)^T = \sum_{i=0}^{+\infty} A_i^T z^i = R(z) D_k(z) Q,$$

$$B_{j+1}^T(z) = \sum_{i=0}^{+\infty} B_{i+1,j+1}^T z^i = R(z) D_j(z) Q$$

for $j = 0, \ldots, k-1$, and where

$$D_j(z) = \mathrm{diag}\{1, \ldots, 1, z, \ldots, z^{m-k+j-1}\}$$

is an $m \times m$ diagonal matrix.

8.2.2 Conditions for Positive Recurrence

Computing the probability invariant vector π of P consists of evaluating the eigenvector, corresponding to the eigenvalue 1, of the nonnegative matrix P^T. A matrix P is said to be nonnegative, and we write $P \geq 0$ if all its entries are nonnegative. (This is distinct from saying P is nonnegative definite, which means $x^* P x \geq 0$ for all vectors x.) For finite Markov chains, the theory of nonnegative matrices [Ste94], and more specifically the Perron–Frobenius theorem, guarantees the existence of a nonnegative eigenvector π such that (8.2.2) holds. The uniqueness of π, and thus the positive recurrence of the finite Markov chain, holds if the matrix P is not reducible. (A matrix A is said to be reducible if there exists a permutation of rows and columns that transforms A by similarity in the following way:

$$\Pi A \Pi^T = \begin{bmatrix} A_{1,1} & A_{1,2} \\ O & A_{2,2} \end{bmatrix}, \tag{8.2.7}$$

where the blocks $A_{1,1}$, $A_{2,2}$ are square matrices and Π is a permutation matrix.)

The computation of π can be carried out by solving the homogeneous linear system

$$(I - P^T)\pi = 0,$$

where I is the identity matrix, by means of the customary techniques such as Gaussian elimination. The matrix of the above system is a singular M-matrix [Var63] since the spectral radius of P^T, i.e., the maximum modulus of the eigenvalues, is equal to 1. A matrix of the form $\alpha I - B$ is said to be an M-matrix if $B \geq 0$ and α is greater than or equal to the spectral radius of B.

From the theory of M-matrices it follows that both the LU (lower upper triangular) and the UL (upper lower triangular) factorizations of $I - P^T$ always exist [FP81], [VC81]. Such factorizations can be used for the computation of π. Moreover, due to the properties of M-matrices, this computation is numerically stable provided that the diagonal adjustment technique of [GTH85], [Oci93] is employed.

For infinite matrices of the form (8.2.3) we can give explicit conditions for the existence and uniqueness of a solution π to (8.2.2) in the case where P and $\sum_{i=0}^{+\infty} A_i$ are not reducible. Observe that the definition of a reducible matrix can be extended naturally to infinite matrices where the blocks $A_{1,1}$ and $A_{2,2}$ in (8.2.7) may have infinite size.

Let us now introduce $e = \text{col}\{1, 1, \ldots, 1\}$ and the m-dimensional vectors a, $b = \text{col}\{b_0, b_1, \ldots, b_{m-1}\}$ such that

$$a = \sum_{i=1}^{+\infty} i A_i e, \quad \sum_{i=0}^{+\infty} A_i^T b = b, \quad \sum_{i=0}^{m-1} b_i = 1.$$

Then the corresponding Markov chain is positive recurrent if and only if $\rho = b^T a < 1$ [Neu89].

8.2.3 Computation of the Probability Invariant Vector

In order to devise efficient algorithms for the computation of π in (8.2.2) it is fundamental to take advantage of the Toeplitz-like structure of the transition probability matrix P.

For positive recurrent infinite Markov chains (8.2.3), the vector π that solves (8.2.2) can be computed by means of a recursive and numerically stable formula (known as Ramaswami's formula [Ram88]). The formula first requires that we obtain the solution of the following nonlinear matrix equation:

$$X = \sum_{i=0}^{+\infty} X^i A_i = A_0 + X A_1 + X^2 A_2 + \cdots, \tag{8.2.8}$$

where X is $m \times m$. It is possible to establish that for positive recurrent Markov chains, (8.2.8) has a unique nonnegative solution G such that G^T is stochastic [Neu89].

Now define the matrices

$$\bar{A}_i \triangleq \sum_{j=i}^{+\infty} G^{j-i} A_j, \quad \bar{B}_i \triangleq \sum_{j=i}^{+\infty} G^{j-i} B_j \quad \text{for } i \geq 1 \tag{8.2.9}$$

and partition the vector π into m-dimensional vectors π_i, $i \geq 0$, according to the block structure of (8.2.3). Then the vector π_0 solves the system of equations

$$\begin{cases} \bar{B}_1 \pi_0 = \pi_0, \\ \left(e^T + e^T (I - \sum_{i=1}^{+\infty} \bar{A}_i)^{-1} \sum_{i=2}^{+\infty} \bar{B}_i \right) \pi_0 = 1, \end{cases}$$

while the remaining components of π can be computed by means of the Ramaswami formula [Ram88]:

$$\pi_i = (I - \bar{A}_1)^{-1} \left[\bar{B}_{i+1} \pi_0 + \sum_{j=1}^{i-1} \bar{A}_{i+1-j} \pi_j \right], \quad i \geq 1. \tag{8.2.10}$$

It is also possible to rephrase the matrix equation (8.2.8) in terms of a block Toeplitz block Hessenberg matrix and to reduce the design and analysis of algorithms for solving (8.2.8) to the design and analysis of algorithms for treating the infinite matrix

$$H = \begin{bmatrix} I - A_1 & -A_0 & & \bigcirc \\ -A_2 & I - A_1 & -A_0 & \\ -A_3 & -A_2 & I - A_1 & -A_0 \\ \vdots & \vdots & \ddots & \ddots & \ddots \end{bmatrix}. \tag{8.2.11}$$

Indeed, if G is the unique solution of (8.2.8), then the unique solution of the infinite system of equations

$$\begin{bmatrix} X_1 & X_2 & X_3 & \cdots \end{bmatrix} H = \begin{bmatrix} A_0 & O & O & \cdots \end{bmatrix}, \qquad (8.2.12)$$

where X_i are $m \times m$ matrices, is given by $X_i = G^i$, $i \geq 1$. Therefore, solving (8.2.12) provides the only solution G of (8.2.8) having nonnegative entries.

Observe that in order to compute G it is sufficient to compute the top-leftmost block entry of H^{-1}, which we shall denote by $(H^{-1})_{1,1}$. In fact, it holds that $G = A_0(H^{-1})_{1,1}$.

Observe also that if we consider the finite system obtained by truncating (8.2.12) at the dimension n, say,

$$\begin{bmatrix} X_1^{(n)} & X_2^{(n)} & \cdots & X_n^{(n)} \end{bmatrix} H_n = \begin{bmatrix} A_0 & O & \cdots & O \end{bmatrix}, \qquad (8.2.13)$$

where

$$H_n = \begin{bmatrix} I - A_1 & -A_0 & & & O \\ -A_2 & I - A_1 & -A_0 & & \\ \vdots & \ddots & \ddots & \ddots & \\ -A_{n-1} & \ddots & & I - A_1 & -A_0 \\ -A_n & -A_{n-1} & \cdots & -A_2 & I - A_1 \end{bmatrix}, \qquad (8.2.14)$$

then $\{X_1^{(n)}\}_n$ is a sequence of nonnegative matrices that monotonically converges to G as n tends to infinity [LS96].

We now study how to exploit the Toeplitz structure of H_n in order to speed up the computations.

8.3 EXPLOITATION OF STRUCTURE AND COMPUTATIONAL TOOLS

We start by studying the relations that exist among block Toeplitz matrices, matrix polynomials, and matrix power series. We show that matrix computations involving (infinite) block Toeplitz matrices can be rephrased in terms of matrix polynomials or matrix power series, thus generalizing the correlations between Toeplitz computations and polynomial computations widely investigated in [BP94]. We also introduce some basic algorithms for polynomial (power series) computations and for manipulating block Toeplitz matrices.

The relation between Toeplitz matrices and polynomials has been implicitly used in many fields but only recently pointed out in a detailed way in [BG95], [BP86], [BP93], [BP94], [Gem97]. In particular, computations such as polynomial multiplication, polynomial division (evaluation of quotient and remainder), polynomial g.c.d. and l.c.m., Padé approximation, modular computations, Chinese remainder, and Taylor expansion have their own counterparts formulated in terms of Toeplitz or Toeplitz-like computations and vice versa. Quite surprisingly, almost all the known algorithms for polynomial division match with corresponding algorithms independently devised for the inversion of triangular Toeplitz matrices [BP86]. Also several computations involving matrix algebras strictly related with Toeplitz matrices, such as the circulant class, the τ class, and the algebra generated by a Frobenius matrix, can be rephrased in terms of computations among polynomials modulo a given specific polynomial associated with the algebra [BP94], [BC83], [Boz95].

These results can be extended in a natural way to the case of block Toeplitz matrices, a fact that does not seem to be well known in the literature. For instance, a remark in [Ste95] states that "there are fast algorithms for multiplying Toeplitz matrices by a vector. Unfortunately, they do not generalize to block Toeplitz matrices."

The goal of this section is to derive FFT-based algorithms for performing operations between block Toeplitz matrices, such as computing the product of a block Toeplitz matrix and a block vector (and thus extending the discussion of Sec. 1.4) and computing the inverse of a block Toeplitz block triangular matrix. To achieve these results, we exploit the relations between block Toeplitz matrices and matrix polynomials.

Let z be a scalar indeterminate and consider the *matrix polynomial* $A(z) = \sum_{i=0}^{p} A_i z^i$ of degree p [LT85], where A_i, $i = 0, \ldots, p$, are $m \times m$ matrices having real entries and A_p is not the null matrix. A matrix polynomial can be viewed as a polynomial in z having matrix coefficients or, equivalently, as a matrix having entries that are polynomials. Similarly, a *matrix power series* is a series having matrix coefficients or, equivalently, a matrix having entries that are power series.

A matrix polynomial is fully defined by its matrix coefficients $A_0, \ldots, A_p$ or, equivalently, by the $(p+1) \times 1$ block matrix A having blocks $A_0, \ldots, A_p$. We call *block column vector* any $n \times 1$ block matrix. Similarly we call *block row vector* any $1 \times n$ block matrix. The blocks defining a block (row or column) vector are called *block components*.

8.3.1 Block Toeplitz Matrices and Block Vector Product

Given two matrix polynomials $A(z)$ and $B(z)$ of degrees p and q, respectively, we may consider the matrix polynomial $C(z) = A(z)B(z)$ having degree at most $p+q$, obtained by means of the row-by-column product of $A(z)$ and $B(z)$. If we denote $C(z) = \sum_{i=0}^{p+q} C_i z^i$, then we have $C_0 = A_0 B_0$, $C_1 = A_0 B_1 + A_1 B_0$, $C_2 = A_0 B_2 + A_1 B_1 + A_2 B_0$, ..., $C_{p+q} = A_p B_q$. That is, in matrix form, we have

$$\begin{bmatrix} C_0 \\ C_1 \\ \vdots \\ C_{p+q} \end{bmatrix} = \begin{bmatrix} A_0 & O & \cdots & O \\ A_1 & A_0 & \ddots & \vdots \\ \vdots & \ddots & \ddots & O \\ A_p & \ddots & \ddots & A_0 \\ O & \ddots & \ddots & A_1 \\ \vdots & \ddots & \ddots & \vdots \\ O & \cdots & O & A_p \end{bmatrix} \begin{bmatrix} B_0 \\ B_1 \\ \vdots \\ B_q \end{bmatrix}. \tag{8.3.1}$$

Observe that, by choosing $p = 2n - 2$, $q = n - 1$, the middle n block rows of the matrix equation (8.3.1) yield the following product between a general block Toeplitz matrix and a block column vector:

$$\begin{bmatrix} C_{n-1} \\ C_n \\ \vdots \\ C_{2n-2} \end{bmatrix} = \begin{bmatrix} A_{n-1} & A_{n-2} & \cdots & A_0 \\ A_n & A_{n-1} & \ddots & \vdots \\ \vdots & \ddots & \ddots & A_{n-2} \\ A_{2n-2} & \cdots & A_n & A_{n-1} \end{bmatrix} \begin{bmatrix} B_0 \\ B_1 \\ \vdots \\ B_{n-1} \end{bmatrix}. \tag{8.3.2}$$

This shows that the product of a block Toeplitz matrix and a block vector can be viewed in terms of the product of two matrix polynomials. More specifically, (8.3.1)

Section 8.3. Exploitation of Structure and Computational Tools 219

can be used together with an evaluation-interpolation technique at the roots of unity to efficiently compute the product (8.3.2), as we now clarify.

For this purpose, let us introduce some notation and definitions concerning DFTs. Let $\hat{\imath}$ be the imaginary unit such that $\hat{\imath} = \sqrt{-1}$ and denote

$$\omega_N = \cos\frac{2\pi}{N} + \hat{\imath}\sin\frac{2\pi}{N}, \tag{8.3.3}$$

a primitive Nth root of unity such that the powers ω_N^j, $j = 0, \ldots, N-1$, are all the Nth roots of unity. Moreover, let z^* denote the complex conjugate of the complex number z.

For N-dimensional complex vectors

$$\boldsymbol{a} = \text{col}\{a_0, a_1, \ldots, a_{N-1}\}, \quad \boldsymbol{b} = \text{col}\{b_0, b_1, \ldots, b_{N-1}\}$$

such that

$$b_j = \sum_{k=0}^{N-1} a_k \omega_N^{kj} \tag{8.3.4}$$

or, equivalently,

$$a_j = \frac{1}{N} \sum_{k=0}^{N-1} \left(\omega_N^{kj}\right)^* b_k, \tag{8.3.5}$$

we denote $\boldsymbol{b} = \text{DFT}(\boldsymbol{a})$, the DFT of $\boldsymbol{a}$ of order N, and $\boldsymbol{a} = \text{IDFT}(\boldsymbol{b})$, the inverse DFT of $\boldsymbol{b}$ of order N. We recall that both DFT and IDFT can be computed in $O(N \log N)$ operations by means of FFT algorithms [ER82].

Observe that evaluating $\boldsymbol{b} = \text{DFT}(\boldsymbol{a})$ corresponds to computing the values that the polynomial $a(z) = \sum_{k=0}^{N-1} a_k z^k$ takes at the Nth roots of unity. Similarly, computing $\boldsymbol{a} = \text{IDFT}(\boldsymbol{b})$ corresponds to solving an interpolation problem, viz., that of computing the coefficients of a polynomial $a(z)$ given its values at the Nth roots of unity.

In summary, the evaluation-interpolation technique for computing a product of the form (8.3.2) proceeds according to the following scheme:

1. Evaluate $A(z)$ at the Nth roots of unity, ω_N^j, $j = 0, \ldots, N-1$, for a choice of N that satisfies $N > 3n - 3$, since the product $C(z)$ has degree at most $3n - 3$. This requires that we evaluate all m^2 entries of $A(z)$ at the roots of unity, and this computation can be performed by applying m^2 DFTs, each of order N.

2. Evaluate $B(z)$ at the Nth roots of unity, again by performing m^2 DFTs, each of order N.

3. Compute the N matrix products $C(\omega_N^j) = A(\omega_N^j)B(\omega_N^j)$, $j = 0, \ldots, N-1$. The total cost of this step is $O(m^3 N)$ operations.

4. Interpolate the values of the entries of $C(\omega_N^j)$ by means of m^2 IDFTs, each of order N, and recover the coefficients of the m^2 polynomials, i.e., the blocks C_i.

The total cost of the above procedure is $O(m^2 N \log N + m^3 N)$ operations, where $O(m^2 N \log N)$ is due to the FFTs while $O(m^3 N)$ is the cost of stage 3. Here N is of the order of n. This cost is below the customary figure of $O(m^3 N^2)$ operations for carrying out the matrix multiplication (8.3.2).

We may in fact devise a more efficient algorithm involving FFTs of lower order for computing the product between a block Toeplitz matrix and a block vector if we consider computations modulo the polynomial $z^N - 1$. Indeed, given matrix polynomials $P(z), Q(z), R(z)$ of degree at most $N - 1$ such that

$$R(z) = P(z)Q(z) \bmod z^N - 1, \tag{8.3.6}$$

we may similarly rephrase the above equation in matrix form in the following way:

$$\begin{bmatrix} R_0 \\ R_1 \\ \vdots \\ R_{N-1} \end{bmatrix} = \begin{bmatrix} P_0 & P_{N-1} & \cdots & P_1 \\ P_1 & P_0 & \ddots & \vdots \\ \vdots & \ddots & \ddots & P_{N-1} \\ P_{N-1} & \cdots & P_{k-1} & P_0 \end{bmatrix} \begin{bmatrix} Q_0 \\ Q_1 \\ \vdots \\ Q_{N-1} \end{bmatrix}. \tag{8.3.7}$$

The matrix on the right-hand side of (8.3.7) is a *block circulant* matrix, namely, a matrix whose block entries in the kth block row and in the jth block column depend on $j - k$ mod N.

The blocks R_i can be efficiently computed, given the blocks P_i and Q_i, by exploiting the polynomial relation (8.3.6). In fact, from (8.3.6) we deduce that $R(\omega_N^j) = P(\omega_N^j)Q(\omega_N^j)$, $j = 0, \ldots, N-1$. Therefore, the blocks R_i can be computed by means of the evaluation-interpolation technique at the Nth roots of unity.

Now, given an $n \times n$ block Toeplitz matrix $A = (A_{i-j+n-1})_{i,j=1,\ldots,n}$ it is possible to embed A into an $N \times N$ block circulant matrix H, $N = 2n$, defined by its first block column having blocks $A_{n-1}, A_n, \ldots, A_{2n-2}, O, A_0, \ldots, A_{n-2}$, i.e.,

$$H = \left[\begin{array}{cccc|cccc} A_{n-1} & A_{n-2} & \cdots & A_0 & O & A_{2n-2} & \cdots & A_n \\ A_n & A_{n-1} & \ddots & \vdots & A_0 & O & \ddots & \vdots \\ \vdots & \ddots & \ddots & A_{n-2} & \vdots & \ddots & \ddots & A_{2n-2} \\ A_{2n-2} & \cdots & A_n & A_{n-1} & A_{n-2} & \cdots & A_0 & O \\ \hline O & A_{2n-2} & \cdots & A_n & A_{n-1} & A_{n-2} & \cdots & A_0 \\ A_0 & O & \ddots & \vdots & A_n & A_{n-1} & \ddots & \vdots \\ \vdots & \ddots & \ddots & A_{2n-2} & \vdots & \ddots & \ddots & A_{n-2} \\ A_{n-2} & \cdots & A_0 & O & A_{2n-2} & \cdots & A_n & A_{n-1} \end{array} \right].$$

The product of H and the block column vector defined by the blocks

$$\{B_0, B_1, \ldots, B_{N-1}\},$$

where $B_j = O$ for $j \geq n$, delivers a block column vector of N block components $C_0, C_1, \ldots, C_{N-1}$ such that

$$H \begin{bmatrix} B_0 \\ \vdots \\ B_{n-1} \\ \hline O \\ \vdots \\ O \end{bmatrix} = \begin{bmatrix} C_0 \\ \vdots \\ C_{n-1} \\ \hline C_n \\ \vdots \\ C_{N-1} \end{bmatrix}.$$

Since the leading principal block submatrix of H of block size n coincides with A, the blocks $C_0, C_1, \ldots, C_{n-1}$ define the block column vector C such that $C = AB$, where B is the block column vector defined by $B_0, B_1, \ldots, B_{n-1}$. In this way we arrive at the following algorithm for the multiplication of a block Toeplitz matrix and a block vector.

Section 8.3. Exploitation of Structure and Computational Tools

Algorithm 8.3.1 (Block Toeplitz and Vector Multiplication).

- Input: The $m \times m$ matrices $A_0, A_1, \ldots, A_{2n-2}$ defining the $n \times n$ block Toeplitz matrix $A = (A_{i-j+n-1})_{i,j=1,\ldots,n}$; the $m \times m$ matrices $B_0, B_1, \ldots, B_{n-1}$ defining the block vector B.

- Output: The $m \times m$ matrices $C_0, C_1, \ldots, C_{n-1}$ defining the block vector C such that $C = AB$.

- Computation:

  1. Evaluate the matrix polynomial
  $$\alpha(z) = A_{n-1} + A_n z + \cdots + A_{2n-2} z^{n-1} + A_0 z^{n+1} + \cdots + A_{n-2} z^{2n-1}$$
  at the $2n$ roots of 1, by means of m^2 DFTs of order $2n$ each, and obtain the matrices $\alpha(\omega_{2n}^j)$, $j = 0, \ldots, 2n-1$.

  2. Evaluate the matrix polynomial
  $$\beta(z) = B_0 + B_1 z + \cdots + B_{n-1} z^{n-1}$$
  at the $2n$ roots of 1, by means of m^2 DFTs of order $2n$ each, and obtain the matrices $\beta(\omega_{2n}^j)$, $j = 0, \ldots, 2n-1$.

  3. Compute the products $\gamma(\omega_{2n}^j) = \alpha(\omega_{2n}^j)\beta(\omega_{2n}^j)$, $j = 0, \ldots, 2n-1$.

  4. Interpolate $\gamma(\omega_{2n}^j)$ by means of m^2 IDFTs of order $2n$ each, obtain the coefficients $\gamma_0, \gamma_1, \ldots, \gamma_{2n-1}$ such that
  $$\gamma(z) = \sum_{i=0}^{2n-1} \gamma_i z^i = \alpha(z)\beta(z) \bmod z^{2n} - 1,$$
  and output $C_i = \gamma_i$, $i = 0, \ldots, n-1$.

  $\diamond$

8.3.2 Inversion of Block Triangular Block Toeplitz Matrices

We can also devise efficient algorithms for the inversion of block triangular block Toeplitz matrices. For this purpose, observe that given three matrix power series $A(z) = \sum_{i=0}^{+\infty} A_i z^i$, $B(z) = \sum_{i=0}^{+\infty} B_i z^i$, and $C(z) = \sum_{i=0}^{+\infty} C_i z^i$, the relation $C(z) = A(z)B(z)$ can be rewritten equivalently in matrix form, in a way similar to (8.3.1), as

$$\begin{bmatrix} C_0 \\ C_1 \\ \vdots \end{bmatrix} = \begin{bmatrix} A_0 & & \bigcirc \\ A_1 & A_0 & \\ \vdots & & \ddots \end{bmatrix} \begin{bmatrix} B_0 \\ B_1 \\ \vdots \end{bmatrix}.$$

Analogously, the same functional relation modulo z^n, i.e., $C(z) = A(z)B(z) \bmod z^n$, can be rewritten as the finite lower block triangular block Toeplitz system

$$\begin{bmatrix} C_0 \\ \vdots \\ C_{n-1} \end{bmatrix} = \begin{bmatrix} A_0 & & \bigcirc \\ \vdots & \ddots & \\ A_{n-1} & \cdots & A_0 \end{bmatrix} \begin{bmatrix} B_0 \\ \vdots \\ B_{n-1} \end{bmatrix}. \qquad (8.3.8)$$

In this way, the product of two matrix power series modulo z^n can be viewed as the product of an $n \times n$ lower block triangular block Toeplitz matrix and a block vector. Now since the inversion of a block triangular block Toeplitz matrix can be viewed as the inversion of a matrix power series $A(z)$ modulo z^n, that is, as the computation of the coefficients of the matrix polynomial $B(z)$ such that

$$A(z)B(z) = I \bmod z^n, \qquad (8.3.9)$$

we see that the inverse of a block triangular block Toeplitz matrix is itself a block triangular block Toeplitz matrix.

We now describe an algorithm for the inversion of a block triangular block Toeplitz matrix that has been derived for scalar entries in [Laf75]. In the matrix polynomial framework, this algorithm extends to matrix polynomials the so-called Sieveking–Kung algorithm, which is based on Newton's iteration for inverting a polynomial [BP94], [Knu81].

Let us denote by T_n the coefficient matrix in (8.3.8) and assume for simplicity that $n = 2^q$ with q a positive integer. We further partition T_n as follows:

$$T_n = \begin{bmatrix} T_{n/2} & O \\ H_{n/2} & T_{n/2} \end{bmatrix},$$

where all four blocks are $(n/2) \times (n/2)$ block Toeplitz matrices. Moreover, let $B_0, \ldots, B_{n-1}$ denote the block components of the first block column of T_n^{-1}, i.e., the solution of the linear system of equations

$$T_n \begin{bmatrix} B_0 \\ B_1 \\ \vdots \\ B_{n-1} \end{bmatrix} = \begin{bmatrix} I \\ O \\ \vdots \\ O \end{bmatrix}. \qquad (8.3.10)$$

Now note that, in view of the block lower triangular structure of T_n, we have

$$T_n^{-1} = \begin{bmatrix} T_{n/2}^{-1} & O \\ -T_{n/2}^{-1} H_{n/2} T_{n/2}^{-1} & T_{n/2}^{-1} \end{bmatrix},$$

which shows that the first block column of T_n^{-1} that solves (8.3.10) can be computed from the first block column of $T_{n/2}^{-1}$ by means of two multiplications between an $(n/2) \times (n/2)$ block Toeplitz matrix and a block vector. More specifically, we have

$$\begin{bmatrix} B_{\frac{n}{2}} \\ B_{\frac{n}{2}+1} \\ \vdots \\ B_{n-1} \end{bmatrix} = -T_{\frac{n}{2}}^{-1} H_{\frac{n}{2}} \begin{bmatrix} B_0 \\ B_1 \\ \vdots \\ B_{\frac{n}{2}-1} \end{bmatrix}. \qquad (8.3.11)$$

This observation leads to the following algorithm, whose cost is $O(m^3 n + m^2 n \log n)$ operations.

Algorithm 8.3.2. (Inversion of a Block Triangular Block Toeplitz Matrix). *This algorithm also solves the congruence relation $A(z)B(z) = I \bmod z^n$.*

- Input: *The $m \times m$ matrices $A_0, A_1, \ldots, A_{n-1}$, $n = 2^q$, $\det A_0 \neq 0$, defining the first block column of the block triangular block Toeplitz matrix T_n (equivalently, defining the matrix polynomial $A(z) = \sum_{i=0}^{n-1} A_i z^i$).*

- Output: *The matrices $B_0, B_1, \ldots, B_{n-1}$ satisfying (8.3.10) or, equivalently, such that the polynomial $B(z) = \sum_{i=0}^{n-1} B_i z^i$ solves the congruence $A(z)B(z) = I \mod z^n$.*

- Computation:

  1. *Compute $B_0 = A_0^{-1}$.*
  2. *For $i = 0, \ldots, q-1$, given the first column $U = (B_0^T, \ldots, B_{2^i-1}^T)^T$ of $T_{2^i}^{-1}$, compute the block vector $V = (B_{2^i}^T, \ldots, B_{2^{i+1}-1}^T)^T$, which defines the remaining blocks of the first column of $T_{2^{i+1}}^{-1}$, by applying (8.3.11) with $n = 2^{i+1}$, where the products $W = H_{2^i} U$ and $V = T_{2^i}^{-1} W$ are computed by means of Alg. 8.3.1.*

$\diamond$

We may remark that the solution of (8.3.9) can also be computed by formally applying the Newton–Raphson algorithm to the equation

$$A(z)^{-1} - B(z) = O,$$

where the unknown is $A(z)$, thus obtaining the functional iteration

$$\phi^{(i+1)}(z) = 2\phi^{(i)}(z) - \phi^{(i)}(z)^2 B(z), \quad i = 0, 1, \ldots, \quad \phi^{(0)}(z) = A_0^{-1}.$$

It is easy to show that

$$\phi^{(i)}(z) = B(z) \mod z^{2^i}.$$

Hence the algorithm obtained by rewriting the above formula as

$$\phi^{(i+1)}(z) = 2\phi^{(i)}(z) - \phi^{(i)}(z)^2 B(z) \mod z^{2^{i+1}}$$

and by implementing the latter equation by means of the evaluation-interpolation procedure at the roots of unity is equivalent to Alg. 8.3.2 (compare with [BP86] for the scalar case).

8.3.3 Power Series Arithmetic

In certain computations related to Markov chains we need to perform several operations (multiplications and matrix inversions) among infinite lower block triangular block Toeplitz matrices or, equivalently, among matrix power series. More specifically, we have to compute rational functions $Y = F(W^{(1)}, \ldots, W^{(h)})$ in the matrix power series $W^{(i)} = W^{(i)}(z)$, $i = 1, \ldots, h$.

Now since all these series are assumed convergent for $|z| = 1$, their block coefficients will tend to zero. Hence we may replace the power series by matrix polynomials and then apply the algorithms of Sec. 8.3.1. However, to truncate a power series $W^{(i)}(z)$ at a degree that results in a negligible remainder, we need to know its numerical degree. For a matrix power series $A(z) = \sum_{i=0}^{+\infty} A_i z^i$, we define its ϵ-degree as the minimum integer d such that $e^T \sum_{i=d+1}^{+\infty} |A_i| < \epsilon e^T$. When ϵ is the machine precision, then d is said to be the *numerical degree* of the matrix power series.

In this way, the evaluation of a function F by means of a *coefficientwise arithmetic* requires that we apply several FFTs for all the products and inversions involved. Even when the numerical degree of the output is rather small, the degrees of the intermediate power series might be large depending on the number of operands and on the computations performed. For this reason, the fast coefficientwise arithmetic and the fast Toeplitz matrix computations described in the previous section may be inadequate to achieve highest performance.

An alternative way of computing the coefficients of the matrix power series F is the use of *pointwise arithmetic*. In this approach, assuming knowledge of the numerical degree d of F, it is sufficient first to evaluate all the individual matrix power series $W^{(i)}(z)$ at the $(d+1)$ roots of unity and then to evaluate $(d+1)$ times the function F at these values, thus obtaining $Y(\omega_{d+1}^j)$, $j = 0, 1, \ldots, d$.

In this way, by means of a single interpolation stage at the $(d+1)$ roots of unity, it is possible to recover all the coefficients of the matrix power series Y. This strategy allows us to reduce the number of FFTs to $m^2(h+1)$, and it is particularly convenient in the case where the numerical degree of the output is smaller than the numerical degree of the input or of the intermediate matrix power series.

To arrive at an efficient implementation of this technique, a criterion for the dynamical evaluation of the numerical degree is needed. The design and analysis of such a criterion is performed in Sec. 8.5.4, where the specific properties of the function F and of the power series are used. For now, we simply assume that the following test function is available: TEST(Y, A) is true if the numerical degree of Y is less than or equal to the degree d of the matrix polynomial $A(z)$ that interpolates Y at the $(d+1)$ roots of unity.

A dynamic evaluation of the matrix power series Y may proceed according to the following scheme:

Set $d = 0$.

Repeat

Set $d = 2d+1$, compute $W^{(i)}(z)$ at the $(d+1)$ roots of unity, apply the pointwise evaluation of F, and compute the coefficients of the matrix polynomial $A(z)$ of degree d that interpolates Y.

Until TEST(Y, A) is true.

Set $Y = A$.

It is worth observing that to compute the values of $W^{(i)}(z)$ at the $(d+1)$ roots of unity once the values of the same power series have been computed at the $(\frac{d-1}{2} + 1)$ roots of unity, it is not necessary to apply afresh the FFTs of order $d+1$. The same observation applies to the computation of the interpolation stage. Algorithms for performing these computations, where part of the output has been precomputed, are described in [BM97a].

8.4 DISPLACEMENT STRUCTURE

For our applications in Markov chains we shall adopt a definition of displacement structure that seems to be particularly suitable for dealing with block Toeplitz matrices in block Hessenberg form (compare with [KVM78], [KKM79a], [BP94], [HR84], and Ch. 1).

We define the $n \times n$ block down-shift matrix

$$Z_{n,m} = \begin{bmatrix} O & & & \\ I & O & & \\ & \ddots & \ddots & \\ & & I & O \end{bmatrix},$$

Section 8.4. Displacement Structure

where the blocks have dimension m, and consider the block displacement operator

$$\nabla_{n,m} H = Z_{n,m} H - H Z_{n,m}$$

defined for any $n \times n$ block matrix H. We also denote by $\mathcal{L}_n(W)$ the $n \times n$ lower block triangular block Toeplitz matrix defined by its first block column W.

For the sake of notational simplicity, if the dimensions are clear from the context, we use the notation ∇H instead of $\nabla_{n,m} H$, Z instead of $Z_{n,m}$, and $\mathcal{L}(W)$ instead of $\mathcal{L}_n(W)$.

We also introduce the following notation: the block vectors $E_n^{(1)} = [I, O, \ldots, O]^T$, $E_n^{(2)} = [O, \ldots, O, I]^T$ denote $mn \times m$ matrices made up by the first and the last m columns of the identity matrix of order mn, respectively.

Observe that for a general block Toeplitz matrix A the displacement ∇A is zero except for the entries in the first block row and in the last block column. Hence the rank of ∇A is at most $2m$.

Following the discussions in Ch. 1, we shall say that the block matrix H has *block displacement rank* r if r is the minimum integer such that there exist block column vectors $U^{(i)}$ and block row vectors $V^{(i)}$, $i = 1, \ldots, r$, satisfying the equation $\nabla H = \sum_{i=1}^{r} U^{(i)} V^{(i)}$. For an $n \times n$ block Toeplitz matrix A we obtain

$$\nabla A = -E_n^{(1)} E_n^{(1)T} A Z + Z A E_n^{(2)} E_n^{(2)T}. \tag{8.4.1}$$

An interesting property of $\nabla(H)$ is that the block displacement of the inverse matrix can be explicitly related to the block displacement of the matrix itself; viz., if H is nonsingular, then

$$\nabla(H^{-1}) = -H^{-1}(\nabla H) H^{-1}. \tag{8.4.2}$$

The following result can be easily proved by extending to block matrices the same proof given in [Bin83], [BP94] for the scalar case.

Theorem 8.4.1 (Displacement Representation). *Let K_n be an $n \times n$ block matrix such that $\nabla K_n = \sum_{i=1}^{r} U^{(i)} V^{(i)}$, where $U^{(i)}$ and $V^{(i)}$ are n-dimensional block column and block row vectors, respectively. Then we have*

$$K_n = \mathcal{L}(K_n E_n^{(1)}) - \sum_{i=1}^{r} \mathcal{L}(U^{(i)}) \mathcal{L}^T(Z V^{(i)T}).$$

◇

The above result allows us to represent any matrix K_n as a sum of products of lower and upper block triangular block Toeplitz matrices defined by the first block column of K_n and by the block vectors $U^{(i)}$, $V^{(i)}$ associated with the block displacement of K_n.

If the matrix K_n is nonsingular, then the above representation theorem can be applied to K_n^{-1} in the light of (8.4.2), thus leading to

$$K_n^{-1} = \mathcal{L}(K_n^{-1} E_n^{(1)}) + \sum_{i=1}^{r} \mathcal{L}(K_n^{-1} U^{(i)}) \mathcal{L}^T(Z K_n^{-T} V^{(i)T}). \tag{8.4.3}$$

For the $n \times n$ block Toeplitz matrix H_n in lower block Hessenberg form (8.2.14) we can easily verify that

$$\nabla H_n = \begin{bmatrix} A_0 & O & \cdots & O \\ O & O & \ddots & \vdots \\ \vdots & \ddots & O & O \\ O & \cdots & O & -A_0 \end{bmatrix}$$

and, hence,

$$\nabla H_n = E_n^{(1)} A_0 E_n^{(1)T} - E_n^{(2)} A_0 E_n^{(2)T}. \qquad (8.4.4)$$

This formula is the basis of the algorithm developed in Sec. 8.5.2.

Equations (8.4.3), (8.4.1), and (8.4.4) allow us to write useful inversion formulas for a generic block Toeplitz matrix A and for the block Hessenberg block Toeplitz matrix H_n of (8.2.14). We have, in fact,

$$A^{-1} = \mathcal{L}(A^{-1}E_n^{(1)})(I - \mathcal{L}^T(ZA^{-T}Z^T A^T E_n^{(1)})) + \mathcal{L}(A^{-1}ZAE_n^{(2)})\mathcal{L}^T(ZA^{-T}E_n^{(2)}) \quad (8.4.5)$$

and

$$H_n^{-1} = \mathcal{L}(C_n^{(1)})\mathcal{L}^T(E_n^{(1)} + ZR_n^{(1)T}A_0^T) - \mathcal{L}(C_n^{(2)})\mathcal{L}^T(ZR_n^{(2)T}A_0^T), \qquad (8.4.6)$$

where $C_n^{(1)}$, $C_n^{(2)}$ denote the first and the last block columns, respectively, of H_n^{-1} while $R_n^{(1)}$, $R_n^{(2)}$ denote the first and the last block rows, respectively, of the matrix H_n^{-1}.

8.5 FAST ALGORITHMS

In this section we develop efficient algorithms for the solution of the linear system of (8.2.2), where P is given by (8.2.6) and (8.2.3), as well as the solution of the matrix equation (8.2.8) by means of the finite or infinite systems of (8.2.13) or (8.2.12).

We start by providing a novel interpretation of the Ramaswami formula (8.2.10) in terms of Toeplitz computations. We also provide an algorithm for the evaluation of this formula using FFTs [Mei97b].

In Sec. 8.5.2 we present a doubling method [LS96] for solving a sequence of the finite systems of (8.2.13) and, by exploiting displacement structure, we further improve the performance of the method. More specifically, we explicitly relate the inverse of an $n \times n$ block Hessenberg block Toeplitz matrix H_n to the inverse of its $\frac{n}{2} \times \frac{n}{2}$ leading principal submatrix $H_{\frac{n}{2}}$. This fact provides a means for computing the inverses of H_{2^i}, $i = 0, 1, \ldots, \log_2 n$, in $O(m^2 n \log n + m^3 n)$ operations. The algorithm is then used for solving block Hessenberg block Toeplitz systems and for solving the matrix equation (8.2.8). The cases of block tridiagonal matrices and of Toeplitz blocks are also discussed.

In Sec. 8.5.3 we apply the cyclic reduction algorithm [BM96a] for finite block Hessenberg block Toeplitz-like systems (8.2.2), where P^T is given in (8.2.6). We prove that the Schur complement obtained after one step of cyclic reduction is still a block Hessenberg block Toeplitz matrix except for its first block column and its last block row. This leads to an algorithm for solving block Hessenberg block Toeplitz-like systems in $O(m^2 n \log n + m^3 n)$ operations.

In the case of infinite matrices, by means of the correlation between matrix power series and block Toeplitz matrices, we rephrase the properties of the Schur complement in functional form and provide a fast and efficient algorithm for the solution of the infinite system (8.2.12) based on a pointwise evaluation of the functions defining the Schur complements. We also analyze the case of block tridiagonal matrices and show

Section 8.5. Fast Algorithms

that the cyclic reduction procedure in this case is equivalent to the method of Graeffe for squaring the roots of a polynomial.

In Sec. 8.5.5 we consider the problem of solving (8.2.12) in the case of non-skip-free matrices, where the M/G/1 matrix (8.2.3) is obtained by partitioning into $mk \times mk$ blocks the block Toeplitz-like matrix having the generalized block Hessenberg form (8.2.4). Although the blocks obtained after a cyclic reduction step are no longer block Toeplitz, they still exhibit displacement structure. This property allows us to devise a fast algorithm for the solution of banded Toeplitz systems and for the computation of the matrix G that solves (8.2.8). The algorithm, based on the LU factorization of an M-matrix and on computing FFTs, has shown a good numerical stability.

8.5.1 The Fast Ramaswami Formula

Observe that the relation (8.2.10) can be rewritten equivalently in terms of the UL factorization of the infinite block Hessenberg block Toeplitz matrix H of (8.2.11), $H = UL$, where

$$U = \begin{bmatrix} I & -G & & & \\ & I & -G & & \\ & & I & -G & \\ & & & \ddots & \ddots \end{bmatrix}, \quad L = \begin{bmatrix} I - \bar{A}_1 & & & \\ -\bar{A}_2 & I - \bar{A}_1 & & \\ -\bar{A}_3 & -\bar{A}_2 & I - \bar{A}_1 & \\ \vdots & \ddots & \ddots & \ddots \end{bmatrix},$$

G is the solution of (8.2.8), and $\bar{A}_i$ are defined in (8.2.9). Ramaswami's formula (8.2.10) can now be derived by solving the system of equations

$$UL \begin{bmatrix} \pi_1 \\ \pi_2 \\ \pi_3 \\ \vdots \end{bmatrix} = \begin{bmatrix} B_2 \\ B_3 \\ B_4 \\ \vdots \end{bmatrix} \pi_0.$$

In fact, by multiplying the above equation by the left inverse of U, we obtain that

$$L \begin{bmatrix} \pi_1 \\ \pi_2 \\ \pi_3 \\ \vdots \end{bmatrix} = \begin{bmatrix} \bar{B}_2 \\ \bar{B}_3 \\ \bar{B}_4 \\ \vdots \end{bmatrix} \pi_0. \tag{8.5.1}$$

Hence, by solving the lower block triangular system (8.5.1) by forward substitution, we arrive at (8.2.10).

In this way, the computation of the vector π is reduced to solving the lower block triangular block Toeplitz infinite system (8.5.1). In [Mei97b] a fast Ramaswami formula based on Algs. 8.3.1 and 8.3.2 has been devised with a substantial reduction of the asymptotic computational cost. More specifically, the computational cost to calculate p block components of the probability invariant vector π is roughly $p(7m^2 + 40 \log n_0)$ arithmetic operations, where n_0 is the numerical degree of $A(z) = \sum_{i=0}^{+\infty} A_i z^i$, whereas the computational cost of the customary Ramaswami formula is $2pn_0 m^2$ arithmetic operations.

8.5.2 A Doubling Algorithm

Consider the $n \times n$ block Toeplitz matrix H_n in the block Hessenberg form (8.2.14) that is obtained by truncating the infinite matrix (8.2.11). Let us assume for simplicity that

$n = 2^q$ for a positive integer q. Suppose that $\det H_{2^j} \neq 0$, $j = 0, 1, \ldots, q$ (this condition is satisfied for a positive recurrent Markov chain), and partition the matrix H_n in the following way:

$$H_n = \begin{bmatrix} H_{\frac{n}{2}} & U_{\frac{n}{2}} V_{\frac{n}{2}}^T \\ T_{\frac{n}{2}} & H_{\frac{n}{2}} \end{bmatrix},$$

where

$$U_{\frac{n}{2}} = \begin{bmatrix} O \\ \vdots \\ O \\ I \end{bmatrix}, \quad V_{\frac{n}{2}} = \begin{bmatrix} -A_0^T \\ O \\ \vdots \\ O \end{bmatrix}, \quad T_{\frac{n}{2}} = \begin{bmatrix} -A_{\frac{n}{2}+1} & -A_{\frac{n}{2}} & \cdots & -A_2 \\ -A_{\frac{n}{2}+2} & -A_{\frac{n}{2}+1} & \ddots & \vdots \\ \vdots & \ddots & \ddots & -A_{\frac{n}{2}} \\ -A_n & \cdots & -A_{\frac{n}{2}+2} & -A_{\frac{n}{2}+1} \end{bmatrix}.$$

By applying the Sherman–Morrison–Woodbury matrix inversion formula (compare with [GV96, p. 3]; see also App. A) to the decomposition

$$H_n = \begin{bmatrix} H_{\frac{n}{2}} & O \\ T_{\frac{n}{2}} & H_{\frac{n}{2}} \end{bmatrix} + \begin{bmatrix} O & U_{\frac{n}{2}} V_{\frac{n}{2}}^T \\ O & O \end{bmatrix} = S_n + M_n N_n^T,$$

$$M_n = \begin{bmatrix} U_{\frac{n}{2}} \\ O \end{bmatrix}, \quad N_n = \begin{bmatrix} O \\ V_{\frac{n}{2}} \end{bmatrix},$$

we immediately find the following expression for the matrix inverse of H_n:

$$H_n^{-1} = S_n^{-1} - S_n^{-1} M_n (I + N_n^T S_n^{-1} M_n)^{-1} N_n^T S_n^{-1},$$

where

$$S_n^{-1} = \begin{bmatrix} H_{\frac{n}{2}}^{-1} & O \\ -H_{\frac{n}{2}}^{-1} T_{\frac{n}{2}} H_{\frac{n}{2}}^{-1} & H_{\frac{n}{2}}^{-1} \end{bmatrix}.$$

These relations have been used in [LS96], [Ste95] to devise a doubling algorithm for the solution of the linear system (8.2.12), truncated at a finite system of block dimension n, in $O(m^3 n \log^2 n)$ operations. The algorithm can be further simplified by exploiting displacement structure, as shown in [BM98a].

Indeed, observe that for the matrix H_n^{-1} of (8.2.14) we have a relation of the form (8.4.6). Hence the inverse of H_n can be explicitly determined as a sum of products of block triangular block Toeplitz matrices that are defined by the block A_0, by the block rows $R_n^{(1)}$, $R_n^{(2)}$, and by the block columns $C_n^{(1)}$, $C_n^{(2)}$.

The matrix inversion formula allows us to further relate the block vectors $C_n^{(1)}$, $C_n^{(2)}$, $R_n^{(1)}$, $R_n^{(2)}$ defining the matrix H_n^{-1} and the block vectors $C_{\frac{n}{2}}^{(1)}$, $C_{\frac{n}{2}}^{(2)}$, $R_{\frac{n}{2}}^{(1)}$, $R_{\frac{n}{2}}^{(2)}$ defining the matrix $H_{\frac{n}{2}}^{-1}$. Moreover, since such relations involve only operations between block Toeplitz matrices and block vectors, we may devise an efficient scheme for their implementation that is based on Alg. 8.3.1. This leads to a procedure for the computation of the inverses of H_{2^i}, $i = 0, 1, \ldots, q$, that requires $O(m^3 n + m^2 n \log n)$ arithmetic operations for $n = 2^q$ and a low storage cost; in fact, only four auxiliary block vectors need to be allocated to carry out our algorithm.

The following result provides the desired correlation among block rows and columns of H_n^{-1} and $H_{\frac{n}{2}}^{-1}$.

Section 8.5. Fast Algorithms   229

Theorem 8.5.1 (H_n^{-1} and $H_{\frac{n}{2}}^{-1}$). *The first and last block columns $C_n^{(1)}$, $C_n^{(2)}$ and the first and last block rows $R_n^{(1)}$, $R_n^{(2)}$ of H_n^{-1} satisfy the relations*

$$C_n^{(1)} = \begin{bmatrix} C_{\frac{n}{2}}^{(1)} \\ -H_{\frac{n}{2}}^{-1} T_{\frac{n}{2}} C_{\frac{n}{2}}^{(1)} \end{bmatrix} - \begin{bmatrix} C_{\frac{n}{2}}^{(2)} \\ -H_{\frac{n}{2}}^{-1} T_{\frac{n}{2}} C_{\frac{n}{2}}^{(2)} \end{bmatrix} Q R_{\frac{n}{2}}^{(1)} T_{\frac{n}{2}} C_{\frac{n}{2}}^{(1)},$$

$$C_n^{(2)} = \begin{bmatrix} O \\ C_{\frac{n}{2}}^{(2)} \end{bmatrix} + \begin{bmatrix} C_{\frac{n}{2}}^{(2)} \\ -H_{\frac{n}{2}}^{-1} T_{\frac{n}{2}} C_{\frac{n}{2}}^{(2)} \end{bmatrix} Q R_{\frac{n}{2}}^{(1)} E_{\frac{n}{2}}^{(2)},$$

$$R_n^{(1)} = A_0 [R_{\frac{n}{2}}^{(1)}, O] - A_0 R_{\frac{n}{2}}^{(1)} E_{\frac{n}{2}}^{(2)} Q [R_{\frac{n}{2}}^{(1)} T_{\frac{n}{2}} H_{\frac{n}{2}}^{-1}, -R_{\frac{n}{2}}^{(1)}],$$

$$R_n^{(2)} = A_0 [-R_{\frac{n}{2}}^{(2)} T_{\frac{n}{2}} H_{\frac{n}{2}}^{-1}, R_{\frac{n}{2}}^{(2)}] + A_0 R_{\frac{n}{2}}^{(2)} T_{\frac{n}{2}} C_{\frac{n}{2}}^{(2)} Q [R_{\frac{n}{2}}^{(1)} T_{\frac{n}{2}} H_{\frac{n}{2}}^{-1}, -R_{\frac{n}{2}}^{(1)}],$$

where $Q = (I + A_0 R_{\frac{n}{2}}^{(1)} T_{\frac{n}{2}} C_{\frac{n}{2}}^{(2)})^{-1} A_0$.

$\diamond$

Once the block vectors $\{R_n^{(1)}, R_n^{(2)}, C_n^{(1)}, C_n^{(2)}\}$ have been computed, the solution x of a system $H_n x = b$ can be obtained by means of (8.4.6) and Thm. 8.5.1, leaving unchanged the asymptotic cost $O(m^3 n + m^2 n \log n)$.

For block tridiagonal matrices H_n, like the ones arising from QBD problems, the formulas of Thm. 8.5.1 are simplified and the cost becomes $O(m^3 n)$.

For non-skip-free matrices, H_n is obtained by reblocking the matrix (8.2.4) leading to the structure (8.2.5). In this case, it has been proved in [GHT97] that the matrix G can be represented as $G = F^k$, where F is the $k \times k$ block Frobenius matrix

$$F = \begin{bmatrix} O & \cdots & O & G_{1,1} \\ I & \ddots & \vdots & G_{2,1} \\ & \ddots & O & \vdots \\ O & & I & G_{k,1} \end{bmatrix}$$

that is defined by the first block column of $G = (G_{i,j})$. In particular, the block displacement rank of G is 1 with respect to the operator $\nabla_{k,m}$.

Here we show that, for the non-skip-free case, our algorithm also can be further simplified. In fact, since H_n is an $nk \times nk$ block Toeplitz matrix, in light of (8.4.6) we may rewrite H_n^{-1} as

$$H_n^{-1} = \mathcal{L}(u_n^{(1)}) \mathcal{L}^T(v_n^{(1)T}) - \mathcal{L}(u_n^{(2)}) \mathcal{L}^T(v_n^{(2)T})$$

for suitable kn-dimensional block vectors $u_n^{(i)}$, $v_n^{(i)}$, $i = 1, 2$.

In this way it is sufficient to relate the block vectors $u_n^{(i)}$, $v_n^{(i)}$ with $u_{\frac{n}{2}}^{(i)}$, $v_{\frac{n}{2}}^{(i)}$ for $i = 1, 2$. This relation is implicitly provided by Thm. 8.5.1. We observe that the computation of $u_n^{(i)}$, $v_n^{(i)}$ is reduced to performing a finite number of products of block Toeplitz matrices and block vectors of block dimension nk except for the computation of the inverse of Q. For this purpose we have the following result [BM98a].

Theorem 8.5.2 (Displacement Rank of Q). *The block displacement rank of Q, with respect to the operator $\nabla_{k,m}$, is at most 6.*

◇

From Thms. 8.5.1 and 8.5.2, it follows that the inverse of Q can be represented as the sum of at most seven products of $nk \times nk$ lower and upper block triangular block Toeplitz matrices. Thus, its inverse can be computed fast in $O(k^2 m^3)$ arithmetic operations. Hence, each doubling step of size 2^i requires $O(m^2)$ FFTs of order $k2^i$ and the inversion of a matrix having block displacement rank at most 6. Therefore, the total cost is $O(m^2 kn \log(kn)) + O(knm^3)$.

8.5.3 Cyclic Reduction

We now describe a method for the numerical solution of (8.2.2), introduced in [BM96a], which is based on the block LU factorization of the $n \times n$ block matrix $\Pi H \Pi^T$, where $H = I - P^T$ is the block Hessenberg block Toeplitz-like matrix of (8.2.6) and Π is a suitable permutation matrix.

This method relies on a technique originally introduced for solving certain block tridiagonal block Toeplitz systems arising from the numerical treatment of elliptic equations [BGN70] and rediscovered in [LR93]. This technique is based on the reduction of the block tridiagonal matrix into a new block tridiagonal matrix of half the size. The reduction is repeated cyclically until a system of size 1 is obtained. This technique of *cyclic reduction* was called *successive state reduction* in [LR93].

Let $q \geq 2$ be an integer such that $n = 2^q$ and consider the matrix in block Hessenberg form, that is, block Toeplitz except for its first block column and its last block row,

$$H = H^{(0)} = I - P^T = \begin{bmatrix} \widehat{H}_1 & H_0 & & & \bigcirc \\ \widehat{H}_2 & H_1 & H_0 & & \\ \vdots & \vdots & \ddots & \ddots & \\ \widehat{H}_{n-1} & H_{n-2} & \cdots & H_1 & H_0 \\ \widetilde{H}_n & \widetilde{H}_{n-1} & \cdots & \widetilde{H}_2 & \widetilde{H}_1 \end{bmatrix}, \qquad (8.5.2)$$

uniquely defined by the blocks $H_0 = -A_0$, $H_1 = I - A_1$, $\widehat{H}_1 = I - B_1$, $\widetilde{H}_1 = I - C_1$, $H_i = -A_i$, $\widehat{H}_i = -B_i$, $\widetilde{H}_i = -C_i$, $i = 2, \ldots, n-2$, $\widehat{H}_{n-1} = -B_{n-1}$, $\widetilde{H}_n = -C_n$, $\widetilde{H}_{n-1} = -C_{n-1}$.

By interchanging block rows and columns of $H^{(0)} = H$ according to the odd-even permutation $(1, 3, 5, \ldots, n-1, 0, 2, 4, 6, \ldots, n-2)$ we obtain the matrix

$$\Pi^{(0)} H^{(0)} \Pi^{(0)T} = \begin{bmatrix} T_1^{(0)} & W^{(0)} \\ Z^{(0)} & T_2^{(0)} \end{bmatrix}, \qquad (8.5.3)$$

where $\Pi^{(0)}$ is the block odd-even permutation matrix, and $T_1^{(0)}$, $T_2^{(0)}$, $Z^{(0)}$, and $W^{(0)}$ are $(n/2) \times (n/2)$ block Toeplitz-like matrices defined by

Section 8.5. Fast Algorithms

$$W^{(0)} = \begin{bmatrix} \widehat{H}_2 & H_0 & & \bigcirc \\ \widehat{H}_4 & H_2 & \ddots & \\ \vdots & \vdots & \ddots & H_0 \\ \widetilde{H}_n & \widetilde{H}_{n-2} & \cdots & \widetilde{H}_2 \end{bmatrix}, \quad Z^{(0)} = \begin{bmatrix} H_0 & & & \bigcirc \\ H_2 & H_0 & & \\ \vdots & \ddots & \ddots & \\ H_{n-2} & \cdots & H_2 & H_0 \end{bmatrix},$$

$$T_1^{(0)} = \begin{bmatrix} H_1 & & & & \bigcirc \\ H_3 & H_1 & & & \\ \vdots & \vdots & \ddots & & \\ H_{n-3} & H_{n-5} & \cdots & H_1 & \\ \widetilde{H}_{n-1} & \widetilde{H}_{n-3} & \cdots & \widetilde{H}_3 & \widetilde{H}_1 \end{bmatrix}, \quad (8.5.4)$$

$$T_2^{(0)} = \begin{bmatrix} \widehat{H}_1 & & & & \bigcirc \\ \widehat{H}_3 & H_1 & & & \\ \vdots & & \ddots & \ddots & \\ \widehat{H}_{n-3} & \cdots & & H_3 & H_1 \\ \widehat{H}_{n-1} & H_{n-3} & \cdots & H_3 & H_1 \end{bmatrix}.$$

By applying one step of block Gaussian elimination (see Ch. 1) to the 2×2 block matrix (8.5.3) we find that

$$\Pi^{(0)} H^{(0)} \Pi^{(0)T} = \begin{bmatrix} I & 0 \\ K^{(0)} & I \end{bmatrix} \begin{bmatrix} T_1^{(0)} & W^{(0)} \\ 0 & H^{(1)} \end{bmatrix},$$
$$K^{(0)} = Z^{(0)} T_1^{(0)^{-1}}, \quad H^{(1)} = T_2^{(0)} - K^{(0)} W^{(0)}. \quad (8.5.5)$$

Now we show that the Schur complement $H^{(1)}$ has the same structure as $H^{(0)}$ in (8.5.2). For this purpose, we define the block column vectors $H_{odd} = (H_{2i+1})_{i=0,n/2-2}$, $H_{even} = (H_{2i})_{i=0,n/2-2}$ and consider the $(n/2-1) \times (n/2-1)$ block matrices

$$F_0^{(0)} = \mathcal{L}(Z_{n/2-1,m} H_{odd}), \quad F_1^{(0)} = \mathcal{L}(H_{even}), \quad F_2^{(0)} = \mathcal{L}(H_{odd}).$$

Let us partition $H^{(1)}$ as

$$H^{(1)} = \begin{bmatrix} U^{(1)} & R^{(1)} \\ S^{(1)} & V^{(1)} \end{bmatrix},$$

where $R^{(1)}$ is an $(n/2-1) \times (n/2-1)$ block submatrix. Then from (8.5.5) and (8.5.4) it follows that

$$R^{(1)} = F_0^{(0)} - F_1^{(0)} F_2^{(0)^{-1}} F_1^{(0)},$$
$$U^{(1)} = \begin{bmatrix} \widehat{H}_1 \\ \widehat{H}_3 \\ \vdots \\ \widehat{H}_{n-3} \end{bmatrix} - F_1^{(0)} F_2^{(0)^{-1}} \begin{bmatrix} \widehat{H}_2 \\ \widehat{H}_4 \\ \vdots \\ \widehat{H}_{n-2} \end{bmatrix}, \quad (8.5.6)$$
$$[S^{(1)}, V^{(1)}] = [\widehat{H}_{n-1}, H_{n-3}, \ldots, H_1] - [H_{n-2}, H_{n-4}, \ldots, H_0] T_1^{(0)^{-1}} W^{(0)}.$$

Since the linear space of lower block triangular block Toeplitz matrices is closed under multiplication and inversion, i.e., it constitutes a matrix algebra, we deduce that $R^{(1)}$ is a block triangular block Toeplitz matrix. Hence the Schur complement $H^{(1)}$ has the same structure as (8.5.2); i.e., $P^{(1)T} = I - H^{(1)}$ is still a block Toeplitz-like matrix in block Hessenberg form, where $H^{(1)}$ is uniquely defined by the matrices $H_0^{(1)}, \ldots, H_{n/2-2}^{(1)}$, $\widehat{H}_1^{(1)}, \ldots, \widehat{H}_{n/2-1}^{(1)}$, and $\widetilde{H}_1^{(1)}, \ldots, \widetilde{H}_{n/2}^{(1)}$ such that

$$R^{(1)} = \mathcal{L}(Q^{(1)}),$$
$$U^{(1)} = [\widehat{H}_1^{(1)T}, \widehat{H}_2^{(1)T}, \ldots, \widehat{H}_{n/2-1}^{(1)T}]^T, \qquad (8.5.7)$$
$$[S^{(1)}, V^{(1)}] = [\widetilde{H}_{n/2}^{(1)}, \widetilde{H}_{n/2-1}^{(1)}, \ldots, \widetilde{H}_1^{(1)}],$$

where $Q^{(1)} = (H_i^{(1)})_{i=0,\ldots,n/2-2}$. Moreover, it is easy to check that $P^{(1)}$ is a stochastic matrix. Therefore, the cyclic reduction process can be recursively applied $q-1$ times until the $2m \times 2m$ matrix $H^{(q-1)}$ is computed. The resulting algorithm, which computes the block LU factorization of a matrix obtained by suitably permuting rows and columns of H, is described by the formulas (8.5.2)–(8.5.7) adjusted to the generic jth step. This algorithm outputs the blocks $H_i^{(j+1)}$, $i = 0, \ldots, 2^{q-j-1} - 2$, $\widetilde{H}_i^{(j+1)}$, $i = 1, \ldots, 2^{q-j-1}$, and $\widehat{H}_i^{(j+1)}$, $i = 1, \ldots, 2^{q-j-1} - 1$, defining the block matrices $T_1^{(j)}$, $W^{(j)}$, $K^{(j)}$, $H^{(j+1)}$, $j = 0, 1, \ldots, q-2$.

Now consider the problem of solving the system (8.2.2) and partition the vector π into blocks of length m according to the block structure of H, i.e., set $\pi^T = [\pi_0^T, \pi_1^T, \ldots, \pi_{n-1}^T]$. Moreover, denote by $\pi_-^{(j)}$ the vector having blocks π_{i2^j}, $i = 0, \ldots, 2^{q-j} - 1$, $j = 0, 1, \ldots, q-1$, where $n = 2^q$, $q \geq 2$. Similarly, denote by $\pi_+^{(j)}$ the vector having blocks $\pi_{(2i+1)2^{j-1}}$, $i = 0, \ldots, 2^{q-j} - 1$, for $j = 1, \ldots, q-1$. In this way, at the jth recursive step of the cyclic reduction algorithm applied to $H^{(0)}\pi = 0$ we obtain the system $H^{(j)}\pi_-^{(j)} = 0$, $j = 0, \ldots, q-1$. In fact, after the odd-even permutation on the block rows and the block columns and after performing one step of block Gaussian elimination we obtain the system of equations

$$\begin{bmatrix} T_1^{(j)} & W^{(j)} \\ O & H^{(j+1)} \end{bmatrix} \begin{bmatrix} \pi_+^{(j+1)} \\ \pi_-^{(j+1)} \end{bmatrix} = 0, \qquad (8.5.8)$$
$$H^{(j+1)} = T_2^{(j)} - Z^{(j)}{T_1^{(j)}}^{-1} W^{(j)}$$

(compare with (8.5.5)). At the end of the cyclic reduction algorithm we have to solve the $2m \times 2m$ homogeneous system

$$H^{(q-1)}\pi_-^{(q-1)} = 0, \quad \pi_-^{(q-1)} = \begin{pmatrix} \pi_0 \\ \pi_{2^{(q-1)}} \end{pmatrix},$$

and we may recover the remaining components of the vector π by means of back substitution by using the following relation derived by (8.5.8):

$$\pi_+^{(j+1)} = -{T_1^{(j)}}^{-1} W^{(j)} \pi_-^{(j+1)}, \quad j = q-2, \ldots, 0.$$

The algorithm thus obtained for the computation of the probability invariant vector π can be carried out in the following way.

Algorithm 8.5.1 (Cyclic Reduction for the Computation of π).

- Input: *Positive integers m, q, n, $n = 2^q$, and the nonnegative $m \times m$ matrices A_i, $i = 0, 1, \ldots, n-2$, B_i, $i = 1, \ldots, n-1$, C_i, $i = 1, \ldots, n$, defining the stochastic matrix P of (8.2.6).*

Section 8.5. Fast Algorithms

- Output: *The solution π of system (8.2.2).*
- Computation:

    1. Cyclic reduction stage
       Let $H^{(0)} = I - P^T$ and, for $j = 1, \ldots, q-1$, recursively compute the $m \times m$ matrices $H_i^{(j)}$, $\widehat{H}_{i+1}^{(j)}$, $i = 0, 1, \ldots, n_j - 2$, and $\widetilde{H}_{i+1}^{(j)}$, $i = 0, 1, \ldots, n_j - 1$, $n_j = n/2^j$, defining the $n_j \times n_j$ block matrices $H^{(j)} = T_2^{(j-1)} - Z^{(j-1)} T_1^{(j-1)^{-1}} W^{(j-1)}$ by means of the formulas (8.5.6)–(8.5.8) represented for $j = 0$ and here adjusted for the recursive jth step of the cyclic reduction algorithm as follows:

$$R^{(j+1)} = F_0^{(j)} - F_1^{(j)} F_2^{(j)^{-1}} F_1^{(j)},$$

$$U^{(j+1)} = \begin{bmatrix} \widehat{H}_1^{(j)} \\ \widehat{H}_3^{(j)} \\ \vdots \\ \widehat{H}_{n_j-3}^{(j)} \end{bmatrix} - F_1^{(j)} F_2^{(j)^{-1}} \begin{bmatrix} \widehat{H}_2^{(j)} \\ \widehat{H}_4^{(j)} \\ \vdots \\ \widehat{H}_{n_j-2}^{(j)} \end{bmatrix},$$

$$[S^{(j+1)}, V^{(j+1)}] = [\widehat{H}_{n_j-1}^{(j)}, H_{n_j-3}^{(j)}, \ldots, H_1^{(j)}]$$
$$- [H_{n_j-2}^{(j)}, H_{n_j-4}^{(j)}, \ldots, H_0^{(j)}] T_1^{(j)^{-1}} W^{(j)},$$

where $F_0^{(j)} = \mathcal{L}(Z H_{odd}^{(j)})$, $F_1^{(j)} = \mathcal{L}(H_{even}^{(j)})$, $F_2^{(j)} = \mathcal{L}(H_{odd}^{(j)})$.

    2. Back-substitution stage
       Solve, by means of LU or UL factorization, the $2m \times 2m$ system of equations $H^{(q-1)} \pi_-^{(q-1)} = \mathbf{0}$.
       Compute $\pi_+^{(j+1)} = -T_1^{(j)^{-1}} W^{(j)} \pi_-^{(j+1)}$ for $j = q-2, \ldots, 0$.

    3. Normalization stage
       Normalize the vector π.

◇

The most expensive part of each recursive step of the above algorithm is to compute the blocks of the matrix $H^{(j)}$. This computation is reduced to performing operations among block triangular block Toeplitz matrices. In fact, observe that $F_1^{(0)}$, $F_2^{(0)}$, and $F_2^{(0)^{-1}}$ are block triangular block Toeplitz matrices. Thus we may use the algorithms described in Sec. 8.3.1. In this way the cost of the jth step is $O(m^2 n_j \log n_j + m^3 n_j)$ arithmetic operations and the overall cost of the algorithm to compute π by means of cyclic reduction is $O(m^2 n \log n + m^3 n)$ arithmetic operations. On the other hand, it can easily be verified that the computational cost incurred by applying the customary block Gaussian elimination is $O(m^3 n^2)$.

In the case where the matrix H is block tridiagonal, i.e., when the Markov chain comes from a QBD problem, the whole computation can be carried out in a simpler form and we arrive at the finite-dimensional analogue of the algorithm of [LR93] (see also [YL91]). In fact, let

$$H = \begin{bmatrix} \widehat{H}_1 & H_0 & & & \bigcirc \\ \widehat{H}_2 & H_1 & H_0 & & \\ & H_2 & \ddots & \ddots & \\ & & \ddots & H_1 & H_0 \\ \bigcirc & & & \widetilde{H}_2 & \widetilde{H}_1 \end{bmatrix};$$

then the block tridiagonal matrix $H^{(j)}$ obtained at the jth recursive step of the cyclic reduction procedure, defined by the blocks $H_i^{(j)}$, $i = 0, 1, 2$, $\widehat{H}_i^{(j)}$, $\widetilde{H}_i^{(j)}$, $i = 1, 2$, $j = 0, \ldots, \log_2 n - 1$, is such that

$$\begin{aligned}
H_1^{(j+1)} &= H_1^{(j)} - (H_2^{(j)} H_1^{(j)^{-1}} H_0^{(j)} + H_0^{(j)} H_1^{(j)^{-1}} H_2^{(j)}), \\
H_0^{(j+1)} &= -H_0^{(j)} H_1^{(j)^{-1}} H_0^{(j)}, \quad H_2^{(j+1)} = -H_2^{(j)} H_1^{(j)^{-1}} H_2^{(j)}, \\
\widehat{H}_1^{(j+1)} &= \widehat{H}_1^{(j)} - H_0^{(j)} H_1^{(j)^{-1}} \widehat{H}_2^{(j)}, \\
\widetilde{H}_1^{(j+1)} &= H_1^{(j)} - (H_0^{(j)} \widetilde{H}_1^{(j)^{-1}} \widetilde{H}_2^{(j)} + H_2^{(j)} H_1^{(j)^{-1}} H_0^{(j)}), \\
\widetilde{H}_2^{(j+1)} &= H_2^{(j+1)}, \quad \widehat{H}_2^{(j)} = -H_2^{(j)} H_1^{(j)^{-1}} \widehat{H}_2^{(j)},
\end{aligned}$$

where $H_1^{(0)} = I - A_1$, $H_0^{(0)} = -A_0$, $H_2^{(0)} = -A_2$, $\widehat{H}_1^{(0)} = I - B_1$, $\widetilde{H}_1^{(0)} = I - C_1$, $\widehat{H}_2^{(0)} = -B_2$, and $\widetilde{H}_2^{(0)} = -C_2$.

It can be verified that the overall cost for the computation of π in the QBD case is reduced to $O(m^3 \log n + m^2 n)$ operations, against the $O(m^3 n)$ cost of Gaussian elimination.

8.5.4 Cyclic Reduction for Infinite Systems

The technique of successive state reduction, discussed in the previous section, can be successfully applied even to infinite systems. In this case, at each stage of the cyclic reduction the size of the problem does not decrease since we obtain a sequence of infinite block Hessenberg block Toeplitz-like matrices. However, the sequence of problems that we obtain in this way converges quadratically to a block bidiagonal block Toeplitz system that can be solved easily. A sort of a back-substitution step allows us to recover the solution of the starting problem. We now consider the problem of solving (8.2.12).

By performing an odd-even permutation of the block rows and block columns in (8.2.12) we find that

$$[G^2, G^4, \ldots \mid G, G^3, \ldots] \begin{bmatrix} T_1^{(0)} & W^{(0)} \\ Z^{(0)} & T_2^{(0)} \end{bmatrix} = [O, O, \ldots \mid A_0, O, \ldots], \quad (8.5.9)$$

where $T_1^{(0)}$, $T_2^{(0)}$, and $Z^{(0)}$ are infinite block triangular block Toeplitz matrices and $W^{(0)}$ is an infinite block Hessenberg block Toeplitz matrix (compare with (8.5.4)). Applied to the 2×2 block system (8.5.9), one step of block Gaussian elimination yields

$$[G, G^3, G^5, \ldots] H^{(1)} = [A_0, O, O, \ldots], \quad (8.5.10)$$

where $H^{(1)} = T_2^{(0)} - Z^{(0)} T_1^{(0)^{-1}} W^{(0)}$ is the Schur complement of $T_2^{(0)}$. It is interesting to observe that $Q^{(1)} = I - H^{(1)}$ is a nonnegative block Hessenberg matrix which, except for the first block column, has the block Toeplitz structure of the matrix of (8.2.11). In fact, $T_1^{(0)}$, $T_2^{(0)}$, and $Z^{(0)}$ are infinite block triangular block Toeplitz matrices and $W^{(0)}$ is an infinite block Hessenberg block Toeplitz matrix. Hence $H^{(1)}$ is uniquely determined by the blocks $\widehat{A}_i^{(1)}$, $i \geq 1$, $A_i^{(1)}$, $i \geq 0$, defining the first two block columns of $Q^{(1)}$.

We may recursively apply the same reduction (cyclic reduction) to the matrix equation (8.5.10) thus obtaining the sequence of systems

$$[G^{2^j+1}, G^{3 \cdot 2^j+1}, \ldots \mid G, G^{2 \cdot 2^j+1}, G^{4 \cdot 2^j+1}, \ldots] \begin{bmatrix} T_1^{(j)} & W^{(j)} \\ Z^{(j)} & T_2^{(j)} \end{bmatrix}$$
$$= [O, O, \ldots \mid A_0, O, \ldots]$$

Section 8.5. Fast Algorithms

such that
$$H^{(j)} = T_2^{(j-1)} - Z^{(j-1)}T_1^{(j-1)^{-1}}W^{(j-1)}, \quad (8.5.11)$$
$$[G, G^{2^j+1}, G^{2\cdot 2^j+1}, \ldots]H^{(j)} = [A_0, O, O, \ldots].$$

The matrix $\{H^{(j)}\}$ is such that $Q^{(j)} = I - H^{(j)}$ is a nonnegative matrix having, except for the first block column, the same block Hessenberg and Toeplitz structure of the matrix in (8.2.11). Each matrix $Q^{(j)}$ is uniquely determined by the blocks $\widehat{A}_i^{(j)}$, $i \geq 1$, $A_i^{(j)}$, $i \geq 0$, defining its first two block columns.

Due to the correlation between infinite block triangular block Toeplitz matrices and matrix power series, the block entries $\{A_i^{(j+1)}\}_{i\geq 0}$, $\{\widehat{A}_i^{(j+1)}\}_{i\geq 1}$, obtained at step $j+1$, can be related to the block entries $\{A_i^{(j)}\}_{i\geq 0}$, $\{\widehat{A}_i^{(j)}\}_{i\geq 1}$ that are obtained at step j by means of functional relations.

More specifically, for any $j \geq 0$, let us associate with the matrix sequences $\{A_i^{(j)}\}_{i\geq 0}$, $\{\widehat{A}_i^{(j)}\}_{i\geq 1}$ the formal matrix power series

$$A^{(j)}(z) = \sum_{i=0}^{+\infty} A_i^{(j)} z^i, \quad \widehat{A}^{(j)}(z) = \sum_{i=0}^{+\infty} \widehat{A}_{i+1}^{(j)} z^i,$$

respectively, where $A_i^{(0)} = \widehat{A}_i^{(0)} = A_i$, $i \geq 1$, $A_0^{(0)} = A_0$. Then we can write

$$\begin{cases} A^{(j+1)}(z) = zA_{odd}^{(j)}(z) + A_{even}^{(j)}(z)\big(I - A_{odd}^{(j)}(z)\big)^{-1} A_{even}^{(j)}(z), \\ \widehat{A}^{(j+1)}(z) = \widehat{A}_{odd}^{(j)}(z) + A_{even}^{(j)}(z)\big(I - A_{odd}^{(j)}(z)\big)^{-1} \widehat{A}_{even}^{(j)}(z), \end{cases} \quad (8.5.12)$$

where
$$A_{even}^{(j)}(z) = \sum_{i=0}^{+\infty} A_{2i}^{(j)} z^i, \quad A_{odd}^{(j)}(z) = \sum_{i=0}^{+\infty} A_{2i+1}^{(j)} z^i,$$
$$\widehat{A}_{even}^{(j)}(z) = \sum_{i=0}^{+\infty} \widehat{A}_{2(i+1)}^{(j)} z^i, \quad \widehat{A}_{odd}^{(j)}(z) = \sum_{i=0}^{+\infty} \widehat{A}_{2i+1}^{(j)} z^i.$$

The relations (8.5.12), in addition to expressing in compact form the recursions of the cyclic reduction method, provide a tool for the efficient computation of the matrices $\{A_i^{(j)}\}_{i\geq 0}$, $\{\widehat{A}_i^{(j)}\}_{i\geq 1}$, by using the algorithms of Sec. 8.3.

The following results (see [BM96a], [BM96b], [BM97a]) are fundamental for devising an efficient algorithm that is based on cyclic reduction.

Theorem 8.5.3 (Representation of G). *The blocks $\{A_i^{(j)}\}_{i\geq 0}$, $\{\widehat{A}_i^{(j)}\}_{i\geq 1}$ are nonnegative matrices such that $\sum_{i=0}^{+\infty} A_i^{(j)T}$, $A_0^T + \sum_{i=1}^{+\infty} \widehat{A}_i^{(j)T}$ are stochastic. Moreover, if the matrix $I - \sum_{i=0}^{+\infty} G^{i\cdot 2^j} \widehat{A}_{i+1}^{(j)}$ is nonsingular, then*

$$G = A_0 \left(I - \sum_{i=0}^{+\infty} G^{i\cdot 2^j} \widehat{A}_{i+1}^{(j)}\right)^{-1}. \quad (8.5.13)$$

$\diamond$

Under mild conditions, usually satisfied in applications, the block entries $A_i^{(j)}$ and $\widehat{A}_i^{(j)}$ converge quadratically to zero for $i \geq 2$ and for $j \to \infty$ [BM96a], [BM96b], [BM97a].

Theorem 8.5.4 (Convergence Properties). *Let $G' = \lim_{j \to \infty} G^j$. Then the following convergence properties hold:*

1. $\lim_{j \to \infty} \widehat{A}_i^{(j)} = 0$ *for $i \geq 2$.*

2. *If the entries of the matrix $(I - \sum_{i=1}^{+\infty} A_i^{(j)})^{-1}$ are bounded above by a constant, then the sequence of matrices $R^{(j)} = A_0^{(j)}(I - \sum_{i=1}^{+\infty} A_i^{(j)})^{-1}$ converges quadratically to the matrix G'.*

3. *If the solution G of (8.2.8) is irreducible, then $\lim_{j \to \infty} A_0^{(j)}(I - A_1^{(j)})^{-1} = G'$ and $\lim_{j \to \infty} A_i^{(j)} = 0$, $i \geq 2$.*

$\diamond$

Under the assumptions of Thms. 8.5.3 and 8.5.4, the following algorithm for the numerical computation of the matrix G can be applied.

Algorithm 8.5.2 (Computation of the Matrix G).

- Input: *Positive integers q_0, n_0, m, $n_0 = 2^{q_0}$, an error bound $\epsilon > 0$, and the nonnegative $m \times m$ matrices A_i, $i = 0, 1, \ldots, n_0$, where n_0 is the numerical degree of $A(z) = \sum_{i=0}^{+\infty} A_i z^i$.*

- Output: *An approximation of the solution G of (8.2.8).*

- Computation:

  1. *Apply the cyclic reduction procedure to (8.2.12), using (8.5.12), and thus obtain the sequence (8.5.11) of infinite systems defined by the blocks $A_i^{(j)}$, $\widehat{A}_i^{(j)}$, $j = 1, 2, \ldots, r$, until one of the following conditions is satisfied:*

     (C1) $|R^{(r)} - R^{(r-1)}| < \epsilon E$,

     (C2) $e^T(I - A_0^{(r)}(I - A_1^{(r)})^{-1}) < \epsilon e^T$,

     (C3) $e^T(I - A_0(I - \widehat{A}_1^{(r)})^{-1}) < \epsilon e^T$,

     where, at each step j, the matrix $R^{(j)}$ is defined by Thm. 8.5.4 and E is the $m \times m$ matrix having all entries equal to 1.

  2. *Compute an approximation of the matrix G:*

     (a) *If condition (C1) or condition (C2) is verified, compute an approximation of G by replacing, in the right-hand side of (8.5.13) for $j = r$, the positive powers of G with $R^{(r)}$ and by stopping the summation to the numerical degree of the series $\widehat{A}^{(r)}(z)$.*

     (b) *If condition (C3) is verified, an approximation of G is given by $A_0(I - \widehat{A}_1^{(r)})^{-1}$.*

$\diamond$

The effectiveness of Alg. 8.5.2 relies on the possibility of computing the blocks $A_i^{(j)}$, $\widehat{A}_i^{(j)}$, at each step j, in an efficient way. We may truncate the power series $A^{(j)}(z)$ and $\widehat{A}^{(j)}(z)$ to polynomials having ϵ-degree n_j and $\widehat{n}_j$, respectively, according to the definition given in Sec. 8.3.3. In this way, the matrices $\sum_{i=0}^{n_j} A_i^{(j)T}$ and $A_0^T + \sum_{i=1}^{\widehat{n}_j} \widehat{A}_i^{(j)T}$

Section 8.5. Fast Algorithms

are ϵ-stochastic. (A nonnegative matrix A is said to be ϵ-*stochastic* if $|(I - A)e| < \epsilon e$. If ϵ is the machine precision, A is said to be *numerically stochastic*.)

With this truncation, we may reduce the computation of the cyclic reduction steps to the multiplication of matrix polynomials and to the inversion of matrix polynomials modulo z^n for values of n that can be dynamically adjusted step by step according to the numerical degrees of the power series involved. In this way we obtain an algorithm similar to the one described in Sec. 8.5.4 in the finite case but which does not require the truncation of the infinite matrices to a finite size. The cost of this computation, based on the coefficientwise polynomial arithmetic described in Sec. 8.3.1, amounts to $O(m^3 n + m^2 n \log n)$ operations.

A more efficient technique consists of using the pointwise evaluation-interpolation procedure at the roots of unity of the series involved in (8.5.12). This approach consists of performing the following steps at stage $j + 1$ of the cyclic reduction procedure:

1. Evaluate the series $A_{odd}^{(j)}(z)$, $A_{even}^{(j)}(z)$, $\widehat{A}_{odd}^{(j)}(z)$, $\widehat{A}_{even}^{(j)}(z)$ at the n_jth roots of unity, where $n_j - 1 = 2^q - 1$ is an upper bound to the ϵ-degree of the above series.

2. Perform a pointwise evaluation of (8.5.12) at the n_jth roots of unity.

3. Compute the coefficients of the matrix polynomials $P(z)$ and $\widehat{P}(z)$ of degree $n_j - 1$, which interpolate the values of the matrix series $A^{(j+1)}(z)$ and $\widehat{A}^{(j+1)}(z)$ of (8.5.12).

4. Check whether the matrix polynomials $P(z)$ and $\widehat{P}(z)$ are good approximations of the series $A^{(j+1)}(z)$, $\widehat{A}^{(j+1)}(z)$, respectively.

5. If the polynomials $P(z)$ and $\widehat{P}(z)$ are poor approximations of $A^{(j+1)}(z)$, $\widehat{A}^{(j+1)}(z)$, set $n_j = 2n_j$ and repeat steps 1–5 until the required accuracy of the approximation is reached.

Due to the properties of the FFT in each doubling step, part of the results is already available at no cost. Moreover, unlike in the version based on coefficientwise polynomial arithmetic, the computation of the reciprocal of a polynomial is avoided and the order of the involved DFT and IDFT is kept to its minimum value, thus substantially reducing the computational cost per iteration.

The following properties [BM97a] of cyclic reduction and of the FFT provide a good test for checking the accuracy of the approximations $P(z)$, $\widehat{P}(z)$ of the series $A^{(j+1)}(z)$, $\widehat{A}^{(j+1)}(z)$ needed at step 4.

Theorem 8.5.5 (Two Recursive Relations). *For any $j \geq 0$, let*

$$\alpha^{(j)T} = e^T \sum_{i=1}^{+\infty} i A_i^{(j)}, \quad \widehat{\alpha}^{(j)T} = e^T \sum_{i=1}^{+\infty} i \widehat{A}_{i+1}^{(j)}.$$

Then the following recursive relations hold:

$$\alpha^{(j+1)T} = \left(e^T + \alpha^{(j)T} - (e^T - \alpha^{(j)T})(I - A_{odd}^{(j)}(1))^{-1} A_{even}^{(j)}(1) \right) / 2,$$

$$\widehat{\alpha}^{(j+1)T} = \left(\widehat{\alpha}^{(j)T} - (e^T - \alpha^{(j)T})(I - A_{odd}^{(j)}(1))^{-1} \widehat{A}_{even}^{(j)}(1) \right) / 2.$$

(8.5.14)

◊

Theorem 8.5.6 (Two Inequalities). *At step j, let $P^{(n)}(z) = \sum_{i=0}^{n-1} P_i z^i$ and $\widehat{P}^{(n)} = \sum_{i=0}^{n-1} \widehat{P}_i z^i$ be the matrix polynomials of degree $n-1$ interpolating the series $A^{(j)}(z)$, $\widehat{A}^{(j)}(z)$ at the nth roots of unity. Then the following inequalities hold:*

$$e^T \sum_{i=n}^{+\infty} A_i^{(j)} \leq \alpha^{(j)T} - e^T \sum_{i=1}^{n-1} i P_i,$$

$$e^T \sum_{i=n+1}^{+\infty} \widehat{A}_i^{(j)} \leq \widehat{\alpha}^{(j)T} - e^T \sum_{i=1}^{n-1} i \widehat{P}_i.$$

◇

Theorems 8.5.5 and 8.5.6 provide a good test with which to check the accuracy of the approximations of the series $A^{(j)}(z)$, $\widehat{A}^{(j)}(z)$ at each step j. Indeed, suppose we know the coefficients of the series $A^{(j)}(z)$, $\widehat{A}^{(j)}(z)$ and compute the coefficients P_i, $\widehat{P}_i$, $i = 0, \ldots, n-1$, of the approximations $P^{(n)}(z) = \sum_{i=0}^{n-1} P_i z^i$, $\widehat{P}^{(n)}(z) = \sum_{i=0}^{n-1} \widehat{P}_i z^i$ of the series $A^{(j+1)}(z)$, $\widehat{A}^{(j+1)}(z)$ by interpolating the functional relations (8.5.12) at the nth roots of unity. From Thm. 8.5.6 it follows that, if

$$\alpha^{(j+1)T} - e^T \sum_{i=1}^{n-1} i P_i \leq \epsilon e^T \tag{8.5.15}$$

and

$$\widehat{\alpha}^{(j+1)T} - e^T \sum_{i=1}^{n-1} i \widehat{P}_i \leq \epsilon e^T, \tag{8.5.16}$$

then the matrices $\sum_{i=0}^{n-1} A_i^{(j+1)T}$ and $A_0^T + \sum_{i=1}^{n} \widehat{A}_i^{(j+1)T}$ are ϵ-stochastic. Hence the series $A^{(j+1)}(z)$, $\widehat{A}^{(j+1)}(z)$ have ϵ-degree $n-1$ and the matrix coefficients of $P^{(n)}(z)$ and $\widehat{P}^{(n)}(z)$ are approximations of the corresponding coefficients of $A^{(j+1)}(z)$, $\widehat{A}^{(j+1)}(z)$ within the error ϵ. It is important to point out that (8.5.15) and (8.5.16) can be easily applied without knowing the coefficients of the series $A^{(j+1)}(z)$, $\widehat{A}^{(j+1)}(z)$. In fact, $\alpha^{(j+1)}$ and $\widehat{\alpha}^{(j+1)}$ can be obtained explicitly by means of (8.5.14) at the cost of $O(m^3)$ arithmetic operations. This provides an efficient tool to check the accuracy of the approximations $P^{(n)}(z)$, $\widehat{P}^{(n)}(z)$ to $A^{(j+1)}(z)$, $\widehat{A}^{(j+1)}(z)$.

Algorithm 8.5.3 (Computation of $A^{(j+1)}(z)$, $\widehat{A}^{(j+1)}(z)$).

- **Input:** *An error bound $\epsilon > 0$, nonnegative integers n_j, q_j, and the matrix power series $A^{(j)}(z)$, $\widehat{A}^{(j)}(z)$ having numerical degree bounded above by $n_j = 2^{q_j}$.*

- **Output:** *The matrix power series $A^{(j+1)}(z)$, $\widehat{A}^{(j+1)}(z)$ and an upper bound $n_{j+1} = 2^{q_{j+1}}$ to their numerical degrees.*

- **Computation:**

    1. *Set $q_{j+1} = q_j - 1, n_{j+1} = 2^{q_{j+1}}$.*

    2. *Compute $\alpha^{(j+1)}$ and $\widehat{\alpha}^{(j+1)}$ by means of (8.5.14).*

    3. *Evaluate the functions $A_{odd}^{(j)}(z)$, $A_{even}^{(j)}(z)$ and $\widehat{A}_{odd}^{(j)}(z)$, $\widehat{A}_{even}^{(j)}(z)$ at the (n_{j+1})th roots of unity by means of DFTs.*

Section 8.5. Fast Algorithms

4. *Apply equations (8.5.12) and obtain the coefficients of the matrix polynomials $P(z)$ and $\widehat{P}(z)$ interpolating $A^{(j+1)}(z)$, $\widehat{A}^{(j+1)}(z)$ at the (n_{j+1})th roots of unity.*

5. *Apply the tests (8.5.15) and (8.5.16) to check whether $P(z)$ and $\widehat{P}(z)$ are good approximations of the series. If the inequalities (8.5.15) and (8.5.16) are satisfied, then skip to the next stage. Otherwise, set $n_{j+1} = 2n_{j+1}$, $q_{j+1} = q_{j+1} + 1$ and repeat from stage 3.*

6. *Set $A^{(j+1)}(z) = P(z)$, $\widehat{A}^{(j+1)}(z) = \widehat{P}(z)$.*

$\diamond$

In the case of QBD processes, where P is a block tridiagonal matrix, the functions $A^{(j)}(z)$ and $\widehat{A}^{(j)}(z)$ are matrix polynomials of degree 2 and 1, respectively. By comparing terms of the same degree, we obtain the simple relations (compare [LR93]):

$$A_0^{(j+1)} = A_0^{(j)}(I - A_1^{(j)})^{-1} A_0^{(j)},$$

$$A_1^{(j+1)} = A_1^{(j)} + A_0^{(j)}(I - A_1^{(j)})^{-1} A_2^{(j)} + A_2^{(j)}(I - A_1^{(j)})^{-1} A_0^{(j)},$$

$$A_2^{(j+1)} = A_2^{(j)}(I - A_1^{(j)})^{-1} A_2^{(j)},$$

$$\widehat{A}_1^{(j+1)} = \widehat{A}_1^{(j)} + A_0^{(j)}(I - A_1^{(j)})^{-1} \widehat{A}_2^{(j)},$$

$$\widehat{A}_2^{(j)} = A_2^{(j)}.$$

Moreover, it is surprising to observe that the cyclic reduction step is equivalent to the squaring step in the Graeffe algorithm, which is used for factoring polynomials [BP94], [Ost40]. In fact, the first functional relation of (8.5.12) can be rewritten equivalently as

$$z^2 I - A^{(j+1)}(z^2) = -(zI - A^{(j)}(z))(I - A_1^{(j)})^{-1}(-z - A^{(j)}(-z)).$$

By evaluating the determinants of both sides of the above equation we obtain

$$\phi^{(j+1)}(z^2) = -\phi^{(j)}(z)\phi^{(j)}(-z)/\det(I - A_1^{(j)}), \qquad (8.5.17)$$

where $\phi^{(j)}(z) = \det(zI - A^{(j)}(z))$. The latter relation extends to matrix polynomials the Graeffe iteration, which is formally obtained from (8.5.17) for $m = 1$.

8.5.5 Cyclic Reduction for Generalized Hessenberg Systems

Since a non-skip-free matrix can be reblocked into an M/G/1 matrix, we may apply the cyclic reduction technique for solving problems with the structure (8.2.4). However, in this way we would not exploit the additional structure of the problem, more specifically the fact that the blocks of the matrix P, being block Toeplitz matrices, have block displacement rank at most 2 and the fact that the matrix G that solves the equation (8.2.8) has block displacement rank 1. In this section we present new results that allow us to fully exploit the problem structure.

So consider the problem of solving the infinite system (8.2.12). (The same technique can be applied to solve any generalized block Hessenberg block Toeplitz system, for instance, banded block Toeplitz systems [BM97b].)

Let $\mathcal{A}_i$ of (8.2.5) denote the matrices that are obtained by reblocking the matrix (8.2.4) and consider the sequence of matrix power series $\mathcal{A}^{(j)}(z)$, $\widehat{\mathcal{A}}^{(j)}(z)$ that are obtained by means of the functional relations (8.5.12), where each A is replaced with $\mathcal{A}$. We note that the matrix power series $\mathcal{H}^{(0)}(z) = \sum_{i=0}^{+\infty} \mathcal{H}_i^{(0)} z^i = zI - \mathcal{A}^{(0)}(z)$ and $\widehat{\mathcal{H}}^{(0)}(z) = \sum_{i=0}^{+\infty} \widehat{\mathcal{H}}_i^{(0)} z^i = I - \widehat{\mathcal{A}}^{(0)}(z)$ are block Toeplitz matrices.

A direct inspection further shows that the Toeplitz structure is generally lost by the matrix power series $\mathcal{H}^{(j)}(z) = \sum_{i=0}^{+\infty} \mathcal{H}_i^{(j)} z^i = zI - \mathcal{A}^{(j)}(z)$ and $\widehat{\mathcal{H}}^{(j)}(z) = \sum_{i=0}^{+\infty} \widehat{\mathcal{H}}_i^{(j)} z^i = I - \widehat{\mathcal{A}}^{(j)}(z)$ for $j \geq 1$. However, the displacement structure is preserved by the matrix power series $\mathcal{H}^{(j)}(z)$ and $\widehat{\mathcal{H}}^{(j)}(z)$. This fact allows us to devise an FFT-based implementation of the cyclic reduction algorithm [BM97b].

Theorem 8.5.7 (Displacement of $\mathcal{H}^{(j)}(z)$, $\widehat{\mathcal{H}}^{(j)}(z)$). *For the matrix power series $\mathcal{H}^{(j)}(z) = zI - \mathcal{A}^{(j)}(z)$, $\widehat{\mathcal{H}}^{(j)}(z) = I - \widehat{\mathcal{A}}^{(j)}(z)$ generated at jth step of cyclic reduction we have*

$$\nabla_{k,m}(\mathcal{H}^{(j)}(z)) = (\mathcal{H}^{(j)}(z) E_k^{(1)}) U^{(j)}(z) - V^{(j)}(z)(E_k^{(2)T} \mathcal{H}^{(j)}(z)),$$

$$\nabla_{k,m}(\widehat{\mathcal{H}}^{(j)}(z)) = -E_k^{(1)}(E_k^{(2)T} \mathcal{A}_0^{(0)}) - (\mathcal{H}^{(j)}(z) E_k^{(1)}) \widehat{U}^{(j)}(z)$$
$$- V^{(j)}(z)(E_k^{(2)T} \widehat{\mathcal{H}}^{(j)}(z))$$

for suitable block row vectors $U^{(j)}(z)$, $\widehat{U}^{(j)}(z)$ and block column vector $V^{(j)}(z)$.
◇

As a consequence, the matrix power series $\mathcal{H}^{(j)}(z)$, $\widehat{\mathcal{H}}^{(j)}(z)$ have block displacement rank not greater than 2 and 3, respectively. Moreover, from the above theorem and from Thm. 8.4.1, we can derive a suitable representation formula for the matrix power series $\mathcal{H}^{(j)}(z)$ and $\widehat{\mathcal{H}}^{(j)}(z)$.

The explicit equations relating the block vectors at two consecutive steps of the cyclic reduction algorithm can be derived by generalizing the analogous relations provided in [BM97b] for banded block Toeplitz matrices. Such relations, expressed in functional form, consist of performing products and inversions of matrix power series. Hence, the computational cost of performing the jth step of cyclic reduction by using FFTs reduces to $O(n_j m^3 k \log^2 k + m^2 k n_j \log n_j)$, where n_j is an upper bound to the numerical degree of the matrix power series $\mathcal{A}^{(j)}(z)$ and $\widehat{\mathcal{A}}^{(j)}(z)$.

In the case where $\mathcal{A}_i = O$ for $i > 2$, i.e., when the reblocked matrix P is block tridiagonal, the above results can be simplified. We can give explicit expressions for the blocks $\mathcal{H}_0^{(j)} = -\mathcal{A}_0^{(j)}$, $\mathcal{H}_1^{(j)} = I - \mathcal{A}_1^{(j)}$, $\mathcal{H}_2^{(j)} = -\mathcal{A}_2^{(j)}$, $\widehat{\mathcal{H}}_1^{(j)} = I - \widehat{\mathcal{A}}_1^{(j)}$ by means of the following result.

Theorem 8.5.8 (Displacement of $\mathcal{H}_i^{(j)}$). *If $\mathcal{A}_i = O$ for $i > 2$, then for the matrices $\mathcal{H}_0^{(j)}, \mathcal{H}_1^{(j)}, \mathcal{H}_2^{(j)}, \widehat{\mathcal{H}}_1^{(j)}$, $j \geq 0$, generated by the cyclic reduction (8.5.12) we have*

$$\nabla(\mathcal{H}_0^{(j)}) = \mathcal{C}_0^{(j)} U_0^{(j)} - V_0^{(j)} \mathcal{R}_0^{(j)},$$

$$\nabla(\mathcal{H}_1^{(j)}) = \mathcal{C}_0^{(j)} U_1^{(j)} + \mathcal{C}_1^{(j)} U_0^{(j)} - V_0^{(j)} \mathcal{R}_1^{(j)} - V_1^{(j)} \mathcal{R}_0^{(j)},$$

$$\nabla(\mathcal{H}_2^{(j)}) = \mathcal{S}^{(j)} U_1^{(j)} - V_1^{(j)} \widehat{\mathcal{R}}^{(j)},$$

$$\nabla(\widehat{\mathcal{H}}_1^{(j)}) = -E_k^{(1)} \mathcal{R}_0^{(0)} - \mathcal{C}_0^{(j)} U_1^{(j)} - V_0^{(j)} \widehat{\mathcal{R}}^{(j)}$$

for suitable block row vectors $\widehat{\mathcal{R}}^{(j)}$, $U_i^{(j)}$, $\mathcal{R}_i^{(j)}$, $i = 0, 1$, and block column vectors $\mathcal{S}^{(j)}$, $V_i^{(j)}$, $\mathcal{C}_i^{(j)}$, $i = 0, 1$.

$\diamond$

For this case, the computational cost per step is reduced to $O(m^3 k \log^2 k)$ operations. Moreover, the quadratic convergence properties of the blocks $A_i^{(j)}$, $\widehat{A}_i^{(j)}$ of the algorithms of Sec. 8.5.4 can be directly extended to the blocks $\mathcal{A}_i^{(j)}$, $\widehat{\mathcal{A}}_i^{(j)}$. In particular it holds that the block $\mathcal{A}_i^{(j)}$, $i > 1$, tend to zero and the block $\mathcal{A}_1^{(j)}$ tends to a matrix of block displacement rank 2.

The algorithm devised in this way is more efficient than the linearly convergent method of [GHT97], particularly when the block dimension k is large. In fact, the computational cost of one step of the latter method is $O(m^3 kn)$ and many iterations may need to be computed in order to reach a good approximation of G.

Due to the structure of the blocks $\mathcal{A}_i$, some interesting relations hold between the zeros of the analytic functions $\phi(z) = \det \mathcal{H}(z) = \det(zI - \mathcal{A}(z))$ and $\psi(z) = \det(z^k I - A(z))$. In fact, in [GHT97] it is proved that

$$\phi(z^k) = \prod_{i=0}^{k-1} \psi(z \omega_k^i). \tag{8.5.18}$$

It then follows that if ξ is zero of the analytic function $\psi(z)$, then ξ^k is zero of $\phi(z)$. Conversely, if η is a zero of $\phi(z)$, then there exists a kth root of η which is zero of $\psi(z)$.

For positive recurrent Markov chains, the analytic function $\phi(z)$ has exactly $km - 1$ zeros lying in the open unit circle and one zero equal to 1. This property, together with relations (8.5.18) and (8.5.17), yields the following convergence result [BM98b].

Theorem 8.5.9 (Convergence Speed). *Let $\mathcal{A}_i = 0$ for $i > 1$. If ξ_i, $i = 1, 2, \ldots$, are the zeros of $\phi(z)$ ordered such that $|\xi_1| \le |\xi_2| \le \cdots \le |\xi_{mk}| = 1 < |\xi_{mk+1}| \le \cdots$ and if $A_i = O$ for $i > 2$, then $\|\mathcal{A}_2^{(j)}\| = O((|\xi_{mk+1}|^{-1} + \epsilon)^{k 2^j})$ for any matrix norm and for any $\epsilon > 0$.*

$\diamond$

The above theorem is a special case of a more general convergence result provided in [BM97b], where cyclic reduction is used for solving a banded Toeplitz system.

8.6 NUMERICAL EXPERIMENTS

The algorithms described in this chapter for the numerical solution of Markov chains have been implemented and tested in [ALM97], [BM96a], [BM96b], [BM97a], [Mei97b]. Here we report the most significant results.

In Fig. 8.2 we compare the time needed for the computation of the Ramaswami formula by means of the fast and the customary techniques for a problem investigated in [ALM97].

Tables 8.1 and 8.2 display the CPU time in seconds, the number of iterations, and the residual error of the pointwise cyclic reduction (CR) algorithm and of the fast functional iteration (FI) method usually used in applications for the computation of G [Mei97a]. The problem, which has been solved, arises from the modeling of a Metaring MAC protocol [ALM97]. Its solution depends on a parameter ρ, related to the positive recurrence, and involves blocks of size $m = 16$ and numerical degrees less than 265.

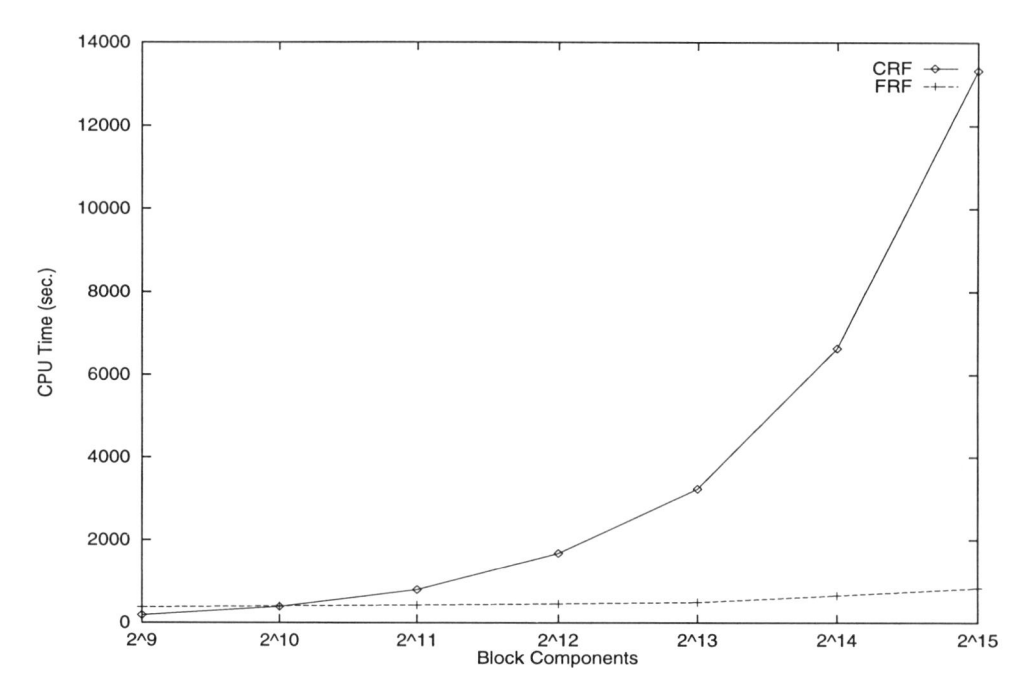

242   Fast Algorithms with Applications to Markov Chains and Queueing Models   Chapter 8

Figure 8.2. Fast and customary Ramaswami formula.

The acceleration of the Latouche–Stewart (LS) algorithm, in view of the displacement rank (DR) properties, is shown in Table 8.3, where the algorithms have been tested on the same Metaring MAC protocol problem for $\rho = 0.8$.

The non-skip-free version of cyclic reduction (NSF-CR) has been tested on block tridiagonal problems of different block sizes k and compared with the ordinary CR and with the algorithm of [GHT97]. The results are summarized in Table 8.4, where the order of magnitude of the residual error is shown. An asterisk (∗) in the tables means failure of the algorithm due to lack of memory.

Table 8.1. Cyclic reduction.

ρ	Time (s.)	Iterations	Residual
0.1	0.9	9	$1.8 \cdot 10^{-13}$
0.8	1.5	13	$5.4 \cdot 10^{-14}$
0.9	2.3	14	$1.5 \cdot 10^{-14}$
0.95	2.4	16	$1.8 \cdot 10^{-14}$
0.96	2.4	17	$2.3 \cdot 10^{-14}$
0.97	2.5	20	$4.2 \cdot 10^{-14}$

Table 8.2. Functional iteration method.

ρ	Time (s.)	Iterations	Residual	FI/CR
0.1	0.3	22	$2.2 \cdot 10^{-14}$	0.3
0.8	3.9	148	$1.1 \cdot 10^{-13}$	2.6
0.9	10.8	373	$1.2 \cdot 10^{-13}$	4.7
0.95	44.4	1534	$1.3 \cdot 10^{-13}$	18.5
0.96	91.4	3158	$1.3 \cdot 10^{-13}$	38.1
0.97	96.8	3336	$1.3 \cdot 10^{-13}$	38.7

Section 8.6. Numerical Experiments

Table 8.3. Fast and customary doubling algorithm.

	DR		LS		
n	Time	Residual	Time	Residual	Ratio
256	8.7	$2.5 \cdot 10^{-3}$	38.3	$2.5 \cdot 10^{-3}$	4.4
512	18.1	$4.0 \cdot 10^{-4}$	103.5	$4.0 \cdot 10^{-4}$	5.7
1024	39.2	$1.7 \cdot 10^{-5}$	264.9	$1.7 \cdot 10^{-5}$	6.8
2048	89.3	$3.4 \cdot 10^{-8}$	*	*	*
4096	193.4	$1.3 \cdot 10^{-13}$	*	*	*

Table 8.4. Non-skip-free Markov chains.

	NSF-CR		CR		GHT	
k	Time	Residual	Time	Residual	Time	Residual
16	14.4	10^{-16}	1.1	10^{-16}	6.1	10^{-11}
32	19.2	10^{-15}	9.8	10^{-15}	13.3	10^{-11}
64	37.7	10^{-13}	136.3	10^{-14}	60.4	10^{-11}
128	89.5	10^{-11}	*	*	555.5	10^{-11}
256	146.4	10^{-15}	*	*	816.4	10^{-11}
512	448.1	10^{-11}	*	*	5830.3	10^{-4}

Chapter 9

TENSOR DISPLACEMENT STRUCTURES AND POLYSPECTRAL MATCHING

Victor S. Grigorascu

Phillip A. Regalia

9.1 INTRODUCTION

This chapter studies the extension of the notion of structured matrices to tensors. These are multi-indexed arrays, in contrast to matrices, which are two-indexed arrays. Such arrays arise while considering higher-order cumulants and the corresponding polyspectra in applications, particularly in blind model identification and approximation problems.

While matrices are adequate representations for second-order statistics, higher-order cumulants are more naturally (and more completely) studied in a tensor setting. In this chapter, we examine the displacement rank concept of Ch. 1 for tensors. After a semitutorial presentation of Tucker products and cumulant representations of linear systems, we show links between interpolation of polyspectral values by a linear model and the Tucker factorability of a certain Pick tensor. We also develop a particular higher-order extension of a Schur-type algorithm, based on a novel outer product of tensors. This leads to a pyramidal factorization approach for tensors, which specializes to triangular factorization in the matrix case.

9.2 MOTIVATION FOR HIGHER-ORDER CUMULANTS

Recent years have witnessed increasing interest in higher-order cumulants, which convey more information about an underlying stochastic process than second-order statistics, including non-Gaussianity, phase information, nonlinearities, and so forth.

An example arises in the blind identification problem, in which one considers a process $\{y(\cdot)\}$ generated by

$$y(n) = h_1 u(n-1) + h_2 u(n-2) + h_2 u(n-3) + \cdots = \sum_{i=1}^{\infty} h_k u(n-i),$$

where $\{y(\cdot)\}$ is observable; $\{u(\cdot)\}$ is an unobserved but independent, identically distributed (i.i.d.) stochastic process; and $\{h_i\}$ denote the impulse responses of an unknown channel. The transfer function associated with the channel is

$$H(z) = \sum_{i=1}^{\infty} h_i z^i, \qquad |z| < 1,$$

where in this chapter we are using z (instead of z^{-1}) to denote the delay operator, viz., $z[u(n)] = u(n-1)$. A basic problem in this setting is to estimate the impulse response $\{h_i\}$ or the transfer function $H(z)$, given the output sequence $\{y(\cdot)\}$.

Second-order statistics of the output process $\{y(\cdot)\}$ allow one to determine the magnitude $|H(e^{j\omega})|$ of the channel but not its phase, whereas higher-order statistics of the output process allow one to deduce both the magnitude and the phase of the channel frequency response. This added informational content served as the impetus for a revived interest in higher-order statistics in signal processing in the early 1990s [Men91].

Despite numerous intriguing developments in this field, including the ability to separate minimum-phase from nonminimum-phase components of a signal [GS90] and linear from nonlinear components [TE89], or the ability to locate more sources than sensors in an array processing context [Car90], practical interest in algorithm development for signal processing applications has dwindled rapidly. This phenomenon may be attributed to two basic obstacles underlying cumulant-based signal processing.

The first concerns the computational complexity of estimating cumulants from a given time series. Although empirical estimation formulas are available, they tend to be computationally expensive, and in some cases they converge more slowly than estimators for second-order statistics.

The second obstacle concerns the successful extraction of desired information from higher-order statistics. Although such statistics often are touted for carrying phase information, they also convey information on potential nonlinear mechanisms. This is problematic in applications where the underlying process $\{y(\cdot)\}$ *is* linear, since any estimation errors can result in higher-order (estimated) statistics that are suddenly incompatible with *any* linear process. (By a "linear process," we mean the output of a linear time-invariant system when driven by an i.i.d. process.)

To appreciate this problem further, let us turn momentarily to second-order statistics. Suppose $\{y(\cdot)\}$ is a real-valued wide-sense stationary stochastic process. We introduce a finite number of autocorrelation lags:

$$r_i = E[y(n)\, y(n-i)], \qquad i = 0, 1, \ldots, M.$$

Under the mild constraint that the Toeplitz matrix

$$R = \begin{bmatrix} r_0 & r_1 & \cdots & r_M \\ r_1 & r_0 & \ddots & \vdots \\ \vdots & \ddots & \ddots & r_1 \\ r_M & \cdots & r_1 & r_0 \end{bmatrix}$$

be positive definite, the familiar Yule–Walker equations, in which the unknowns $\{\sigma^2, a_1, \ldots, a_M\}$ are obtained according to

$$R \begin{bmatrix} 1 \\ a_1 \\ \vdots \\ a_M \end{bmatrix} = \begin{bmatrix} \sigma^2 \\ 0 \\ \vdots \\ 0 \end{bmatrix},$$

Section 9.2. Motivation for Higher-Order Cumulants 247

allow one to deduce a candidate linear model for the data $\{y(\cdot)\}$. In particular, choosing

$$\widehat{H}(z) = \frac{\sigma}{1 + a_1 z + \cdots + a_M z^M}$$

yields a stable autoregressive transfer function such that, when driven by unit-variance white noise, the resulting output sequence $\{\hat{y}(\cdot)\}$ is compatible with the given second-order statistics, i.e.,

$$E[\hat{y}(n)\,\hat{y}(n-i)] = r_i, \qquad i = 0, 1, \ldots, M.$$

Whether the initial process $\{y(\cdot)\}$ is autoregressive, or even linear, is irrelevant to the validity of this result.

Many attempts to generalize such relations to higher-order cumulants may be found in [GM89], [GS90], [JK92], [NM93], [SM90a], [SM90b], under the hypothesis that the underlying (non-Gaussian) process $\{y(\cdot)\}$ is linear and generated from a rational transfer function of known degree. In cases where the process *is* linear, but the degree of the underlying model is underestimated, the equations so solved do not in general lead to a model that replicates the cumulant values used for its determination. The incompatibility between the resulting model and the cumulant values used to determine it implies that such methods do not correctly capture the structure of the data.

One of the few results establishing compatibility of higher-order cumulants with a linear process is given by Tekalp and Erdem [TE89]. Introduce the kth-order cumulant lags of a process $\{y(\cdot)\}$ as

$$c_{i_1, i_2, \ldots, i_{k-1}} \triangleq \mathrm{cum}[y(n-i_1), y(n-i_2), \ldots, y(n-i_{k-1}), y(n)],$$

where $\mathrm{cum}[\cdots]$ denotes the cumulant value of the k random variables that form its argument. (A nice tutorial overview of cumulants in signal processing may be found in [Men91].) Since our process $\{y(\cdot)\}$ is assumed stationary, the cumulant value here depends only on the relative lags $i_1, \ldots, i_{k-1}$. The kth-order polyspectrum of the process $\{y(\cdot)\}$ is a $(k-1)$-dimensional z-transform of the sequence $\{c_{i_1,\ldots,i_{k-1}}\}$, defined as [Men91]

$$R(z_1, \ldots, z_{k-1}) \triangleq \sum_{i_1 = -\infty}^{+\infty} \cdots \sum_{i_{k-1} = -\infty}^{+\infty} c_{i_1,\ldots,i_{k-1}} z_1^{i_1} \cdots z_{k-1}^{i_{k-1}},$$

whenever the infinite sum converges on the unit polycircle $|z_1| = \cdots = |z_{k-1}| = 1$. A well-known relation [Men91], [NP93] shows that whenever $\{y(\cdot)\}$ is the output process of a linear system with transfer function $H(z)$, which in turn is driven by an i.i.d. sequence, the polyspectrum assumes the form

$$R(z_1, \ldots, z_{k-1}) = \gamma_k \cdot H(z_1) \cdots H(z_{k-1}) H((z_1 \cdots z_{k-1})^{-1}),$$

where γ_k is the kth-order cumulant of the i.i.d. input sequence (assumed nonzero).

The polycepstrum is defined as the logarithm [NP93], [TE89] of the polyspectrum which, for the linear case, gives the separable structure

$$\log[R(z_1, \ldots, z_{k-1})] = \log \gamma_k + \log H(z_1) + \cdots + \log H(z_{k-1}) + \log H((z_1 \cdots z_{k-1})^{-1}).$$

Assuming $H(z)$ has no poles or zeros on the unit circle $|z| = 1$, we may develop a multidimensional z-transform expansion of the polycepstrum as

$$\log[R(z_1, \ldots, z_k)] = \sum_{i_1 = -\infty}^{+\infty} \cdots \sum_{i_{k-1} = -\infty}^{+\infty} \hat{c}_{i_1,\ldots,i_{k-1}} z_1^{i_1} \cdots z_{k-1}^{i_{k-1}},$$

in which the terms $\{\hat{c}_{i_1,\ldots,i_{k-1}}\}$ are the polycepstral coefficients. The process $\{y(\cdot)\}$ is then linear if and only if the polycepstral coefficients are nonzero only on the principal axes (only one index nonzero) and the main diagonal ($i_1 = i_2 = \cdots = i_{k-1}$), with elementary symmetry relations connecting the nonzero coefficients [TE89]. Since this result involves infinitely many cumulant lags, its practical application is limited to cases where the cumulant lags are finite in duration or decay sufficiently rapidly in all indices as to render truncation effects negligible [NP93].

Similar in spirit to the cumulant matching approach of [Tug87], [Tug95], a generic problem statement that motivates the present work is the following: Given a finite number of cumulant lags, or possibly a finite number of evaluations of a polyspectrum, under what conditions can a linear process be fit to such values?

For second-order statistics, this problem is solved. Various formulations are possible, including the Yule–Walker equations, the closely connected Levinson recursion, the Kalman–Yakubovich–Popov lemma (e.g., [FCG79]), and deeper approaches connected with the Schur algorithm [DD84], Darlington synthesis [DVK78], and interpolation problems among the class of Schur functions [Dym89a]. Many of these approaches admit matrix analogues by way of matrix displacement structure theory [KS95a], and we examine candidate extensions of displacement structure relations to higher-order cumulants.

Many algorithmic contributions in recent years aim to manipulate cumulant information by way of basic matrix algebra. Since a matrix is a two-indexed structure, while higher-order cumulants involve more than two indices, a tensorial formulation for cumulants, where tensor here refers simply to a multi-indexed array, would seem a more natural setting for capturing cumulant-based structures [McC87].

Some recent works have reinforced the utility of tensorial representations of higher-order statistics. For example, Delathauwer, DeMoor, and Vandewalle [DMV99] have developed a multilinear singular value decomposition, in which a kth-order tensor is reindexed into k different "matrix unwindings," each of whose left singular vectors may be computed. The overall scheme is then equivalent to applying k unitary transformations (one for each index dimension) to the tensor to expose a core tensor—not, in general, diagonal—verifying certain norm and orthogonality properties.

Cardoso and Comon [CC96a] and Comon and Mourrain [CM96] have shown the role of independent component analysis in many signal processing problems, particularly source separation. This notion specializes to principal component analysis when applied to second-order statistics.

Cardoso [Car90], [Car95] has developed supersymmetric tensor diagonalization, motivated by earlier work involving quadricovariance structures defined from fourth-order cumulants. Just as a second-order tensor (or matrix) can be understood as an operator between first-order tensor (or vector) spaces, a fourth-order cumulant structure may be treated as an operator between matrix spaces, leading to many fruitful extensions of eigendecompositions familiar in matrix theory.

Our approach aims to exploit displacement structure in a multi-indexed setting, with the chapter organized as follows. Sec. 9.3 presents a brief overview of displacement structure in second-order statistical modeling, so that various higher-order extensions may appear more recognizable. Sec. 9.4 then presents a tutorial overview of a particular multilinear matrix product (sometimes called the Tucker product), followed by its relation to cumulant representations in system theory. Sec. 9.6 then introduces displacement structure for cumulant tensors, along with relations connecting displacement residues with polyspectra; the relations so studied are valid for all cumulant orders. From these relations we show in Sec. 9.7 that the existence of a linear model compatible with a

Section 9.3. Second-Order Displacement Structure 249

given set of cumulant or polyspectral values implies the Tucker-factorability of a certain Pick tensor defined from the data. Sec. 9.8 then presents a candidate extension of a Schur algorithm to higher-order tensors, based on an apparently novel outer product involving tensors of successive degrees.

Concluding remarks are made in Sec. 9.9, including some open problems that arise throughout our presentation.

9.3 SECOND-ORDER DISPLACEMENT STRUCTURE

We present a brief review of displacement structure in second-order stochastic modeling to motivate subsequent extensions to higher-order arrays. Further details can be found in [KS95a] and the references therein as well as in Ch. 1 of this book.

Consider a wide-sense real stationary time series $\{y(\cdot)\}$ with autocorrelation coefficients

$$E[y(n)\,y(n-k)] = r_k$$

and the corresponding autocorrelation matrix

$$R = E\left\{\begin{bmatrix} y(n) \\ y(n-1) \\ y(n-2) \\ \vdots \end{bmatrix} \begin{bmatrix} y(n) & y(n-1) & y(n-2) & \cdots \end{bmatrix}\right\} = \begin{bmatrix} r_0 & r_1 & r_2 & \cdots \\ r_1 & r_0 & r_1 & \ddots \\ r_2 & r_1 & r_0 & \ddots \\ \vdots & \ddots & \ddots & \ddots \end{bmatrix}$$

of infinite dimensions for now, which assumes a celebrated Toeplitz structure.

Let Z denote the shift matrix with ones on the subdiagonal and zeros elsewhere. The matrix ZRZ^T relates to R by shifting all elements one position diagonally; the Toeplitz structure of R implies that the displacement residue

$$R - ZRZ^T = \begin{bmatrix} r_0 & r_1 & r_2 & \cdots \\ r_1 & 0 & 0 & \cdots \\ r_2 & 0 & 0 & \cdots \\ \vdots & \vdots & \vdots & \ddots \end{bmatrix} \quad (9.3.1)$$

vanishes except along the borders of the matrix.

Consider now the two-variable (generating function) form

$$\begin{bmatrix} 1 & z_1 & z_1^2 & \cdots \end{bmatrix} \begin{bmatrix} r_0 & r_1 & r_2 & \cdots \\ r_1 & r_0 & r_1 & \ddots \\ r_2 & r_1 & r_0 & \ddots \\ \vdots & \ddots & \ddots & \ddots \end{bmatrix} \begin{bmatrix} 1 \\ z_2 \\ z_2^2 \\ \vdots \end{bmatrix} = \sum_{i_1=0}^{\infty} \sum_{i_2=0}^{\infty} r_{|i_1-i_2|} z_1^{i_1} z_2^{i_2}$$

$$\triangleq R(z_1, z_2).$$

By way of the displacement residue equation (9.3.1), we see that the function $R(z_1, z_2)$ satisfies

$$(1 - z_1 z_2) R(z_1, z_2) = R_+(z_1) + r_0 + R_+(z_2), \quad (9.3.2)$$

where

$$R_+(z) \triangleq \sum_{i=1}^{\infty} r_i z^i.$$

Setting $z_2 = z_1^{-1}$ gives the power spectral density function

$$R_+(z_1) + r_0 + R_+(z_1^{-1}) = \sum_{i=-\infty}^{\infty} r_{|i|} z_1^i, \qquad |z_1| = 1.$$

Since this function along the unit circle $|z_1| = 1$ is simply the real part of $r_0 + 2R_+(z_1)$, the positivity of the power spectrum at (almost) all points on the unit circle reveals $r_0 + 2R_+(z_1)$ as a positive real function, i.e., one that may be continued analytically to all points in $|z_1| < 1$ with positive real part.

The spectral factorization problem may be advantageously treated by considering a dyadic decomposition of the displacement residue from (9.3.1), namely,

$$\begin{bmatrix} r_0 & r_1 & r_2 & \cdots \\ r_1 & 0 & 0 & \cdots \\ r_2 & 0 & 0 & \cdots \\ \vdots & \vdots & \vdots & \ddots \end{bmatrix} = \underbrace{\begin{bmatrix} \sqrt{r_0} \\ r_1/\sqrt{r_0} \\ r_2/\sqrt{r_0} \\ \vdots \end{bmatrix}}_{\triangleq\, a} [\cdot]^T - \underbrace{\begin{bmatrix} 0 \\ r_1/\sqrt{r_0} \\ r_2/\sqrt{r_0} \\ \vdots \end{bmatrix}}_{\triangleq\, b} [\cdot]^T, \qquad (9.3.3)$$

in which $[\cdot]$ means "repeat the previous vector." The two-variable form (9.3.2) induced by the displacement residue (9.3.1) may then be rewritten as

$$(1 - z_1 z_2) R(z_1, z_2) = a(z_1) a(z_2) - b(z_1) b(z_2),$$

in which

$$b(z) = R_+(z)/\sqrt{r_0}, \qquad a(z) = \sqrt{r_0} + b(z). \qquad (9.3.4)$$

According to a celebrated result, whose origins go back to the contributions of Toeplitz, Carathéodory, and Schur, the Toeplitz matrix R that induces $R(z_1, z_2)$ is positive (semi-) definite if and only if there exists a Schur function $S(z)$ (meaning that $S(z)$ is analytic in $|z| < 1$ and strictly bounded by unit magnitude there) that maps $a(z)$ into $b(z)$:

$$b(z) = S(z) a(z).$$

By way of (9.3.4), we see that $S(z)$ must relate to the positive real function $r_0 + 2R_+(z)$ according to

$$r_0 + 2R_+(z) = r_0 \frac{1 + S(z)}{1 - S(z)},$$

which is simply the Cayley transform. By a well-known property of this transform, $S(z)$ will indeed be a Schur function if and only if $r_0 + 2R_+(z)$ is a positive real function.

The virtue of this approach is best appreciated if we consider the case in which only partial information on the power spectrum is available. To this end, suppose we know (or have estimated) r_0 as well as $R_+(z)$ at N distinct points $z = \lambda_1, \ldots, \lambda_N$ inside the unit disk $0 < |z| < 1$. With the convention $\lambda_0 = 0$, this then determines, again by way of (9.3.4), the value pairs

$$[a(\lambda_0), b(\lambda_0)] = [\sqrt{r_0}, 0],$$
$$[a(\lambda_i), b(\lambda_i)] = [\sqrt{r_0} + R_+(\lambda_i)/\sqrt{r_0}, R_+(\lambda_i)/\sqrt{r_0}], \quad i = 1, 2, \ldots, N.$$

There then exists a Schur function $S(z)$ fulfilling the system of equations

$$b(\lambda_i) = S(\lambda_i) a(\lambda_i), \qquad i = 0, 1, \ldots, N,$$

Section 9.4. Tucker Product and Cumulant Tensors

if and only if a certain Pick matrix P, written elementwise as

$$P_{i_1,i_2} = \frac{a(\lambda_{i_1})\,a(\lambda_{i_2}^*) - b(\lambda_{i_1})\,b(\lambda_{i_2}^*)}{1 - \lambda_{i_1}\lambda_{i_2}^*} = R(\lambda_{i_1}, \lambda_{i_2}^*), \qquad (9.3.5)$$

is positive (semi-) definite. If positive semidefinite and singular, then $S(z)$ becomes a rational allpass function of degree equal to the rank of P. If positive definite, infinitely many solutions exist; they may be parametrized by various recursive constructive procedures (e.g., [DVK78], [Dym89a], [KS95a], [SKLC94]).

The recursive procedures for constructing $S(z)$ so cited also place in evidence a complementary Schur function, call it $Q(z)$, fulfilling

$$S(z)\,S(z^{-1}) + Q(z)\,Q(z^{-1}) = 1.$$

When P is positive definite, the solution set for $S(z)$ always includes choices fulfilling the constraint $1 - S(z) \neq 0$ for all $|z| = 1$. In this case, $S(z)$ and its complement $Q(z)$ yield

$$\widehat{H}(z) = \sqrt{r_0}\,\frac{Q(z)}{1 - S(z)}$$

as a stable and causal function, providing a candidate model for the correlation data $\{r_0, R_+(\lambda_i)\}$. This means that if the system $\widehat{H}(z)$ is driven by unit-variance white noise, its output sequence $\{\hat{y}(\cdot)\}$ fulfills the correlation matching properties

$$E[\hat{y}^2(n)] = r_0,$$

$$\sum_{k=1}^{\infty} E[\hat{y}(n)\,\hat{y}(n-k)]\,\lambda_i^k = R_+(\lambda_i), \quad i = 1, 2, \ldots, N.$$

A higher-order extension of this problem will be addressed in Sec. 9.7.

9.4 TUCKER PRODUCT AND CUMULANT TENSORS

Second-order cumulants reduce to conventional second-order statistics [Men91], i.e., $\mathrm{cum}[y(n-i_1), y(n-i_2)] = E[y(n-i_1)\,y(n-i_2)]$ with $E[\cdot]$ the expectation operator. This quantity depends on only two indices i_1 and i_2 such that calculations involving second-order cumulants reduce to basic operations on two-indexed arrays (i.e., matrices). Because higher-order cumulants are multi-indexed quantities, they may be profitably treated using tools of multi-indexed arrays, or tensors. Cumulants are also multilinear functions of their arguments [Men91], so it is useful to introduce some basic concepts of multilinear algebra applied to multi-indexed arrays. A particularly useful tool in this regard, to be reviewed in this section, is a multilinear matrix product called the Tucker product, in view of its early application to three-mode factor analysis in [Tuc64], [Tuc66]. Illustrations of its utility in cumulant analysis of system theory are included as well. For notational convenience, all vectors, matrices, and tensors will be indexed starting from zero rather than one.

Consider k matrices $\{A_i\}_{i=1}^k$, each of dimensions $M_i \times L$. A kth-order tensor $\mathcal{D}$, of dimensions $M_1 \times M_2 \times \cdots \times M_k$, may be defined from a Tucker product as

$$\mathcal{D}_{i_1,i_2,\ldots,i_k} = \sum_{l=0}^{L-1} (A_1)_{i_1,l}(A_2)_{i_2,l}\cdots(A_k)_{i_k,l}$$

$$\stackrel{\triangle}{=} A_1 \star A_2 \star \cdots \star A_k.$$

Example 1. Suppose each matrix A_i reduces to a column vector. The summation in the above definition becomes superfluous, and $\mathcal{D}$ may be written elementwise as

$$\mathcal{D}_{i_1,i_2,\ldots,i_k} = (A_1)_{i_1}(A_2)_{i_2}\cdots(A_k)_{i_k}.$$

The reader may think of this as a kth-order "outer product" since, if we consider the case $k = 2$, the tensor $\mathcal{D}_{i_1,i_2}$ becomes a matrix and the relation $\mathcal{D}_{i_1,i_2} = (A_1)_{i_1}(A_2)_{i_2}$ implies that the matrix $\mathcal{D}$ is the outer product $A_1 A_2^T$.

Example 2. Suppose instead that each matrix A_i is a row vector. The above definition yields the scalar

$$\mathcal{D}_{0,0,\ldots,0} = \sum_{l=0}^{L-1} (A_1)_l (A_2)_l \cdots (A_k)_l.$$

The reader may think of this as a kth-order "inner product" since, for the case $k = 2$, we recognize the sum as the the standard inner product of two real vectors A_1 and A_2.

$\diamond$

When all the factors A_i are matrices, the resulting tensor $\mathcal{D}$ may be considered as an array collecting all possible kth-order inner products of the rows of each factor or as the sum of L higher-order outer products.

Example 3. Consider $k = 3$ matrices A, B, and C, each having $L = 2$ columns. Partition these matrices columnwise as

$$A = [a_1 \ a_2], \quad B = [b_1 \ b_2], \quad C = [c_1 \ c_2].$$

Their third-order Tucker product may be written as

$$\mathcal{D} = A \star B \star C = (a_1 \star b_1 \star c_1) + (a_2 \star b_2 \star c_2)$$

involving $L = 2$ vector outer products.

$\diamond$

One can also consider a weighted version, using a kth-order tensor $\mathcal{T}$ as a kernel. The $\mathcal{T}$-product of matrices A_i, $i = 1, \ldots, k$, is the kth-order tensor

$$\mathcal{D}_{i_1,i_2,\ldots i_k} = \sum_{l_1=0}^{L_1-1} \sum_{l_2=0}^{L_2-1} \cdots \sum_{l_k=0}^{L_k-1} (A_1)_{i_1,l_1}(A_2)_{i_2,l_2}\cdots(A_k)_{i_k,l_k}(\mathcal{T})_{l_1,l_2,\ldots,l_k},$$
$$\stackrel{\triangle}{=} A_1 \stackrel{\mathcal{T}}{\star} A_2 \stackrel{\mathcal{T}}{\star} \cdots \stackrel{\mathcal{T}}{\star} A_k,$$

where all dimensions are assumed compatible. One may check that if $\mathcal{T}$ is the identity tensor $[\mathcal{T}_{i_1,\ldots,i_k} = \delta(i_1,\ldots,i_k)]$, the weighted Tucker product reduces to the standard Tucker product.

Example 4. Suppose we are given three column vectors v, w, x containing random variables, whose third-order cross cumulants are collected into the tensor $\mathcal{T}$:

$$\mathcal{T}_{i_1,i_2,i_3} = \text{cum}[v_{i_1}, w_{i_2}, x_{i_3}].$$

Suppose each vector undergoes a linear transformation, using matrices A, B, and C:

$$v' = Av, \quad w' = Bw, \quad x' = Cx.$$

Section 9.4. Tucker Product and Cumulant Tensors

Let $\mathcal{D}$ be the new third-order cross-cumulant tensor, i.e.,

$$\mathcal{D}_{i_1,i_2,i_3} = \text{cum}[v'_{i_1}, w'_{i_2}, x'_{i_3}].$$

Cumulants are multilinear functions of their arguments, and the new tensor $\mathcal{D}$ relates to the old one $\mathcal{T}$ by the multilinear transformation

$$\mathcal{D} = A \overset{\mathcal{T}}{\star} B \overset{\mathcal{T}}{\star} C,$$

using the weighted Tucker product. $\diamond$

Some further properties are summarized for the reader's convenience:

1. When specialized to a second-order tensor (or matrix) T,

$$A_1 \overset{T}{\star} A_2 = A_1 \, T \, A_2^T,$$

in which T denotes matrix or vector transposition, with the usual matrix product interpretation on the right-hand side.

2. If $x = [x_1, x_2, \ldots]$ is a row vector and I is the identity matrix, then

$$\left(I \overset{\mathcal{T}}{\star} \cdots \overset{\mathcal{T}}{\star} I \overset{\mathcal{T}}{\star} x\right)_{i_1,\ldots,i_{k-1}} = \sum_l x_l \, \mathcal{T}_{i_1,\ldots,i_{k-1},l}$$

yields a tensor of order $k-1$.

3. If $e_{i_1}, \ldots, e_{i_k}$ are k unit row vectors each having a 1 in the position indexed i_k, then

$$\mathcal{T}_{i_1,i_2,\ldots,i_k} = e_{i_1} \overset{\mathcal{T}}{\star} e_{i_2} \overset{\mathcal{T}}{\star} \cdots \overset{\mathcal{T}}{\star} e_{i_k}.$$

4. If $\text{vec}(\cdot)$ is the operator which rearranges a tensor into a vector according to

$$\text{vec}(\mathcal{T}) = \begin{bmatrix} \mathcal{T}_{00\ldots 0} \\ \mathcal{T}_{10\ldots 0} \\ \vdots \\ \mathcal{T}_{01\ldots 0} \\ \mathcal{T}_{11\ldots 0} \\ \vdots \end{bmatrix},$$

then the equation

$$\mathcal{S} = A_1 \overset{\mathcal{T}}{\star} A_2 \overset{\mathcal{T}}{\star} \cdots \overset{\mathcal{T}}{\star} A_k$$

is equivalent to

$$\text{vec}(\mathcal{S}) = \left(A_1 \otimes A_2 \otimes \cdots \otimes A_k\right) \text{vec}(\mathcal{T}),$$

where $\otimes$ denotes the conventional Kronecker product of matrices [Bre78], [RM89].

5. *Composition property.* If $\mathcal{T} = B_1 \overset{\mathcal{D}}{\star} B_2 \overset{\mathcal{D}}{\star} \cdots \overset{\mathcal{D}}{\star} B_k$ with $\mathcal{D}$ some kth-order tensor, then $\mathcal{S} = A_1 \overset{\mathcal{T}}{\star} A_2 \overset{\mathcal{T}}{\star} \cdots \overset{\mathcal{T}}{\star} A_k$ implies that

$$\mathcal{S} = (A_1 B_1) \overset{\mathcal{D}}{\star} (A_2 B_2) \overset{\mathcal{D}}{\star} \cdots \overset{\mathcal{D}}{\star} (A_k B_k). \tag{9.4.1}$$

9.5 EXAMPLES OF CUMULANTS AND TENSORS

We now show some simple examples relating the cumulants of the output process of a linear system to tensors constructed from the Tucker product. We set

$$y(n) = h_1 u(n-1) + h_2 u(n-2) + h_3 u(n-3) + \cdots,$$

where $\{u(\cdot)\}$ is an i.i.d. sequence and the transfer function $H(z) = \sum_i h_i z^i$ is strictly causal. (If $H(z)$ were causal but not strictly causal, the system $zH(z)$ would be strictly causal and would generate the same output cumulants; the strictly causal constraint on $H(z)$ leads to simpler relations later on.)

Example 5. Consider a strictly causal system initially at rest. The output sequence becomes

$$\begin{bmatrix} y(0) \\ y(1) \\ y(2) \\ \vdots \end{bmatrix} = \underbrace{\begin{bmatrix} 0 & 0 & 0 & \cdots \\ h_1 & 0 & 0 & \ddots \\ h_2 & h_1 & 0 & \ddots \\ \vdots & \vdots & \vdots & \ddots \end{bmatrix}}_{\triangleq H} \begin{bmatrix} u(0) \\ u(1) \\ u(2) \\ \vdots \end{bmatrix},$$

where H is the convolution matrix of the system. If $\{u(\cdot)\}$ is an i.i.d. sequence, its kth-order cumulants become

$$\mathrm{cum}[u(i_1), u(i_2), \ldots, u(i_k)] = \begin{cases} \gamma_k, & i_1 = i_2 = \cdots = i_k, \\ 0 & \text{otherwise.} \end{cases}$$

The cumulant tensor built from such an i.i.d. sequence is clearly $\gamma_k \mathcal{I}$ (where $\mathcal{I}$ is the identity tensor). The kth-order cumulant tensor $\mathcal{T}$ with elements indexed from zero,

$$(\mathcal{T}_1)_{i_1, i_2, \ldots, i_k} = \mathrm{cum}[y(i_1), y(i_2), \ldots, y(i_k)],$$

then becomes

$$\mathcal{T}_1 = \gamma_k \cdot H \star H \star \cdots \star H.$$

This tensor is, of course, symmetric (i.e., invariant to any permutation of the indices) since cumulants are symmetric functions of their arguments [Men91].

Example 6. Consider rewriting the input-output relation in the form

$$\begin{bmatrix} y(n) \\ y(n-1) \\ y(n-2) \\ \vdots \end{bmatrix} = \underbrace{\begin{bmatrix} 0 & h_1 & h_2 & \cdots \\ 0 & 0 & h_1 & \cdots \\ 0 & 0 & 0 & \cdots \\ \vdots & \ddots & \ddots & \ddots \end{bmatrix}}_{H^T} \begin{bmatrix} u(n) \\ u(n-1) \\ u(n-2) \\ \vdots \end{bmatrix}.$$

We suppose that n is sufficiently large for any initial conditions to have died out, thus yielding a stationary process for $\{y(\cdot)\}$. Taking now the kth-order output cumulant tensor as

$$(\mathcal{T}_2)_{i_1, i_2, \ldots, i_k} = \mathrm{cum}[y(n-i_1), y(n-i_2), \ldots, y(n-i_k)],$$

with elements again indexed from zero, we obtain

$$\mathcal{T}_2 = \gamma_k \cdot H^T \star H^T \star \cdots \star H^T.$$

Section 9.5. Examples of Cumulants and Tensors

Note that this tensor is Toeplitz (or invariant along any diagonal: $(T_2)_{i_1,\ldots,i_k} = (T_2)_{i_1+l,\ldots,i_k+l}$), due to the stationarity of the process $\{y(\cdot)\}$.

$\Diamond$

We shall give special attention to the Toeplitz tensor of Ex. 6. Consideration of the structured tensor of Ex. 5, however, leads to the following interesting identity. For any cumulant of order k, we have [Gri96]

$$\begin{aligned}\left(T_2 - T_1\right)/\gamma_k &= H^T \star \cdots \star H^T - H \star \cdots \star H \\ &= \Gamma_H \star \cdots \star \Gamma_H,\end{aligned} \qquad (9.5.1)$$

where Γ_H is the infinite Hankel matrix

$$\Gamma_H = \begin{bmatrix} h_1 & h_2 & h_3 & \cdots \\ h_2 & h_3 & h_4 & \cdots \\ h_3 & h_4 & h_5 & \cdots \\ \vdots & \vdots & \vdots & \vdots \end{bmatrix}.$$

Hankel matrices take a special significance in system theory [AAK71], [Glo84]. For now we note that, since $H \star \cdots \star H$ vanishes along all faces (where any index equals zero), the faces of $H^T \star \cdots \star H^T$ coincide with those of $\Gamma_H \star \cdots \star \Gamma_H$, which will prove convenient in what follows.

When specialized to second-order arrays, the identity (9.5.1) reads as

$$H^T H - H H^T = \Gamma_H \Gamma_H, \quad \text{or} \quad H^T H = H H^T + \Gamma_H \Gamma_H.$$

This implies the existence of an orthogonal matrix Q (satisfying $QQ^T = Q^TQ = I$) fulfilling

$$\begin{bmatrix} H \\ O \end{bmatrix} = Q \begin{bmatrix} H^T \\ \Gamma_H \end{bmatrix}.$$

One is naturally led to inquire whether there exist square matrices that appear "orthogonal" with respect to higher-order Tucker products, i.e., square matrices Q for which $Q \star Q \star \cdots \star Q = \mathcal{I}$. If Q is an infinite matrix, it is readily verified that the choice $Q = Z^T$ (the "up-shift" matrix) yields $Z^T \star \cdots \star Z^T = \mathcal{I}$, the kth-order identity tensor, for any order $k \geq 2$. Similarly, choosing Q as any permutation matrix likewise leads to $Q \star \cdots \star Q = \mathcal{I}$, for any order $k \geq 2$. And, for k even, choosing Q as any signed permutation matrix (i.e., having a sole entry of ± 1 in each row) still works.

The following result shows that, in finite dimensions, the list of "higher-order orthogonal" matrices is short.

Theorem 9.5.1 (Higher-Order Orthogonal Matrices). *A square matrix Q of finite dimensions fulfills the kth-order orthogonality*

$$\underbrace{Q \star Q \star \cdots \star Q}_{k \geq 3 \text{ terms}} = \mathcal{I} \qquad (9.5.2)$$

if and only if Q is a permutation matrix (k odd) or a signed permutation matrix (k even).

Proof: Suppose Q has dimensions $L \times L$, with L arbitrary, and write out the matrix as

$$Q = \begin{bmatrix} q_1^T \\ q_2^T \\ \vdots \\ q_L^T \end{bmatrix} = \begin{bmatrix} q_{11} & q_{12} & \cdots & q_{1L} \\ q_{21} & q_{22} & \cdots & q_{2L} \\ \vdots & \vdots & \ddots & \vdots \\ q_{L1} & q_{L2} & \cdots & q_{LL} \end{bmatrix}.$$

If $v^T = [v_1, \ldots, v_L]$ and $w^T = [w_1, \ldots, w_L]$ are two row vectors, their Hadamard (or componentwise) product will be denoted as

$$v^T * w^T = [v_1 w_1, \ldots, v_L w_L].$$

Now, the constraint (9.5.2) can be written in vector inner product form as

$$\left(\underbrace{q_{i_1} * \cdots * q_{i_m}}_{m \text{ terms}} \right)^T \left(\underbrace{q_{i_{m+1}} * \cdots * q_{i_k}}_{k - m \text{ terms}} \right) = \delta(i_1, i_2, \ldots, i_k) \tag{9.5.3}$$

for any $1 \leq m < k$. Upon choosing $i_1 = i_2 = \cdots = i_k$, we see immediately that none of the row vectors q_l^T can be the zero vector.

Let us show next that the row vectors must be linearly independent. First note from (9.5.3) that

$$\left(\underbrace{q_1 * \cdots * q_1}_{k - 1 \text{ terms}} \right)^T q_1 = 1 \quad \text{and} \quad \left(\underbrace{q_1 * \cdots * q_1}_{k - 1 \text{ terms}} \right)^T q_l = 0, \quad l = 2, 3, \ldots, L.$$

Suppose to the contrary that the vectors are linearly dependent. We can then find nonzero constants $\alpha_1, \ldots, \alpha_L$ such that

$$\alpha_1 q_1 + \cdots + \alpha_L q_L = 0.$$

If only one of the terms α_l were nonzero, the corresponding vector q_l would be zero, in contradiction with all vectors being distinct from the zero vector. Suppose then that two or more terms from $\alpha_1, \ldots, \alpha_L$ are nonzero. By permuting the indices if necessary, we may suppose that $\alpha_1 \neq 0$ and $\alpha_2 \neq 0$ (and possibly others as well). We may then write q_1 as

$$q_1 = -\frac{\alpha_2}{\alpha_1} q_2 - \frac{\alpha_3}{\alpha_1} q_3 - \cdots.$$

This yields a contradiction as

$$1 = \left(\underbrace{q_1 * \cdots * q_1}_{k - 1 \text{ terms}} \right)^T q_1$$

$$= \left(\underbrace{q_1 * \cdots * q_1}_{k - 1 \text{ terms}} \right)^T \left(-\frac{\alpha_2}{\alpha_1} q_2 - \frac{\alpha_3}{\alpha_1} q_3 - \cdots \right) = 0.$$

Accordingly, the vectors $q_1, \ldots, q_L$ must be linearly independent.

Now, from (9.5.3) we can write

$$\text{for all } i \neq j, \quad \left(\underbrace{q_i * \cdots * q_i}_{k - n \text{ terms}} * \underbrace{q_j * \cdots * q_j}_{n - 1 \text{ terms}} \right)^T q_l = 0, \quad l = 1, 2, \ldots, L,$$

for any choice of n between 2 and $k-1$. Since the vectors $q_1, \ldots, q_L$ are linearly independent, they span $\mathbb{R}^L$. The only vector in $\mathbb{R}^L$ orthogonal to $\mathbb{R}^L$ is, of course, the zero vector. The previous expression then implies that

$$\text{for all } i \neq j, \quad \underbrace{q_i * \cdots * q_i}_{k-n \text{ terms}} * \underbrace{q_j * \cdots * q_j}_{n-1 \text{ terms}} = 0,$$

which reads componentwise as

$$(q_{im})^{k-n}(q_{jm})^{n-1} = 0 \quad \text{for all } i \neq j.$$

This simplifies to

$$\text{if } q_{im} \neq 0 \text{ then } q_{jm} = 0 \quad \text{for all } j \neq i.$$

As such, each column of Q can have only one nonzero entry. The same must now apply to each row of Q, for if a given row were to have two or more nonzero entries, then another row would be left with no nonzero entries, giving a zero vector. From the constraint

$$\sum_{l=1}^{L} q_{il}^k = 1,$$

it follows easily that the sole nonzero entry of each row q_i^T must be $+1$ if k is odd, or ± 1 if k is even, giving Q as a (signed) permutation matrix.

$\diamond$

9.6 DISPLACEMENT STRUCTURE FOR TENSORS

In this section we develop various relations that connect the displacement structure of a cumulant tensor to polyspectral functions. Relations to cumulant interpolation will follow in Sec. 9.7.

Let $\mathcal{T}$ be a given kth-order tensor and let Z still denote the shift matrix with ones on the subdiagonal and zeros elsewhere. The kth-order tensor

$$\mathcal{D} = \underbrace{Z \stackrel{T}{\star} Z \stackrel{T}{\star} \cdots \stackrel{T}{\star} Z}_{k \text{ terms}}$$

relates to $\mathcal{T}$ as

$$\mathcal{D}_{i_1,\ldots,i_k} = \begin{cases} 0 & \text{if } i_1 = 0 \text{ and/or} \ldots \text{and/or } i_k = 0, \\ \mathcal{T}_{i_1-1,\ldots,i_k-1} & \text{otherwise.} \end{cases}$$

Example 7. If we take for $\mathcal{T}$ the Toeplitz tensor of Ex. 6, then its displacement residue

$$\mathcal{T} - Z \stackrel{T}{\star} Z \stackrel{T}{\star} \cdots \stackrel{T}{\star} Z$$

will coincide with $\mathcal{T}$ along all faces (when at least one index equals zero) and will vanish at all interior points (where all indices are nonzero).

$\diamond$

If we instead consider a Hankel-based tensor, i.e.,

$$\mathcal{T} = \Gamma_H \star \Gamma_H \star \cdots \star \Gamma_H, \tag{9.6.1}$$

we can obtain an interesting relation for the up-shifted displacement residue, using the up-shift matrix Z^T.

Lemma 9.6.1 (Displacement Residue). *The tensor T from (9.6.1) fulfills*

$$T - Z^T \overset{T}{\star} Z^T \overset{T}{\star} \cdots \overset{T}{\star} Z^T = h \star h \star \cdots \star h$$

with $h = [h_1, h_2, h_3, \ldots]^T$.

Proof: We recall that a Hankel matrix satisfies (by definition of Hankel) the shift equation

$$Z^T \Gamma_H = \Gamma_H Z.$$

Since $T = \Gamma_H \star \cdots \star \Gamma_H$, we see by a direct calculation that

$$\begin{aligned}
T - Z^T \overset{T}{\star} Z^T \overset{T}{\star} \cdots \overset{T}{\star} Z^T &= \Gamma_H \star \cdots \star \Gamma_H - \left((Z^T \Gamma_H) \star \cdots \star (Z^T \Gamma_H)\right) \\
&= \Gamma_H \star \cdots \star \Gamma_H - \left((\Gamma_H Z) \star \cdots \star (\Gamma_H Z)\right) \\
&= \Gamma_H \star \cdots \star \Gamma_H - \left(\Gamma_H \overset{J}{\star} \cdots \overset{J}{\star} \Gamma_H\right),
\end{aligned}$$

in which the final line comes from the composition property with $J = Z \star \cdots \star Z$. This latter tensor reads elementwise as

$$(J)_{i_1,\ldots,i_k} = \begin{cases} 1, & i_1 = \cdots = i_k \geq 1, \\ 0 & \text{otherwise.} \end{cases}$$

This allows us to continue as

$$\left(\Gamma_H \star \cdots \star \Gamma_H\right) - \left(\Gamma_H \overset{J}{\star} \cdots \overset{J}{\star} \Gamma_H\right) = \Gamma_H \overset{I-J}{\star} \cdots \overset{I-J}{\star} \Gamma_H,$$

in which $I - J$ vanishes everywhere except in the leading entry, which equals one, thus giving $I - J = e_0^T \star \cdots \star e_0^T$, in which e_0^T is the unit column vector with a 1 in the leading entry. This then gives, again by the composition property,

$$\Gamma_H \overset{I-J}{\star} \cdots \overset{I-J}{\star} \Gamma_H = (\Gamma_H e_0^T) \star \cdots \star (\Gamma_H e_0^T) = h \star \cdots \star h$$

as claimed. $\diamond$

9.6.1 Relation to the Polyspectrum

We return now to the Toeplitz tensor

$$T_{i_1,i_2,\ldots,i_k} = \operatorname{cum}[y(n-i_1), y(n-i_2), \ldots, y(n-i_k)]$$

with the assumption that $\{y(\cdot)\}$ is a stationary process, although not necessarily a linear process. Its cumulant lags of order k involve the relative lags of the first $k-1$ arguments with respect to the final argument, i.e.,

$$c_{i_1,i_2,\ldots,i_{k-1}} = \operatorname{cum}[y(n-i_1), y(n-i_2), \ldots, y(n-i_{k-1}), y(n)].$$

These are simply the elements of the final face of T, i.e.,

$$\left(I \overset{T}{\star} \cdots \overset{T}{\star} I \overset{T}{\star} e_0\right)_{i_1,\ldots,i_{k-1}} = c_{i_1,\ldots,i_{k-1}}.$$

The kth-order polyspectrum is defined as the bilateral $(k-1)$-dimensional Fourier transform of the cumulants,

$$R(z_1, z_2, \ldots, z_{k-1}) \qquad (9.6.2)$$

Section 9.6. Displacement Structure for Tensors

$$\triangleq \sum_{i_1=-\infty}^{+\infty} \sum_{i_2=-\infty}^{+\infty} \cdots \sum_{i_{k-1}=-\infty}^{+\infty} c_{i_1,i_2,\ldots,i_{k-1}} \, z_1^{i_1}, z_2^{i_2} \cdots z_{k-1}^{i_{k-1}},$$

whenever the sum converges along the unit polycircle $|z_1| = \cdots = |z_{k-1}| = 1$.

Introduce the infinite row vector

$$\mathbf{z}_i \triangleq \begin{bmatrix} 1 & z_i & z_i^2 & z_i^3 & \cdots \end{bmatrix}, \qquad |z_i| < 1,$$

containing successive powers of the complex variable z_i. We may then introduce the k-variable scalar "generating function," whose coefficients are the elements of the tensor $\mathcal{T}$, as

$$T(z_1, z_2, \ldots, z_k) = \mathbf{z}_1 \overset{\mathcal{T}}{\star} \mathbf{z}_2 \overset{\mathcal{T}}{\star} \cdots \overset{\mathcal{T}}{\star} \mathbf{z}_k = \sum_{i_1=0}^{\infty} \sum_{i_2=0}^{\infty} \cdots \sum_{i_k=0}^{\infty} \mathcal{T}_{i_1,i_2,\ldots,i_k} z_1^{i_1} z_2^{i_2} \cdots z_k^{i_k}.$$

Note that this function depends on k complex variables, whereas the polyspectrum from (9.6.2) involves only $k-1$ complex variables. We pursue now how to reconcile these two functions.

Introducing the displacement residue

$$\mathcal{S} = \mathcal{T} - Z \overset{\mathcal{T}}{\star} \cdots \overset{\mathcal{T}}{\star} Z,$$

its multivariable function becomes

$$\begin{aligned} S(z_1, \ldots, z_k) &= \mathbf{z}_1 \overset{\mathcal{S}}{\star} \cdots \overset{\mathcal{S}}{\star} \mathbf{z}_k \\ &= \sum_{i_1=0}^{\infty} \cdots \sum_{i_k=0}^{\infty} \mathcal{S}_{i_1,\ldots,i_k} z_1^{i_1} \cdots z_k^{i_k} \\ &= (1 - z_1 z_2 \cdots z_k) T(z_1, z_2, \ldots, z_k). \end{aligned}$$

Because $\mathcal{T}$ is a Toeplitz tensor, its displacement residue $\mathcal{S}$ vanishes at all interior points. We shall call $S(z_1, \ldots, z_k)$ the polyspectral residue function, based on the following identity.

Lemma 9.6.2 (Polyspectral Residue Function). *With*

$$S(z_1, \ldots, z_k) = (1 - z_1 \cdots z_k) T(z_1, \ldots, z_k),$$

the polyspectrum is obtained by setting $z_k = (z_1 \cdots z_{k-1})^{-1}$:

$$R(z_1, \ldots, z_{k-1}) = S(z_1, \ldots, z_{k-1}, (z_1 \cdots z_{k-1})^{-1}).$$

Proof: This identity comes from exploiting various symmetry relations linking cumulants of stationary processes. We illustrate the proof for third-order cumulants, as the verification for higher-order cumulants is quite similar.

Introduce the constant, one-dimensional causal, and two-dimensional causal parts of $S(z_1, z_2, z_3)$ as

$$c_{00} = S(0,0,0),$$

$$S_+(z_1) = \sum_{i_1=1}^{\infty} c_{i_1,0} z_1^{i_1} = S(z_1, 0, 0) - c_{00},$$

$$S_{2+}(z_1, z_2) = \sum_{i_1=1}^{\infty} \sum_{i_2=1}^{\infty} c_{i_1,i_2} z_1^{i_1} z_2^{i_2} = S(z_1, z_2, 0) - c_{00} - S_+(z_1) - S_+(z_2).$$

Now, $S(z_1, z_2, z_3)$ is a symmetric function of the complex variables z_1, z_2, and z_3 and may be expressed as

$$S(z_1, z_2, z_3) = c_{00} + S_+(z_1) + S_+(z_2) + S_+(z_3) + S_{2+}(z_1, z_2) + S_{2+}(z_2, z_3) + S_{2+}(z_1, z_3).$$

Setting $z_3 = (z_1 z_2)^{-1}$ gives

$$\begin{aligned} S(z_1, z_2, (z_1 z_2)^{-1}) &= c_{00} + S_+(z_1) + S_+(z_2) + S_+((z_1 z_2)^{-1}) \\ &\quad + S_{2+}(z_1, z_2) + S_{2+}(z_2, (z_1 z_2)^{-1}) \\ &\quad + S_{2+}(z_1, (z_1 z_2)^{-1}). \end{aligned} \qquad (9.6.3)$$

By exploiting stationarity, we see that

$$c_{i,0} = \text{cum}[y(n-i), y(n), y(n)] = \text{cum}[y(n), y(n+i), y(n+i)] = c_{-i,-i},$$

so that

$$S_+((z_1 z_2)^{-1}) = \sum_{i=1}^{\infty} c_{i,0} z_1^{-i} z_2^{-i} = \sum_{i=1}^{\infty} c_{-i,-i} z_1^{-i} z_2^{-i},$$

which coincides with the z-transform of the negative diagonal slice $c_{-i,-i}$.

In a similar way, stationarity again gives

$$\begin{aligned} c_{i_1, i_2} &= \text{cum}[y(n-i_1), y(n-i_2), y(n)] \\ &= \text{cum}[y(n-i_1+i_2), y(n), y(n+i_2)] = c_{i_2-i_1, -i_2}, \end{aligned}$$

so that

$$S_{2+}(z_1, (z_1 z_2)^{-1}) = \sum_{i_1=1}^{\infty} \sum_{i_2=1}^{\infty} c_{i_1, i_2} z_1^{i_1} [(z_1 z_2)^{-1}]^{i_2} = \sum_{i_1=1}^{\infty} \sum_{i_2=1}^{\infty} c_{i_2-i_1, -i_2} z_1^{i_1-i_2} z_2^{-i_2}$$

and, in the same way,

$$S_{2+}(z_2, (z_1 z_2)^{-1}) = \sum_{i_1=1}^{\infty} \sum_{i_2=1}^{\infty} c_{-i_1, i_1-i_2} z_1^{-i_1} z_2^{i_2-i_1}.$$

Figure 9.1 illustrates the (i_1, i_2)-plane, in which each point represents a sample value c_{i_1, i_2} and the dashed lines indicate which samples enter into which sum from (9.6.3). The sum from (9.6.3) is seen to incorporate the doubly two-sided sequence c_{i_1, i_2}, i.e.,

$$S(z_1, z_2, (z_1 z_2)^{-1}) = \sum_{i_1=-\infty}^{+\infty} \sum_{i_2=-\infty}^{+\infty} c_{i_1, i_2} z_1^{i_1} z_2^{i_2},$$

yielding the bispectrum as claimed.

$\diamond$

Remark. The decomposition into $S_+(z_1)$ and $S_{2+}(z_1, z_2)$ can be considered, for this third-order case, a type of analytic continuation into the unit bidisk ($|z_1| < 1$, $|z_2| < 1$) of the bispectrum, with the bispectrum obtained along the boundary $|z_1| = |z_2| = 1$ by the symmetry relation (9.6.3). An open problem here is to determine the set of admissible functions for $S_+(z_1)$ and $S_{2+}(z_1, z_2)$ for which (9.6.3) yields a *valid* bispectrum, i.e., corresponding to *some* stationary process. An analogous open question applies to higher orders as well; for second-order statistics, admissibility reduces to a positive real constraint.

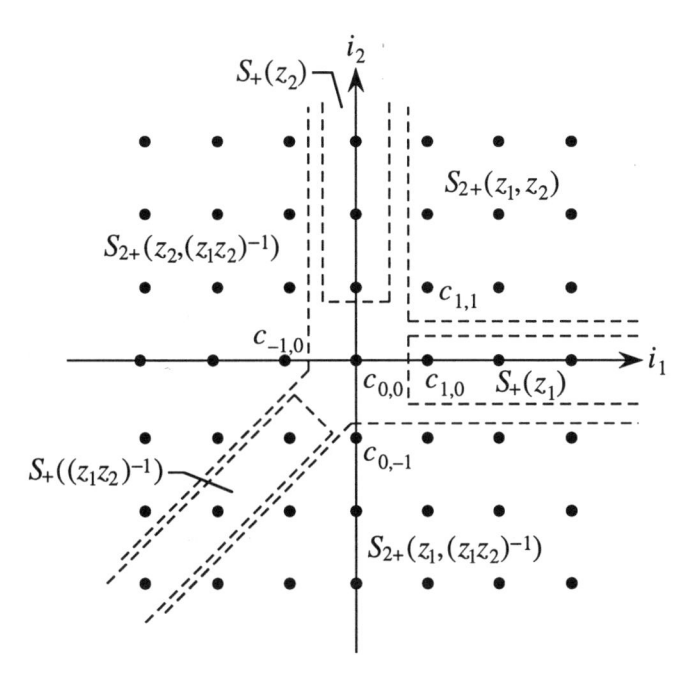

Section 9.6. Displacement Structure for Tensors 261

Figure 9.1. Illustrating cumulant sample values c_{i_1,i_2} in the (i_1,i_2)-plane and which terms enter into which sum from (9.6.3).

9.6.2 The Linear Case

In this section we further examine the structure of the polyspectral residue function for the special case in which the Toeplitz tensor $\mathcal{T}$ is obtained from the cumulants of a linear process. We recall from Ex. 6 that the Toeplitz tensor $\mathcal{T}$ is Tucker factorable as

$$\mathcal{T} = \gamma_k \cdot \underbrace{H^T \star \cdots \star H^T}_{k \text{ terms}},$$

in which H is the convolution matrix of the linear system and γ_k is the kth-order cumulant of the i.i.d. driving sequence to the system. We shall study the $(k-1)$-variable function obtained from $T(z_1, \ldots, z_k)$ by setting the final complex variable z_k to zero:

$$T(z_1, \ldots, z_{k-1}, 0) = \sum_{i_1=0}^{\infty} \cdots \sum_{i_{k-1}=0}^{\infty} c_{i_1,\ldots,i_{k-1}} z_1^{i_1} \cdots z_{k-1}^{i_{k-1}}.$$

Observe that this function involves unilateral z-transforms in each index and differs from the polyspectrum of (9.6.2), which involves bilateral z-transforms in each index. We seek a closed-form expression for $T(z_1, \ldots, z_{k-1}, 0)$ in terms of the system $H(z)$, when this transfer function is rational.

We exploit the fact that the faces of the Toeplitz tensor $\mathcal{T}$ coincide with those of the Hankel-based tensor $\gamma_k \cdot \Gamma_H \star \cdots \star \Gamma_H$ [cf. (9.5.1)], i.e.,

$$(\mathcal{T})_{i_1,\ldots,i_{k-1},0} = \left(\gamma_k \cdot H^T \star \cdots \star H^T\right)_{i_1,\ldots,i_{k-1},0} = \left(\gamma_k \cdot \Gamma_H \star \cdots \star \Gamma_H\right)_{i_1,\ldots,i_{k-1},0},$$

whose multidimensional z-transform is easier to treat.

Suppose now that $H(z)$ is rational; this means that we have a realization of the form

$$x(n+1) = Ax(n) + bu(n),$$
$$y(n) = cx(n),$$

in which $H(z) = zc(I - zA)^{-1}b$. We let M denote the state vector dimension. The Hankel matrix Γ_H can then be decomposed as

$$\Gamma_H = \underbrace{\begin{bmatrix} c \\ cA \\ cA^2 \\ \vdots \end{bmatrix}}_{\mathcal{O}} \underbrace{\begin{bmatrix} b & Ab & A^2 & \cdots \end{bmatrix}}_{\mathcal{C}}$$

in terms of the infinite horizon observability and controllability matrices, $\mathcal{O}$ and $\mathcal{C}$, respectively. The full kth-order Hankel-based tensor becomes

$$\gamma_k \cdot \Gamma_H \star \cdots \star \Gamma_H = \gamma_k \cdot (\mathcal{OC}) \star \cdots \star (\mathcal{OC})$$
$$= \mathcal{O} \overset{\mathcal{P}}{\star} \cdots \overset{\mathcal{P}}{\star} \mathcal{O}$$

using the composition property in the second line, in which $\mathcal{P}$ is the kth-order tensor

$$\mathcal{P} = \gamma_k \cdot \mathcal{C} \star \cdots \star \mathcal{C}. \tag{9.6.4}$$

The following lemma is in direct analogy with the second-order case.

Lemma 9.6.3 (Higher-Order Lyapunov Equation). *The kth-order tensor $\mathcal{P}$ from (9.6.4) fulfills the (higher-order) Lyapunov equation*

$$\mathcal{P} - \underbrace{A \overset{\mathcal{P}}{\star} A \overset{\mathcal{P}}{\star} \cdots \overset{\mathcal{P}}{\star} A}_{k \text{ terms}} = \gamma_k \cdot \underbrace{b \star b \star \cdots \star b}_{k \text{ terms}}. \tag{9.6.5}$$

If $\lambda_1, \ldots, \lambda_M$ are the eigenvalues of A, then this equation admits a unique solution $\mathcal{P}$ provided

$$\lambda_{i_1} \lambda_{i_2} \cdots \lambda_{i_k} \neq 1 \quad \text{for all } i_1, \ldots, i_k. \tag{9.6.6}$$

With respect to the state equation $x(n+1) = Ax(n) + bu(n)$, with A stable ($|\lambda_i| < 1$), $\mathcal{P}$ is the state cumulant tensor

$$\mathcal{P}_{i_1,\ldots,i_k} = \text{cum}[x_{i_1}(n), \ldots, x_{i_k}(n)].$$

Proof: The verification follows closely that familiar from second-order statistics [AM79] and is included for completeness. To begin, with $\mathcal{P} = \gamma_k \cdot \mathcal{C} \star \cdots \star \mathcal{C}$, the composition property gives

$$A \overset{\mathcal{P}}{\star} \cdots \overset{\mathcal{P}}{\star} A = \gamma_k \cdot (A\mathcal{C}) \star \cdots \star (A\mathcal{C}).$$

Here we observe that

$$A\mathcal{C} = A \begin{bmatrix} b & Ab & A^2b & \cdots \end{bmatrix}$$
$$= \begin{bmatrix} b & Ab & A^2b & \cdots \end{bmatrix} Z = \mathcal{C} Z,$$

Section 9.6. Displacement Structure for Tensors

so that

$$P - A \overset{P}{\star} \cdots \overset{P}{\star} A = \gamma_k \cdot \left(C \star \cdots \star C \right) - \gamma_k \left((CZ) \star \cdots \star (CZ) \right)$$
$$= \gamma_k \cdot C \overset{\mathcal{J}}{\star} \cdots \overset{\mathcal{J}}{\star} C, \tag{9.6.7}$$

in which $\mathcal{J} = \mathcal{I} - Z \star \cdots \star Z$. Since $\mathcal{J}$ has a 1 in the leading entry and vanishes elsewhere, we can write

$$\mathcal{J} = e_0^T \star \cdots \star e_0^T,$$

where e_0^T is the unit column vector with a 1 in its leading entry. This combines with (9.6.7) to give

$$P - A \overset{P}{\star} \cdots \overset{P}{\star} A = \gamma_k \cdot (Ce_0^T) \star \cdots \star (Ce_0^T) = \gamma_k \cdot b \star \cdots \star b,$$

yielding the Lyapunov equation (9.6.5).

For existence and uniqueness, the vectorized tensor vec($\mathcal{P}$) fulfills

$$(I - A \otimes \cdots \otimes A) \, \text{vec}(\mathcal{P}) = \gamma_k \cdot b \otimes \cdots \otimes b.$$

With $\{\lambda_i\}$ denoting the eigenvalues of A, those of its k-term Kronecker product $A \otimes \cdots \otimes A$ become $\lambda_{i_1} \cdots \lambda_{i_k}$ as the indices $i_1, \ldots, i_k$ range over all M^k possibilities. The relation (9.6.6) is then equivalent to invertibility of $I - A \otimes \cdots \otimes A$, which in turn is equivalent to existence and uniqueness of a solution vec($\mathcal{P}$) and hence of $\mathcal{P}$ itself.

For the final part, (asymptotic) stationarity implies that

$$\text{cum}[x_{i_1}(n+1), x_{i_2}(n+1), \ldots, x_{i_k}(n+1)] = \text{cum}[x_{i_1}(n), x_{i_2}(n), \ldots, x_{i_k}(n)].$$

It suffices to show that these values build a state cumulant tensor which indeed satisfies the given Lyapunov equation. Now, $x(n)$ depends only on past values $u(n-1)$, $u(n-2), \ldots$ of the input. By the i.i.d. assumption on $\{u(\cdot)\}$, cross cumulants involving $x(n)$ and $u(n)$ vanish, and a simple calculation shows that the state cumulant tensor satisfies the given Lyapunov equation.

$\diamond$

Let $\mathcal{T}^{(0)}$ denote the face of the Toeplitz tensor $\mathcal{T}$, i.e.,

$$\mathcal{T}^{(0)}_{i_1,\ldots,i_{k-1}} = \mathcal{T}_{i_1,\ldots,i_{k-1},0} = c_{i_1,\ldots,i_{k-1}}.$$

This face coincides with that of its Hankel-based counterpart, giving

$$\mathcal{T}^{(0)} = \mathcal{O} \overset{P}{\star} \cdots \overset{P}{\star} \mathcal{O} \overset{P}{\star} c.$$

In particular, an expression for each output cumulant contained on the face $\mathcal{T}^{(0)}$ becomes

$$c_{i_1,i_2,\ldots,i_{k-1}} = \mathcal{T}^{(0)}_{i_1,i_2,\ldots,i_{k-1}} = (cA^{i_1}) \overset{P}{\star} (cA^{i_2}) \overset{P}{\star} \cdots \overset{P}{\star} (cA^{i_{k-1}}) \overset{P}{\star} c.$$

Analogous formulas are found in [SM90b], using conventional Kronecker product formalisms.

The multidimensional z-transform of the face of $\mathcal{T}$ is then readily computed as

$$T(z_1, \ldots, z_{k-1}, 0) = \sum_{i_1=0}^{\infty} \cdots \sum_{i_{k-1}=0}^{\infty} c_{i_1,\ldots,i_{k-1}} z_1^{i_1} \cdots z_{k-1}^{i_{k-1}}$$
$$= [c(I - z_1 A)^{-1}] \overset{P}{\star} \cdots \overset{P}{\star} [c(I - z_{k-1} A)^{-1}] \overset{P}{\star} c.$$

This shows, in particular, that whenever $\{y(\cdot)\}$ is a rational process, the polyspectral function $T(z_1, \ldots, z_{k-1}, 0)$ will likewise be rational with a separable denominator of the form $A(z_1) \cdots A(z_{k-1})$, where $A(z) = \det(I - zA)$ is the denominator of $H(z)$. This fact has been used in numerous works [GM89], [JK92], [SM90a], [SM92] to extract the poles of the model from a one-dimensional cumulant "slice," obtained by varying only one index. The z-transform of such a slice appears as

$$\sum_{i_1=0}^{\infty} c_{i_1,i_2,\ldots,i_k} z_1^{i_1} = \frac{\partial^{i_2}}{i_2!(\partial z_2)^{i_2}} \cdots \frac{\partial^{i_{k-1}}}{i_{k-1}!(\partial z_{k-1})^{i_{k-1}}} S(z_1, \ldots, z_{k-1}, 0) \bigg|_{z_2=0;\ldots;z_{k-1}=0}.$$

This function may suffer pole-zero cancellations in certain cases [Men91], such that certain system poles are hidden from the cumulant slice in question and in some cases no matter which cumulant slice is taken [Men91]. As shown in [RG94], however, this phenomenon is limited to very special classes of systems $H(z)$.

9.7 POLYSPECTRAL INTERPOLATION

We consider some explicit solutions to higher-order Lyapunov equations and how such equations relate to specific evaluations of the polyspectral residue function $S(z_1, \ldots, z_k)$. We then establish a necessary condition for the existence of a linear process compatible with these polyspectral evaluations.

Let F be a square ($M \times M$) matrix with all eigenvalues in the open unit disk and g an $M \times 1$ column vector, and suppose (F, g) is a controllable pair, i.e., the M rows of the infinite horizon controllability matrix

$$\begin{bmatrix} g & Fg & F^2g & \cdots \end{bmatrix}$$

are linearly independent. We suppose in what follows that the eigenvalues of F are distinct for ease of presentation, although the various relations to follow extend readily to the case of repeated eigenvalues. By controllability of the pair (F, g), there exists an invertible matrix W, which renders the transformed pair $(W^{-1}FW, W^{-1}g)$ in canonic parallel form [Kai80], i.e.,

$$W^{-1}FW = \Lambda = \begin{bmatrix} \lambda_1 & & & \\ & \lambda_2 & & \\ & & \ddots & \\ & & & \lambda_M \end{bmatrix}, \quad W^{-1}g = \mathbf{1} \triangleq \begin{bmatrix} 1 \\ 1 \\ \vdots \\ 1 \end{bmatrix}.$$

The controllability matrix in this parallel coordinate system is simply

$$\begin{bmatrix} \mathbf{1} & \Lambda\mathbf{1} & \Lambda^2\mathbf{1} & \cdots \end{bmatrix} = \begin{bmatrix} 1 & \lambda_1 & \lambda_1^2 & \cdots \\ 1 & \lambda_2 & \lambda_2^2 & \cdots \\ \vdots & \vdots & \vdots & \cdots \\ 1 & \lambda_M & \lambda_M^2 & \cdots \end{bmatrix}. \tag{9.7.1}$$

A simple calculation then shows that the solution to the Lyapunov equation

$$\mathcal{D} - \underbrace{\Lambda \overset{\mathcal{D}}{\star} \cdots \overset{\mathcal{D}}{\star} \Lambda}_{k \text{ terms}} = \underbrace{\mathbf{1} \star \cdots \star \mathbf{1}}_{k \text{ terms}}$$

Section 9.7. Polyspectral Interpolation

is given by (indexed from one)

$$\mathcal{D}_{i_1,i_2,\ldots,i_k} = \sum_{l=0}^{\infty} (\lambda_{i_1}\lambda_{i_2}\cdots\lambda_{i_k})^l = \frac{1}{1-\lambda_{i_1}\lambda_{i_2}\cdots\lambda_{i_k}}.$$

Since

$$[g \quad Fg \quad F^2g \quad \cdots] = W[1 \quad \Lambda 1 \quad \Lambda^2 1 \quad \cdots],$$

the solution to the Lyapunov equation $\mathcal{P} - F \overset{\mathcal{P}}{\star} \cdots \overset{\mathcal{P}}{\star} F = g \star \cdots \star g$ relates to $\mathcal{D}$ by the congruence transformation

$$\mathcal{P} = W \overset{\mathcal{D}}{\star} W \overset{\mathcal{D}}{\star} \cdots \overset{\mathcal{D}}{\star} W.$$

Note that although the elements of $\mathcal{P}$ are real whenever F and g are real, the elements of $\mathcal{D}$ will in general be complex.

Consider now the state recursion

$$\xi(n+1) = F\xi(n) + gy(n),$$

where $\{y(\cdot)\}$ is a stationary (possibly nonlinear) process, F is a stable matrix, and the time index n is sufficiently large for $\xi(\cdot)$ to be a stationary vector process. With $\bar{\xi}(n) = W^{-1}\xi(n)$, we have an equivalent parallel realization of the form

$$\bar{\xi}(n+1) = \Lambda\bar{\xi}(n) + \mathbf{1}\,y(n).$$

We examine in the remainder of this section state cumulant tensors from such recursions and how they relate to evaluations of the polyspectral residue function $S(z_1, \ldots, z_k)$ obtained from $\{y(\cdot)\}$ at specific points in the open unit polydisk $|z_1| < 1$, $\ldots, |z_k| < 1$. This will lead to a necessary condition in Thm. 9.7.1 for the existence of a linear process which is compatible with (or replicates) a set of polyspectral evaluations. We begin with the following identity.

Lemma 9.7.1 (An Identity). *Let $\mathcal{D}$ be the $M \times M \times \cdots \times M$ tensor (indexed from one)*

$$\mathcal{D}_{i_1,i_2,\ldots,i_k} = \mathrm{cum}[\bar{\xi}_{i_1}(n+1), \bar{\xi}_{i_2}(n+1), \ldots, \bar{\xi}_{i_k}(n+1)]. \tag{9.7.2}$$

Then $\mathcal{D}$ can be written as

$$\mathcal{D}_{i_1,i_2,\ldots,i_k} = \frac{S(\lambda_{i_1}, \lambda_{i_2}, \ldots, \lambda_{i_k})}{1 - \lambda_{i_1}\lambda_{i_2}\cdots\lambda_{i_k}}. \tag{9.7.3}$$

Proof: To verify the identity (9.7.3), we have that

$$\bar{\xi}(n+1) = \underbrace{[1 \quad \Lambda 1 \quad \Lambda^2 1 \quad \cdots]}_{\mathcal{C}_p} \begin{bmatrix} y(n) \\ y(n-1) \\ y(n-2) \\ \vdots \end{bmatrix},$$

in which $\mathcal{C}_p$ denotes the controllability matrix in the parallel coordinate system. The cumulant tensor $\mathcal{D}$ from (9.7.2) then becomes

$$\mathcal{D} = \mathcal{C}_p \overset{\mathcal{T}}{\star} \cdots \overset{\mathcal{T}}{\star} \mathcal{C}_p,$$

in which $\mathcal{T}$ is the Toeplitz cumulant tensor constructed from the stationary process $\{y(\cdot)\}$. Consider now the displaced tensor

$$\mathcal{E} = \Lambda \stackrel{\mathcal{D}}{\star} \cdots \stackrel{\mathcal{D}}{\star} \Lambda,$$

which reads elementwise as

$$\mathcal{E}_{i_1, i_2, \ldots, i_k} = \lambda_{i_1} \lambda_{i_2} \cdots \lambda_{i_k} \cdot \mathcal{D}_{i_1, i_2, \ldots, i_k}. \tag{9.7.4}$$

Using the relation $\Lambda \mathcal{C}_p = \mathcal{C}_p Z$, we see that

$$\mathcal{D} - \mathcal{E} = \mathcal{D} - \Lambda \stackrel{\mathcal{D}}{\star} \cdots \stackrel{\mathcal{D}}{\star} \Lambda = \left(\mathcal{C}_p \stackrel{\mathcal{T}}{\star} \cdots \stackrel{\mathcal{T}}{\star} \mathcal{C}_p \right) - \left((\mathcal{C}_p Z) \stackrel{\mathcal{T}}{\star} \cdots \stackrel{\mathcal{T}}{\star} (\mathcal{C}_p Z) \right)$$
$$= \mathcal{C}_p \stackrel{\mathcal{S}}{\star} \cdots \stackrel{\mathcal{S}}{\star} \mathcal{C}_p,$$

in which

$$\mathcal{S} = \mathcal{T} - Z \stackrel{\mathcal{T}}{\star} \cdots \stackrel{\mathcal{T}}{\star} Z$$

is the displacement residue of the Toeplitz tensor $\mathcal{T}$. Now, the multidimensional z-transform of the elements of $\mathcal{S}$ gives $S(z_1, \ldots, z_k)$. Considering the special structure of $\mathcal{C}_p$ exposed in (9.7.1), we see that $\mathcal{D} - \mathcal{E}$ may be written elementwise as

$$(\mathcal{D} - \mathcal{E})_{i_1, i_2, \ldots, i_k} = \sum_{n_1 = 0}^{\infty} \cdots \sum_{n_k = 0}^{\infty} \mathcal{S}_{n_1, \ldots, n_k} \lambda_{i_1}^{n_1} \cdots \lambda_{i_k}^{n_k} = S(\lambda_{i_1}, \lambda_{i_2}, \ldots, \lambda_{i_k}).$$

The relation (9.7.4) connecting $\mathcal{E}$ to $\mathcal{D}$ then allows us to solve for $\mathcal{D}$ as in (9.7.3).
◇

Remark. If we let

$$\mathcal{P}_{i_1, \ldots, i_k} = \text{cum}[\xi_{i_1}(n+1), \ldots, \xi_{i_k}(n+1)]$$

be the state cumulant tensor in the original (real) coordinate system, then again it relates to $\mathcal{D}$ by the congruence transformation

$$\mathcal{P} = W \stackrel{\mathcal{D}}{\star} \cdots \stackrel{\mathcal{D}}{\star} W$$

with $\mathcal{P}$ now containing all real entries. The reader may wish to check that, for the second-order case ($k = 2$), the expression (9.7.3) reduces to the Pick matrix from (9.3.5).
◇

Note that the M eigenvalues $\lambda_1, \ldots, \lambda_M$ contained in Λ lead in fact to M^k evaluations of the polyspectral residue function $S(z_1, \ldots, z_k)$. A natural question is whether these evaluations might display some form of redundancy, allowing their determination from a reduced set. The following lemma shows that setting successive complex variables to zero (which simplifies the corresponding z-transform evaluations) suffices for retrieving the M^k evaluations of the previous lemma.

Lemma 9.7.2 (Determining Polyspectral Values). *The polyspectral values*

$$S(\lambda_{i_1}, \ldots, \lambda_{i_k})$$

are uniquely determined from the set

$$S(\lambda_{i_1}, 0, \ldots, 0), \; S(\lambda_{i_1}, \lambda_{i_2}, 0, \ldots, 0), \; \cdots, \; S(\lambda_{i_1}, \ldots, \lambda_{i_{k-1}}, 0), \tag{9.7.5}$$

as each index i_l ranges over its M possibilities.

Section 9.7. Polyspectral Interpolation

Remark. This reduces the number of evaluations of $S(z_1, \ldots, z_k)$ from M^k to $M + M^2 + \cdots + M^{k-1}$.

Proof: Set $\bar{\xi}_0(n) = y(n)$ and introduce the augmented vector $\begin{bmatrix} y(n) \\ \bar{\xi}(n) \end{bmatrix}$; its cumulant tensor (now indexed from zero) is denoted $\overline{\mathcal{D}}$. Its interior elements (all indices greater than zero) yield the elements of $\mathcal{D}$ from (9.7.2), since by stationarity

$$\overline{\mathcal{D}}_{i_1,\ldots,i_k} = \mathrm{cum}[\bar{\xi}_{i_1}(n), \ldots, \bar{\xi}_{i_k}(n)]$$
$$= \mathrm{cum}[\bar{\xi}_{i_1}(n+1), \ldots, \bar{\xi}_{i_k}(n+1)] = \mathcal{D}_{i_1,\ldots,i_k} \qquad (9.7.6)$$

whenever all indices are greater than zero. The elements on the faces of $\overline{\mathcal{D}}$ become

$$\mathcal{D}_{i_1,\ldots,i_l,0,\ldots,0} = \mathrm{cum}[\bar{\xi}_{i_1}(n), \ldots, \bar{\xi}_{i_l}(n), \underbrace{y(n), \ldots, y(n)}_{k-l \text{ times}}]$$

$$= \sum_{n_1=1}^{\infty} \cdots \sum_{n_l=1}^{\infty} \mathrm{cum}[y(n-n_1), \ldots, y(n-n_l), y(n), \ldots, y(n)] \lambda_{i_1}^{n_1} \cdots \lambda_{i_l}^{n_l}$$

$$= \lambda_{i_1} \cdots \lambda_{i_l} S(\lambda_{i_1}, \ldots, \lambda_{i_l}, 0, \ldots, 0), \qquad (9.7.7)$$

which is one of the values from the set (9.7.5) multiplied by the scale factor $\lambda_{i_1} \cdots \lambda_{i_l}$.

Observe now that

$$\begin{bmatrix} 0 \\ \bar{\xi}(n+1) \end{bmatrix} = \begin{bmatrix} 0 & 0^T \\ 1 & \Lambda \end{bmatrix} \begin{bmatrix} y(n) \\ \bar{\xi}(n) \end{bmatrix} \qquad (9.7.8)$$

so that the cumulant tensor formed from $\begin{bmatrix} 0 \\ \bar{\xi}(n+1) \end{bmatrix}$ relates to $\overline{\mathcal{D}}$ by the congruence transformation

$$\begin{bmatrix} 0 & 0^T \\ 1 & \Lambda \end{bmatrix} \overline{\mathcal{D}} \star \cdots \star \overline{\mathcal{D}} \begin{bmatrix} 0 & 0^T \\ 1 & \Lambda \end{bmatrix}.$$

This tensor, in turn, has interior elements coinciding with those of $\overline{\mathcal{D}}$ in view of (9.7.6) and vanishes on all faces because the leading entry of the vector (9.7.8) is zero. We deduce that $\overline{\mathcal{D}}$ satisfies the Lyapunov equation

$$\overline{\mathcal{D}} - \begin{bmatrix} 0 & 0^T \\ 1 & \Lambda \end{bmatrix} \overline{\mathcal{D}} \star \cdots \star \overline{\mathcal{D}} \begin{bmatrix} 0 & 0^T \\ 1 & \Lambda \end{bmatrix} = \partial \mathcal{D},$$

in which $\partial \mathcal{D}$ vanishes at all interior points and has faces coinciding with those of $\overline{\mathcal{D}}$. Since $\begin{bmatrix} 0 & 0 \\ 1 & \Lambda \end{bmatrix}$ is a stable matrix, the existence claim of Lemma 9.6.3 implies that $\overline{\mathcal{D}}$ is uniquely determined from the evaluation points $\{\lambda_i\}$, which build up Λ, and the face values gathered in (9.7.5), which generate $\partial \mathcal{D}$.

◊

Theorem 9.7.1 (A Pick Condition). *Given the polyspectral values $S(\lambda_{i_1}, \ldots, \lambda_{i_k})$, a linear process may be fit to these values only if the Pick tensor from (9.7.3) is Tucker factorable.*

Proof: To see this, suppose that

$$\hat{y}(n) = \hat{h}_1 u(n-1) + \hat{h}_2 u(n-2) + \cdots$$

is a linear process whose polyspectral function $\widehat{S}(z_1,\ldots,z_k)$ fulfills

$$\widehat{S}(\lambda_{i_1},\ldots,\lambda_{i_k}) = S(\lambda_{i_1},\ldots,\lambda_{i_k}).$$

We know that the cumulant tensor $\widehat{\mathcal{D}}$ generated from $\widehat{S}(\lambda_{i_1},\ldots,\lambda_{i_k})$ can be written as

$$\widehat{\mathcal{D}} = \mathcal{C}_p \stackrel{\widehat{\mathcal{T}}}{\star} \cdots \stackrel{\widehat{\mathcal{T}}}{\star} \mathcal{C}_p,$$

where $\widehat{\mathcal{T}}$ is the cumulant tensor built from the sequence $\{\hat{y}(\cdot)\}$. By design, $\widehat{\mathcal{T}}$ is Tucker factorable as

$$\widehat{\mathcal{T}} = \hat{\gamma}_k \cdot \widehat{H}^T \star \cdots \star \widehat{H}^T$$

because the process $\{\hat{y}(\cdot)\}$ is linear, and this gives $\mathcal{D} = \widehat{\mathcal{D}}$ as

$$\mathcal{D} = (\mathcal{C}_p \widehat{H}^T) \star \cdots \star (\mathcal{C}_p \widehat{H}^T),$$

which is Tucker factorable.

$\diamond$

One may be tempted to conjecture a result in the converse direction; let us pinpoint a difficulty here. As remarked at the end of Sec. 9.6.1, admissibility conditions for $S(z_1,\ldots,z_k)$ to be a valid polyspectral residue function are not known. Without this, one is confronted with the difficulty of how to verify whether a candidate solution is valid.

9.8 A SCHUR-TYPE ALGORITHM FOR TENSORS

We develop now a candidate procedure for a Schur-type algorithm adapted to higher-order arrays. For the benefit of the nonexpert, we review first the algorithm for second-order arrays, which consists of subtracting off vector outer products to expose the Cholesky factor of a symmetric factorable (or positive-definite) matrix.

We then introduce a tensorial outer product which replicates the faces of a symmetric tensor in terms of a tensor of one lower dimension. Successive subtraction operations annihilate successive faces of a tensor, leading to a type of pyramidal decomposition that reduces to a Cholesky decomposition in the second-order case. The relations with displacement residues conclude this section.

9.8.1 Review of the Second-Order Case

Consider a symmetric matrix R, assumed positive definite and hence factorable in the form $R = L \star L = LL^T$. Let us partition R in the form

$$R = \begin{bmatrix} r_0 & r^T \\ r & R_1 \end{bmatrix},$$

where r_0 is a scalar, r is a column vector, and R_1 is a submatrix. Upon setting

$$a = \begin{bmatrix} \sqrt{r_0} \\ r/\sqrt{r_0} \end{bmatrix}, \tag{9.8.1}$$

one verifies that the outer product aa^T coincides with R on the borders of the matrix and when subtracted from R reveals

$$R - aa^T = \begin{bmatrix} 0 & 0^T \\ 0 & R_1 - rr^T/r_0 \end{bmatrix},$$

Section 9.8. A Schur-Type Algorithm for Tensors

in which the lower right block contains the Schur complement $R_1 - rr^T/r_0$ with respect to the leading entry (see also Sec. 1.6.1).

Now, if R is positive definite, we may write $R = LL^T$, in which L is a lower triangular Cholesky factor of R. The vector a from (9.8.1) is simply the first column of L.

The determination of successive columns of the Cholesky factor L has an intimate connection with the displacement structure of R and the Schur algorithm (see, e.g., Ch. 1 and [KS95a]). Consider the displacement residue of a matrix R, written as the sum and difference of vector dyads:

$$R - Z \overset{R}{\star} Z = R - ZRZ^T = \sum_{i=1}^{p} a_i a_i^T - \sum_{i=1}^{q} b_i b_i^T$$

$$= \underbrace{\begin{bmatrix} a_1 & \cdots & a_p & b_1 & \cdots & b_q \end{bmatrix}}_{G} \underbrace{\begin{bmatrix} I_p & \\ & -I_q \end{bmatrix}}_{J} G^T.$$

The generator vectors $\{a_i\}$ and $\{b_i\}$ are said to be proper (see, e.g., [LK84] and Ch. 1) provided that a_1 is the sole vector that is nonzero in its leading entry. One checks readily that the border of R must then be $a_1 a_1^T$, such that a_1 yields the first column of the Cholesky factor of R.

To obtain the remaining columns of the Cholesky factor, let $P = R_1 - rr^T/r_0$ denote the Schur complement. It turns out, when the generator G is proper, that P satisfies an analogous displacement equation [KS95a], viz.,

$$\begin{bmatrix} 0 & 0^T \\ 0 & P \end{bmatrix} - Z \begin{bmatrix} 0 & 0^T \\ 0 & P \end{bmatrix} Z^T$$

$$= \underbrace{\begin{bmatrix} Za_1 & a_2 & \cdots & a_p & b_1 & \cdots & b_q \end{bmatrix}}_{G'} J(G')^T, \qquad (9.8.2)$$

whose generator matrix G' relates to G by a down-shift operation on the leading column. (The matrix G' now has zeros on the top row.)

Now, if Θ is any J-unitary matrix, i.e., fulfilling $\Theta J \Theta^T = J$, then $G'\Theta$ remains a generator matrix for the displacement structure of (9.8.2). Whenever the leading entry of the Schur complement P is positive, then one can always determine a J-unitary matrix Θ which renders $G'\Theta$ in proper form, i.e., for which only the first column vector of $G'\Theta$ has a nonzero leading entry (occuring now in the second position); see Ch. 1. The leading column of the resulting $G'\Theta$ then generates the next column of the Cholesky factor L. Successive shift and rotate operations are then applied to yield the successive columns of L. We refer the reader to Ch. 1 and [KS95a], and the references therein, for more detail and applications of these recursions.

We turn now to a candidate extension of this procedure for higher-order tensors.

9.8.2 A Tensor Outer Product

A vector outer product, in the form $a_1 a_2^T = D$, generates a matrix D (i.e., a second-order tensor) obtained from two vectors a_1 and a_2 (i.e., first-order tensors), by projecting the indices onto the respective entries: $R_{i_1,i_2} = (a_1)_{i_1}(a_2)_{i_2}$. An analogous operation is to consider k tensors of order $k - 1$, to generate a kth-order tensor by the formulation in the following definition.

Definition 9.8.1 (Tensor Outer Product). *Given k tensors $\mathcal{E}_1, \ldots, \mathcal{E}_k$, each of order $k-1$, their outer product, denoted*

$$\mathcal{D} = \mathcal{E}_1 \odot \mathcal{E}_2 \odot \cdots \odot \mathcal{E}_k,$$

is the kth-order tensor with elements

$$\mathcal{D}_{i_1,i_2,\ldots,i_k} = (\mathcal{E}_1)_{i_2,\ldots,i_k}(\mathcal{E}_2)_{i_1,i_3,\ldots,i_k}\cdots(\mathcal{E}_k)_{i_1,\ldots,i_{k-1}}.$$

◇

If $\mathcal{E}_1$ and $\mathcal{E}_2$ are column vectors, then $(\mathcal{E}_1 \odot \mathcal{E}_2)_{i_1,i_2} = (\mathcal{E}_1)_{i_2}(\mathcal{E}_2)_{i_1} = (\mathcal{E}_2\mathcal{E}_1^T)_{i_1,i_2}$, which reduces to the conventional outer product of vectors. If $\mathcal{E}_1$, $\mathcal{E}_2$, and $\mathcal{E}_3$ are three matices, the generation of the third-order tensor $\mathcal{E}_1 \odot \mathcal{E}_2 \odot \mathcal{E}_3$ is as illustrated in Fig. 9.2. Each matrix is set adjacent to a face of the cube, and each element of the cube is obtained by projecting the coordinates onto the three faces and multiplying the matrix elements occuring on the three faces.

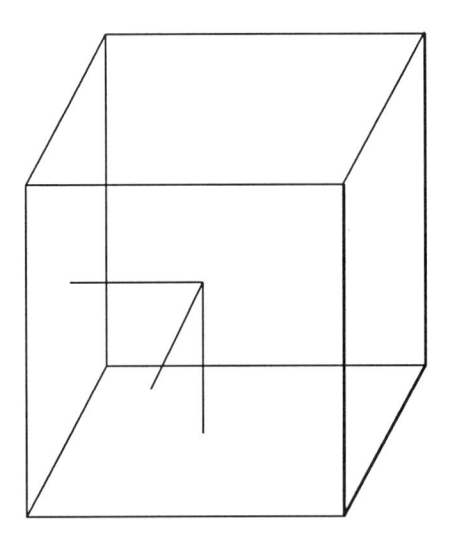

Figure 9.2. Geometric interpretation of the outer product of three matrices: Each matrix occupies one face of the cube (front, left, and bottom), and each interior element of the tensor is obtained by projecting its coordinates onto the three faces and multiplying the resulting elements.

The utility of this product can be appreciated by returning to the Toeplitz tensor $\mathcal{T}$ containing output cumulants. Consider first the third-order case, i.e.,

$$\mathcal{T}_{i_1,i_2,i_3} = \text{cum}[y(n-i_1), y(n-i_2), y(n-i_3)],$$

with $\mathcal{T}_{i_1,i_2,0} = c_{i_1,i_2}$ (the third-order cumulant with lags i_1 and i_2). The displacement residue $\mathcal{T} - Z \overset{T}{\star} Z \overset{T}{\star} Z$ coincides with $\mathcal{T}$ along the faces and vanishes at all interior points. The displacement residue can be expressed as

$$\mathcal{T} - Z \overset{T}{\star} Z \overset{T}{\star} Z = \mathcal{E}_1 \odot \mathcal{E}_1 \odot \mathcal{E}_1 - \mathcal{E}_2 \odot \mathcal{E}_2 \odot \mathcal{E}_2,$$

Section 9.8. A Schur-Type Algorithm for Tensors

in which

$$(\mathcal{E}_1)_{i_1,i_2} = \begin{cases} \sqrt[3]{c_{0,0}}, & i_1 = i_2 = 0, \\ \sqrt{\dfrac{c_{i_1,0}}{(\mathcal{E}_1)_{00}}}, & i_1 > 0 \text{ and } i_2 = 0, \\ \sqrt{\dfrac{c_{0,i_2}}{(\mathcal{E}_1)_{00}}}, & i_1 = 0 \text{ and } i_2 > 0, \\ \dfrac{c_{i_1,i_2}}{(\mathcal{E}_1)_{i_1,0}(\mathcal{E}_1)_{0,i_2}} & \text{elsewhere}, \end{cases}$$

and

$$(\mathcal{E}_2)_{i_1,i_2} = \begin{cases} 0, & i_1 = 0 \text{ and/or } i_2 = 0, \\ (\mathcal{E}_1)_{i_1,i_2} & \text{elsewhere}. \end{cases}$$

The first term $\mathcal{E}_1 \odot \mathcal{E}_1 \odot \mathcal{E}_1$ generates the faces of $\mathcal{T}$, whereas the second term $\mathcal{E}_2 \odot \mathcal{E}_2 \odot \mathcal{E}_2$ vanishes along each face while replicating the interior terms of $\mathcal{E}_1 \odot \mathcal{E}_1 \odot \mathcal{E}_1$. Observe that $\mathcal{E}_1$ also can be written directly in terms of cumulant values c_{i_1,i_2} as

$$(\mathcal{E}_1)_{i_1,i_2} = c_{i_1,i_2} \dfrac{\sqrt[3]{c_{00}}}{\sqrt{c_{i_1,0}\, c_{0,i_2}}}.$$

This decomposition extends readily to high-order tensors as well. If $\mathcal{T}$ is a kth-order Toeplitz cumulant tensor, its displacement residue can be decomposed as

$$\mathcal{T} - Z \overset{\mathcal{T}}{\star} Z \overset{\mathcal{T}}{\star} \cdots \overset{\mathcal{T}}{\star} Z = \underbrace{\mathcal{E}_1 \odot \cdots \odot \mathcal{E}_1}_{k \text{ terms}} - \underbrace{\mathcal{E}_2 \odot \cdots \odot \mathcal{E}_2}_{k \text{ terms}}, \qquad (9.8.3)$$

where now

$$(\mathcal{E}_2)_{i_1,\ldots,i_{k-1}} = \begin{cases} 0, & i_1 = 0 \text{ and/or } \ldots i_{k-1} = 0, \\ (\mathcal{E}_1)_{i_1,\ldots,i_{k-1}} & \text{elsewhere}, \end{cases} \qquad (9.8.4)$$

and [Gri96]

$$\begin{aligned}
(\mathcal{E}_1)_{i_1,\ldots,i_{k-1}} &= c_{i_1,\ldots,i_{k-1}} \\
&\times [c_{i_1,0,\ldots,0}\, c_{i_2,0,\ldots,0} \cdots c_{i_{k-1},0,\ldots,0}]^{-1/2} \\
&\times [c_{i_1,i_2,0,\ldots,0}\, c_{i_2,i_3,0,\ldots,0} \cdots c_{i_{k-1},i_1,0,\ldots,0}]^{1/3} \\
&\times \cdots \times [c_{0,\ldots,0}]^{(-1)^{k+1}/k}.
\end{aligned} \qquad (9.8.5)$$

When specialized to the matrix case, the decomposition reduces to the outer product decomposition of the displacement structure of a Toeplitz matrix, as illustrated in (9.3.3). Some potential weaknesses of this higher-order extension, however, are worth noting. First, the generation of $\mathcal{E}_1$ involves various division and rooting operations, and a potential division by zero is not to be discarded immediately, indicating that this decomposition need not always exist. For the second-order case by contrast [cf. (9.3.3)], all divisions are by $\sqrt{r_0}$, whose positivity is assured whenever the stochastic process $\{y(\cdot)\}$ is nontrivial. Second, even if $\mathcal{T}$ has all real entries, those of $\mathcal{E}_1$ and $\mathcal{E}_2$ may be complex, due to the various radicals involved in their generation. Finally, the transform domain relation is more complicated with this product. To illustrate, consider the third-order case, for which $\mathcal{E}_1$ becomes a matrix. Let us set

$$\mathcal{E}(z_1, z_2) = \sum_{i_1=0}^{\infty} \sum_{i_2=0}^{\infty} \mathcal{E}_{i_1,i_2}\, z_1^{i_1}\, z_2^{i_2}$$

and $\mathcal{D} = \mathcal{E} \odot \mathcal{E} \odot \mathcal{E}$. The function $\mathcal{D}(z_1, z_2, z_3) = \sum \mathcal{D}_{i_1,i_2,i_3} z_1^{i_1} z_2^{i_2} z_3^{i_3}$ may then be expressed as the convolutional formula [Gri96]

$$\mathcal{D}(z_1, z_2, z_3)$$
$$= \frac{1}{(2\pi j)^3} \oint_{|w_1|=1} \oint_{|w_2|=1} \oint_{|w_3|=1} \mathcal{E}(w_1, w_2) \, \mathcal{E}\left(\frac{z_3}{w_3}, w_1\right) \mathcal{E}\left(\frac{z_1}{w_1}, \frac{z_2}{w_2}\right) \frac{dw_1}{w_1} \frac{dw_2}{w_2} \frac{dw_3}{w_3}.$$

For the second-order case, by contrast, one finds that $\mathcal{D} = \mathcal{E} \odot \mathcal{E}$ induces the much simpler multiplicative structure $\mathcal{D}(z_1, z_2) = \mathcal{E}(z_1) \mathcal{E}(z_2)$.

Despite these complications, some interesting relations with displacement generators do fall out, which we now address.

9.8.3 Displacement Generators

It is natural to consider a "Schur complement" of a tensor as that obtained by subtracting from a given symmetric tensor an outer product of lower-order tensors that eliminates the face elements. Although the expressions to be developed likewise apply to nonsymmetric tensors [Gri96], the symmetric case pursued here affords simpler notations.

For third-order symmetric tensors, this Schur complement operation appears as

$$(\mathcal{T}^{(1)})_{i_1,i_2,i_3} = (\mathcal{T})_{i_1,i_2,i_3} - (\mathcal{T}_{000} \mathcal{T}_{i_100}^{-1} \mathcal{T}_{0i_20}^{-1} \mathcal{T}_{00i_3}^{-1}) \mathcal{T}_{0i_2i_3} \mathcal{T}_{i_10i_3} \mathcal{T}_{i_1i_20}$$

or

$$\mathcal{T}^{(1)} = \mathcal{T} - \mathcal{E} \odot \mathcal{E} \odot \mathcal{E},$$

in which

$$\mathcal{E}_{i_1,i_2} = \mathcal{T}_{i_1,i_2,0} \frac{\sqrt[3]{\mathcal{T}_{000}}}{\sqrt{\mathcal{T}_{i_1,0,0} \mathcal{T}_{i_2,0,0}}},$$

thereby eliminating the faces of $\mathcal{T}$. For higher-order tensors, the operation appears as

$$(\mathcal{T}^{(1)})_{i_1,i_2,\ldots,i_k} = (\mathcal{T})_{i_1,i_2,\ldots,i_k} - \prod_{l=0}^{k} \left(\prod_{\sigma} \mathcal{T}_{j_1,j_2,\ldots,j_l,0,\ldots,0} \right)^{(-1)^{l+k+1}},$$

where $\sigma = \begin{pmatrix} i_1 & i_2 & \cdots & i_l & i_{l+1} & \cdots & i_k \\ j_1 & j_2 & \cdots & j_l & j_{l+1} & \cdots & j_k \end{pmatrix}$ is a circular permutation of indices.

Suppose now that the symmetric tensor $\mathcal{T}$ has as displacement structure the outer product decomposition

$$\mathcal{T} - Z \overset{\mathcal{T}}{\star} \cdots \overset{\mathcal{T}}{\star} Z = \sum_{l=1}^{L} \pm \mathcal{E}_l^{\odot k}, \tag{9.8.6}$$

in which $\mathcal{E}_l^{\odot k}$ denotes the k-term product $\mathcal{E}_l \odot \cdots \odot \mathcal{E}_l$. In analogy with the second-order case, the generator tensors $\{\mathcal{E}_l\}$ will be termed proper provided that $\mathcal{E}_1$ is the only generator that is nonzero on its faces. The displacement decomposition (9.8.3)-(9.8.5) for a Toeplitz tensor is proper, for example. The face elements of $\mathcal{T}$ then come from the contribution of $\mathcal{E}_1$ alone, such that the Schur complement of $\mathcal{T}$, by the above definition, becomes $\mathcal{T}^{(1)} = \mathcal{T} - \mathcal{E}_1^{\odot k}$.

Extraction of the next Schur complement appears as

$$\mathcal{T}^{(2)} = \mathcal{T}^{(1)} - (\mathcal{E}_1^{(1)})^{\odot k},$$

Section 9.8. A Schur-Type Algorithm for Tensors

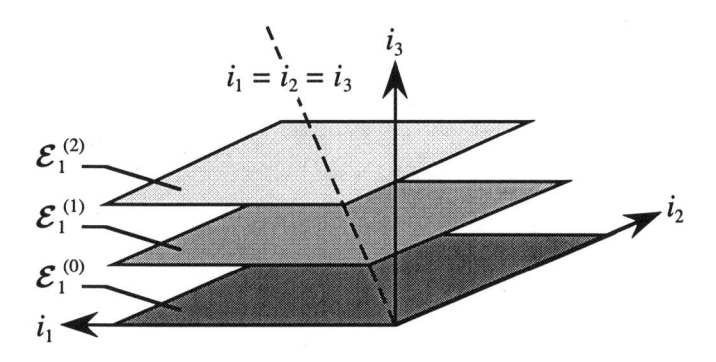

Figure 9.3. Illustrating a pyramidal structure for a third-order tensor.

in which $(\mathcal{E}_1^{(1)})^{\odot k}$ generates each first nonzero face of $\mathcal{T}^{(1)}$, such that $\mathcal{T}^{(2)}$ now vanishes in its first subfaces as well. Upon iterating this process, we generate successive $(k-1)$-dimensional tensors $\mathcal{E}_1^{(l)}$, vanishing in the first l subfaces and such that the tensor difference

$$\mathcal{T} - \sum_{l=1}^{n} (\mathcal{E}_1^{(l)})^{\odot k}$$

vanishes whenever all indices are less than n. A new kth-order tensor, defined as

$$\mathcal{D}_{i_1,\ldots,i_{k-1},l} = (\mathcal{E}_1^{(l)})_{i_1,\ldots,i_{k-1}} \qquad (9.8.7)$$

for successive values of l, then assumes a "pyramidal" structure, which reduces to a triangular (or Cholesky) structure when specialized to second-order tensors (or matrices). Figure 9.3 illustrates the pyramidal structure for third-order tensors.

We now relate successive subtensors of $\mathcal{D}$ from (9.8.7) to the displacement structure of (9.8.6). Thus, suppose that the generator tensors in (9.8.6) are proper, i.e., only $\mathcal{E}_1$ is nonzero along any face. Define a shifted first generator $\mathcal{E}'_1$ by shifting all elements of $\mathcal{E}_1$ one position along its main diagonal, i.e.,

$$\mathcal{E}'_1 = \underbrace{Z \overset{\mathcal{E}_1}{\star} \cdots \overset{\mathcal{E}_1}{\star} Z}_{k-1 \text{ terms}}.$$

We then have the following result.

Lemma 9.8.1 (Structure of Schur Complements). *The Schur complement* $\mathcal{T}^{(1)} = \mathcal{T} - \mathcal{E}_1 \odot \cdots \odot \mathcal{E}_1$ *satisfies the displacement equation*

$$\mathcal{T}^{(1)} - Z \overset{\mathcal{T}^{(1)}}{\star} \cdots \overset{\mathcal{T}^{(1)}}{\star} Z = (\mathcal{E}'_1)^{\odot k} + \sum_{l=2}^{L} \pm \mathcal{E}_l^{\odot k}$$

obtained by shifting the first generator of a proper set.

Proof: Note that shifting each entry of $\mathcal{E}_1$ by one index simply shifts each entry of the outer product $\mathcal{E}_1^{\odot k}$ by one index, so that

$$(\mathcal{E}'_1)^{\odot k} = \underbrace{Z \overset{\mathcal{E}_1^{\odot k}}{\star} \cdots \overset{\mathcal{E}_1^{\odot k}}{\star} Z}_{k \text{ terms}}.$$

We then find by direct calculation that

$$T^{(1)} - Z \overset{T^{(1)}}{\star} \cdots \overset{T^{(1)}}{\star} Z = \left(T - Z \overset{T}{\star} \cdots \overset{T}{\star} Z\right) - \left(\mathcal{E}_1^{\odot k} - Z \overset{\mathcal{E}_1^{\odot k}}{\star} \cdots \overset{\mathcal{E}_1^{\odot k}}{\star} Z\right)$$

$$= \left(\mathcal{E}_1^{\odot k} + \sum_{l=2}^{L} \pm \mathcal{E}_l^{\odot k}\right) - \left(\mathcal{E}_1^{\odot k} - (\mathcal{E}_1')^{\odot k}\right)$$

$$= (\mathcal{E}_1')^{\odot k} + \sum_{l=2}^{L} \pm \mathcal{E}_l^{\odot k}$$

as claimed.

$\diamond$

The next step in the algorithm is to transform the resulting generators $\mathcal{E}_1'$ and $\{\mathcal{E}_l\}_{l \geq 2}$ into a proper set, since the leading generator tensor would then be identified as the next subtensor $\mathcal{E}_1^{(1)}$ of the pyramidal factor $\mathcal{D}$ from (9.8.7).

At this point a major difference arises compared to the second-order (or matrix) case. In the second-order case, the transformation amounts to arranging the generator vectors into a matrix, which is then multiplied by a J-unitary transformation to zero out preassigned terms. The higher-order analogy of this operation instead involves nonlinear operations, which we shall illustrate with a simplified example adapted from [Gri96].

Suppose we begin with a third-order Toeplitz tensor for T, and let $\nabla T^{(1)} = T^{(1)} - Z \overset{T^{(1)}}{\star} Z \overset{T^{(1)}}{\star} Z$ be the displacement residue from the first Schur complement. By construction, this tensor vanishes along all faces, so we consider only nonzero indices. For the Toeplitz case considered, the displacement equation involves only two generators, i.e.,

$$\nabla T^{(1)} = (\mathcal{E}_1')^{\odot 3} - \mathcal{E}_2^{\odot 3}.$$

We now seek a pair of *proper* generators $\mathcal{F}_1$ and $\mathcal{F}_2$, compatible with $\nabla T^{(1)}$, i.e.,

$$\nabla T^{(1)} = \mathcal{F}_1^{\odot 3} - \mathcal{F}_2^{\odot 3}.$$

We require that $\mathcal{F}_2$ vanish along its first two faces and hence that only $\mathcal{F}_1$ be nonzero along its first face. From the equation

$$(\nabla T^{(1)})_{111} = (\mathcal{E}_1')_{11}^3 - (\mathcal{E}_2)_{11}^3 = (\mathcal{F}_1)_{11}^3,$$

we deduce the first nonzero element of $\mathcal{F}_1$ as

$$(\mathcal{F}_1)_{11} = \sqrt[3]{(\mathcal{E}_1')_{11}^3 - (\mathcal{E}_2)_{11}^3}.$$

The conditions

$$(\nabla T^{(1)})_{1,1,i} = (\mathcal{E}_1')_{1,1}(\mathcal{E}_1')_{1,i}^2 - (\mathcal{E}_2)_{1,1}(\mathcal{E}_2)_{1,i}^2 = (\mathcal{F}_1)_{1,1}(\mathcal{F}_1)_{1,i}^2$$

give the elements of the first nonzero row and column of $\mathcal{F}_1$ as

$$(\mathcal{F}_1)_{1,i} = (\mathcal{F}_1)_{i,1} = \sqrt{\frac{(\mathcal{E}_1')_{1,1}(\mathcal{E}_1')_{1,i}^2 - (\mathcal{E}_2)_{1,1}(\mathcal{E}_2)_{1,i}^2}{(\mathcal{F}_1)_{1,1}}}.$$

To obtain the remaining elements of $\mathcal{F}_1$, let us set

$$\alpha_i = \frac{(\mathcal{E}_1')_{1,i}}{(\mathcal{F}_1)_{1,i}} \quad \text{and} \quad \beta_i = \frac{(\mathcal{E}_2)_{1,i}}{(\mathcal{F}_1)_{1,i}}.$$

Using the general relation

$$(\nabla \mathcal{T}^{(1)})_{i_1,i_2,1} = (\mathcal{E}'_1)_{i_1,1}(\mathcal{E}'_1)_{1,i_2}(\mathcal{E}'_1)_{i_1,i_2} - (\mathcal{E}_2)_{i_1,1}(\mathcal{E}_2)_{1,i_2}(\mathcal{E}_2)_{i_1,i_2}$$
$$= (\mathcal{F}_1)_{i_1,1}(\mathcal{F}_1)_{1,i_2}(\mathcal{F}_1)_{i_1,i_2},$$

we obtain

$$\mathcal{F}_{i_1,i_2} = \frac{(\mathcal{E}'_1)_{i_1,1}(\mathcal{E}'_1)_{1,i_2}(\mathcal{E}'_1)_{i_1,i_2} - (\mathcal{E}_2)_{i_1,1}(\mathcal{E}_2)_{1,i_2}(\mathcal{E}_2)_{i_1,i_2}}{(\mathcal{F}_1)_{i_1,1}(\mathcal{F}_1)_{1,i_2}}$$
$$= \alpha_{i_1} \alpha_{i_2} (\mathcal{E}'_1)_{i_1,i_2} - \beta_{i_1} \beta_{i_2} (\mathcal{E}_2)_{i_1,i_2}.$$

A similar procedure may be carried out for $\mathcal{F}_2$, whose first nonzero elements begin with indices 2 or greater, since it must vanish along its first two faces. Starting now with the pivot $(\nabla \mathcal{T}^{(1)})_{2,2,2}$, we have that

$$(\nabla \mathcal{T}^{(1)})_{2,2,2} = (\mathcal{F}_1)^3_{2,2} - (\mathcal{F}_2)^3_{2,2}$$

or

$$(\mathcal{F}_2)_{2,2} = \sqrt[3]{(\mathcal{F}_1)^3_{2,2} - (\nabla \mathcal{T}^{(1)})_{2,2,2}},$$

which gives the leading entry. From the relation

$$(\nabla \mathcal{T}^{(1)})_{2,2,i} = (\mathcal{F}_1)_{2,2}(\mathcal{F}_1)^2_{2,i} - (\mathcal{F}_2)_{2,2}(\mathcal{F}_2)^2_{2,i}$$

we deduce the elements of the first nonzero row and column of $\mathcal{F}_2$ as

$$(\mathcal{F}_2)_{2,i} = (\mathcal{F}_2)_{i,2} = \sqrt{\frac{(\mathcal{F}_1)_{2,2}(\mathcal{F}_1)^2_{2,i} - (\nabla \mathcal{T}^{(1)})_{2,2,i}}{(\mathcal{F}_2)_{2,2}}}.$$

Finally, from the general relation

$$(\nabla \mathcal{T}^{(1)})_{i_1,i_2,2} = (\mathcal{F}_1)_{i_1,2}(\mathcal{F}_1)_{2,i_2}(\mathcal{F}_1)_{i_1,i_2} - (\mathcal{F}_2)_{i_1,2}(\mathcal{F}_2)_{2,i_2}(\mathcal{F}_2)_{i_1,i_2}$$

we obtain the formula for the remaining elements of $\mathcal{F}_2$ as

$$(\mathcal{F}_2)_{i_1,i_2} = \frac{(\mathcal{F}_1)_{i_1,2}(\mathcal{F}_1)_{2,i_2}(\mathcal{F}_1)_{i_1,i_2} - (\nabla \mathcal{T}^{(1)})_{i_1,i_2,2}}{(\mathcal{F}_2)_{i_1,2}(\mathcal{F}_2)_{2,i_2}}.$$

We observe that obtaining a proper generator set from a nonproper set does not reduce to linear transformations. Whether a more expedient procedure to that outlined above may be obtained, and whether some physically relevant interpretation may be attached to the intermediate terms of this procedure, are topics which require further study.

9.9 CONCLUDING REMARKS

We have presented a semitutorial account of tensorial representations for cumulants in system theory, with special emphasis on Tucker factorability for linear process. The key result concerning the Tucker factorability of a Pick tensor for the linear case is apparently one of the few results establishing compatibility of cumulants with a linear process given only partial information. Usable conditions guaranteeing Tucker factorability of a given tensor require further study, as do methods for reliably deducing such a factor when one exists. Further study is likewise required to establish "admissibility" conditions for higher-order spectra.

Another avenue worthy of further study relates to the faces of a Toeplitz cumulant tensor coinciding with its Hankel-based counterpart in the linear case. Given thus the faces of a Toeplitz tensor, a useful query asks how to reconstruct candidate interior points compatible with a Hankel-based tensor. If such a procedure could be rendered successful, then Lemma 9.6.1 shows that a simple displacement operation reveals a rank 1 tensor built from the system impulse response.

A candidate Schur algorithm for pyramidal factorization of higher-order tensors has also been proposed which, when specialized to second-order arrays, reduces to a recursive algorithm for triangular factorization. Whether the given procedure may have some utility in checking for Tucker factorability is not immediately clear. Similarly, whether deeper connections with modeling filter synthesis in the linear case [LK84] are inherited by this procedure remains to be investigated.

Acknowledgments

The authors would like to thank P. Comon and L. Delathauwer for their critical comments on some earlier versions of this work. They are also grateful to Professors A. H. Sayed and T. Kailath for their assistance in adapting this work to the present volume.

Chapter 10

MINIMAL COMPLEXITY REALIZATION OF STRUCTURED MATRICES

Patrick Dewilde

10.1 INTRODUCTION

The earlier chapters considered the class of matrices that satisfy displacement equations (cf. Ch. 1) and, hence, have small displacement ranks. There are also other kinds of structured matrices. As a general working definition, we propose "matrices whose entries satisfy class generic constraints that reduce the number of algebraically free parameters."

Class generic constraints on the entries can be of several kinds:

- Linear constraints between entries. Examples are the following:

    (i) Toeplitz, Hankel, or even Cauchy matrices.

    (ii) Their generalizations to matrices of *low displacement rank*, as studied extensively by the Kailath school and its many ramifications (see Ch. 1). This is the class of matrices studied in the earlier chapters.

- Hard value constraints on entries. Examples are the following:

    (i) Banded or multibanded matrices.

    (ii) Inverses of banded matrices and (possibly continuous) products of banded matrices with inverses of banded matrices.

- Matrices described by a low-complexity time-varying state-space model.

- Nonlinear algebraic constraints. (Unitary matrices may seem to be of this type, but they can be brought into the class with linear constraints via the transformation $U = e^{iH}$ in which H is a Hermitian matrix and $i = \sqrt{-1}$.)

There are connections among the types described above. A banded matrix or its inverse has a low-complexity state-space realization; the collection of matrices described by a low-order state-space model is a generalization of the "banded" case. Products of these may also have low-complexity state-space realizations. An upper triangular Toeplitz matrix can be interpreted as a partial transfer operator of a time-varying linear system and has a state-space model derived from it. Some generic constraints do not reduce the number of parameters involved. Positivity in one form or the other is one; the fact that a parameter or an algebraic expression involving parameters is restricted to an interval does not decrease the "algebraic freedom," at least not in infinite precision arithmetic. We shall not be concerned with such cases.

10.2 MOTIVATION OF MINIMAL COMPLEXITY REPRESENTATIONS

Why are we interested in structured matrices? We are interested for at least two reasons:

1. Structured matrices may be represented by (often many) fewer parameters.

2. Computations involving structured matrices may be much more efficient, sometimes at the cost of numerical accuracy or stability, but in important cases even improving on these two factors (see, e.g., the discussions in Sec. 1.13 and in Chs. 2, 3, and 4 in this book).

Two important additional reasons may be the following:

3. The reduced complexity is indicative of an underlying physical structure which is interesting in its own right.

4. The reduced complexity may lead to approximations and "model reduction," which reduce the number of necessary parameters even further.

The present chapter treats the combination of two entirely different methods of using matrix structure for parameter reduction: low displacement rank on the one hand and representation by low-order time-varying state models on the other. The first type has been pioneered by Kailath and his coworkers (Ch. 1 of this book gives a recent survey), while the second type was the subject of [VD94]. In the case of low-displacement-rank matrices, one computational advantage derives from the fact that in many cases the matrix or its inverse can be represented by a small sum of by-products of Toeplitz matrices. If the FFT algorithm is used to execute the product of a Toeplitz matrix with a vector, then the overall computational complexity of the matrix-vector multiplication is reduced to $\alpha n k \log n$, where α is the "displacement rank" and k is a small number depending on the type of FFT algorithm chosen. (See [Bla84] for detailed information—see also the discussion in Secs. 1.4 and 8.3.1 of this book.) On the other hand, matrices with low state representations (e.g., single band matrices) also give rise to reduced matrix-vector computations either with the original matrix or with its inverse, the computational complexity now being $2\delta n$, where δ is the maximal state complexity. We shall see further in the theory that matrices with low state representations may aptly be called "matrices with low Hankel rank," a term which we shall use in this chapter. (Another expression would be "with low local degree".)

Matrices with low displacement rank are not the same as matrices with low Hankel rank. One can easily exhibit examples of matrices which score high for one and low for

Section 10.3. Displacement Structure

the other characteristic. For example, the Toeplitz matrix defined by

$$H \triangleq \begin{bmatrix} 1 & \frac{1}{2} & \frac{1}{3} & \frac{1}{4} & \cdots \\ & 1 & \frac{1}{2} & \frac{1}{3} & \ddots \\ & & 1 & \frac{1}{2} & \ddots \\ & & & 1 & \ddots \\ & & & & \ddots \end{bmatrix}$$

has low displacement rank but does not have a useful low-order system representation, since each such representation would either decay exponentially or not decay at all with increasing index, while the original decays as $1/n$, just like the Maclaurin series for $\log(1+z)$. For matrices that score high for one of the criteria, it just pays to use the corresponding representation method. However, for matrices in the middle category, it may be advantageous to combine the two techniques. This may be reason enough to study the combination; there are more reasons, however, which we shall consider in the concluding section.

10.3 DISPLACEMENT STRUCTURE

Let R be an $n \times n$ positive-definite matrix (the entries of R may actually be $N \times N$ blocks; R is then a positive-definite $nN \times nN$ matrix overall), and let us define the lower triangular shift matrix Z with ones (or unit matrices) on the first subdiagonal and zeros elsewhere:

$$Z \triangleq \begin{bmatrix} 0 & & & \\ I & \ddots & & \\ & \ddots & \ddots & \\ & & I & 0 \end{bmatrix}.$$

We consider the displacement of R with respect to Z (cf. [KKM79a]—see also Ch. 1),

$$\nabla_Z R \triangleq R - ZRZ^*,$$

where $\cdot^*$ denotes Hermitian transpose, and assume that it has inertia $(p, 0, q)$. This means that there exist matrices (the a_i are the rows of the matrix G)

$$G = \begin{bmatrix} a_0 \\ a_1 \\ \vdots \\ a_{n-1} \end{bmatrix}, \quad J = \begin{bmatrix} I_p & \\ & -I_q \end{bmatrix}$$

of dimensions $n \times (p+q)$ and $(p+q) \times (p+q)$, respectively, such that

$$R - ZRZ^* = GJG^* = \begin{bmatrix} a_0 \\ a_1 \\ \vdots \\ a_{n-1} \end{bmatrix} J \begin{bmatrix} a_0^* & a_1^* & \cdots & a_{n-1}^* \end{bmatrix}, \quad (10.3.1)$$

in which G has full (column) rank. It is convenient to split each entry a_k according to the inertia formula

$$a_k = \begin{bmatrix} \overbrace{a_{k1}}^{p} & \overbrace{a_{k2}}^{q} \end{bmatrix}.$$

The integer $\alpha \stackrel{\Delta}{=} p + q$ is called the *displacement rank* of R. If it is small compared with n, then R is said to be of low displacement rank and one can expect great simplifications of calculus with such matrices.

Another notion leading to low complexity representations of matrices is that of "low Hankel rank," defined in [DV93]. It leads to reduced state-space models for matrices. The derivation of such a model from the matrix viewed as an input-output operator is called a "realization theory."

10.4 REALIZATION THEORY FOR MATRICES

Let $T = [t_{ij}]$ be an upper triangular matrix. Such a matrix often represents a linear computation, say, of the type $y = uT$. The matrix T is applied linearly to an input row vector u to produce an output row vector y. Any computation, including the linear computation under consideration, will happen in stages. A major, but often hidden, assumption is that the input vector is presented in sequence; it takes the character of a signal that flows in the computation and is used sequentially. As soon as sufficient data are present, a partial calculation can start, produce an intermediate result, store it, output whatever data it has been able to generate (also in sequence), and then move to input new data, engage in a new partial calculation, and so on. Viewed in this way, a linear computation becomes what we would traditionally call a linear system.

Let us analyze such a computing system. We assume that at time k ($k = 1, \ldots, n$) the component u_k of the input vector together with some stored information gleaned from previous samples is used to compute the component y_k of the output vector. If we collect the relevant information from stage k as a vector x_k, which we call the *state*, then a data flow scheme of our computation would appear as in Fig. 10.1.

For example, we can write the ordinary vector-matrix multiplication $y = uT$ with scalar series u and y as

$$\begin{aligned} y_0 &= u_0 t_{00}, \\ y_1 &= u_0 t_{01} + u_1 t_{11}, \\ y_2 &= u_0 t_{02} + u_1 t_{12} + u_2 t_{22}, \\ \vdots &= \vdots \end{aligned} \qquad (10.4.1)$$

As soon as u_0 is available, y_0 can be computed and outputted. For the computation of u_1 one needs to remember u_0, so the state at $t = 1$ must contain u_0, but then, as soon as u_1 becomes available, y_1 can be computed and outputted; for the computation of y_2, u_0 and u_1 may be needed, etc. If this continues, then the dimension of the state will quickly "explode." In many cases (as we shall see soon), a more clever choice of state leads to a more efficient choice of state vector at each time point.

The linear scheme of computations at each stage is shown in Fig. 10.2.

In the case of the straight vector-matrix multiplication shown in (10.4.1), we have

1. $x_1 = u_0$, $y_0 = u_0 t_{00}$; hence

$$B_0 = [1], \quad D_0 = [t_{00}],$$

while A_0 and C_0 are empty since there is no initial state.

Section 10.4. Realization Theory for Matrices

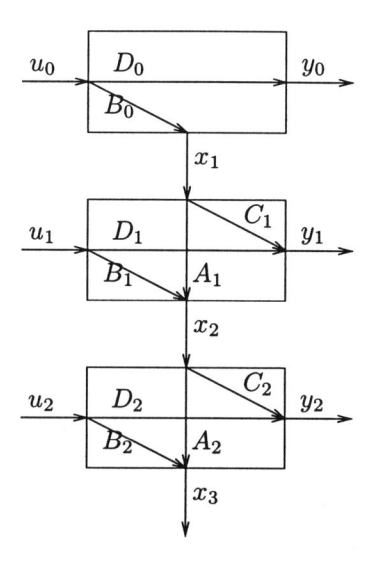

Figure 10.1. The realization of a linear computation.

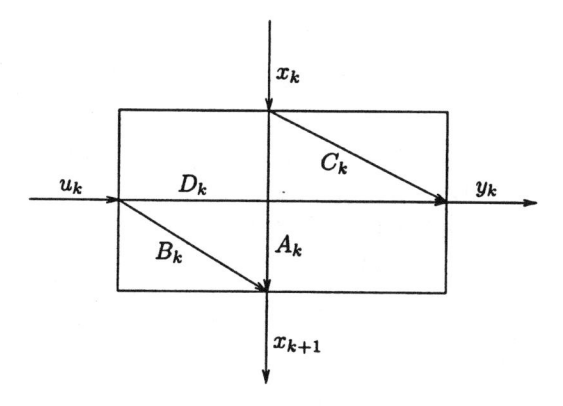

Figure 10.2. The local linear computing scheme.

2. $x_2 = [u_0 \ u_1] = x_1[1 \ 0] + u_1[0 \ 1]$ and $y_1 = x_1 t_{01} + u_1 t_{11}$; hence

$$A_1 = [1 \ 0], \ B_1 = [0 \ 1], \ C_1 = [t_{01}], \ D_1 = [t_{11}].$$

3. $x_3 = [u_0 \ u_1 \ u_2] = x_2 \begin{bmatrix} 1 & 0 & 0 \\ 0 & 1 & 0 \end{bmatrix} + u_2[0 \ 0 \ 1]$ and $y_2 = x_2 \begin{bmatrix} t_{02} \\ t_{12} \end{bmatrix} + u_2 t_{22}$; hence

$$A_2 = \begin{bmatrix} 1 & 0 & 0 \\ 0 & 1 & 0 \end{bmatrix}, \ B_2 = [0 \ 0 \ 1], \ C_2 = \begin{bmatrix} t_{02} \\ t_{12} \end{bmatrix}, \ D_2 = [t_{22}].$$

The principle should be clear! In any case, at each stage of the procedure linear computations take place connecting the present state x_k and input u_k with the next state x_{k+1} and output y_k:

$$\begin{cases} x_{k+1} &= x_k A_k + u_k B_k, \\ y_k &= x_k C_k + u_k D_k. \end{cases} \tag{10.4.2}$$

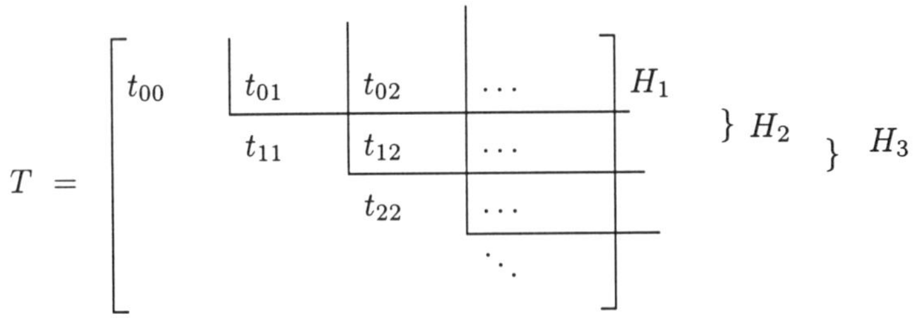

$$T = \begin{bmatrix} t_{00} & t_{01} & t_{02} & \cdots & \\ & t_{11} & t_{12} & \cdots & \\ & & t_{22} & \cdots & \\ & & & \ddots & \end{bmatrix} \begin{matrix} \} H_1 \\ \} H_2 \\ \} H_3 \end{matrix}$$

Figure 10.3. Collection of Hankel matrices of T.

However, there is no reason why the state cannot be a linear combination of past inputs, rather than the inputs themselves. There is also no reason why the calculations should be restricted to scalar inputs and outputs. In principle, all dimensions may vary; the input dimensions form a sequence j_0, j_1, j_2, ... and likewise the output dimensions, o_0, o_1, o_2, ..., as well as the state dimensions, $\delta_0 = 0$, δ_1, δ_2, ... Zero dimensions means that the entry is empty. (We agree, by definition, that the matrix multiplication of an empty matrix of dimension $m \times 0$ with one of dimension $0 \times n$ yields a zero matrix of dimension $m \times n$.) In the case of interest here, however, we work in a framework in which the input dimensions and output dimensions are the same for all k ($j_k = o_k = N$), in which N is a fixed number. (We keep all formulas as general as possible.)

The purpose of realization theory is to find a scheme of minimal state dimensions which computes $y = uT$. It turns out that such a scheme exists and that the minimal dimension of the state at stage k is given by the rank of a certain submatrix of T called the Hankel matrix H_k [VD94], which we now define. Our utilization of the term "Hankel matrix" here is not the traditional one (a matrix with second diagonals consisting of equal entries), but it is in the sense of mathematical system theory: a matrix that maps past inputs to future outputs. We define the *collection of Hankel matrices of T* as the set of matrices H_i represented by the scheme of Fig. 10.3.

More explicitly, each H_i is $(j_0 + j_1 + \cdots j_{i-1}) \times (o_i + o_{i+1} + \cdots + o_n)$ and given by

$$H_i = \begin{bmatrix} t_{0,i} & t_{0,i+1} & \cdots & t_{0,n-1} \\ \vdots & \vdots & \vdots & \vdots \\ t_{i-1,i} & \cdots & \cdots & t_{i-1,n-1} \end{bmatrix}. \qquad (10.4.3)$$

We make the diagonal an exception in the definition. In most cases the diagonal is special or plays a special role, and it could be included in the calculation by moving all diagonals one notch up and introducing a new main diagonal consisting exclusively of zeros.

The important role that Hankel matrices play in realization theory can be deduced from a reconstruction of the matrix T, which is actually the transfer operator of the computational scheme of Fig. 10.1, based on the computation model

$$T = \begin{bmatrix} D_0 & B_0 C_1 & B_0 A_1 C_2 & B_0 A_1 A_2 C_3 & \cdots \\ & D_1 & B_1 C_2 & B_1 A_2 C_3 & \cdots \\ & & D_2 & B_2 C_3 & \cdots \\ & & & \ddots & \vdots \end{bmatrix},$$

Section 10.4.   Realization Theory for Matrices

and hence
$$H_k = \begin{bmatrix} \vdots \\ B_{k-3}A_{k-2}A_{k-1} \\ B_{k-2}A_{k-1} \\ B_{k-1} \end{bmatrix} \begin{bmatrix} C_k & A_k C_{k+1} & \cdots \end{bmatrix}.$$

We see that the realization induces a factorization of each Hankel operator. A direct conclusion is that their ranks are at most equal to the dimensions of the respective local state spaces, rank$(H_k) = \delta_k$, where δ_k is the minimal dimension of x_k. The converse appears true as well, and it is also true that *any* minimal factorization of each of the Hankel matrices induces a specific realization, so that the corresponding $\{A_k, B_k, C_k, D_k\}$ can be recovered from them. A "physical interpretation" of this fact goes back to the celebrated Nerode state equivalence theory, which is briefly reviewed next.

10.4.1 Nerode Equivalence and Natural State Spaces

At each time point k, the Hankel operator maps input signals with support on time points up to and including $k-1$ to the restriction of output signals on the interval $[k, \infty)$. If T is the transfer operator concerned and $\mathbf{P}_{[k,\infty)}$ indicates projection on the ℓ_2 space based on the interval $[k, \infty)$ (we consider the general case), then H_k is given by

$$H_k = \mathbf{P}_{[k,\infty)}(T) \mid_{\ell_2(-\infty,k-1]}. \qquad (10.4.4)$$

The image $\mathcal{H}_{ok}$ of H_k is the set of natural responses that the system is able to generate at time k, while the image $\mathcal{H}_k$ of H_k^* is the orthogonal complement of the nullspace at time k—the space of strict past inputs that generate the zero state. It is a space of equivalent classes, called *Nerode equivalent classes*, each of which represents a class of strictly past input signals that generate the same state, while the output space of natural responses is actually isomorphic to a natural state space. (See [KFA70] for an account of the original theory.) Hence, the state dimension is given by the dimension δ_k of H_k. To find an $\{A, C\}$ realization pair, we choose a basis for each $\mathcal{H}_{ok}$ and collect all those base vectors in one observability operator, as shown in Fig. 10.4.

If each block row in Fig. 10.4 is indeed a basis, then it is also left invertible and we see that the choice determines each A_k and C_k. The corresponding B_k and D_k then follow straightforwardly from knowledge of the transfer map T. The choice of a basis either in $\mathcal{H}_0$ or dually $\mathcal{H}$ determines the realization.

10.4.2 Algorithm for Finding a Realization

An algorithm for finding a minimal realization for T then simply proceeds as follows.

Algorithm 10.4.1 (Time Varying System Realization of T). *Consider an upper triangular matrix $T = [t_{ij}]$ and define its Hankel matrices as in (10.4.3). A realization (A_k, B_k, C_k, D_k) can be found as follows:*

1. *The D_k are obtained from the diagonal entries of T.*

2. *Find a minimal factorization of H_k as $H_k = \mathcal{R}_k \mathcal{O}_k$.*

3. *Put $B_{k-1} = [\mathcal{R}_k]_{k-1}$ (last block entry of $\mathcal{R}_k$).*

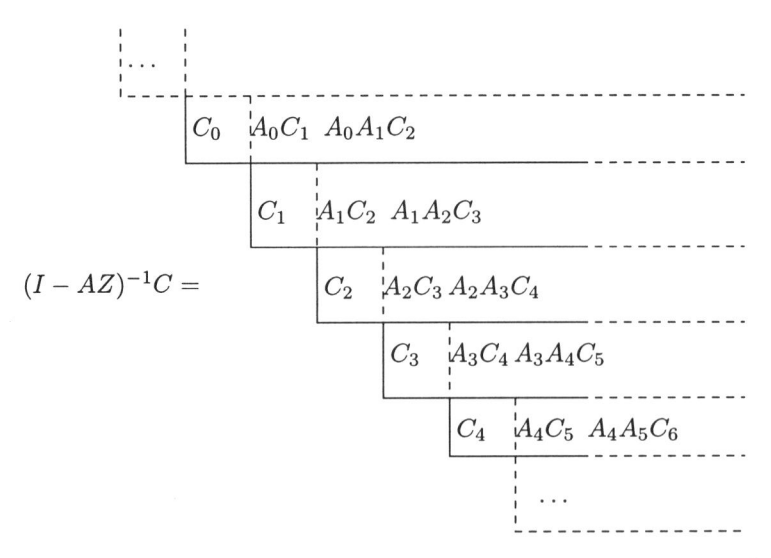

284   Minimal Complexity Realization of Structured Matrices   Chapter 10

$$(I - AZ)^{-1}C = \begin{bmatrix} C_0 & A_0 C_1 & A_0 A_1 C_2 & \cdots \\ & C_1 & A_1 C_2 & A_1 A_2 C_3 & \cdots \\ & & C_2 & A_2 C_3 & A_2 A_3 C_4 & \cdots \\ & & & C_3 & A_3 C_4 & A_3 A_4 C_5 & \cdots \\ & & & & C_4 & A_4 C_5 & A_4 A_5 C_6 & \cdots \\ & & & & & & \cdots \end{bmatrix}$$

Figure 10.4. Choosing and representing a basis for the space of natural responses at each time point.

4. Put $C_k = [\mathcal{O}_k]_1$ (first block entry of $\mathcal{O}_k$).

5. Find A_k so that
$$\begin{bmatrix} [\mathcal{O}_k]_2 & [\mathcal{O}_k]_3 & \cdots \end{bmatrix} = A_k \mathcal{O}_{k+1}. \tag{10.4.5}$$

◇

The matrix A_k is uniquely determined by the condition (10.4.5), since $\mathcal{O}_{k+1}$ is right invertible by the assumption of minimal factorization. The matrices $\mathcal{R}_k$ and $\mathcal{O}_k$ play a central role in system theory and are called the *reachability* and *observability* matrices of the realization. (For discussion on controllability and observability, see [KFA70], [Kai80], [DV93].)

The proof that the algorithm works requires us to show that if the realization is given by the algorithm, then it reproduces the entries $T_{k\ell} = B_k A_{k+1} \cdots A_{\ell-1} C_\ell$ exactly for all $0 \leq k < \ell$ (in which expression some of the A_i factors can disappear when $\ell - k \leq 2$). This can (fairly simply) be done as a recursion on $\ell - k$. Note first that the algorithm defines the entries of all the observability matrices $\mathcal{O}_k$: the $[\mathcal{O}_k]_1$ are given directly, while $[\mathcal{O}_k]_i$ follows from the definition of A_{i-1} and the value just below it, $[\mathcal{O}_{k+1}]_{i-1}$. Since all the values of the B_{k-1} also are known, we now have all the bottom rows of the H_k specified and hence all the upper off diagonal entries of T. (As stated above, the diagonal entries are assumed known, while the lower entries are all zero.) It is now easy to check that all the reachability matrices are well defined (just put $[\mathcal{R}]_i = B_{k-i} A_{k-i+1} \cdots A_{k-1}$ for $i > 1$) and that the H_k factor is as expected.

We can also obtain nonminimal realizations through nonminimal factorizations of the H_k, but then we have to be a little more careful. Examination of the proof in the previous paragraph shows that one way could be by producing a sequence of well-defined observability matrices and that this can be done by ensuring that for all k, the rows of $[[\mathcal{O}_k]_2, [\mathcal{O}_k]_3, \ldots]$ lie in the row space of the subsequent $\mathcal{O}_{k+1}$. Then an A_k can be found for each k (although now it is not necessarily unique), and all the entries of the observability matrices follow recursively.

Section 10.4. Realization Theory for Matrices

Dually, a realization could be based on the reachability matrices rather than on the observability matrices. It should be clear that once the choice for one has been made, the other follows automatically. Clearly, even minimal realizations are not unique. Each different factorization will produce a different realization: there is a one-to-one correspondence between the choice of bases for the observability (or dually reachability) spaces and to be minimal realizations. We say that a realization is in *output normal form* if the bases of all the observability spaces have been chosen to be orthonormal. In that case, the corresponding $\{A_k, C_k\}$ will be isometric, i.e., they will satisfy (for all $k \geq 0$)

$$A_k A_k^* + C_k C_k^* = I, \qquad (10.4.6)$$

and vice versa. If (10.4.6) is satisfied, then the corresponding basis for the observability spaces is orthonormal. (The recursive proof is not difficult; we skip it for the sake of brevity.) The transformation of one minimal realization to another is accomplished via a transformation of the state at each point k. If we write, for each point k, $x'_k = T_k x_k$, in which T_k is an invertible matrix, then the state equation in the primed quantities becomes

$$\begin{cases} x'_{k+1} &= x'_k T_k A_k T_{k+1}^{-1} + u_k B_k T_{k+1}^{-1}, \\ y_k &= x'_k T_k C_k + u_k D_k, \end{cases} \qquad (10.4.7)$$

and the transformed realization is given by $\{T_k A_k T_{k+1}^{-1}, B_k T_{k+1}^{-1}, T_k C_k, D_k\}$. In particular, suppose that we are given a realization and that we wish to bring it to normal form. Then we should find a collection $\{T_k\}$ such that the transformed $\{A'_k, C'_k\}$ satisfy (10.4.6). If we define $\Lambda_k = T_k^{-1}(T_k^*)^{-1}$, then this amounts to satisfying the recursive equation

$$A_k \Lambda_{k+1} A_k^* + C_k C_k^* = \Lambda_k. \qquad (10.4.8)$$

In the remainder of the chapter we shall treat cases where this equation can indeed be satisfied uniquely by a (uniformily) invertible collection of $\{\Lambda_k\}$. It is known that the existence of such a solution to (10.4.8) requires uniform exponential stability of the sequence $\{A_k\}$. This is known as the Lyapunov condition, and we shall put ourselves in a situation where this condition is automatically satisfied.

Once a realization for an upper triangular operator T is obtained, it is easy to derive a realization for its inverse. If T is invertible, then that will also be the case for its main diagonal. If $\{A_k, B_k, C_k, D_k\}$ is a realization for T, then each $D_k = T_{kk}$ will also be invertible, and from the state equations we obtain

$$\begin{cases} x_{k+1} &= x_k(A_k - C_k D_k^{-1} B_k) + y_k D_k^{-1} B_k, \\ u_k &= -x_k C_k D_k^{-1} + y_k D_k^{-1}; \end{cases} \qquad (10.4.9)$$

hence $\{A_k - C_k D_k^{-1} B_k, D_k^{-1} B_k, -C_k D_k^{-1}, D_k^{-1}\}$ provides a realization for T^{-1} of the same state complexity as the original.

Generalizing our framework, suppose that the original operator T is not upper triangular in the traditional sense. Then we have a number of options at our disposal to make it upper triangular in a generalized sense:

- We can shift the $(0,0)$th position to the bottom left corner. This strategy requires the introduction of a more general numbering scheme than that used so far; see the next section.

- We can additively decompose T as the sum of a lower triangular and an upper triangular component and realize each of them separately. Needless to say, this strategy will not be very useful when our actual purpose is to compute the inverse of T, but it may be very useful in other circumstances.

- We can also try to do a multiplicative decomposition of T into a lower triangular matrix that multiplies an upper triangular one (or vice versa); this strategy would yield good results when we wish to invert T subsequently.

The important point is that the low complexity representation technique remains valid for the components.

In the next section we shall discuss realizations for the additive and the multiplicative decompositions of a positive-definite matrix R, which presumably is of low displacement rank.

10.5 REALIZATION OF LOW DISPLACEMENT RANK MATRICES

The goal of the next two sections is the derivation of low-complexity representations for the additive and the multiplicative decomposition of a positive-definite matrix R. Let us write $R = [r_{ij}]$ as

$$R = U^*U = \frac{1}{2}(F + F^*), \tag{10.5.1}$$

in which U and F are upper triangular matrices. Then

$$F = \begin{bmatrix} r_{00} & 2r_{01} & 2r_{02} & \cdots \\ & r_{11} & 2r_{12} & \cdots \\ & & r_{22} & \cdots \\ & & & \ddots \end{bmatrix}.$$

If a low state dimension realization exists for F, then one can be found for U as well. Although this fact can be derived in general (it is a form of a spectral factorization result), we shall rederive it and specialize the calculation for the case at hand.

Let us write for simplicity $R - ZRZ^* \stackrel{\Delta}{=} X$; then it is easy to see that R can be recovered from X via the formula

$$R = X + ZXZ^* + \cdots + Z^{n-1}X(Z^*)^{n-1}.$$

The contribution of each term to the Hankel operators for F is easy to evaluate. Indeed, consider the Hankel operator H_k for F. Then the contributions of the individual terms to H_k are

$$H_k(X) = \begin{bmatrix} a_0 \\ \vdots \\ a_{k-1} \end{bmatrix} J \begin{bmatrix} a_k^* & \cdots & a_{n-1}^* \end{bmatrix},$$

$$H_k(ZXZ^*) = \begin{bmatrix} 0 \\ a_0 \\ \vdots \\ a_{k-2} \end{bmatrix} J \begin{bmatrix} a_{k-1}^* & \cdots & a_{n-2}^* \end{bmatrix},$$

$$H_k(Z^{k-1}X(Z^*)^{k-1}) = \begin{bmatrix} 0 \\ \vdots \\ 0 \\ a_0 \end{bmatrix} J \begin{bmatrix} a_1^* & \cdots & a_{n-k}^* \end{bmatrix}.$$

Section 10.5. Realization of Low Displacement Rank Matrices

Putting these terms together and using the outer product representation of a matrix, we get

$$H_k(F) = 2 \begin{bmatrix} a_0 J & 0 & \cdots & 0 \\ a_1 J & a_0 J & \ddots & \vdots \\ \vdots & \ddots & \ddots & 0 \\ a_{k-1} J & \cdots & \cdots & a_0 J \end{bmatrix} \begin{bmatrix} a_k^* & \cdots & \cdots & a_{n-1}^* \\ \vdots & & & \vdots \\ a_2^* & \cdots & \cdots & a_{n-k+1}^* \\ a_1^* & a_2^* & \cdots & a_{n-k}^* \end{bmatrix},$$

which is of the form (traditional) Toeplitz matrix times (traditional) Hankel matrix. (The second matrix seems to be like a traditional Toeplitz matrix also, but it is actually of the classical Hankel type since it maps a past input sequence to a past output sequence. We recover the classical Hankel type when we reverse the order of the rows. The difference between the two types is essential for the discussion here; see the explanation in Sec. 10.4.1 for added emphasis.) The rank of the Hankel matrix $H_k(F)$ (the term now refers to its more general meaning) is the essential parameter in the derivation of the state realization, and we obtain

$$\operatorname{rank}(H_k(F)) \leq \operatorname{rank} \begin{bmatrix} a_1^* & a_2^* & \cdots & a_{n-1}^* \\ a_2^* & a_3^* & \ddots & \vdots \\ \vdots & \ddots & \ddots & \vdots \\ a_k^* & \ddots & \ddots & a_{n-k}^* \end{bmatrix},$$

which is a submatrix of the global (linear time invariant (LTI)) Hankel operator for the system

$$a_0^* + a_1^* z + a_2^* z^2 + a_3^* z^3 + \cdots,$$

which is given by

$$\begin{bmatrix} a_1^* & a_2^* & \cdots & \cdots \\ a_2^* & a_3^* & \ddots & \cdots \\ \vdots & \ddots & \ddots & \cdots \\ \vdots & \vdots & \vdots & \ddots \end{bmatrix}.$$

A (standard) realization for that LTI system can be used as a starting point for the realization of F. Assuming that the dimension of the state space needed is δ, we find matrices α, β, γ of dimensions $\delta \times \delta, (p+q) \times \delta, \delta \times N$ such that, for $i \geq 1$,

$$a_i^* = \beta \alpha^{i-1} \gamma. \tag{10.5.2}$$

We choose the realization in output normal form, which means that the matrix $[\alpha \ \gamma]$ is isometric, i.e., $\alpha \alpha^* + \gamma \gamma^* = 1$. The realization $\{\alpha, \beta, \gamma\}$ may even be an adequate approximation to the system of a_k^*'s. Use your favorite approximation theory, based either on Hankel approximation theory in the style of [AAK71] or on balanced realizations [Kun78]. Notice that in the case of scalar inputs or outputs, the a_k^*'s just form a single z-dependent column. The relevant Hankel matrix for the series $\{a_i^*\}$ is now

$$\begin{bmatrix} a_k^* & \cdots & a_{n-1}^* \\ \vdots & & \vdots \\ a_1^* & \cdots & a_{n-k}^* \end{bmatrix} = \begin{bmatrix} \beta \alpha^{k-1} \\ \vdots \\ \beta \alpha \\ \beta \end{bmatrix} [\gamma \ \alpha \gamma \ \cdots] \begin{bmatrix} I_{n-k} \\ 0 \end{bmatrix}, \tag{10.5.3}$$

in which the last matrix cuts out the first $n-k$ components from an otherwise infinite series.

The kth Hankel matrix for F is now

$$H_k(F) = 2 \begin{bmatrix} a_0 J & & 0 \\ \vdots & \ddots & \\ a_{k-1}J & \cdots & a_0 J \end{bmatrix} \begin{bmatrix} \beta \alpha^{k-1} \\ \vdots \\ \beta \alpha \\ \beta \end{bmatrix} [\gamma \; \alpha\gamma \; \cdots] \begin{bmatrix} I_{n-k} \\ 0 \end{bmatrix}$$

and we find a realization for F with $A = \alpha$ and $C = \gamma$ already determined and, from the last row,

$$\begin{aligned} B_{k-1} &= 2a_{k-1}J\beta\alpha^{k-1} + \cdots + 2a_0 J\beta \\ &= 2\gamma^*[(\alpha^*)^{k-2}\beta^*J\beta\alpha^{k-1} + \cdots + \beta^*J\beta\alpha] + 2a_0 J\beta. \end{aligned} \quad (10.5.4)$$

Let us define

$$M_k \triangleq (\alpha^*)^{k-1}\beta^*J\beta\alpha^{k-1} + \cdots + \beta^*J\beta; \quad (10.5.5)$$

then M_k satisfies the recursive Lyapunov equation

$$M_k = \alpha^* M_{k-1} \alpha + \beta^* J\beta, \quad (10.5.6)$$

and B_k can easily be computed from M_k via

$$B_k = 2\gamma^* M_k \alpha + 2a_0 J\beta. \quad (10.5.7)$$

Similarly,

$$\begin{aligned} D_k &= a_k J a_k^* + \cdots + a_0 J a_0^* \\ &= a_k J a_k^* + D_{k-1} \quad \text{for } k \geq 1, \end{aligned} \quad (10.5.8)$$

and we have found a low rank recursive realization for F.

Algorithm 10.5.1 (Realization of F). *Given a symmetric positive-definite matrix R with displacement structure (10.3.1), a state-space realization (A, B_k, C, D_k) for the upper triangular additive component F in (10.5.1) can be found as follows:*

1. $A = \alpha$, $C = \gamma$ from the LTI system (10.5.2).

2. $B_k = 2C^* M_k \alpha + 2a_0 J\beta$, where $M_1 = \beta^* J\beta$ and $M_k = \alpha^* M_{k-1}\alpha + \beta^* J\beta$ when $k \geq 1$.

3. $D_k = D_{k-1} + a_k J a_k^*$ for $k \geq 1$ and $D_0 = a_0 J a_0^*$.

$\diamond$

This realization is not necessarily (locally) minimal; it can be trimmed at the borders if needed. (The detailed procedure may be worthwhile but would lead us too far astray here—see [VD94].) A final observation is that the scheme gradually converges to a time-invariant realization when the operator R, now viewed as semi-infinite for positive indices, is bounded, since M_k, D_k, B_k converge as $k \to \infty$.

10.6 A REALIZATION FOR THE CHOLESKY FACTOR

We had before
$$R = \frac{1}{2}(F + F^*) = U^*U.$$

To find a realization for the Cholesky factor U, we keep $\{A, C\}$ and compute new b_k, d_k from the realization $\{A, B_k, C, D_k\}$ of F of the preceding section. First we show how this can be done in a general way; we deduce the algorithm and we show its correctness.

At this point it is advantageous to introduce block diagonal matrices to represent time-varying state-space representations. Let

$$\hat{A} \triangleq \text{diag}\left\{\boxed{A_0}, A_1, A_2, \ldots\right\},$$
$$\hat{B} \triangleq \text{diag}\left\{\boxed{B_0}, B_1, B_2, \ldots\right\},$$
$$\hat{C} \triangleq \text{diag}\left\{\boxed{C_0}, C_1, C_2, \ldots\right\},$$
$$\hat{D} \triangleq \text{diag}\left\{\boxed{D_0}, D_1, D_2, \ldots\right\}.$$

The first transition matrix A_0 is usually empty because there is no incoming state in the calculation—see Fig. 10.3. Let us assume that the sequence of state dimensions is $\{\Delta_1, \Delta_2, \ldots\}$ (we take $\Delta_0 = 0$!); then $\hat{A}$ consists of a sequence of diagonal blocks of dimensions $0 \times \Delta_1, \Delta_1 \times \Delta_2, \Delta_2 \times \Delta_3, \ldots$. It is a block diagonal matrix for which the first block is empty. (As indicated before, we write matrix-vector multiplication usually as row vector × matrix: $y = uA$.)

In addition to block diagonal matrices we introduce the (causal) shift matrix as

$$\mathcal{Z} \triangleq \begin{bmatrix} \ddots & \ddots & & & \\ & 0 & I & & \\ & & 0 & I & \\ & & & 0 & I \\ & & & & \ddots & \ddots \end{bmatrix}.$$

$\mathcal{Z}$ will shift rows if applied to the left of a matrix and will shift columns when applied to the right. It is also a block matrix where the first off diagonal is filled with unit matrices of possibly varying dimensions. $\mathcal{Z}$ actually stands for a collection of block matrices, because the dimensions of the various blocks may be different. For example, if $\mathcal{Z}$ is applied to the right of matrix $\hat{A}$ with block column dimensions $\Delta_1 + \Delta_2 + \Delta_3 + \cdots$, it will also have that sequence of (block) rows, while its sequence of (block) columns will be $\Delta_0 + \Delta_1 + \Delta_2 + \cdots$. It is understood that $\Delta_0 = 0$ in this case but that an empty column is there as a placeholder (and actually defines the location of the main diagonal). The underlying matrix when the block structure is stripped is just a unit matrix (which would not be the case if T had been doubly infinite to start with). We find in this way that the computing scheme "realizes" the operator

$$T = \hat{D} + \hat{B}\mathcal{Z}(I - \hat{A}\mathcal{Z})^{-1}\hat{C}. \tag{10.6.1}$$

We show in Fig. 10.5 a semigraphical illustration of how the block matrix mechanics of (10.6.1) work starting at $t = 0$. Because of the start-up condition, the state dimension δ_0 at $t = 0$ is zero. The various matrices of importance to the reasoning are also shown

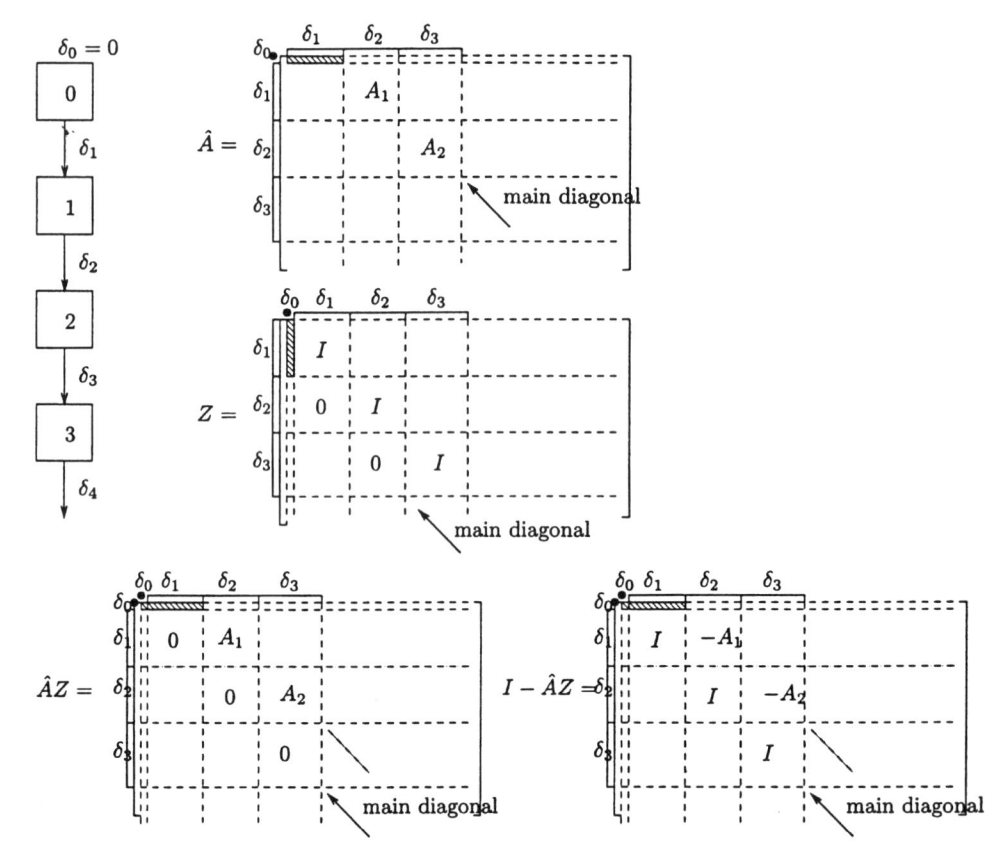

290 Minimal Complexity Realization of Structured Matrices Chapter 10

Figure 10.5. How the operator $I - \hat{A}\mathcal{Z}$ originates.

in the figure. We remark further that

$$I - \hat{A}\mathcal{Z} = \begin{bmatrix} I & -A_1 & & 0 \\ & I & -A_2 & \\ & & \ddots & \ddots \\ 0 & & & \ddots \end{bmatrix}.$$

Let us now try to find a realization for U with the same $\hat{A}$ and $\hat{C}$ as before but a new $\hat{b}$ and $\hat{d}$. Then we should have

$$U^*U = \hat{d}^*\hat{d} + \hat{C}^*(I - \mathcal{Z}^*\hat{A}^*)^{-1}\mathcal{Z}^*\hat{b}^*\hat{d} + \hat{d}^*\hat{b}\mathcal{Z}(I - \hat{A}\mathcal{Z})^{-1}\hat{C} \\ + \hat{C}^*(I - \mathcal{Z}^*\hat{A}^*)^{-1}\mathcal{Z}^*\hat{b}^*\hat{b}\mathcal{Z}(I - \hat{A}\mathcal{Z})^{-1}\hat{C}.$$

The last term in this expression is quadratic. It can be subjected to a partial fraction expansion, which in this generalized context works as follows.

Let us define the diagonal shift on any block matrix $\hat{M}$ (a shift of one block down the main diagonals in the southeast direction):

$$\hat{M}^{(1)} \triangleq \mathcal{Z}^*\hat{M}\mathcal{Z}.$$

Section 10.6. A Realization for the Cholesky Factor

Then

$$\begin{aligned}(I - \mathcal{Z}^*\hat{A}^*)^{-1}(\hat{b}^*\hat{b})^{(1)}(I - \hat{A}\mathcal{Z})^{-1} &= (I - \mathcal{Z}^*\hat{A}^*)^{-1}\hat{m} + \hat{m}(I - \hat{A}\mathcal{Z})^{-1} - \hat{m} \\ &= \hat{m} + \hat{m}\hat{A}\mathcal{Z}(I - \hat{A}\mathcal{Z})^{-1} \\ &\quad + (I - \mathcal{Z}^*\hat{A}^*)^{-1}\mathcal{Z}^*\hat{A}^*\hat{m}\end{aligned}$$

if the equation for the block diagonal matrix $\hat{m}$,

$$\hat{m} = (\hat{b}^*\hat{b} + \hat{A}^*\hat{m}\hat{A})^{(1)}, \tag{10.6.2}$$

has a solution. Checking is immediate by pre- and postmultiplication of the expression with $(I - \mathcal{Z}^*\hat{A}^*)$ and $(I - \hat{A}\mathcal{Z})$, respectively.

This equation is known as a recursive Lyapunov–Stein equation, and in the present context it has a (unique) solution which can be computed recursively, provided that $b_k^* b_k$ is known at each step. Moreover, $\hat{m}$ is a matrix with square diagonal blocks of dimensions $\Delta_0 \times \Delta_0$, $\Delta_1 \times \Delta_1$, $\Delta_2 \times \Delta_2$, ..., in which the Δ_i are the block row dimensions of $\hat{A}$ and the first block $\Delta_0 \times \Delta_0$ is empty (row and column dimensions are zero). Let us write $\hat{m} = \text{diag}(m_0 \dotplus m_1 \dotplus m_2 \cdots)$ in which m_0 is empty; then the recursion (10.6.3) says

$$\begin{aligned}(1) \quad m_1 &= b_0^* b_0, \\ (2) \quad m_2 &= b_1^* b_1 + A_1^* m_1 A_1, \\ (3) \quad m_3 &= b_2^* b_2 + A_2^* m_2 A_2, \\ \vdots \quad &= \vdots\end{aligned}$$

When the partial fraction decomposition is now introduced in the equation for U^*U above, and we identify the strictly upper triangular, diagonal, and strictly lower triangular parts, then we see that the block diagonal matrices $\hat{b}$ and $\hat{d}$ must now satisfy the set of equations

$$\begin{cases} \frac{1}{2}(\hat{D} + \hat{D}^*) &= \hat{d}^*\hat{d} + \hat{C}^*\hat{m}\hat{C}, \\ \frac{1}{2}\hat{B} &= \hat{d}^*\hat{b} + \hat{C}^*\hat{m}\hat{A}, \\ \hat{m}^{(-1)} &= \hat{b}^*\hat{b} + \hat{A}^*\hat{m}\hat{A}. \end{cases} \tag{10.6.3}$$

This set of equations clearly leads to a recursive algorithm if consistent.

Algorithm 10.6.1 (Realization of the Cholesky Factor). *Given a symmetric positive-definite matrix R with displacement structure (10.3.1), a state-space realization (A, b_k, C, d_k) for the Cholesky factor U in (10.5.1) can be found as follows:*

1. *Keep the (A, C) from Alg. 10.5.1 and consider the (B_k, D_k) from the same algorithm.*

2. *Step 0. Set $d_0 = [\frac{1}{2}(D_0 + D_0^*)]^{1/2}$, $b_0 = \frac{1}{2}d_0^{-*}B_0$, and $m_1 = b_0^* b_0$.*

3. *Step i. Now assume m_i is known! Then set $d_i = [\frac{1}{2}(D_i + D_i^*) - C^* m_i C]^{1/2}$ (we shall show that the positive square root exists), $b_i = d_i^{-*}[\frac{1}{2}B_i - C^* m_i A]$, and $m_{i+1} = b_i^* b_i + A^* m_i A$.*

$\diamond$

One may think that a solution must exist, almost by construction (since the starting point of the recursion is well known—$m_0 = \emptyset$, the empty set) or by the theory of spectral factorization for time-varying systems, but because the realization for F is not guaranteed minimal, there is reasonable doubt that at the kth step the equation for d_k,

$$d_k^* d_k = \frac{1}{2}(D_k + D_k^*) - C_k^* m_k C_k,$$

cannot be satisfied because the second member is possibly not positive definite. It is instructive to show that this cannot happen. In doing so we also give an alternative proof of the spectral factorization theorem for a time-varying R, and we show that it amounts to a Cholesky factorization. We construct the proof by looking at the Cholesky factorization of R in a Crout–Doolittle fashion—the classical method for solving a system of linear equations; see [Ste73]. The general Crout–Doolittle method consists of a recursive construction of a tableau for the lower or upper factorization of a general matrix $T = LU$ (in which we take U upper with unit diagonal entries and L lower). It has the form (taking u_{ij} and l_{ij} as the entries of U and L, respectively, and assuming no pivoting is necessary)

$$\begin{bmatrix} u_{00} & u_{01} & u_{02} & \cdots \\ (l_{10}) & u_{11} & u_{12} & \cdots \\ (l_{20}) & (l_{21}) & u_{22} & \cdots \\ \vdots & \vdots & \vdots & \ddots \end{bmatrix}.$$

It turns out that an entry, say, u_{ij}, of this tableau can be computed from the entries of the original matrix and the entries of the tableau with lower indices k, ℓ with either $k < i$ and $\ell \leq j$ or vice versa. In the next paragraph we give the details for our case.

The Cholesky modification of the Crout–Doolittle tableau for R looks as follows (in which the u_{ij} are the entries of U):

$$\begin{bmatrix} r_{00} & r_{01} & r_{02} & \cdots \\ r_{10} & r_{11} & r_{12} & \cdots \\ r_{20} & r_{21} & r_{22} & \cdots \\ \vdots & \vdots & \vdots & \ddots \end{bmatrix} \Rightarrow \begin{bmatrix} u_{00} & u_{01} & u_{02} & \cdots \\ (u_{01}^*) & u_{11} & u_{12} & \cdots \\ (u_{02}^*) & (u_{12}^*) & u_{22} & \cdots \\ \vdots & \vdots & \vdots & \ddots \end{bmatrix}. \quad (10.6.4)$$

The right-hand side is not really a useable matrix since its strictly lower part belongs to the matrix U^* and not to U, but it is customary and useful to include it in the tableau. Moreover, we remark that the entries can be matrices themselves. Filling the Cholesky tableau recursively then proceeds as follows:

- Step 0. $u_{00} = r_{00}^{1/2}$, $u_{0i} = u_{00}^{-*} r_{0i}$.

- Step i.
$$\begin{array}{ll} [\text{pivot}] & u_{ii}^* u_{ii} = r_{ii} - \sum_{k=0}^{i-1} u_{ki}^* u_{ki}, \\ (j > i) & u_{ij} = u_{ii}^{-*}[r_{ij} - \sum_{k=0}^{i-1} u_{ki}^* u_{kj}]. \end{array}$$

The central property in the algorithm is that the pivot is positive definite when R is, so that its square root can be taken in the case of scalar as well as matrix block entries. A proof for this fact is found by looking at a partial factorization of R up to the ith step and is of course classical.

In our case we have, thanks to the realization for F,

$$R = \begin{bmatrix} \frac{1}{2}[D_0 + D_0^*] & \frac{1}{2}B_0\gamma & \frac{1}{2}B_0 A\gamma & \frac{1}{2}B_0 A^2\gamma & \cdots \\ \frac{1}{2}\gamma^* B_0^* & \frac{1}{2}[D_1 + D_1^*] & \frac{1}{2}B_1\gamma & \frac{1}{2}B_1 A\gamma & \cdots \\ \frac{1}{2}\gamma^* A^* B_0^* & \frac{1}{2}\gamma^* B_1^* & \frac{1}{2}[D_2 + D_2^*] & \frac{1}{2}B_2\gamma & \cdots \\ \vdots & \vdots & \vdots & \vdots & \ddots \end{bmatrix}.$$

We now show that the recursion (10.6.2) in effect generates the (modified) Crout–Doolittle recursion.

- Step 0. $m_0 = \emptyset$, $\frac{1}{2}[D_0 + D_0^*] = d_0^* d_0$, $\frac{1}{2}B_0 = d_0^* b_0$ are of course solvable and produce the first row of U as

$$d_0 \quad b_0\gamma \quad b_0 A\gamma \quad b_0 A^2\gamma \quad \cdots.$$

- Step i. Let us assume that the first i rows (i.e., with indices $0,\ldots,i-1$) are computed. We have to show that $d_i^* d_i$ is well defined (i.e., the expression for it is positive definite) and also that the rest of the row with index i is correct. The Crout–Doolittle scheme applies and, thanks to the induction hypothesis, says that

$$\frac{1}{2}[D_i + D_i^*] - \sum_{k=0}^{i-1} \gamma^*[A^*]^{i-1-k} b_k^* b_k A^{i-k-1}\gamma$$

is positive definite. The recursion for $\hat{m}$ on the other hand gives an expression for the sum, so that the formula is in fact

$$\frac{1}{2}[D_i + D_i^*] - \gamma^* m_i \gamma,$$

which is hence positive definite and can be factored as $d_i^* d_i$. A further identification with the Crout–Doolittle scheme produces for $j > i$,

$$\begin{aligned} u_{ij} &= d_i^{-*}\{\tfrac{1}{2} B_i A^{j-i-1}\gamma - \sum_{k=0}^{i-1}(b_k A^{i-1-k}\gamma)^*(b_k A^{j-1-k}\gamma)\} \\ &= d_i^{-*}[\tfrac{1}{2} B_i - \gamma^* m_i A] A^{j-i-1}\gamma, \end{aligned}$$

an equation that will be satisfied if (the more demanding) equation

$$\frac{1}{2} B_i = d_i^* b_i + \gamma^* m_i A$$

is. We may conclude that the scheme given by (10.6.2) always produces a positive-definite expression for

$$\frac{1}{2}[D_i + D_i^*] - \gamma^* m_i \gamma$$

when the original R is positive definite.

This concludes the proof of the existence of the realization for U as given by the algorithm, and we see that it is of the same complexity as the realization for F. In the following section we shall see that this realization also leads to an attractive computational scheme for U^{-1}, again of the same complexity.

10.7 DISCUSSION

The theory presented here is of course a specialization of a theory that can handle more general types of operators beyond matrices, e.g., general time-varying, time-discrete systems. For a reasonably complete account see [DV98]. The situation considered here is much simpler for two reasons: (1) matrices have a starting index, and equations become recursive with a well-defined initial condition; (2) there is an underlying time-invariant system that can be handled by classical techniques, especially concerning approximation. The more general case, however, does have some interest even here. Conceivably, the

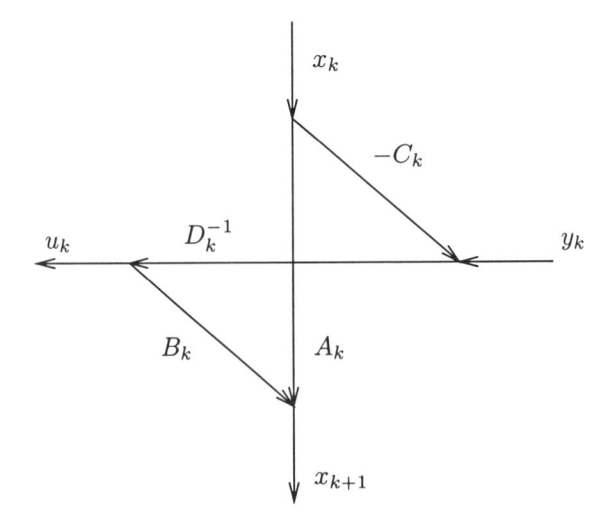

Figure 10.6. Simple local computation scheme for the inverse of a system.

matrices that we handle can be very large, but even more interesting, they may consist of subsequent "slices" of different low displacement rank systems. In that case we have a global time-varying but local low displacement behavior, but the approximation and complexity reduction theory will work roughly along the same lines as set out above, now with the use of the general theory.

A legitimate question, already announced in the introductory sections of this chapter, is, What do we gain in complexity reduction of the calculations if we apply the realization theory detailed in this chapter? A meaningful answer to such a question requires an understanding of what we mean by "the calculations." We consider two cases: calculations aiming at the construction of a model for the system or its inverse and calculations that aim at applying the model to an input. Both the low displacement rank and the low Hankel degree will contribute in both cases and in the expected manner. The low displacement rank allows for realizations of F and U in which only the matrices B_k and D_k vary from one point to the next using simple update equations, depending only on the actual a_k, which is itself dependent only on time-invariant data. If the Hankel rank is δ and the original system has scalar inputs and outputs, then the complexity of the realization $\{\alpha, \beta, \gamma\}$ is of the order of $(p+q)\delta$. Hence we end up with a parameter update scheme which can be very efficient depending on the precise values of the three parameters. The computational efficiency of vector-matrix products realized by a computational scheme as shown in Fig. 10.1 is directly proportional to the size of the state δ. As for the inverse (say, of U), we also face two types of computation: updates and the application of the computing scheme to inputs. Again, the update of the realization matrices for the inverse is a purely local matter dependent only on the actual a_k or their realization, via the formulas given by (10.4.9), but the computation can be restricted to the computation of D_k^{-1} since the other realization matrices can be used directly by graph inversion, as shown in Fig. 10.6. (More sophisticated schemes in which only δ scalar entries must be inverted exist; see [Vee93].)

Of course, the usage of a model for computation as shown in Fig. 10.1 precludes the utilization of the FFT as a complexity reducing engine. An FFT scheme, however, requires a complete shuffle of the data, either at the input side, or in the course of the computations. It is (in some variations) the computational scheme that uses the smallest number of multiplications and additions possible but at the cost of maximal shuffling of data. It also does not utilize the fact that relevant impulse responses can have a lot of structure or can be approximated with very efficient data. In selective applications, accuracy will suffer. This is the reason why, in many signal processing applications, filtering algorithms are the preferred mode of implementation, although they coexist with the FFT. Even intermediate forms are possible, utilized in subband or multiresolution coding schemes, in which some shuffling of data takes place, combined with classical filtering. Therefore, a clear-cut statement concerning the advantage of one or the other is hard to make outside a specific application domain. This holds true even for the Toeplitz case. Here, Hankel realization theory reduces to the classical LTI realization theory, and the displacement rank may be just 1, so that vector-matrix multiplication reduces to a single FFT. The relative computational efficiency then pitches the system's degree δ against the logarithm of the time sequence, $\ln n$, which might appear to be to the advantage of the latter. But then, not all items in the complexity calculation have been included! For example, the "pipeline" (space) complexity of the FFT is again n against δ, which may be very disadvantageous in concrete cases. And if selective accuracy is included in the considerations, then the length of the FFT and the wordlength to be used may be impractical.

Appendix A

USEFUL MATRIX RESULTS

Thomas Kailath

Ali H. Sayed

Useful Matrix Results — Appendix A

We collect in this appendix several matrix facts and formulas, where we assume that inverses exist as needed.

A.1 SOME MATRIX IDENTITIES

(i) Block Gaussian Elimination and Schur Complements

Consider a block matrix

$$M = \begin{bmatrix} A & B \\ C & D \end{bmatrix}$$

that we wish to triangularize by a (block) Gaussian elimination procedure. For this, note that

$$\begin{bmatrix} I & 0 \\ X & I \end{bmatrix} \begin{bmatrix} A & B \\ C & D \end{bmatrix} = \begin{bmatrix} A & B \\ XA+C & XB+D \end{bmatrix},$$

so that choosing $X = -CA^{-1}$ gives

$$\begin{bmatrix} I & 0 \\ -CA^{-1} & I \end{bmatrix} \begin{bmatrix} A & B \\ C & D \end{bmatrix} = \begin{bmatrix} A & B \\ 0 & \Delta_A \end{bmatrix},$$

where

$$\Delta_A \triangleq D - CA^{-1}B$$

is called the *Schur complement of A in M*. Similarly we can find that

$$\begin{bmatrix} A & B \\ C & D \end{bmatrix} \begin{bmatrix} I & -A^{-1}B \\ 0 & I \end{bmatrix} = \begin{bmatrix} A & 0 \\ C & \Delta_A \end{bmatrix}.$$

Thus we also can obtain

$$\begin{bmatrix} I & -BD^{-1} \\ 0 & I \end{bmatrix} \begin{bmatrix} A & B \\ C & D \end{bmatrix} = \begin{bmatrix} \Delta_D & 0 \\ C & D \end{bmatrix}$$

and

$$\begin{bmatrix} A & B \\ C & D \end{bmatrix} \begin{bmatrix} I & 0 \\ -D^{-1}C & I \end{bmatrix} = \begin{bmatrix} \Delta_D & B \\ 0 & D \end{bmatrix},$$

where $\Delta_D = A - BD^{-1}C$ is the *Schur complement* of D in M.

(ii) Determinants

Using the product rule for determinants, the results in (i) give

$$\det \begin{bmatrix} A & B \\ C & D \end{bmatrix} = \det A \det (D - CA^{-1}B) = \det A \det \Delta_A \quad (A.1.1)$$

$$= \det D \det (A - BD^{-1}C) = \det D \det \Delta_D. \quad (A.1.2)$$

Section A.1. Some Matrix Identities

(iii) Block Triangular Factorizations

The results in (i) can be combined to block diagonalize M:

$$\begin{bmatrix} I & 0 \\ -CA^{-1} & I \end{bmatrix} \begin{bmatrix} A & B \\ C & D \end{bmatrix} \begin{bmatrix} I & -A^{-1}B \\ 0 & I \end{bmatrix} = \begin{bmatrix} A & 0 \\ 0 & \Delta_A \end{bmatrix}$$

and

$$\begin{bmatrix} I & -BD^{-1} \\ 0 & I \end{bmatrix} \begin{bmatrix} A & B \\ C & D \end{bmatrix} \begin{bmatrix} I & 0 \\ -D^{-1}C & I \end{bmatrix} = \begin{bmatrix} \Delta_D & 0 \\ 0 & D \end{bmatrix}.$$

Then by using the easily verified formula

$$\begin{bmatrix} I & 0 \\ P & I \end{bmatrix}^{-1} = \begin{bmatrix} I & 0 \\ -P & I \end{bmatrix},$$

we can obtain the direct factorization formulas

$$\begin{bmatrix} A & B \\ C & D \end{bmatrix} = \begin{bmatrix} I & 0 \\ CA^{-1} & I \end{bmatrix} \begin{bmatrix} A & 0 \\ 0 & \Delta_A \end{bmatrix} \begin{bmatrix} I & A^{-1}B \\ 0 & I \end{bmatrix}$$

$$= \begin{bmatrix} I & BD^{-1} \\ 0 & I \end{bmatrix} \begin{bmatrix} \Delta_D & 0 \\ 0 & D \end{bmatrix} \begin{bmatrix} I & 0 \\ D^{-1}C & I \end{bmatrix}.$$

(iv) Recursive Triangularization and LDU Decomposition

An alternative way of writing the above formulas is

$$\begin{bmatrix} A & B \\ C & D \end{bmatrix} = \begin{bmatrix} A \\ C \end{bmatrix} A^{-1} \begin{bmatrix} A & B \end{bmatrix} + \begin{bmatrix} 0 & 0 \\ 0 & \Delta_A \end{bmatrix} \qquad (A.1.3)$$

$$= \begin{bmatrix} B \\ D \end{bmatrix} D^{-1} \begin{bmatrix} C & D \end{bmatrix} + \begin{bmatrix} \Delta_D & 0 \\ 0 & 0 \end{bmatrix}, \qquad (A.1.4)$$

which also serves to *define* the Schur complements Δ_A and Δ_D. The above formulas can be used recursively to obtain, respectively, the block lower upper and block upper lower triangular factorizations of the matrix on the left-hand side.

In particular, by choosing A to be scalar and proceeding recursively we can obtain the important LDU decomposition of a *strongly* regular matrix, i.e., one whose leading minors are all nonzero. To demonstrate this so-called Schur reduction procedure, let R be an $n \times n$ strongly regular matrix whose individual entries we denote by r_{ij}. Let l_0 and u_0 denote the first column and the first row of R, respectively. In view of (A.1.3), we see that if we subtract from R the rank 1 matrix $l_0 r_{00}^{-1} u_0$, then we obtain a new matrix whose first row and column are zero,

$$R - l_0 r_{00}^{-1} u_0 = \begin{bmatrix} 0 & 0 \\ 0 & R_1 \end{bmatrix}.$$

The matrix R_1 is the Schur complement of R with respect to its $(0,0)$ entry r_{00}. Now, let $\{r_{ij}^{(1)}, l_1, u_1\}$ denote the entries, the first column, and the first row of R_1, respectively, and repeat the above procedure. In general, we can write for the jth step

$$R_j - l_j \left[r_{00}^{(j)} \right]^{-1} u_j = \begin{bmatrix} 0 & 0 \\ 0 & R_{j+1} \end{bmatrix}.$$

We conclude that we can express R in terms of the successive $\{l_i, u_i, r_{00}^{(i)}\}$ as follows:

$$R = l_0 r_{00}^{-1} u_0 + \begin{bmatrix} 0 \\ l_1 \end{bmatrix} \left[r_{00}^{(1)}\right]^{-1} \begin{bmatrix} 0 & u_1 \end{bmatrix} + \begin{bmatrix} 0 \\ 0 \\ l_2 \end{bmatrix} \left[r_{00}^{(2)}\right]^{-1} \begin{bmatrix} 0 & 0 & u_2 \end{bmatrix} + \cdots$$

$$\triangleq LD^{-1}U,$$

where L is lower triangular, D^{-1} is diagonal, and U is upper triangular. The nonzero parts of the columns of L are the $\{l_i\}_{i=0}^{n-1}$, while the nonzero parts of the rows of U are the $\{u_i\}_{i=0}^{n-1}$. Likewise, the entries of D are the $\{r_{00}^{(i)}\}_{i=0}^{n-1}$. We can further normalize the diagonal entries of L and U and define $\bar{L} = LD^{-1}$ and $\bar{U} = D^{-1}U$. In this case, we obtain $R = \bar{L}D\bar{U}$ and the diagonal entries of $\bar{L}$ and $\bar{U}$ are unity.

It is also immediate to verify that the LDU factorization of a strongly regular matrix is unique. Indeed, assume there exist two decompositions of the form $R = L_1 D_1 U_1 = L_2 D_2 U_2$, where $\{L_1, L_2\}$ are lower triangular with unit diagonal, $\{D_1, D_2\}$ are diagonal, and $\{U_1, U_2\}$ are upper triangular with unit diagonal. Then it must hold that

$$L_2^{-1} L_1 = D_2 U_2 U_1^{-1} D_1^{-1}.$$

Now the left-hand matrix in the above equality is lower triangular, while the right-hand matrix is upper triangular. Hence, equality holds only if both matrices are diagonal. But since the diagonal entries of $L_2^{-1} L_1$ are unity, it follows that we must have

$$L_2^{-1} L_1 = D_2 U_2 U_1^{-1} D_1^{-1} = I, \quad \text{the identity matrix,}$$

from which we conclude that $L_1 = L_2$, $D_1 = D_2$, and $U_1 = U_2$.

(v) **Inverses of Block Matrices**

When the block matrix is invertible, we can use the factorizations in (iii) to write

$$\begin{bmatrix} A & B \\ C & D \end{bmatrix}^{-1} = \begin{bmatrix} I & -A^{-1}B \\ 0 & I \end{bmatrix} \begin{bmatrix} A^{-1} & 0 \\ 0 & \Delta_A^{-1} \end{bmatrix} \begin{bmatrix} I & 0 \\ -CA^{-1} & I \end{bmatrix}$$

$$= \begin{bmatrix} A^{-1} + A^{-1} B \Delta_A^{-1} C A^{-1} & -A^{-1} B \Delta_A^{-1} \\ -\Delta_A^{-1} C A^{-1} & \Delta_A^{-1} \end{bmatrix}. \quad \text{(A.1.5)}$$

Alternatively, we can write

$$\begin{bmatrix} A & B \\ C & D \end{bmatrix}^{-1} = \begin{bmatrix} I & 0 \\ -D^{-1}C & I \end{bmatrix} \begin{bmatrix} \Delta_D^{-1} & 0 \\ 0 & D^{-1} \end{bmatrix} \begin{bmatrix} I & -BD^{-1} \\ 0 & I \end{bmatrix}$$

$$= \begin{bmatrix} \Delta_D^{-1} & -\Delta_D^{-1} B D^{-1} \\ -D^{-1} C \Delta_D^{-1} & D^{-1} + D^{-1} C \Delta_D^{-1} B D^{-1} \end{bmatrix}. \quad \text{(A.1.6)}$$

By equating the (1,1) and (2,2) elements in the right-hand sides of (A.1.5) and (A.1.6), we note that

$$\Delta_D^{-1} = A^{-1} + A^{-1} B \Delta_A^{-1} C A^{-1},$$
$$\Delta_A^{-1} = D^{-1} + D^{-1} C \Delta_D^{-1} B D^{-1}.$$

Section A.1. Some Matrix Identities

(vi) More Inverse Formulas

Another useful set of formulas can be obtained from the formulas in (v) (and a little algebra):

$$\begin{bmatrix} A & B \\ C & D \end{bmatrix}^{-1} = \begin{bmatrix} I & -\Delta_D^{-1}BD^{-1}\Delta_A \\ -D^{-1}C & I \end{bmatrix} \begin{bmatrix} \Delta_D^{-1} & 0 \\ 0 & \Delta_A^{-1} \end{bmatrix}$$

$$= \begin{bmatrix} I & -A^{-1}B \\ -D^{-1}C & I \end{bmatrix} \begin{bmatrix} \Delta_D^{-1} & 0 \\ 0 & \Delta_A^{-1} \end{bmatrix},$$

and similarly

$$\begin{bmatrix} A & B \\ C & D \end{bmatrix}^{-1} = \begin{bmatrix} \Delta_D^{-1} & 0 \\ 0 & \Delta_A^{-1} \end{bmatrix} \begin{bmatrix} I & -BD^{-1} \\ -CA^{-1} & I \end{bmatrix}.$$

We also have formulas analogous to (A.1.3) and (A.1.4):

$$\begin{bmatrix} A & B \\ C & D \end{bmatrix}^{-1} = \begin{bmatrix} A^{-1} & 0 \\ 0 & 0 \end{bmatrix} + \begin{bmatrix} -A^{-1}B \\ I \end{bmatrix} \Delta_A^{-1} \begin{bmatrix} -CA^{-1} & I \end{bmatrix}, \quad (A.1.7)$$

$$\begin{bmatrix} A & B \\ C & D \end{bmatrix}^{-1} = \begin{bmatrix} 0 & 0 \\ 0 & D^{-1} \end{bmatrix} + \begin{bmatrix} I \\ -D^{-1}C \end{bmatrix} \Delta_D^{-1} \begin{bmatrix} I & -BD^{-1} \end{bmatrix}. \quad (A.1.8)$$

(vii) The Matrix Inversion Lemma

For convenience of recall, replacing C by $-D$ and D by C^{-1}, we can rewrite the above formula for Δ_D^{-1} as

$$(A + BCD)^{-1} = A^{-1} - A^{-1}B(C^{-1} + DA^{-1}B)^{-1}DA^{-1},$$

which is often called the modified matrices formula or the matrix inversion lemma.

(viii) Hermitian Matrices

The Hermitian conjugate A^* of a matrix A is the complex conjugate of its transpose. Hermitian matrices are (necessarily square) matrices obeying $A^* = A$. Such matrices have real eigenvalues, say, $\{\lambda_i\}$, and a full set of orthonormal eigenvectors, say, $\{p_i\}$. The so-called spectral decomposition of a Hermitian matrix is the representation

$$A = P\Lambda P^* = \sum_{i=1}^n \lambda_i p_i p_i^*,$$

where

$$\Lambda = \operatorname{diag}\{\lambda_1, \ldots, \lambda_n\}, \quad P = \begin{bmatrix} p_1 & \cdots & p_n \end{bmatrix}, \quad Ap_i = \lambda_i p_i, \; i = 1, \ldots, n.$$

For strongly regular Hermitian matrices, the LDU decomposition takes the form

$$A = LDL^*, \quad L = \text{lower triangular with unit diagonal}.$$

The proof is instructive. If $A = LDU$, then $A^* = U^*D^*L^* = U^*DL^*$, since D is real valued. But by uniqueness of triangular factorization, we must have $U = L^*$.

(ix) Inertia Properties

Since the eigenvalues of a Hermitian matrix $A = A^*$ are real, we can define the inertia of A as the triple $In\{A\} = \{n_+, n_-, n_0\}$, where n_+ is the number of positive (> 0) eigenvalues of A, n_- is the number of negative (< 0) eigenvalues of A, and n_0 is the number of zero eigenvalues of A. Note that $n_+ + n_- = $ the rank of A, while n_0 is often called the *nullity of* A. The *signature* of A is the pair $\{n_+, n_-\}$. We shall define

$$S_A \triangleq \text{the signature matrix of } A$$
$$= \text{a diagonal matrix with } n_+ \text{ ones } (+1) \text{ and}$$
$$n_- \text{ minus ones } (-1) \text{ on the diagonal.}$$

It is not necessary to compute the eigenvalues of A to determine its inertia or its signature matrix. The following property shows that it suffices to compute the LDL^* decomposition of A.

Lemma A.1.1 (Sylvester's Law of Inertia). *For any nonsingular matrix B, $In\{A\} = In\{BAB^*\}$.*

◇

The matrices A and BAB^* are said to be *congruent* to each other, so Sylvester's law states that congruence preserves inertia. The following useful result follows easily from the above and the factorizations in (iii).

Lemma A.1.2 (Inertia of Block Hermitian Matrices). *Let*

$$M = \begin{bmatrix} A & C^* \\ C & D \end{bmatrix}, \quad A = A^*, \quad D = D^*.$$

If A is nonsingular, then

$$In\{M\} = In\{A\} + In\{\Delta_A\}, \tag{A.1.9}$$

where $\Delta_A \triangleq D - CA^{-1}C^*$, the Schur complement of A in M. If D is nonsingular, then

$$In\{M\} = In\{D\} + In\{\Delta_D\}, \tag{A.1.10}$$

where $\Delta_D \triangleq A - C^*D^{-1}C$, the Schur complement of D in M.

◇

(x) Positive-Definite Matrices

An $n \times n$ Hermitian matrix A is positive semidefinite (p.s.d.) or nonnegative definite (n.n.d.), written $A \geq 0$, if it satisfies

$$x^*Ax \geq 0 \quad \text{for all } x \in \mathbb{C}^n.$$

It is strictly positive definite (p.d.), written $A > 0$, if $x^*Ax > 0$ except when $x = 0$.

Among the several characterizations of $A \geq 0$, we note the nonnegativity of all its eigenvalues and the fact that *all* minors are nonnegative. For strict positive definiteness it is necessary and sufficient that the leading minors be positive. An often more computationally useful characterization is that n.n.d. matrices can be factored as LDL^* or UDU^*, where all entries of the diagonal matrix D are nonnegative.

From the results of (ix), we note that a Hermitian block matrix

$$M = \begin{bmatrix} A & C^* \\ C & D \end{bmatrix}$$

is positive definite if and only if either $A > 0$ and $\Delta_A > 0$ or $D > 0$ and $\Delta_D > 0$.

A.2 THE GRAM–SCHMIDT PROCEDURE AND THE QR DECOMPOSITION

A fundamental step in many algorithms is that of replacing a collection of linearly independent vectors by a collection of orthonormal vectors that span the same column space.

Given n independent columns $\{a_i \in \mathbb{C}^N\}$, the so-called Gram–Schmidt procedure finds n orthonormal column vectors $\{q_i \in \mathbb{C}^N\}$ such that, for any $0 \leq j < n$, the column span of $\{q_0, \ldots, q_j\}$ coincides with the column span of $\{a_0, \ldots, a_j\}$. These vectors are determined recursively as follows. Start with $q_0 = a_0/\sqrt{a_0^* a_0}$. Now assume for step i that we have already found the orthonormal vectors $\{q_0, q_1, \ldots, q_{i-1}\}$. We project a_i onto the space spanned by these vectors and determine the residual vector r_i,

$$r_i = a_i - (q_0^* a_i) q_0 - (q_1^* a_i) q_1 - \cdots - (q_{i-1}^* a_i) q_{i-1}.$$

We further scale r_i to have unit norm and take the result to be q_i:

$$q_i = r_i/\sqrt{r_i^* r_i}.$$

(The fact that the vectors $\{a_k\}$ are linearly independent guarantees a nonzero r_i.) It follows from this construction that each a_i can be expressed as a linear combination of the resulting $\{q_0, q_1, \ldots, q_i\}$, viz.,

$$a_i = (q_0^* a_i) q_0 + (q_1^* a_i) q_1 + \cdots + (q_{i-1}^* a_i) q_{i-1} + \sqrt{r_i^* r_i}\, q_i.$$

If we now introduce the $N \times n$ matrices

$$A = \mathrm{col}\{a_0, a_1, \ldots, a_{n-1}\}, \quad \bar{Q} = \mathrm{col}\{q_0, q_1, \ldots, q_{n-1}\},$$

we conclude that the above construction leads to the so-called reduced QR factorization of A,

$$A = \bar{Q}\bar{R},$$

where $\bar{R}$ is $n \times n$ upper triangular,

$$\bar{R} = \begin{bmatrix} \sqrt{r_0^* r_0} & q_0^* a_1 & q_0^* a_2 & \cdots & q_0^* a_{n-1} \\ & \sqrt{r_1^* r_1} & q_1^* a_2 & \cdots & q_1^* a_{n-1} \\ & & \ddots & & \vdots \\ & & & \ddots & \vdots \\ & & & & \sqrt{r_{n-1}^* r_{n-1}} \end{bmatrix}.$$

A *full* QR factorization of A can be obtained by appending an additional $N-n$ orthonormal columns to $\bar{Q}$ so that it becomes a unitary $N \times N$ matrix. Likewise, we append rows of zeros to $\bar{R}$ so that it becomes an $N \times n$ matrix:

$$A = QR \equiv \begin{bmatrix} \bar{Q} & q_n & \cdots & q_{N-1} \end{bmatrix} \begin{bmatrix} \bar{R} \\ 0 \end{bmatrix}.$$

The orthogonalization procedure so described is not reliable numerically due to the accumulation of round-off errors in finite precision arithmetic. A so-called modified Gram–Schmidt procedure has better numerical properties. It operates as follows:

1. We again start with $q_0 = a_0/\sqrt{a_0^* a_0}$ but now project the remaining column vectors $\{a_1, a_2, \ldots, a_{n-1}\}$ onto q_0. The corresponding residuals are denoted by $a_j^{(1)} = a_j - (q_0^* a_j) q_0$. This step therefore replaces all the original vectors $\{a_0, \ldots, a_{n-1}\}$ by the new vectors $\{q_0, a_1^{(1)}, a_2^{(1)}, \ldots, a_{n-1}^{(1)}\}$.

2. We then take $q_1 = a_1^{(1)}/\sqrt{a_1^{*(1)} a_1^{(1)}}$ and project the remaining column vectors $\{a_2^{(1)}, \ldots, a_{n-1}^{(1)}\}$ onto q_1. The corresponding residuals are denoted by $a_j^{(2)} = a_j^{(1)} - (q_1^* a_j^{(1)}) q_1$. This step replaces $\{q_0, a_1^{(1)}, a_2^{(1)}, \ldots, a_{n-1}^{(1)}\}$ by $\{q_0, q_1, a_2^{(2)}, a_3^{(2)}, \ldots, a_{n-1}^{(2)}\}$.

3. We now take $q_2 = a_2^{(2)}/\sqrt{a_2^{*(2)} a_2^{(2)}}$ and proceed as above.

For both variants of the Gram–Schmidt algorithm, we can verify that the computational cost involved is $O(2Nn^2)$ flops. We should further add that the QR factorization of a matrix can also be achieved by applying a sequence of numerically reliable rotations to the matrix (as explained, for example, in App. B).

A.3 MATRIX NORMS

The 2-induced norm of a matrix A, also known as the spectral norm of the matrix, is defined by

$$\|A\|_2 \triangleq \max_{\|x\| \neq 0} \frac{\|Ax\|}{\|x\|} = \max_{\|z\|=1} \|Az\|,$$

where $\|x\|$ denotes the Euclidean norm of the vector x. It can be shown that $\|A\|_2$ is also equal to the maximum singular value of A. More specifically, the following two conclusions can be established. Let $\sigma_{\max}$ denote the largest singular value and let $\sigma_{\min}$ denote the smallest singular value. Then

$$\sigma_{\max} = \max_{\|x\|=1} \|Ax\| \quad \text{and} \quad \sigma_{\min} = \min_{\|x\|=1} \|Ax\|.$$

The Frobenius norm of a matrix $A = [a_{ij}]$ is defined by

$$\|A\|_{\mathrm{F}} \triangleq \sqrt{\sum_{i=0}^{M} \sum_{j=0}^{m} |a_{ij}|^2}. \tag{A.3.1}$$

In terms of the singular values of A, it is easy to verify that if A has rank p with nonzero singular values $\{\sigma_1, \ldots, \sigma_p\}$, then

$$\|A\|_{\mathrm{F}} = \sqrt{\mathrm{trace}(A^* A)} = \sqrt{\sum_{i=1}^{p} \sigma_i^2}.$$

A.4 UNITARY AND J-UNITARY TRANSFORMATIONS

The following result plays a key role in the derivation of many array algorithms. One proof uses the SVDs of the involved matrices.

Lemma A.4.1 (Basis Rotation). *Given two $n \times m$ ($n \le m$) matrices A and B. Then $AA^* = BB^*$ if and only if there exists an $m \times m$ unitary matrix Θ ($\Theta\Theta^* = I = \Theta^*\Theta$) such that $A = B\Theta$.*

Proof: One implication is immediate. If there exists a unitary matrix Θ such that $A = B\Theta$, then $AA^* = (B\Theta)(B\Theta)^* = B(\Theta\Theta^*)B^* = BB^*$. One proof for the converse implication follows by invoking the SVDs of A and B, say,

$$A = U_A \begin{bmatrix} \Sigma_A & 0 \end{bmatrix} V_A^*, \quad B = U_B \begin{bmatrix} \Sigma_B & 0 \end{bmatrix} V_B^*,$$

where U_A and U_B are $n \times n$ unitary matrices, V_A and V_B are $m \times m$ unitary matrices, and Σ_A and Σ_B are $n \times n$ diagonal matrices with nonnegative entries. The squares of the diagonal entries of Σ_A (Σ_B) are the eigenvalues of AA^* (BB^*). Moreover, U_A (U_B) can be constructed from an orthonormal basis for the right eigenvectors of AA^* (BB^*). Hence, it follows from the identity $AA^* = BB^*$ that we have $\Sigma_A = \Sigma_B$ and $U_A = U_B$. Let $\Theta = V_B V_A^*$. We then get $\Theta\Theta^* = I$ and $B\Theta = A$.

◇

We can establish a similar result when the equality $AA^* = BB^*$ is replaced by $AJA^* = BJB^*$ for some signature matrix J. More specifically, we have the following statement.

Lemma A.4.2 (J-Unitary Transformations). *Let A and B be $n \times m$ matrices (with $n \le m$), and let $J = (I_p \oplus -I_q)$ be a signature matrix with $p+q = m$. If $AJA^* = BJB^*$ is full rank, then there exists a J-unitary matrix Θ such that $A = B\Theta$.*

Proof: Since AJA^* is Hermitian and invertible,[9] we can factor it as $AJA^* = RSR^*$, where $R \in \mathbb{C}^{n \times n}$ is invertible and $S = (I_\alpha \oplus -I_\beta)$ is a signature matrix (with $\alpha + \beta = n$). We normalize A and B by defining $\bar{A} = R^{-1}A$ and $\bar{B} = R^{-1}B$. Then $\bar{A}J\bar{A}^* = \bar{B}J\bar{B}^* = S$.

Now consider the block triangular factorizations

$$\begin{bmatrix} S & \bar{A} \\ \bar{A}^* & J \end{bmatrix} = \begin{bmatrix} I & \\ \bar{A}^*S & I \end{bmatrix} \begin{bmatrix} S & \\ & J - \bar{A}^*S\bar{A} \end{bmatrix} \begin{bmatrix} I & \\ \bar{A}^*S & I \end{bmatrix}^*$$

$$= \begin{bmatrix} I & \bar{A}J \\ & I \end{bmatrix} \begin{bmatrix} \underbrace{S - \bar{A}J\bar{A}^*}_{=0} & \\ & J \end{bmatrix} \begin{bmatrix} I & \bar{A}J \\ & I \end{bmatrix}^*.$$

Using the fact that the central matrices must have the same inertia, we conclude that $In\{J - \bar{A}^*S\bar{A}\} = In\{J\} - In\{S\} = \{p - \alpha, q - \beta, n\}$. Similarly, we can show that $In\{J - \bar{B}^*S\bar{B}\} = \{p - \alpha, q - \beta, n\}$.

Define the signature matrix $J_1 \triangleq (I_{p-\alpha} \oplus -I_{q-\beta})$. The above inertia conditions then mean that we can factor $(J - \bar{A}^*S\bar{A})$ and $(J - \bar{B}^*S\bar{B})$ as

$$J - \bar{A}^*S\bar{A} = XJ_1X^*, \quad J - \bar{B}^*S\bar{B} = YJ_1Y^*, \quad X,Y \in \mathbb{C}^{m \times m-n}.$$

---
[9] This argument was suggested by Professor T. Constantinescu.

Finally, introduce the square matrices

$$\Sigma_1 = \begin{bmatrix} \bar{A} \\ X^* \end{bmatrix}, \quad \Sigma_2 = \begin{bmatrix} \bar{B} \\ Y^* \end{bmatrix}.$$

It is easy to verify that these matrices satisfy $\Sigma_1^*(S \oplus J_1)\Sigma_1 = J$ and $\Sigma_2^*(S \oplus J_1)\Sigma_2 = J$. Moreover, $\Sigma_1 J \Sigma_1^* = (S \oplus J_1)$ and $\Sigma_2 J \Sigma_2^* = (S \oplus J_2)$. These relations allow us to relate Σ_1 and Σ_2 as $\Sigma_1 = \Sigma_2[J\Sigma_2^*(S \oplus J_1)\Sigma_1]$. If we set $\Theta \triangleq [J\Sigma_2^*(S \oplus J_1)\Sigma_1]$, then it is immediate to check that Θ is J-unitary and, from the equality of the first block row of $\Sigma_1 = \Sigma_2\Theta$, that $\bar{A} = \bar{B}\Omega$. Hence, $A = B\Theta$.

$\diamond$

In the above statement, the arrays A and B are either square or fat ($n \leq m$). We can establish a similar result when $n \geq m$ instead. For this purpose, first note that if A is an $n \times m$ and full-rank matrix, with $n \geq m$, then its SVD takes the form

$$A = U \begin{bmatrix} \Sigma \\ 0 \end{bmatrix} V^*,$$

where Σ is $n \times n$ and invertible. The left inverse of A is defined by

$$A^\dagger \triangleq V \begin{bmatrix} \Sigma^{-1} & 0 \end{bmatrix} U^*,$$

and it satisfies $A^\dagger A = I_m$, the identify matrix of size m.

Lemma A.4.3 (J-Unitary Transformations). *Let A and B be $n \times m$ full-rank matrices (with $n \geq m$) and let $J = (I_p \oplus -I_q)$ be a signature matrix with $p + q = m$. The relation $AJA^* = BJB^*$ holds if and only if there exists a unique $m \times m$ J-unitary matrix Θ such that $A = B\Theta$.*

Proof: The "if" statement is immediate. For the converse, note that since A and B are assumed full rank, there exist left inverses $A^\dagger$ and $B^\dagger$ such that $A^\dagger A = I_m$ and $B^\dagger B = I_m$. Now define $\Theta = B^\dagger A$. We claim that Θ is J-unitary and maps B to A, as desired.

The proof that $\Theta J \Theta^* = J$ is immediate from the equality $AJA^* = BJB^*$. Just multiply it from the left by $B^\dagger$ and from the right by $(B^\dagger)^*$ and use $B^\dagger B = I_m$.

To prove that $B\Theta = A$, for the above choice of Θ, we start with $AJA^* = BJB^*$ again and insert the term $B^\dagger B$ into the right-hand side to get

$$AJA^* = B(B^\dagger B)JB^* = BB^\dagger(BJB^*) = BB^\dagger AJA^*.$$

Multiplying from the right by $(A^\dagger)^*$ and using $A^\dagger A = I_m$ we obtain $BB^\dagger(AJ) = AJ$. Since J is invertible and its inverse is J, we conclude by multiplying by J from the right that $B(B^\dagger A) = A$, which is the desired result. That is, Θ is J-unitary and maps B to A.

To show that Θ is unique, assume $\bar{\Theta}$ is another J-unitary matrix that maps B to A and write $B\Theta = B\bar{\Theta}$. Now multiply by $B^\dagger$ from the left to conclude that $\Theta = \bar{\Theta}$.

$\diamond$

A.5 Two Additional Results

Finally, we state two matrix results that are needed in Chs. 5 and 8. The first theorem is cited in Ch. 5. Its statement was provided by the authors of that chapter.

Section A.5. Two Additional Results

Theorem A.5.1 (Cauchy Interlace Theorem) (see [Par80]). *Let A, W, and Y be symmetric matrices and $A = W + Y$. Let the eigenvalues of the matrices be ordered as*

$$\lambda_1 \leq \lambda_2 \leq \cdots \lambda_n$$

or

$$\lambda_{-n} \leq \cdots \leq \lambda_{-2} \leq \lambda_{-1}.$$

For any i, j satisfying $1 \leq i + j - 1 \leq n$, the following inequalities hold:

$$\lambda_i(W) + \lambda_j(Y) \leq \lambda_{i+j-1}(A)$$

and

$$\lambda_{-(i+j-1)}(A) \leq \lambda_{-i}(W) + \lambda_{-j}(Y).$$

◇

The next theorem is cited in Ch. 8. Its statement was provided by the authors of that chapter.

Theorem A.5.2 (Perron–Frobenius). *Let $A = (a_{i,j})$ be an $n \times n$ matrix with nonnegative entries and denote ρ its spectral radius, that is, the maximum modulus of its eigenvalues. Then*

1. *there exists an eigenvalue λ of A such that $\rho = \lambda$;*

2. *there exists an eigenvector v of A with nonnegative components corresponding to λ;*

3. *if the matrix is not reducible then $\lambda > 0$ and v has positive components; moreover, λ and v are unique. (A matrix A is said to be reducible if there exists a permutation of rows and columns that transforms A by similarity in the following way:*

$$PAP^T = \begin{bmatrix} A_{1,1} & A_{1,2} \\ O & A_{2,2} \end{bmatrix},$$

where the blocks $A_{1,1}$, $A_{2,2}$ are square matrices and P is a permutation matrix.)

◇

Appendix B

ELEMENTARY TRANSFORMATIONS

Thomas Kailath

Ali H. Sayed

B.1 ELEMENTARY HOUSEHOLDER TRANSFORMATIONS

Suppose we wish to simultaneously annihilate several entries in a row vector, for example, to transform an n-dimensional vector $x = \begin{bmatrix} x_1 & x_2 & \ldots & x_{n-1} \end{bmatrix}$ into the form $\begin{bmatrix} \alpha & 0 & 0 & 0 \end{bmatrix}$, where, for general complex data, the resulting α may be complex as well.

One way to achieve this transformation is to employ a so-called Householder reflection Θ: it takes a row vector x and aligns it along the direction of the basis vector $e_0 = \begin{bmatrix} 1 & 0 & \ldots & 0 \end{bmatrix}$. More precisely, it performs the transformation

$$\begin{bmatrix} x_1 & x_2 & \ldots & x_{n-1} \end{bmatrix} \Theta = \alpha \, e_0 \qquad (B.1.1)$$

for some α to be determined. Since, as we shall promptly verify, the transformation Θ that we shall employ is unitary and also Hermitian (i.e., $\Theta\Theta^* = I = \Theta^*\Theta$ and $\Theta = \Theta^*$), we can be more specific about the resulting α. In particular, it follows from (B.1.1) that the magnitude of α must be equal to $\|x\|$, i.e., $|\alpha| = \|x\|$. This is because $x\Theta\Theta^*x^* = \|x\|^2 = |\alpha|^2$. Moreover, it also follows from (B.1.1) that $x\Theta x^* = \alpha x_1^*$. But since Θ will be Hermitian, we conclude that $x\Theta x^*$ is a real number and, hence, αx_1^* must be real as well.

This means that by rotating a vector x with a unitary and Hermitian transformation Θ we can achieve a postarray of the form $\begin{bmatrix} \alpha & 0 & \ldots & 0 \end{bmatrix}$, where α in general will be a complex number whose magnitude is the norm $\|x\|$ and whose phase is such that αx_1^* is real. For example, $\alpha = \pm\|x\|e^{j\phi_{x_1}}$ are the possible values for α, where ϕ_{x_1} denotes the phase of x_1. (For real data, $\pm\|x\|$ are the possible values for α.)

Now, assume we define

$$\Theta \triangleq I - 2\frac{g^*g}{gg^*}, \quad \text{where} \quad g = x + \alpha \, e_0 \qquad (B.1.2)$$

and α is a complex number that is chosen as above, $\alpha = \pm\|x\|e^{j\phi_{x_1}}$. It can be verified by direct calculation that, for any g, Θ is a unitary matrix, i.e., $\Theta\Theta^* = I = \Theta^*\Theta$. It is also Hermitian.

Lemma B.1.1 (Complex Householder Transformation). *Given a row vector x with leading entry x_1, define Θ and g as in (B.1.2), where α is any complex number that satisfies the following two requirements: $|\alpha| = \|x\|$ and αx_1^* is real. Then it holds that $x\Theta = -\alpha e_0$. That is, x is rotated and aligned with e_0; the leading entry of the postarray is equal to $-\alpha$.*

(**Algebraic**) **proof:** We shall provide a geometric proof below. Here we verify our claim algebraically. Indeed, direct calculation shows that

$$gg^* = \|x\|^2 + \alpha^* x_1 + \alpha x_1^* + |\alpha|^2$$
$$= 2\|x\|^2 + 2\alpha x_1^*, \quad \text{since } |\alpha|^2 = \|x\|^2 \text{ and } \alpha^* x_1 = \alpha x_1^*.$$

Section B.1. Elementary Householder Transformations

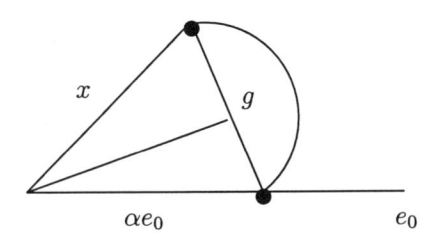

Figure B.1. Geometric interpretation of the Householder transformation.

Likewise,

$$\begin{aligned}xg^*g &= x\|x\|^2 + \alpha\|x\|^2 e_0 + \alpha^* x_1 x + |\alpha|^2 x_1 e_0 \\ &= x\|x\|^2 + \alpha\|x\|^2 e_0 + \alpha^* x_1 x + \alpha(\alpha^* x_1) e_0 \\ &= x\|x\|^2 + \alpha\|x\|^2 e_0 + \alpha^* x_1 x + \alpha(\alpha x_1^*) e_0, \\ xgg^* &= 2x\|x\|^2 + 2\alpha x_1^* x,\end{aligned}$$

and we obtain

$$x\Theta = \frac{xgg^* - 2xg^*g}{gg^*} = \frac{-(2\|x\|^2 + 2\alpha x_1^*)\alpha e_0}{2\|x\|^2 + 2\alpha x_1^*} = -\alpha e_0.$$

◇

In other words, by defining

$$g \stackrel{\Delta}{=} x \pm e^{j\phi_{x_1}} \|x\| e_0, \qquad (B.1.3)$$

we obtain

$$x\Theta = \mp e^{j\phi_{x_1}} \|x\| e_0. \qquad (B.1.4)$$

The choice of the sign in (B.1.4) depends on the choice of the sign in the expression for g. Usually, the sign in the expression for g is chosen so as to avoid a vector g of small Euclidean norm, since this norm appears in the denominator of the expression defining Θ. (In the real case, this can be guaranteed by choosing the sign in the expression for g to be the same as the sign of the leading entry of the row vector x, viz., the sign of x_1.)

A Geometric Derivation

The result of the above lemma has a simple geometric interpretation: given a vector x, we would like to rotate it and align it with the vector e_0. (The careful reader will soon realize that the argument applies equally well to alignments along other vector directions.) This rotation should keep the norm of x unchanged. Hence, the tip of the vector x should be rotated along a circular trajectory until it becomes aligned with e_0. The vector aligned with e_0 is equal to αe_0. Here, as indicated in Fig. B.1, we are assuming that the rotation is performed in the clockwise direction. The triangle with sides x and αe_0 and base $g = x - \alpha e_0$ is then an isosceles triangle.

We thus have $\alpha e_0 = x - g$. But we can also express this in an alternative form. If we drop a perpendicular (denoted by $g^\perp$) from the origin of x to the vector g, it will divide g into two equal parts. Moreover, the upper part is nothing but the projection of the vector x onto the vector g and is thus equal to $\langle x, g \rangle \|g\|^{-2} g$. Therefore,

$$\alpha e_0 = x - 2xg^*(gg^*)^{-1}g = x\underbrace{\left[I - 2\frac{g^*g}{gg^*}\right]}_{\Theta} = x - 2 <x,g> \|g\|^{-2} g.$$

A similar argument holds for the choice $g = \alpha e_0 + x$. The Householder transformation *reflects* the vector x across the line $g^{\perp}$ to the vector αe_0, so it is often called a Householder reflection.

To represent the transformation in matrix form we have two choices, depending upon whether we represent vectors as row $(1 \times n)$ matrices or column $(n \times 1)$ matrices. In the first case, we have $\langle x, g \rangle = xg^*$ and $\|g\|^2 = gg^*$, so that

$$\alpha e_0 = x - 2(xg^*)(gg^*)^{-1}g = x\left(I - 2\frac{g^*g}{gg^*}\right),$$

as in (B.1.4) earlier.

If we represent vectors by columns, then $\langle x, g \rangle = g^*x$ and $\|g\|^2 = g^*g$, and we shall have

$$\alpha e_0 = x - 2(g^*x)(g^*g)^{-1}g = \left(I - 2\frac{gg^*}{g^*g}\right)x.$$

Triangularizing a Matrix

A sequence of Householder transformations of this type can be used to triangularize a given $m \times n$ matrix, say, A. For this we first find a transformation Θ_0 to rotate the first row to lie along e_0, so that we have $A\Theta_0$ of the form (where α denotes entries whose exact values are not of current interest):

$$A\Theta_0 = \begin{bmatrix} \sigma_1 & 0 & 0 & 0 & 0 \\ \alpha & & & & \\ \alpha & & A_1 & & \\ \alpha & & & & \end{bmatrix}.$$

Now apply a transformation of the type $(1 \oplus \Theta_1)$, where Θ_1 rotates the first row of A_1 so that it lies along e_0 in an $(n-1)$-dimensional space, and so on. This so-called Householder reduction of matrices has been found to be an efficient and stable tool for displaying rank information via matrix triangularization and it is widely used in numerical analysis (see, e.g., [GV96], [Hig96]).

B.2 ELEMENTARY CIRCULAR OR GIVENS ROTATIONS

An elementary 2×2 unitary rotation Θ (also known as Givens or circular rotation) takes a 1×2 row vector $x = \begin{bmatrix} a & b \end{bmatrix}$ and rotates it to lie along the basis vector $e_0 = \begin{bmatrix} 1 & 0 \end{bmatrix}$. More precisely, it performs the transformation

$$\begin{bmatrix} a & b \end{bmatrix} \Theta = \begin{bmatrix} \alpha & 0 \end{bmatrix}, \tag{B.2.1}$$

where, for general complex data, α may be complex as well. Furthermore, its magnitude needs to be consistent with the fact that the prearray, $\begin{bmatrix} a & b \end{bmatrix}$, and the postarray, $\begin{bmatrix} \alpha & 0 \end{bmatrix}$, must have equal Euclidean norms since

$$\begin{bmatrix} a & b \end{bmatrix} \underbrace{\Theta\Theta^*}_{I} \begin{bmatrix} a^* \\ b^* \end{bmatrix} = \begin{bmatrix} \alpha & 0 \end{bmatrix} \begin{bmatrix} \alpha^* \\ 0 \end{bmatrix}.$$

Section B.2. Elementary Circular or Givens Rotations

In other words, α must satisfy $|\alpha|^2 = |a|^2 + |b|^2$, and its magnitude should therefore be $|\alpha| = \sqrt{|a|^2 + |b|^2}$.

An expression for Θ that achieves the transformation (B.2.1) is given by

$$\Theta = \frac{1}{\sqrt{1+|\rho|^2}} \begin{bmatrix} 1 & -\rho \\ \rho^* & 1 \end{bmatrix}, \quad \text{where} \quad \rho = \frac{b}{a}, \quad a \neq 0. \tag{B.2.2}$$

Indeed, if we write a in polar form, say, $a = |a|e^{j\phi_a}$, then it can be verified by direct calculation that we can write

$$\begin{bmatrix} a & b \end{bmatrix} \Theta = \begin{bmatrix} \pm e^{j\phi_a}\sqrt{|a|^2 + |b|^2} & 0 \end{bmatrix}.$$

That is, the above Θ leads to a postarray with a complex value α that has the same magnitude as the Euclidean norm of the prearray but with a phase factor that is determined by the phase of a up to a sign change. (Note in particular that αa^* is real.)

For real data $\{a, b\}$, and hence $\rho = \rho^*$, the same argument will show that we get a postarray of the form

$$\begin{bmatrix} a & b \end{bmatrix} \Theta = \begin{bmatrix} \pm\sqrt{|a|^2 + |b|^2} & 0 \end{bmatrix}.$$

In any case, the main issue is that once a and b are given, real or complex, a unitary rotation Θ can be defined that reduces the prearray $\begin{bmatrix} a & b \end{bmatrix}$ to the form $\begin{bmatrix} \alpha & 0 \end{bmatrix}$ for some α.

In the trivial case $a = 0$, we simply choose Θ to be the permutation matrix

$$\Theta = \begin{bmatrix} 0 & 1 \\ 1 & 0 \end{bmatrix}.$$

We finally note that, in the special case of real data, a general unitary rotation as in (B.2.2) can be expressed in the alternative form

$$\Theta = \begin{bmatrix} c & -s \\ s & c \end{bmatrix},$$

where the so-called cosine and sine parameters, c and s, respectively, are defined by

$$c = \frac{1}{\sqrt{1+|\rho|^2}}, \quad s = \frac{\rho}{\sqrt{1+|\rho|^2}}.$$

This justifies the name *circular rotation* for Θ, since the effect of Θ is to rotate a vector x along a circle of radius $\|x\|$, by an angle θ that is determined by the inverse of the above cosine or sine parameters, $\theta = \tan^{-1} \rho$, in order to align it with the basis vector $\begin{bmatrix} 1 & 0 \end{bmatrix}$. The trivial case $a = 0$ corresponds to a 90 degrees rotation in an appropriate clockwise (if $b \geq 0$) or anticlockwise (if $b < 0$) direction.

Triangularizing a Matrix

Matrix triangularization can also be effected by a product of Givens transformations, each of which introduces a zero in a particular location. For example, suppose that $x = [\ldots, x_i, \ldots, x_j, \ldots]$, and we wish to null out x_j using x_i. All entries are possibly complex. Then let $\rho = x_j/x_i$, and define

$$\Theta = \begin{bmatrix} 1 & & & & & & & \\ & 1 & & & & & & \\ & & \frac{1}{\sqrt{1+|\rho|^2}} & & & \frac{-\rho}{\sqrt{1+|\rho|^2}} & & \\ & & & 1 & & & & \\ & & & & 1 & & & \\ & & \frac{\rho^*}{\sqrt{1+|\rho|^2}} & & & \frac{1}{\sqrt{1+|\rho|^2}} & & \\ & & & & & & 1 & \\ & & & & & & & 1 \end{bmatrix}.$$

Except for the ρ terms, all off-diagonal entries are 0. Then we can see that

$$x\Theta = [\ldots, \alpha, \ldots, 0, \ldots],$$

where the entries indicated by ... are arbitrary and unchanged by Θ, while the resulting α will be of the general form

$$\alpha = \pm e^{j\phi_{x_i}} \sqrt{|x_i|^2 + |x_j|^2}.$$

To systematically triangularize a $p \times p$ matrix A, apply a sequence of $p-1$ such transformations to zero all entries in the first row of A expect for the first element. Proceed to the second row of the thus transformed A matrix and apply a sequence of $p-2$ transformations to zero all entries after the second one. The first row has a zero in every column affected by this sequence of transformations, so it will be undisturbed. Continuing in this fashion for all rows except the last one, we will transform A to lower triangular form.

In general, the Givens method of triangularization requires more computations than the Householder method. It requires about 30% more multiplications, and it requires one scalar square root per zero produced as opposed to one per column for the Householder method. However, the Givens method is more flexible in preserving zeros already present in the A matrix and can require fewer computations than the Householder method when A is nearly triangular to begin with (see [Gen73]). Moreover, there is a fast version, presented next, that uses 50% fewer multiplications.

B.3 HYPERBOLIC TRANSFORMATIONS

In many cases, it is necessary to use hyperbolic transformations rather than unitary transformations. We therefore exhibit here the necessary modifications.

Elementary Hyperbolic Rotations

An elementary 2×2 hyperbolic rotation Θ takes a row vector $x = \begin{bmatrix} a & b \end{bmatrix}$ and rotates it to lie either along the basis vector $e_0 = \begin{bmatrix} 1 & 0 \end{bmatrix}$ (if $|a| > |b|$) or along the basis vector $e_1 = \begin{bmatrix} 0 & 1 \end{bmatrix}$ (if $|a| < |b|$). More precisely, it performs either of the transformations

$$\begin{bmatrix} a & b \end{bmatrix} \Theta = \begin{bmatrix} \alpha & 0 \end{bmatrix} \quad \text{if } |a| > |b|, \tag{B.3.1}$$

$$\begin{bmatrix} a & b \end{bmatrix} \Theta = \begin{bmatrix} 0 & \alpha \end{bmatrix} \quad \text{if } |a| < |b|, \tag{B.3.2}$$

Section B.3. Hyperbolic Transformations

where, for general complex data, α may be complex as well. Furthermore, its magnitude needs to be consistent with the fact that the prearray, $[\,a\ \ b\,]$, and the postarray, $[\,\alpha\ \ 0\,]$, must have equal Euclidean J-norms; e.g., when $|a| > |b|$ we get

$$[\,a\ \ b\,]\underbrace{\Theta J \Theta^*}_{J}\begin{bmatrix} a^* \\ b^* \end{bmatrix} = [\,\alpha\ \ 0\,]J\begin{bmatrix} \alpha^* \\ 0 \end{bmatrix},$$

where $J = (1 \oplus -1)$. By the J-norm of a row vector x we mean the indefinite quantity xJx^*, which can be positive, negative, or even zero. Hence, for $|a| > |b|$, α must satisfy $|\alpha|^2 = |a|^2 - |b|^2$, and its magnitude should therefore be $|\alpha| = \sqrt{|a|^2 - |b|^2}$. When $|b| > |a|$ we should get $|\alpha| = \sqrt{|b|^2 - |a|^2}$.

An expression for a J-unitary hyperbolic rotation Θ that achieves (B.3.1) or (B.3.2) is given by

$$\Theta = \frac{1}{\sqrt{1 - |\rho|^2}}\begin{bmatrix} 1 & -\rho \\ -\rho^* & 1 \end{bmatrix}, \quad \text{where } \rho = \frac{b}{a},\ a \neq 0\ \text{ if } |a| > |b|, \quad \text{(B.3.3)}$$

$$\Theta = \frac{1}{\sqrt{1 - |\rho|^2}}\begin{bmatrix} 1 & -\rho \\ -\rho^* & 1 \end{bmatrix}, \quad \text{where } \rho^* = \frac{a}{b},\ b \neq 0\ \text{ if } |a| < |b|. \quad \text{(B.3.4)}$$

It can be verified by direct calculation that these transformations lead to postarrays of the form

$$[\,a\ \ b\,]\Theta = [\,\pm e^{j\phi_a}\sqrt{|a|^2 - |b|^2}\ \ 0\,] \quad \text{when } |a| > |b|,$$

$$[\,a\ \ b\,]\Theta = [\,0\ \ \pm e^{j\phi_b}\sqrt{|b|^2 - |a|^2}\,] \quad \text{when } |b| > |a|.$$

For real data, a general hyperbolic rotation as in (B.3.3) or (B.3.4) can be expressed in the alternative form

$$\Theta = \begin{bmatrix} ch & -sh \\ -sh & ch \end{bmatrix},$$

where the so-called hyperbolic cosine and sine parameters, ch and sh, respectively, are defined by

$$ch = \frac{1}{\sqrt{1 - |\rho|^2}}, \quad sh = \frac{\rho}{\sqrt{1 - |\rho|^2}}.$$

This justifies the name *hyperbolic rotation* for Θ, since the effect of Θ is to rotate a vector x along the *hyperbola* of the equation

$$x^2 - y^2 = |a|^2 - |b|^2$$

by an angle θ that is determined by the inverse of the above hyperbolic cosine or sine parameters, $\theta = \tanh^{-1}\rho$, in order to align it with the appropriate basis vector. Note also that the special case $|a| = |b|$ corresponds to a row vector $x = [\,a\ \ b\,]$ with zero hyperbolic norm since $|a|^2 - |b|^2 = 0$. It is then easy to see that there does not exist a hyperbolic rotation that will rotate x to lie along the direction of one basis vector or the other.

There exist alternative implementations of the hyperbolic rotation Θ that exhibit better numerical properties. Here we briefly mention two modifications.

Mixed Downdating

Assume we apply a hyperbolic rotation Θ to a row vector $\begin{bmatrix} x & y \end{bmatrix}$, say,

$$\begin{bmatrix} x_1 & y_1 \end{bmatrix} = \begin{bmatrix} x & y \end{bmatrix} \frac{1}{\sqrt{1-|\rho|^2}} \begin{bmatrix} 1 & -\rho \\ -\rho^* & 1 \end{bmatrix}. \quad (B.3.5)$$

Then, more explicitly,

$$x_1 = \frac{1}{\sqrt{1-|\rho|^2}} [x - \rho^* y], \quad (B.3.6)$$

$$y_1 = \frac{1}{\sqrt{1-|\rho|^2}} [-\rho x + y]. \quad (B.3.7)$$

Solving for x in terms of x_1 from the first equation and substituting into the second equation we obtain

$$y_1 = -\rho x_1 + \sqrt{1-|\rho|^2}\, y. \quad (B.3.8)$$

An implementation that is based on (B.3.6) and (B.3.8) is said to be in mixed downdating form. It has better numerical stability properties than a direct implementation of Θ as in (B.3.5)—see [BBDH87]. In the above mixed form, we first evaluate x_1 and then use it to compute y_1. We can obtain a similar procedure that first evaluates y_1 and then uses it to compute x_1. For this purpose, we solve for y in terms of y_1 from (B.3.7) and substitute into (B.3.6) to obtain

$$x_1 = -\rho^* y_1 + \sqrt{1-|\rho|^2}\, x. \quad (B.3.9)$$

Equations (B.3.7) and (B.3.9) represent the second mixed form.

The OD Method

The OD procedure is based on using the SVD of the hyperbolic rotation Θ. Assume ρ is real and write $\rho = b/a$, where $|a| > |b|$. Then it is straightforward to verify that any hyperbolic rotation of this form admits the following eigendecomposition:

$$\Theta = \frac{1}{\sqrt{2}} \begin{bmatrix} 1 & 1 \\ -1 & 1 \end{bmatrix} \begin{bmatrix} \sqrt{\frac{a+b}{a-b}} & 0 \\ 0 & \sqrt{\frac{a-b}{a+b}} \end{bmatrix} \begin{bmatrix} 1 & -1 \\ 1 & 1 \end{bmatrix} \frac{1}{\sqrt{2}} \triangleq QDQ^T, \quad (B.3.10)$$

where the matrix

$$Q = \frac{1}{\sqrt{2}} \begin{bmatrix} 1 & 1 \\ -1 & 1 \end{bmatrix}$$

is orthogonal ($QQ^T = I$) and T denotes transposition.

Due to the special form of the factors (Q, D), a real hyperbolic rotation with $|\rho| < 1$ can then be applied to a row vector $\begin{bmatrix} x & y \end{bmatrix}$ to yield $\begin{bmatrix} x_1 & y_1 \end{bmatrix}$ as follows (note that the first and last steps involve simple additions and subtractions):

$$\begin{bmatrix} x' & y' \end{bmatrix} \leftarrow \begin{bmatrix} x & y \end{bmatrix} \begin{bmatrix} 1 & 1 \\ -1 & 1 \end{bmatrix},$$

Section B.3. Hyperbolic Transformations

$$[\begin{array}{cc} x'' & y'' \end{array}] \leftarrow [\begin{array}{cc} x' & y' \end{array}] \begin{bmatrix} \frac{1}{2}\sqrt{\frac{a+b}{a-b}} & 0 \\ 0 & \frac{1}{2}\sqrt{\frac{a-b}{a+b}} \end{bmatrix},$$

$$[\begin{array}{cc} x_1 & y_1 \end{array}] \leftarrow [\begin{array}{cc} x'' & y'' \end{array}] \begin{bmatrix} 1 & -1 \\ 1 & 1 \end{bmatrix}.$$

This procedure is numerically stable, as shown in [CS96] (and also Ch. 2). An alternative so-called H-procedure is described in the same reference. It is costlier than the OD method, but it is more accurate and can be shown to be "forward" stable, which is a desirable property for finite precision implementations.

Hyperbolic Householder Transformations

One can also use hyperbolic or J-unitary Householder reflections to simultaneously annihilate several entries in a row, e.g., to transform $[\begin{array}{cccc} x & x & x & x \end{array}]$ directly into the form $[\begin{array}{cccc} x' & 0 & 0 & 0 \end{array}]$.

Let J be an $n \times n$ signature matrix such as $J = (I_p \oplus -I_q)$ with $p + q = n$. We are now interested in a J-unitary Householder transformation Θ that takes a $1 \times n$ row vector x and aligns it either along the basis vector $e_0 = [\begin{array}{cc} 1 & 0 \end{array}]$ (if $xJx^* > 0$) or along the basis vector $e_{n-1} = [\begin{array}{cc} 0 & 1 \end{array}]$ (if $xJx^* < 0$). (One can also require Θ to align x along the direction of some other basis vector depending on the sign of xJx^* and on the order of the sequence of ± 1's in J. We shall, without loss of generality, focus here on the special directions e_0 and e_{n-1} and assume that J is of the form $J = (I_p \oplus -I_q)$.)

Hence, we require Θ to perform either of the transformations

$$x\Theta = \pm\alpha\, e_0 \quad \text{if} \quad xJx^* > 0, \tag{B.3.11}$$

$$x\Theta = \pm\alpha\, e_{n-1} \quad \text{if} \quad xJx^* < 0, \tag{B.3.12}$$

where, for general complex data, the resulting α may be complex as well.

When $xJx^* > 0$, we define

$$\Theta = I - 2\frac{Jg^*g}{gJg^*}, \quad \text{where} \quad g = x + \alpha\, e_0 \tag{B.3.13}$$

and α is a complex number that satisfies $|\alpha|^2 = xJx^*$ and αx_1^* is real. It can be verified by direct calculation that Θ is J-unitary, i.e., $\Theta J \Theta^* = J = \Theta^* J \Theta$. When $xJx^* < 0$, we use the same expression for Θ but with

$$g = x + \alpha\, e_{n-1}, \tag{B.3.14}$$

where α is a complex number that satisfies $|\alpha|^2 = -xJx^*$ and αx_{n-1}^* is real.

Lemma B.3.1 (Complex Hyperbolic Householder Transformation). *Given a row vector x with leading entry x_1 and $xJx^* > 0$, define Θ and g as in (B.3.13) where α is any complex number that satisfies the following two requirements (see below): $|\alpha| = \sqrt{xJx^*}$ and αx_1^* is real. Then it holds that $x\Theta = -\alpha e_0$. That is, x is rotated and aligned with e_0; the leading entry of the postarray is equal to $-\alpha$.*

For a vector x that satisfies instead $xJx^* < 0$, and with trailing entry x_{n-1}, we choose g as in (B.3.14), where α is any complex number that satisfies $|\alpha| = \sqrt{|xJx^*|}$ and αx_{n-1}^* is real. Then it holds that $x\Theta = -\alpha e_{n-1}$.

(Algebraic) proof: We prove the first statement only since the second one follows from a similar argument. Direct calculation shows that

$$gJg^* = 2xJx^* + 2\alpha x_1^*,$$
$$xJg^*g = x(xJx^*) + \alpha(xJx^*)e_0 + \alpha^* x_1 x + \alpha(\alpha x_1^*)e_0,$$
$$xgJg^* = 2x(xJx^*) + 2\alpha x_1^* x.$$

Therefore,

$$x\Theta = \frac{xgJg^* - 2xJg^*g}{gJg^*} = -\alpha e_0.$$

$\diamond$

Specific choices for α, and hence g, are

$$g = \begin{cases} x \pm e^{j\phi_{x_1}} \sqrt{xJx^*}\, e_0 & \text{when } xJx^* > 0, \\ x \pm e^{j\phi_{x_{n-1}}} \sqrt{|xJx^*|}\, e_{n-1} & \text{when } xJx^* < 0, \end{cases}$$

and they lead to

$$x\Theta = \begin{cases} \mp e^{j\phi_{x_1}} \sqrt{xJx^*}\, e_0 & \text{when } xJx^* > 0, \\ \mp e^{j\phi_{x_{n-1}}} \sqrt{|xJx^*|}\, e_{n-1} & \text{when } xJx^* < 0. \end{cases}$$

Geometric Derivation

The geometric derivation presented earlier for Householder transformations still applies provided we use "J-inner products," i.e., provided we interpret

$$\langle x, g \rangle_J = xJg^* \quad \text{when } \{x, g\} \text{ are rows},$$
$$\langle x, g \rangle_J = g^*Jx \quad \text{when } \{x, g\} \text{ are columns}.$$

Then using rows, we can write, for example, when $\|x\|_J = \sqrt{xJx^*} > 0$,

$$\mp \alpha e_0 = x - 2\langle x, g \rangle_J \|g\|_J^{-2}\, g = x\left(I - 2\frac{Jg^*g}{gJg^*}\right),$$

where $g \triangleq x \pm \alpha\, e_0$. Table B.1 collects the expressions for the several rotations that we have considered in the earlier discussion.

Section B.3. Hyperbolic Transformations

Table B.1. Unitary and hyperbolic rotations.

Rotation	Expression	Effect
Circular or Givens	$\Theta = \frac{1}{\sqrt{1+|\rho|^2}} \begin{bmatrix} 1 & -\rho \\ \rho^* & 1 \end{bmatrix}$ $\rho = \frac{b}{a}$, $a \neq 0$	$\begin{bmatrix} a & b \end{bmatrix} \Theta =$ $\begin{bmatrix} \pm e^{j\phi_a}\sqrt{|a|^2+|b|^2} & 0 \end{bmatrix}$
Permutation	$\Theta = \begin{bmatrix} 0 & 1 \\ 1 & 0 \end{bmatrix}$	$\begin{bmatrix} 0 & b \end{bmatrix} \Theta = \begin{bmatrix} b & 0 \end{bmatrix}$
Hyperbolic I	$\Theta = \frac{1}{\sqrt{1-|\rho|^2}} \begin{bmatrix} 1 & -\rho \\ -\rho^* & 1 \end{bmatrix}$ $\rho = \frac{b}{a}$, $a \neq 0$, $|a| > |b|$	$\begin{bmatrix} a & b \end{bmatrix} \Theta =$ $\begin{bmatrix} \pm e^{j\phi_a}\sqrt{|a|^2-|b|^2} & 0 \end{bmatrix}$
Hyperbolic II	$\Theta = \frac{1}{\sqrt{1-|\rho|^2}} \begin{bmatrix} 1 & -\rho \\ -\rho^* & 1 \end{bmatrix}$ $\rho^* = \frac{a}{b}$, $b \neq 0$, $|a| < |b|$	$\begin{bmatrix} a & b \end{bmatrix} \Theta =$ $\begin{bmatrix} 0 & \pm e^{j\phi_b}\sqrt{|b|^2-|a|^2} \end{bmatrix}$
Unitary Householder	$\Theta = I_n - 2\frac{g^*g}{gg^*}$ $g = x \pm e^{j\phi_{x_1}}\|x\| e_0$	$\begin{bmatrix} x_1 & \ldots & x_{n-1} \end{bmatrix} \Theta =$ $\mp e^{j\phi_{x_1}}\|x\| e_0$
Hyperbolic Householder I	$\Theta = I - 2\frac{Jg^*g}{gJg^*}$ $g = x \pm e^{j\phi_{x_1}}\sqrt{|xJx^*|} e_0$ $xJx^* > 0$	$\begin{bmatrix} x_1 & \ldots & x_{n-1} \end{bmatrix} \Theta =$ $\mp e^{j\phi_{x_1}}\sqrt{|xJx^*|} e_0$ $e_0 = \begin{bmatrix} 1 & 0 & \ldots & 0 \end{bmatrix}$
Hyperbolic Householder II	$\Theta = I - 2\frac{Jg^*g}{gJg^*}$ $g = x \pm e^{j\phi_{x_{n-1}}}\sqrt{|xJx^*|} e_{n-1}$ $xJx^* < 0$	$\begin{bmatrix} x_1 & \ldots & x_{n-1} \end{bmatrix} \Theta =$ $\mp e^{j\phi_{x_{n-1}}}\sqrt{|xJx^*|} e_{n-1}$ $e_{n-1} = \begin{bmatrix} 0 & \ldots & 0 & 1 \end{bmatrix}$

BIBLIOGRAPHY

[AA86] A. C. ANTOULAS AND B. D. O. ANDERSON, *On the scalar rational interpolation problem*, IMA J. Math. Control Inform., 3, pp. 61–88, 1986.

[AAK71] V. M. ADAMJAN, D. Z. AROV, AND M. G. KREĬN, *Analytic properties of Schmidt pairs for a Hankel operator and the generalized Schur-Takagi problem*, Math. USSR Sbornik, 15, pp. 31–73, 1971 (transl. of Iz. Akad. Nauk Armjan. SSR Ser. Mat., 6 (1971)).

[AB84] O. AXELSSON AND V. BARKER, *Finite Element Solution of Boundary Value Problems, Theory and Computation*, Academic Press, Orlando, FL, 1984.

[Ack91] R. ACKNER, *Fast Algorithms for Indefinite Matrices and Meromorphic Functions*, Ph.D. dissertation, Stanford University, Stanford, CA, 1991.

[AD86] D. ALPAY AND H. DYM, *On applications of reproducing kernel spaces to the Schur algorithm and rational J-unitary factorization*, Oper. Theory: Adv. Appl., 18, pp. 89–159, Birkhäuser, Boston, 1986.

[AD92] D. ALPAY AND H. DYM, *On a new class of reproducing kernel spaces and a new generalization of Iohvidov laws*, Linear Algebra Appl., 178, pp. 109–183, 1992.

[ADD89] D. ALPAY, P. DEWILDE, AND H. DYM, *On the existence and construction of solutions to the partial lossless inverse scattering problem, with applications to estimation theory*, IEEE Trans. Inform. Theory, 35, pp. 1184–1205, 1989.

[AE87] J. ABBISS AND P. EARWICKER, *Compact operator equations, regularization and superresolution*, in Mathematics in Signal Processing, T. Durrani, J. Abbiss, T. Durrani, J. Hudson, R. Madan, J. McWriter, and T. Moore, eds., Clarendon Press, Oxford, UK, 1987.

[AG88] G. S. AMMAR AND W. B. GRAGG, *Superfast solution of real positive definite Toeplitz systems*, SIAM J. Matrix Anal. Appl., 9, pp. 61–76, 1988.

[AG89] G. S. AMMAR AND P. GADER, *New decomposition of the inverse of a Toeplitz matrix*, Proc. Int. Symp. MTNS, vol. III, pp. 421–428, Birkhäuser, Boston, 1989.

[Akl89] S. AKL, *The Design and Analysis of Parallel Algorithms*, Prentice–Hall, Englewood Cliffs, NJ, 1989.

[AL86] O. AXELSSON AND G. LINDSKOG, *The rate of convergence of the conjugate gradient method*, Numer. Math., 48, pp. 499–523, 1986.

[ALM97] G. ANASTASI, L. LENZINI, AND B. MEINI, *Performance evaluation of a worst case model of the MetaRing MAC protocol with global fairness*, Performance Evaluation, 29, pp. 127–151, 1997.

[AM79] B. D. O. ANDERSON AND J. B. MOORE, *Optimal Filtering*, Prentice–Hall, Englewood Cliffs, NJ, 1979.

[APP88] S. T. ALEXANDER, C.-T. PAN, AND R. J. PLEMMONS, *Analysis of a recursive least-squares hyperbolic rotation algorithm for signal processing*, Linear Algebra Appl., 98, pp. 3–40, 1988.

[AS99] N. AL-DHAHIR AND A. H. SAYED, *A computationally efficient FIR MMSE-DFE for multi-user communications*, in Proc. Asilomar Conference on Signals, Systems, and Computers, Pacific Grove, CA, 1999, to appear.

[Atk78] K. E. ATKINSON, *An Introduction to Numerical Analysis*, John Wiley, New York, 1978.

[Avr88] F. AVRAM, *On bilinear forms on Gaussian random variables and Toeplitz matrices*, Probab. Theory Related Fields, 79, pp. 37–45, 1988.

[Bar69] E. H. BAREISS, *Numerical solution of linear equations with Toeplitz and vector Toeplitz matrices*, Numer. Math., 13, pp. 404–424, 1969.

[BBDH87] A. W. BOJANCZYK, R. P. BRENT, P. VAN DOOREN, AND F. R. DE HOOG, *A note on downdating the Cholesky factorization*, SIAM J. Sci. Statist. Comput., 8, pp. 210–220, 1987.

[BBH86] A. W. BOJANCZYK, R. P. BRENT, AND F. R. DE HOOG, *QR factorization of Toeplitz matrices*, Numer. Math., 49, pp. 81–94, 1986.

[BBH95] A. W. BOJANCZYK, R. P. BRENT, AND F. R. DE HOOG, *Stability analysis of a general Toeplitz systems solver*, Numer. Algorithms, 10, pp. 225–244, 1995.

[BBHS95] A. W. BOJANCZYK, R. P. BRENT, F. R. DE HOOG, AND D. R. SWEET, *On the stability of the Bareiss and related Toeplitz factorization algorithms*, SIAM J. Matrix Anal. Appl., 16, pp. 40–57, 1995.

[BC83] D. BINI AND M. CAPOVANI, *Spectral and computational properties of band symmetric Toeplitz matrices*, Linear Algebra Appl., 52, pp. 99–126, 1983.

[BCK88] A. M. BRUCKSTEIN, T. K. CITRON, AND T. KAILATH, *On inverse scattering and partial realizations*, Internat. J. Control, 48, pp. 1537–1550, 1988.

[BD90] D. BINI AND F. DI BENEDETTO, *A new preconditioner for the parallel solution of positive definite Toeplitz systems*, in Proc. Second ACM Symp. on Parallel Algorithms and Architectures, Crete, Greece, pp. 220–223, 1990.

[BD91] P. BROCKWELL AND R. DAVIS, *Time Series: Theory and Methods*, 2nd ed., Springer-Verlag, New York, 1991.

[BF93] D. BINI AND P. FAVATI, *On a matrix algebra related to the discrete Hartley transform*, SIAM J. Matrix Anal. Appl., 14, pp. 500–507, 1993.

[BG95] D. BINI AND L. GEMIGNANI, *Fast parallel computation of the polynomial remainder sequence via Bezout and Hankel matrices*, SIAM J. Comput., 24, pp. 63–77, 1995.

[BG97] A. BÖTTCHER AND S. M. GRUDSKY, *Estimates for the condition numbers of large Toeplitz matrices*, preprint.

[BGN70] B. L. BUZBEE, G. H. GOLUB, AND C. W. NIELSON, *On direct methods for solving Poisson's equation*, SIAM J. Numer. Anal., 7, pp. 627–656, 1970.

[BGR90] J. A. BALL, I. GOHBERG, AND L. RODMAN, *Interpolation of Rational Matrix Functions*, Oper. Theory Adv. Appl. 45, Birkhäuser, Boston, 1990.

[BGY80] R. P. BRENT, F. G. GUSTAVSON, AND D. Y. Y. YUN, *Fast solution of Toeplitz systems of equations and computation of Padé approximants*, J. Algorithms, 1, pp. 259–295, 1980.

[Bin83] D. BINI, *On a Class of Matrices Related to Toeplitz Matrices*, Tech. Rep. 83-5, State University of New York, Albany, NY, 1983.

[Bjo87] A. BJÖRCK, *Stability analysis of the method of semi-normal equations for linear least squares problems*, Linear Algebra Appl., 88/89, pp. 31–48, 1987.

[Bjo91] A. BJÖRCK, *Error analysis of least squares algorithms*, in Numerical Linear Algebra, Digital Signal Processing and Parallel Algorithms, G. H. Golub and P. Van Dooren, eds., Springer-Verlag, Berlin, New York, pp. 41–73, 1991.

[BK87a] A. BRUCKSTEIN AND T. KAILATH, *An inverse scattering framework for several problems in signal processing*, IEEE ASSP Magazine, pp. 6–20, January 1987.

[BK87b] A. BRUCKSTEIN AND T. KAILATH, *Inverse scattering for discrete transmission-line models*, SIAM Rev., 29, pp. 359–389, 1987.

[BK87c] A. BRUCKSTEIN AND T. KAILATH, *On discrete Schrodinger equations and their two component wave-equation equivalents*, J. Math. Phys., 28, pp. 2914–2924, 1987.

[BK95] E. BOMAN AND I. KOLTRACHT, *Fast transform based preconditioners for Toeplitz equations*, SIAM J. Matrix Anal. Appl., 16, pp. 628–645, 1995.

[BKLS98a] T. BOROS, T. KAILATH, H. LEV-ARI, AND A. H. SAYED, *A generalized Schur-type algorithm for the joint factorization of a structured matrix and its inverse: Part I—Nondegenerate case*, preprint.

[BKLS98b] T. BOROS, T. KAILATH, H. LEV-ARI, AND A. H. SAYED, *A generalized Schur-type algorithm for the joint factorization of a structured matrix and its inverse: Part II—General case*, preprint.

[Bla84] R. E. BLAHUT, *Fast Algorithms for Digital Signal Processing*, Addison–Wesley, Reading, MA, 1984.

[BM96a] D. BINI AND B. MEINI, *On cyclic reduction applied to a class of Toeplitz-like matrices arising in queueing problems*, in Computations with Markov Chains, W. J. Stewart, ed., Kluwer Academic Publishers, Norwell, MA, pp. 21–38, 1996.

[BM96b] D. BINI AND B. MEINI, *On the solution of a nonlinear matrix equation arising in queueing problems*, SIAM J. Matrix Anal. Appl., 17, pp. 906–926, 1996.

[BM97a] D. BINI AND B. MEINI, *Improved cyclic reduction for solving queueing problems*, Numer. Algorithms, 15, pp. 57–74, 1997.

[BM97b] D. A. BINI AND B. MEINI, *Effective methods for solving banded Toeplitz systems*, SIAM J. Matrix Anal. Appl., 20, pp. 700–719, 1999.

[BM98a] D. BINI AND B. MEINI, *Inverting block Toeplitz matrices in block Hessenberg form by means of displacement operators: Application to queueing problems*, Linear Algebra Appl., 272, pp. 1–16, 1998.

[BM98b] D. BINI AND B. MEINI, *Using displacement structure for solving non-skip-free M/G/1 type Markov chains*, in Advances in Matrix Analytic Methods, A. Alfa and S. Chakravarthy, eds., Notable Publications, Neshanic Station, NJ, 1998, pp. 17–37.

[Boy68] C. A. BOYER, *A History of Mathematics*, John Wiley, New York, 1968.

[Boz95] E. BOZZO, *Algebras of higher dimension for displacement decompositions and computations with Toeplitz plus Hankel matrices*, Linear Algebra Appl., 230, pp. 127–150, 1995.

[BP86] D. BINI AND V. PAN, *Polynomial division and its computational complexity*, J. Complexity, 2, pp. 179–203, 1986.

[BP93] D. BINI AND V. Y. PAN, *Improved parallel computations with Toeplitz-like and Hankel matrices*, Linear Algebra Appl., 188–189, pp. 3–29, 1993.

[BP94] D. BINI AND V. Y. PAN, *Matrix and Polynomial Computations, Vol. 1: Fundamental Algorithms*, Birkhäuser, Boston, 1994.

[Bre91] R. P. BRENT, *Parallel algorithms for Toeplitz systems*, in Numerical Linear Algebra, Digital Signal Processing and Parallel Algorithms, G. H. Golub and P. Van Dooren, eds., Springer-Verlag, Berlin, New York, pp. 75–92, 1991.

[Bre78] J. W. BREWER, *Kronecker products and matrix calculus in system theory*, IEEE Trans. Circuits Systems, 25, pp. 772–781, 1978.

[Bre97] R. P. BRENT, *Numerical stability of some fast algorithms for structured matrices*, in Proc. Workshop on Scientific Computing, Hong Kong, March 1997, Springer-Verlag, Berlin, New York, 1998.

[BS88] A. W. BOJANCZYK AND A. O. STEINHARDT, *Matrix downdating techniques for signal processing*, Proc. SPIE Conference on Advanced Algorithms and Architectures for Signal Processing, San Diego, 975, pp. 68–75, 1988.

[BS91] A. W. BOJANCZYK AND A. O. STEINHARDT, *Stability analysis of a Householder-based algorithm for downdating the Cholesky factorization*, SIAM J. Sci. Statist. Comput., 12, pp. 1255–1265, 1991.

[BSK94] T. BOROS, A. H. SAYED, AND T. KAILATH, *Structured matrices and unconstrained rational interpolation*, Linear Algebra Appl., 203–204, pp. 155–188, 1994.

[BSK99] T. BOROS, A. H. SAYED, AND T. KAILATH, *A recursive method for solving unconstrained tangential interpolation problems*, IEEE Trans. Automat. Control, 44, pp. 454–470, 1999.

[BSLK96] T. BOROS, A. H. SAYED, H. LEV-ARI, AND T. KAILATH, *A generalized Schur-type algorithm for the joint factorization of a structured matrix and its inverse*, Calcolo, 33, pp. 131–145, 1996.

[BS90] A. BÖTTCHER AND B. SILBERMANN, *Analysis of Toeplitz Operators*, Springer-Verlag, Berlin, New York, 1990.

[BT89] D. BERTSEKAS AND J. TSITSIKLIS, *Parallel and Distributed Computation: Numerical Methods*, Prentice–Hall, Englewood Cliffs, NJ, 1989.

[Bun85] J. BUNCH, *Stability of methods for solving Toeplitz systems of equations*, SIAM J. Sci. Statist. Comput., 6, pp. 349–364, 1985.

[Bun87] J. BUNCH, *The weak and strong stability of algorithms in numerical linear algebra*, Linear Algebra Appl., 88/89, pp. 49–66, 1987.

[Bun92] J. BUNCH, *Matrix properties of the Levinson and Schur algorithms*, J. Numer. Linear Algebra Appl., 1, pp. 183–198, 1992.

[Bur75] J. P. BURG, *Maximum Entropy Spectral Analysis*, Ph.D. thesis, Stanford University, Stanford, CA, 1975.

[Car90] J. CARDOSO, *Eigen-structure of the fourth-order cumulant tensor with application to the blind source separation problem*, in Proc. ICASSP, Albuquerque, NM, 1990, pp. 2655–2658.

[Car95] J. CARDOSO, *A tetradic decomposition of 4th-order tensors: Application to the source separation problem*, in SVD and Signal Processing, III, M. Moonen and B. D. Moor, eds., Elsevier Science Publishers, Amsterdam, 1995.

[CC82] C. CHUI AND A. CHAN, *Application of approximation theory methods to recursive digital filter design*, IEEE Trans. Acoustics, Speech Signal Process., 30, pp. 18–24, 1982.

[CC92] R. CHAN AND T. CHAN, *Circulant preconditioners for elliptic problems*, Numer. Linear Algebra Appl., 1, pp. 77–101, 1992.

[CC96a] J. CARDOSO AND P. COMON, *Independent component analysis, a survey of some algebraic methods*, in Proc. ISCAS, 1996.

[CC96b] R. CHAN AND W. CHING, *Toeplitz-circulant preconditioners for Toeplitz systems and their applications to queueing networks with batch arrivals*, SIAM J. Sci. Comput., 17, pp. 762–772, 1996.

[CCW95] R. CHAN, T. CHAN, AND C. WONG, *Cosine transform based preconditioners for total variation minimization problems in image processing*, in Iterative Methods in Linear Algebra, II, 3, S. Margenov and P. Vassilevski, eds., IMACS Series in Computational and Applied Mathematics, Proc. Second IMACS International Symposium on Iterative Methods in Linear Algebra, Bulgaria, pp. 311–329, 1995.

[CCW96] R. CHAN, W. CHING, AND C. WONG, *Optimal trigonometric preconditioners for elliptic problems and queueing problems*, SEA Bull. Math., 20, pp. 110–117, 1996.

[CCZ97] W. CHING, R. CHAN, AND X. ZHOU, *Circulant preconditioners for Markov modulated Poisson processes and their applications to manufacturing systems*, SIAM J. Matrix. Anal. Appl., 18, pp. 464–481, 1997.

[CDH97] R. CHAN, T. DELILLO, AND M. HORN, *The numerical solution of the biharmonic equation by conformal mapping*, SIAM J. Sci. Comput., 18, pp. 1571–1582, 1997.

[CDH98] R. CHAN, T. DELILLO, AND M. HORN, *Superlinear convergence estimates for a conjugate gradient method for the biharmonic equation*, SIAM J. Sci. Comput., 19, pp. 139–147, 1998.

[CH92a] T. F. CHAN AND P. C. HANSEN, *A look-ahead Levinson algorithm for indefinite Toeplitz systems*, SIAM J. Matrix Anal. Appl. 13, pp. 490–506, 1992.

[CH92b] T. F. CHAN AND P. C. HANSEN, *A look-ahead Levinson algorithm for general Toeplitz systems*, IEEE Trans. Signal Process., 40, pp. 1079–1090, 1992.

[Cha88] T. CHAN, *An optimal circulant preconditioner for Toeplitz systems*, SIAM J. Sci. Statist. Comput., 9, pp. 766–771, 1988.

[Cha89a] R. CHAN, *Circulant preconditioners for Hermitian Toeplitz systems*, SIAM J. Matrix Anal. Appl., 10, pp. 542–550, 1989.

[Cha89b] R. CHAN, *The spectrum of a family of circulant preconditioned Toeplitz systems*, SIAM J. Numer. Anal., 26, pp. 503–506, 1989.

[Cha91] R. CHAN, *Toeplitz preconditioners for Toeplitz systems with nonnegative generating functions*, IMA J. Numer. Anal., 11, pp. 333–345, 1991.

[Chu89] J. CHUN, *Fast Array Algorithms for Structured Matrices*, Ph.D. dissertation, Stanford University, Stanford, CA, 1989.

[CJY91a] R. CHAN, X. JIN, AND M. YEUNG, *The circulant operator in the Banach algebra of matrices*, Linear Algebra Appl., 149, pp. 41–53, 1991.

[CJY91b] R. CHAN, X. JIN, AND M. YEUNG, *The spectra of super-optimal circulant preconditioned Toeplitz systems*, SIAM J. Numer. Anal., 28, pp. 871–879, 1991.

[CK91a] J. CHUN AND T. KAILATH, *Divide-and-conquer solutions of least-squares problems for matrices with displacement structure*, SIAM J. Matrix Anal. Appl., 12, pp. 128–145, 1991.

[CK91b] J. CHUN AND T. KAILATH, *Displacement structure for Hankel, Vandermonde, and related (derived) matrices*, Linear Algebra Appl., 151, pp. 199–227, 1991.

[CKL87] J. CHUN, T. KAILATH, AND H. LEV-ARI, *Fast parallel algorithms for QR and triangular factorization*, SIAM J. Sci. Statist. Comput., 8, pp. 899–913, 1987.

[CKM82] G. CARAYANNIS, N. KALOUPTSIDIS, AND D. MANOLAKIS, *Fast recursive algorithms for a class of linear equations*, IEEE Trans. Acoustics Speech Signal Process., 30, pp. 227–239, 1982.

[CM96] P. COMON AND B. MOURRAIN, *Decomposition of quantics in sums of powers of linear forms*, Signal Process., 53, pp. 93–107, 1996.

[CN93a] R. CHAN AND M. NG, *Fast iterative solvers for Toeplitz-plus-band systems*, SIAM J. Sci. Comput., 14, pp. 1013–1019, 1993.

[CN93b] R. CHAN AND M. NG, *Toeplitz preconditioners for Hermitian Toeplitz systems*, Linear Algebra Appl., 190, pp. 181–208, 1993.

[CN96] R. CHAN AND M. NG, *Conjugate gradient methods for Toeplitz systems*, SIAM Rev., 38, pp. 427–482, 1996.

[CNP93] R. CHAN, J. NAGY, AND R. PLEMMONS, *FFT-based preconditioners for Toeplitz-block least squares problems*, SIAM J. Numer. Anal., 30, pp. 1740–1768, 1993.

[CNP94a] R. CHAN, J. NAGY, AND R. PLEMMONS, *Circulant preconditioned Toeplitz least squares iterations*, SIAM J. Matrix Anal. Appl., 15, pp. 80–97, 1994.

[CNP94b] R. CHAN, J. NAGY, AND R. PLEMMONS, *Displacement preconditioner for Toeplitz least squares iterations*, Electron. Trans. Numer. Anal., 2, pp. 44–56, 1994.

[CNP96] R. CHAN, M. NG, AND R. PLEMMONS, *Generalization of Strang's preconditioner with applications to Toeplitz least squares problems*, Numer. Linear Algebra Appl., 3, pp. 45–64, 1996.

[CNW96] R. CHAN, M. NG, AND C. WONG, *Sine transform based preconditioners for symmetric Toeplitz systems*, Linear Algebra Appl., 232, pp. 237–259, 1996.

[CO94] T. CHAN AND J. OLKIN, *Circulant preconditioners for Toeplitz-block matrices*, Numer. Algorithms, 6, pp. 89–101, 1994.

[Col60] L. COLLATZ, *The Numerical Treatment of Differential Equations*, 3rd ed., Springer-Verlag, Berlin, New York, 1960.

[Con73] J. CONWAY, *Functions of One Complex Variable*, Springer-Verlag, Berlin, 1973.

[Con96] T. CONSTANTINESCU, *Schur Parameters, Factorization and Dilation Problems*, Birkhäuser, Basel, 1996.

[Coo72] R. COOPER, *Introduction to Queueing Theory*, 2nd ed., Macmillan, New York, 1972.

[CS89] R. CHAN AND G. STRANG, *Toeplitz equations by conjugate gradients with circulant preconditioner*, SIAM J. Sci. Statist. Comput., 10, pp. 104–119, 1989.

[CS96] S. CHANDRASEKARAN AND A. H. SAYED, *Stabilizing the generalized Schur algorithm*, SIAM J. Matrix Anal. Appl., 17, pp. 950–983, 1996.

[CS98] S. CHANDRASEKARAN AND A. H. SAYED, *A fast stable solver for nonsymmetric Toeplitz and quasi-Toeplitz systems of linear equations*, SIAM J. Matrix Anal. Appl., 19, pp. 107–139, 1998.

[CSK94] T. CONSTANTINESCU, A. H. SAYED, AND T. KAILATH, *A recursive Schur-based approach to the four-block problem*, IEEE Trans. Automat. Control, 39, pp. 1476–1481, 1994.

[CSK95] T. CONSTANTINESCU, A. H. SAYED, AND T. KAILATH, *Displacement structure and completion problems*, SIAM J. Matrix Anal. Appl., 16, pp. 58–78, 1995.

[CSK99] T. CONSTANTINESCU, A. H. SAYED, AND T. KAILATH, *Displacement structure and H_∞ problems*, in Advances in System Theory, T. Djaferis, ed., Kluwer Academic Publishers, Norwell, MA, 1999, to appear.

[CT65] J. COOLEY AND J. TUKEY, *An algorithm for the machine calculation of complex Fourier series*, Math. Comp., 19, pp. 297–301, 1965.

[CT94] R. CHAN AND P. TANG, *Fast band-Toeplitz preconditioners for Hermitian Toeplitz systems*, SIAM J. Sci. Comput., 15, pp. 164–171, 1994.

[CXT94] Y. M. CHO, G. XU, AND T. KAILATH, *Fast identification of state-space models via exploitation of displacement structure*, IEEE Trans. Automat. Control, 39, pp. 2004–2017, 1994.

[CY92] R. CHAN AND M. YEUNG, *Circulant preconditioners constructed from kernels*, SIAM J. Numer. Anal., 29, pp. 1093–1103, 1992.

[CY93] R. CHAN AND M. YEUNG, *Circulant preconditioners for complex Toeplitz matrices*, SIAM J. Numer. Anal., 30, pp. 1193–1207, 1993.

[Cyb80] G. CYBENKO, *The numerical stability of the Levinson-Durbin algorithm for Toeplitz systems of equations*, SIAM J. Sci. Statist. Comput., 1, pp. 303–319, 1980.

[Cyb83] G. CYBENKO, *A general orthogonalization technique with applications to time series analysis and signal processing*, Math. Comp., 40, pp. 323–336, 1983.

[Cyb87] G. CYBENKO, *Fast Toeplitz orthogonalization using inner products*, SIAM J. Sci. Statist. Comput., 8, pp. 734–740, 1987.

[Dan67] J. DANIEL, *The conjugate gradient method for linear and nonlinear operator equations*, SIAM J. Numer. Anal., 4, pp. 10–26, 1967.

[Dav79] P. DAVIS, *Circulant Matrices*, John Wiley, New York, 1979.

[DD84] P. DEWILDE AND H. DYM, *Lossless inverse scattering, digital filters, and estimation theory*, IEEE Trans. Inform. Theory, 30, pp. 644–662, 1984.

[Del82] J.-M. DELOSME, *Algorithms and Implementations for Linear Least-Squares Estimation*, Ph.D. dissertation, Stanford University, Stanford, CA, 1982.

[DFS93] F. DI BENEDETTO, G. FIORENTINO, AND S. SERRA, *C.G. preconditioning for Toeplitz matrices*, Comput. Math. Appl., 25, pp. 35–45, 1993.

[DGK85] P. DELSARTE, Y. V. GENIN, AND Y. G. KAMP, *A generalisation of the Levinson algorithm for Hermitian Toeplitz matrices with any rank profile*, IEEE Trans. Acoustics Speech Signal Process., 33, pp. 964–971, 1985.

[DI86] J.-M. DELOSME AND I. C. F. IPSEN, *Parallel solution of symmetric positive definite systems with hyperbolic rotations*, Linear Algebra Appl., 77, pp. 75–111, 1986.

[DiB95] F. DI BENEDETTO, *Analysis of preconditioning techniques for ill-conditioned Toeplitz matrices*, SIAM J. Sci. Comput., 16, pp. 682–697, 1995.

[DM85] L. DELVES AND J. MOHAMED, *Computational Methods for Integral Equations*, Cambridge University Press, Cambridge, UK, 1985.

[DMV99] L. DELATHAUWER, B. DEMOOR, AND J. VANDEWALLE, *A multilinear singular value decomposition*, SIAM J. Matrix Anal. Appl., to appear.

[Dur59] J. DURBIN, *The fitting of time-series models*, Rev. Int. Stat. Inst., 28, pp. 229–249, 1959.

[DV93] P. M. DEWILDE AND A. J. VAN DER VEEN, *On the Hankel-norm approximation of upper-triangular operators and matrices*, Integral Equations Operator Theory, 17, pp. 1–45, 1993.

[DV98] P. DEWILDE AND A. J. VAN DER VEEN, *Time-Varying Systems and Computations*, Kluwer Academic Publishers, Boston, MA, 1998.

[DVK78] P. DEWILDE, A. C. VIEIRA, AND T. KAILATH, *On a generalized Szegő-Levinson realization algorithm for optimal linear predictors based on a network synthesis approach*, IEEE Trans. Circuits Systems, 25, pp. 663–675, 1978.

[Dym89a] H. DYM, *J-Contractive Matrix Functions, Reproducing Kernel Hilbert Spaces, and Interpolation*, CBMS Regional Conf. Ser. in Math. 71, AMS, Providence, RI, 1989.

[Dym89b] H. DYM, *On reproducing kernel spaces, J-unitary matrix functions, interpolation and displacement rank*, Oper. Theory Adv. Appl. 41, pp. 173–239, Birkhäuser, Basel, 1989.

[Edw82] R. E. EDWARDS, *Fourier Series*, Vols. 1 and 2, 2nd ed., Springer-Verlag, Berlin, New York, 1982.

[ER82] D. F. ELLIOTT AND K. R. RAO, *Fast Transform Algorithms, Analyses, Applications*, Academic Press, New York, 1982.

[FCG79] P. FAURRE, M. CLERGET, AND F. GERMAIN, *Opérateurs Rationnels Positifs*, Dunod, Paris, 1979.

[FF90] C. FOIAS AND A. E. FRAZHO, *The Commutant Lifting Approach to Interpolation Problems*, Oper. Theory Adv. Appl. 44, Birkhäuser, Basel, 1990.

[Fie85] M. FIEDLER, *Hankel and Loewner matrices*, Linear Algebra Appl., 58, pp. 75–95, 1985.

[FKML78] B. FRIEDLANDER, T. KAILATH, M. MORF, AND L. LJUNG, *Extended Levinson and Chandrasekhar equations for general discrete-time linear estimation problems*, IEEE Trans. Automat. Control, 23, pp. 653–659, 1978.

[FM67] G. E. FORSYTHE AND C. B. MOLER, *Computer Solution of Linear Algebraic Systems*, Prentice–Hall, Englewood Cliffs, NJ, 1967.

[FP81] R. E. FUNDERLIC AND R. J. PLEMMONS, *LU decomposition of M-matrices by elimination without pivoting*, Linear Algebra Appl., 41, pp. 99–110, 1981.

[Fre94] R. W. FREUND, *A look-ahead Bareiss algorithm for general Toeplitz matrices*, Numer. Math., 68, pp. 35–69, 1994.

[FS95] G. FIORENTINO AND S. SERRA, *Tau preconditioners for (high order) elliptic problems*, in Proc. 2nd IMACS Conf. on Iterative Methods in Linear Algebra, Vassilevski, ed., pp. 241–252, Blagoevgrad, Bulgaria, 1995.

[FZ93a] R. W. FREUND AND H. ZHA, *Formally biorthogonal polynomials and a look-ahead Levinson algorithm for general Toeplitz systems*, Linear Algebra Appl., 188/189, pp. 255–303, 1993.

[FZ93b] R. W. FREUND AND H. ZHA, *A look-ahead algorithm for the solution of general Hankel systems*, Numer. Math., 64, pp. 295–321, 1993.

[Gem97] L. GEMIGNANI, *Schur complement of Bezoutians with applications to the inversion of block Hankel and block Toeplitz matrices*, Linear Algebra Appl., 253, pp. 39–59, 1997.

[Gen73] M. GENTLEMAN, *Least squares computations by Givens transformations*, J. Inst. Math. Appl., 12, pp. 329–336, 1973.

[Ger54] L. Y. GERONIMUS, *Polynomials orthogonal on a circle and their applications*, Amer. Math. Soc. Transl., 3, pp. 1–78, 1954 (in Russian, 1948).

[GF74] I. GOHBERG AND I. FEL'DMAN, *Convolution equations and projection methods for their solution*, Transl. Math. Monogr., 41, AMS, Providence, RI, 1974.

[GGM92] A. GREENBAUM, L. GREENGARD, AND A. MAYO, *On the numerical solution of the biharmonic equation in the plane*, Physica D, 60, pp. 216–225, 1992.

[GH93a] M. H. GUTKNECHT AND M. HOCHBRUCK, *Look-ahead Levinson and Schur algorithms for non-Hermitian Toeplitz Systems*, IPS Research Report 93-11, ETH, Zürich, 1993.

[GH93b] M. H. GUTKNECHT AND M. HOCHBRUCK, *The stability of inversion formulas for Toeplitz matrices*, IPS Research Report 93-13, ETH, Zürich, 1993.

[GHKT94] H. R. GAIL, S. L. HANTLER, A. G. KONHEIM, AND B. A. TAYLOR, *An analysis of a class of telecommunications models*, Performance Evaluation, 21, pp. 151–161, 1994.

[GHT97] H. R. GAIL, S. L. HANTLER, AND B. A. TAYLOR, *Non-skip-free M/G/1 and G/M/1 type Markov chains*, Adv. Appl. Probab., 29, pp. 733–758, 1997.

[Gia90] G. G. GIANNAKIS, *On the identifiability of non-Gaussian models using cumulants*, IEEE Trans. Automat. Control, 35, pp. 18–26, 1990.

[GK93] I. GOHBERG AND I. KOLTRACHT, *Mixed, componentwise and structured condition numbers*, SIAM J. Matrix Anal. Appl., 14, pp. 688–704, 1993.

[GKO95] I. GOHBERG, T. KAILATH, AND V. OLSHEVSKY, *Fast Gaussian elimination with partial pivoting for matrices with displacement structure*, Math. Comp., 64, pp. 1557–1576, 1995.

[GKX94] I. GOHBERG, I. KOLTRACHT, AND D. XIAO, *Condition and accuracy of algorithms for computing Schur coefficients of Toeplitz matrices*, SIAM J. Matrix Anal. Appl., 15, pp. 1290–1309, 1994.

[GL55] I. GELFAND AND B. LEVITAN, *On the determination of a differential equation from its spectral function*, Amer. Math. Soc. Transl., 1, pp. 253–304, 1955.

[Glo84] K. GLOVER, *All optimal Hankel-norm approximations to linear multivariable systems and their L^∞-error bounds,* Internat. J. Control, 39, pp. 1115–1193, 1984.

[GM89] G. G. GIANNAKIS AND J. M. MENDEL, *Identification of nonminimum phase systems using higher order statistics*, IEEE Trans. Acoustics Speech Signal Process., 37, pp. 360–377, 1989.

[GO92] I. GOHBERG AND V. OLSHEVSKY, *Circulant displacements and decomposition of matrices*, Integral Equations Operator Theory, 15, pp. 730–743, 1992.

[GO94c] I. GOHBERG AND V. OLSHEVSKY, *Complexity of multiplication with vectors for structured matrices*, Linear Algebra Appl., 202, pp. 163–192, 1994.

[Goh86] I. GOHBERG, ED., I. *Schur Methods in Operator Theory and Signal Processing*, Oper. Theory Adv. Appl. 18, Birkhäuser, Basel, 1986.

[Gol65] G. H. GOLUB, *Numerical methods for solving linear least squares problems*, Numer. Math., 7, pp. 206–216, 1965.

[Gou91] N. GOULD, *On growth in Gaussian elimination with complete pivoting*, SIAM J. Matrix Anal. Appl., 12, pp. 354–361, 1991.

[GR70] G. H. GOLUB AND C. REINSCH, *Singular value decomposition and least squares solutions*, Numer. Math., 14, pp. 403–420, 1970.

[Gri96] V. S. GRIGORASCU, *Tenseurs Structurés, Produits d'Ordre Supérieur et Cumulants*, Ph.D. dissertation, University of Paris, Orsay, 1996.

[Gro84] C. GROETSCH, *The Theory of Tikhonov Regularization for Fredholm Equations of the First Kind*, Pitman Publishing, London, 1984.

[GS84] U. GRENANDER AND G. SZEGŐ, *Toeplitz Forms and Their Applications*, 2nd ed., Chelsea Publishing, New York, 1984.

[GS90] G. G. GIANNAKIS AND A. M. SWAMY, *On estimating noncausal nonminimum phase ARMA models of non-Guassian processes*, IEEE Trans. Acoustics Speech Signal Process., 38, pp. 478–495, 1990.

[GS94] I. GOHBERG AND L. A. SAKHNOVICH, ED., *Matrix and Operator-Valued Functions— V. P. Potapov Memorial Volume*, Oper. Theory Adv. Appl. 72, Birkhäuser, Basel, 1994.

[GT83] D. GILBARG AND N. S. TRUDINGER, *Elliptic Partial Differential Equations of Second Order*, 2nd ed., Springer-Verlag, Berlin, New York, 1983.

[GTH85] W. K. GRASSMAN, M. I. TAKSAR, AND D. P. HEYMAN, *Regenerative analysis and steady state distribution for Markov chains*, Oper. Res., 33, pp. 1107–1116, 1985.

[Gu95a] M. GU, *Stable and efficient algorithms for structured systems of linear equations*, SIAM J. Matrix Anal. Appl., 19, pp. 279–306, 1998.

[Gu95b] M. GU, *New Fast Algorithms for Structured Least Squares Problems*, Tech. Rep. LBL-37878, Lawrence Berkeley Laboratory, 1995.

[Gut93] M. H. GUTKNECHT, *Stable row recurrences for the Padé table and generically superfast lookahead solvers for non-Hermitian Toeplitz systems*, Linear Algebra Appl., 188/189, pp. 351–422, 1993.

[GV96] G. GOLUB AND C. VAN LOAN, *Matrix Computations*, 3rd ed., The Johns Hopkins University Press, Baltimore, MD, 1996.

[GW66] G. H. GOLUB AND J. H. WILKINSON, *Note on iterative refinement of least squares solution*, Numer. Math., 9, pp. 139–148, 1966.

[Hay96] S. HAYKIN, *Adaptive Filter Theory*, 3rd ed., Prentice–Hall, Englewood Cliffs, NJ, 1996.

[Hei95] G. HEINIG, *Inversion of generalized Cauchy matrices and other classes of structured matrices*, Linear Algebra Signal Process., IMA Vol. Math. Appl. 69, pp. 95–114, 1995.

[Hel87] J. W. HELTON, *Operator Theory, Analytic Functions, Matrices and Electrical Engineering*, Conference Board of the Mathematical Sciences, AMS, Providence, RI, 1987.

[HG93] P. C. HANSEN AND H. GESMAR, *Fast orthogonal decomposition of rank deficient Toeplitz matrices*, Numer. Algorithms, 4, pp. 151–166, 1993.

[HH77] L. L. HIRSCHMAN AND D. E. HUGHES, *Extreme Eigen Values of Toeplitz Operators*, Lecture Notes in Math., Springer-Verlag, Heidelberg, 1977.

[HH89] N. J. HIGHAM AND D. J. HIGHAM, *Large growth factors in Gaussian elimination with pivoting*, SIAM J. Matrix Anal. Appl., 10, pp. 155–164, 1989.

[HH92] D. J. HIGHAM AND N. J. HIGHAM, *Backward error and condition of structured linear systems*, SIAM J. Matrix Anal. Appl., 13, pp. 162–175, 1992.

[Hig96] N. J. HIGHAM, *Accuracy and Stability of Numerical Algorithms*, SIAM, Philadelphia, 1996.

[Hil94] D. HILBERT, *Ein Beitrag zur Theorie des Legendre'schen Polynoms*, Acta Math., 18, pp. 155–160, 1894.

[HJ85] R. A. HORN AND C. R. JOHNSON, *Matrix Analysis*, Cambridge University Press, Cambridge, UK, 1985.

[HN94] M. HANKE AND J. NAGY, *Toeplitz approximate inverse preconditioner for banded Toeplitz matrices*, Numer. Algorithms, 7, pp. 183–199, 1994.

[HR84] G. HEINIG AND K. ROST, *Algebraic Methods for Toeplitz-like Matrices and Operators*, Akademie-Verlag, Berlin, Birkhäuser, Boston, 1984.

[HS52] M. HESTENES AND E. STIEFEL, *Methods of conjugate gradients for solving linear systems*, J. Res. National Bureau of Standards, Sec. B, 49, pp. 409–436, 1952.

[Huc93] T. HUCKLE, *Some aspects of circulant preconditioners*, SIAM J. Sci. Comput., 14, pp. 531–541, 1993.

[Huc94] T. HUCKLE, *Iterative methods for Toeplitz-like matrices*, Report SCCM-94-05, Computer Science Dept., Stanford University, Stanford, CA, 1994.

[HY93] J. HSUE AND A. YAGLE, *Fast algorithms for close-to-Toeplitz-plus-Hankel systems and two-sided linear prediction*, IEEE Trans. Signal Process., 41, pp. 2349–2361, 1993.

[IK66] E. ISAACSON AND H. B. KELLER, *Analysis of Numerical Methods*, John Wiley, New York, 1966.

[Ioh82] I. S. IOHVIDOV, *Hankel and Toeplitz Forms: Algebraic Theory*, Birkhäuser, Boston, 1982.

[Jai89] A. JAIN, *Fundamentals of Digital Image Processing*, Prentice–Hall, Englewood Cliffs, NJ, 1989.

[JK92] B. JELONNEK AND K.-D. KAMMEYER, *Improved methods for blind system identification using higher order statistics*, IEEE Trans. Signal Process., 40, pp. 2947–2960, 1992.

[JW77] M. JANKOWSKI AND M. WOZNIAKOWSKI, *Iterative refinement implies numerical stability*, BIT, 17, pp. 303–311, 1977.

[Kai73] T. KAILATH, *Some new algorithms for recursive estimation in constant linear systems*, IEEE Trans. Inform. Theory, 19, pp. 750–760, 1973.

[Kai80] T. KAILATH, *Linear Systems*, Prentice–Hall, Englewood Cliffs, NJ, 1980.

[Kai85] T. KAILATH, *Signal processing in the VLSI era*, in VLSI and Modern Signal Processing, S. Y. Kung, H. J. Whitehouse, and T. Kailath, eds., pp. 5–24, Prentice–Hall, Englewood Cliffs, NJ, 1985.

[Kai86] T. KAILATH, *A theorem of I. Schur and its impact on modern signal processing*, Oper. Theory Adv. Appl., 18, pp. 9–30, Birkhäuser, Basel, 1986.

[Kai87] T. KAILATH, *Signal processing applications of some moment problems*, in Moments in Mathematics 37, H. Landau, ed., pp. 71–109, AMS, Providence, RI, 1987.

[Kai91] T. KAILATH, *Remarks on the origin of the displacement-rank concept*, Appl. Math. Comput., 45, pp. 193–206, 1991.

[Kat76] Y. KATZNELSON, *An Introduction to Harmonic Analysis*, 2nd ed., Dover Publications, New York, 1976.

[KC94] T. KAILATH AND J. CHUN, *Generalized displacement structure for block-Toeplitz, Toeplitz-block, and Toeplitz-derived matrices*, SIAM J. Matrix Anal. Appl., 15, pp. 114–128, 1994.

[KFA70] R. E. KALMAN, P. L. FALB, AND M. A. ARBIB, *Topics in Mathematical System Theory*. Int. Ser. Pure Appl. Math. McGraw–Hill, New York, 1970.

[KH83] S. Y. KUNG AND Y. H. HU, *A highly concurrent algorithm and pipelined architecture for solving Toeplitz systems*, IEEE Trans. Acoustics Speech Signal Process., 31, pp. 66–76, 1983.

[KK92] T. KU AND C. KUO, *Design and analysis of Toeplitz preconditioners*, IEEE Trans. Signal Process., 40, pp. 129–141, 1992.

[KK93a] T. KU AND C. KUO, *Preconditioned iterative methods for solving Toeplitz-plus-Hankel systems*, SIAM J. Numer. Anal., 30, pp. 824–845, 1993.

[KK93b] T. KU AND C. KUO, *Spectral properties of preconditioned rational Toeplitz matrices*, SIAM J. Matrix Anal. Appl., 14, pp. 146–165, 1993.

[KK93c] T. KU AND C. KUO, *Spectral properties of preconditioned rational Toeplitz matrices: The nonsymmetric case*, SIAM J. Matrix Anal. Appl., 14,, pp. 521–544, 1993.

[KKM79a] T. KAILATH, S. Y. KUNG, AND M. MORF, *Displacement ranks of matrices and linear equations*, J. Math. Anal. Appl., 68, pp. 395–407, 1979.

[KKM79b] T. KAILATH, S. Y. KUNG, AND M. MORF, *Displacement ranks of a matrix*, Bull. Amer. Math. Soc., 1, pp. 769–773, 1979.

[KLM78] T. KAILATH, L. LJUNG, AND M. MORF, *Generalized Krein-Levinson equations for efficient calculation of Fredholm resolvents of nondisplacement kernels*, in Topics in Functional Analysis, I. Gohberg and M. Kac, eds., pp. 169–184, Academic Press, New York, 1978.

[Knu81] D. E. KNUTH, *The Art of Computer Programming: Seminumerical Algorithms*, 2, Addison–Wesley, Reading, MA, 1981.

[KO95] T. KAILATH AND V. OLSHEVSKY, *Displacement structure approach to Chebyshev-Vandermonde and related matrices*, Integral Equations Operator Theory, 22, pp. 65–92, 1995.

[KO96] T. KAILATH AND V. OLSHEVSKY, *Displacement structure approach to discrete-trigonometric-transform based preconditioners of G. Strang type and T. Chan type*, Calcolo, 33, pp. 191–208, 1996.

[KO98] T. KAILATH AND V. OLSHEVSKY, *Diagonal pivoting for partially reconstructible Cauchy-like matrices, with applications to Toeplitz-like linear equations and to boundary rational matrix interpolation problems*, Linear Algebra Appl., 254, pp. 251–302, 1997.

[Kol41] A. N. KOLMOGOROV, *Interpolation and extrapolation of stationary random sequences*, Izv. Akad. Nauk SSSR, 5, pp. 3–11, 1941 (in Russian); German summary, pp. 11–14.

[KR86] A. G. KONHEIM AND M. REISER, *The moveable-boundary multiplexor: Stability and Decomposability*, in Teletraffic Analysis and Computer Performance Evaluation, O. J. Boxma, J. W. Cohen, and H. C. Tijms, eds., North–Holland, Amsterdam, pp. 375–394, 1986.

[KS91] T. KAILATH AND A. H. SAYED, *Fast algorithms for generalized displacement structures*, in Proc. Internat. Symposium Math. Theory of Networks and Systems, H. Kimura and S. Kodama, eds., 2, pp. 27–32, Kobe, Japan, 1991.

[KS95a] T. KAILATH AND A. H. SAYED, *Displacement structure: Theory and applications*, SIAM Rev., 37, pp. 297–386, 1995.

[KS95b] T. KAILATH AND A. H. SAYED, *On lossless cascades in structured matrix factorization*, Arch. Für Elektronik und Übertragungstechnik, 49, pp. 307–312, 1995.

[KSH99] T. KAILATH, A. H. SAYED, AND B. HASSIBI, *State-Space Estimation*, Prentice–Hall, Englewood Cliffs, NJ, 1999.

[Kun78] S. Y. KUNG, *A new identification and model reduction algorithm via singular value decomposition*, in Proc. Asilomar Conf. on Circuits, Systems and Comp., pp. 705–714, Asilomar, CA, 1978.

[KVM78] T. KAILATH, A. VIEIRA, AND M. MORF, *Inverses of Toeplitz operators, innovations and orthogonal polynomials*, SIAM Rev., 20, pp. 106–119, 1978.

[LBK91] H. LEV-ARI, Y. BISTRITZ, AND T. KAILATH, *Generalized Bezoutians and families of efficient zero-location procedures*, IEEE Trans. Circuits Systems, 38, pp. 170–185, 1991.

[Laf75] J. C. LAFON, *Base tensorielle des matrices des Hankel (ou de Toeplitz), applications*, Numer. Math., 23, pp. 349–361, 1975.

[LK84] H. LEV-ARI AND T. KAILATH, *Lattice filter parametrization and modeling of nonstationary processes*, IEEE Trans. Inform. Theory, 30, pp. 2–16, 1984.

[LK86] H. LEV-ARI AND T. KAILATH, *Triangular factorization of structured Hermitian matrices*, Oper. Theory Adv. Appl. 18, pp. 301–324, 1986.

[LK92] H. LEV-ARI AND T. KAILATH, *State-space approach to factorization of lossless transfer functions and structured matrices*, Linear Algebra Appl., 162–164, pp. 273–295, 1992.

[Lev47] N. LEVINSON, *The Wiener RMS (Root-Mean-Square) error criterion in filter design and prediction*, J. Math. Phys., 25, pp. 261–278, 1947.

[Lev83] H. LEV-ARI, *Nonstationary Lattice-Filter Modeling*, Ph.D. dissertation, Stanford University, Stanford, CA, 1983.

[Lev97] H. LEV-ARI, *Displacement structure: Two related perspectives*, in Communications, Computation, Control, and Signal Processing, A. Paulraj, V. Roychowdhury, and C. D. Schaper, eds., Kluwer, Norwell, MA, pp. 233–241, 1997.

[LG77] J. LEROUX AND C. GUEGUEN, *A fixed-point computation of parcor coefficients*, IEEE Trans. Acoustics Speech Signal Process., 25, pp. 257–259, 1977.

[LM85] S. Q. LI AND J. W. MARK, *Performance of voice/data integration on a TDM switch*, IEEE Trans. Comm., 33, pp. 1265–1273, 1985.

[LQ87] F. T. LUK AND S. QIAO, *A fast but unstable orthogonal triangularization technique for Toeplitz matrices*, Linear Algebra Appl., 88/89, pp. 495–506, 1987.

[LR93] G. LATOUCHE AND V. RAMASWAMI, *A logarithmic reduction algorithm for Quasi-Birth-Death processes*, J. Appl. Probab., 30, pp. 650–674, 1993.

[LS96] G. LATOUCHE AND G. STEWART, *Numerical methods for M/G/1 type queues*, in Computations with Markov Chains, W. J. Stewart, ed., Kluwer Academic Publishers, Norwell, MA, pp. 571–581, 1996.

[LT85] P. LANCASTER AND M. TISMENETSKI, *The Theory of Matrices*, Academic Press, New York, 1985.

[Mar80] L. MARPLE, *A new autoregressive spectrum analysis algorithm*, IEEE Trans. Acoustics Speech Signal Process., 28, pp. 441–454, 1980.

[Mar81] L. MARPLE, *Efficient least squares FIR system identification*, IEEE Trans. Acoustics Speech Signal Process., 29, pp. 62–73, 1981.

[Mar82] L. MARPLE, *Fast algorithms for linear prediction and system identification filters with linear phase*, IEEE Trans. Acoustics Speech Signal Process., 30, pp. 942–953, 1982.

[Mas69] J. L. MASSEY, *Shift-register synthesis and BCH decoding*, IEEE Trans. Inform. Theory, 15, pp. 122–127, 1969.

[McC87] P. MCCULLAGH, *Tensor Methods in Statistics*, Chapman and Hall, London, 1987.

[Mei97a] B. MEINI, *New convergence results on functional iteration techniques for the numerical solution of M/G/1 type Markov chains*, Numer. Math., 78, pp. 39–58, 1997.

[Mei97b] B. MEINI, *An improved FFT-based version of Ramaswami's formula*, Comm. Statist. Stochastic Models, 13, pp. 223–238, 1997.

[Men91] J. M. MENDEL, *Tutorial on higher-order statistics (spectra) in signal processing and system theory: Theoretical results and some applications*, Proc. IEEE, 79, pp. 278–305, 1991.

[Mil68] L. MILNE-THOMSON, *Theoretical Hydrodynamics*, 5th ed., Macmillan Press, London, 1968.

[Mor70] M. MORF, personal communication, 1970.

[Mor74] M. MORF, *Fast Algorithms for Multivariable Systems*, Ph.D. thesis, Stanford University, Stanford, CA, 1974.

[Mor80] M. MORF, *Doubling algorithms for Toeplitz and related equations*, in Proc. IEEE Internat. Conf. on Acoustics, Speech and Signal Process., Denver, CO, pp. 954–959, 1980.

[MSK74] M. MORF, G. S. SIDHU, AND T. KAILATH, *Some new algorithms for recursive estimation in constant, linear, discrete-time systems*, IEEE Trans. Automat. Control, 19, pp. 315–323, 1974.

[MT96] M. MIRANDA AND P. TILLI, *Block Toeplitz matrices and preconditioning*, Calcolo, 33, pp. 79–86, 1996.

[Mus53] N. MUSKHELISHVILI, *Some Basic Problems of the Mathematical Theory of Elasticity*, P. Noordhoff Ltd., Groningen, Holland, 1953.

[MW80] W. MILLER AND C. WRATHALL, *Software for Roundoff Analysis of Matrix Algorithms*, Academic Press, New York, 1980.

[Neu89] M. F. NEUTS, *Structured Stochastic Matrices of M/G/1 Type and Their Applications*, Marcel Dekker, New York, 1989.

[Ng94] M. NG, *Fast iterative methods for solving Toeplitz-plus-Hankel least squares problems*, Electron Trans. Numer. Anal., 2, pp. 154–170, 1994.

[NM93] C. NIKIAS AND J. MENDEL, *Signal processing with higher-order spectra*, IEEE Signal Process. Magazine, 10, pp. 10–57, 1993.

[NP93] C. NIKIAS AND A. PETROPULU, *Higher-Order Spectra Analysis. A Nonlinear Signal Processing Framework*, Prentice–Hall, Englewood Cliffs, NJ, 1993.

[NP96] M. NG AND R. PLEMMONS, *Fast RLS adaptive filtering by FFT-based conjugate gradient iterations*, SIAM J. Sci. Comput., 7, pp. 920–941, 1996.

[NPT96] J. NAGY, R. PLEMMONS, AND T. TORGERSEN, *Iterative image restoration using approximate inverse*, IEEE Trans. Image Process., 5, pp. 1151–1162, 1996.

[Oci93] C. A. O'CINNEIDE, *Entrywise perturbation theory and error analysis for Markov chains*, Numer. Math., 65, pp. 109–120, 1993.

[Oda91] T. ODA, *Moment analysis for traffic associated with Markovian queueing systems*, IEEE Trans. Comm., 39, pp. 737–745, 1991.

[Olk86] J. OLKIN, *Linear and Nonlinear Deconvolution Problems*, Ph.D. thesis, Rice University, Houston, TX, 1986.

[Ost40] A. M. OSTROWSKI, *Recherches sur la methode de Graeffe et les zeros des polynomes et des series de Laurent*, Acta Math., 72, pp. 99–257, 1940.

[Pai73] C. C. PAIGE, *An error analysis of a method for solving matrix equations*, Math. Comp., 27, pp. 355–359, 1973.

[Pal90] D. PAL, *Fast Algorithms for Structured Matrices with Arbitrary Rank Profile*, Ph.D. dissertation, Stanford University, Stanford, CA, 1990.

[Pan90] V. Y. PAN, *Computations with dense structured matrices*, Math. Comp., 55, pp. 179–190, 1990.

[Pan92a] V. Y. PAN, *Parallel solution of Toeplitz-like linear systems*, J. Complexity, 8, pp. 1–21, 1992.

[Pan92b] V. Y. PAN, *Parametrization of Newton's iteration for computation with structured matrices and applications*, Comput. Math., 24, pp. 61–75, 1992.

[Pan93a] V. Y. PAN, *Concurrent iterative algorithms for Toeplitz-like linear systems*, IEEE Trans. Parallel Distributive Systems, 4, 5, pp. 592–600, 1993.

[Pan93b] V. Y. PAN, *Decreasing the displacement rank of a matrix*, SIAM J. Matrix Anal. Appl., 14, pp. 118–121, 1993.

[Par80] B. PARLETT, *The Symmetric Eigenvalue Problem*, Prentice–Hall, Englewood Cliffs, NJ, 1980.

[Par86] S. V. PARTER, *On the distribution of the singular values of Toeplitz matrices*, Linear Algebra Appl., 80, pp. 115–130, 1986.

[PK93] D. PAL AND T. KAILATH, *Fast triangular factorization and inversion of Hermitian, Toeplitz, and related matrices with arbitrary rank profile*, SIAM J. Matrix Anal. Appl., 14, pp. 1016–1042, 1993.

[PS91] V. Y. PAN AND R. SCHREIBER, *An Improved Newton iteration for the generalized inverse of a matrix with applications*, SIAM J. Sci. Statist. Comput., 12, pp. 1109–1131, 1991.

[PZHD97] V. Y. PAN, A. L. ZHENG, X. H. HUANG, AND O. DIAS, *Newton's iteration for inversion of Cauchy-like and other structured matrices*, J. Complexity, 13, pp. 108–124, 1997.

[Qia88] S. QIAO, *Hybrid algorithm for fast Toeplitz orthogonalization*, Numer. Math., 53, pp. 351–366, 1988.

[Ram88] V. RAMASWAMI, *A stable recursion for the steady state vector in Markov chains of $M/G/1$ type*, Comm. Statist. Stochastic Models, 4, pp. 183–188, 1988.

[RG94] P. A. REGALIA AND V. S. GRIGORASCU, *Analytic criteria underlying the full-rank cumulant slice problem*, 10th IFAC Symp. System Identification, Copenhagen, pp. 1071–1075, 1994.

[Ris73] J. RISSANEN, *Algorithms for triangular decomposition of block Hankel and Toeplitz matrices with application to factoring positive matrix polynomials*, Math. Comp., 27, pp. 147–154, 1973.

[RK84] S. K. RAO AND T. KAILATH, *Orthogonal digital filters for VLSI implementation*, IEEE Trans. Circuit Systems, 31, pp. 933–945, 1984.

[RM89] P. A. REGALIA AND S. K. MITRA, *Kronecker products, unitary matrices, and signal processing applications*, SIAM Rev., 31, pp. 586–613, 1989.

[ROF92] L. RUDIN, S. OSHER, AND E. FATEMI, *Nonlinear total variation based noise removal algorithms*, Phys. D, 60, pp. 259–268, 1992.

[Saa96] Y. SAAD, *Iterative Methods for Sparse Linear Systems*, PWS Publishing Company, Boston, MA, 1996.

[Sav76] J. E. SAVAGE, *The Complexity of Computing*, John Wiley, New York, 1976.

[Say92] A. H. SAYED, *Displacement Structure in Signal Processing and Mathematics*, Ph.D. dissertation, Stanford University, Stanford, CA, 1992.

[SB95] D. R. SWEET AND R. P. BRENT, *Error analysis of a fast partial pivoting method for structured matrices*, Proc. SPIE, 2563, Advanced Signal Processing Algorithms, Bellingham, WA, pp. 266–280, 1995.

[Sch17] I. SCHUR, *Über potenzreihen die im Inneren des Einheitskreises beschränkt sind*, J. Reine Angew. Math., 147, pp. 205–232, 1917 (English translation in *Oper. Theory Adv. Appl.* 18, pp. 31–88, 1986).

[Sch33] G. SCHULTZ, *Iterative berechnung der reziproken matrix*, Z. Angew. Math. Mech., 13, pp. 57–59, 1933.

[SCK94] A. H. SAYED, T. CONSTANTINESCU, AND T. KAILATH, *Time-variant displacement structure and interpolation problems*, IEEE Trans. Automat. Control, 39, pp. 960–976, 1994.

[SCK95] A. H. SAYED, T. CONSTANTINESCU, AND T. KAILATH, *Square-root algorithms for structured matrices, interpolation, and completion problems*, IMA Vol. Math. Appl. 69, Springer-Verlag, New York, pp. 153–184, 1995.

[SD97b] M. STEWART AND P. VAN DOOREN, *Stability issues in the factorization of structured matrices*, SIAM J. Matrix Anal. Appl., 18, pp. 104–118, 1997.

[Sei90] A. SEILA, *Multivariate estimation of conditional performance measure in regenerative simulation*, Amer. J. Math. Management Sci., 10, pp. 17–45, 1990.

[Sil83] B. SILBERMANN, *On the limiting set of singular values of Toeplitz matrices*, Linear Algebra Appl., 182, pp. 35–43, 1983.

[SK92] A. H. SAYED AND T. KAILATH, *Recursive solutions to rational interpolation problems*, Proc. IEEE Internat. Symposium on Circuits and Systems, 5, pp. 2376–2379, San Diego, 1992.

[SK94a] A. H. SAYED AND T. KAILATH, *Extended Chandrasekhar recursions*, IEEE Trans. Automat. Control, 39, pp. 619–623, 1994.

[SK94b] A. H. SAYED AND T. KAILATH, *A state-space approach to adaptive RLS filtering*, IEEE Signal Process. Magazine, 11, pp. 18–60, 1994.

[SK95a] A. H. SAYED AND T. KAILATH, *Fast algorithms for generalized displacement structures and lossless systems*, Linear Algebra Appl., 219, pp. 49–78, 1995.

[SK95b] A. H. SAYED AND T. KAILATH, *A look-ahead block Schur algorithm for Toeplitz-like matrices*, SIAM J. Matrix Anal. Appl., 16, pp. 388–413, 1995.

[SKLC94] A. H. SAYED, T. KAILATH, H. LEV-ARI, AND T. CONSTANTINESCU, *Recursive solutions of rational interpolation problems via fast matrix factorization*, Integral Equations Operator Theory, 20, pp. 84–118, 1994.

[SLK94a] A. H. SAYED, T. KAILATH, AND H. LEV-ARI, *Generalized Chandrasekhar recursions from the generalized Schur algorithm*, IEEE Trans. Automat. Control, 39, pp. 2265–2269, 1994.

[SLK94b] A. H. SAYED, H. LEV-ARI, AND T. KAILATH, *Time-variant displacement structure and triangular arrays*, IEEE Trans. Signal Process., 42, pp. 1052–1062, 1994.

[SM90a] A. SWAMY AND J. M. MENDEL, *ARMA parameter estimation using only output cumulants*, IEEE Trans. Acoustics Speech Signal Process., 38, pp. 1257–1265, 1990.

[SM90b] A. SWAMY AND J. M. MENDEL, *Time and lag recursive computation of cumulants from a state space model*, IEEE Trans. Automat. Control, 35, pp. 4–17, 1990.

[SM92] A. SWAMY AND J. M. MENDEL, *Identifiability of the AR parameters of an ARMA process using only output cumulants*, IEEE Trans. Automat. Control, 38, pp. 268–273, 1992.

[ST98] S. SERRA AND P. TILLI, *Extreme eigenvalues of multilevel Toeplitz matrices*, preprint.

[Ste73] G. W. STEWART, *Introduction to Matrix Computations*. Academic Press, New York, 1973.

[Ste77] G. W. STEWART, *Perturbation bounds for the QR factorization of a matrix*, SIAM J. Numer. Anal., 14, pp. 509–518, 1977.

[Ste79] G. W. STEWART, *The effect of rounding error on an algorithm for downdating a Cholesky factorization*, J. Inst. Math. Appl., 23, pp. 203–213, 1979.

[Ste94] W. J. STEWART, *Introduction to the Numerical Solution of Markov Chains*, Princeton University Press, Princeton, NJ, 1994.

[Ste95] G. W. STEWART, *On the solution of block Hessenberg systems*, Numer. Linear Algebra Appl., 2, pp. 287–296, 1995.

[Ste98] M. STEWART, *Stable pivoting for the fast factorization of Cauchy-like matrices*, preprint.

[Str86] G. STRANG, *A proposal for Toeplitz matrix calculations*, Stud. Appl. Math., 74, pp. 171–176, 1986.

[SV86] A. VAN DER SLUIS AND H. A. VAN DER VORST, *The rate of convergence of conjugate gradients*, Numer. Math., 48, pp. 543–560, 1986.

[SVS83] K. SRIRAM, P. K. VARSHNEY, AND J. G. SHANTHIKUMAR, *Discrete-time analysis of integrated voice/data multiplexers with and without speech activity detectors*, IEEE J. Selected Areas Comm., 1, pp. 1124–1132, 1983.

[Swa87] P. SWARZTRAUBER, *Multiprocessor FFTs*, Parallel Comput., 5, pp. 197–210, 1987.

[Swe82] D. R. SWEET, *Numerical Methods for Toeplitz Matrices*, Ph.D. thesis, University of Adelaide, Adelaide, Australia, 1982.

[Swe84] D. R. SWEET, *Fast Toeplitz orthogonalization*, Numer. Math., 43, pp. 1–21, 1984.

[Swe93] D. R. SWEET, *The use of pivoting to improve the numerical performance of algorithms for Toeplitz matrices*, SIAM J. Matrix Anal. Appl., 14, pp. 468–493, 1993.

[Sze39] G. SZEGŐ, *Orthogonal Polynomials*, Amer. Math. Soc. Colloq. Publ., 23, AMS, Providence, RI, 1939.

[TB97] L. N. TREFETHEN AND D. BAU, *Numerical Linear Algebra*, SIAM, Philadelphia, PA, 1997.

[TE89] M. A. TEKALP AND A. T. ERDEM, *Higher-order spectrum factorization in one and two dimensions with applications in signal modelling and nonminimum phase system identification*, IEEE Trans. Acoustics Speech Signal Process., 37, pp. 1537–1549, 1989.

[Til96] P. TILLI, *Some spectral properties of non-hermitian block Toeplitz matrices*, Calcolo, 1996.

[Til97a] P. TILLI, *Clustering properties of eigen and singular values of block multilevel Hankel matrices*, preprint.

[Til97b] P. TILLI, *On the asymptotic spectrum of Hermitian block Toeplitz matrices with Toeplitz blocks*, Math. Comp., 66, pp. 1147–1159, 1997.

[Til98a] P. TILLI, *Singular values and eigenvalues of non-Hermitian block Toeplitz matrices*, Linear Algebra Appl., 272, pp. 59–89, 1998.

[Til98b] P. TILLI, *Locally Toeplitz sequences: Spectral properties and applications*, Linear Algebra Appl., 278, pp. 91–120, 1998.

[Til98c] P. TILLI, *A note on the spectral distribution of Toeplitz matrices*, Linear and Multilinear Algebra, 45, pp. 147–159, 1998.

[TM99] P. TILLI AND M. MIRANDA, *Asymptotic spectra of Hermitian block Toeplitz matrices and preconditioning results*, SIAM J. Matrix Anal. Appl., to appear.

[Tis91] M. TISMENETSKY, *A decomposition of Toeplitz matrices and optimal circulant preconditioning*, Linear Algebra Appl., 154/156, pp. 105–121, 1991.

[TP91] A. TEKALP AND G. PAVLOVIĆ, *Restoration of scanned photographic images*, in Digital Image Restoration, A. Katsaggelos, ed., Springer-Verlag, Berlin, 1991.

[Tre64] W. F. TRENCH, *An algorithm for the inversion of finite Toeplitz matrices*, J. SIAM, 12, pp. 515–522, 1964.

[Tre86] W. F. TRENCH, *Solution of systems with Toeplitz matrices generated by rational functions*, Linear Algebra Appl., 74, pp. 191–211, 1986.

[Tre90] L. N. TREFETHEN, *Approximation theory and numerical linear algebra*, in Algorithms for Approximation II, J. Mason and M. Cox, eds., Chapman and Hall, London, 1990.

[Tuc64] L. R. TUCKER, *The extension of factor analysis to three-dimensional matrices*, in Contributions to Mathematical Psychology, H. Gullikson and N. Frederiksen, eds., pp. 109–127, Holt, Rinehart and Winston, New York, 1964.

[Tuc66] L. R. TUCKER, *Some mathematical notes on three-mode factor analysis*, Psychometrika, 31, pp. 279–311, 1966.

[Tug87] J. K. TUGNAIT, *Identification of linear stochastic systems via second- and fourth-order cumulant matching*, IEEE Trans. Inform. Theory, 33, pp. 393–407, 1987.

[Tug95] J. K. TUGNAIT, *Parameter estimation for noncausal ARMA models of non-Gaussian signals via cumulant matching*, IEEE Trans. Signal Process., 43, pp. 886–893, 1995.

Bibliography

[Tyr91] E. E. TYRTYSHNIKOV, *Cauchy-Toeplitz matrices and some applications*, Linear Algebra Appl., 149, pp. 1–18, 1991.

[Tyr92a] E. E. TYRTYSHNIKOV, *Singular values of Cauchy-Toeplitz matrices*, Linear Algebra Appl., 161, pp. 99–116, 1992.

[Tyr92b] E. E. TYRTYSHNIKOV, *Optimal and superoptimal circulant preconditioners*, SIAM J. Matrix Anal. Appl., 13, pp. 459–473, 1992.

[Tyr94a] E. E. TYRTYSHNIKOV, *Influence of matrix operations on the distribution of eigenvalues and singular values of Toeplitz matrices*, Linear Algebra Appl., 207, pp. 225–249, 1994.

[Tyr94b] E. E. TYRTYSHNIKOV, *How bad are Hankel matrices?*, Numer. Math., 67, pp. 261–269, 1994.

[Tyr95] E. E. TYRTYSHNIKOV, *Circulant preconditioners with unbounded inverses*, Linear Algebra Appl., 216, pp. 1–24, 1995.

[Tyr96a] E. E. TYRTYSHNIKOV, *A unifying approach to some old and new theorems on distribution and clustering*, Linear Algebra Appl., 232,, pp. 1–43, 1996.

[Tyr97] E. E. TYRTYSHNIKOV, *A Brief Introduction to Numerical Analysis*, Birkhäuser, Boston, 1997.

[TZ97] E. E. TYRTYSHNIKOV AND N. ZAMARASHKIN, *Spectra of multilevel Toeplitz matrices: Advanced theory via simple matrix relationships*, to appear in Linear Algebra Appl.

[Var63] R. S. VARGA, *Matrix Iterative Analysis*, Prentice–Hall, Englewood Cliffs, NJ, 1963.

[Var92] J. M. VARAH, *Backward error estimates for Toeplitz systems*, preprint, Computer Science Department, University of British Columbia, Vancouver, 1992.

[Var93] J. M. VARAH, *The prolate matrix*, Linear Algebra Appl., 187, pp. 269–278, 1993.

[Vav91] Z. VAVRIN, *A unified approach to Loewner and Hankel matrices*, Linear Algebra Appl., 143, pp. 171–222, 1991.

[VC81] R. S. VARGA AND D.-Y. CAI, *On the LU factorization of M-matrices*, Numer. Math., 38, pp. 179–192, 1981.

[VD94] A. J. VAN DER VEEN AND P. M. DEWILDE, *On low-complexity approximation of matrices*, Linear Algebra Appl., 205/206, pp. 1145–1201, 1994.

[Vee93] A. J. VAN DER VEEN, *Time-Varying System Theory and Computational Modeling: Realization, Approximation, and Factorization*. Ph.D. thesis, Delft University of Technology, Delft, The Netherlands, 1993.

[VO96] C. VOGEL AND M. OMAN, *Iterative methods for total variation denoising*, SIAM J. Sci. Comput., 17, pp. 227–238, 1996.

[WH31] N. WIENER AND E. HOPF, *On a class of singular integral equations*, Proc. Prussian Acad. Math.—Phys. Ser., p. 696, 1931.

[Wid73] H. WIDOM, *Toeplitz determinants with singular generating functions*, Amer. J. Math., 95, pp. 333–383, 1973.

[Wid74] H. WIDOM, *Asymptotic behaviour of block Toeplitz matrices and determinants*, Adv. Math., 13, pp. 284–322, 1974.

[Wid75] H. WIDOM, *On the limit of block Toeplitz determinants*, Proc. Amer. Math. Soc., 50, pp. 167–173, 1975.

[Wid80] H. WIDOM, *Szegő limit theorem: The higher dimensional matrix case*, J. Funct. Anal., 39, pp. 182–198, 1980.

[Wie49] N. WIENER, *Extrapolation, Interpolation and Smoothing of Stationary Time Series, with Engineering Applications*, Technology Press and Wiley, New York, 1949.

[Wil61] J. H. WILKINSON, *Error analysis of direct methods of matrix inversion*, J. Assoc. Comput. Mach., 8, pp. 281–330, 1961.

[Wil63] J. H. WILKINSON, *Rounding Errors in Algebraic Processes*, Prentice–Hall, Englewood Cliffs, NJ, 1963.

[Wil65] J. H. WILKINSON, *The Algebraic Eigenvalue Problem*, Oxford University Press, London, 1965.

[Wri91] S. WRIGHT, *Parallel algorithms for banded linear systems*, SIAM J. Sci. Statist. Comput., 12, pp. 824–842, 1991.

[Yag91] A. YAGLE, *New analogues of split algorithms for arbitrary Toeplitz-plus-Hankel matrices*, IEEE Trans. Signal Process., 39, pp. 2457–2463, 1991.

[YL91] J. YE AND S.-Q. LI, *Analysis of multi-media traffic queues with finite buffer and overload control—Part I: Algorithm*, in Proc. IEEE Infocom 91, Bal Harbour, FL, pp. 1464–1474, 1991.

INDEX

adaptive filtering, 53
algorithm
    array, 18, 59, 62, 86
    Bareiss, 5, 59, 102
    CG, 118
    generalized Schur, 17, 18, 62, 86, 112
    hybrid Schur–Levinson, 30, 109
    inversion, 37
    Levinson–Durbin, 4, 102, 245
    PCG, 122
    Schur, 28, 102, 245
    tensor Schur, 265

back substitution, 33
backward stability, 58, 85, 105
banded block Toeplitz system, 237, 239
banded matrix, 274
Bareiss algorithm, 5, 59, 102
    error analysis, 59, 112
biharmonic equation, 141
Blaschke matrix, 18, 26, 69, 113
block circulant matrix, 218
block displacement operator, 223
block displacement rank, 223, 227, 228, 238
block Hessenberg form, 211, 214, 224, 225, 228
block Toeplitz matrix, 169, 173, 209, 211, 214, 216, 218, 223–225
block tridiagonal matrix, 211, 227, 231, 237, 238
boundary value problem, 156

Carathéodory function, 10
Cauchy interlace theorem, 302
Cauchy matrix, 6, 61, 102, 108, 274

Cauchy-like matrix, 8, 49, 57, 108, 109, 205
Cayley transform, 247
CG method, 116, 117, 120, 152, 153
Chandrasekhar equations, 53
Chebyshev–Vandermonde matrix, 110
Cholesky factorization, 58, 59, 63, 64, 73, 107, 112
circulant matrix, 6, 50, 122
clustered eigenvalues, 119
coding theory, 56
condition number, 92, 104
congruence, 298
Crout–Doolittle recursion, 289
cumulants, 242, 244, 248
cyclic reduction, 228, 230–232, 237, 238

Darlington synthesis, 245
deconvolution, 147
deflation, 15
digital filter, 2, 56
direct methods, 53, 116
displacement
    for tensors, 254
    fundamental properties, 13–15
    generalized, 9
    inertia, 3
    rank, 2, 103, 107, 274, 277
    structure, 2, 6–11, 60, 157, 222, 246, 276
    time-variant, 53
divided difference matrix, 10
doubling algorithm, 225
downdating, 59, 112, 113

elementary section, 23
embedding, 31, 58, 85, 114
entropy, 2

equation
    displacement, 7, 8, 11, 12, 18, 84, 89, 94, 270, 271
    Fredholm, 2
    Lyapunov, 11, 259, 260, 285
    Lyapunov–Stein, 288
    seminormal, 102
    Stein, 11
    Wiener–Hopf, 2
    Yule–Walker, 30, 243, 245
explicit structure, 1

factorization
    block triangular, 35
    modified QR, 85
    QR, 32, 85, 89, 113
    triangular, 2, 5, 6, 15, 58, 61, 62, 85, 86, 242, 273
f-circulant matrix, 196
FFT, 13, 217, 235, 238, 275, 291
floating point processor, 60
four-block problem, 54
Frobenius norm, 300

Gaussian elimination, 5, 16, 48, 57, 102, 105, 108, 294
generalized Hessenberg systems, 237
generalized Schur algorithm, 17–18, 58
    derivation, 18–23
    error analysis, 59, 64–73, 112
    for tensors, 265
    proper form, 25–27, 62, 86
    pseudocode, 81
generating function, 120, 161
generator
    growth, 75, 110
    matrix, 3, 60–62, 107
    nonminimal, 3
Givens rotation, 307
Gohberg–Semencul formula, 13
Gram–Schmidt procedure, 299

Hankel matrix, 1, 8, 61, 102, 274
Hankel rank, 275
Hankel-like matrix, 7, 47
Hessenberg matrix, 209
higher-order statistics, 243
Hilbert matrix, 103
homotopy technique, 196
Householder matrix

algebraic derivation, 305, 313
complex case, 305, 312
geometric derivation, 306, 313
hyperbolic case, 312
hybrid Schur–Levinson algorithm, 30, 32, 37, 109
hyperbolic rotation, 65, 113, 309
    H procedure, 68
    mixed downdating, 66, 311
    OD procedure, 67, 311

IEEE standards, 60
ill-conditioned matrix, 96, 104
image restoration, 146
implicit structure, 1
inertia of a matrix, 298
inflation, 37
input-output model, 53
interpolation, 2, 11, 54, 245
    Carathéodory, 54
    Hermite–Fejér, 54
    Lagrange, 55
    Nevanlinna–Pick, 54
    Padé, 55
    polyspectral, 261
invariance property, 13
inverse scattering, 2, 55
inversion algorithm, 37
iterative methods, 53, 104, 116, 120
iterative refinement, 76

J-lossless system, 54
J-unitary matrix, 3, 87, 88, 301

Krylov subspace, 117

Levinson–Durbin algorithm, 4, 37, 102, 111, 245
    error analysis, 4, 58, 112
linear convergence, 119, 190
linear phase filtering, 139
locally Toeplitz matrix, 174–185
Loewner matrix, 8
look-ahead algorithm, 104
look-ahead Schur algorithm, 34
lossless system, 55
Lyapunov condition, 282

MAC protocol, 239
machine precision, 60, 92, 96, 98, 104, 112

Index

Markov chain, 210–215
    M/G/1 type, 211
matrix completion, 11
matrix inversion lemma, 297
matrix polynomial, 216
matrix power series, 216, 219–222, 233, 238
matrix-vector product, 12, 123
method
    CG, 117
    iterative, 53, 116
    Newton's, 187, 188
    PCG, 122
modified Gram–Schmidt, 300
multibanded matrix, 274
multilevel Toeplitz matrix, 165, 173

Nerode equivalence, 280
network traffic, 212
Newton's iteration, 187–190
Newton–Toeplitz iteration, 192–196
norm of a matrix, 300
numerical stability, 51, 57, 85, 103
    backward, 52, 58, 85, 105
    strong, 105
    weak, 5, 104, 106

observability matrix, 281
orthogonal polynomials, 4

PCG method, 116, 122, 187
permutation, 308
Perron–Frobenius theorem, 303
perturbation analysis, 64
Pick matrix, 1, 6, 32, 44, 61
Pick tensor, 242
pivoting, 48, 57, 73
    complete, 48, 57
    partial, 48, 57, 105
polyspectrum, 242, 255
positive recurrence, 210
power series arithmetic, 221
preconditioner, 54, 116, 121
    band-Toeplitz, 129
    circulant, 124
    for structured matrices, 132
    Strang's, 124
    T. Chan's, 126
    Toeplitz-circulant, 131
probability invariant vector, 210

probability matrix, 209, 211
proper form, 25, 42, 62, 87

QBD problem, 211, 227, 231, 237
QR factorization, 32, 59, 84, 89–100, 107, 113, 299
    fast stable algorithm, 114
quadratic convergence, 190
quasi-Toeplitz matrix, 59, 61, 85
queueing network, 143, 212

Ramaswami's formula, 210, 225
reachability matrix, 281
realization theory, 277
reflection coefficient, 4, 37, 103
regularization, 147
residual
    correction, 188, 198
    error, 4, 58, 106, 239, 240
    matrix, 190
    norm, 118, 122, 195
    normalized, 106
    vector, 106, 117
Riccati equation, 2
Riccati recursion, 53
Riemann sum, 160, 181
Riemann–Lebesgue lemma, 158
rounding error, 64, 103

Schur algorithm, 5, 28–30, 102, 104
Schur complement, 14–17, 21, 30, 31, 63, 71, 85, 88, 89, 96, 224, 229, 232, 269, 270, 294
Schur construction, 37
Schur reduction, 15, 295
second-order statistics, 242, 243, 245
seminormal equations, 114
shift invariance, 156
shift matrix, 3
shift-structured matrix, 61, 84, 89
sparse matrix, 1
spectral decomposition, 297
spectral distribution, 120, 152–156
spectral norm, 300
spectrum, 116
stable algorithm, 105
state-space structure, 52, 274
stochastic matrix, 210
structured perturbation, 103
superlinear convergence, 126

Sylvester equation, 11
Sylvester's law, 13, 298
Szegő formula, 158, 159, 162, 163, 181

tensor, 242, 248
time-variant structure, 11, 53
Toeplitz matrix, 1, 2, 37, 61, 102, 108, 116, 274
Toeplitz-like matrix, 7, 45, 109, 116, 132, 190
Toeplitz-plus-band matrix, 116, 138
Toeplitz-plus-Hankel matrix, 102, 110, 116, 136
total variation, 148
transformation to Cauchy-like, 50
transmission line, 27
transmission zero, 24
triangular factorization, 2, 5, 6, 9, 16, 58, 61, 86, 295
Tucker product, 248

unitary matrix, 301

Vandermonde matrix, 1, 6, 7, 61, 102
Vandermonde-like matrix, 205

weak stability, 104
well-conditioned matrix, 92, 104
Wiener–Hopf technique, 5

Yule–Walker equations, 4, 243, 245